AF717824

Advanced JavaScript™

Third Edition

Chuck Easttom

Wordware Publishing, Inc.

Library of Congress Cataloging-in-Publication Data

Easttom, Chuck.
Advanced JavaScript / by Chuck Easttom. -- 3rd ed.
p. cm.
Includes index.
ISBN-13: 978-1-59822-033-9 (pbk.)
ISBN-10: 1-59822-033-0
1. JavaScript (Computer program language). I. Title.
QA76.73.J39E37 2007
005.13'3--dc22 2007012641
CIP

© 2008, Wordware Publishing, Inc.
All Rights Reserved

1100 Summit Avenue, Suite 102
Plano, Texas 75074

No part of this book may be reproduced in any form or by any means without permission in writing from Wordware Publishing, Inc.

Printed in the United States of America

ISBN-10: 1-59822-033-0
ISBN-13: 978-1-59822-033-9
10 9 8 7 6 5 4 3 2 1
0708

JavaScript is a trademark of Sun Microsystems, Inc. in the United States and other countries.

Other brand names and product names mentioned in this book are trademarks or service marks of their respective companies. Any omission or misuse (of any kind) of service marks or trademarks should not be regarded as intent to infringe on the property of others. The publisher recognizes and respects all marks used by companies, manufacturers, and developers as a means to distinguish their products.

This book is sold as is, without warranty of any kind, either express or implied, respecting the contents of this book and any disks or programs that may accompany it, including but not limited to implied warranties for the book's quality, performance, merchantability, or fitness for any particular purpose. Neither Wordware Publishing, Inc. nor its dealers or distributors shall be liable to the purchaser or any other person or entity with respect to any liability, loss, or damage caused or alleged to have been caused directly or indirectly by this book.

All inquiries for volume purchases of this book should be addressed to Wordware Publishing, Inc., at the above address. Telephone inquiries may be made by calling:

(972) 423-0090

Contents Summary

Contents

Acknowledgments

This book was a wonderful project and one I was eager to do for some time. The first two editions of *Advanced JavaScript* had been well received, but it was time for an update. I would like to take the time to thank several people who were indispensable in making this project happen:

Tim McEvoy and the wonderful people at Wordware Publishing who labored through this with me.

And of course my wife, Misty, who did not complain at all when I was spending hours in my den typing away.

Introduction

The Third Edition

Several things have been updated in this book. First, the text in general has been updated due to changes in the Internet and web development since the last edition. I have also dropped a few items that are outdated (such as hiding scripts from older browsers) and expanded coverage of topics like the Document Object Model. I think this book is even better than the last edition, and it is my hope it will help take your JavaScript to a new level.

Prerequisites

JavaScript is a scripting language designed to be used within HTML documents. For this reason a basic working knowledge of HTML is required before you can learn or use JavaScript. For those readers either lacking this basic knowledge or requiring a refresher course, Appendix A is a basic HTML primer that will teach you all of the skills you will need.

How to Read This Book

As the title suggests, this book focuses on advanced JavaScript programming and has the experienced JavaScript programmer in mind. However, the first few chapters and Appendix A do provide basic primers on both HTML and JavaScript. Those with limited JavaScript experience should carefully study the first few chapters, while more experienced programmers may want to skim these chapters or skip them entirely.

The Structure of This Book

It's important to understand how the book is structured so you can plan your learning experience in the best possible way. The table of contents lists the chapters by name. If you are an experienced JavaScript programmer just looking for a reference on a particular subject, feel free to skip directly to the relevant chapter.

JavaScript is a viable scripting language for both Netscape and Internet Explorer, so I will use examples from both browsers and will point out any differences. If you have the latest version of either Netscape or Internet Explorer, then virtually all the examples should work fine for you. Older versions of both browsers, particularly 3.0 and earlier, lacked support for some JavaScript features.

Programming Style

As both an aid to the reader and to illustrate good programming practices, I use a uniform style throughout this entire text and in all the sample code you will find in the companion files (available at www.wordware.com/files/java0330). For example, all variables are in Hungarian notation, meaning the variable is preceded by one to three letters designating the type of variable it is. That is, an integer being used as a loop counter might be named `intcounter`, and a float that holds an account balance might be named `fltbalance`. I also have a tendency to comment very heavily; some would say too much. This comes from teaching and creating code samples for students. I hope you will find this helpful:

```
for (var intcounter = 0; intcounter < 10; ++intcounter)
{
   [JavaScript statements]
}// end of for loop
```

Some JavaScript scripters prefer to use a different style:

```
for (var num = 0; num < 10; ++num)
{
   [JavaScript statements]
}
```

A lot of my style preferences are just that—preferences. It is hard to call one style right and another wrong. However, I strongly suggest that when you are writing code you consider the fact that other programmers will probably need to read your code at some point. They will have absolutely no idea what you were thinking when you wrote your code. I try to write code in such a way that even a novice programmer with no prior knowledge of the project at hand could easily deduce the intended purpose of the code.

Reading Examples

It seems obvious but read the examples thoroughly. Make sure you have a firm understanding of how and why they work. It is also helpful to actually run them. If you don't wish to run them, at least read them thoroughly and make certain that you fully understand every line of code and what it does.

Encouragement for Nonprogrammers

Learning a scripting language is a lot easier than learning a full programming language such as Java or C++. Fortunately, JavaScript is enough like Java that you will find it relatively easy to leverage your JavaScript skills into Java programming as well. Just remember that computers do exactly what we tell them to do, which may not always be exactly what we intended them to do. Most programming errors (called "bugs") stem from simple mistakes. I have an axiom that I believe is true: "Any error that takes more than 15 minutes to find will turn out to be something simple." In my experience, complex or fundamental errors are easy to find, though they may be quite hard to fix. Errors that take a long time to find are almost invariably simple mistakes.

Warning for Programmers

If your programming experience has been in strictly procedural languages such as C and Pascal, hold on tight. JavaScript, like Java, is object oriented. This will be a whole new approach to programming for you. But not to worry—this book will walk you through it step by step. However, if you are an experienced object-oriented programmer, especially a C++ or Java programmer, then this book should be a pretty easy read for you.

Chapter 1
Introduction to JavaScript

The World Wide Web

With each passing year the Internet becomes a more integral part of our lives, and web pages (along with e-mail) are probably the most common way we use the Internet. Twenty years ago there were few web pages, and not many people using them. Most of those web pages were very plain, simple text with an occasional inserted image, all done with simple HTML. As more and more end users discovered the Internet, however, web page developers found those users had quite an appetite for expanded graphics and functionality.

Simple, plain HTML web pages were no longer attractive to end users. New technologies emerged to help enhance web pages, and JavaScript has been, for the past decade, one of the most common enhancements to HTML web pages. With JavaScript you can take a static HTML page and make it dynamic and interactive. You can add real functionality, calculations, and even some interesting image effects.

Competition on the Web

With the explosion in the number of web sites available, competition for visitors is every bit as intense as the competition among television networks, radio stations, and other media. Since on any given topic there are a plethora of sites vying for your attention, simply having a web site is not enough. Having a popular web site is the goal now.

Site popularity is usually measured by the number of visits, or "hits," a web site receives. Major sites such as www.yahoo.com can receive tens of thousands of hits per day. Less popular sites may only receive a few hundred hits a day, while personal web pages may only receive a few hits per week or month. The competition to get visitors to sites is becoming quite fierce. In fact, advertising dollars are now pouring in to sites that can attract a significant number of visitors. Entire businesses are now based entirely on the web. Book sellers like www.amazon.com, search engines like www.google.com, and informative pages like www.kbb.com (Kelly Blue

Book) are all conducting business entirely online. Without traffic, they have no business at all. Even those businesses that do not entirely conduct their business online are often dependent upon the web for at least some of their customers.

The obvious way to get visitors to a site is to add content, both informational/functional and purely decorative. By informational content, I mean content that provides some valuable information to the visitor. Information is the reason people go to the web, and for your site to be popular it must contain usable, easily searchable information. Even without large advertising budgets, robust content and "word of mouth" can drive traffic to your web site. This is an area for which JavaScript is ideally suited. Your web site is truly useless if people do not visit it. There are several ways to attract readers to a site:

- **Advertising.** You can advertise your web site on pages that belong to other companies or individuals by placing some text or images on their page. For example, the user sees a banner at the top of the page; when he or she clicks the banner, the advertiser's site is loaded. Many large companies also tend to advertise via traditional methods such as newspapers, magazines, television, and radio. Although this method is somewhat less efficient, it works surprisingly well for well-established companies and has become a quite common practice. Web sites with high traffic (like www.yahoo.com) make substantial revenue via advertising other sites.
- **Submission.** Once you have a web site, people should know that it exists. Most people and small businesses do not have enough resources to advertise via banners that can cost up to tens of thousands of dollars a month. The most common free promotion method is to submit the URL and description of a web page to search engines and directories. Those services provide an easy way of retrieving desired web pages. For example, a search engine returns URLs of pages that are related to a specific topic that the user searched for. Google and Lycos are just some examples of such search engines; there are hundreds available on the web. Directories such as Yahoo! gather web pages by subject so the user can find pages related to a given subject.
- **Attractive site.** The most important way to attract users to your site is by creating an engaging site. Most readers tend to stick to sites that they have visited before and where they have found interesting, new material every visit. The most "effective" way to deter people from revisiting your site is by allowing it to become stale. Consider retail businesses. They all work hard to have the exterior of the business as attractive and convenient for their target customers as possible. You should use the same philosophy in your web sites.

Extending HTML

HTML is the heart of all web programming, but it is a somewhat limited document-formatting language. It is based on *tags*, which instruct the browser how to display a chunk of text or an image. As such, the HTML is limited to a static, one-way interaction with the user. The web page can be as sophisticated and attractive to the surfer's eyes as it can possibly be, but the user cannot interact with the page. Put another way, HTML simply lays there, much like a newspaper or book. The author has produced content and that content will be the same no matter how many times you read it, and it will be the same for all readers.

Interactive or dynamic web sites bring more enriched content and personalization to the web. Interaction cannot be static—it requires constructs such as if statements and for loops, which are not part of the HTML syntax.

These missing constructs needed to make interactive web pages are found in JavaScript. This object-oriented language provides web page authors with the power to reach a very high level of interaction between the user and the document. The power of the language is best shown by its long tenure in the arena of web development tools. JavaScript has been a standard in web developers' toolboxes for over ten years, and most web development jobs today still require a strong working knowledge of JavaScript. Some technologies come and go before we even realize what they were (Jazz drives and Virtual Reality Modeling Language come to mind), but JavaScript has earned a cornerstone place in web development. It is truly difficult to imaging a competent web developer who is not well versed in JavaScript.

Plug-ins, Applets, and ASP

Web page authoring consists of applying various techniques and technologies. This is often conceptualized as developing the web site in layers. The more powerful the layer, the more complex it is to program. The most fundamental layer is HTML. HTML is used to create the basic web page. Most other web technologies are used to enhance and expand that basic HTML page. As we explained earlier, JavaScript extends HTML to a dynamic user/page interaction. Plug-ins and applets extend JavaScript's capabilities even more.

Plug-ins

Another way to extend browser capabilities is by plugging an application into it. You have already seen plug-ins if you have ever visited a web page that had a Flash animation or video in it. We will discuss plug-ins in depth in Chapter 25, which is dedicated to these mechanisms and their powerful connections with JavaScript.

Java Applets

There are cases where one may find plug-ins just not up to the task. Let's say you want to place a rotating globe on your page. Sun Microsystems answered this need with the Java programming language. While Java can certainly be used for other tasks, Java applets are a common application of the Java language. Programmers can use Java to build small applications (applets) that are downloaded to the browser upon hitting the appropriate page and then automatically discarded from memory when a new page is loaded. The applet concept is similar to the image file concept. Like the way a .gif file is loaded upon hitting a page that calls the appropriate image, an applet is loaded upon the browser's request. The applet, though, is more than a static combination of pixels; it is an independent program that executes when the page loads and is automatically terminated when the page unloads. The applet is a self-sustained, independent module, without any possibilities for user interaction during its execution.

One classic example of an applet is a scrolling LED banner, similar to the scrolling sign at Times Square. This is a common method used to inform your visitors about changes you have made to your page. You can change your banner whenever you want to bring new items to the user's attention. This touch of animation can bring your page to life and create the perception of a dynamic, up-to-date site.

For a browser company to support Java applets, it needs to license the technology from Sun and build the proper hooks in the browser. The first one to do so was Sun itself, with its HotJava browser. Netscape incorporated it later, as did Microsoft. More recently Mozilla Firefox supports Java applets. In recent years Microsoft has quit supporting Java directly; however, Microsoft does provide links to external web sites where one can get Java. The following web sites also contain Java downloads: http://www.microsoft.com/mscorp/java/ and http://www.java.com/en/download/index.jsp.

Note: You have probably asked yourself about the origin of Java. The Java language is derived from C and C++ and is targeted for more experienced programmers. Therefore, many web page authors and casual programmers cannot adopt the language as easily as they have adopted HTML or Visual Basic. JavaScript was created to answer this exact need; however, you will find the syntax of JavaScript very much like that of Java or C.

ASP and ASP.Net

There are some tasks that cannot be accomplished by the browser on the client side. Tasks such as building a common database for an engineering department must rely on a server accepting data and requests from all users and storing it for future access and processing. Such applications were formerly written almost exclusively in Common Gateway Interface; however, more web sites today use ASP or ASP .NET for such tasks. ASP is a Microsoft technology that must run on a Microsoft Internet Information Server (IIS) web server, but can be viewed from any browser on any platform (Windows, Linux, Mac, etc.). ASP stands for Active Server Pages. The name itself tells you something about how it works. The ASP pages are on the server side, not the client, and they are active and dynamic. If your goal is professional web development, then at some point you should consider learning ASP/ASP .NET. Unfortunately, ASP and ASP .NET are far beyond the scope of this book. There are other technologies in use such as Ruby on Rails and JavaServer pages. But as of this writing, JavaScript is the most commonly used client-side scripting language and ASP/ASP.Net have become the most commonly used server-side tools.

What Is JavaScript?

We have talked about the various major web development technologies and given you an idea of where JavaScript fits in, but what exactly is JavaScript? JavaScript is an easy-to-use object-oriented scripting language designed for creating dynamic online applications that link together objects and resources on both clients and servers. While Java is used by programmers to create new objects and applets, JavaScript is designed for use by HTML page authors and enterprise application developers to dynamically script the behavior of objects running on either the client or the server. JavaScript's design and concepts represent the next generation of software for the Internet. JavaScript is:

- Designed for creating network-centric applications
- Complementary to and integrated with Java
- Complementary to and integrated with HTML
- Open and cross-platform

This means that JavaScript works hand in hand with HTML, and will work on any platform (Windows, Linux, Mac, etc.). It is also important to note that you don't need any special tools to use JavaScript. You can simply write scripts in any text editor, as we will do throughout most of this book. We will, in a much later chapter, look at editors that make writing JavaScript much easier; however, you can certainly write JavaScript without the use of such editors.

With JavaScript, an HTML page might contain a form that processes data on the client side. A server-side JavaScript might pull data out of a relational database and format it in HTML on the fly. A page might contain JavaScript scripts that run on both the client and the server.

Who Can Benefit from JavaScript?

Generally speaking, the people who visit your web site benefit most from JavaScript, because they have the opportunity to enjoy the language's capabilities in the form of games, animation, interaction, and so forth. Netscape Communications benefited from JavaScript early on, because it gave them a competitive advantage over other web browsers. And of course you, the web developer, benefit since you can create more dynamic web content.

The History of JavaScript

JavaScript was originated by Netscape as LiveScript, developed in parallel with LiveWire server software. LiveScript was developed for several applications—we'll discuss two of them here. The first application is to enhance web pages in a way that HTML cannot. The classic example is verifying a user's form entries. Instead of sending the data as is to the server and validating the data types there, the client handles all the validation and only then sends the data to the server for further processing. Another application for LiveScript (JavaScript) is as the communication glue between HTML documents and Java applets. A scrolling banner, for example, can use information from the user's customized settings, sent to the applet by LiveScript. This data exchange is transparent to the server and, since there is no server-client communication, there is no response time penalty.

In December 1995, Sun Microsystems took over LiveScript development and changed its name to JavaScript. On the one hand, JavaScript is related to Java in its C++ object flavor. On the other hand, JavaScript's vernacular is much reduced compared to Java, in order to make it suitable for less experienced programmers and scripters. JavaScript's first and foremost advantage is in its ease of learning. Additionally, its features and capabilities are important for web page interactivity as well as for customizing solutions around prewritten applets.

In 1996 Microsoft introduced its first JavaScript-enabled browser, Internet Explorer 3.0. Netscape followed up a week later with another JavaScript-enabled browser, Netscape Navigator. Internet Explorer was far from reaching Navigator 3.0's level in terms of JavaScript support and lacked many important features and capabilities. In early 1997 the beta version of Netscape Navigator version 4.0 (Communicator) was released. Microsoft Internet Explorer was still far from reaching Navigator 3.0's level at that point. Versions of Internet Explorer and Navigator as early as 5.5 and 6.0, respectively, fully support JavaScript.

JavaScript in a Browser

Client-side JavaScript

Client-side JavaScript is the most common form of the language. The script should be included in or referenced by an HTML document for the code to be interpreted by the browser. Suppose you load a web page with a JavaScript-generated banner. The browser begins interpreting the HTML code and then encounters a JavaScript script. If the script has no syntax errors, it is executed by the browser's built-in interpreter. This is the most common method of implementing JavaScript because it is the easiest. Just write your scripts directly into the HTML and you are done.

The JavaScript client-side mechanism features many advantages over traditional CGI server-side scripts. For example, you might use JavaScript to check if the user has entered a valid e-mail address in a form field. The JavaScript function is executed when the user submits the form, and only if the entry is a valid e-mail address (includes an @) is the form transmitted to the server for further processing, database storage, and so on. In this case, the user does not need to wait until the form is submitted over the network to the server and back to the client, only to be informed that a required character is missing.

Browser Objects

JavaScript uses a built-in object model that is mostly based on the HTML content of the given web page. This object model, called the Document Object Model (or DOM), is used by many web technologies to access the content of HTML documents as well as the browser itself. The tight interaction between JavaScript and other browser objects (such as forms, browser windows, frames, and images) provides full control over various page elements and enables the programmer to create a link between "external" objects and "internal" ones. A classic example for such linking is a JavaScript script that invokes a Java applet from an HTML form.

JavaScript exposes objects and properties related to the browser's window, history list, status bar, frames, forms, links, and so forth. All of these are part of that Document Object Model. Furthermore, JavaScript can be used to trap user-initiated events such as button clicks, link navigation, and other actions that the user explicitly or implicitly initiates. You can create a distinct script for each event, enabling a smooth, logical interaction with the user.

What Can JavaScript Do?

In this section we take a look at a few interesting effects and programs created entirely with JavaScript. At this point we will only focus on client-side JavaScript that is embedded in or referenced by an HTML document. Consider these items a preview of things to come in this book.

Image Effects

It is very easy to create interesting image effects with JavaScript. Effects such as image rollovers are common on many web sites. You will see later in this book just how easy these are to implement in JavaScript.

Games

You can create many interesting games with JavaScript. During our JavaScript programming experience we have written tic-tac-toe games, a mastermind game, a Tetris game, and many others. There are basically two types of games you can create via JavaScript:

- Static games
- Dynamic games

Static games are usually logical ones, and thus do not require much action or immediate responses. For example, you can play tic-tac-toe without any live action, because even reloading the entire page for each move does not interfere with the game itself (although it might be very boring). Static games do not require image replacements or animation. Dynamic games, on the other hand, require real-time action and animation. For example, a Tetris game requires that the blocks will fall down the screen smoothly without having to wait each time for the screen to be refreshed. Dynamic games are often resource intensive and therefore must be programmed with efficiency in mind. Small, simple games are usually embedded in existing web pages, whereas large, complex games are most often placed on a separate page.

Banners

JavaScript is a full scripting language, so you can create an infinite number of distinct scripts. Nevertheless, some implementations became more popular than others due to the fact that they are easy to use and create interesting effects. Banners are a classic example of such scripts. A banner is a script that displays text in the browser's status bar or in a form's text field. The most common banners are those that scroll and those that type in messages sequentially.

Form Validation

JavaScript is tightly connected to browser objects, including forms and their elements; therefore, it provides a great amount of control over forms. Form validation is one of the most common applications of JavaScript, and one we will certainly be using in this book. A classic form-related script is one that validates a form's fields before it is submitted and cancels the submission to the server if an error is found in one of the fields. The advantage of using JavaScript in this particular example is that client-side validation is much faster than validation via transmission to the server and back to the client. For example, suppose you have a form that accepts data from the user, including his or her e-mail address. Let's assume that the e-mail address is essential, and that a string containing an "@" character is assumed to be a valid e-mail address. There are two options:

- You can choose not to validate the entries. In that case, when the user clicks the Submit button, the form is submitted to the server where a CGI script checks if the e-mail address field is valid and then processes the form. If the e-mail address does not contain an "@" character, the submission is denied and the appropriate message is returned to the user.
- You can choose to use client-side validation via JavaScript. In that case the validating script is loaded as plain text (JavaScript code embedded in the HTML code). When the user clicks the Submit button, a JavaScript function is triggered to validate the form. If the e-mail address seems valid, the form is submitted to the server; otherwise, an appropriate message is immediately displayed and the submission is canceled. Note that the user does not have to wait for the form to be submitted to the server and back to the client, only to receive a message informing him or her that the e-mail address field contains an invalid entry.

Miscellaneous

I have covered the most important JavaScript implementations. However, as with all other languages, it is obviously impossible to cover all or most of the possible scripts. You can use JavaScript to create almost anything you desire. For example, you can create an LED sign, which once could be created only with Java.

Bear in mind that client-side JavaScript is executed on the user's machine. That is, you do not have any direct access to the server's properties with client-side JavaScript. Although that may seem to be a disadvantage, it is sometimes very convenient to have access to client-side properties rather than server-side ones. For example, you can create a digital clock that shows the current time in the client's time zone, because JavaScript extracts the time from the client's operating system, be it Windows, Macintosh, Unix, or any other OS.

The full control over browser objects is what makes client-side JavaScript so powerful. You can pop up windows and use them as remote controls linked to the original window. (Pop-up windows have been drastically overused, however, and many web developers tend to avoid them now.) You can use one link to perform several operations or load various documents in separate frames simultaneously. You can also use JavaScript to create an online calculator or to draw graphs and curves. To attract visitors, you can enhance a web page with JavaScript in many different ways.

We have introduced a few client-side JavaScript scripts in this section. Although client-side JavaScript is by far the most important and useful, there are many other implementations of the language. For example, you can use JavaScript for server-side applications using the LiveWire compiler. Server-side JavaScript is actually an alternative to traditional CGI programming via Perl and C++. JavaScript is a very convenient language; thus, it is used alongside many other languages and for various purposes. Another example of using JavaScript is for automatic proxy configuration. As you might already know, Netscape Navigator enables you to connect through a proxy server. You can configure the proxies manually by entering the correct values or entering the URL of an automatic proxy configuration script, which is actually a JavaScript code. The JavaScript code is located in a text file on the server but is not compiled like server-side JavaScript. As you can see, there is plenty to do with JavaScript, and JavaScript is now one of the most important languages for web development. We will cover the most important implementations of the language in this book.

JavaScript and Java

JavaScript Resembles Java

JavaScript supports most of Java's expression syntax and basic control flow constructs. Take a look at the following JavaScript code segment:

```
for (var i = 0; i < 10; ++i)
{
   /* statements come here */
}
```

Now take a look at the Java equivalent:

```
for (int i = 0; i < 10; ++i)
{
   /* statements come here */
}
```

Notice the similarity. The only difference is the variable declaration (JavaScript is loosely typed).

JavaScript and Java are both based on objects, but their implementations differ. In both languages, many built-in functions are implemented as properties and methods of various objects.

JavaScript Differs from Java

JavaScript resembles Perl in that it is interpreted, not compiled. Java is referred to as a compiled language. Unlike most other programming languages, though, Java is not compiled to a native machine code, but rather to a Java byte code. Java byte code is an architecture-neutral byte-code compiled language. That is, an applet is compiled to Java byte code and then run by a machine-dependent run-time interpreter. Therefore, Java is much slower than general programming languages such as C++. Since Java is compiled, the common user cannot see the actual code behind the program. When a user comes across a JavaScript script, he or she can generally see and even copy (legally or illegally) the code simply by using the browser to view the HTML source that contains the script (unless it is an external script). A compiled language has many other advantages. For example, a compiled program is much more efficient than one that is always interpreted directly from a text file, such as Perl and JavaScript. On the other hand, there are more than enough reasons to prefer an interpreted language over a compiled one. It is much easier and more convenient to debug and modify a program by simply modifying its text file rather than having to recompile it. Furthermore, most scripts and applets implemented in Java or JavaScript for web usage do not require efficiency and do not demand resources. Therefore, an interpreted language is somewhat more convenient.

Both Java and JavaScript are based on objects. However, their implementations of objects are different. JavaScript is an object-based language. It supports built-in, extensible objects, but no classes or inheritance. Its object hierarchy is not an inheritance hierarchy as in Java. JavaScript features two types of objects:

- Static objects—objects that combine general functions (methods) and data constructs (properties). The values of such objects' properties are usually read-only. A static object is a single object, and thus does not enable you to create instances of it. For example, the `Math` object in JavaScript is a static one, because you cannot create instances according to its template. Its methods are common mathematical functions, whereas its properties are mostly mathematical constants.
- Dynamic objects—objects by which instances are created. A dynamic object resembles a template. You do not touch or use the object directly. In order to take advantage of such an object, you must create an instance of it. For example, the `Date` object is a dynamic object in JavaScript. An instance of that object is associated with a given date. You can create as many instances of a dynamic object as needed.

Java is fully extensible. A programmer can create numerous classes that group objects together. A *class* is a term used in object-oriented programming vernacular to refer to a set of related objects that share common characteristics. Java programmers create their own extensions to the base set of tools or classes. JavaScript's object model is somewhat simpler than Java's equivalent, so JavaScript's object implementation is much easier to accommodate than Java's model.

Another difference between Java and JavaScript is their time of binding. JavaScript features dynamic binding, so all object references are checked at run time. Java, on the other hand, is based on static binding, meaning that all object references must exist and be valid at compile time. However, an object-oriented language may require dynamic method bindings because polymorphism allows multiple definitions of methods sharing a common name, and calling such polymorphic methods often cannot be resolved until run time. The most obvious reason for this difference is that JavaScript is not compiled, so checking object references at compile time has no meaning. If you are not familiar with Java, you should pay no attention to these confusing terms—simply bear in mind that the object implementation in JavaScript varies widely from that in Java.

When you write a script, you likely need to use variables. In order to use a variable, you must declare it. Another difference between Java and JavaScript is that Java is strongly typed, as opposed to JavaScript, which is loosely typed. That is, when you declare a variable in Java, you must specify its data type. For example, when you create a variable to contain integer values you must use the `int` keyword. In JavaScript, all variables are declared in the same way. Furthermore, a variable of one data type can contain a value of a different data type elsewhere in the script. This behavior resembles other popular languages such as Perl, and is discussed in Chapter 3.

I have intentionally left the most critical difference to the end. You may have noticed that all differences discussed thus far are related to the language itself. A very important difference between Java and JavaScript is that JavaScript is integrated with, and embedded in, HTML.

I have spoken with many people who believe that JavaScript is a scaled-down version of Java. As you should already know, that is not true. JavaScript cannot perform many tasks that Java can, whereas Java cannot do most things that JavaScript is capable of doing.

JavaScript is supported by many companies. At the same time Netscape Communications and Sun Microsystems announced JavaScript, more than 28 companies also announced that they would be endorsing JavaScript as the open scripting standard for the Internet, and many indicated that they were considering licensing the technology to include it in their own products.

A web page designer simply cannot afford to ignore JavaScript if he wants to compete in the field. Nevertheless, JavaScript has limits and cannot perform every task. A few classic JavaScript-based solutions are as follows:

- User interaction with form elements (input fields, text areas, buttons, radio buttons, check boxes, and selection lists)
- Distributing small collections of database-like information with friendly interfaces to that data
- Processing the data on the client side before submission to the server
- Animation and live image swapping

This list is obviously an abbreviated one and does not include all possible uses of JavaScript.

Summary

In this chapter you have seen an overview of JavaScript as well as comparisons to other web development technologies. This should give you a clear understanding of what JavaScript is used for and how it relates to those other technologies. The most important point to remember is that JavaScript is perhaps the most widely used web technology (after HTML of course), and it is therefore imperative that any web developer have a grasp of it.

Chapter 2
Getting Started with JavaScript

I am a big believer in getting students and readers actually working with the technology they are attempting to learn as soon as possible Therefore, in this chapter we are going to just dive right in and write a few simple scripts with JavaScript. The idea is to get you working with JavaScript right away. The sooner you feel comfortable with the basics, the better. Of course if you are proficient in JavaScript and wish to move on to more advanced topics, feel free to skip this chapter.

Essential Authoring Tools

The good news about JavaScript is that you won't need any special tools or software to start using it. In fact, you probably have everything you need on your computer right now. In order to begin writing scripts, you simply need any standard text editor. You should not have any problem getting a text editor for your computer since most operating systems include a text editor (Windows ships with both Notepad and WordPad). Most Linux distributions include several text editors.

Of course you can find specialized editors that help you sort out the syntax and debug your JavaScript. We will discuss some of these toward the end of this book in Chapter 28. However, you can work with just a basic text editor, and many professional web developers do just that.

Choosing a Text Editor

If you are using Windows, then you already have Notepad and WordPad on your PC; both are fine for doing HTML and JavaScript. The advantage of using standard text editors is that they are free. The disadvantage is that they do not offer any debugging tools to help you with the JavaScript. We will discuss editors that help you with JavaScript syntax in Chapter 24.

Choosing a Browser

Besides the basic programming tool, you need to be able to run your scripts and view their output. In order to run JavaScript, you need a compatible browser. Many years ago this was a problem, as not all browsers supported JavaScript and some only supported portions of JavaScript. However, it has been quite a few years since this was an issue. Any version of Microsoft Internet Explorer, Netscape Navigator, or Mozilla Firefox produced in the past five years will support JavaScript. Many lesser-known browsers such as Galleon and Opera also support JavaScript. As I stated earlier, it has become a standard for web development and one would be hard pressed to find a browser that did not support JavaScript, so it doesn't really matter which browser you choose.

Note: With most web development technologies (JavaScript, ASP .NET, etc.) things don't always look the same in different browsers. For this reason, most professional web developers use multiple browsers to test their code. I would recommend you have at least Internet Explorer and Mozilla Firefox. Since almost all browsers are free downloads, keeping multiple browsers should not be a problem.

Basic JavaScript Structure

In order to run client-side JavaScript, you must embed the code in the HTML document. Obviously, you cannot place JavaScript statements in the source code in just any location. There are several different ways to embed JavaScript scripts in HTML:

- As statements and functions using the <SCRIPT> tag
- As event handlers using HTML tag attributes
- As short statements resembling URLs

The <SCRIPT> Tag

Internal Scripts

The <SCRIPT> tag is used to enclose JavaScript code in HTML documents. Here is the general syntax:

```
<SCRIPT LANGUAGE="JavaScript">
[JavaScript statements...]
</SCRIPT>
```

The <SCRIPT LANGUAGE="JavaScript"> tag acts like all other HTML tags. Notice that it must be followed by its closing counterpart, </SCRIPT>. Every statement you put between the two tags is interpreted as JavaScript code. This is probably the most common method for inserting JavaScript into HTML documents.

The LANGUAGE attribute is used to specify the scripting language. At present, the <SCRIPT> tag supports various languages including JavaScript and VBScript. JavaScript is the default scripting language, so the LANGUAGE definition is not required. When the browser comes across the name of the language, it loads the built-in JavaScript interpreter and then interprets the script. However, it is always best to explicitly name the scripting language you are using. This ensures that your script will work the same in future versions of HTML and in a variety of browsers.

JavaScript is case sensitive, but HTML is not. It does not matter whether you write <SCRIPT> or <script>, but try to be consistent. Personally I use all capitals in my HTML. Even though it does not matter to the browser, it does to the person reading my HTML code. Remember that HTML and JavaScript are no different from any programming language in that you should always strive to make sure your code is readable.

External Scripts

Many years ago JavaScript added the <SCRIPT> tag, which enables the use of external scripts; that is, you can use a JavaScript script that is located in another file. This is now supported by all browsers that support JavaScript (which means every browser you are likely to encounter). Some people prefer to have their scripts in external files for a few reasons. First, your script is not as immediately and easily viewable as your HTML. (In most browsers one can simply choose View>Source to see the HTML source code.) Also, some web developers have common scripts they use on multiple pages. I rarely use external scripts in this book, but you should remember that they exist as you may find them helpful. External scripts are useful when you need to integrate a long, sophisticated JavaScript script into an HTML file.

Here are some disadvantages of using an external file:

- **No back references.** JavaScript scripts are mainly driven by user-initiated events. A click on a button calls a function, a selection of a form element executes another function, and so on. If you design your entire script in an external file, you will have difficulties in referring to the HTML definitions in the original file. For this reason, place only general functions in an external script.
- **Additional processing.** The JavaScript interpreter evaluates all functions found in your script header, including those defined in the external file, and stores them in memory. Loading unneeded functions in an external file degrades the script performance.
- **Additional server access.** You know how irritating it is to wait until another page loads in the window, especially with slow connections. That is the problem with the SRC attribute. When the browser comes across the tag that tells it to interpret JavaScript code in another file, it must first load that file. Such an action is time consuming. Most programmers say that efficiency is not as important as maintainability and clarity. However, with web page development, appearance is everything

and a slow-loading web site is unlikely to be successful. Always keep in mind that unnecessary HTTP hits to the server should be avoided.

Enough theory. Here is the syntax for defining an external script in the <SCRIPT> tag:

```
<SCRIPT LANGUAGE="JavaScript" SRC="yourFile.js">
[additional JavaScript statements...]
</SCRIPT>
```

Note that the extension of the external file must be .js, just as the extension of an HTML file must be .html or .htm. The name of the file does not have to include the full path; a relative (virtual) path is enough. The .js, obviously, stands for JavaScript.

Suppose abc1.js contains the following code:

```
var counter = 100
function alertMe(message)
{
   alert(message)
}
function writeMe(message)
{
   document.write(message)
}
```

At this point, the meaning of the JavaScript statements themselves is unimportant. They are all explained in the following chapters. Here's the basic HTML file:

```
<HTML>
<HEAD>
<TITLE>Using external files</TITLE>
<SCRIPT LANGUAGE="JavaScript" SRC="abc1.js">
<!--
var digit = 8
alertMe("Hello!")
writeMe("Howdy!")
// -->
</SCRIPT>
</HEAD>
</HTML>
```

The preceding structure is equivalent to the following HTML document:

```
<HTML>
<HEAD>
<TITLE>Equivalent Script</TITLE>
<SCRIPT LANGUAGE="JavaScript">
<!--
var counter = 100
function alertMe(message)
{
   alert(message)
}
```

```
function writeMe(message)
{
  document.write(message)
}
var digit = 8
alertMe("Hello!")
writeMe("Howdy!")
// -->
</SCRIPT>
</HEAD>
</HTML>
```

Both scripts produce the output shown in Figure 2-1.

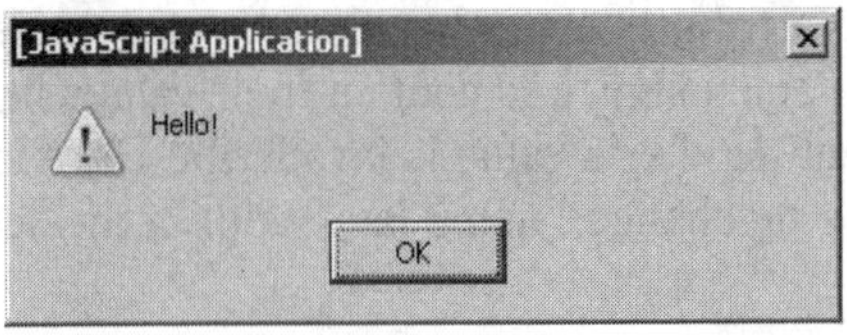

Figure 2-1. *An alert box*

When you press the OK button, you are taken to the image shown in Figure 2-2.

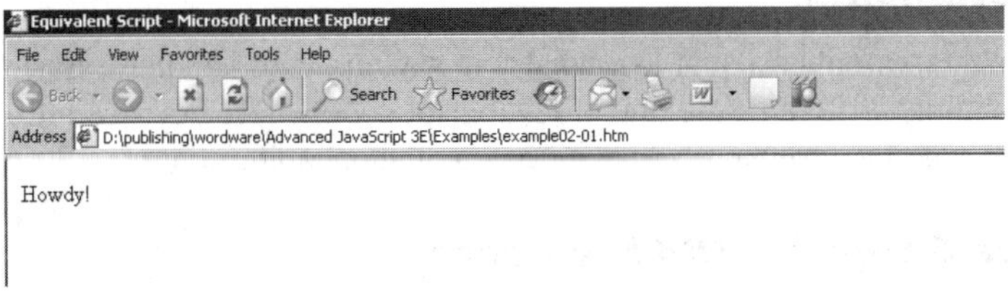

Figure 2-2. *Document.Write*

It is important to understand the way external scripts are interpreted, because many different rules apply to JavaScript and HTML layout. Just keep in mind that an external script is actually interpreted as if it precedes the local script (enclosed by the <SCRIPT> and </SCRIPT> tags).

JavaScript-only files should have the filename suffix .js, and the server must map the .js suffix to the MIME type application/x-javascript, which it sends back in the HTTP header. If the server does not map the .js filename extension to application/x-javascript, Navigator will not properly load the JavaScript file specified by the SRC attribute. In short, your server must be configured to reflect the proper MIME type; otherwise, the browser does not respond properly with the data coming back in the HTTP response to the SRC-initiated request.

Event Handlers

You can place JavaScript right into event handlers. Event handlers are HTML tag attributes that refer to a specific action which takes place in reference to that form element. For example, it might be onclick for an HTML button or onload for the HTML document itself. Event handlers are used to control when the JavaScript is executed. With an event handler, the script in question will execute when the event occurs. A good example of this is an image rollover, where an image changes when the mouse pointer moves over it. Event handlers are why JavaScript is able to interact with the end user. Some commonly used event handlers include onMouseOver, onMouseOut, onLoad, onSubmit, and onClick.

Like any other HTML tag attribute, event handlers belong inside an HTML tag, are followed by an equal sign, and contain their values in quotes. The difference is that the event handler's value is JavaScript. Here is an example of an image source being changed using JavaScript in the actual event of the link tag:

```
<a href="x.html" onMouseOver="document.mainimage.src='mypic.gif'" >
```

You will see event handlers used in this manner quite frequently. It is a very popular technique with JavaScript programmers.

Short Statements

Short statements are just like what you saw in event handlers. Essentially, you simply write a single line of JavaScript code where you need it. In fact, event handlers are simply special cases of short statements.

Hiding the Script for Old Browsers

You have probably asked yourself what happens when someone loads your page with an old browser that does not support JavaScript. Since all major browsers have supported JavaScript for many years and browsers are free downloads, the chances are almost nonexistent that someone will come to your web site with a browser that is five or more years out of date. While many JavaScript programmers still put in code for handling outdated browsers, it is more out of habit than necessity. So we will not be discussing this issue, though it was covered in previous versions of this book.

Important Notes about JavaScript

Since the first edition of this book was written quite a few years ago, the Internet has grown tremendously. We now have tens of thousands of web sites on every conceivable topic. Most people use the Internet in their daily lives to look up information, do banking, order goods, book vacations, search for jobs, and more. However, with this incredible expansion of online information available to everyone at the click of a mouse, there has also been an incredible increase in danger on the Internet. Viruses, phishing, and spyware are all very real dangers on the Internet. It would be difficult to find any computer user today who has not, in some way or another, been adversely affected by some type of malware. For this reason it is becoming more common for browsers to block any content that might be used in any adverse way.

As you will see in later chapters of this book, JavaScript can be used to place cookies (small files with information) on the client computer to gather information about that client such as their IP address and what kind of browser they are using. For this reason many browsers have optional higher security levels that will block JavaScript. If someone is using Internet Explorer with high security and visits your web site that has JavaScript in it, they will see a warning message similar to what is shown in Figure 2-3.

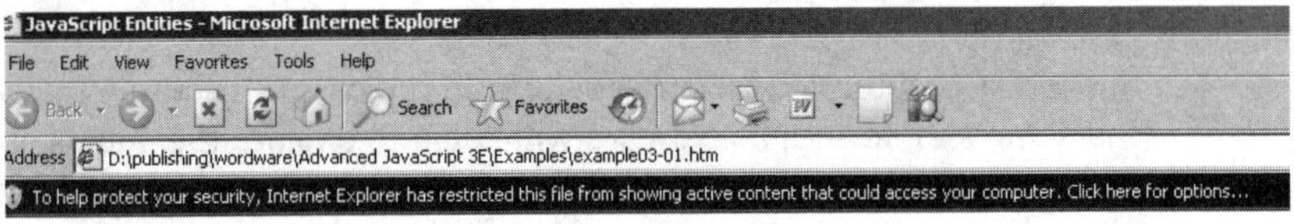

Figure 2-3. *Internet Explorer security message*

This message states that the browser has restricted content in the file and allows the user to choose whether or not to allow the activity.

This is not a major problem. The person merely needs to click on the pop-up window and he or she will be able to view your JavaScript. If you are creating a web site for personal purposes, you really don't need to do anything about this. However, some companies are beginning to place privacy statements/policies on their main page. These policies tell the visitor about any cookies that might be placed on their machine and exactly what sort of data might be collected about them. It is probably a good idea to implement this in any business web site. It is my opinion that in the very near future you will find visitors to your web site becoming more and more security and privacy conscious. If you are not able to alleviate their concerns, you will find yourself with far fewer web site visitors.

Summary

Our goal in this chapter was to get you writing simple scripts in JavaScript. This should begin to give you a feel for how JavaScript works. After this chapter you should understand the basic structure of JavaScript and be able to insert a JavaScript script into your HTML page.

Chapter 3
JavaScript Fundamentals

"Building" a Script

In the last chapter you were introduced to the basic structure of JavaScript and some simple scripts. Now we will begin to explore the details of JavaScript. In this chapter you will learn all the basic elements of JavaScript. As we begin to cover the basics of JavaScript, it is important to remember that it has many fundamental concepts in common with all programming languages, including its basic elements. So if you have worked with any other programming languages, this won't be difficult to learn. It has variables that hold data, it has expressions or statements, and it has functions. These building blocks are used to construct your JavaScript script. I will explain each of these elements in this chapter.

Data Types in JavaScript

Variables hold information that usually must be of a specific type. These types are referred to as *data types*. Note that JavaScript will allow you to create a generic variable and put any data you wish into it, which is why JavaScript is often referred to as a "loosely typed language." Other languages (Java, C, C++, etc.) will not let you create a generic variable of an unspecified type. These languages are referred to as "strongly typed languages." Even though you don't have to use typed variables in JavaScript, many programmers find that using specific data types makes their code more readable, and thus more maintainable.

If you are going to use specific typed data variables, then it is important to use the proper data type to store your information. For example, a number is a type of information that JavaScript recognizes. There are four specific data types in JavaScript: numbers, strings, Booleans, and null values. As opposed to other languages, a variable data type is not declared explicitly but rather implicitly according to its initial value assignment. Also unique to JavaScript, there is no explicit distinction between integers and real-valued numbers.

All of these data types are specified in Table 3-1.

Table 3-1. Data types in JavaScript

Type	Description	Examples
number	Any number without quotes	`42` or `16.3` or `2e-16`
string	A series of characters enclosed in quote marks	`"Hello!"` or `"10"` or `''` or `""`
Boolean	A logical value	`true` or `false`
null	A keyword meaning no value	`null`

The Value Null

The value null is often used to initialize variables that do not have any special meaning (see "Variable Declaration" later in the chapter). You assign it to a variable using the standard assignment statement:

```
var name = null
```

The null value is special in that it is automatically converted to initial values of other data types. When used as a number it becomes 0, when used as a string it becomes `""`, and when used as a Boolean value it becomes `false`. Since the source of many JavaScript errors is uninitialized variables, one of the common debugging techniques is to initialize all uninitialized variables, including the meaningless ones, with a null value.

The JavaScript interpreter uses the null value on two occasions: (1) built-in functions return null under certain circumstances, and (2) nonexistent properties evaluate to null. When checking for a null value, you should check if it is false or if it is equal to null.

Variables

At some level all programs hold data, at least for a short time, and data is stored, temporarily, in variables. Therefore, it is not an overstatement to claim that variables are the cornerstone of most programming and scripting languages. They serve as a link between simple words in your script and the computer allocated memory. There is a limit to the amount of memory you can use, but it would be virtually impossible for you to even approach that limit. JavaScript applications are not heavy resource demanders and modern PCs typically have a great deal of memory. As of this writing, it is hard to buy a PC with less than 512 megabytes of memory, so exceeding available memory is probably an indication of a bug in the browser or a major flaw in your program (such as an unexpected infinite loop).

Because you do not deal directly with the memory allocation, you should think of variables as baskets that contain different data. You can put an item in a basket, take it out, or replace it with another. A script that does not use any variables at all probably does not accomplish much. So you should definitely get comfortable with variables, as you will be using them throughout this book.

Identifiers

Each variable is identified by a *variable name*, also known as an *identifier*. Each variable name is associated with a specific memory location, and the interpreter uses it to determine its location. There are strict rules for naming variables and you will need to learn them:

- The first character of an identifier must be either a letter (uppercase or lowercase) or an underscore (_).
- All other characters can be letters, underscores, or digits (0 to 9).
- An identifier cannot be one of the language's reserved words. Reserved words consist of all JavaScript keywords as well as other tokens reserved for future versions.

An identifier length is not limited, and you should take advantage of this feature to select meaningful names. JavaScript is case sensitive (uppercase letters are distinct from lowercase letters). For example, `counter`, `Counter`, and `COUNTER` are names of three different variables. While those three variable names are legal, and would create three separate and distinct variables, using such similar names would cause a great deal of confusion for yourself or anyone else who may need to read or modify your JavaScript. You should always avoid using such similar identifiers in the same script. However, you will want to use variable names that are related to the data they contain. For example, if you have a string variable that holds a person's last name, you might wish to name it LastName.

The following identifiers are legal:

```
loopCounter
_AccountNumber
_123456789_
customer_name
OfficeNumber6
```

but the following ones are illegal:

```
with               // reserved word
^fastTimer         // first character is illegal
911phoneNumber     // cannot start with a digit
04-825-6408        // first character is illegal
                   // "-" is an illegal character
***important***    // * is not a legal character
10_guesses         // first character cannot be a digit
```

Keywords are words that have special meanings in a programming language. You cannot use keywords to name variables or functions you create in a script (such as variables, functions, etc.). The list of keywords is the basic vocabulary of the language. The word `if`, for example, is a keyword. You do not have to memorize the list, because you will gradually remember it as you use the words in your scripts.

Naming Conventions

There are a number of generally accepted conventions in JavaScript:

- A variable name is normally written in lowercase letters.
- The variable name indicates its purpose and use in a program.
- In a multiword identifier, either place an underscore between words or capitalize the first letter of each embedded word.

The following are examples of multiword identifiers.

```
all_done        // underscores
allDone         // capitalized letters
```

Avoid similar variable names. The following illustrates a poor choice of variable names:

```
digit           // current digit
digits          // number of digits in the number
```

A much better set of variables is:

```
current_digit  // current digit
num_of_digits  // number of digits in the number
```


Variable Declaration

You have seen how to name a variable, and know why you need variables, but how do you create them? Before you use a variable, you need to create it. JavaScript is a loosely typed language, which means that you do not have to explicitly specify the data type of a variable when you create it. As needed, data types are converted automatically during the course of the script execution. In strongly typed languages, the variable must be created of a specific type.

There are two ways to create a variable, and fortunately both are very simple. The first type of declaration includes the `var` keyword followed by the name of the variable:

```
var variableName
```

The second method is simply to use the variable name and set it equal to an initial value without the use of the `var` keyword. While this will work, it is not recommended, as it can be confusing for someone reading the script.

When interpreting this statement, the browser creates a link between the name of the variable and its memory address, so successive references can be done by name. Unlike some programming languages, declarations are not limited to a specific zone but can be done anywhere throughout the script.

The action of assigning an initial value to a variable is called *initialization*. You give the variable a value using the most common *assignment operator*—the equal sign:

```
var variableName = initialValue
```

You only need to use the `var` keyword when you create the variable. When you want to refer to the variable, you only use its name. Assign a value to a variable (after it has been declared) in the following fashion:

```
variableName = anyValue
```

You use `var` only once per variable. A global variable can be created simply by assigning it a value without the `var` keyword. Local variables inside functions, on the other hand, must be declared with the `var` keyword. As in many other programming languages, JavaScript allows you to declare numerous variables in the same statement by using a comma to separate them:

```
var variableName1 = initialValue1, variableName2 = initialValue2, ...
```

JavaScript Entities

JavaScript entities can be assigned to HTML attributes. This attribute substitution enables creation of more flexible HTML constructions, without the writing overhead of full JavaScript scripts.

You are probably familiar with HTML character entities with which you can display a character by its numerical code or name. You precede a name or a number with an ampersand (&) and terminate it with a semicolon (;). Here are a few examples:

```
&gt;
&lt;
&#169;
```

These HTML entities evaluate to the following characters:

> (greater than)
< (less than)
© (copyright)

JavaScript entities also start with an ampersand and end with a semicolon. Instead of a name (as in the first two examples) or a number (as in the third example), you use a JavaScript expression enclosed in curly braces ({ and }). Note that you can use JavaScript entities to assign HTML attributes only. Consider the following HTML document:

```
<HTML>
<HEAD>
<TITLE>JavaScript Entities</TITLE>
<SCRIPT LANGUAGE="JavaScript">
<!-- hide content from old browsers
var fontSize = "+4"
var fontColor = "red"
// end hiding content-->
</SCRIPT>
</HEAD>
<BODY>
<FONT COLOR="&{fontColor};" SIZE="&{fontSize};">
Flexible attributes with JavaScript entities
```

```
</FONT>
</BODY>
</HTML>
```

Example 3-1 (ex3-1.htm)

When you execute this script you will see something similar to what is shown in Figure 3-1.

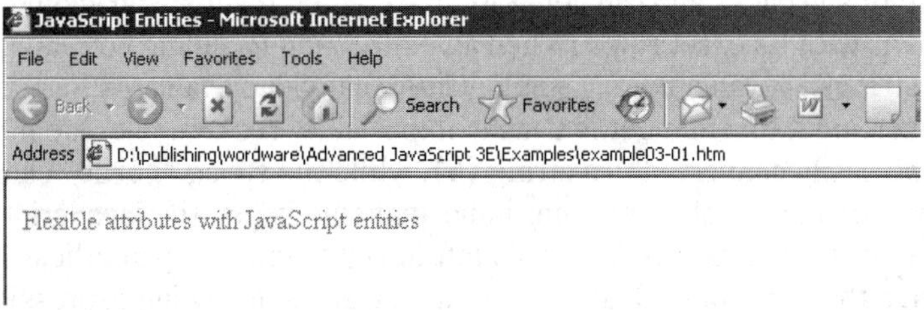

Figure 3-1. *JavaScript entities*

The entity `&{fontColor};` is replaced by the current value of `fontColor` and `&{fontSize};` is replaced by the current value of `fontSize`. Since JavaScript can only use values that are stored in memory at the time of page layout, JavaScript entities should be used only after calling the script that assigns their value.

Once layout is complete, the display of the page can change only if you reload the page. Even if the value of the JavaScript entity variable changes, the entity itself does not change until you reload the page.

Unlike HTML character entities, which can be used in any script statement, JavaScript entities can be used only in a tag statement. Another difference is that, while HTML character entities may substitute for any HTML element, JavaScript entities are limited to HTML attribute substitution only. For example, you cannot specify the entity `"&{text};"` with the variable `text = "<H1>Hi!</H1>"`—it is not a valid value for a tag attribute.

Type Conversion

As mentioned above, data types are converted automatically as needed during the course of script execution. This can be quite convenient, and many other programming languages do not allow this. A variable may hold a numeric value at one point of the script and a string at another. The following statements constitute a valid JavaScript script:

```
var myVar = 12
myVar = "university"
```

The first statement assigns a numeric value to `myVar`, and the second one assigns it a string. Such conversions are not allowed in strictly typed languages such as C++ and Java. While they are possible in JavaScript, they are not recommended. Using this technique makes for very sloppy programming.

Mixing Strings and Numbers

Mixing strings and numbers is sometimes necessary for certain operations. Since this is tricky and can generate unexpected results, you should be familiar with its exact rules. When an expression including both numbers and strings is evaluated to a single value, that value evaluates to a string. Converting it to a number is usually impossible. For example, the number `6` can be easily converted to a string `(6)`, while the string `"horse"` cannot be converted to a number. Another important rule is that the JavaScript interpreter evaluates expressions from left to right, and only parentheses can change the order of evaluation. Take a look at the following expressions, numbered by line.

```
/* 1 */  8 + 8        // 16
/* 2 */  "8" + 8      // "88"
/* 3 */  8 + "8"      // "88"
/* 4 */  "8" + "8"    // "88"
/* 5 */  8 + 8 + "8"  // "168"
/* 6 */  8 + "8" + 8  // "888"
```

These expressions all use the string concatenation operator, which is also the numeric plus operator. (Operators are covered later in this chapter.)

The first expression simply adds up two numbers using a numeric format. It uses the standard plus operator and evaluates to the sum of its operands. The second expression is quite different. Its first operand is a string rather than a number. In order to add a number to a string, the number is converted to its matching string and the strings are then concatenated. The third and fourth expressions are similar in that they also include at least one string operand. The fifth expression is a bit trickier. The first two operands are added up because they are numbers. The expression now evaluates to `16 + "8"` which, as you already know, evaluates to `"168"`. Using parentheses can change the result. For example:

```
8 + (8 + "8") // "888"
```

In this expression, the content in the parentheses is evaluated first to `"88"` and the entire expression evaluates to `"888"`. Comparing the sixth expression to the fifth one clearly demonstrates what left-to-right evaluation means.

Whenever a string is found during the expression evaluation, the accumulated value thus far is converted to a string. The remaining numeric values on the right-hand side are automatically converted to strings when concatenated to this accumulated value.

If you want to convert a single number to a string, you can use one of the following three methods:

```
var newVar = " " + numericValue
var newVar = new String(numericValue)
var newVar = numericValue.toString()
```

The first method is simple. You use the concatenation operator, which instructs JavaScript to convert the number to a string and then append it to a null string. The other methods are discussed later in the book.

Literals

Literals are fixed values that you literally provide in your application source, and that are not variables or any other data structure. The same concept in other programming languages is often called a *constant*. They are notations for constant values and therefore do not change throughout the script. A literal gives you a value instead of merely representing possible values. Unlike C++ and Java, which have five literal types, JavaScript has only four: integer, floating-point, Boolean, and string. Character literals are simply considered strings with a length of 1.

Integer Literals

Integer literals, also called *whole numbers*, are numbers that have no decimal point or fractional part. Here are some integer literals:

```
49
16
0
-18
-42
```

An integer can be positive, negative, or zero. JavaScript, like most other programming languages, supports integers of three types or bases: decimal, octal, and hexadecimal.

Decimal Integers

Decimal integers, also known as *base-10 integers*, are the common integers we use daily. They are written with the digits 0, 1, 2, 3, 4, 5, 6, 7, 8, and 9. Except for the number 0 itself, a decimal integer cannot have a leading 0 digit. It makes no sense to write the current year as 02007, and, indeed, JavaScript will not evaluate it as 2007.

Octal Integers

Octal integers, also known as *base-8 integers*, use only eight digits: 0, 1, 2, 3, 4, 5, 6, 7. Octal digits are written with a leading 0 digit (that's a zero, not the letter "o"). If you want to reference the octal integer 12 (equal to 10 in the decimal system), you would have to write it as 012.

Hexadecimal Integers

Hexadecimal integers are commonly used in programming environments because each hexadecimal digit represents four binary bits. A *hexadecimal number* is any sequence of these digits: 0, 1, 2, 3, 4, 5, 6, 7, 8, 9, A, B, C, D, E, F. The integers are called hexadecimal because they are based on 16 different digits. Case sensitivity rules do not apply to numbers, so you can use lowercase letters as well. The prefix for hexadecimal numbers is 0x or 0X.

Hexadecimal numbers might look familiar to HTML authors. In early versions of Netscape Navigator and Internet Explorer, colors were specified in a *hexadecimal triplet* format. Although the latest versions of Netscape Navigator and Internet Explorer let you specify colors by their names, some people continue to use the hexadecimal notation. The following tag sets the background color to the default gray (even for users who changed their default to white):

```
<BODY BGCOLOR="#c0c0c0">
```

You probably know that monitor screen colors differ in the relative contributions of red, green, and blue. The hexadecimal triplet combines three hexadecimal numbers of two digits each (2 digits = 16 * 16 = 256 possibilities).

Converting from Decimal to Other Bases

You can use a calculator to convert a decimal integer to a different base. But what happens when the calculator is broken?! It is surprisingly simple to do the conversion with a pencil and a piece of paper. You start by dividing the decimal number by the target base (e.g., 2 for binary, 8 for octal, 16 for hexadecimal). Write down the remainder. Now do the same with the quotient, writing the new remainder to the left of that from the previous operation. Keep looping until the quotient is less than the target base. The following table shows the conversion of the decimal number 747 to a hexadecimal notation:

Table 3-2. *A base conversion example*

Operation and Integer Quotient	Remainder (decimal)	Remainder (hex)
747 / 16 = 46	11	B
46 / 16 = 2	14	E
no operation	2	2

Take a look at the table's far-right column. Reading it bottom up, we get $2EB_{16}$, which is exactly 747_{10}.

The same process converts decimal integers to any base.

Converting from a Specified Base to Decimal

It is equally easy to convert a number from a specified base to a decimal notation. First, let's analyze a number in decimal notation, say 276:

$$276 = (6 * 10^0) + (7 * 10^1) + (2 * 10^2) = 6 + 70 + 200$$

Each digit contributes the value `digit * base`$^{\texttt{digitPlaceFromRight}}$, where `digit` is the current digit, `digitPlaceFromRight` is the digit's position (starting at the right-hand side 0 position), and `base` is the current base. The number is equal to the sum of all contributed values. Conversion from a given base to a decimal notation uses the same technique, except that each digit is worth its value in decimal notation. Let's convert 14728 (octal) to a decimal base:

$$(2 * 8^0) + (7 * 8^1) + (4 * 8^2) + (1 * 8^3) = 2 + 56 + 256 + 512 = 826^{10}$$

We use these techniques to create automatic conversion functions later in the book.

Referring to Octal and Hexadecimal Integers

Octal integers have a leading 0 character. Hexadecimal integers have a leading 0x or 0X prefix. Decimal integers are normal integers with no prefixes. So how do we work with these prefixes?

JavaScript refers to all integers as decimal. So if you write 0x2EB, JavaScript stores the number and refers to it as 747 in decimal notation. The same rule applies to octal integers. They are stored, displayed, and handled according to their decimal value. The computer obviously stores them as binary numbers, but to the JavaScript programmer, it seems as if they are handled in decimal form.

Floating-Point Literals

Floating-point numbers (sometimes called *real numbers*) have a fractional part. JavaScript uses a decimal point to distinguish between floating-point numbers and integers. Literally, a number such as 16.0 is a floating-point number, whereas 16 is an integer. Additionally, a floating-point number may include an exponent specification of the form e±exp. Since there is no explicit declaration of data types in JavaScript, the floating-point format is implicitly determined by the literals that are assigned to the variables. Here are some floating-point numbers, with some explanations:

```
-13.3
0.056
4.2e19   // equal to 4.2 * 10_19
-3.1E12  // equal to -3.1 * 10_12
.1e12    // equal to 0.1 * 10_12
2E-12    // equal to 2 * 10_-12
```

Notice that the exponent specification can be in uppercase or lowercase characters.

Floating-point math is much more difficult than integer math and is the source of many bugs. *Overflow* describes the situation in which the exponent of a floating-point number exceeds the upper limit. *Underflow* occurs when the exponent is below the lower one. You should avoid calculations that are likely to result in an overflow or an underflow.

A more common problem with floating-point numbers is the *roundoff error.* Everyone knows that 5 + 5 is 10, but is 1/3 + 1/3 equal to 2/3? The answer is: not always. Take a look at the following to find out why:

1/3 as floating point is 3.333E–1 (rounded off).

2/3 as floating point is 6.667E–1 (rounded off).

```
      3.333E-1
+     3.333E-1
=     6.666E-1
```

As you can see, the result is different from the normal value of 2/3 because 6.666E–1 ≠ 6.667E–1.

Every computer has a similar problem with floating-point values. The fraction 0.2, for example, has no exact binary representation. For this reason, always round off your floating-point values before doing calculations in order to avoid these inaccuracies.

Boolean Literals

Boolean values, also called *logical values,* are basically true or false. They are usually used in conditional expressions and statements. If you are familiar with C++, you probably recognize these terms as 1 and 0, 1 representing true and 0 representing false. JavaScript officially uses the true and false values to express Boolean values, but 1 and 0 are acceptable in most situations. The true value, or 1, can usually be replaced by any nonzero integer. Avoid using these numeric values as Boolean, because Netscape has not officially recognized this kind of usage and may opt to invalidate it in future versions of the browser. Usage of integer values to represent Boolean values, as in other programming languages, can cause data type confusion and should not be done at all by novice programmers.

String Literals

String literals are delimited by either single or double quotes. You must terminate the string with the same type of quote you used to open it, so `"Hi'` is not a legal string in JavaScript. Unlike strings in most programming languages and shells, JavaScript does not distinguish between single and double quotes. They serve exactly the same purposes. Strings in JavaScript are not subject to variable interpolation, i.e., you cannot embed variables directly in the string and expect them to be replaced by the value they hold. Perl, for example, features variable interpolation (or variable substitution) because variables can be identified by the preceding $ character.

The alternative delimiters `q/string/` and `qq/string/` are not supported in JavaScript. You must always use the traditional quotes to delimit strings.

Nested strings are widely used in JavaScript. A nested string consists of a string inside another one. Alternating quotes enables proper interpretation of nested string constructions. The following statement demonstrates how to alternate quote types:

```
document.write("<FONT COLOR='red' SIZE=4>")
```

The `document.write()` statement requires quotes, and so does the `COLOR` attribute of the `<FONT>` tag. You may use single quotes for the string `red` and double quotes for the longer enclosing string. You may also use escape quotes, as explained below.

Be careful to place the trailing quote at the end of the string. If you forget it, the relevant error will be reported only after JavaScript runs into the end of the file or finds a matching quote character in another line. Fortunately, such errors will be detected immediately as syntax errors on the following line. Sometimes, though, the error message does not give any clue about the runaway string, so paying extra attention when dealing with strings is a good strategy.

Strings often include *escape sequences*, also called *escape characters*, *special characters*, or *control characters*. Such sequences have special purposes. For example, `\t` is the tab character. They are usually used to express nonprintable characters or other problematic ones. The following table outlines the escape sequences:

Table 3-3. *Escape sequences in JavaScript*

Escape Sequence	Character	Meaning
\ddd*	0ddd	octal character
\xdd*	0xdd	hexadecimal character
\\	\	backslash
\'	'	single quote
\"	"	double quote
\b	BS	backspace
\f	FF	form feed
\n	NL or LF	new line (or line feed)
\r	CR	carriage return
\t	HT	horizontal tab
\	<new line>	continuation

* The *d* character represents a digit.

Be sure to use these inline characters only where needed. You should use the standard HTML tags for line breaks (`<BR>`) and paragraph breaks (`<P>`). The carriage return escape sequence creates a new line only in dialog boxes and text area objects. Most of the escape sequences act the same way. Do not expect them to format the look of the page, because layout relies solely on HTML.

Here are some strings that take advantage of escape sequences:

```
"\x2499.99" // $99.99 (the hex value of the $ char is 24)
'c:\\games\\sc2000\\' // c:\games\sc2000\
'Let\'s learn JavaScript...' // Let's learn JavaScript...
"line1\rline2"
```

To see the effect of a carriage return character, try displaying the last string in an alert box.

Operators

Every programming language has operators. An *operator* is simply a symbol that tells the compiler (or interpreter) to perform a certain action. The most obvious operators are the math operators. The basic arithmetic operators are common to most programming languages. These are addition (+), subtraction (–), multiplication (*), and division (/). These should be very familiar to most people. The order of precedence of operators follows the standard mathematical rules of multiplication, division, addition, and subtraction. However, when your code has multiple operations in a single line, it is usually a good idea to use parentheses to clarify what you want to occur: 3 * 4/2 + 1 can be ambiguous, whereas 3 * ((4/2) + 1) is very clear.

C, C++, and Java programmers will already be familiar with the increment and decrement operators. The increment operator is formed by placing two plus signs after a variable, such as this:

```
var somenumber
somenumber++
```

This line of code increments the value of `somenumber` by one. Had we written:

```
somenumber--
```

it would have decreased the value by one.

It is very important that you realize that where you place increment and decrement operators is critical. If you place the increment operator after a variable, such as:

```
var somenumber = 10
var someothernumber
someothernumber = somenumber++
```

The assignment operation will take place before the evaluation operation. In other words, first `someothernumber` will be set equal to the value of `somenumber`, then the value of `somenumber` will be incremented. In our example, that means that `someothernumber` will equal 10 and `somenumber` will equal 11. If you wish to rewrite the statement so that the increment takes place first, just reposition the increment sign:

```
someothernumber = ++somenumber
```

In this case, `somenumber` is incremented to 11 and then that value is assigned to `someothernumber`.

You've already learned how to assign a value to a variable or to initialize it using the equal assignment operator. As the following piece of code demonstrates, you can also perform calculations when you assign a value:

```
/* 1 */ var answer
/* 2 */ answer = 4 * 2 + 9
/* 3 */ document.write(answer)
```

Line 1 includes the declaration of the variable `answer`. The second line shows how the variable `answer` is assigned the result of a simple mathematical expression. At this point, the variable holds a value of 17. Referring to the variable `answer` is the same as referring to the number 17. For this reason, the statement on line 3 prints the number 17.

Caution: A very common mistake is to use the single equal sign for equality check. In Visual Basic, for example, "=" is an equality test operator as well as an assignment operator. However, in JavaScript, like in C++ and Java, "=" (the equal sign operator) is an assignment operator, while "==" (two equal signs) is an equality test operator.

This is just a cursory examination of the simplest operators in JavaScript. A thorough discussion of operators is given in Chapter 6. However, your understanding of this chapter and the next two chapters depends on a brief introduction to operators.

Statements

Now that we have thoroughly examined data types, let's look at statements. A *statement* is a line of code that performs some specific task. For example, all of the following are statements:

```
yourAge = 32
for(x=1;x<10,x++)
myname= "Chuck"
```

Multiple Statements

The JavaScript interpreter accepts multiple statements on the same line. If you choose to use this method, you must separate the statements with semicolons (;). The last statement of the line does not have to be followed by a semicolon. Such a line looks like this:

```
statement1; statement2; statement3; ...
```

The browser interprets these statements as if they were listed on separate lines:

```
statement1
statement2
statement3
```

Although this is possible with JavaScript, I certainly do not recommend it. Placing multiple statements on a single line makes for very unreadable code.

Even though JavaScript does not require semicolons after each statement (unless they are on the same line), it does not generate an error if you place them at the end of each statement. So if it is one of your programming habits, you may terminate all statements with semicolons.

```
statement1;
statement2;
statement3;
```

Remember, however, this is not required in JavaScript as it is in C, Java, and C++.

Nested Statements

A *command block* is a unit of statements enclosed by curly braces. It is very important to understand that a block should be used as a single statement. The statements inside the block are called *nested statements*:

```
{
   nested statement1
   nested statement2
   nested statement3
}
```

command block (one statement)

A loop that includes many statements is actually one statement with many nested statements. This rule applies to functions, if-else statements, and other language elements.

Evaluating Expressions

Now that you know how to create a variable, you need to know how to use it. As mentioned earlier, variables hold values of different types. What does "holding a value" mean? This term refers to expression *evaluation*. A variable always evaluates to its value. When you perform an operation on a variable, you are actually performing the operation on the current value associated with the variable. Let's assume you created a variable named `firstNumber` using the following statement:

```
var firstNumber = 120 // declaration and initialization
```

At this point, if you refer to the variable `firstNumber`, its value, 120, is returned. That is, `firstNumber` is evaluated to 120. The following statement outlines an evaluation of `firstNumber`:

```
secondNumber = firstNumber * 6
```

The `secondNumber` variable now holds the value 720, because `firstNumber` evaluates to 120. Bear in mind that no link between the memory locations of the variables is established. Therefore, `secondNumber` now holds a value of 720, which does not change even if the value of `firstNumber` changes. A variable can evaluate to a value of any type (see Table 3-1).

Testing Evaluation

A hidden feature of Netscape Navigator (and several other browsers) enables you to experiment with evaluation in the browser's window. You can reach this window by simply entering `javascript:` in the Location box. Another way to do this is by choosing Open Location from the File menu. Then type `javascript:` to open the evaluation window.

The evaluation window contains two frames. The field in the bottom frame is used to accept your input, and the upper frame displays the Navigator's computation results. To experiment with this tool, enter the following statements at the javascript typein field at the bottom:


```
var firstNumber = 120
var secondNumber = firstNumber - 60
firstNumber
secondNumber
var finalAverage = (firstNumber + secondNumber) / 2
finalAverage
secondNumber = firstNumber
finalAverage
finalAverage > secondNumber
```

Before you enter these expressions, try to figure out what they evaluate to. Then type them in the field in the bottom frame, with a carriage return (Enter) after each statement.

Functions

Function Definition

Functions are groupings of statements organized in a block with a common name. Good functions work to perform a single goal. For example, a function might calculate the monthly payments on a mortgage given a certain principal and interest rate. Just like variables, you must define a function before you can call it.

Functions are defined using the keyword `function`, followed by the name of the function. The same rules that apply to variable names apply to functions. Since a function usually does something besides storing a value, it is common to include a verb in its name. The function's parameters are written in brackets after the name. A command block follows the parameters. The syntax of a function definition is:

```
function functionName([parameters])
{
   [statements]
}
```

Parameters are local variables that are assigned values when the function is called. Essentially a parameter is the raw materials the function will process. In our earlier example of a function that calculates mortgage payments, the principal and interest rate would be parameters for that function. Another word you will often hear used for parameters is *argument*. Arguments and parameters are synonymous in programming. At this point, you should always give a name to every parameter.

In a formal syntax specification, the square brackets ([]) usually denote optional elements. Since a function does not have to have parameters or statements, both are enclosed in such brackets. The curly braces enclosing the function body can be placed anywhere following the parameter section. The following functions are valid:

```
function functionName([parameters]) {[statement1]; [statement2]; ...}
```

```
function functionName([parameters])
{
   [statement1]
   [statement2]
}
```

The following example demonstrates a function declaration:

```
<HTML>
<HEAD>
<SCRIPT LANGUAGE="JavaScript">
function square(number)
{
   document.write("The call passed ",
                  number, // the function's parameter
                  " to the function.<BR>",
                  number, // the function's parameter
                  " square is ",
                  number * number,
                  ".<BR>")
}
// *** add function call
</SCRIPT>
</HEAD>
<BODY>
</BODY>
</HTML>
```

Example 3-2 (ex3-2.htm). *A function definition (deferred code)*

Example 3-2 does not print anything to the browser's window, nor does it generate any other form of output. The reason is that the function is only defined in the script but is never called. When the browser locates a function, it loads its statements into memory, ready to be executed later.

Calling Functions

In order to execute the set of statements located in the function block, you must call the function. The syntax of a function call is:

```
functionName([arguments])
```

By adding the statement `square(5)` to Example 3-2, at the specified place, we call the function. The statements in the function are executed, and the following message is output:

```
The call passed 5 to the function.
5 square is 25.
```


You can also call a function from within another function, as the following example demonstrates:

```
<HTML>
<HEAD>
<TITLE>Calling a function from within another function</TITLE>
<SCRIPT LANGUAGE="JavaScript">
function makeBar()
{
   var output = "<HR ALIGN='left' WIDTH=400>"
   document.write(output)
}
function makeHeader(text, color, size)
{
   var output = "<FONT COLOR='" + color + "' SIZE=" +
                size + ">" + text + "</FONT>"
   document.write(output)
   makeBar()
}
makeHeader("JavaScript Examples", "red", "+4")
</SCRIPT>
</HEAD>
<BODY>
</BODY>
</HTML>
```

Example 3-3 (ex3-3.htm). *A function call in a function block*

Example 3-3 summarizes many of the terms discussed in this chapter. It includes two function definitions. In both functions, the output is assigned to a variable (output) and then printed to the client window using the `document.write()` method. Assigning strings to variables before printing them is extremely useful when the string is long (i.e., you want to print a lot of data). You can see the result of Example 3-3 in Figure 3-2.

Figure 3-2. *Example 3-3 output*

Control Structures

Dialog Boxes

Before we discuss the control structures in JavaScript, we need some basic user-interaction devices. These will allow us to create both useful and helpful examples for demonstration purposes. Dialog boxes are only introduced in this chapter. They will be discussed later in further detail.

JavaScript provides the ability to create small windows called *dialog boxes*. You can create alert boxes, confirm boxes, and even prompt boxes. These boxes let you generate output and receive input from the user.

Alert Boxes

An alert box is the most simple dialog box. It enables you to display a short message to the user in a separate window. Take a look at the following script and its corresponding output:

```
alert("Click OK to continue...")
```

The generic form of this function is `alert(`*`message`*`)`. The function `alert()` is actually a method of the `window` object. It is not necessary to specify that because `window` is the default object. The same applies to all dialog boxes.

You can also display messages using data structures. For example:

```
var message = "Click OK to continue"
alert(message)
```

As you can see, the alert box is often used to pause the execution of a script until the user approves its continuation.

Confirm Boxes

Confirm boxes are different from alert boxes in that they evaluate to a value based on a decision made by the user. Rather than a simple OK button, the confirm box includes both OK and Cancel buttons.

Like the alert box, `confirm` is also a method of the `window` object. This method returns a Boolean value, because there are two options. You can use confirmation boxes to ask the user a yes-or-no question, or to confirm an action. Here is an example:

```
var reply = confirm("OK to continue?")
```

`reply` is assigned a true value if the user chooses OK, and false if the user selects Cancel.

The generic form of this function is `confirm(message)`.

Prompt Boxes

The `prompt()` method displays a prompt dialog box with a message and an input field. You can use these boxes to receive input from the user. It is similar to the confirm box, except that it returns the value of the input field, rather than true or false. Here is an example:

```
var name = prompt("Enter your name:", "anonymous")
```

The method returns a value of null if the user chooses Cancel. Figure 3-3 shows a typical prompt box.

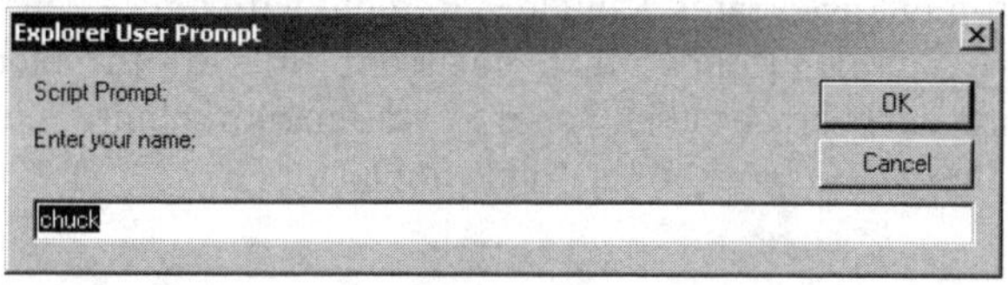

Figure 3-3. *The prompt box*

Chapter 3

The value of the field is always a string. If the user enters 16 in the form, the string `"16"` is returned rather than the number 16. When you want to prompt the user for a number, you must convert the input into a numeric value. JavaScript features a built-in function that does this—`parseInt()`. You can use the following statement to ask the user for a number:

```
var number = parseInt(prompt("Enter a number:", 0))
```

or

```
var number = prompt("Enter a number:", 0)
number = parseInt(number)
```

The generic form of this function is `prompt(message[, inputDefault])`.

You can see that this function works by using the `typeof` operator for testing:

```
var number = prompt("Enter a number:", 0)
alert(number + " is a " + typeof(number)) // "... is a string"
number = parseInt(number)
alert(number + " is a " + typeof(number)) // "... is a number"
```

The input must be of a numeric type, of course (e.g., 99).

Conditional Statements

Conditional statements are key to all programming languages. They allow your program (or script in this case) to execute different code segments based on varying conditions.

if Statement

```
if (condition)
   statement
```

The `if` statement lets you put decision making in your scripts. A script without any decisions does the same procedure each time it is executed. Such linear structures limit your scripts to simple algorithms. JavaScript enables decision making using an `if` statement. `if` statements associate a single statement with a true condition. That statement is only executed if the conditional expression is true; otherwise, it is not executed at all. The condition must evaluate to a Boolean value: true or false. Numeric values are also acceptable as an alternative to a Boolean condition. 0 is equivalent to false, and all other values are equivalent to true.

The `if` statement associates a single statement with a true condition. A statement can be anything from a simple `document.write()` to a block of statements, using curly braces ({}). Some `if` statements require multiple statements, so they use a block in the following form:

```
if (condition)
{
   statement1
   statement2
   statement3
}
```

A nested statement can be any legal statement, including an additional `if` statement. Here is a simple example demonstrating the `if` statement:

```
<HTML>
<HEAD>
<TITLE>A simple if statement</TITLE>
<SCRIPT LANGUAGE="JavaScript">
<!--
var age = parseInt(prompt("Please enter your age:", 15))
if (age < 21)
   alert("Sorry, you are too young to enter")
// -->
</SCRIPT>
</HEAD>
<BODY>
</BODY>
</HTML>
```

Example 3-4 (ex3-4.htm). *A script with one conditional statement*

At first, the script asks the user for his or her age.

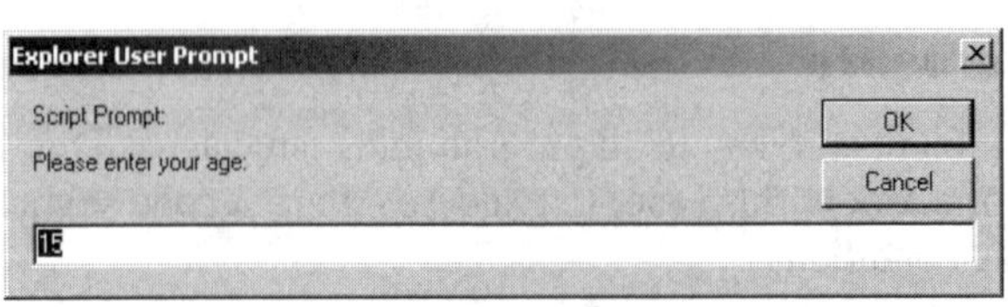

Figure 3-4. *A prompt box that requests the user's age*

The age is stored in numeric format in the variable `age`. The `if` statement checks if the user's age is less than 21. If so, the expression `age < 21` evaluates to true. Because the condition is true, the next statement is executed, and an alert box is displayed. Note that if the value of `age` is greater than or equal to 21, no statements are executed. The remedy to this problem is presented in the next section.

Here is another example using multiple statements associated with a true condition:

```
<HTML>
<HEAD>
<TITLE>An if statement with a command block</TITLE>
<SCRIPT LANGUAGE="JavaScript">
<!--
var name = prompt("Enter your name:", "John Doe")
// draw a horizontal rule of the specified width
function drawRule(width)
{
   document.write("<HR WIDTH=" + width + "%>")
}
var message = "Click OK if you are using Netscape 3.0 or above, or Internet
               Explorer 4.0 or above"
if (!confirm(message))
{
   document.write("<CENTER><B>")
   document.write("Hello " + name + "!<BR>")
   drawRule(50)
   document.write("Please download the latest ",
                  "version of Netscape Navigator or Internet Explorer")
   document.write("</B></CENTER>")
}
// -->
</SCRIPT>
</HEAD>
<BODY>
</BODY>
</HTML>
```

Example 3-5 (ex3-5.htm). *A conditional statement associated with a command block*

If you enter this code properly into your editor and view the web page in either Netscape or Internet Explorer, you should see something similar to Figure 3-5 or Figure 3-6.

Figure 3-5. *A prompt box that requests the user's name*

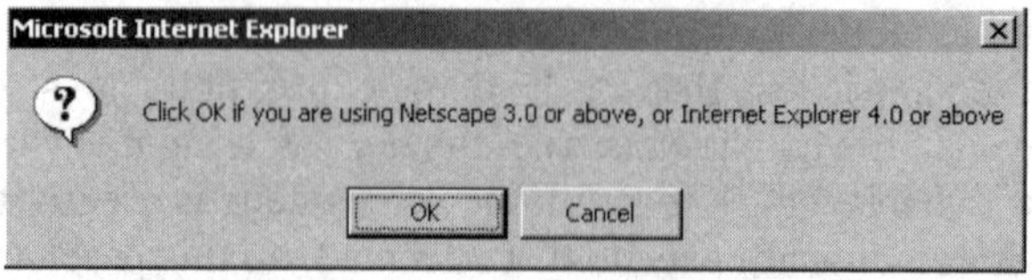

Figure 3-6. *A confirm box verifying the browser version number*

Example 3-5 features an `if` statement with a set of statements grouped together in a command block. Notice the function that prints a horizontal rule of a specified width. In this example, the user must reply to two dialog boxes. If the user responds by clicking Cancel to the confirm dialog box, the page looks like this:

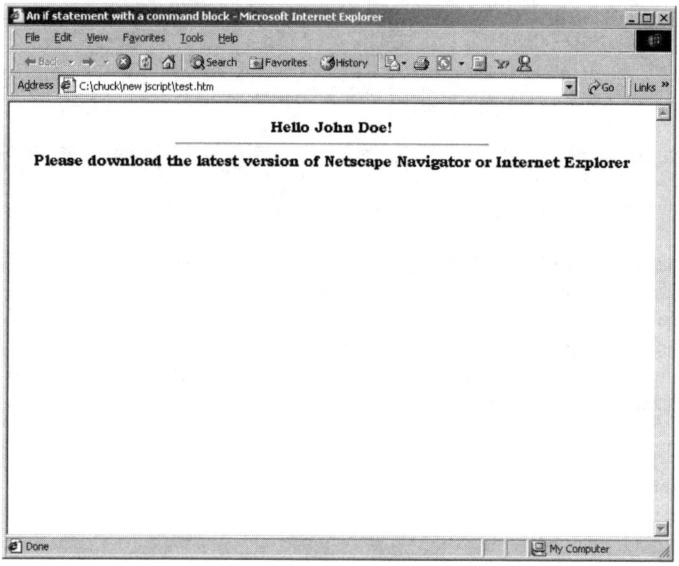

Figure 3-7. *JavaScript-generated HTML content that depends on the user's input*

else Statement

```
if (condition)
   statement1
else
   statement2
```

You might feel limited with the structure of the `if` statement, because it only lets you execute a statement when the condition is true. The additional `else` statement specifies a statement that is executed when the condition is false. This construction covers all possibilities, because a condition can be either true or false. Here is a script segment extracted from Example 3-4 and improved with an `else` statement:

```
var age = parseInt(prompt("Please enter your age:", 120))
if (age < 21)
   alert("Sorry, you are too young to enter")
else
   alert("Welcome in...")
```

If the user's age is greater than 21, he receives a welcoming message.

Nested if-else Statements

An `if` statement can execute any legal statement. Obviously, a simple `if` statement meets this requirement. Statements inside a command block are called *nested statements*.

Consider the following function:

```
function testChar(ch)
{
   if (ch >= "A" && ch <= "Z")
      alert("An uppercase letter")
   else
      if (ch >= "a" && ch <= "z")
         alert("A lowercase letter")
      else
         alert("Not a letter")
}
```

The function accepts a character (a one-character string) as its argument. If the character is greater than A and less than Z, it must be an uppercase letter, and an appropriate message is displayed. Only if the character is not an uppercase letter does the execution continue. If it is a lowercase letter, the appropriate message is provided. Once again, only if it is not a lowercase letter (meaning it is not a letter at all) does the execution proceed. No more tests are performed, so the last message is generated.

This function demonstrates simple nested `if-else` statements. Only if the condition is false does the execution continue. If, for example, `ch` is `"H"`, only the first expression is evaluated. The message "An uppercase letter" is displayed, and the other tests are not performed.

Although it is not required, try to put the condition that is most likely to be true as the top condition. If the condition is true, the other tests are not even performed. Such a practice will make your scripts more efficient, especially if the tests are complex.

C++ requires a semicolon after the first statement (*statement1*). JavaScript is friendly—it lets you choose.

```
   statement1
else
   if (switchingVariable == value2)
      statement2
   else
      if (switchingVariable == value3)
         statement3
      else
         statement4 // default case
```

Chapter 3

Loop Statements

Loops are control structures that perform a set of actions more than once. Everyone agrees that a computer can calculate faster than a human. Using loops you can repeat calculations and take advantage of the computer's ability to do them faster. Theoretically, a loop repeats only one statement. However, you already know that a statement can be a block of statements, allowing the repetition of many statements or perhaps the whole program. JavaScript features two basic loop types:

- The `for` loop
- The `while` loop

Each loop type has its own advantages. However, the `for` loop is the most commonly used loop, and thus we will focus primarily on it in this chapter.

for Statement

```
for ([initialExpression;] [condition;] [operation])
   statement
```

Because a loop usually repeats more than one statement, you use a command block in the following format:

```
for ([initialExpression;] [condition;] [operation])
{
   statements
}
```

`initialExpression` is usually a statement or a variable declaration. It should evaluate to a single value and is typically used to initialize a counter variable. This expression may optionally declare new variables with the `var` keyword.

`condition` is a condition that is evaluated before each successive pass through the loop. The statement is executed only if the condition evaluates to true.

`operation` is a statement that is executed after each consecutive pass through the loop's body. It is typically used to update or increment the `counter` variable, which counts the number of passes through the loop.

Consider the following looping script fragment:

```
var number1 = 1
var number2 = 1
for (var counter = 1; counter <= 10; counter++)
{
   document.write(number1 + " ")
   number2 = number2 + number1
   number1 = number2 – number1
}
```

This piece of code prints the first ten numbers of the Fibonacci sequence. The Fibonacci sequence is a sequence of numbers that is commonly used in computer science and is intriguing from a mathematical point of view because of certain natural phenomena that exhibit a Fibonacci sequence. The Fibonacci sequence includes the following numbers:

1 1 2 3 5 8 13 21 34 55 89 144 . . . ($f_1 = 1, f_2=1, f_x = f_{x-1} + f_{x-2}$)

Each number is equal to the sum of the two preceding numbers. The first two numbers are both equal to 1.

Take a look at the script. `number1` and `number2` are initialized to 1, because $f_1 = 1$ and $f_2=1$. The `for` statement prints the numbers in the Fibonacci sequence. The initial expression of the loop is `var counter = 1`, which declares the loop counter and initializes its value to 1. The condition `counter <= 10` means that the loop executes while the value of `counter` is less than or equal to 10. Note that the condition is evaluated only at the end of the loop. Incrementing the value of the loop counter is the action in this example, and is typical of `for` loops. In short, this loop's attributes cause it to execute exactly ten times. The net effect is that it computes and prints the first ten numbers of the Fibonacci sequence.

Understanding the content of the loop is just plain math. After the current number is printed, `number2` is assigned the sum of its two preceding numbers in the sequence. `number1` should hold the value of `number2` before the assignment statement. The following explains how this is done (`number2'` is the value of `number2` before the assignment statement):

```
number1 = number2 – number1 == (number2' + number1) – number1 ==
number2'
```

Although you do not need to associate a command block with a loop if its body consists of only one statement, it is a common practice in this book. The `counter` variable is a regular variable. Its value can change during the execution of the loop.

You can create infinite executing loops with the `for` statement. The `break` statement, which is discussed later, makes such loops meaningful by providing a way to terminate their execution. The basic structure of an infinite loop is:

```
for ( ; ; )
   statement
```

You can also create nested `for` loops. The following loop prints a rectangle of asterisks (25 x 10):

```
for (var i = 1; i <= 10; i++)
{
   for (var j = 1; j <= 25; j++)
   {
      document.write("*")
   }
   document.write("<BR>")
}
```

while Statement

Here is the basic structure of the `while` loop:

```
while (condition)
   {
   ...statements...
   }
```

As you can see it is actually a bit simpler than the `for` loop. There is no loop counter, nor need to increment that loop counter. However, it can also be a problem since it is quite easy to accidentally get into an infinite loop.

Here is an example using the `while` loop:

```
<SCRIPT LANGUAGE="javascript">
var i = 0;
do
{
document.write("Testing Do-While loop");
}
while(i! = 0)
</SCRIPT>
```

You can do almost all the looping you need with a `for` loop, but it is important that you realize the `while` loop is there and available to you should you choose to use it.

Summary

This chapter is a pivotal chapter, and a rather long one. It provided you with all the fundamentals of JavaScript. Before you can continue with all the interesting things we will be doing in later chapters, it is critical that you master the concepts in this chapter. If you are not totally comfortable with this material, it is probably a good idea to reread it. You might also want to experiment with the examples, changing them slightly so that you will understand the elements of those examples better.

Chapter 4
Object-Oriented Programming

Objects

Object-oriented concepts are everywhere in modern programming. If you have worked with .NET (C# or VB .NET), C++, or Java, then you should already be familiar with objects and object-oriented programming. If you are not, then this chapter will both introduce you to that topic conceptually and show you how to use it in JavaScript.

An *object* is a programming abstraction that groups data with the code that operates on it. All programs contain data of different types. Variables, as well as functions, were introduced separately in the previous chapter. I defined functions, and I defined variables, but I did not connect them in any way. An object encapsulates related data and functions into a single cohesive unit.

Originally in procedural programming (Cobol, C, Basic, etc.), code and data were kept apart. For example, in the C language, units of code are called functions, while units of data are known as structures. Functions and structures are not formally connected in C. A C function can operate on numerous data structures, and more than one function can operate on the same structure. In *object-oriented* (OO) and *object-based* programming, code and data are merged into an object, which is a single indivisible "object."

An *object* is simply data and the functions that work on that data placed together in a single package. Objects typically have both properties that are represented by variables, and methods that are essentially functions that are part of the object.

Properties

Any physical object has its own unique characteristics. A car, for example, has a size, a weight, a model, a color, a price, and many other attributes. The full set of attributes distinguishes a car from all other objects. These features are called *properties* or *fields* in the OO (object-oriented) vernacular. An object's property stores data related to the object.

Properties are usually named according to their meaning. For instance, a property that holds the color of the car would be named `color`. It is possible to extend an object by adding new properties to it; this was first supported by Netscape Navigator 3.0. Although it is possible to add new properties to an existing object, it is not always possible to modify the value of a static built-in object. For example, the `PI` property of the `Math` object cannot be modified, for obvious reasons.

JavaScript supports two different types of objects:

- Predefined built-in objects, such as the `Math` object
- User-defined objects

An object can also be a property of another object, thus creating an object hierarchy. An object hierarchy is essentially an object that has other objects as parts of it. The object models of most applications, including Microsoft Office, are constructed in a hierarchy.

Figure 4-1 illustrates an object hierarchy, similar to a family tree. A is only an object, while D, E, F, G, and H are only properties. B and C are both objects and properties, and therefore they are located between the other levels of the hierarchy.

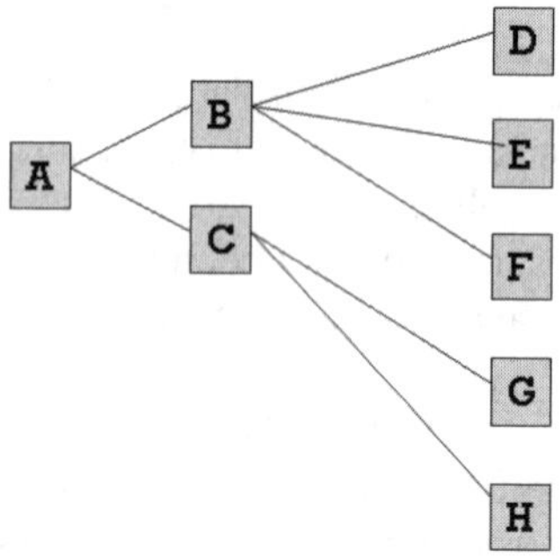

Figure 4-1. *Object hierarchy*

Syntax

An object's properties hold its data. Obviously you will want to refer to that data at some point, either to put new data in or to get out what the object's property contains. You can refer to properties using the following syntax:

```
objectReference.propertyName
```

`objectReference` is the name of the object that the property belongs to, or any other valid reference to the object. For example, you can assign an object to a variable and then refer to its properties using this variable, followed by the property specification. *`propertyName`* is the name of the property (data field).

A dot separates each object from its property. A hierarchical object structure, with objects and properties at different levels, uses the same syntax:

```
object1.object2Property1.object3Property2.property3
```

Notice that all the elements in the middle are both objects and properties. Referring again to Figure 4-1, let's assume that the elements of the structure have the following values:

```
d ⇒ 16
e ⇒ 42
f ⇒ true
g ⇒ "king"
h ⇒ 13
i ⇒ 10
```

The following statements demonstrate referencing elements of a hierarchical object structure:

```
var tempVar = ""
tempVar = a.b.d
document.write(tempVar) // prints 16
tempVar = a.b.e
document.write(tempVar) // prints 42
tempVar = a.c.f
document.write(tempVar) // prints true
tempVar = a.c.g
document.write(tempVar) // prints king
tempVar = a.c.h
document.write(tempVar) // prints 13
tempVar = a.c.i
document.write(tempVar) // prints 10
```

Another important concept is that a property belongs to an object, and to only one object. Different objects may have properties of the same name and type, but they are not the same property. Even though two different people might own identical high-definition televisions, the televisions are still separate entities. That is, the same location in memory cannot be associated with two different objects. A property must always be associated with an object. Therefore, the following statements are legal:

```
var d = a.b.d
document.write(d) // prints 16
var e = a.b.e
document.write(e) // prints 42
var f = a.c.f
document.write(f) // prints true
var g = a.c.g
document.write(g) // prints king
var h = a.c.h
document.write(h) // prints 13
var i = a.c.i
document.write(i) // prints 10
```

As you can see, a variable may be named exactly like a property of an object. This is possible because properties are not of the same scope as variables. However, a variable cannot have the same name as an object at the same level. For example, the statement `var a = a.b.d` is not valid (actually it is valid, but the value of a is lost). The main object is at the same scope of the variable because they are not properties of any other object. As a matter of fact, an object is a variable, and two variables that have the exact same name are associated with the same location in memory. The statement `var a = a.b.d` converts a to a simple variable containing the value 16, and not an object. It is generally a good practice to avoid naming variables by an object's property or method, at least until you feel comfortable with objects and properties.

The output of the statement `document.write(a)` might be `[object create]` because that is the object's string equivalent.

Methods

Properties hold the data of an object, and methods are what execute the actions of an object. If you think about it for just a moment you will realize that *method* is just another word for a function, if that function is part of an object. During execution of a JavaScript script, an object may invoke one or more methods to accomplish a task. As you know, objects consist of both data (properties) and functions that handle the data. These functions are called methods. Methods enable an object to perform different actions, mostly on its own properties.

Methods, as previously stated, are simply functions that are part of the object. However, since they are part of the object they have access to the properties of the object, including private properties that cannot otherwise be accessed.

Most advantages of OOP (object-oriented programming) are associated with methods. JavaScript does not completely support external libraries (other than the `SRC` attribute of the `<SCRIPT>` tag), so the following features apply mostly to built-in objects:

- Because an object encapsulates related data and functions (methods) into a single cohesive unit, it is easy to perform maintenance activities.
- Every language paradigm influences its application design. Therefore, scripts developed in JavaScript often make use of objects. Although you can design your scripts in a traditional procedural way, you will find it a great deal easier to use objects and methods. You will notice the difference between the traditional style and the OO style as soon as you start writing complex scripts.

JavaScript's implementation of objects is not as powerful as that of Java, C++, or .NET, so some OO programming advantages that apply to Java do not apply to JavaScript.

Syntax

A method can exist at different levels of an object's hierarchy. You can invoke a method using the same syntax you use to reference a property, i.e., the "dot" syntax. Methods are actually functions associated with objects. Therefore, they resemble functions in many aspects. A method is called in the following fashion:

```
objectReference.methodName([arguments])
```

objectReference is the name of the object, or any other reference. *methodName* is the name of the method, and *arguments* are the arguments that the method accepts.

Because a method is a function, the name of the method is always followed by a pair of parentheses. This rule also applies to methods that do not accept arguments.

You probably find this syntax familiar. We have been using `document.write ([expression])` to print HTML expressions to the page. `write()` is a method belonging to the built-in `document` object.

Using the Array Notation

You can refer to properties and methods using either the "dot" syntax or the array notation. In array notation, square brackets replace the dots. For example, the following expression refers to `a.b.d`:

```
a["b"]["d"]
```

You can use the array notation for both properties and methods. The general syntax is:

```
objectReference["propertyName"]
objectReference["methodName"]([arguments])
```

It is important to understand this alternative syntax, because you cannot always use the traditional dot syntax. For example, the first character of a property name cannot be a digit when using the dot syntax. When you create an array using the built-in `Array` object, you can only refer to the elements of the array via the array notation (e.g., `myArray[0]`, `myArray[99]`). You must always use double quotes when you refer to a property of an object that is not an array. Here are some examples for using the array notation to reference methods and properties:

```
document["write"]("hello!")
window["alert"]("howdy!") // note: alert() == window.alert()
Math["PI"]
```

Sometimes you can only use the array notation. Suppose the variable `str` holds the string `"write"`. You can use the following syntax instead of `document.write()`:

```
document[str]()
```

However, you cannot use `document.str()` because that is equivalent to `document["str"]()`. Another situation in which you should use the array notation is when you want to name a property not according to the identifier rules. For example, `myObject["*"]` is possible only with the array notation. When you use the array notation, the value in the square brackets should be a string, because the content is evaluated.

Object Oriented vs. Object Based

JavaScript is based on a simple object-oriented paradigm. This paradigm is often called object based, as opposed to object oriented. If you are used to a truly object-oriented language such as C#, Java, or C++, you will find much of that functionality is missing in JavaScript. For example, classes do not exist in JavaScript (all objects belong to one "class"), nor do packages (because a package groups classes together). The object hierarchy in JavaScript is a containment hierarchy, not an inheritance hierarchy as in Java and C++. That is, an object does not inherit from other objects, but it can be contained by another object if it is a property of that object. Most object-oriented languages require static resolution of objects at compile time. If all this talk of inheritance hierarchies seems foreign to you, don't worry. The purpose of this section is to explain to readers who are used to true object-oriented programming what is not available to them in JavaScript.

However, an object-oriented language may require dynamic method bindings because polymorphism allows multiple definitions of methods sharing a common name. Calling such polymorphic methods often cannot be resolved until run time. JavaScript is completely based on dynamic binding. That is, object references are checked at run time. There are many other differences between the object paradigm in JavaScript and the one in full object-oriented languages (such as Java and C++).

Summary

This chapter discussed the basics of object-based programming, based on JavaScript's object model. Its purpose is to introduce you to general object-oriented and object-based terminology and to a bit of JavaScript syntax. Every language paradigm heavily influences the design of applications in that language. Therefore, scripts written in JavaScript are typically object-based systems. Procedural scripting is possible in JavaScript, but object-based scripting has many advantages. Because JavaScript has a large set of built-in objects, including very useful methods and properties, a basic understanding of the object structure is necessary. If you are a beginner and find objects difficult to understand, don't be too concerned. I promise that you will understand these concepts as we move on, mostly by studying examples.

Chapter 5

Functions and Variable Scope

Variable Scope and Storage Class

Remember that JavaScript is a programming language, and as such, it shares certain characteristics common to all programming languages. The concepts of variables and functions are two such shared characteristics. A *variable* is basically a segment of memory set aside to hold data. That memory segment is referenced by a name that you assign, thus allowing you to put things into it and take them out when you wish.

All JavaScript variables have two attributes:

- Scope
- Storage class

JavaScript implements these characteristics slightly differently than other programming languages, but the concepts are similar. As we will see in this book, the attribute of scope is the most important of the two.

Variable Scope

The *scope* of a variable describes the area of the script where the variable is valid. You can refer to the variable only in this area—it does not exist elsewhere. The scope of a global variable is the entire script. You can access it anywhere between the `<SCRIPT>` and `</SCRIPT>` tags and in other scripts that are executed after the variable definition (including preceding event handler scripts). In JavaScript, you can declare global variables with or without the keyword `var`. It does not affect the scope of the variable at all.

A *local variable* is declared in a function. It can only be referenced by statements inside that function. Therefore, a global variable may have the same name as a given local variable. In the scope of a local variable (the function where it is defined), only the local variable exists. Outside that function, only the global one exists. A local variable must be declared inside a function using the keyword `var`. If the keyword is omitted, the variable is assumed to be global. The following script segments show how a variable's scope influences various results:

```
// Script 1
function test()
{
   age = 43
}
age = 11
test()
document.write(age + "<BR>")
```

```
// Script 2
function test()
{
   var age = 43
}
age = 11
test()
document.write(age + "<BR>")
```

The only difference between these scripts is the statement inside the function. In the second script segment, we use `var` to define the variable `age`, whereas in the first statement we simply state the desired variable name.

The output of the first script is:

```
43
```

and the output of the second script is:

```
11
```

Take another look at the first script and try following the execution thread. The value `11` is assigned to the global variable `age` and the function is invoked. Notice that the word `var` is not used inside the function. Therefore, the variable `age` in the function is assumed to be global, and the value `43` is assigned to the global `age`. Thus, the result is `43`.

In the second script, we assign the value `11` to the variable `age`, and then call the function. The `var` keyword means that the variable `age`, which is defined inside the function, is local. It does not exist beyond the function, so the value of the global variable `age` (the one defined before the function call) is not modified by the assignment statement inside the function. The last statement of the script prints the value of the global variable `age`, because it is the only variable named `age` in that scope. Therefore, the script's output is 11—the global variable's initial value.

Once declared with the `var` keyword, additional statements referring to the variable should not use that prefix. The `var` tells JavaScript that you are about to declare a variable. After that, you have already declared the variable and don't need the keyword `var` any more. Here is the previous script with an additional statement inside the function:

```
// Script 2 (additional statement in function)
function test()
```

```
{
    var age = 43
    age = 58
}
age = 11
test()
document.write(age + "<BR>")
```

Once again, the output of the script is `11`. The variable inside the function is declared with the keyword `var`. From that point on, the scope of the variable is only the function `test()`. It does not exist outside the boundaries of that function, so the script's output is the value of the global variable named `age`, not the local one. It is absolutely critical that you keep the concept of scope in mind. A variable only exists, and can only be used, within the scope with which it was defined.

Note that the statement:

```
age = 11
```

in the previous script segment is equivalent to:

```
var age = 11
```

because the `var` keyword is optional for global variables.

Here's another script segment that deals with various scopes:

```
function test()
{
    age = 5
}
test()
document.write(age + "<BR>")
```

The script's output is 5, because the variable `age` is declared inside the function as global (without `var`), so its scope is the entire script. The next script generates quite an unexpected output:

```
function test()
{
    var age = 5
}
test()
document.write(age + "<BR>")
```

Rather than generating an output, this script generates an error because `age` is a local variable and the printing statement is not located in its scope.

Variable Storage Class

The variable's storage class is a bit more complicated than scope. But the good news is that if you want, you can ignore this attribute and JavaScript will just use defaults. In fact, many people use JavaScript on a regular basis and are not even aware that there is a storage class attribute for a variable.

The variable's storage class may be either permanent or temporary. You cannot modify this attribute directly the way you can declare the variable as static in other languages such as C# or C++. The storage class of a variable in JavaScript depends only on its scope. Local variables are temporary, while global variables are permanent. Permanent variables exist throughout the script and even in other scripts. Even after a script has terminated, the global variable remains, and is only discarded when the page unloads. Temporary variables are allocated on the *stack* (a section of memory) when a function is called. The space used by a function's local (temporary) variable is returned to the stack at the end of the function execution. After a local variable "dies," it leaves free memory space for other variables and objects to come.

Avoid declaring large local data structures such as arrays (discussed in later chapters). If you try to allocate too many temporary variables or extremely large ones, you are likely to receive an error (usually called *stack overflow*). For the same reason, avoid passing large data structures to a function. It is better to use global variables for such tasks.

Function Parameters

Function parameters are identical to local variables. They exist only inside the function, and do not affect any variable outside it. You can refer to function parameters as if they were variables that you declared at the beginning of the function and initialized with appropriate values. The following script segment demonstrates this:

```
function test(age)
{
   age = 5
   document.write(age + "<BR>")
}
test(6)
```

The printed value is 5, because it is assigned to the variable `age` (which is the function's parameter).

JavaScript lacks a couple of features found in other languages:

- A function's parameter cannot behave as a global variable.
- Nested functions, such as those in Pascal, are not supported. You cannot declare a function inside another one.

Take a look at the following script. (Note that the line numbers are for your benefit; you would not have line numbers in a real script.)

```
/* 1  */  function goFirst(pineapple)
/* 2  */  {
/* 3  */     var banana = 3
/* 4  */     pineapple = 6
/* 5  */     apple = 4
/* 6  */     goSecond()
/* 7  */     var peach = goThird()
/* 8  */     document.write(apple + "<BR>")
```

```
/* 9  */ }
/* 10 */ function goSecond()
/* 11 */ {
/* 12 */    var apple = 2
/* 13 */    document.write(apple + "<BR>")
/* 14 */ }
/* 15 */ function goThird() {
/* 16 */       var peach = apple
/* 17 */       document.write(peach + "<BR>")
/* 18 */       return peach
/* 19 */ }
/* 20 */ var pineapple = 8
/* 21 */ goFirst(5)
/* 22 */ document.write("apple = " + apple)
/* 23 */ document.write(", pineapple = " + pineapple)
```

As you can see, it is impossible to construct scripts without a deep understanding of variable scopes and storage classes.

The output of the preceding script is:

```
2
4
4
apple = 4, pineapple = 8
```

Table 5-1 keeps track of the variables' values throughout the course of the script execution.

Table 5-1. *A classic table to keep track of variable values*

Line Number	pineapple	apple	banana	peach
20	8 (g)			
1	8 (g)			
	5 (goFirst)			
3	8 (g)		3 (goFirst)	
	5 (goFirst)			
4	8 (g)		3 (goFirst)	
	6 (goFirst)			
5	8 (g)	4 (g)	3 (goFirst)	
	6 (goFirst)			
12	8 (g)	4 (g)	3 (goFirst)	
	6 (goFirst)	2 (goSecond)		
16	8 (g)	4 (g)	3 (goFirst)	4 (goThird)
	6 (goFirst)			
7	8 (g)	4 (g)	3 (goFirst)	4 (goFirst)
	6 (goFirst)			
22	8 (g)	4 (g)		

(g) stands for global, (*functionName*) stands for local in the function named *functionName*.

This technique is very useful because JavaScript does not have a decent debugger. You can find some third-party tools used for editing and debugging JavaScript, but you have to go search for them and they have varying levels of efficacy. Make sure you understand every value in the table. If you don't have much programming background, Table 5-1 might seem confusing. However, all you must do to use the table is locate the line where the printing statements are placed and extract the variables' values from the table. For example, suppose you want to find what the statement prints on Line 13. The last line expressed in the table before Line 13 is Line 12. We are trying to find out what the value of `apple` is, so you should first check to see if there is a local variable with the corresponding name, because a local variable rules if it exists. As you can see, the value of the local variable `apple` is `2`. Therefore, JavaScript prints that value on Line 13, followed by a line break.

The following script's output might surprise you a little:

```
var num = 4
function funct1()
{
   alert(num)
   var num = 2
}
funct1()
```

The output of this script is illustrated in Figure 5-1:

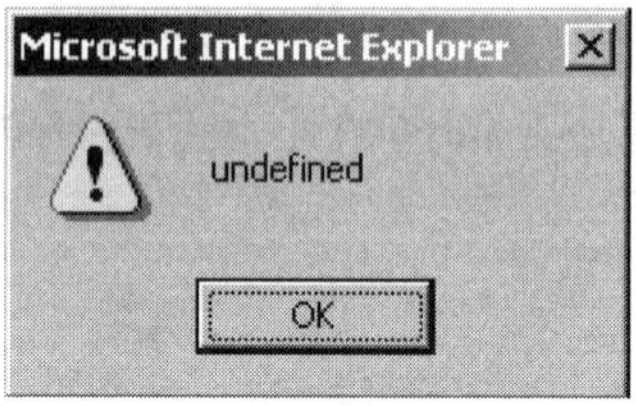

Figure 5-1. *The "undefined" alert box*

The term "undefined" means that a variable does not have a value at the desired point, although it has previously been declared. Generally speaking, JavaScript scans the entire script before any execution begins. During this scan, also called *parsing*, JavaScript evaluates each line of code, testing it for basic syntax errors. It also determines the scope of each variable, regardless of whether or not it is in a function. If it encounters a variable declaration with the keyword `var`, that variable is considered local, even if a global variable with the same name exists. A variable's scope can be either the entire script or just one function. In the preceding script segment, a global variable `num` is declared by initializing it to `4`. The function consists of one local variable declaration. Note that the variable `num` inside the function has no connection to the global variable `num`. The function is executed, as usual, from top to bottom. The first statement instructs JavaScript to display the value of `num`, the local variable inside the function. JavaScript already knows that the local variable is declared inside the function, so it does not generate an error. However, at that point, the variable does not retain any value, so it is undefined.

The following definitions of a function are equivalent:

```
// #1
function functionName
{
   [JavaScript statements...]
   var varName = initialValue
   [JavaScript statements...]
}
```

```
// #2
function functionName
{
   var varName
   [JavaScript statements...]
   varName = initialValue
   [JavaScript statements...]
}
```

Some programmers find it easier to use the second form. Each form has its own advantages and disadvantages, so you should choose the one that is most convenient for you. In this book, we use the first form because we prefer to use the `var` keyword in an assignment statement.

If you declare global variables inside a function, you must assign an initial value to the variable; otherwise, JavaScript returns an error. The following script segment and screen capture demonstrate this fact:

```
function foo()
{
   // local variable declarations
   var a          // without initialization
   var b = 0      // with initialization
   // global variable declarations
   c              // without initialization - error!
   d = 0          // with initialization
}
foo()
```

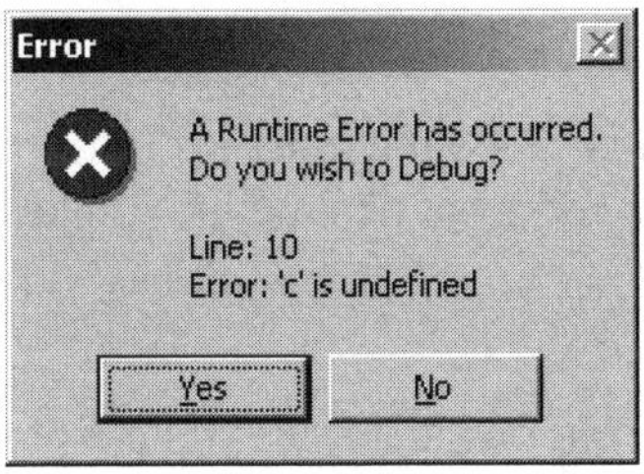

Figure 5-2. *The error message returned when a global variable is declared without an initial value*

Notice that the variable does not hold an undefined value as it would if the declaration used the `var` keyword—it causes an error instead.

The var keyword is used to "officially" declare variables. JavaScript only remembers the scope of variables that are declared in that fashion. It recognizes other variables during the execution of the script, and automatically refers to them as global variables. Although it does not really matter whether or not you use var to declare global variables in the main script, it might affect the result of the script under certain circumstances. If you do not use var and, when the variable is still undefined, you use it in a value-requiring statement, an error will occur. But this is an easy problem to fix because you will get a message. The problem with the var declaration is that not all statements that require a variable with a meaningful value use the undefined string when the variable has no value. The basic document.write() statement may print nothing at all if the variable is undefined.

What Are Functions?

We have been using functions in this book already, but have not really defined them. Basically, a *function* is a logical grouping of code statements that perform some task. For example, a function might calculate a mortgage payment or how many days since you were born.

Functions group a sequence of statements to perform a specific task or a function. JavaScript features many built-in functions that are presented later in the book. Such functions are predefined for you to use. In this chapter we will focus on those functions you build for yourself.

Defining and Calling Functions

Before you can use a function you must define it. You have already seen function definitions in this book, although we have not explicitly identified them as such. The general syntax of a function definition is:

```
function functionName([parameters])
{
   statements
}
```

and the form of a function call is:

```
functionName(arguments)
```

The first line of the function definition is called the *signature* of the function. It tells you what the function's name is and what parameters it takes.

Function Parameters

Parameters, also called *arguments*, are the raw materials you pass to a function. The function should then be able to use these values to perform a specific task. When you define a function, you should specify the names by which you refer to the custom values handed off to the function from outside. These names must follow the same rules that apply to identifiers in the language. Think of it like this: a parameter is something you must give the function in order for it to produce the results you need. For example, if you are creating a function that calculates mortgage payments, you would have to give it the principal, interest rate, and length of loan. So those would be three parameters you would pass to that function.

Parameters become local variables for the function, so they exist only inside the function where they are defined. Therefore, a parameter may use the same name as a global variable or a local variable in a different function. I don't recommend that, however, as using the same names will just confuse anyone reading your code. You can manipulate and modify the value of a parameter as if it were a common variable. There is no need to explicitly declare a parameter inside the function's body as you would with a regular variable.

JavaScript is loosely typed, so you do not specify the data type of the arguments as in C++, Java, Pascal, and other strictly typed programming languages. Both variables and literals can be passed to a function. All parameters in a function definition header should be delimited by the comma operator (,). Here is a simple JavaScript function with two parameters:

```
function printName(name, ruleWidth)
{
   document.write("<CENTER><H1>" + name + "</H1></CENTER>")
   document.write("<HR WIDTH=" + ruleWidth + "%>")
}
```

You can call this function with a simple function call, such as:

```
printName(prompt("Enter your name:", "John Doe"), 60)
```

Using the arguments Array

JavaScript supports functions that accept a variable number of arguments. The first argument is *functionName*`.arguments[0]`, the second one is *functionName*`.arguments[1]`, the third one is *functionName*`.arguments[2]`, and so on. The number of arguments handed to the function is stored in the `length` property of the `arguments` object:

functionName`.arguments.length`

The following script demonstrates this concept:

```
function calc()
{
   document.write("The first argument is ", calc.arguments[0], "<BR>")
   document.write("The fourth argument is ", calc.arguments[3], "<BR>")
   document.write("There are ", calc.arguments.length, " arguments<BR>")
}
var company = "Yahoo"
calc(2, 999, "internet", company, 0.0)
```

The script's output is:

```
The first argument is 2
The fourth argument is Yahoo
There are 5 arguments
```

The scope of the `arguments` object's properties is the current function, so it can only be used inside a function. You can use loop statements to print a list of arguments handed to a function:

```
function createList()
{
   var result = ""
   for (var i = 0; i < createList.arguments.length; ++i)
   {
      result += createList.arguments[i] + "\r"
   }
   alert(result)
}
```

Here is a simple function call:

```
createList("C", "H", "U", "C", "K")
```

When invoked with the preceding statement, the function generates the following dialog box:

Figure 5-3. *Each line displayed is a distinct argument handed to the* `createList()` *function.*

Creating Functions with Default Arguments

JavaScript does not support functions with default arguments. In C++, these are the values supplied to the parameters in a function's prototype. There are, however, ways you can "fake it" and make JavaScript behave as if it used default parameters. Calling the following function at the beginning of a function is a simple workaround you can use in JavaScript:

```
function checkDefault(parameter, defaultValue)
{
   if (typeof parameter == "undefined")
      return defaultValue
   /* else */
      return parameter
}
```

The appropriate call to this function is:

```
parameterName = checkDefault(parameterName, defaultValue)
```

The parameter is assigned its default value only if the function is called without specifying the required argument. The following function uses this technique to print a row of a given character; an asterisk is the default character, and 30 characters is the default length:

```
function checkDefault(parameter, defaultValue)
{
   if (typeof parameter == "undefined")
      return defaultValue
   /* else */
      return parameter
}
function drawLine(character, numOfChars)
{
   character = checkDefault(character, "*")
   numOfChars = checkDefault(numOfChars, 30)
   for (var i = 0; i < numOfChars; i++)
   {
      document.write(character)
   }
}
```

Here are some function calls and their corresponding output:

```
drawLine() // prints 30 asterisks
```

```
******************************
```

```
drawLinc("-") // prints 30 equal signs
```

```
==============================
```

```
drawLine("-", 10) // prints 10 dashes
```

```
----------
```

It is also possible to specify the second argument without providing the first by using an undefined variable (just declare it before with `var`, without initializing it).

Returning a Value

Sometimes a function will simply do whatever task you programmed it to do and end; other times it will return a value. This value is often the answer to some calculation. A function can return a value, so it is possible to use a function call as a valid JavaScript value. Use this feature to create general functions for usage by other scripts. For example, you can use a function that accepts a number in one base and returns it in a different representation. This function can be used in creating a base-conversion table, a dialog box, or additional calculations.

Use the following syntax to return a value from within a function:

```
return value
```

The `return` statement returns a value and terminates the function, similar to the way `break` terminates a loop. Take a look at the following function:

```
function sum(op1, op2)
{
   return op1 + op2
}
var answer = sum(3, 5)
alert(answer)
```

The value returned by the function is the sum of its arguments. As you can see, the function evaluates to a value. A function may only return one value—a variable, a literal, or any other valid data structure.

A function with a return value can also generate an output. When you use the function in an expression, it automatically runs, executing all statements until it returns a value that is used in the expression. The preceding function can also display the sum of its arguments inside the function itself, provided that the `alert()` statement precedes the `return` statement (which terminates the function):

```
function sum(op1, op2)
{
   var result = op1 + op2
   alert(result)
   return result
}
var answer = sum(3, 5)
```

Be sure that the `return` statement is placed after the statements that should be executed, since it terminates the function and no additional statements of the function are executed afterward.

You can use nested `if` constructions without `else` statements, provided that each `if` statement calls a `return` statement if the condition is true. Eliminating the `else` statements does not affect the efficiency of the function, because the function terminates immediately after a true condition is met. The following function converts hexadecimal digits (not numbers) to their equivalent decimal values:

```
function getValue(dig)
{
   if (dig == "A") return 10
   if (dig == "B") return 11
   if (dig == "C") return 12
   if (dig == "D") return 13
   if (dig == "E") return 14
   if (dig == "F") return 15
   return dig
   // the return statement terminates the function,
   // so there is no need for else statements
}
```

If the digit is from 0 to 9, none of the conditions evaluate to true, so the function returns the same digit it accepts:

```
return dig
```

Recursion

Recursion is an advanced topic, and you can certainly write JavaScript without using it. However in many situations, including some of the more interesting examples later in this book, recursion is useful. A *recursive* function is usually one that calls itself. It is similar to a loop with or without a terminating condition. Some programming functions lend themselves to recursive algorithms, such as the factorial one. The factorial is a classic recursive algorithm because it is very obvious. A simple mathematical definition of the factorial operation is:

```
fact(0) = 1
fact(n) = n * fact(n–1)
```

Factorial is commonly represented by the exclamation mark (!).

With this algorithm, let's calculate 3!:

1. `fact(3) - 3 * fact(2)`
2. `fact(2) = 2 * fact(1)`
3. `fact(1) = 1 * fact(0)`
4. `fact(0) - 1`

As you can see, the algorithm works its way down from the given number to zero, so when it gets to `fact(0)` it must work its way back up to the numbers.

We know that `fact(0) = 1`.

```
fact(1) = 1 * fact(0) = 1 * 1 = 1
fact(2) = 2 * fact(1) = 2 * 1 = 2
fact(3) = 3 * fact(2) = 3 * 2 = 6
```

We have reached the desired answer using a recursive algorithm. In JavaScript this is:

```
function fact(num)
{
   if (num == 0)
      return 1
   /* else */
      return num * fact(num – 1)
}
```

You can call the function in the following way:

```
var fiveFactorial = fact(5) // 120
```

Notice that the `else` statement is commented because it is not necessary.

The `fact()` function satisfies two rules. First, it has an ending point. Second, it simplifies the problem because `fact(num – 1)` is simpler than `fact(num)`. Recursive functions should always follow these two rules.

Recursive functions have a few advantages:

- Invariably, recursive functions are clearer, simpler, shorter, and easier to understand than their nonrecursive counterparts.
- The program directly reflects the abstract solution strategy (algorithm). The recursive factorial function, for example, uses the common mathematical strategy to solve the problem.

At first, it may seem that recursive functions are more difficult, but they become easier with practice.

Recursion can also be used to compute a value in the Fibonacci sequence (1, 1, 2, 3, 5, 8, 13, ...). The basic algorithm is:

```
getVal(1) = 1
getVal(2) = 1
getVal(place) = getVal(place – 1) + getVal(place – 2)
```

Summary

In this chapter we have discussed variables and functions, which are fundamental programming concepts. You can certainly create simple web pages and effects (like image rollovers) with only a cursory knowledge of these two topics. But for more advanced work, a full understanding is absolutely required.

Chapter 6
Utilizing JavaScript Operators

Operator Categories

An *operator*, as the name suggest, performs some action. Programming languages would be virtually useless if they did not provide the programmer with operators to use. JavaScript has many operators, most of them borrowed from C and Java. The wide variety of operators makes it necessary to divide them into the following categories:

- Mathematical operators
- String operators
- Bitwise operators
- Assignment operators
- Relational operators
- Short-circuit logical operators
- More logical operators
- Data type operator
- Void operator

In this chapter we will discuss JavaScript's operators, grouped by the above categories. Operators in each category are divided into two groups:

- Unary operators—operators that operate on a single operand
- Binary operators—operators that operate on two operands

Mathematical Operators

The most obvious category of operators is mathematical operators. *Mathematical operators*, also called *arithmetic operators*, perform basic mathematical operations. Table 6-1 lists the mathematical operators in JavaScript:

Table 6-1. Mathematical operators

Syntax	Name	Type
+	Addition (plus)	Binary
–	Subtraction (minus)	Binary
*	Multiplication (multiply)	Binary
/	Division (divide)	Binary
%	Modulus (modulo)	Binary
++	Increment	Unary
– –	Decrement	Unary
–	Negation	Unary
+=	Add then assign	Binary
=	Assignment	Binary
= =	Evaluation	Binary

Arithmetic operators take numeric literals, variables, or properties of existing objects as their operands. They always return a single numeric value, based on their operands' values.

Addition

```
operand1 + operand2
```

The addition operator is a simple mathematical operator. It adds two numbers of any type and evaluates to their sum.

```
-5 + 3      // evaluates to -2
2.4 + 3.6   // evaluates to 6
1.1 + 7.8   // evaluates to 8.9
```

Subtraction

```
operand1 – operand2
```

Another simple mathematical operator is the subtraction operator. It subtracts one number from another.

```
8 - 2        // evaluates to 6
16.3 - 56    // evaluates to -39.7
13.3 - 13.3 // evaluates to 0
```

Multiplication

```
operand1 * operand2
```

The multiplication operator takes two numbers as its operands, and performs the usual arithmetic conversion.

```
4 * 3       // evaluates to 12
1.2 * 30    // evaluates to 36
20.4 * 6.7  // evaluates to 136.68
```

Division

```
operand1 / operand2
```

The division operator also performs the usual arithmetic conversion. However, since JavaScript is loosely typed, this operator does not act exactly as in C, Perl, and other strictly typed programming languages. In those languages, integer division is different from floating-point division in that the result of integer division is always an integer number. JavaScript, on the other hand, does not explicitly distinguish between integers and real-valued numbers, and therefore, the result of a division operation is not guaranteed to be an integer number. In fact, most floating-point numbers are the result of a division operator. While debugging a script, it may be helpful to remember that the division operation in JavaScript generates the same value as your pocket calculator. You should also remember that the remainder of a division operation is never discarded.

When the operands are floating-point numbers and cannot be represented in binary notation, division expressions often evaluate to inaccurate results. The following demonstrates the behavior of JavaScript's division operator:

```
3 / 4         // evaluates to 0.75
3.6 / 0.1     // evaluates to 36
-20 / 4       // evaluates to -5
11.1 / 2.22   // evaluates to 4.999999999999999
```

Modulus

```
operand1 % operand2
```

The modulus operator returns the remainder of a division operation. The division is performed, but only the remainder is kept. The sign of the result is the sign of the quotient. The modulus operator in JavaScript is also different from the one in other programming languages. It operates not only on integers but also on floating-point numbers. You should be aware that the modulus operator occasionally returns inaccurate results. The modulus' inaccuracies stem from the division operation, which sometimes returns inaccurate results:

```
12 % 5         // evaluates to 2
12.3 % 4       // evaluates to 0.3000000000000007 (inaccuracy)
0 % 99         // evaluates to 0
12.75 % 4.25   // evaluates to 0
11.1 % 2.22    // evaluates to 2.219999999999999
```


The Nonexistent Integral Division Operator

JavaScript does not feature an integral division (also called `div`) operator. In fact, many JavaScript programmers get by just fine without it. However, if you feel the absolute need to create such an operator, you can do so with the following function:

```
function div(op1, op2)
{
   return (op1 / op2 - op1 % op2 / op2)
{
```

The keyword `return` instructs the function to return a value, so the function call itself evaluates to a value, just like an expression consisting of an operator.

Now we can define the newly created `div` syntax:

```
div(operand1, operand2)
```

Here are a few examples:

```
var a = div(23, 3)    // a is assigned 7
var b = div(12, 4)    // b is assigned 3
```

The function evaluates to the quotient of its arguments, with the remainder discarded. The sign of the result is the sign of the quotient.

Caution: Various operations on floating-point numbers return inaccurate results. This may seem strange, but such inaccuracies are a common phenomenon in computers. You should avoid floating-point values when possible, because such inaccuracies often result in unexpected behavior. Above all, debugging scripts that fail to work due to inaccurate calculations is nearly impossible.

Increment

```
operand1++
```

```
++operand1
```

The increment operator is a unary operator that can be used in either suffix or prefix notations. It increments the operand's value by 1. If used after the operand (suffix), the operator returns the value of the operand before incrementing it. If used before the operand (prefix), the operator returns the value of the operand after incrementing it. Understanding these differences is important when you use such operations as side effects of other statements, such as assignment statements. The following set of statements outlines this concept:

```
var a = 1
var b = ++a                                  // prefix
document.write("a is ", a, ", b is ", b)  // a is 2, b is 2
```

The first statement assigns the value 1 to a. The second statement performs two different actions:

- Increments a to 2
- Assigns a's new value to b

The increment operator in suffix notation performs the actions in reverse order, and therefore the results differ. Suffix notation is demonstrated in the following code:

```
var a = 1
var b = a++                                // suffix
document.write("a is ", a, ", b is ", b)  // a is 2, b is 1
```

b is assigned the value of a, and then a is incremented.

Dual actions in one statement are discussed at the end of this chapter in the section named "Side Effects." Generally, you should avoid using such side effects. The previous code would be simpler had it looked like:

```
var a = 1
var b = a
a++
document.write("a is ", a, ", b is ", b)  // a is 2, b is 1
```

The increment operator can only be used with a variable or a property of an existing object, but not on a literal.

It is natural to come to a conclusion that incrementing is the same as adding 1 to the value:

```
var a = 1
var b = 1
a++
b = b + 1   // equivalent to b += 1 (see assignment operators)
```

This is true as far as correctness of the script is concerned. It is incorrect if performance is important. The advantage of incrementing is that it is much faster than standard assignment (fourth line in above code section). You should always increment when you want to add 1 to a variable (or to a property of an object). It is not so important when the addition operation is done a few times. You will definitely feel the difference when you have 100,000 addition operations. Another benefit of the increment operator is that it is much easier to understand a statement like `countTemp++` than `countTemp = countTemp + 1`.

It is important to remember that Boolean expressions are equivalent to 1 and 0 in certain situations. The following statements show the effect of incrementing Boolean variables:

```
var a = true
var b = false
a++
b++
document.write("a is ", a, ", b is ", b)  // a is 2, b is 1
```

Decrement

```
operand1--
```

```
--operand1
```

The decrement operator is similar to the increment operator. It decreases the value of the operand by 1, whereas the increment operator increases it by 1.

Negation

```
–operand1
```

Negation is the programming equivalent to shouting "IS NOT!" and can be quite handy. The negation operator precedes a numeric value (a variable, a property of an existing object, or a numeric literal). By placing this operator before its operand (do not insert any space characters), JavaScript evaluates a positive number as its corresponding negative number and vice versa. As before, you might think that this operator can be replaced by a statement in which the operand is multiplied by –1. Once again, this is a mistake. Due to the internal structure of the JavaScript interpreter, and the negation operator specifically, negating a numeric value using the negation operator is faster than multiplying it by –1. If you are a traditional Pascal programmer, it might take you a while to get used to the negation and increment operators, but it is worth the effort!

```
var a = 3
var b = 9
-a + b       // evaluates to 6
-b           // evaluates to -9
```

String Concatenation

Concatenation is a very common string operation, and works as shown here:

```
operand1 + operand2
```

The string operator's syntax is identical to that of the addition operator. They differ in the type of operands they operate on. This operator accepts any values as operands, provided that at least one of them is a string. A string is actually an object, so it can be said that the string operator operates on string objects. It joins them together, as in:

```
"Ladies " + "and " + "gentlemen"
```

The string operator can operate on more than two operands, but it is still a binary operator because of the way it works. It concatenates the first two strings, then concatenates the third string to the accumulated string, and so on. If one of the operands is not a string, it is automatically cast to a string. The string operator is also called a *concatenation* operator.

An expression consisting of numerous string operators evaluates to a single string. Based on that, here are two different statements:

```
document.write("I have " + 2 + " cookies.")
document.write("I have ", 2, " cookies.")
```

At first, you might think that these statements are equivalent. They aren't, because the first one uses the string operator, and the second one uses commas to delimit strings and numbers. They differ more than in style. In the first statement, the expression between the parentheses is evaluated to a single string—"I have 2 cookies." Therefore, the `document.write()` method in this statement prints only one expression. The second statement prints multiple expressions. The literals are not evaluated to a single value as in the first statement but rather are printed independently. Both statements print the same HTML to the page, but they do it in different ways. In order to understand how each statement works, take a look at the following sequences of statements. The first sequence is equivalent to the first statement in the previous set, and the second sequence is equivalent to the second statement.

```
// sequence #1
var stringToPrint = "I have " + 2 + " cookies."
document.write(stringToPrint)
```

```
// sequence #2
document.write("I have ")
document.write(2)
document.write(" cookies.")
```

A common mistake made by beginners is to forget spaces in strings. A space is a character just like any other. Forgetting a space character is not a severe error, because you can easily locate where to add it. You should use one of the following statements to print two consecutive numbers with a separating space character in between:

```
document.write(16 + " " + 18) // first possibility
document.write(16, " ", 18)   // second possibility
```

The first statement is valid because of the automatic casting method used by JavaScript's interpreter.

Tip: The plus (+) operator in JavaScript does not convert string operands to numeric values. The reason behind this is that the string concatenation operator and the plus operator use the same character: +. If only one operand is a string, the other is converted to a string value and then the operator concatenates the strings. In Perl, the plus (addition) and minus (subtraction) operators convert their arguments from strings to numeric values if necessary, and return a numeric result. This feature is made possible because the string concatenation operator in Perl is . (dot), not +, which is shared with another operator (addition) in JavaScript. C++ and Pascal feature a function that concatenates strings.

Bitwise Operators

First, let me state that bitwise operations can be confusing for many programmers. I should also note that a great many programmers work for years without ever having to use them. You can be a successful JavaScript programmer even if this section does not quite make sense to you. However, I would have been remiss not to have included it.

Bitwise operators are the operators used in bit-oriented operations. A *bit* is the smallest unit of information, usually represented by 0 or 1. Bit manipulations are used to control the machine at the lowest level. If you plan to program at a higher level, this section may be safely skipped. In JavaScript you won't be using bitwise operators to control the machine at a low level but rather for other purposes such as encrypting and encoding.

Eight consecutive bits form a byte. There are 256 (2^8) byte variations. That is, a byte can be one of 256 eight-bit sequences. For example, 11010001 is one of these 256 possibilities. A byte is represented by a character in programming languages that support character data types, such as C, C++, and Pascal.

Hexadecimal notation is convenient for representing binary data because each hexadecimal digit represents four binary bits. Table 6-2 lists the hexadecimal values from 0 to F along with the equivalent binary values.

Table 6-2. *Hexadecimal and binary equivalents*

Hexadecimal	Binary	Hexadecimal	Binary
0	0000	8	1000
1	0001	9	1001
2	0010	A	1010
3	0011	B	1011
4	0100	C	1100
5	0101	D	1101
6	0110	E	1110
7	0111	F	1111

Bitwise operators enable the scripter to work on individual bits. The bitwise (bit) operators in JavaScript are listed in Table 6-3.

Table 6-3. *Bitwise operators in JavaScript*

Syntax	Name	Type
&	Bitwise AND	binary
|	Bitwise OR	binary
^	Bitwise XOR (exclusive OR)	binary
~	Bitwise NOT	unary
<<	Left shift	binary
>>	Right shift	binary
>>>	Zero-fill right shift	binary

Bitwise AND

```
operand1 & operand2
```

The bitwise AND operator compares two bits. The only situation in which the result is 1 is when both bits are 1. The truth table for this operator is shown in Table 6-4.

Table 6-4. *Bitwise AND truth table*

Bit1	Bit2	Bit1 & Bit2
0	0	0
0	1	0
1	0	0
1	1	1

Important Note: A *truth table* is a concept borrowed from mathematics and is used to graphically demonstrate the truth of a combination of statements.

The AND operator, like all other bitwise operators, can take only a numeric value as its operand.

Although you will probably never use bitwise operators, let's learn how the results are calculated. All calculations will be performed in hexadecimal and binary bases, because they are most convenient for the task. Remember that hexadecimal numbers have a "0x" prefix.

Let's take a look at the following numbers, and how the bitwise AND operates on them:

	0x23	00100011_2
&	0x72	01110010_2
=	0x22	00100010_2

```
0x23 & 0x72 // evaluates to 34 (= 0x22 = 2216)
```

The bitwise AND operator is similar to the logical AND operator, which is discussed later in this chapter.

You can use the bitwise AND operator to test whether a number is even or odd. In binary (base-2), the last digit of an odd number is 1, and the last digit of an even number is 0. The following function uses the bitwise AND operator to determine whether the number is odd or even. It returns true if `decimalNumber` is even, and false if it is odd.

```
function checkEven(decimalNumber)
{
   return (decimalNumber & 1 == 0)
}
```

Don't worry if you are not familiar with the "==" equality operator. It is introduced later in this chapter. Come back to this script after we discuss the equality operator.

Bitwise OR

```
operand1 | operand2
```

The OR operator, also known as the *inclusive OR operator,* compares its operands. It returns 1 if at least one of the compared bits is 1. Table 6-5 shows the operator's truth table.

Table 6-5. *Bitwise OR truth table*

Bit1	Bit2	Bit1 | Bit2
0	0	0
0	1	1
1	0	1
1	1	1

When operating on bytes:

	0x46	01000110_2
|	0x79	01111001_2
=	0x7F	01111111_2

Bitwise XOR

```
operand1 ^= operand2
```

The XOR is a very interesting and useful operator. It is the *exclusive* OR. In other words, it asks if there is a 1 in one or the other number but not in both. Table 6-6 shows the operator's truth table.

Table 6-6. *Bitwise XOR truth table*

Bit1	Bit2	Bit1 ^= Bit2
0	0	0
0	1	1
1	0	1
1	1	0

Take a look at the following example:

	0x2C	00101100_2
^	0xA3	10100011_2
=	0x8F	10001111_2

The bitwise XOR operator is used in a simple cipher technique called *XORing*, which will be covered later in this book.

Bitwise NOT

The bitwise NOT operator returns the reverse of its operand. Therefore, it is also called the *bit flip operator* or the *invert operator.* All 1s are converted to 0s, and all 0s are converted to 1s. Here is the truth table:

Table 6-7. *Bitwise NOT truth table*

Bit	~Bit
0	1
1	0

For example,

~	70	$00000000000000000000000001000110_2$
=	–71	$11111111111111111111111110111001_2$

Note that this operator refers to all operands (integers) as 32 bits. If they are not 32-bit integers, they are converted for the operation and then converted back to their initial form.

Shift Operators

The shift operators take two operands:

- The quantity (value) to be shifted
- The number of bit positions to shift the first operand

Shift operators convert their operands to 32-bit integers, and return a result of the same type as the left operator. There are three shift operators:

- Left shift (<<)
- Right shift (>>)
- Zero-fill right shift (>>>)

Left Shift

```
operand1 << operand2
```

The left shift operator shifts the first operand the specified number of bits to the left. All bits that are shifted out (to the left) are discarded. New bits coming in from the right are zeros. In the following example, └──┘ represents 4 bytes (32 bits):

179 ⇒ 0xB3 ⇒ 10110011_2

179 << 0 ⇒ 00000000000000000000000010110011

179 << 2 ⇒ 00000000000000000000000010110011

empty space filled with 0s

⇒ 00000000000000000000001011001100

⇒ 1011001100_2 ⇒ 0x2CC ⇒ 716

You now know that 179 << 2 is 716. You might realize that 179 * 4 is also 716—this is no coincidence. In general, x << n is the same as $x * 2^n$. Shifting left n places is the same as multiplying by 2^n. This rule applies also to negative numbers—the sign is always preserved. Thus, you can choose between two different methods to multiply by a power of two. Although shifting is faster, it is also less clear to the reader and should be avoided.

Right Shift

```
operand1 >> operand2
```

The right shift operator is also called *sign-propagating right shift* because it preserves the sign of the initial operand. Like the left shift operator, the right shift operator shifts the first operand the specified number of bits to the right. Excess bits shifted off at the right are discarded. The sign of an integer is stored in the first bit (from the left). In order to preserve the sign, the first bit remains as is. The other 31 bits are shifted to the right. New bits coming in from the left are either 0s or 1s, depending on the sign. If the first bit was a 0, all new bits are 0s, and vice versa. Therefore, if the number was positive, the operation will also return a positive number; if it was negative, the operation evaluates to a negative number. It is important to remember that this operator, like all shift operators, converts the first operand to a 32-bit integer, and after shifting returns it to its initial representation. Here is a simple example:

176 ⇒ 0xB0 ⇒ 10110000_2

176 >> 0 ⇒ 00000000000000000000000010110000

176 >> 3 ⇒ 0 00000000000000000000000000010110000

⇒ 00000000000000000000000000010110

⇒ 10110_2 ⇒ 0x16 ⇒ 22

Let's see how this operator works on a negative number, say, –17.

```
-17 ⇒ 11111111111111111111111111101111₂

-17 >> 0 ⇒      11111111111111111111111111101111

-17 >> 3 ⇒      1   11111111111111111111111111101111

⇒               11111111111111111111111111111101

⇒ 11111111111111111111111111111101₂ ⇒ -3
```

You can refer to the right shift operator as the opposite of the left shift operator. While the left shift operator is equivalent to multiplying by a power of 2, the right shift operation is equivalent to dividing by a power of 2. `176 >> 3` is equal to `176 / 2`^{3}. In general, `x << n` is the same as `x / 2`^{n}.

Zero-fill Right Shift

```
operand1 >>> operand2
```

The zero-fill right shift operator shifts the first operand the specified number of bits to the right. Like the sign-propagating right shift, the zero-fill right shift discards excess bits that are shifted off to the right. However, the bits shifted in from the left are always zeros. The number's sign is lost because the leftmost bit is always 0. Here is the simple example from the previous section, this time with the zero-fill right shift:

```
-17 ⇒ 11111111111111111111111111101111₂

-17 >>> 0 ⇒      11111111111111111111111111101111

-17 >>> 3 ⇒         11111111111111111111111111101111

⇒                00011111111111111111111111111101

⇒ 11111111111111111111111111101₂ ⇒ 536870909
```

Don't worry if the bitwise shift operators seem difficult. One can program in JavaScript for many years without needing to use bitwise operators, so having some difficulty grasping them is not going to be a problem.

Assignment Operators

```
operand1 □ = operand2
```

Assignment operators are binary operators handling arithmetic, string, or bitwise operators. They perform the regular operation on the operands and assign the result to the first operand. The assignment operators are as follows:

***Table 6-8.** Assignment operators*

Syntax	Name
=	Equal
+=	Add/concatenate by value
−=	Subtract by value
*=	Multiply by value
/=	Divide by value
%=	Modulo by value
&=	Bitwise AND by value
|=	Bitwise OR by value
^=	Bitwise XOR
<<=	Left shift by value
>>=	Right shift by value
>>>=	Zero-fill right shift by value

You already know what the simple = assignment operator does—it stores the value of the expression in the data structure. For all the other operators, JavaScript pretends that

```
var1 □ = var2
```

is

```
var1 = var1 □ var2
```

For example:

```
counter =>> 2
```

shifts the value of `counter` two positions to the right, and

```
text += " Gates"
```

attaches the word `Gates` to the end of the string stored in `text`. The same rule applies to all assignment operators listed in Table 6-8.

Since the assignment statements are evaluated from right to left, you can use multiple operators in the same statement. The rule is that the value to the right of the operator is evaluated and then assigned to the variable to the left of the operator.

```
num1 = num2 = num3 = num4 = num5
```

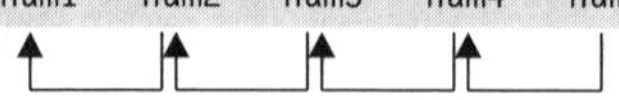

The value of `num5` is assigned to `num4`, the value of `num4` is assigned to `num3`, and so on. After such an operation, all five variables hold the same value.

Relational Operators

operand1 □ *operand2*

Relational operators, also called comparison operators, compare two values and return a Boolean result. All relational operators are binary, because they compare two values. These operators are often used in conditional statements. Here is the complete list of JavaScript's relational operators:

***Table 6-9.** Relational operators*

Syntax	Name
==	Equal
!=	Not equal
<	Less than
<=	Less than or equal to
>	Greater than
>=	Greater than or equal to

These operators take numeric or string values as their operands. Numeric comparison is usually very simple:

```
2 == 1      // evaluates to false
99.0 == 99  // evaluates to true
2 != 1      // evaluates to true
3 < 2.5     // evaluates to false
2 <= 2      // evaluates to true
9 > 9       // evaluates to false
9 >= -10    // evaluates to false
```

String operands are compared according to the ASCII value of their characters. This comparison is similar to the one by which words are placed in a dictionary. The only difference is that instead of using a single set of letters, JavaScript uses 256 different characters. As you know, each character has a numeric value. This value determines if a character is greater than, equal to, or less than another one.

When you compare multicharacter strings, the first character of the first operand is compared with the first character of the second operand. The second characters are compared only if the comparison of the first ones indicates equality. The process continues until the corresponding characters are not equal, or until the end of one of the strings is reached. Here are some characters and their ASCII values:

0 – 48	A – 65	a – 97
9 – 57	Z – 90	z – 122

You can find the full ASCII table in Appendix C.

Here is an example:

```
"computerA" > "computerB"
"c" == "c"
"o" == "o"
"m" == "m"
"p" == "p"
"u" == "u"
"t" == "t"
"e" == "e"
"r" == "r"
"A" < "B"      ⇒      ("computerA" > "computerB" ⇒ false)
```

Take a look at the following results for a better understanding:

```
"JavaScript" == "javascript"  // evaluates to false
"bill" != "bill"              // evaluates to false
" " < "  "                    // ([one space] < [two spaces]) evaluates to true
16 <= "16"                    // evaluates to true
"luck" > "Work"               // evaluates to true!
"XT" >= "pentium pro    "     // evaluates to false
```

Equality and Inequality

As you can see, the Boolean equality operator (==) is similar to the assignment operator (=). This similarity is the source of many programming errors, not only in JavaScript but also in other languages such as C, C++, and Java. Equality operators are often used in `if-else` statements, where the assignment operator cannot be used. (JavaScript does not allow side effects in a conditional statement.) In this case, the interpreter produces a meaningful error saying: "test for equality (==) mistyped as assignment (=)? Assuming equality test." However, in some other situations, both the equality and assignment operators are valid and the browser, rightly so, does not generate any errors. This is why such errors are very difficult to debug. The following example demonstrates a situation in which both operators are acceptable:

```
var i = 1
document.write(i = 2)
var j = 1
document.write(j == 2)
```

The first printing statement prints 2, because an assignment expression evaluates to the assigned value. The second printing statement prints `false` under Netscape Navigator, and 0 on Internet Explorer (Internet Explorer converts the Boolean value false to 0 for printing), because 1 is not equal to 2. In a long script, if you accidentally replaced one operator with the other, you would have a hard time finding the mistake.

Another problem with the equality operator has to do with the way a computer deals with floating-point numbers. This problem is especially difficult when you try to store integer numbers in the form of floating-point numbers (e.g., 3.0). Depending on the underlying machine, the results may differ. You might find out that (`5. == 5.00`) evaluates to false, and (`5.0 == 4.99999999`) evaluates to true. Therefore, avoid using equality operators with floating-point values. The solution for this problem is presented later in the chapter.

Short-Circuit Logical Operators

Short-circuit logical operators, also called Boolean operators or logical operators, are binary operators that accept Boolean values as their operands. They group multiple relational expressions together. There are three logical operators:

Table 6-10. *Logical operators*

Syntax	Name	Type
||	Logical OR	binary
&&	Logical AND	binary
!	Logical NOT	unary

Logical OR

```
operand1 || operand2
```

The logical OR operator accepts two Boolean values as its operands and evaluates to a single Boolean value. It evaluates to true if at least one of the operands is true; in other words, the only situation in which it evaluates to false is when both operands are false. Take a look at Table 6-11.

Table 6-11. *Logical OR truth table*

Operand1	Operand2	Operand1 || Operand2
true	true	true
true	false	true
false	true	true
false	false	false

Here are a few examples:

```
2 > 1 || 3 < 4                     // true
1 == 1 || 99 >= 98                 // true
"mouse" > "elephant" || 6 < 5      // true
1 == 2 || 5 <= 4                   // false
```

Be careful not to confuse the logical OR operator with the bitwise OR due to their similar meaning and syntax (`||` vs. `|`). The only difference in meaning is that the first handles Boolean operands while the second handles numeric ones.

The logical OR operator is *short-circuit* evaluated. As you can see from the truth table, if the first operand is true, it is certain that the expression will evaluate to true. Checking the second operand in such a situation is unnecessary and is avoided by JavaScript.

Logical AND

```
operand1 && operand2
```

The logical AND operator is similar to the logical OR operator, except both operands must be true for the expression to evaluate to a true value. This operator is similar to the bitwise AND operator, except that the operand types are different, and the logical AND operator operates on the whole operand at once rather than on a small segment (bit).

Logical AND expressions are also short-circuit evaluated. If the first operand is false, the expression will obviously be false, so the second operand is not evaluated.

Here are some examples:

```
2 > 1 && 3 < 4                    // true
1 == 1 && 99 >= 98                // true
"mouse" > "elephant" && 6 < 5     // false
1 == 2 && 5 <= 4                  // false
```

Logical NOT

```
!operand1
```

The logical NOT operator is a simple unary operator that accepts a Boolean value and negates it. This operator is similar to the negation operator, which negates a number (changes its sign). It is even more similar to the bitwise NOT operator (~), which converts all 1 bits to 0 bits, and 0 bits to 1 bits. Although the truth table is obvious, here it is for your reference:

Table 6-12. *Logical NOT truth table*

Operand	!Operand
true	false
false	true

Because this is a unary operator, short-circuit evaluation is not relevant.

Here are some examples:

```
!true       // evaluates to false
!(2 > 4)    // evaluates to true
!(7 == 7)   // evaluates to false
!false      // evaluates to true
```

Caution: Short-circuit evaluation is mostly useful because it makes your scripts more efficient. However, there are times when this method of evaluation is harmful. For example, you finish writing a complicated script and you want to test it. Depending on certain decisions in the script, short-circuit evaluation is performed, and the interpreter ignores the second operand of various expressions. You might think that the script works perfectly fine, even if there is a data mistype or a syntax error in the second operand. This type of evaluation can mislead you in such situations, but it is unavoidable.

Testing Equality for Floating-Point Numbers

We mentioned earlier that the equality operator (==) is not suitable for floating-point numbers due to inaccuracy issues. Using logical AND and OR operators, you can check if the number is close to the specified value. For example, if you want to evaluate the expression `x == 10.0` you use a *fuzzy comparison* using one of the following expressions, in which ∝ represents a small number (such as 0.001).

```
(x - 10.0) < ∝ || (10.0 - x) < ∝
```

or

```
x > (10.0 - ∝) && x < (10.0 + ∝)
```

More Logical Operators

The conditional operator and the comma operator are also logical operators.

Conditional Operator

```
condition ? trueAlternative : falseAlternative
```

The conditional operator is unique because it is trinary (takes three operands) and because it returns values of all types. It can return a numeric value, a string, a Boolean value, and so on. The first operand is the condition. The condition must be an expression that evaluates to a Boolean value, either true or false. The second operator holds the value that the operator should return if the condition is true. The third operand is the value that the expression evaluates to if the condition is false. The conditional operator is often used with an assignment operator. For example:

```
var level = (points > 500) ? "Second Level" : "First Level"
```

The variable `level` is assigned either `"First Level"` or `"Second Level"`, depending on the value of the Boolean expression `points > 500`. If the value of `points` is greater than 500, the conditional expression evaluates to the string `"Second Level"`, which in turn is assigned to the variable `level`. If the value of `points` does not exceed 500, the string `"First Level"` is assigned to the variable. The first operand (the condition) must be Boolean (a single Boolean value or an expression that evaluates to a single Boolean value). The other operands can be of any type.

Comma Operator

```
operand1, operand2, operand3, ...
```

The comma operator is rarely used. You can use it to force the evaluation of a set of expressions. The comma operator is also called a *parameter delimiter* because it does just that. You probably recall that we used the comma operator in functions when we wanted a function to accept multiple arguments.

In this example, the comma operator delimits the method's arguments:

```
var beerNum = 99
document.write(beerNum, " bottles of beer on the wall")
```

Here is another example:

```
var a = (b = "Hello", alert("Hi"), "Howdy")
```

The comma operator forces the evaluation of all expressions in the statement. Only the last expression is returned, so the value of a would be "Howdy". This statement is equivalent to the following set of statements:

```
b = "Hello"
alert("Hi")
var a = "Howdy"
```

Data Type Operator

```
typeof operand1
```

or

```
typeof (operand1)
```

JavaScript provides an operator to check the data type of its operand. The operand can be either a literal or a data structure such as a variable, a function, or an object. The operator returns the data type. The expression includes the word typeof followed by the literal or identifier. Here are some examples:

```
typeof foo == "undefined"       // when foo is undefined
typeof eval == "function"       // eval is a built-in function
typeof null == "object"         // null is an object
typeof 3.14 == "number"
typeof true == "Boolean"
typeof "a string" == "string"
// all of the expressions are true, of course
```

The typeof operator is very useful for debugging. Until strong debugging tools are available, you must do all debugging by hand, and detecting the data type of a structure is sometimes essential.

Void Operator

```
void operand1
void (operand1)
```

or

```
javascript:void operand1
javascript:void (operand1)
```

The `void` operator, like `typeof`, is quite extraordinary. It specifies an expression to be evaluated without returning a value. Take a look at the following script:

```
function foo()
{
   alert("Function entered")
   return true
}
alert(foo())
```

The preceding script segment displays two alert boxes with the following strings:

- `Function entered`
- `true`

Now take a look at another function and call:

```
function foo()
{
   alert("Function entered")
   return true
}
alert(void foo())
```

This script also generates two alerts, but the second one reads "undefined" because the `void` operator evaluates the function without returning a value. A more important use of this operator comes with hypertext links, where it is used to evaluate a JavaScript expression. The expression is evaluated but is not loaded in place of the current document.

The following link does nothing because the expression 0 has no effect in JavaScript:

```
<A HREF="javascript:void(0)">Click here to do nothing</A>
```

The following code generates an alert box when the link is clicked:

```
<A HREF="javascript:void(alert('Wow'))">Click here to display message</A>
```

The parentheses are optional, so it's up to you to decide whether to use them. Some scripters specify them in HTML and omit them in JavaScript for no particular reason.

Operator Precedence

You probably remember that 2 + 6 * 9 is 56 and not 72, because multiplication precedes addition. That is exactly the meaning of *operator precedence*. It is not necessary to remember the precedence rules because parentheses can be used to force evaluation in the desired order. The expressions are evaluated according to the precedence rules. Operators at the same level are evaluated from left to right. The following table will help you when you want to define complex expressions.

Table 6-13. *Operator precedence*

Level	Operators	Notes
1	() [] .	call, member (including typeof and void)
2	! ~ − ++ −−	negation, increment
3	* / %	multiply/divide
4	+ −	addition/subtraction
5	<< >> >>>	bitwise shift
6	< <= > >=	relational
7	== !=	equality
8	&	bitwise AND
9	^	bitwise XOR
10	|	bitwise OR
11	&&	logical AND
12	||	logical OR
13	?:	conditional
14	= += −= *= /= %= <<= >>= >>>= &= ^= |=	assignment
15	,	comma

Expressions

The term *expression* has been mentioned dozens of times throughout this chapter. An expression is any valid set of literals, variables, operators, and other expressions that evaluates to a single value. The value may be a number, a string, or a Boolean value. Conceptually, there are two types of expressions:

- Those that assign a value to a variable (or another data structure)
- Those that have a value

The following are expressions:

```
a = "Dog"
"Netscape"
256
false
b = true
```

The first type of expression is a bit more difficult to understand. In such expressions, an assignment is performed. The entire specification, including both operands of the assignment operator and the operator itself, is evaluated to the assigned value. Consider the following statement:

```
document.write(x = "Texas")
```

This statement prints `Texas`, because the whole expression evaluates to the assigned value. The next section discusses side effects, which take advantage of such expressions.

Side Effects

A *side effect* is an operation performed in addition to the main one. Take a look at the following statements:

```
number = 3
answer = ++number
```

The first line is a simple assignment statement. The second line is a bit more complicated. It performs two actions in the following order:

- Increments `number` (side effect)
- Assigns the value of `number` (4) to `answer` (main operation)

Remembering the order in which the actions take place is not necessary. You could break down the side effect and use two different statements instead:

```
number = 3
number++
answer = number
```

This set of statements is easy to follow. The only "advantage" of the first method is that the code is compact. Compact code is a holdover from the early days of computing, when storage was expensive and programmers used various compacting techniques to save disk space. The situation is different today, because the number one rule in programming is to keep programs clear and simple. It comes even before efficiency, especially in simple programs like the ones written in JavaScript (you will not find any 500,000-line scripts in this advanced book).

Other side effects are not related to the increment and decrement operators. Consider the following JavaScript statement:

```
document.write(myName = "Chuck")
```

You already know that this statement prints `Chuck`. The assignment operation also takes place in this statement, so `myName` holds the value `Chuck` after the statement. The assignment operation is the side effect, and the printing action is the main action. The preceding statement should be split into two separate statements:

```
myName = "Chuck"
document.write(myName)
```

Here are some more statements you should avoid (they will keep you busy for a while…):

```
number = 0
answer = (number++ – 2) * (--number – 1)
document.write(number = answer++)
```

This set of statements prints 2. Let's analyze it:

1.
   1.1 number is assigned the value 0.
2.
   2.1. (number++ – 2) is evaluated to –2.
   2.2. number is incremented to 1.
   2.3. number decrements to 0.
   2.4. (--number – 1) evaluates to –1.
   2.5. answer is assigned 2 (because (–1) * (–2) yields 2).
3.
   3.1. number is assigned the value of answer (2).
   3.2. The value of number is printed.
   3.3. answer increments to 3.

The final result:

- number holds the value 2.
- answer holds the value 3.
- The number 2 is printed to the document.

The following script is longer, but it is definitely better:

```
number = 0
answer = number – 2
number++
number--
answer *= number – 1
number = answer
document.write(number)
number = amswer
answer++
```

Summary

This chapter brought you information on a key piece of serious JavaScript programming: operators. You could write a script that had no operators, but it would probably not be particularly useful or interesting. This information, combined with Chapter 5's coverage of variables and functions, should help you understand some basic programming fundamentals as they apply to JavaScript. You will see these concepts in various scripts as we proceed through this book.

Chapter 7
Events in JavaScript

Events

While HTML is the bedrock of all web pages, it is very static. HTML cannot respond to user input and it provides a limited set of features. When browsing an HTML-based web page you can read the text, look at the graphics, and possibly listen to the sound it plays. All of these actions are static in that the user has no control over the actions the web page takes. Such pages remind us of art masterpieces seen in a museum. You can look at them, maybe take a picture, but you cannot interact with the paintings. We use JavaScript to produce dynamic, interactive content in our HTML web pages. One of the best way to do this is to use events.

Events are actions that occur in response to a specific user action on the web site. For example, clicking on a form element will trigger a `click` event. The events occur regardless of whether you provide code to respond to them. JavaScript provides you with a method to respond to these events and to take action based on them. In this way your web page becomes very dynamic, responding to user interaction. The events supported by JavaScript are listed in Table 7-1.

Table 7-1. *Events in JavaScript*

Event	Description
abort	Occurs when the user aborts loading an image.
blur	Occurs when focus is removed from a form element (when the user clicks outside the form element). It also occurs when the user removes focus from a browser window.
change	Occurs when the user changes the value of a form field.
click	Occurs when the user clicks on a link, an image map area, or a form element.
error	Occurs if there is an error loading an image.
focus	Occurs when the user gives input focus to a form element or a window.
load	Occurs when a page or image has finished loading into the browser window.

Event	Description
mouseOut	Occurs when the user moves the mouse pointer from inside a link or image map area's bounding box to its outside.
mouseOver	Occurs when the user moves the pointer over a hypertext link or an image map area.
select	Occurs when the user selects a form field.
submit	Occurs when the user submits a form via the "submit" button.
unload	Occurs when the user exits a page.

Not all actions that take place in your browser are events. Events are only actions that occur in the area of the HTML page, such as loading images and selecting form elements. If an action occurs directly in the boundary of the browser's display zone, it is an event as well. In short, what I am saying is that an event is only concerned with action on the web page itself, not on the browser. Take a look at Figure 7-1.

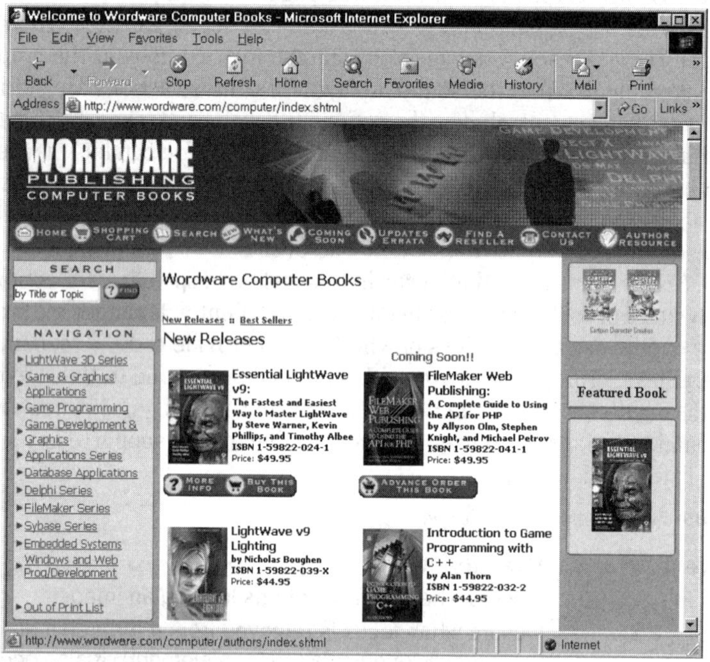

Figure 7-1. A browser

In this case, a browser displays the web site at www.wordware.com. You know that this window consists of two parts: the HTML page and the browser. You already know that many actions can occur in the environment illustrated in Figure 7-1. Some are events, while others are nonevent actions. The main part of the window is the HTML page, the content window without the surrounding menus and buttons.

All actions that take place in the area that actually contains the web site itself are the events. The user loads, unloads, clicks links, and causes many other events in this zone. The rest of the image contains the browser's features, such as the menu bar, the scroll bar, and other elements seen in Figure 7-2.

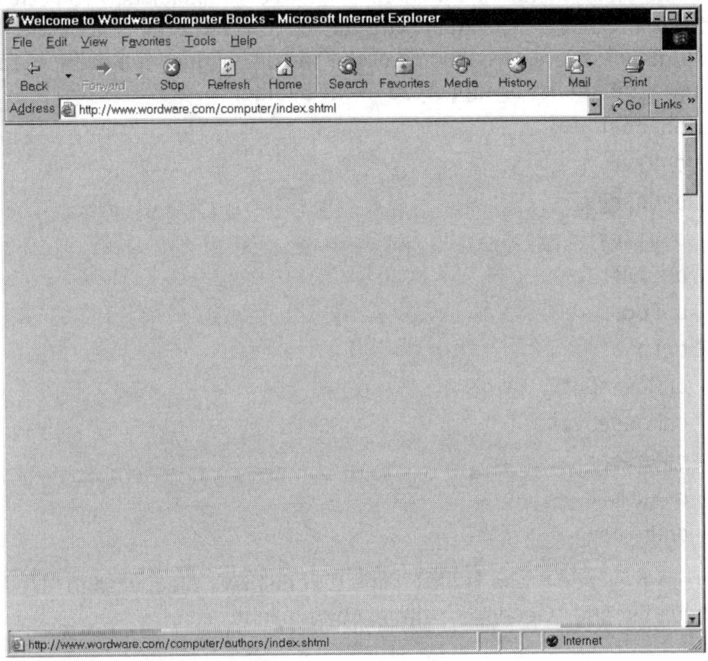

Figure 7-2. *The browser without a web page*

This figure is exactly the same as the one presented in Figure 7-1, except that the HTML page is excluded. No events occur outside of the HTML page. For example, pressing any of the buttons shown in Figure 7-2 will not trigger an event, nor will scrolling up and down the window. Even if you change the appearance of an HTML page, you are not triggering an event. It is very important to realize the difference between events and other actions because JavaScript can only handle events, not other actions.

Event Handlers

Event handlers correspond to their associated events. They are functions that execute automatically when events occur. Many JavaScript functions are called by event handlers. You saw earlier that events are actions that do not have any direct influence; they only serve the event handlers. Each event handler is associated with an event.

Event handlers are embedded in documents as attributes of HTML tags to which you assign JavaScript code. The general syntax is:

```
<TAG eventHandler="JavaScript Code">
```

You can use event handlers to embed any JavaScript code. You can place a 500-line script including functions as an event handler tag. You can also use more than one event handler with the same HTML tag. The names of the event handlers are constructed of the word "on" plus the name of the event. Here is the full list of supported event handlers:

- onAbort
- onBlur
- onChange
- onClick
- onError
- onFocus
- onLoad
- onMouseOut
- onMouseOver
- onSelect
- onSubmit
- onUnload

Here is the code for an HTML page that displays the message "Hello" when you load it, and "Goodbye" when you unload it.

```
<HTML>
<HEAD>
<TITLE>Hello / Goodbye</TITLE>
</HEAD>
<BODY onLoad="alert('Hello')" onUnLoad="alert('Goodbye')">
</BODY>
</HTML>
```

Example 7-1 (ex7-1.htm). *An event handler*

Event handlers are not case sensitive. For example, you can use either `ONLOAD` or `onLoad`. Although event handlers are related to JavaScript, the event handler itself is normally used as an HTML attribute, and HTML is not case sensitive. What this means is that event handlers are technically part of HTML, not JavaScript. However, you can put JavaScript into an event handler. It is still a good practice to use identifier-like naming conventions for event handlers.

Example 7-2 is a classic script that takes advantage of event handlers.

```
<HTML>
<HEAD>
<TITLE>Example 7-2</TITLE>
</HEAD>
<BODY>
```

```
<A HREF="http://www.wordware.com/"
     onMouseOver="window.status = 'Wordware Publishing'; return true"
                                  >Wordware</A>
</BODY>
</HTML>
```

***Example 7-2 (ex7-2.htm).** An event handler example*

It is sometimes problematic to execute statements directly in an event handler script. For example, if you want to include a long script, placing it in the event handler script makes the HTML page cumbersome, and maintenance becomes difficult. Another case in which difficulties can arise is when you want to correlate a script containing strings—quotation marks—to an event handler. The quotation marks themselves can cause a problem. As you can see in Example 7-2, the event handler requires quotation marks to delimit the specified JavaScript code from the surrounding HTML content. JavaScript requires alternation of quotation types, single and double, so you will probably find it annoying to write scripts with an emphasis on quotes. Event handlers accept any JavaScript script as long as it is valid. For that reason, you should associate functions with event handlers. The only statement you need in the event handler script is the function call.

You should normally place all functions at the top of the page, or more accurately, in the <HEAD></HEAD> portion of the document. This action forces JavaScript to evaluate your functions before it continues laying out the page. With this practice you guarantee that when the browser comes across an event handler in the HTML portion of the page, it will succeed in calling the function associated with that event if it occurs. The only restriction is that you do not place any event handlers to pick up events before the JavaScript script in the <HEAD></HEAD> portion. Such a restriction applies also to external files implemented via the SRC attribute of the <SCRIPT> tag. The basic structure of such a page is:

```
<HTML>
<HEAD>
<TITLE>The title of the page</TITLE>
<SCRIPT LANGUAGE="JavaScript" [SRC="path.js"]>
<!--
function functionName(parameters)
{
   statement1
   statement2
   statement3
}
// -->
</SCRIPT>
</HEAD>
<BODY>
<TAG otherAttributes eventHandler="functionName(arguments)">
</BODY>
</HTML>
```

It is very easy to find the associated functions if you always place their definitions in the <HEAD></HEAD> portion of the page. The HTML portion of the page stays as simple as it was before JavaScript was even invented. Another important advantage of using functions with event handlers is that you can use the same function many times in the same HTML page. For example, if you have a form with four text fields, you can validate each one of them using the same function by calling this function upon occurrence of an event that is specific to one of the fields.

You may have noticed that the title is specified before the <SCRIPT> tag. Although the title is specified via an HTML tag, it has no event handlers that could possibly invoke a function defined later. You probably won't have any problems if you do not follow this rule, although it is still a good practice because it contributes to the neat organization of the page and guarantees that you will never have any layout problems.

onLoad and onUnload

Two very important event handlers are onLoad and onUnload. Their corresponding events, load and unload, are triggered by those actions. When the page has finished loading, the load event takes place. When the user exits a page in any way, the unload event occurs. These are the most simple event handlers because they are related to the most basic <BODY> tag, and are specified as attributes of this tag. The following document welcomes the user via an alert box when entering the page, and says goodbye when the user exits, also via an alert box:

```
<HTML>
<HEAD>
<TITLE>onLoad and onUnload event handlers</TITLE>
</HEAD>
<BODY onLoad="alert('Welcome to our page!')" onUnload="alert('Goodbye,
and don\'t forget to come back!')">
</BODY>
</HTML>
```

The onLoad event handler is widely used to call deferred scripts—functions. Placing a function call as the event handler's script enables you to control the timing of the execution, so the script executes only when the page is fully laid out.

onError

The onError event handler expands JavaScript's ability to interact with the user according to errors that occur when loading a window or an image. This event handler was not supported by early browsers (such as Internet Explorer 3.0) but is now widely supported by most modern browsers. In this section we discuss window loading errors.

The onError event handler executes a JavaScript script when an error event occurs.

The `onError` event handler is extremely useful due to the fact that it can be set to one of three values:

- null—suppresses all error dialogs. Setting `window.onerror` to null means your users won't see JavaScript errors caused by your own code.
- A function that handles errors—replaces the standard dialog boxes used by JavaScript to report errors.
- Variable that contains null or a valid function reference.

The following JavaScript statement disables JavaScript error dialogs:

```
window.onerror = null
```

You should place this statement in its *own script* directly after the <HEAD> tag to be on the safe side, using the following HTML document structure:

```
<HTML>
<HEAD>
<SCRIPT LANGUAGE="JavaScript">
<!--
window.onerror = null
// -->
</SCRIPT>
</HEAD>
<BODY>
</BODY>
</HTML>
```

The same rule applies to all values you assign to this event handler explicitly.

The following document does not display any error dialog, although an error is encountered. (If you can't fish it out, you may want to review the previous chapters, or just look at the `alert()` method's argument for a clue.)

```
<HTML>
<HEAD>
<SCRIPT LANGUAGE="JavaScript">
window.onerror = null
</SCRIPT>
</HEAD>
<BODY>
<SCRIPT LANGUAGE="JavaScript">
alert(Quotes missing)
</SCRIPT>
</BODY>
</HTML>
```

It is a good practice to set the `onError` event handler to null when your script runs on a public page. However, it makes no sense when writing the script, because it makes debugging impossible.

Here is another document that disables errors and therefore avoids a stack overflow error from being reported:

```
<HTML>
<HEAD>
<TITLE>Disabling error messages</TITLE>
<SCRIPT LANGUAGE="JavaScript">
<!--
// disable error reports
window.onerror = null
// create an error-generating function (infinite recursion)
function testErrorFunction()
{
   testErrorFunction()
}
// -->
</SCRIPT>
</HEAD>
<BODY onload="testErrorFunction()">
</BODY>
</HTML>
```

An error occurs with or without assigning null to the event handler. The difference is that no response to the error on the browser's behalf is generated. See "Calling Event Handlers Explicitly" later in this chapter for a discussion on assigning values to event handlers via JavaScript.

Another option is to write a function to handle errors in place of the standard JavaScript error-reporting dialog boxes. The function should accept three arguments:

- The error message
- The URL of the script that caused the error
- The error line number

The function intercepts JavaScript errors. It must return the value true.

Here is a classic set of functions and statements for error handling:

```
<HTML>
<HEAD>
<SCRIPT LANGUAGE="JavaScript">
<!--
// assign user-defined function to intercept errors
window.onerror = myOnError
// create array to hold error messages
messageArray = new Array(0)
// create array to hold URLs of errors
urlArray = new Array(0)
// create array to hold line numbers of errors
lineNumberArray = new Array(0)
// error-intercepting function
function myOnError(msg, url, lno)
{
   // assign message of current error to the array element following
         the last element
   messageArray[messageArray.length] = msg
   // assign URL of current error to the array element following the
         last element
```

```
   urlArray[urlArray.length] = url
   // assign line number of current error to the array element
          following the last element
   lineNumberArray[lineNumberArray.length] = lno
   // return true to intercept JavaScript errors
   return true
}
function displayErrors()
{
   // open new browser window to report errors
   errorWindow = window.open('','errors','scrollbars=yes')
   // write header to window
   errorWindow.document.write('<B>Error Report</B><P>')
   // loop to print all error data
   for (var i = 0; i < messageArray.length; ++i)
   {
      errorWindow.document.write('<B>Error in file:</B> ' +
             urlArray[i] + '<BR>')
      errorWindow.document.write('<B>Line number:</B> ' +
             lineNumberArray[i] + '<BR>')
      errorWindow.document.write('<B>Message:</B> ' +
             messageArray[i] + '<P>')
   }
   // close data stream
   errorWindow.document.close()
}
// -->
</SCRIPT>
</HEAD>
<BODY>
<FORM>
<INPUT TYPE="button" onClick="displayErrors()" VALUE="display errors">
</FORM>
</BODY>
</HTML>
```

Example 7-3 (ex7-3.htm). *A complex event handler example*

At first, the function reference is assigned to `window.onerror`. Three arrays are then created; each holds a different piece of data associated with errors that might occur. The length of each array is set to 0, because no errors have occurred thus far. The function that intercepts the JavaScript errors is `myOnError()`. Its arguments are the error message, URL, and line number, respectively.

You do not need to understand the functions at this stage because they use concepts that have not been discussed yet, such as arrays and windows. The only point you should be aware of is that the function returns true to instruct JavaScript that it is intended to intercept the standard JavaScript errors. In general, a list of the JavaScript errors generated by the script is printed in another window when the user clicks the button. See the section "Calling Event Handlers Explicitly" for more details on the event handler implementation demonstrated in Example 7-3 (`window.onerror`).

Emulating Events via Methods

We mentioned earlier that each event belongs to a specific object. Some events are associated with more than one object. Another characteristic of objects is methods. They are functions that usually work on the data related to that object, the properties. Some methods of objects that include event handlers actually emulate those events. You can use such a method to cause an event to occur. These methods are usually called *event methods*. Although we will discuss them in depth later, here are some common methods:

- `blur()`
- `click()`
- `focus()`
- `select()`
- `submit()`

Events generated with these methods are like any other method. Most importantly, they do not invoke their corresponding event handlers.

When you emulate an event, it is important that you do so only after the browser has finished laying out the page, or at least the object (usually a form element) with which the method is associated. The following page generates an error:

```
<HTML>
<HEAD>
<TITLE>Emulating an event of a nonexistent (thus far) form</TITLE>
<SCRIPT LANGUAGE="JavaScript">
document.form1.field1.focus()
</SCRIPT>
</HEAD>
<BODY>
<FORM NAME="form1" METHOD=POST>
<INPUT TYPE="text" NAME="field1">
</FORM>
</BODY>
</HTML>
```

The error message is shown in Figure 7-3.

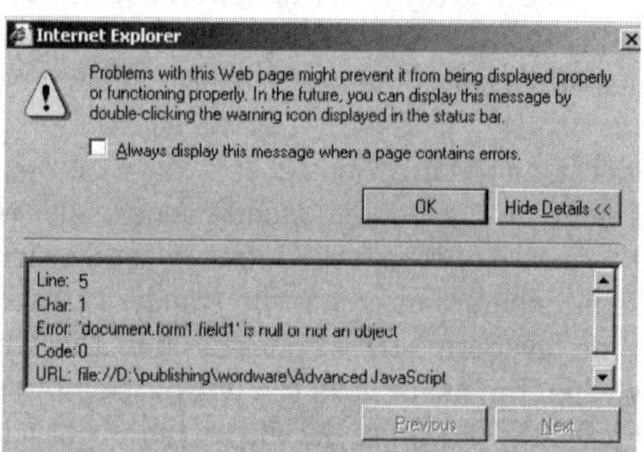

Figure 7-3. *Error message*

This error is not guaranteed to be exactly the same on all platforms. Emulating an object's event that has not yet been laid out is just one example that creates such an error. Generally speaking, you cannot refer to any element of a page that has not yet been laid out. A deferred script is allowed to refer to an object laid out after the script, provided that you do not execute that script before the object has been laid out. We will discuss this issue in depth throughout the book.

Calling Event Handlers Explicitly

You can set an event handler from within a JavaScript script. Here is a short example:

```
<HTML>
<HEAD>
<TITLE>Emulating an event of a nonexistent (thus far) form</TITLE>
<SCRIPT LANGUAGE="JavaScript">
<!--
function alert1()
{
   alert("This is the first function.")
}
function alert2()
{
   alert("This is the second function.")
}
// -->
</SCRIPT>
</HEAD>
<BODY>
<FORM NAME="form1" METHOD=POST>
<INPUT TYPE="button" NAME="button1" VALUE="button1" onClick="alert1()">
</FORM>
<SCRIPT LANGUAGE="JavaScript">
<!--
document.form1.button1.onclick = alert2
// -->
</SCRIPT>
</BODY>
</HTML>
```

Example 7-4 (ex7-4.htm). *You can call a JavaScript script via an event handler*

Try loading this page and clicking the button. If you are using an earlier version of Netscape Navigator, an alert box displays the message "This is the second function," despite the fact that the event handler associates the `click` event with the first function, `alert1()`. Notice the script placed directly after the form. It associates a different function with the `click` event of `button1` in `form1`.

Note: Event handlers are function references as opposed to function calls. Therefore, you must assign `alert2`, not `alert2()`, which is primarily a function call, evaluating to the type and value the function returns. Also, since the event handler HTML attributes are literal function bodies, you cannot use `<INPUT ... onClick=alert2>` in the HTML source. You must call the function instead.

You are probably wondering why we used `onclick` rather than `onClick`. The reason is that JavaScript is case sensitive and understands `onclick` (all lowercase), whereas HTML is case insensitive. In HTML, you may use all lowercase, all uppercase, or any other convention you choose.

Calling event handlers explicitly enables flexible event handlers, because you can modify them anywhere in the script. You can create a customized page, allowing the user to determine what a certain button should do when clicked.

An event handler does not have to exist when you use this technique. The preceding script would work exactly the same if you omitted the event handler specification in the HTML source and used the following line instead:

```
<INPUT TYPE="button" NAME="button1" VALUE="button1">
```

In this case you are actually defining a new event handler to correspond with an event.

Also note that the above method is the only way to assign a function reference to an event handler. You cannot use any of the following structures:

```
<SCRIPT LANGUAGE="JavaScript">
<!--
document.form1.button1.onclick = "alert2()"
// -->
```

```
<SCRIPT LANGUAGE="JavaScript">
<!--
document.form1.button1.onclick = alert2()
// -->
```

```
<SCRIPT LANGUAGE="JavaScript">
<!--
document.form1.button1.onclick = "var counter = 5"
// -->
```

Such attempts to assign statements that are not function references result in an error upon clicking the button.

Canceling Events

Netscape Navigator, Internet Explorer, and Firefox all make it possible to cancel a `click` event, either with a hypertext link or a client-side image map. The `onClick` event handler can return false to cancel the action normally associated with a `click` event. Here is an example:

```
<HTML>
<HEAD>
<TITLE>Canceling events in onClick</TITLE>
</HEAD>
<BODY>
<A HREF="http://www.mozilla.org/" onClick="return confirm('Load
        Mozilla home page?')">Mozilla</a>
</BODY>
</HTML>
```

Example 7-5 (ex7-5.htm). *Try running this script to cancel the event*

When you click the hypertext link, a confirm box pops up. If you click OK, the method evaluates to true, the event qualifies, and the new page (Firefox's home page) loads. If the user selects Cancel, the method returns false, and the new page, which is associated with the `click` event, does not load.

Summary

In this chapter you discovered events and event handlers. JavaScript is designed to add interaction to web pages, meaning you can respond to actions that the user performs. Events describe such actions, whereas event handlers take care of them. They give JavaScript programmers the ability to interact with the user. Only rarely do you find scripts on the web that do not take advantage of this unique feature. Although interaction is not exclusive to event handlers (we've seen dialog boxes before), they are probably the most important means of interaction in JavaScript. They extend the capability of web pages, as you might have noticed while surfing the net. We did not present any events or event handlers in detail in this chapter, excluding `onLoad` and `onUnload`, for they will be discussed individually in depth later in the book. Each event and its corresponding handler has significant features. As you will see later, all events are associated with specific objects, so it is important that you be introduced to these objects before we discuss their event handlers.

Chapter 8

Building and Extending Objects

Creating Instances

We introduced the concepts of object-oriented programming in Chapter 4, so you should already realize that not only does JavaScript support only limited object-oriented programming, but that some terms used here might not be used the same way they are in other languages (such as C++, C#, or Java). In JavaScript, an *object* is the template from which you make *instances*. In purely object-oriented languages, an object is the instance made from a class. If you have experience in true object-oriented languages, don't let this terminology throw you off.

For example, suppose you have defined an employee object that includes some methods and properties of an employee, such as his or her social security number and address. This definition has no effect on the script, because no new entity has been changed or created. Only when you apply the object's definition to a specific person, say John Doe, is a new entity created—an instance of that object. The number of instances you create with a single object definition is unlimited. The object definition can be either one you define with a function or a built-in one. Creating an instance of a built-in object is relatively simple because the object is predefined. Unlike C++ and Java, you cannot create your own objects (what would be called classes in C++ and Java). You can only use the ones built into JavaScript.

You should use the following syntax to create an instance:

```
var name = new objectname([arguments])
```

So, if you want to create an instance of the `String` object, you can use the following statement:

```
var str1 = new String("Hello!")
```

This statement creates an instance named `str1` and passes it the literal `"Hello!"`. You can create another instance if you like:

```
var str2 = new String("Hi!")
```

Most objects, `String` included, have what is called a constructor. A *constructor* is a function that fires automatically when an instance is created of that object. When you pass a parameter to an object when creating an instance, you are actually passing that parameter to the object's constructor function. The reason you have constructors is that some actions need to take place before anything else can take place. For example, with the `String` object, it really needs a string of characters in it before you can do anything with it. Therefore, that string of characters is passed via the `String` object's constructor function.

In the previous examples, the instances `str1` and `str2` act pretty much like regular variables. In fact, you can think of them as variables of the `"String"` type. You can pass them on to functions as in:

```
function printValue(val)
{
   document.write("*** " + val + " ***")
}
printValue(str1)
```

You can also return objects:

```
function printValue(obj)
{
   return obj
}
```

Remember that objects work just like any other variables. That means that if you create an instance of an object inside a function, it is considered local; i.e., it is visible only inside the function during the function's current execution course. If you declare the instance outside a function, it is preferable that you use the `var` keyword. When you create an instance of an object inside a function without `var`, it is a global structure. Bear in mind that if you create a global instance, or even a simple variable inside a function, you must execute the function before that global data structure exists in the script. From that point on you can refer to it freely anywhere in the document.

When you create an instance of an object via the `new` operator, you are actually declaring a specific data type according to the object's definition and allocating the appropriate amount of memory for that data type. All properties referenced in the constructor function are accessible as properties of the object's instance.

After you have created an instance of an object, you do not have to use the keyword `new` anymore when referring to that instance. However, if you want one of the instance's properties to be an instance of its own, you must use `new` again to create the new object. An instance of an object also features its methods. A *method* is essentially a function that is found inside of an object.

Take a look at the following example:

```
var current = new Date()   // the current date
var minutes = current.getMinutes()

var current2 = new Date()  // the current date
var minutes2 = current2.getMinutes()
```

As you can see, both instances have methods. A method belongs to a specific instance of an object. In other words, the `getMinutes()` associated with `current` object is a separate function from the `getMinutes()` associated with the `current2` object. Both functions are made from the same template and perform the same action.

Constructor Functions

We already gave you a brief definition of a constructor. Remember we said that it is a function that is called (i.e., "fires") as soon as the object is instantiated. However, this definition leaves much to be desired. Let's try a more complete description and discussion of constructors. A *constructor function* is a function that defines the properties and methods of the instance you are creating from an object. It fires automatically when an instance of the object is created. You can think of built-in objects as objects whose constructor functions are predefined in JavaScript, so you do not need to write them on your own.

A constructor function resembles a cookie cutter. You provide it some dough and it gives the dough the proper shape. The cookie cutter is like the constructor function because they both receive a simple structure and change it according to a specified template.

Defining Object Properties

The keyword `this` is probably the most important word related to objects in JavaScript (as well as many other object-oriented languages). It refers to the current instance of the object you are in. Inside a constructor function it refers to the instance for which the function was called. Take a look at the following function:

```
function student(name, age, avgGrade)
{
   this.name = name
   this.age = age
   this.grade = avgGrade
}
```

This function accepts three arguments. It defines an object type of a student in a class. The properties are `name`, `age`, and `grade`, and they are initialized by the values passed on to the function. You can use the following statement to create an instance of this object—a student in a class:

```
var student1 = new student("Sharon", 16, 85)
```

Now you can refer to these properties in the following fashion:

```
alert(student1.name + " is a cute " + student1.age + " - year old.)
```

It is also possible to add properties to an object once it has been created. Such properties exist only in the specific instance to which they are assigned. The following script segment demonstrates this:

```
function student(name, age, avgGrade)
{
   this.name = name
   this.age = age
   this.grade = avgGrade
}
var student1 = new student("Sharon", 16, 85)
student1.sex = "female"
var message = student1.name + " is a cute " + student1.age
message += " - year old "
message += (student1.sex == "female") ? "girl." : "boy."
alert(message)
```

The problem with the preceding script is that it adds the new property only to one instance, `student1`. Because constructor functions are just like any other function, you can use valid JavaScript statements in them. Therefore, you can use the following constructor function to add the new property to all instances of the `student` object:

```
function student(name, age, avgGrade, sex)
{
   this.name = name
   this.age = age
   this.grade = avgGrade
   this.description = (sex == "female") ? "girl" : "boy"
}
```

Now you can create instances that will include the "girl" or "boy" description:

```
var student2 = new student("Joe", 16, 91, "male")
```

Based on the exact definition of the word `this`, some JavaScript tends to use alternative structures for construction functions. Here is the preceding example in a different form:

```
function student(name, age, avgGrade, sex)
{
   obj = this
   obj.name = name
   obj.age = age
```

```
    obj.grade = avgGrade
    obj.description = (sex == "female") ? "girl" : "boy"
}
```

Notice that the calling object, referred to as `this`, is assigned to a variable. This variable must be global because a constructor function's purpose is to create an instance for use outside of that function. A local variable does not have any effect outside the function where it is declared. Personally, I never use this method and don't see it used very often. I simply include it here so that you will not be confused if you see it somewhere.

You now know how to define properties via constructor functions. If you only want to create one instance of an object, you must also use a constructor function.

You can use the following function to view the properties of an object:

```
function getProps(obj, objName)
{
   var result = ""   // initialize output string
   for (var i in obj)
   {
      result += objName + "." + i + " = " + obj[i] + "<BR>"
   }
   result += "<HR>"  // add horizontal rule to output string
   return(result)    // return output string
}
```

To invoke this method, use a statement such as:

```
document.write(getProps(student1, "student1"))
```

Note that the arguments are not always the same. For example, if you use this statement from within another function that accepts the instance `student1` as the parameter `person`, you should use the following statement instead:

```
document.write(getProps(person, "student1"))
```

If a property of an object holds a null value, it does not exist. Assigning a null value to a property will cause the function `getProps()` to count out that property. Keep this in mind, especially when you are debugging a script.

Nested Objects

JavaScript supports nested objects. A *nested object* is an object that is also a property of another object. Or put another way, it is a case where an object has other objects inside of it. If you think about this it should not be too much of a surprise. Remember that objects have properties, and inside the object those properties are simply variables. Also recall that an object is just a complex type of variable. When you put those two facts together, having objects contain other objects is really not surprising at all. There are a few ways to create nested objects. Take a look at the following script segment:

```
function student(name, age, grade, father, mother)
{
   this.name = name
   this.age = age
   this.grade = grade
   this.parents = new parents(father, mother)
}
function parents(father, mother)
{
   this.father = father
   this.mother = mother
}
var student1 = new student("Sharon", 16, 85, "Mark", "Stacy")
```

This script consists of two functions. The function `parents()` creates an instance containing two properties, `father` and `mother`. It accepts both values as arguments.

The first function, `student()`, creates a function consisting of four properties. The first three are simple properties like the ones you have seen earlier in this chapter. The fourth property is an instance of an object. This instance is created by the `parents()` function, as described earlier. You can refer to all elements of an object with the "dot" syntax:

```
student1.name
student1.age
student1.grade
student1.parents.father
student1.parents.mother
```

To print the properties of a general object you can use the following recursive function:

```
function getProps(obj, objName)
{
   // initialize accumulative variable
   var result = ""
   // loop through properties
   for (var i in obj)
   {
      // if current property is an object, call function for it
      if (typeof obj[i] == "object")
         result += getProps(obj[i], objName + "." + i)
      else
         result += objName + "." + i + " = " + obj[i] + "<BR>"
   }
   // return final result
   return result
}
```

The function's algorithm is fairly simple. It loops through the properties of the main object. If the current property, represented by `i`, is an object, the function is called once again with the property `obj[i]` as the object, and the property's name attached to the object's name with a separating dot (`objName + "." + i`). Each call to the function returns the string listing the properties at the current level. The value returned by a recursive call is assigned to the variable result, which is local in the calling function. Here is an entire HTML document and its output to help you understand this concept:

```
<HTML>
<HEAD>
<TITLE>Printing properties of nested objects</TITLE>
<SCRIPT LANGUAGE="JavaScript">
<!--
function student(name, age, grade, father, mother)
{
   this.name = name
   this.age = age
   this.grade = grade
   this.parents = new parents(father, mother)
}
function parents(father, mother)
{
   this.father = father
   this.mother = mother
}
var student1 = new student("Sharon", 16, 85, "Mark", "Stacy")
function getProps(obj, objName)
{
   var result = ""
   for (var i in obj)
   {
      if (typeof obj[i] == "object")
         result += getProps(obj[i], objName + "." + i)
      else
         result += objName + "." + i + " = " + obj[i] + "<BR>"
   }
   return result
}
document.write(getProps(student1, "student1"))
// -->
</SCRIPT>
</HEAD>
<BODY>
</BODY>
</HTML>
```

Example 8-1 (ex8-1.htm). *A script that uses the getProps() function to analyze the structure of an object*

The output for that script looks like Figure 8-1.

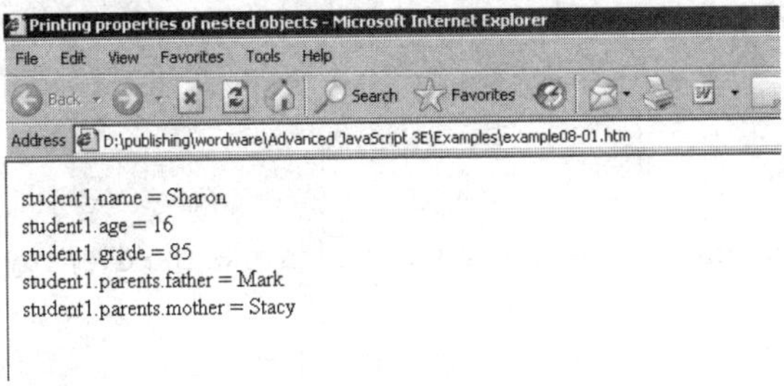

Figure 8-1. *Script output*

Defining Methods

Objects group data and functions that process that data. Data appears in the form of properties. A method is simply a function associated with an object. Consider the following function:

```
function displayStudent()
{
   var result = ""
   result += this.name + " -- "
   result += "a " + this.age + " - year old "
   result += this.grade + "% average student.<BR>"
   result += this.name + "'s parents -- "
   result += this.parents.father + ", " + this.parents.mother
   result += ".<BR>"
   document.write(result)
}
```

You need to include a reference to this function in the constructor function. This is done exactly like you define properties:

```
function displayStudent()
{
   var result = ""
   result += this.name + " -- "
   result += "a " + this.age + " - year old "
   result += this.grade + "% average student.<BR>"
   result += this.name + "'s parents -- "
   result += this.parents.father + ", " + this.parents.mother
   result += ".<BR>"
   document.write(result)
}
function student(name, age, grade, father, mother)
{
   this.name = name
   this.age = age
   this.grade = grade
   this.parents = new parents(father, mother)
   this.display = displayStudent
}
```

```
function parents(father, mother)
{
   this.father = father
   this.mother = mother
}
```

The following statements create an instance and invoke the `display()` method:

```
var student1 = new student("Sharon", 16, 85, "Mark", "Stacy")
student1.display()
```

Notice the extensive use of the keyword `this` inside the function to refer to the object. The main characteristic of a method is that it usually processes the data of its object. You can even create a "constructor method" in the following fashion:

```
function construct(name, val)
{
   this[name] = val
}
function student(name, age, grade, father, mother)
{
   this.construct = construct
   this.name = name
   this.age = age
   this.grade = grade
   this.parents = new parents(father, mother)
}
function parents(father, mother)
{
   this.father = father
   this.mother = mother
}
var student1 = new student("Sharon", 16, 85, "Mark", "Stacy")
student1.construct("boyfriend", "Tom")
```

Notice that the method (`construct()`) refers to the new property via the array notation. You may recall from Chapter 4, "Object-Oriented Programming," that you must use this notation if you wish to use a data value. You can only use the "dot" syntax when you use literals. In this case, `name` is a data structure, not a literal (a literal is a constant value you can see, such as `"boyfriend"`). Now you can use the recursive function presented earlier to view the elements of an object and to see how it works with methods.

Notice that the recursive function works with methods as well as with properties. The statements of the method are placed on the same line. JavaScript automatically adds semicolons to delimit the statement. It also uses a uniform coding scheme if you did not do so originally in the function, as you should.

A method in JavaScript, like a property, belongs only to one instance. You can only invoke it from that instance. All "communication" with an object is done via methods.

The calling object is considered global inside a method. You can modify the object using the keyword `this`.

Creating Objects—An Example

Let's say you want to create a database-like object structure for a store that sells televisions. Each type of television should be an instance of the same object. The number of televisions of a certain model available in stock should be a property of the object. It should also include the features of that television set. In addition, the object should include two methods: one to be invoked when a customer buys a television set, and another to be invoked when the store owner orders a certain quantity of television sets of a given model.

Example 8-2 demonstrates the most important points.

```
<HTML>
<HEAD>
<SCRIPT LANGUAGE="JavaScript">
<!--
function television(brand, size, price, num)
{
   this.brand = brand     // property
   this.size = size       // property
   this.price = price     // property
   this.num = num         // property
   this.sell = sell       // method
   this.buy = buy         // method
   this.display = display // method
}
function sell(quantity)
{
   if (quantity > this.num)
      alert("Not enough " + this.brand + " " + this.size + "\" sets in stock.")
   else
      this.num -= quantity
   if (quantity < 5)
      alert("Order more " + this.brand + " " + this.size + "\" sets urgently.")
}
function buy(quantity)
{
   this.num += quantity
}
function display()
{
   var result = ""
   result += "<TABLE BORDER=2><TR>"
   result += "<TD WIDTH = 60>" + this.brand + "</TD>"
   result += "<TD WIDTH = 30>" + this.size + "\"</TD>"
   result += "<TD WIDTH = 45>$" + this.price + "</TD>"
   result += "<TD WIDTH = 45>" + this.num + " left</TD>"
   result += "</TR></TABLE>"
   document.write(result)
```

```
}
var tel1 = new television("Sony", 27, 1200, 30)
var tel2 = new television("JVC", 20, 650, 20)
var tel3 = new television("Grundig", 14, 420, 45)
tel1.sell(27)  // 27 "Sony" television sets sold
tel1.buy(16)   // 16 "Sony" television sets ordered (bought)
tel1.display()
tel2.sell(21)  // 21 "JVC" television sets sold -- error!
tel2.sell(1)   // 1 "JVC" television set sold
tel2.display()
tel3.display()
// -->
</SCRIPT>
</HEAD>
<BODY>
</BODY>
</HTML>
```

Example 8-2 (ex8-2.htm). *A script that stores data using instances of a general object*

When you run Example 8-2 you should get the output shown in the following figures:

Sony	27"	$1200	19 left
JVC	20"	$650	19 left
Grundig	14"	$420	45 left

Figure 8-2. *A table showing the inventory of television sets*

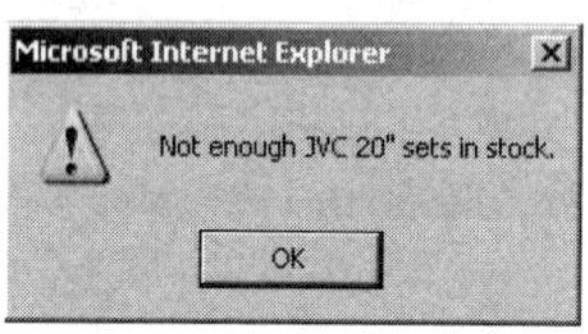

Figure 8-3. *An alert box that notifies the user if there are not enough sets in stock*

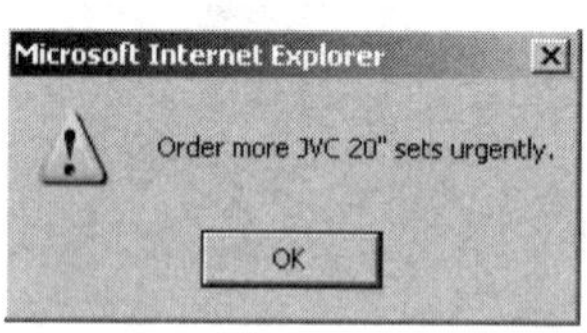

Figure 8-4. *An alert box that tells the user to order more sets*

Example 8-2 features three methods:

- `sell()`—This method modifies the number of television sets of the model number specified in the object. The function's only parameter is one that accepts the number of television sets sold. It checks if there are enough sets in stock, because you cannot sell more than you've got! If there are enough sets of that type in stock, the number is subtracted from the total quantity of that TV available before the transaction.

Lastly, the method checks if there are less than five TV sets of that type left. If so, it sends a message describing that situation.

- `buy()`—This method simply adds the number of television sets to the `num` property of the object, or instance. The only parameter accepted by the method is the one that accepts the number of television sets bought.
- `display()`—This method does not accept any arguments. It simply prints all the properties of the current object in a tabular format.

Notice that the first two methods actually change values of the object. This is another example that shows that methods refer to their calling object as global, so all properties of the object modified inside the function (method) are also affected outside the method.

Prototype and Object Extensions

A *prototype* is a property of any object created with the keyword `new`. A prototype resembles the common e-mail address portion of users sharing the same server. Likewise, a prototype belongs to all instances of the object that the prototype belongs to. Prototypes refer not only to properties, but also to an object's methods. Take a look at the following script segment:

```
var str1 = new String("a"), str2 = new String("b")
function repeat(n, delimiter)
{
   var text = ""
   var str = this.toString()       // make sure the object is string
   while (n >= 0)
   {
      text += str
      text += delimiter
      n--
   }
   return text
}
String.prototype.repeat = repeat // String == name of object
                                 // add a repeat() method to

var str1 ="",str2=""
alert(str1.repeat(5, " ; "))
alert(str1)
alert(str2.repeat(7, " "))
alert(str2.repeat(3))
```

You can see that the function `repeat()` is typical for a method. As a matter of fact, it is implemented as one. The key statement in this script is:

```
String.prototype.repeat = repeat
```

This statement adds a method to all instances of the object (`String`), although they were already created. The word `prototype` is constant, and its role is to merely specify that the following property or method is a prototype. It may seem at first that `repeat()` is a method of a nested object.

However, `prototype` is not actually a property but a specification. Here are some of the alert boxes generated by the preceding script segment:

Figures 8-5a, 8-5b, and 8-5c. *Object prototypes enable extendable objects in JavaScript.*

It is important to know that object prototypes refer to instances of the object created before the definition of the prototype as well as instances that are created later. The prototype exists only from the moment it is defined. Be sure to refer to such prototype properties and methods only after you have created the prototype. Commenting scripts helps assure that you follow this rule.

Up until now you have seen a method used as a prototype. Obviously, properties can also accomplish this task. In the following script we will look at a property as a prototype of a user-defined object. Here is the script:

```
function car(make, model, year)
{
   this.make = make
   this.model = model
   this.year = year
}
var mine1 = new car("Dodge", "Charger", 2007)
car.prototype.wheels = 4                        // no 3-wheelers please!
var mine2 = new car("Jaguar", "X-Type", 2007)
if (mine1.wheels == 4 && mine2.wheels == 4)  // true!
   document.write("Both cars have ", mine2.wheels, " wheels.")
```

The message at the end of the script is printed, because all instances of the `car` object, whether they are created before the definition of the prototype or after it, consist of a property named `wheels`, holding the value 4, which is assigned to the prototype. It is practically useless to create a data property prototype without assigning it a value, or at least a default one, because you will need to refer to that property later, and such a reference automatically creates the property.

Prototypes are probably more useful with built-in objects because they can modify the object. You can create outstanding methods and properties you never dreamed JavaScript would support. We use prototypes in many examples in this book, especially ones dealing with strings, dates, and arrays. The revolutionary concept is that you can add features to the language itself. Note that prototypes can only be added to objects that support instances, as opposed to static objects (such as `Math`), which do not work with prototypes for obvious reasons.

Summary

In this chapter you learned how to create instances of an object. Instances refer to both user-defined objects and built-in ones. You also learned about constructor functions that build objects or object types. As you will see later in the book, such user-defined objects extend the capabilities of the language and enable structured programming. Lastly, I presented object prototypes—properties of all instances of a certain object type. Although it should be clear by now, do not worry too much about how to use them, as they will be used in many examples later on in the book. Objects are the backbone of JavaScript. Many elements of the language are actually objects, although other languages do not refer to them as such. The classic example for such objects are arrays, discussed in depth in the next chapter.

Chapter 9
Arrays

What Is an Array?

The concept of an array is found in all programming languages. *Arrays* are actually variables, just a little more complicated than the standard variables you have encountered so far in this book. You can think about an array as a set of variables with the same name. We use arrays when we want to work with a certain set of related data all of the same data type. An example would be a set of students' ages. These would all be integer values and they would be related. As a programmer, if you want to process an individual item of an array you need to specify the array name and indicate which array element is being referenced. Specific elements are indicated by an index or a subscript.

Some History

Way back in the dark ages of JavaScript (the early 1990s), JavaScript did not have arrays. One reason to point this out is to demonstrate how quickly things change in the world of computers. A time of only 15 to 20 years in the past is ancient history. This is important to realize since, as a JavaScript programmer, you will want to keep up to date with changes.

The first version of JavaScript, the one supported by Navigator 2.x, did not feature arrays. JavaScript scripters had no choice but to come up with a simple workaround. Everyone used (and a few still use) the following function to create arrays:

```
function createArray(n, init)
{
   this.length = n
   for (i = 1 ; i <= n ; i++)
   {
      this[i] = init
   }
}
```

This method is rarely used now and is not necessary. However, you may see it in the field so I am showing it to you so that you are not confused if you do.

Creating Simple Arrays

Okay, you know what an array is, and you are eager to use them, but how do you create one? Arrays in JavaScript are simple built-in objects. You create an array just like an instance of an object, because that is exactly what it is. The formal name of the object is `Array`—notice the capitalized "A." The general syntax is:

```
var arrayObjectName = new Array()
var arrayObjectName = new Array(arrayLength)
```

`arrayObjectName` is the name of a new object, an existing variable, or a property of an existing object.

`arrayLength` is the number of individual elements in the array.

In JavaScript, specifying the length of the array or the number of elements is not vital. An array is an object like any other object. There is no explicit array type in JavaScript.

Here are some arrays:

```
var day = new Array(31)
var month = new Array(12)
var year = new Array() // number of years "not known"
```

All elements of an array are initially null. This is important because such elements do not have any influence on your script. An element with a null value actually does not exist. You can prove this to yourself by running `getProps()` on a new array:

```
function getProps(obj, objName)
{
   var result = ""
   for (var i in obj)
   {
      if (typeof obj[i] == "object")
         result += getProps(obj[i], objName + "[" + i + "]")
      else
         result += objName + "[" + i + "] = " + obj[i] + "<BR>"
   }
   return result
}
var ar = new Array(3)
document.write(getProps(ar, "ar"))
```

This script does not generate any output, because if a property of an object has a null value, it does not exist in the computer memory; thus it is not recognized.

Strongly typed programming languages require that you specify the number of elements in an array. In such languages all elements of an array must contain values of the same type (`int`, `char`, ...). An array is an explicit data structure in those languages. From the moment an array is declared, it takes up the required storage area in memory. It does not matter if you initialized its values or not. JavaScript, however, does not require you to initialize the elements in an array when you create it. Theoretically, if you created an array without specifying the number of elements, it would be as if you created one with zero elements. Extending an array in such languages is usually not possible; therefore, you must specify the length in all array declarations.

The null value is given by default to each element of an array in JavaScript. When the value is null, the element is not stored in the computer's memory. So creating an array with an infinite number of elements is fine in JavaScript. However, doing so is not recommended since it would be confusing to people who read your code, and not particularly useful. Keep in mind that elements holding a null value do not take up space in memory, but they are considered elements in the array, so they are added to the array's `length` property.

With JavaScript (unlike C++), it doesn't matter whether the elements of an array are of the same data type. They can be a mix of numbers, strings, Boolean values, objects, and even arrays (which are actually objects).

Referring to an Array's Elements

Creating an array is fine, but you must be able to use it. To use an array, whether you are putting data in or taking it out, you need to access the elements of that array. Keep in mind that arrays in JavaScript are objects. Like all other objects, they have properties and methods:

```
arrayObjectName[subscript] // ar1[4]
```

The *`subscript`* follows the array name and is enclosed in square brackets. Subscripts are simple integers that start at zero.

Here is a simple array:

```
var ar = new Array(5)
```

This array has five elements: `ar[0]`, `ar[1]`, `ar[2]`, `ar[3]`, and `ar[4]`.

After you create an array you can increase its length by specifying a value for the highest subscript element. The following code creates an array of length zero, then assigns a null value to element 99. This changes the length of the array to 100.

```
accounts = new Array()  // array of zero elements
accounts[99] = null     // array of 100 elements
```

Note that the array does not take up any storage space, even after it is extended.

When referring to an element, the subscript can be either a literal (e.g., 3) or a variable (e.g., num = 3).

An element of an array can be any valid value. It can be a string, a number, a Boolean value, a null value, or even another object. For example, if you want to create an array in which each element is a student object, you can use the following statements:

```
function student()
{  // constructor function
   // properties not initialized to meaningful value
   this.name = ""
   this.age = ""
   this.grade = ""
}
var size = 35                        // num of students in class
var students = new Array(size)       // array is defined
for (var i = 0; i < size; i++)
{
   students[i] = new student()
}
students[0].name = "Mark"
students[32].grade = 88
```

At first, the desired size of the array, the number of students in the class, is assigned to the variable size. An array of that size is then created. All elements of the array, from students[0] to students[34], are then defined using the constructor function student(). In this example, all of the elements in the array are of the same type. An array can also have elements of different types. Here is an example:

```
function student()
{  // constructor function
   // properties not initialized to meaningful value
   this.name = ""
   this.age = ""
   this.grade = ""
}
function teacher(name, age)
{
   this.name = name
   this.age = age
}
var size = 35                          // num of students in class
var students = new Array(size + 1)     // array is defined
students[0] = new teacher("Kate", 45)
for (var i = 1; i < size + 1; i++)
{  // or i <= size
   students[i] = new student()
}
alert("   is the teacher." + students[0].name)
```

In this script segment an array of size + 1 elements is defined, because the first element, students[0], holds an instance of the teacher object.

The most important rule is that the subscript, or index, starts at zero. Although it might seem quite awkward, use this element like all other elements of the array.

Creating Dense Arrays

Recall that we stated earlier that you need not initialize the elements in an array before you use it. However, nothing says you cannot initialize them. This is often referred to as a dense array. A *dense array* is one in which each element has a value. You can construct a dense array of two or more elements starting with index (subscript) 0, if you define initial values for all elements. They are very popular in many scripting languages. You can populate an array by specifying the values of its elements:

```
var bb = "baseball"
var sports = new Array("football", bb, "basketball", "soccer")
```

You can refer to the elements of this array with the common syntax:

```
sports[0] == "football"
sports[1] == "baseball"
var val = 2
sports[val] == "basketball"
sports[3] == "soccer"
```

JavaScript for early versions of Netscape Navigator had problems with some aspects of dense arrays, but you should not encounter these unless you are using a very old browser:

- You cannot assign a list of elements to an array (except when you create it).
- You cannot assign a range to an array.
- You cannot assign elements of one array's values to another array (the resulting array is an *array slice*).

Array Types

You must keep in mind that JavaScript is a loosely typed language. It should not be surprising, therefore, that elements of an array can be of different types. Some elements of a given array can be strings, while others can be numbers, Boolean values, and even objects. Basically, there are five types of arrays:

- String arrays
- Number arrays
- Boolean arrays
- Object arrays (including null arrays, because null is an object)
- Mixed arrays

Sometimes you want to know what type of array you are dealing with. JavaScript does not include any tool to facilitate this. However, using a prototype we can add a property to all arrays (remember, arrays are objects by which you can create instances) that will return the type of the array. Here is the desired method:

```
function getType()
{
   var arrayType = typeof this[0]
   for (var i = 1; i < this.length; ++i)
   {
      if (typeof this[i] != arrayType)
   {
         arrayType = "mixed"
         break
      }
   }
   return arrayType
}
Array.prototype.getType = getType
```

The following script segment is based on the preceding prototype definition:

```
var ar1 = new Array(3)
ar1[0] = "a"
ar1[1] = "b"
ar1[2] = ""
document.write(ar1.getType()) // string
var ar2 = new Array(2)
ar2[0] = 17
ar2[1] = 15.5
document.write(ar2.getType()) // number
var ar3 = new Array()
document.write(ar3.getType()) // object
var ar4 = new Array(0)
document.write(ar4.getType()) // object
var ar5 = new Array(1)
ar5[9999] = 5
document.write(ar5.getType()) // mixed
```

If you tried out the fifth array, you probably had to wait for a while, because the loop executed 10,000 times! You can use a more efficient function for the same prototype:

```
function getType()
{
   var arrayType = typeof this[0]
   for (var i in this)
   {
      if (typeof this[i] != arrayType)
      {
         arrayType = "mixed"
         break
      }
```

```
   }
   return arrayType
}
Array.prototype.getType = getType
```

The improvement in this function is the type of loop used. The `for...in` construct loops only through the existing properties, or elements, not including the null ones. The function works just like the previous one. At first, the data type of the first element of the array is assigned to `arrayType`. In every iteration of the loop, if a different type of element is found, the value of `arrayType` is changed to `"mixed"` because at least two different data types have been found in the array. Once a `"mixed"` array is detected, the loop is immediately terminated using a `break` statement. The function returns the value held by `arrayType`.

Sometimes you want to refer to all elements of a uniform-type array. The following method is designed to be a prototype of the `Array` object, returning an array of element subscripts where the specified value has been found. Here is the method:

```
function getSubscripts(type)
{
   var ar = new Array()
   var arSub = 0
   for (var i = 0; i < this.length; ++i)
   {
      if (typeof this[i] == type)
      {
         ar[arSub] = this[i]
         ++arSub
      }
   }
   return ar
}
Array.prototype.getSubscripts = getSubscripts
```

You can use the preceding prototype with arrays. For example:

```
var ar1 = new Array(6)
ar1[1] = 5
ar1[2] = 7
ar1[3] = "a"
ar1[4] = 2
ar1[5] = "b"
var ar1Temp = ar1.getSubscripts("number")
alert("There are " + ar1Temp.length + " numeric values in ar1")// 3
alert("The third number of ar1 is " + ar1Temp[2])              // 2
alert(ar1Temp) // 5, 7, 2 (discussed later in this chapter!)
```

This method returns an array. You can refer directly to the returned array:

```
var ar1 = new Array(6)
ar1[1] = 5
ar1[2] = 7
ar1[3] = "a"
ar1[4] = 2
ar1[5] = "b"
alert("The third number of ar1 is " + ar1.getSubscripts("number")[2])
```


Strings in JavaScript are `String` objects, not arrays. There are many useful methods that operate only on strings, so dealing with strings as arrays of characters, as is often the practice in other languages, is useless and almost impossible. Chapter 12 deals with strings in depth.

If you try to print an array, you will see that JavaScript prints the values of all elements in consecutive order, with a delimiting comma in between. You can use a user-defined prototype method to return a string containing all values delimited by a user-provided string:

```
function getList(str)
{
   var text = ""
   for (var i = 0; i < this.length - 1; ++i)
   {
      text += this[i] + str
   }
   text += this[this.length - 1]
   return text
}
Array.prototype.getList = getList
var ar = new Array(5)
ar[1] = 3
ar[3] = "a"
ar[4] = "b b b"
document.write(ar.getList(" ; ")) // null ; 3 ; null ; a ; b b b
```

Notice that the loop in the method executes until `i < this.length - 1`. The reason is that the loop concatenates the delimiter (the method's parameter) after each element of the array. We do not want one placed after the last element, so the last element is concatenated to the accumulated string after the loop terminates.

Array Properties

Although you can add your own properties to the `Array` object, not all tasks can be achieved by high-level programming via JavaScript. The only built-in property of the `Array` object is `length`. Fortunately, this is also the most commonly needed property for any array. When you create an instance of an object (an array), the number of properties (elements) is stored in the `length` property. You can refer to it as a regular property. We have already seen this property in action earlier in this chapter.

Let's say you want to display some messages, one after the other. You should use an array to store the messages:

```
var messages = new Array()
messages[0] = "message 1"
messages[1] = "message 2"
messages[2] = "message 3"
```

You can then use a loop to display the messages successively:

```
for (var i = 0; i < messages.length; i++)
{
   document.write(messages[i] + "<BR>")
}
```

The `length` property can also be modified; that is, you can change the length of the array by assigning the property a value. Here is an example:

```
var ar = new Array(6)
ar[0] = "Mouse"
ar[1] = 8
ar[2] = 18
ar[3] = true
ar[4] = "Dog"
ar[5] = "Cat"
ar.length = 3
alert(ar[2]) // 18
alert(ar[3]) // null
```

The array consisting of six elements was reduced to three. The last three values were chopped off. Be extra careful when you reduce the size of an array because shifted-off values are unrecoverable.

Array Methods

We just dealt with properties, or rather the single property of `length`. In this section we will deal with many array methods and will simulate some array functions in Perl using prototype methods. JavaScript features a number of methods, three of which are built-in methods:

- `join()`
- `reverse()`
- `sort()`

In this section we use the `getList` prototype method, introduced in the section "Array Types," to print arrays.

chop()

The chop() method chops off the last character of all strings that are elements of an array. Here is an example:

```
function chop()
{
   for (var i in this)
   {
      if (typeof this[i] == "string")
         this[i] = this[i].substring(0, this[i].length - 1)
   }
}
Array.prototype.chop = chop
// EXAMPLE
var line = new Array("red", "green", "blue")
line.chop()
document.write(line.getList(" "))
```

The script's output is:

```
re gree blu
```

The general syntax is:

```
arrayInstance.chop()
```

The substring() method is explained in Chapter 12, "Handling Strings."

grep()

The term "grep" is borrowed from the Unix world where grep is a standard search function. We use that same concept here in JavaScript. The grep() method evaluates the expression (*expr*) for each element of the array. It returns another array consisting of those elements for which the expression evaluated to true (the pattern was matched). To understand this method you should know that if string2 is found in string1, string1.indexOf(string2) is not equal to –1. Here is the method:

```
function grep(str)
{
   var ar = new Array()
   var arSub = 0
   for (var i in this)
   {
      if (typeof this[i] == "string" && this[i].indexOf(str) != -1)
      {
         ar[arSub] = this[i]
         arSub++
      }
   }
   return ar
}
Array.prototype.grep = grep
var line = new Array("mask", "Mascot", "mine", "amass", "hot")
```

```
document.write(line.grep("mas").getList(" "))
document.write("<BR>")
document.write(line.grep("mas").length)
```

The output of this script is:

```
mask amass
2
```

The general syntax is:

```
arrayInstance.grep(expr)
```

An important concept used by this method is short-circuit evaluation. If JavaScript evaluates the first conditional expression (`typeof this[i] == "string"`) to false, the final expression (`typeof this[i] == "string" && this[i].indexOf(str) != -1`) is obviously false, so the second expression (`this[i].indexOf(str) != -1`) is not even evaluated. This is critical because the `indexOf()` method works only with strings, and generates an error otherwise. However, if the current element (`this[i]`) is not a string, JavaScript does not evaluate the second expression due to short-circuit evaluation.

join()

The `join()` method is a built-in one in JavaScript. It is equivalent to the same function in Perl. It joins the elements of an array into a single string and separates each element with a given delimiter. This method is exactly like the `getList` method we created earlier, so we will use it from this point on instead.

Its general syntax is:

```
arrayInstance.join(delimiter)
```

The delimiter is automatically cast to a string if it is not already one.

Here is an example using this method:

```
var line = new Array("a", "b", "c", "d", "e")
document.write(line.join(" : "))
var str = line.join(", ")
document.write("<BR>" + str)
```

Its output is shown in Figure 9-1.

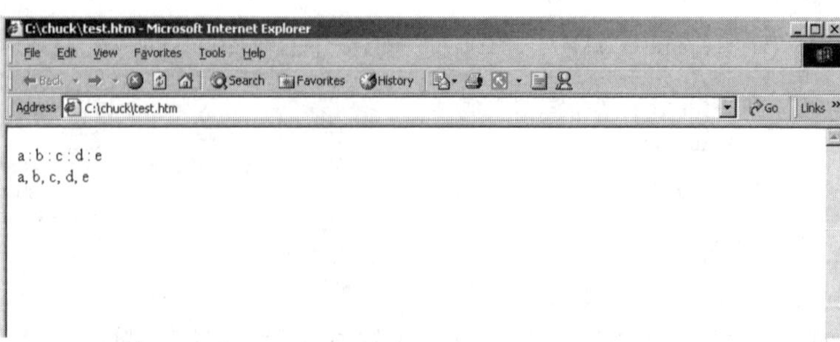

Figure 9-1. *The `join()` method's output*

pop()

The pop() method pops off the last element of an array and returns it. The array size is automatically decreased by one.

The general format is:

```
arrayInstance.pop()
```

This method is not built in, so we need to define it. The following script defines the method as a prototype of the Array object, and demonstrates its use:

```
function pop()
{
   var lastElement = this[this.length - 1]
   this.length--
   return lastElement
}
Array.prototype.pop = pop
```

Here is an example using the pop() method of an array:

```
var names = new Array("Tom", "Mark", "Bart", "John")
var last = names.pop()
document.write(last + "<BR>")
document.write(names.join(" ") + "<BR>")
document.write(names.length)
```

The script's output by rows is shown in Figure 9-2.

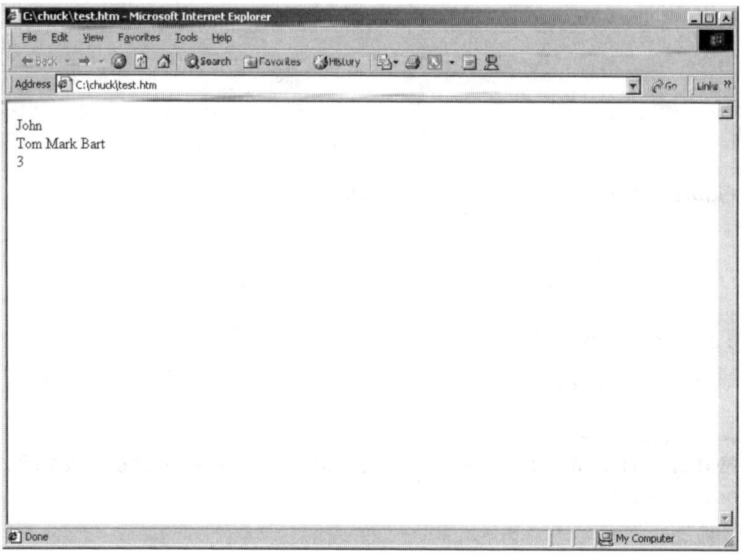

Figure 9-2. *The pop() method's output*

push()

The push() method pushes values onto the end of an array, increasing its length. Here is the method declared as a prototype of the Array object type:

```
function push()
{
   var sub = this.length
   for (var i = 0; i < push.arguments.length; ++i)
   {
      this[sub] = push.arguments[i]
      sub++
   }
}
Array.prototype.push = push
```

Here is an example using the push() method of an array:

```
var names = new Array("Tom", "Mark", "Bart", "John")
names.push("Jim", "Richard", "Tim")
document.write(names.join(" "))
```

The output is shown in Figure 9-3.

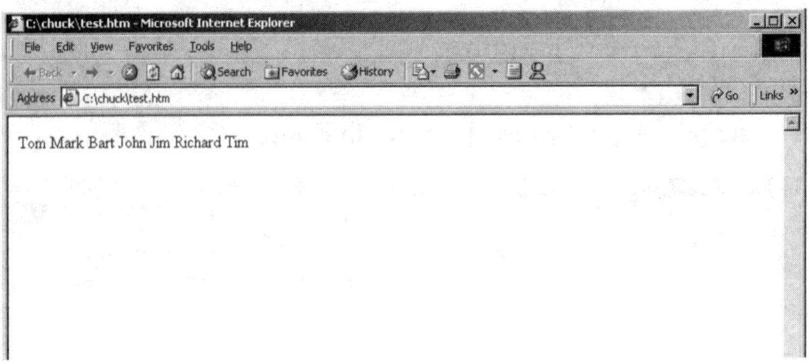

***Figure 9-3.** The push() method's output*

The general syntax is:

```
arrayInstance.push(list)
```

Note: This method was not supported by earlier versions of JavaScript but is now supported.

reverse()

The `reverse()` method transposes the elements of the calling array object. If it was descending, now it is ascending, etc. The last element becomes the first one, and vice versa. This is a built-in method.

The general syntax is:

```
arrayInstance.reverse()
```

Here is a script that illustrates the `reverse()` function:

```
var names = new Array("Tom", "Mark", "Bart", "John")
var colors = new Array("red", "orange", "yellow", "green", "blue", "purple")
document.write("<B>original names: </B>" + names.join(" ") + "<BR>")
names.reverse()
document.write("<B>reversed names: </B>" + names.join(" ") + "<BR>")
document.write("<B>original colors: </B>" + colors.join(" ") + "<BR>")
colors.reverse()
document.write("<B>reversed colors: </B>" + colors.join(" ") + "<BR>")
```

The corresponding output is shown in Figure 9-4.

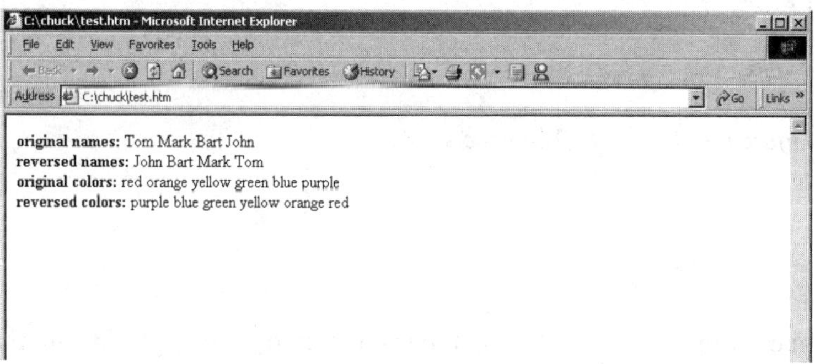

***Figure 9-4.** The `reverse()` method's output*

shift()

The `shift()` method is not defined in JavaScript so we will have to create it. It shifts off and returns the first element of an array, decreasing the size of an array by one element.

The general format of this method call (after defining its prototype) is:

```
arrayInstance.shift()
```

Here is the method along with an example:

```
function shift(str)
{
   var val = this[0]
   for (var i = 1; i < this.length; ++i)
   {
      this[i - 1] = this[i]
```

```
    }
    this.length--
    return val
}
Array.prototype.shift = shift
```

Here is a script that illustrates the use of the `shift()` method:

```
var line = new Array("aaa", "bbb", "ccc", "ddd", "eee")
document.write(line.shift() + "<BR>")
document.write(line.join(" "))
```

The output is shown in Figure 9-5.

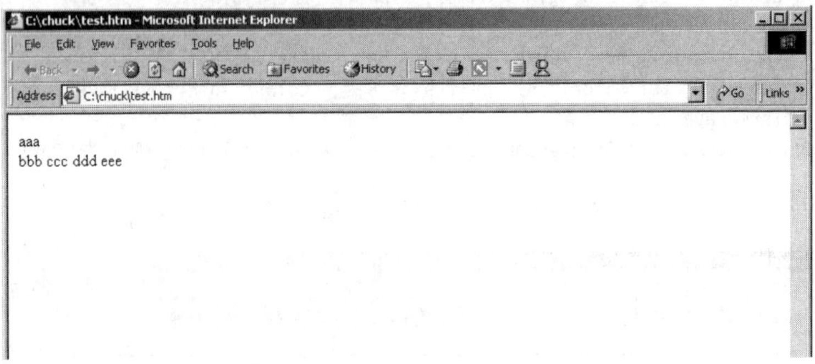

Figure 9-5. *The `shift()` method's output*

sort()

Luckily for us, the `sort()` method is built into JavaScript. This method sorts the elements of an array. It is optional to supply a sorting function. If one is not supplied, the array is sorted lexicographically (comparison order or dictionary order), according to the string conversion of each element. The general syntax of this method is as follows:

```
arrayInstance.sort(compareFunction)
```

If *`compareFunction`* is not supplied, elements are sorted by converting them to strings and comparing the strings in lexicographic order. For example, "10" comes before "9" in lexicographic order, but numeric comparison puts 9 before 10.

The structure of a comparison function is very specific. First of all, it should have two parameters, one for each element being compared. Secondly, it should return a value. If `a` and `b` are the two elements being compared, then:

- If *`compareFunction`*`(a, b)` is less than zero (returns a negative number), sort `b` to a lower index than `a`.

- If *compareFunction*(a, b) returns zero, leave a and b untouched with respect to each other (if a was before b, it will remain before b, and vice versa).
- If *compareFunction*(a, b) is positive (greater than zero), sort b to a higher index than a.

The basic form of a comparison function is:

```
function compare(a, b)
{
   if (a is less than b by some ordering criterion)
      return -1
   if (a is greater than b by the ordering criterion)
      return 1
   // a must be equal to b
   return 0
}
```

The most simple comparison function sorts numbers:

```
function compareNumbers(a, b)
{
   return a - b
}
```

JavaScript uses a *stable sort*, so the relative order of a and b does not change if a and b are equal according to the comparison function.

Here are some comparison functions:

```
// 1. Lexicographic -- built-in
// 2. byIncNum (increasing numbers)
function byIncNum(a, b)
{
   return a - b
}

// 3. byFirstChar (lexicographic order of first char only)
function byFirstChar(a, b)
{
   a += ""
   b += ""
   if (a.charAt(0) < b.charAt(0))
      return -1
   if (a.charAt(0) > b.charAt(0))
      return 1
   return 0
}
```

The following example should make this topic clear:

```
<HTML>
<HEAD>
<TITLE>Sorting arrays</TITLE>
<SCRIPT LANGUAGE="JavaScript">
```

```
<!--

// 1. Lexicographic -- built-in
// 2. byIncNum (increasing numbers)

function incNum(a, b)
{
   return a - b
}

stringArray = new Array("house", "hose", "chair")
numericStringArray = new Array("60", "8", "100")
numberArray = new Array(20, 1, 5, -11, 8)
mixedNumericArray = new Array("70", "9", "600", 3, 40, 70, 250)

function compareNumbers(a, b)
{
   return a - b
}

document.write("<U><B>stringArray</B></U><BR>")
document.write("<B>Original array:</B> " + stringArray.join() +"<BR>")
document.write("<B>Sorted by default:</B> " + stringArray.sort() +"<P>")

document.write("<U><B>numberArray</B></U><BR>")
document.write("<B>Original array:</B> " + numberArray.join() +"<BR>")
document.write("<B>Sorted by default:</B> " + numberArray.sort() +"<BR>")
document.write("<B>Sorted with compareNumbers:</B> " +
               numberArray.sort(compareNumbers) +"<P>")

document.write("<U><B>numericStringArray</B></U><BR>")
document.write("<B>Original array:</B> " + numericStringArray.join() +"<BR>")
document.write("<B>Sorted by default:</B> " + numericStringArray.sort() +"<BR>")
document.write("<B>Sorted with compareNumbers:</B> " +
               numericStringArray.sort(compareNumbers) +"<P>")

document.write("<U><B>mixedNumericArray</B></U><BR>")
document.write("<B>Original array:</B> " + mixedNumericArray.join() +"<BR>")
document.write("<B>Sorted by default:</B> " + mixedNumericArray.sort() +"<BR>")
document.write("<B>Sorted with compareNumbers:</B> " +
               mixedNumericArray.sort(compareNumbers) +"<BR>")
// -->
</SCRIPT>
</HEAD>
<BODY>
</BODY>
</HTML>
```

Example 9-1 (ex9-1.htm). *The built-in* `sort()` *function is a simple replacement for sorting via pointers (used in many languages that feature pointers).*

The results of this script are shown in Figure 9-6.

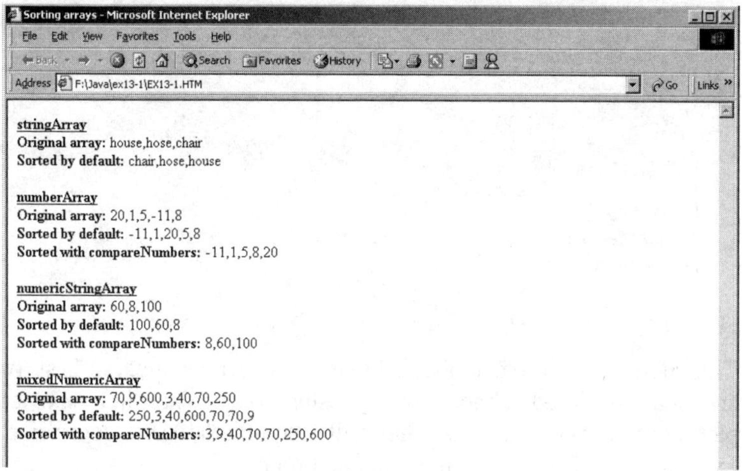

Figure 9-6. *The `sort()` method's output*

splice()

Another method not featured yet by JavaScript is `splice()`. It removes and replaces elements in an array. Its general syntax is:

```
arrayInstance.splice(offset, length, list)
```

`offset` is the starting position from which elements are to be removed. The *`length`* is the number of elements to be removed, starting at `offset`. The *`list`* parameter consists of new elements that are designated to replace the removed ones. Here is the method:

```
function splice(offset, length)
{
   var ar1 = new Array()
   var ar2 = new Array()
   for (i = 0; i < length; ++i)
   {
      ar1[i] = this[i + offset]
   }
   for (i = 0; i < this.length - (offset + length); ++i)
   {
      ar2[i] = this[i + offset + length]
   }
   var args = new Array()
   for (i = 0; splice.arguments[i + 2] != null; ++i)
   {
      args[i] = splice.arguments[i + 2] // second argument
   }
   j = offset
   for (i = 0; i < args.length; ++i)
   {
      this[j] = args[i]
```

```
      j++
   }
   for (i = 0; i < ar2.length; ++i)
   {
      this[j] = ar2[i]
      j++
   }
   this.length = j
   // notice that j is one more than subscript of last element
   return ar1
}
Array.prototype.splice = splice
```

This method is more complicated than the previous ones. At first, two arrays are declared. Although it is possible to calculate their size, it is completely unnecessary because they will accommodate the proper size as we expand them. The first loop in the function is:

```
for (i = 0; i < length; ++i)
{
   ar1[i] = this[i + offset]
}
```

This loop assigns all elements that are to be removed to the array `ar1`, according to the values of the `offset` and `length` parameters. The number of times the loop iterates is exactly the value of `length`, the number of elements specified to be removed. The array `ar1` is populated from the beginning, 0. It is assigned the elements of the calling array (`this`), starting from `offset`, because only elements following `offset` (exactly `length` of them) are to be removed. When the loop terminates, the array `ar1` already consists of elements that should be removed from the calling array. Notice that this array is returned at the end of the function.

Now take a look at the second loop:

```
for (i = 0; i < this.length - (offset + length); ++i)
{
   ar2[i] = this[i + offset + length]
}
```

This loop assigns all elements following the removed ones to the array `ar2`. The loop terminates after it has completed assigning all these elements. `this.length - (offset + length)` is equal to the number of elements following the removed one. The subscript of the first element following the removed set is `offset + length`. Subtracting this number from the full length of the calling array gives the number of elements following the removed set.

The next loop is as follows:

```
for (i = 0; splice.arguments[i + 2] != null; ++i)
{
     args[i] = splice.arguments[i + 2] // second argument
}
```

The preceding loop assigns all items of `list` (the third parameter of the method) to the array `args`. These items are all arguments handed over to the method except for the first two. We use the condition `splice.arguments[i + 2] != null` to terminate the loop due to some unexpected behavior of the `arguments.length` property on some platforms. That is, when the function comes across the first null element of `splice.arguments`, it terminates. This action is based on the fact that the method will never be called to replace an element of the calling array by a null one. This concept is explained later in this chapter in depth. The expression `i + 2` is used because the needed elements of the arguments array are only the third one (`subscript == 2`) on. However, the `args` array created in the function should store the elements starting at subscript 0, so `i` is used as the subscript of that array.

We now have four arrays:

- `this` (the calling array)
- `args`
- `ar2`
- `ar1`

Keep in mind that the `splice()` method needs to modify the calling script. It concatenates the beginning of this array (up to the first removed, exclusively) with `args` and `ar2`, in this order. The last portion of the script does just that:

```
j = offset
for (i = 0; i < args.length; ++i)
{
   this[j] = args[i]
   j++
}
for (i = 0; i < ar2.length; ++i)
{
   this[j] = ar2[i]
   j++
}
this.length = j
```

At first, `j` is set to `offset`, the first value of the array `this` that should be modified (all the existing elements before should remain at the beginning of the array, as they were before calling the method). The following loops assign elements from the other arrays, `args` and `ar2`, respectively, to the calling array (`this`). The variable `j` is important because it holds the subscript of the current element of the calling array throughout both loops. At the end, the length of the calling array (now modified) is set to `j`, so if there were more elements in the original array, they are chopped off.

The last statement of the `splice()` function returns the removed elements in the form of an array, `ar1`.

Now that you have pored over this long and perhaps arduous explanation, it's probably a good idea to see an example:

```
var cols = new Array("red", "orange", "yellow", "green", "blue", "purple")
var newCols = cols.splice(2, 3, "brown", "black")
document.write(newCols.join(" ") + "<BR>")
document.write(cols.join(" ") + "<BR>")

cols = new Array("red", "orange", "yellow", "green", "blue", "purple")

newCols = cols.splice(0, 1, "brown", "black")
document.write(newCols.join(" ") + "<BR>")
document.write(cols.join(" ") + "<BR>")
cols = new Array("red", "orange", "yellow", "green", "blue", "purple")
newCols = cols.splice(3, 0, "brown", "black")
document.write(newCols.join(" ") + "<BR>")
document.write(cols.join(" "))
```

The output of this script segment is shown in Figure 9-7.

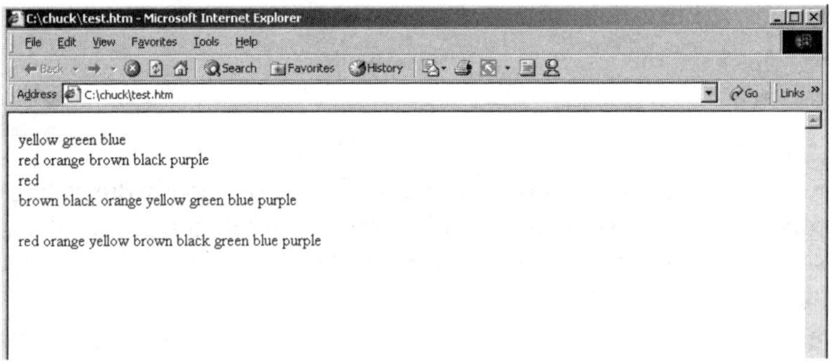

Figure 9-7. *The `splice()` method's output*

The function will not work if you try to remove elements of the array without inserting new ones.

split()

The `split()` method does the opposite of `join()`. It splits up a string (the object) by some delimiter (space by default) and returns an array. To be accurate, this is a method of the `String` object, not the `Array` object, but because it is closely related to arrays, we chose to discuss it in this section. If the delimiter is not supplied or is not found in the entire string, it returns the string itself. This method is built in so you just have to call it. The general format is:

```
stringName.split(delimiter)
```

Here are some examples:

```
var line1 = "a b c d e f"
var ar1 = new Array()
ar1 = line1.split(" ")
document.write(ar1.join(", ")) // a, b, c, d, e, f
document.write("<BR>")
```

```
ar2 = line1.split(";")
document.write(ar2) // a b c d e f
document.write("<BR>")
ar3 = line1.split()
document.write(ar3) // a b c d e f
document.write("<BR>")
ar4 = line1.split("")
document.write(ar4) // [infinite function!]
```


All of these examples follow the rules explained previously, except for the last one, `ar4`. The statement `ar4 = line1.split("")` causes an infinite method execution that will eventually crash the browser, or even the operating system, if you are on a 16-bit version of Windows. The reason for this behavior is obvious—JavaScript tries to split the string with an empty string. Everyone knows that an empty string is found an infinite number of times between two characters, and between two empty strings lies another empty string!

unshift()

The `unshift()` method is the opposite of the `shift()` method. It appends a list of elements to the beginning of an array. Here is the method defined as a prototype of the `Array` object type, along with an example to demonstrate it:

```
function unshift()
{
   for (var i = 0; i < unshift.arguments.length; ++i)
   {
      if (unshift.arguments[i] == null)
         break
   }
   // i = number of arguments! (remember ++i is executed during last loop)
   // i holds the number of arguments
   for (var j = this.length – 1; j >= 0; --j)
   {
      this[j + i] = this[j]
   }
   // j == –1
   // i == number of arguments
   for (j = 0; j < i; ++j)
   {
      this[j] = unshift.arguments[j]
   }
}
Array.prototype.unshift = unshift
```

Here is an example of the `unshift()` function:

```
var line = new Array("ccc", "ddd", "eee")
line.unshift("aaa", "bbb")
document.write(line.join(" "))
```

The arguments Array

The *functionName*`.arguments` array holds the arguments by order that were passed to the function *functionName* when that function was last called. Here is an example:

```
function func()
{
   document.write(func.arguments[2])
}
func(1, 2, 3, 4, 5)
document.write("<BR>")
func()
```

The output of this script is:

```
3
3
```

The second 3 is not an argument passed to the function during the second call, but an argument passed to the function during the first call. It remains an element in the array provided that no argument of a later call replaces it. You can therefore conclude that the *functionName*`.arguments` array has a permanent storage class.

Let's say you want to create a function that accepts string arguments and prints them with a line break after each one. The intuitive function would be:

```
function printList()
{
   for (var i = 0; i < printList.arguments.length; ++i)
   {
      document.write(printList.arguments[i] + "<BR>")
   }
}
```

You can use this function in the following form:

```
printList("message 1", "message 2", "message 3", "message 4")
```

And the output is:

```
message 1
message 2
message 3
message 4
```

You can also use the function twice in a row as in:

```
printList("message 1", "message 2", "message 3", "message 4")
printList("message 5", "message 6", "message 7", "message 8")
```

Once again, the expected output is:

```
message 1
message 2
message 3
message 4
message 5
message 6
message 7
message 8
```

Now let's change the function to the following code:

```
function printList()
{
   document.write("There are " + printList.arguments.length + " arguments.")
   document.write("<BR>")
   document.write("The fourth argument is " + printList.arguments[3] + ".")
   document.write("<BR>")
   for (var i = 0; i < printList.arguments.length; ++i)
   {
      document.write(printList.arguments[i] + "<BR>")
   }
}
```

The function now displays the number of arguments according to the *functionName*`.arguments.length` property. It also displays the fourth argument, whether or not there are four arguments. Consider the following statements:

```
printList("message 1", "message 2", "message 3", "message 4")
printList("message 5", "message 6", "message 7")
```

The output is:

```
There are 4 arguments.
The fourth argument is message 4.
message 1
message 2
message 3
message 4
There are 3 arguments.
The fourth argument is message 4. (!!!)
message 5
message 6
message 7
```

Notice that the function prints the fourth argument passed to the function in each call. However, the second call provides only three arguments! The `arguments.length` property holds the correct value, 3. The fourth argument is actually a leftover from the first function call.

As you can see, the `arguments` array does not follow the rules of arrays that are instances of the `Array` object. The following script demonstrates the difference:

```
var ar = new Array("message 1", "message 2", "message 3")
document.write("The array is: " + ar.join(", ") + "<BR>")
document.write("There are " + ar.length + " elements.<BR>")
document.write("The third element is " + ar[2] + ".<BR>")
ar.length = 2
document.write("There are " + ar.length + " elements.<BR>")
document.write("The third element is " + ar[2] + ".<BR>")
```

The output of this script is:

```
The array is: message 1, message 2, message 3
There are 3 elements.
The third element is message 3.
There are 2 elements.
The third element is null.
```

The simple rule regarding arrays is that the last element's subscript is *`arrayName`*`.length - 1`. When you reduce the size of an array by assigning a smaller number to the `length` property, all elements that were in the range of the array and are now out of range are lost. If you try referring to them, you see that they are null. The *`functionName`*`.arguments` array is different in that its last element has nothing to do with its length.

Multidimensional Arrays

While JavaScript shares many characteristics with traditional programming languages like C++, it is just a scripting language designed for the web. And as such it has some limitations. For example, JavaScript does not feature multidimensional arrays. However, like many other JavaScript limitations you will encounter in this book, you can create your own workaround for this problem. Up to this point we have discussed one-dimensional arrays (1D arrays). Such arrays consist of elements gathered in a row-like structure. The basic structure of a one-dimensional array is outlined in the following illustration:

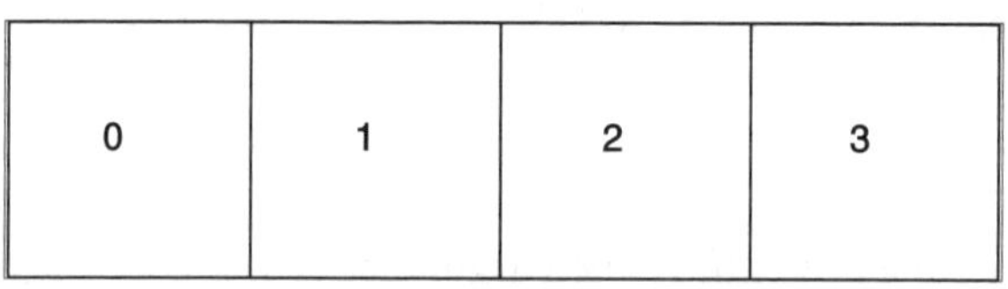

Figure 9-8. *A one-dimensional array*

Let's say you want to store a runner's record times in different years and for different distances. If the array is called `curDis`, the record time for 2005 could be put in `curDis[0]`, the record time for 2006 in `curDis[1]`, the record time for 2007 in `curDis[2]`, and so forth. However, you probably noticed that we can only store the record time for a single distance, such as a 400-meter run. It would be easy to store the record times of various runs in this format using a table or spreadsheet-like array. Such arrays are known as two-dimensional (2D) arrays.

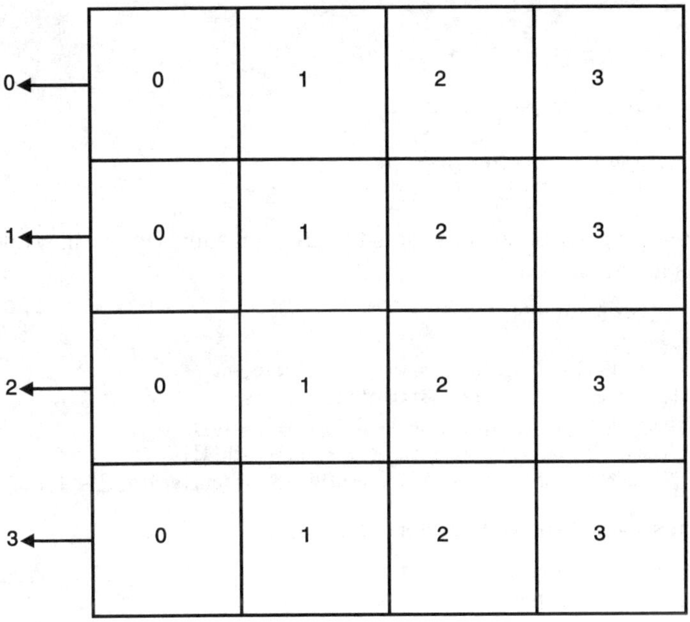

Figure 9-9. *A two-dimensional array*

Remember that JavaScript does not have a built-in two-dimensional array object type. Take a look at the subscripts of the elements. The two-dimensional array is constructed from horizontal arrays (horizontal in the illustration as well), which form an array of their own. That is, the general structure is a regular array of arrays. The main array in the illustration is the vertical one; its subscripts are specified to the left of the arrows.

Note that the dimensions of a multidimensional array do not have to be equal.

The standard reference to elements of a two-dimensional array (2DA) is:

```
ar[1][5]
ar[8][0]
ar[3][3]
```

The first number is the subscript of the first dimension, whereas the second one specifies the subscript of the second dimension.

Creation with a Single Constructor Function

The easiest way to create a two-dimensional array (2DA) is to use a constructor function such as the following:

```
function Array2D(dim1, dim2)
{
   for (var i = 0; i < dim1; ++i)
   {
      this[i] = new Array(dim2)
   }
   this.length = new Array(dim1, dim2)
}
```

The following script demonstrates the creation and usage of an array created by this function:

```
var ar = new Array2D(4,7)
ar[2][1] = 6
ar[0][0] = "Hello"    // this is the "first" element
ar[3][6] = true       // this is the "last" element
alert("Length of first dimension is " + ar.length[0])
alert("Length of second dimension is " + ar.length[1])
alert("\"Last\" element: " + ar[ar.length[0] - 1][ar.length[1] - 1])
```

The messages displayed via alert boxes are:

```
Length of first dimension is 4
Length of second dimension is 7
"Last" element: true
```

The constructor function uses a loop. The first array (`ar`) is not an explicit `Array` object. It is simply a regular object whose properties are specified using the array notation. The built-in methods of the `Array` object type do not operate on this array. The loop executes `dim1` times, the length of the first dimension. Each property (or element) of the calling object is assigned a "real" array consisting of `dim2` elements. Since these are real arrays, you can use the built-in methods and properties of the `Array` object type. For example, `ar[0]` is an array of `dim2` elements, so you can refer to its elements: `ar[0][0]`, `ar[0][1]`, `ar[0][2]`, etc. The 2DA is actually a one-dimensional array of which all elements are one-dimensional arrays. Therefore, you should be careful not to ruin the structure of the 2DA by assigning values to its main array, such as:

```
ar[3] = "Do not do this to a 2DA!"
```

The preceding constructor method also includes a `length` property that is an array of two elements. The first element holds the number of elements in the main array (the specified length of the first dimension), while the second element holds the specified length of the second dimension. The example demonstrates this best. Keep in mind that these are static properties. Assigning a value to an element of the `length` property does not affect the array, but can trip you up when you need the correct values regarding the length of the array's dimensions.

Creation without a Constructor Function

It is possible to create a two-dimensional array without a constructor function. This method is based on creating instances of the Array object:

```
function addDim2(array1D, dim2)
{
   for (var i = 0; i < array1D.length; ++i)
   {
      array1D[i] = new Array(dim2)
   }
   return array1D
}
```

This function alone means almost nothing, so take a look at a working example:

```
var dim1 = 4
var dim2 = 7
var ar = new Array(dim1)
ar = addDim2(ar, dim2)
ar[2][1] = 6
ar[0][0] = "Hello"   // this is the "first" element
ar[3][6] = true      // this is the "last" element
alert("Length of first dimension is " + ar.length)
alert("Length of second dimension is " + ar[0].length)
alert("\"Last\" element: " + ar[ar.length - 1][ar[0].length - 1])
```

At first, the length of the first dimension, 4, is assigned to `dim1`. The length of the second dimension is then assigned to `dim2`. A new array, named `ar`, is created according to the `Array` object type. Its length is the length of the first dimension of the desired array. The function `addDim2` is then called with the array and the length of the second dimension. It returns the final 2DA to the original one-dimensional array, `ar`. The function is based on a simple loop that assigns an array of `dim2` elements to each element of the original one-dimensional array. Since both the first dimension array and the second dimension array are instances of the `Array` object type, you can refer to the length of each dimension in the following way:

```
ar.length == length of first dimension
ar[0].length == length of second dimension == ar[1].length == ...
```

Note that for the second expression to be true, you must not change the length of the 2DA at any time during the script execution. Otherwise, it does not simulate a 2DA anymore.

Associative Arrays

This topic is rather advanced, and one can certainly use JavaScript without mastering this. However, it is very useful in certain situations. *Associative arrays* use strings as subscripts. For example, an element of the array can be:

```
color["yellow"] = "FFFF00"
```

Such arrays group together related data. These arrays are actually objects, except that you use square brackets instead of a dot. Another important difference is that array specification (square brackets) enables you to refer to the value of a variable as the property of method specification rather than the actual literal. For example:

```
var col = "yellow"
color[col] = "FFFF00"
```

Here is another interesting example:

```
var w = "write"
document[w]("Hello!") // prints "Hello!"
```

If you replace the array notation with the regular dot specification you receive an error:

```
var w = "write"
document.w("Hello!")
```

The dot notation requires the actual literal specified, as it does not evaluate the written value. You can use associative arrays to create nested objects resembling multidimensional arrays. For example, you can create an associative array where its subscripts are names of students in a class, so each element of the associative array is an object containing fields such as the student's grade, age, and so on.

Note that associative arrays cannot be created as instances of the built-in `Array` object. You must use a constructor function to create one. Here is an example using students:

```
function studentClass()
{
   for (var i = 0; i < arguments.length; ++i)
   {
      this[studentClass.arguments[i]] = new student()
   }
}
function student()
{
   // this.grade = null
   // this.age = null
}
var students = new studentClass("Bob", "John", "Frank", "Alfred",
                                "Sheila", "Mary")
```

```
students["Bob "].grade = 40
students["John "].age = 11
students["Frank "].grade = "N/A"
alert(students["Frank "].grade)
```

Creating an associative array is not difficult. Array elements are created according to the names of the students accepted as parameters by the function `studentClass()`. The second function is rather strange—it contains no statements. When you create an instance you can use an "empty" constructor function. You may recall from an earlier discussion that objects may be extended by simply assigning values to them. So, the statement `this[studentClass.arguments[i]] = new student()` just makes sure each element of the associative array is an object. The global statements later create the properties simply by assigning them values.

Another important concept to remember is that associative arrays are not explicit arrays. You can also refer to them using the dot syntax, as in:

```
students.John.age
```

Suppose you created a database structure listing all the students in a class with their ages and grades. Assume that both fields are fed with the proper values. You can let the user view these values via a prompt dialog box. For example:

```
var grade = students[prompt("Enter name:", "John Doe")].grade
document.write(grade)
```

In this case you must use the array convention because you are prompting the user for the property name. You can use the dot notation only when you know the property name. If you use the dot notation:

```
students.prompt(...)
```

JavaScript assumes you are referring to a method of the `students` object named `prompt()`, which does not exist at all, of course.

Populating an Associative Array

Creating a dense array is simple when using regular arrays. You simply create the array with the desired values. However, associative arrays require two real values for each element, the key (subscript) and the value. You can create a constructor function to create and populate associative arrays:

```
function AssociativeArray()
{
   for (var i = 0; i < arguments.length - 1; i += 2)
   {
      this[arguments[i]] = arguments[i + 1]
   }
}
```

Chapter 9

You can use this function to create associative arrays in the following format:

```
var ar = new AssociativeArray("red", "FF0000", "green", "00FF00",
                              "blue", "0000FF")
document.write("green = " + ar["green"] + "<BR>")
var col = "blue"
document.write("blue = " + ar[col] + "<BR>")
document.write("red = " + ar.red)
```

The relative output of this script is:

```
green = 00FF00
blue = 0000FF
red = FF0000
```

Let's take a look at the constructor function. It accepts the keys of the array elements followed by their corresponding values. Each key must be followed by its own value. The function loops through the arguments and terminates after it has reached the argument before the last one. During each pass through the function, a property of the calling object is created (an "element" in the array lexicon). The key of the property, or element, is the current argument, whereas its value is extracted from the following argument. The loop counter is advanced by two after each execution of the block, because each element of the associative array is related to two arguments—its key and its value. Although an associative array is primarily a regular object, this constructor must use square brackets, the array notation, for reference and initialization because the values of the keys (subscripts) are not literals, but rather values stored as parameters.

Splitting a String into an Associative Array

The `split()` method splits a string by a specified delimiter into a real instance of an `Array` object. For example:

```
var str = "a;b;c;d;e;f"
var ar = str.split(";") // ar[0] == "a", ar[1] == "b", ar[2] == "c", ...
```

Let's use the `split()` method to create a function named `associativeSplit()` as a prototype of the `String` object:

```
function associativeSplit(del)
{
   var tempAr = new Array()
   tempAr = this.split(del)
   var ar = new Obj()   // not an array, just an object
   for (var i = 0; i < tempAr.length - 1; i += 2)
   {
      ar[tempAr[i]] = tempAr[i + 1]
   }
   return ar
}
function Obj() { }
String.prototype.associativeSplit = associativeSplit
```

Notice the use of an empty function to create an object. At first, the function splits the string via the regular method into a regular array. It then loops through the array, using the next element as the key of an element in the associative array and its following element as the value of the same element in the associative array. Upon completion, the function returns the associative array. The function is then declared as a prototype of the built-in `String` object, applying to all strings.

Now take a look at an example:

```
var str = "a b c d e f"
var ar1 = str.associativeSplit(" ")
document.write(ar1.a + "<BR>")
document.write(ar1.b + "<BR>")
document.write(ar1["c"] + "<BR>")
document.write(ar1["d"] + "<BR>")
// document.write(ar1[e] + "<BR>")
document.write(ar1.f + "<BR>")
```

Note that "associative array" is not a JavaScript term, but rather a regular object. We just prefer to refer to its properties via the array notation.

Summary

This was a complex but very important chapter. In this chapter we learned about arrays in JavaScript. It is important that you remember that in JavaScript an array is an object. We discussed the `Array` object, including its properties and methods. Other important concepts brought together in this chapter were constructor functions and prototypes, used mainly to simulate array methods featured by Perl. By now, you should have a grasp of arrays and constructor functions, two very important elements of the language. You should also know how to create and use two-dimensional arrays, as well as multidimensional ones, although they are rarely used. In this chapter we also introduced the term "associative arrays." Such arrays are regular objects with regular properties, but they remind us of the associative arrays widely used in other languages such as Perl. In following chapters we shall look further into JavaScript's object model, while arrays and constructors will serve as the base of some scripts.

Chapter 10

Time and Date in JavaScript

Working with times and dates is a very common task in web programming. There are a host of scenarios where you will need to use time and date data, such as determining the current date, having the user enter dates for particular items, and even creating online calendars. In this chapter we will explore the time and date functionality built into JavaScript. You will also be shown how to create useful additions to your web page using JavaScript's date and time functions.

The Date Object

Fortunately for JavaScript programmers, JavaScript comes with a built-in `Date` object that allows you to easily work with date and time data and related functions. Both dates and times in JavaScript are derived from the `Date` object, which behaves much like any other object. To implement the current date or time in your script, you must first create a new instance of the object. You can then extract the desired data from that particular instance. JavaScript handles dates in a manner very similar to Java. Many methods are implemented in both languages, resulting in an observable parallelism. All dates are stored as the number of milliseconds since January 1, 1970, 00:00:00. As you will see in this chapter, using the `Date` object is one of the easiest things you have seen so far in JavaScript.

Creating a Date Instance

The `Date` object is a built-in object by which you can create *instances* to store encoded data related to the date and time of a certain moment (recall our discussion of object-oriented programming in Chapter 4). The `Date` object is built in, just like the `Array` object discussed in depth in the previous chapter. It acts as a template when creating instances of the object. The most basic assignment statement regarding the `Date` object is obviously the one that creates an instance according to the default arguments:

```
var dateInstance = new Date()
```

This statement simply assigns an instance of the `Date` object to the data structure named *`dateInstance`*. Take a look at the following script:

```
var now = new Date()
alert(now)
```

The output is shown in Figure 10-1 (the date and time will be different when you try it).

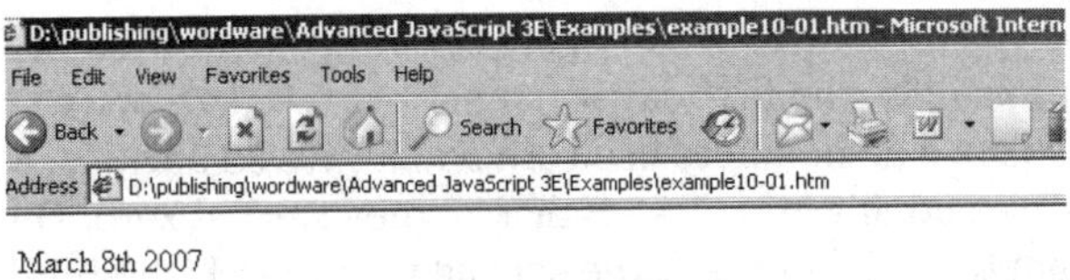

***Figure 10-1.** The* `now` *output*

Although `now` is an identifier of an instance of the `Date` object, it holds a partial string value at its highest level. That is, if you try to print its value, it appears to be a string. However, because it does not belong to the explicit `String` object, string properties and methods do not apply to it.

If you want to refer to an instance of the `Date` object as a string, it is best to convert it to a string explicitly:

```
var newObj = new Date()
var str = newObj.toString()
```

The `toString` method simply converts the object to a `String` object. This is similar to *casting* in other programming languages. You will see many objects have a `toString` method, allowing you to convert them to strings.

Parameters of the Date Constructor

Until now we created instances of the `Date` object without any arguments; that is, we built the instances according to the default arguments. The default is the current date and time on the client's machine. JavaScript enables you to create `Date` instances of specific dates, which you can later use with date arithmetic. For example, you can create an instance of the `Date` object that represents some particular historical date.

Here is an example that creates an instance of a date that occurred in the past:

```
var Xmas2006 = new Date("December 25, 2006 13:30:00")
```

You can also create an instance according to a set of integers of the following format:

year, month, day, hour, minute, seconds

Here is an example using this format:

```
var Xmas2006 = new Date(106,11,25,9,30,0)
```

One important concept is the requirement of year, month, and day specification in both formats (string and integers). If you omit the hours, minutes, or seconds they are set by default to zero. Nonetheless, omitting any of the first three arguments results in an error and even crashes the browser under some operating systems.

Date Numeric Conventions

Dates in JavaScript, as in Java, use integers to specify values that succeed each other. For example, the first day of a month is 1, the second is 2, the third is 3, and so on. The numbers used are not always so obvious. Most date attributes are actually zero-based; that is, they start at zero. For example, the first minute of an hour is 0, the second minute is 1, the third minute is 2, and so on. The following table summarizes the numeric conventions of each attribute of a `Date` instance:

Table 10-1. *Ranges of date attributes*

Date Attribute	Range
seconds	0 - 59
minutes	0 - 59
hours	0 - 23
day	0 - 6
date	1 - 31
month	0 - 11
year	number of years since 1900 (e.g., 107)

Most importantly, when referring to client-side JavaScript, the date and time refer to the client side. All values are the ones passed to the script by the browser. As you might know, especially if you are a Mac or Windows environment programmer, all applications on your computer have access to the machine clock, including the current time and date. If the system clock is not set to the current time and date, JavaScript will use these incorrect values in the script, possibly surprising the user.

Date Method Categories

JavaScript provides JavaScript programmers with a variety of methods to deal with instances of the `Date` object. However, extracting and manipulating their data makes them one of the most important elements of the language.

The whole bulk of methods may seem dazzling if you approach them at once. Therefore, we have chosen to divide them into four groups, according to their operation:

- `get` methods
- `set` methods

- `to` methods
- `parse` methods

The `get` methods return an integer corresponding to the attribute of the instance you desire. You can "get" the year number, the month number, the hour number, and so on. `set` methods enable you to modify the value of a certain attribute of an existing instance. These methods accept integer values rather than returning them. You actually "set" the values of attributes with these statements. `to` methods convert the date into a string according to arguments passed over to the method. You can then take advantage of the string format with string methods and properties, such as the method `split()`. `parse` methods simply interpret date strings. Let's start by exploring the `get` methods.

The get Methods

getYear()

The `getYear()` method returns the current year stored in an instance of the `Date` object type. In the past this was a two-digit date that assumed it to be the 20th century. All major browsers now use four-digit years, so you should not have any concerns over this issue.

```
var now = new Date()
var year = now.getYear()
while (1)
{
   var guessYear = parseInt(prompt("Enter current year:", ""))
   if (guessYear == year)
   {
      alert("That's right!")
      break
   }
   else
      alert("Wrong answer! Try again...")
}
```

The output of this script, assuming you are able to correctly identify the current year, is presented in Figures 10-2 and 10-3.

Figure 10-2. *Script output*

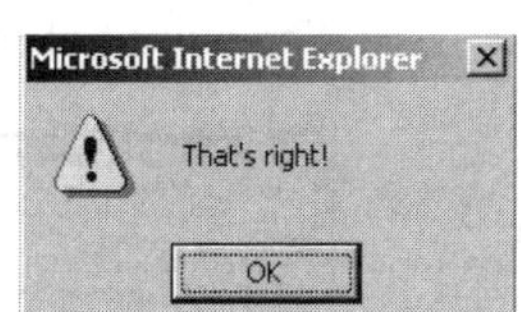

Figure 10-3. *Additional script output*

The current year (based on the system clock) is extracted from the instance `now`, created according to default arguments (current time and date). A loop without a terminating condition is executed next. The user is asked to enter the current year, according to his or her knowledge. Another `if` statement checks if the user entered the correct year. If so, the proper message is displayed, and the loop is broken up with a `break` statement. Otherwise, a message informs the user that his or her input was incorrect, and the loop iterates once more.

The problem with `getYear()` is that Netscape still returns the years since 1900 (thus 2007 is returned as 107), whereas Internet Explorer simply returns the four-digit date (making 2007 return as simply "2007"). You can also use the newer command `getFullYear`, which will get a simple four-digit year in both browsers.

getMonth()

The `getMonth()` method extracts and returns the month of its calling object. Months range from January to December, or more accurately, from 0 to 11. The reason this begins with 0 rather than 1 is that the `Date` object internally stores months as an array, and all arrays start with element zero. Here is a simple example demonstrating this method as well as an array instance:

```
var now = new Date()
var month = now.getMonth()
var ar = new Array(12)
ar[0] = "January"
ar[1] = "February"
ar[2] = "March"
ar[3] = "April"
ar[4] = "May"
ar[5] = "June"
ar[6] = "July"
ar[7] = "August"
ar[8] = "September"
ar[9] = "October"
ar[10] = "November"
ar[11] = "December"
var message = "It is now " + ar[month] + ", my favorite.<BR>"
document.write(message)
```

The output of this script is shown in Figure 10-4.

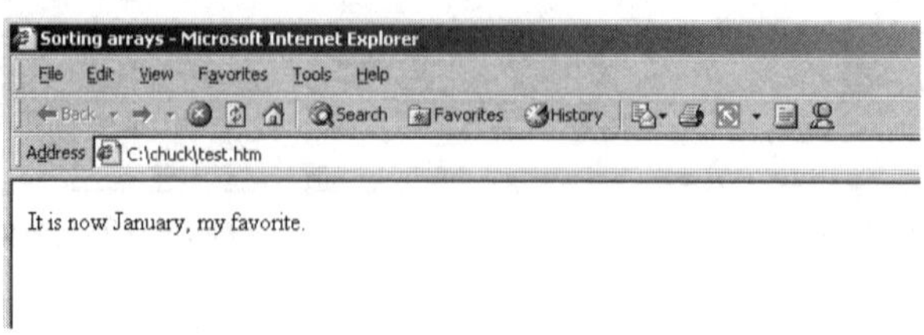

Figure 10-4. *`getMonth()` output*

The current month is extracted from the now instance, which holds the attributes of the current time (after the statement has executed). A static array is then created to hold all months' names (as strings), matching each name to its corresponding number in JavaScript, starting at zero. This obviously fits the default array structure, featuring the first index as zero. Therefore, no math needs to be done, and the current month, by name, is used to construct a message, obviously a string. The message is then printed as plain HTML.

getDate()

The `getDate()` method returns the day of the month as an integer from 1 to 31. Here is an example:

```
<HTML>
<HEAD>
<SCRIPT LANGUAGE = "JavaScript">
function datedemo()
{

var now = new Date()
var year = now.get
Year()
var month = now.getMonth()
var date = now.getDate()
var suf
if (date < 10)
   var lastDigit = date
else
   var lastDigit = date % 10
var exp = ""
// determine suffix
if (lastDigit == 1)
   suf = "st"
else
   if (lastDigit == 2)
      suf = "nd"
   else
      if (lastDigit == 3)
         suf = "rd"
      else
         suf = "th"
// array for name of month
var ar = new Array(12)
ar[0] = "January"
ar[1] = "February"
ar[2] = "March"
ar[3] = "April"
ar[4] = "May"
ar[5] = "June"
ar[6] = "July"
ar[7] = "August"
ar[8] = "September"
```

```
ar[9] = "October"
ar[10] = "November"
ar[11] = "December"
var formDate = date + suf

// build full date such as "May 5th, 2007"
var totalDate
totalDate = ar[month] + " " + formDate + " " + year
document.write(totalDate)
}
</SCRIPT>
</HEAD>
<TITLE> Example 10-01</TITLE>
<BODY bgcolor = white>
<INPUT TYPE = "button" onClick = "datedemo()" VALUE = "Date Demo">
</BODY>
<HTML>
```

Example 10-1 (ex10-1.htm)

The output for this script is shown in Figure 10-5.

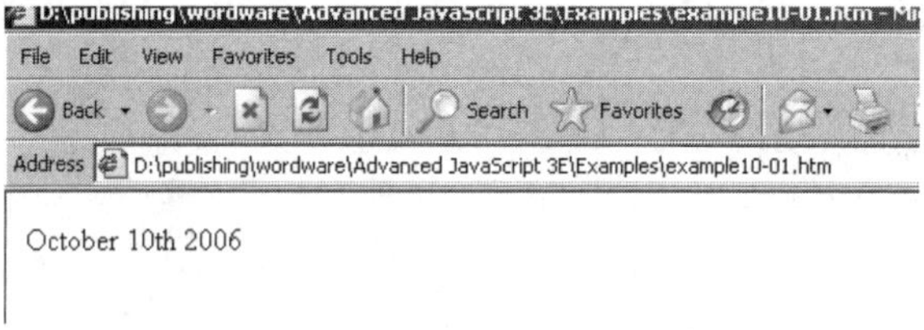

Figure 10-5. `getDate()` *output*

This script segment combines all methods learned so far to display a nicely formatted date. At first, all needed attributes of the previously created instance of the `Date` object are received and assigned to their corresponding variables (e.g., year, month, date). The last digit of the date (1-31) is then assigned to the variable `lastDigit`. According to the value of `lastDigit`, the proper suffix is assigned to `suf` via a nested `if-else` statement. For the digit 1, the suffix is "st" (1st); for the digit 2, the suffix is "nd" (2nd); for the digit 3, it is "rd" (3rd); for all other digits, it is "th" (5th, 6th, ...). Note that the last `else` statement associates the "th" suffix with all digits other than 1, 2, and 3. This suffix even applies to digits ending with a 0. An array of month names is created as before. The current date is then combined with its suffix to create a string such as "27th." This string, along with all the other desired values, is used to build a complete date format, such as "April 24th, 2007." The full string is then printed. If you understand this script, then you have a good understanding of date and time in JavaScript.

getDay()

This method returns the day of the week as an integer from 0 to 6. The day of the week is calculated according to the other attributes, so this method does not have a corresponding `setDay()` method. Here is an example:

```
ar = new Array(7)
ar[0] = "Sunday"
ar[1] = "Monday"
ar[2] = "Tuesday"
ar[3] = "Wednesday"
ar[4] = "Thursday"
ar[5] = "Friday"
ar[6] = "Saturday"
var birthday = new Date("January 3, 1978")
var day = birthday.getDay()
alert("You were born on " + ar[day])
```


getHours()

The `getHours()` function returns the number of hours since midnight. That is, it returns the current hour according to the 24-hour clock. Note that the range is 0 to 23, from midnight (0) to 11 PM (23). Here is an example:

```
var now = new Date()
var hour = now.getHours()
var text = ""
if (hour < 12)
   text = "morning"
else
   if (hour < 16)
      text = "afternoon"
   else
      if (hour < 20)
         text = "evening"
      else
         text = "night"
document.write("Good " + text + "!")
```

This script segment prints a short greeting based on the time of day. For example, if it is between 12:00 (noon) and 16:00 (4 PM), it prints "Good afternoon!" It is based on a nested `if-else` construct.

getMinutes()

The `getMinutes()` method returns the minute attribute of a `Date` instance. The integer returned is always from 0 to 59. Here is a short example to demonstrate the method:

```
var now = new Date()
var minute = now.getMinutes()
var hour = now.getHours()
var text = "Don't you have an appointment for " + (hour + 1)
text += ":00 ?"
```

```
if (minute > 49)
   document.write(text)
```

At first, the message containing the nearest hour is built. For example, if it is currently 15:55, the message is built with the nearest hour, 16:00. The message is printed if the current time is less than ten minutes from the next hour. Note that if it is 23:59, the hour is presented as 24:00, not 00:00.

getSeconds()

This method returns the seconds of a given `Date` instance, from 0 to 59. You can use it in much the same way as you use the `getMinutes()` method.

getTimezoneOffset()

This method returns the time zone offset in minutes for the current locale. The time zone offset is the difference between local time and Greenwich Mean Time (GMT). Daylight savings time prevents this value from being a constant. The returned value is an integer representing the difference in minutes. The following script shows how to use the user's time zone offset to figure out where he or she lives:

```
if (confirm("Are you in the United States?"))
{
   var now = new Date()
   var curOffset = now.getTimezoneOffset()
   curOffset /= 60 // convert from minutes to hours
   var zone = ""
   var prep = ""
   if (curOffset == 8)
   {
      zone = "west coast"
      prep = "on"
   }
   else
      if (curOffset == 7)
      {
         zone = "mid - west"
         prep = "in"
      }
      else
         if (curOffset == 6)
         {
            zone = "mid - east"
            prep = "in"
         }
         else
         {
            zone = "east coast"
            prep = "on"
         }
   alert("I think you live " + prep + " the " + zone + "!")
}
```

```
else
   alert("Sorry, this script is intended for U.S. residents only")
```

The script starts by asking the user if he or she lives in the United States. If not, a message is displayed. Otherwise, the following command block is executed. The area in the United States is determined according to the difference in hours between the local time zone and the GMT. The preceding preposition (e.g., "in", "on") is determined as well in the `if-else` construct. JavaScript then builds an appropriate message based on the current location of the user as well as the proper preposition.

getTime()

The `getTime()` method returns the number of milliseconds since January 1, 1970 00:00:00.

The set Methods

Just as JavaScript provides you with `get` methods so you can retrieve date and time information, it also provides you with `set` methods so you can set the `Date` object to a particular date and time. This can be quite useful. For example, you can set a `Date` object to a person's birthday, then find out what day of the week that was.

setYear()

This method sets the year attribute of a given `Date` instance. The following example computes the day of the current date last year:

```
var now = new Date()
var year = now.getYear()
now.setYear(year - 1)
ar = new Array(7)
ar[0] = "Sunday"
ar[1] = "Monday"
ar[2] = "Tuesday"
ar[3] = "Wednesday"
ar[4] = "Thursday"
ar[5] = "Friday"
ar[6] = "Saturday"
document.write("Last year, the current day was " + ar[now.getDay()])
```

First, an instance of the current date is created, and the current year is assigned to the variable `year`. The `year` attribute of the instance `now` is set to one year behind. The `day` attribute is then extracted from the modified instance, and a message is built based on that day, transformed to a string (via the array).

setMonth()

This method sets the month attribute of a given instance of the Date object. The following script sets the month attribute of the current date to May:

```
var now = new Date()
now.setMonth(4)
```

setDate()

The setDate() method sets the date attribute of a given instance of the Date object. The following script prints the day on which the first day of the month occurred:

```
var now = new Date()
now.setDate(1)
ar = new Array(7)
ar[0] = "Sunday"
ar[1] = "Monday"
ar[2] = "Tuesday"
ar[3] = "Wednesday"
ar[4] = "Thursday"
ar[5] = "Friday"
ar[6] = "Saturday"
document.write("The first day of the month occurred on " + ar[now.getDay()])
```

setHours()

This method sets the hour attribute of a given instance of the Date object. Here is an example:

```
var obj = new Date("December 4, 2006 18:50:59") // JS press release
obj.setHours(obj.getHours() - 2)
alert(obj.getHours())                           // 16
```

setMinutes()

This method sets the minutes of a given Date instance. Here is a simple example:

```
var obj = new Date("December 4, 2006 18:50:59") // JS press release
obj.setMinutes(obj.getMinutes() - 1)
alert(obj.getMinutes())                         // 49
```

setSeconds()

The setSeconds() method sets the seconds of a given instance of the Date object type. The following example demonstrates its usage:

```
var obj = new Date("December 4, 2006 18:50:59") // JS press release
obj.setSeconds(obj.getSeconds() - 9)
alert(obj.getSeconds())                         // 50
```

setTime()

This method sets the number of milliseconds since January 1, 1970 00:00:00. It actually modifies all fields of its calling object. Here is an example:

```
var obj = new Date()
obj.setTime(867999600000)
var date = obj.getDate()
var month = obj.getMonth()
if (date < 10)
   var lastDigit = date
else
   var lastDigit = date % 10
var exp = ""
// determine suffix
if (lastDigit == 1)
   suf = "st"
else
   if (lastDigit == 2)
      suf = "nd"
   else
      if (lastDigit == 3)
         suf = "rd"
      else
         suf = "th"
// array for name of month
var ar = new Array(12)
ar[0] = "January"
ar[1] = "February"
ar[2] = "March"
ar[3] = "April"
ar[4] = "May"
ar[5] = "June"
ar[6] = "July"
ar[7] = "August"
ar[8] = "September"
ar[9] = "October"
ar[10] = "November"
ar[11] = "December"
var text = ar[month] + " " + date + suf
alert(text) // July 4th (setTime modifies the entire instance)
```

The to Methods

toGMTString()

This method converts a date to a string, using the Internet GMT conventions. The conversion is done according to the operating system's time zone offset and returns a string value that is similar to the following form:

```
Tue, 30 Jul 2006 01:03:46 GMT
```

The exact format depends on the platform. Here is a simple example:

```
var now = new Date()
var ar1 = now.toGMTString().split(" ")
document.write("The current time in Greenwich is " + ar1[4])
```

A sample output of this script segment is:

```
The current time in Greenwich is 01:08:21
```

toLocaleString()

This method returns the date in the form of a string, using the current locale's conventions. If you are trying to pass a date using `toLocaleString`, be aware that different locales assemble the string in different ways. Using methods such as `getHours`, `getMinutes`, and `getSeconds` will give more portable results. The following example demonstrates the function:

```
var now = new Date()
var ar1 = now.toLocaleString().split(" ")
document.write("The current time is " + ar1[1])
```

The script's output is:

```
The current time is 18:12:51
```

The general format of the converted string is:

MM/DD/YY HH:MM:SS

The parse Methods

`parse` methods are used to extract one type of information from another. For example, when programming in C, Java, or C++, when you compile your program, the compiler parses your source code looking for commands it recognizes. When you load a web page, the browser parses your HTML looking for specific tags.

parse()

The `parse()` method accepts a date string in the IETF standard and converts it to the number of milliseconds since January 1, 1970 00:00:00. The IETF standard date representation is:

DayAbb, date MonthAbb year HH:MM:SS TimeZoneAbb

An example for this standard is "Mon, 25 Dec 2001 13:30:00 GMT." This method also understands the continental U.S. time zone abbreviations such as PST (Pacific Standard Time) and EST (Eastern Standard Time). However, time zones outside the United States (and their equivalent in Canada, for instance) do not have a standard abbreviation accepted by JavaScript. For such time zones the offset must be specified; that is, you must specify the difference in hours and minutes between the local time zone and Greenwich

Mean Time. For example, in "Mon, 25 Dec 2001 13:30:00 GMT+0430," GMT+0430 is shorthand for 4 hours, 30 minutes west of the Greenwich meridian. If you do not specify a time zone, the local time zone is assumed, according to the settings of the clock in the operating system. If your time zone is not set correctly, you should change it in the control panel, both on Macs and Windows-based machines. GMT is also known as Universal Time Coordinate, or UTC.

The `parse()` method is a static one. It does not belong to a specific instance of the `Date` object, but to the object type itself. Therefore, it is always used as `Date.parse()`. Here is an example for this method:

```
var aDate = "Aug 27 2006"
var birthday = new Date()
birthday.setTime(Date.parse(aDate))
```


UTC()

The `UTC()` method takes a comma-delimited list and returns the number of milliseconds since January 1, 1970 00:00:00, Greenwich Mean Time (GMT, UTC). This is also a static method, so it is called along with the general `Date` object. You cannot use this method to refer to a specific date in the local time zone, because it constantly refers to the Universal Time Coordinate (GMT, UTC). For example, the following statement creates a `Date` object using GMT instead of local time, as it would if the method were not used:

```
gmtDate = new Date(Date.UTC(99, 11, 1, 0, 0, 0))
```

The general syntax of the method is:

```
Date.UTC(year, month, day [, hrs] [, min] [, sec])
```

All attributes should be specified as integers.

Time-Related Methods of Other Objects

setTimeout()

The `setTimeout()` method evaluates an expression after a specified number of milliseconds have elapsed. Its general syntax is:

```
timeoutID = setTimeout(expression, msec)
```

`timeoutID` is an identifier used to identify the current timeout.

`expression` is a string expression or property of an existing object. It is normally a simple statement that is to be executed after the specified time has ticked off.

`msec` is a numeric value, a numeric string, or a property of an existing object in millisecond units.

The `setTimeout()` method evaluates an expression after a specified amount of time. Take a look at the following example:

```
<HTML>
<HEAD>
<TITLE>setTimeout() method</TITLE>
<SCRIPT LANGUAGE = "JavaScript">
function displayAlert()
{
   alert("5 seconds have elapsed since the button was clicked.")
}
</SCRIPT>
</HEAD>
<BODY>
<FORM>
Click the button on the left for a reminder in 5 seconds;
click the button on the right to cancel the reminder before
it is displayed.
<P>
<INPUT TYPE = "button" VALUE = "5-second reminder"
   NAME = "remind_button"
   onClick = "timerID = setTimeout('displayAlert()',5000)">
</FORM>
</BODY>
</HTML>
```

When you click the button, the event handler's script sets a timeout. The timeout specifies that after 5,000 milliseconds, or five seconds, the function `displayAlert()` is called. Therefore, five seconds after you click the button an alert box is displayed.

This method does not repeatedly execute the specified statement. That is, it does not execute it every five seconds. When the time limit specified has ticked down, the statement is executed and the timeout does not exist anymore. `setTimeout()` is a method of the `window` or `frame` object, depending on the basic structure of the HTML document it is used in.

It is common to use the `setTimeout()` method for creating a pause between two consecutive calls to a user-defined recursive function. Take a look at the following script:

```
function alertNumbers(num)
{
   if (num > 10)
      return
   alert(num)
   val = ++num
   timerID = setTimeout("alertNumbers(val)", 3000)
}
alertNumbers(0)
```

This script segment pops up an alert box every three seconds. The displayed message is a number. The first alert box displays the number 0. After three seconds, another one displays the number 1. This process continues until the number 10. If you attempt to print the number to the document rather than displaying it in a window (box), an error is generated. The reason for such an error is that by writing to the document after a delay you are trying to change the layout, which has been completed. Another important point is that if the expression provided to the `setTimeout()` method is a function call, as in this example, and the function requires an argument, then it must be a global variable. Local variables do not work, because `setTimeout()` is a method of a `frame` or the `window` object (`window` is the default value if no object is specified). Nonetheless, you can use a literal as the argument. Bear in mind that `setTimeout()` requires a string-encapsulated expression. You can embed a local variable in this expression as follows:

```
var cmd = "foo(" + num + ")"
timerID = setTimeout(cmd, 2000) // or any other time
```

clearTimeout()

This method cancels a timeout that was set with the `setTimeout()` method. It is also a method of the `frame` or `window` object, so it is discussed later in detail. At this point, it is important that you know how to use it to cancel a timeout. Its general syntax is:

```
clearTimeout(timeoutID)
```

`timeoutID` is a timeout setting that was returned by a previous call to the `setTimeout()` method. It must be exactly the same as the one used in the `setTimeout()` method, because it actually identifies the timeout's settings according to it.

The `setTimeout()` method sets a timeout; that is, it executes a statement after a specified amount of time. If you want to cancel the time "bomb" during its ticking, you clear it via this method. If you want to change the amount of time set by the `setTimeout()` method, you must clear it and then set a new timeout. Here is the previous example enriched by the `clearTimeout()` method:

```
<HTML>
<HEAD>
<TITLE>setTimeout() and clearTimeout() methods</TITLE>
<SCRIPT LANGUAGE = "JavaScript">
function displayAlert()
{
   alert("5 seconds have elapsed since the button was clicked.")
}
</SCRIPT>
</HEAD>
<BODY>
<FORM>
Click the button on the left for a reminder in 5 seconds;
click the button on the right to cancel the reminder before
it is displayed.
<P>
<INPUT TYPE = "button" VALUE = "5-second reminder"
   NAME = "remind_button"
   onClick = "timerID = setTimeout('displayAlert()',5000)">
```

```
<INPUT TYPE = "button" VALUE = "Clear the 5-second reminder"
   NAME = "remind_disable_button"
   onClick = "clearTimeout(timerID)">
</FORM>
</BODY>
</HTML>
```

Time and Date Examples

Throughout this chapter you have explored various time and date functions, and by now you should be comfortable with them. Times and dates are widely used in scripts to achieve many goals and to create various effects. However, what you have looked at so far has not been in the context of a practical real-world example. Now let's take a look at these same functions, but in real-world scenarios. In this section, we shall introduce a few useful scripts that demonstrate the concepts learned in this chapter.

A Simple Digital Clock

The time and date methods are useful for computing time values in JavaScript scripts. The following example shows how to use such values to create an attractive graphical clock on an HTML page. This sort of JavaScript can be immediately useful in your web page.

```
<HTML>
<HEAD>
<TITLE>
Example 10-2
</TITLE>
</HEAD>
<BODY>
<!-- JavaScript immediate script -->
<SCRIPT LANGUAGE="JavaScript">
<!--
document.write(setClock())
function setClock()
{
   // initialize accumulative HTML variable to empty string
   var text = ""
   // set standard convention for digit and punctuation images
   var openImage = "<IMG SRC=\"" + getPath(location.href) + "dg"
   var closeImage = ".gif\" HEIGHT=21 WIDTH=16>"
   // initialize time-related variables with current time settings
   var now = new Date()
   var hour = now.getHours()
   var minute = now.getMinutes()
   now = null
   var ampm = ""

   // validate hour values and set value of ampm
   if (hour >= 12)
```

```
   {
      hour = hour - 12
      ampm = "pm"
   } else
      ampm = "am"
   hour = (hour == 0) ? 12 : hour
   // add zero digit to a one-digit minute as spaceholder
   if (minute < 10)
      minute = "0" + minute // do not parse this number!
   // convert minute and hour values to strings
   minute += ""
   hour += ""
   // assign image tags according to the value of hour
   for (var i = 0; i < hour.length; ++i)
   {
      text += openImage + hour.charAt(i) + closeImage
   }
   // assign image tag of colon separator to text variable
   text += openImage + "c.gif\" HEIGHT=21 WIDTH=9>"
   // assign image tags according to the value of minute
   for (var i = 0; i < minute.length; ++i)
   {
      text += openImage + minute.charAt(i) + closeImage
   }
   // assign am / pm image tag to text variable
   text += openImage + ampm + closeImage
   // return accumulative HTML string
   return text
}
function getPath(url)
{
   lastSlash = url.lastIndexOf("/")
   return url.substring(0, lastSlash + 1)
}
// -->
</SCRIPT>
</BODY>
</HTML>
```

Example 10-2 (ex10-2.htm). *A simple graphical clock based on time and date methods*

The output of this script is shown in Figure 10-6.

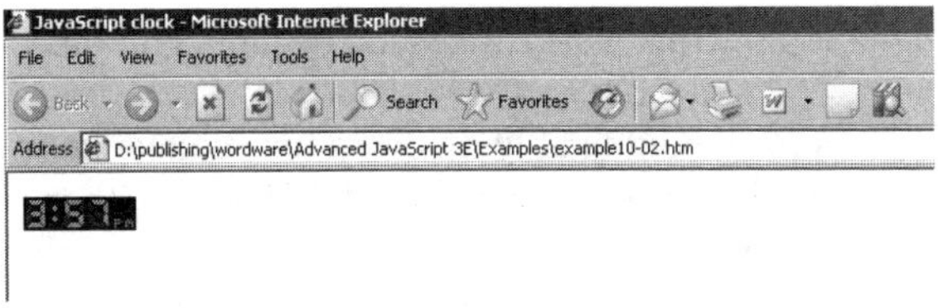

Figure 10-6. *JavaScript digital clock*

The first part of the script is built of the needed images and some instructions. It is important to add these comments to every public-domain script because it is often difficult to guess what a script does and what additional objects are needed, such as images.

The function `getPath()` accepts the URL of the current document. This includes all portions of the URL, including "http://..." and the name of the file. The function returns the URL up to the filename, not including the filename but including the last slash. For example, consider the following URL:

```
http://www.wordware.com/index.html
```

Upon acceptance of this string, the function would return:

```
http://www.wordware.com/
```

The first function in the script, `setClock()`, actually creates the clock, from top to bottom. Notice that each portion of the function is explained by a comment. Take a look at the following statements, taken directly from the function:

```
var openImage = "<IMG SRC =\ "" + getPath(location.href) + "dg"
var closeImage = ".gif\" HEIGHT = 21 WIDTH = 16>"
```

In this script segment, two constant-like variables are declared and initialized a meaningful value. The first is assigned the opening structure of an `<IMG>` tag in HTML. Note that `location.href` is the current URL of the document. Notice also the use of escape sequences (`\"`). The value assigned to `closeImage` is independent of local influences such as the URL of the document. It simply assigns the value `.gif\" HEIGHT = 21 WIDTH = 16>`. The `HEIGHT` and `WIDTH` attributes are based on the actual height and width of the digit images used to display the time.

Here is the following portion of the script:

```
var now = new Date()
var hour = now.getHours()
var minute = now.getMinutes()
now = null
var ampm = ""
```

This section has two important tasks:

1. It assigns the local hour to `hour`.
2. It assigns the minute attribute of the current time to `minute`.

If you do not remember how this works, read the beginning of this chapter again.

The following script segment simply modifies the value of `hour` according to the regular conventions used in the United States and other countries using 12-hour clock systems. First of all, noon is considered PM. Furthermore, midnight is written as 12:00, not 0:00.

Take a look at the following statement:

```
if (minute < 10)
   minute = "0" + minute // do not parse this number!
```

This statement makes sure that the minute attribute holds a two-digit number. That is, if it is originally a one-digit number, a leading "0" digit is added. Notice that this digit is actually a string. Attempting to parse this string with a function such as `parseInt()` would convert it to a numeric type, causing its value to change, because it is written in octal notation (leading 0). It must keep the string value throughout the entire script.

The next two statements in the script cast the value of `minute` and the value of `hour` to strings by concatenating an empty string to them. This is important, because string properties, which can only be used on strings, are used later on in the script.

The following statement is a loop:

```
for (var i = 0; i < hour.length; ++i)
{
   text += openImage + hour.charAt(i) + closeImage
}
```

The loop executes `hour.length` times. That is, if `hour` is a two-digit number, the loop executes twice, once for each digit. During each execution, an image tag corresponding to the current digit in the string, the value of `hour`, is being concatenated to `text`. For example, if the value of `hour` is 12, the loop's command block executes twice. During the first execution, the following string is assigned to `text`:

```
text += '<IMG SRC = "http://www.netscent.com/dg1.gif" HEIGHT = 21
WIDTH = 16>'
```

During the second pass through the loop, this equivalent statement is executed:

```
text += '<IMG SRC = "http://www.netscent.com/dg2.gif" HEIGHT = 21
WIDTH = 16>'
```

If the value of `hour` is a one-character string, the loop obviously executes only once.

The following statement in the script is:

```
text += openImage + "c.gif\" HEIGHT = 21 WIDTH = 9>"
```

This statement simply assigns the tag associated with the colon image. Notice that `closeImage` is not concatenated in this statement because this image's `WIDTH` attribute is different from the other images.

The following loop is exactly like the one described earlier associated with the variable `hour`. It only differs in that it relates to the variable `minute`.

The AM or PM image tag is assigned to `text`, according to the value of `ampm`.

The final statement inside the function instructs JavaScript to return the value of `text`, the accumulative string of all the HTML tags needed to print the clock. The returned value is printed to the document by a global statement—`document.write(text)`.

Chapter 10

Monthly Calendar

The next example outputs a monthly calendar. Before we discuss the code, take a look at some sample output of the function:

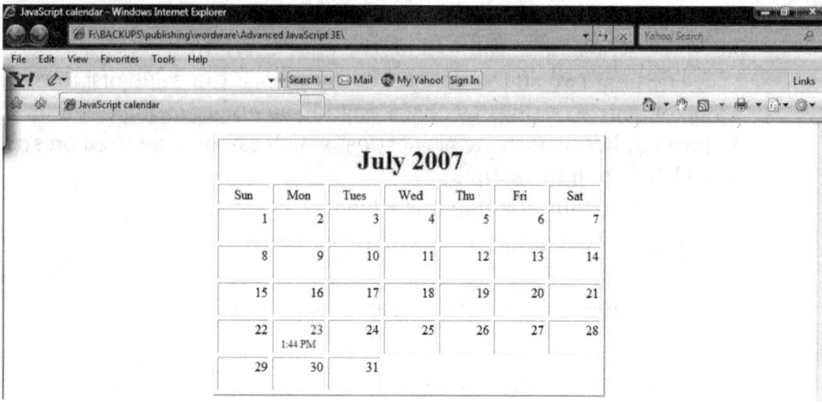

Figure 10-7. *JavaScript calendar*

Now take a look at the script itself:

```
<HTML>
<HEAD>
<TITLE>
JavaScript calendar
</TITLE>
</HEAD>
<BODY>
<!-- JavaScript immediate script -->
<SCRIPT LANGUAGE = "JavaScript">
<!--
setCal()
function getTime()
{
   // initialize time-related variables with current time settings
   var now = new Date()
   var hour = now.getHours()
   var minute = now.getMinutes()
   now = null
   var ampm = ""
   // validate hour values and set value of ampm
   if (hour >= 12)
   {
      hour = hour – 12
      ampm = "PM"
   } else
      ampm = "AM"
   hour = (hour == 0) ? 12 : hour
   // add zero digit to a one-digit minute
   if (minute < 10)
      minute = "0" + minute   // do not parse this number!
```

```
   // return time string
   return hour + ":" + minute + " " + ampm
}
function leapYear(year)
{
   if (year % 4 == 0)   // basic rule
      return true       // is leap year
   /* else */           // else not needed when statement is "return"
      return false      // is not leap year
}

function getDays(month, year)
{
   // create array to hold number of days in each month
   var ar = new Array(12)
   ar[0] = 31  // January
   ar[1] = (leapYear(year)) ? 29 : 28 // February
   ar[2] = 31  // March
   ar[3] = 30  // April
   ar[4] = 31  // May
   ar[5] = 30  // June
   ar[6] = 31  // July
   ar[7] = 31  // August
   ar[8] = 30  // September
   ar[9] = 31  // October
   ar[10] = 30 // November
   ar[11] = 31 // December
   // return number of days in the specified month (parameter)
   return ar[month]
}

function getMonthName(month)
{
   // create array to hold name of each month
   var ar = new Array(12)
   ar[0] = "January"
   ar[1] = "February"
   ar[2] = "March"
   ar[3] = "April"
   ar[4] = "May"
   ar[5] = "June"
   ar[6] = "July"
   ar[7] = "August"
   ar[8] = "September"
   ar[9] = "October"
   ar[10] = "November"
   ar[11] = "December"
   // return name of specified month (parameter)
   return ar[month]
}
function setCal()
{
   // standard time attributes
   var now = new Date()
```

```
   var year = now.getYear()
   var month = now.getMonth()
   var monthName = getMonthName(month)
   var date = now.getDate()
   now = null
   // create instance of first day of month, and extract the day it occurs on
   var firstDayInstance = new Date(year, month, 1)
   var firstDay = firstDayInstance.getDay()
   firstDayInstance = null
   // number of days in current month
   var days = getDays(month, year)
   // call function to draw calendar
   drawCal(firstDay + 1, days, date, monthName, year)
}
function drawCal(firstDay, lastDate, date, monthName, year)
{
   // constant table settings
   var headerHeight = 50      // height of the table's header cell
   var border = 2             // 3D height of table's border
   var cellSpacing = 4        // width of table's border
   var headerColor = "midnightblue" // color of table's header
   var headerSize = "+3"      // size of table's header font
   var colWidth = 60          // width of columns in table
   var dayCellHeight = 25     // height of cells containing days of the week
   var dayColor = "darkblue"  // color of font representing week days
   var cellHeight = 40  // height of cells representing dates in the calendar
   var todayColor = "red"     // color specifying today's date in the calendar
   var timeColor = "purple"   // color of font representing current time

   // create basic table structure
   var text = ""          // initialize accumulative variable to empty string
   text += '<CENTER>'
   text += '<TABLE BORDER = ' + border + ' CELLSPACING = ' + cellspacing + '>'
                          // table settings

   text += '<TH COLSPAN = 7 HEIGHT = ' + headerHeight + '>' // create table
                          // header cell
   text += "<FONT COLOR = " + headerColor + " SIZE = " + headerSize + ">"
                          // set font for table header
   text += monthName + ' ' + year
   text += '</FONT>'      // close table header's font settings
   text += '</TH>'        // close header cell

   // variables to hold constant settings
   var openCol = '<TD WIDTH = ' + colWidth + ' HEIGHT = ' + dayCellHeight + '>'
   openCol = openCol + '<FONT COLOR = "' + dayColor + '">'
   var closeCol = '</FONT></TD>'
   // create array of abbreviated day names
   var weekDay = new Array(7)
   weekDay[0] = "Sun"
   weekDay[1] = "Mon"
   weekDay[2] = "Tues"
```

```
   weekDay[3] = "Wed"
   weekDay[4] = "Thu"
   weekDay[5] = "Fri"
   weekDay[6] = "Sat"
   // create first row of table to set column width and specify week day
   text += '<TR ALIGN = "center" VALIGN = "center">'

   for (var dayNum = 0; dayNum < 7; ++dayNum)
   {
      text += openCol + weekDay[dayNum] + closeCol
   }

   text += '</TR>'
   // declaration and initialization of two variables to help with tables
   var digit = 1
   var curCell = 1
   for (var row = 1; row <= Math.ceil((lastDate + firstDay - 1) / 7); ++row)
   {
      text += '<TR ALIGN = "right" VALIGN = "top">'
      for (var col = 1; col <= 7; ++col)
      {
         if (digit > lastDate)
            break
         if (curCell < firstDay)
         {
            text += '<TD></TD>'
            curCell++
         } else
         {
            if (digit == date)
            { // current cell represent today's date
               text += '<TD HEIGHT = ' + cellHeight + '>'
               text += '<FONT COLOR = "' + todayColor + '">'
               text += digit
               text += '</FONT><BR>'
               text += '<FONT COLOR = "' + timeColor + '" SIZE = 2>'
               text += '<CENTER>' + getTime() + '</CENTER>'
               text += '</FONT>'
               text += '</TD>'
            } else
               text += '<TD HEIGHT = ' + cellHeight + '>' + digit + '</TD>'
            digit++
         }
      }
      text += '</TR>'
   }
   // close all basic table tags
   text += '</TABLE>'
   text += '</CENTER>'
   // print accumulative HTML string
   document.write(text)
}
```

```
// -->
</SCRIPT>
</BODY>
</HTML>
```

Example 10-3 (ex10-3.htm). *A calendar based on HTML tables printed via JavaScript*

Let's follow the script step by step, explaining the task of every function.

getTime()

This function simply returns a string representing the current local time in the following format:

hours : *minutes AM/PM*

Note that there are no spaces between any characters. The function is based on the same algorithm as the first part of `setClock()` in Example 10-2. Refer to the explanation regarding that example for further insights.

leapYear(year)

This function returns true if the current year is a leap year; otherwise, it returns false. The basic rule used for the decision is that a leap year occurs every four years, in the same year of the summer Olympic games. More exactly, if the year is divisible by 4, it is a leap year. Therefore, the modulo operator suits the case perfectly. If `year % 4` is zero, the year is divisible by 4, meaning the current year is a leap year. Otherwise, the year is not divisible by 4, so false is returned. An obvious call to this function is:

```
if (leapYear(current year))
   // is a leap year
else
   // is not a leap year
```

Another possibility is to use the returned value in a conditional statement, or operation (`?:`).

Note that the parameter of the function must accept an integer value, which is reasonable when computing years.

getDays(month, year)

This function accepts two arguments: a month and a year. An array of 12 elements is then created. The array is an instance of the built-in `Array` object. Therefore, the keyword `new` is used. Each element of the array represents the number of days in its corresponding month. `ar[0]` holds the number of days in January (31); `ar[11]` holds the number of days in December. The array is simply assigned the proper data, according to the constant number of days in each month. However, the number of days in February is not constant. In leap years there are 29 days in February, whereas in all other years there are 28 days. The function `leapYear()` is used to decide if the specified year is a leap year. This situation is a typical one for a conditional operator, because one of two values is to be assigned to a variable depending on the value of the condition (the Boolean value returned by the function `leapYear()`). Notice the extensive use of comments to help you understand the script. The value returned by the function is equal to the number of days in the month passed over to the function upon calling. For example, if the value of `month` is 0 (as passed to the function), the value `ar[0] == 31` is returned by the function.

Note that both arguments must be integers. The month must be specified as an integer from 0 to 11, with 0 representing January and 11 representing December.

getMonthName(month)

This function accepts the integer value of a certain month (0 for January, 11 for December) and returns the full name of the function, obviously in the form of a string. This function, like the preceding one, uses an instance of the `Array` object to store constant values. The name of the desired month is retrieved from the array by its index (subscript).

setCal()

At first, the function creates a new instance of the `Date` object, holding the attributes of the current local time. The current year is assigned to `year` via the method `getYear()`, and the current month is assigned to `month` via the method `getMonth()`. The name of the month, returned by `getMonthName()`, is assigned to `monthName`. After the current date is assigned to `date`, the instance `now` is assigned null, a good JavaScript programming practice.

The next statement of the function is:

```
var firstDayInstance = new Date(year, month, 1)
```

It creates a new instance of the `Date` object; this time it is for the first day of the current month. Therefore, the value 1 is used to specify the date. This obviously influences the day of the week on which the date occurred. This value is assigned to `firstDay` in the following statement. The instance `firstDayInstance` is then assigned null. This script segment computes the day of the week (Sunday, Monday, Tuesday, etc.) on which the month started. Another possible way to achieve this goal is to create an instance of the current date as usual:

```
var firstDayInstance = new Date() // not first day yet!
```

You then need to set the date to 1, via the `setDate()` method. You should use the following statement to do so:

```
firstDayInstance.setDate(1)
```

The next portion of the function consists of only one statement. It assigns `days` the number of days in the current month.

The last statement of the function draws the calendar:

```
drawCal(firstDay + 1, days, date, monthName, 1900 + year)
```

The arguments are:

- Integer value of the first day of the month + 1; that is, 1 for Sunday, 2 for Monday, 3 for Tuesday, etc.
- The number of days in the specified month
- The specified date
- The name of the specified month (e.g., "January," "February," "March")
- The specified year, as a four-digit integer (e.g., 2001, 2002)

drawCal(firstDay, lastDate, date, monthName, year)

This function's main task is to print the calendar table. Before it does so, the HTML structure of the table must be constructed. The first part of the function assigns values to attributes associated with the final format of the table. Such attributes are the size of cells, font colors, and more. Here is the full list, including the variable names and their roles:

Table 10-2. *Variables in `drawCal()` and their role in the final format of the calendar*

Variable	Role
headerHeight	The height of the table header's cell. The header cell is the cell containing the name of the month and the year in a large font. The height is specified in pixels.
border	The table's border. You should already know that HTML tables have a `BORDER` attribute. This attribute specifies the three-dimensional height of the border.
cellSpacing	The width of the border. A table border's width can also be set in HTML. This value is the distance between the inner line of the border and its outer line.
headerColor	The color of the header's font. This is the color of the font in the largest cell of the table at the top of the calendar.
headerSize	The size of the header's font (see headerHeight).
colWidth	The width of the table's columns. This is actually the width of each cell, or the width of the widest cell in each column.
dayCellHeight	The height of the cell containing the names of the days ("Sunday," "Monday," "Tuesday," etc.).
dayColor	The color of the font representing the days of the week.
cellHeight	The height of all the regular cells in the table containing the dates of the month.
todayColor	The color specifying the current date in the calendar.
timeColor	The color of the font used with the current time, located in the cell of the current date.

The portion of the function that follows creates the basic table structure, including all general HTML tags referring to the outline of the table. Notice how the variables are implemented in the script. Now take a look at the following two statements of the script:

```
var openCol = '<TD WIDTH = ' + colWidth + ' HEIGHT = ' + dayCellHeight + '>'
openCol += '<FONT COLOR = "' + dayColor + '">'
var closeCol = '</FONT></TD>'
```

These are the tags used to create each of the cells containing the day names. For example, the syntax for "Sunday" using the default values of the variables is:

```
<TD WIDTH = 60 HEIGHT = 25><FONT COLOR = "midnightblue"></FONT></TD>
```

Here are the next two portions of the function for reference:

```
// create array of abbreviated day names
   var weekDay = new Array(7)
   weekDay[0] = "Sun"
   weekDay[1] = "Mon"
   weekDay[2] = "Tues"
   weekDay[3] = "Wed"
   weekDay[4] = "Thu"
   weekDay[5] = "Fri"
   weekDay[6] = "Sat"

   // create first row of table to set column width and specify week day
   text += '<TR ALIGN = "center" VALIGN = "center">'
   for (var dayNum = 0; dayNum < 7; ++dayNum)
   {
      text += openCol + weekDay[dayNum] + closeCol
   }
   text += '</TR>'
```

In the first segment, a regular array is created. It is then assigned the abbreviated names of the days. This array enables us to refer to each name via a number. The following portion, where a cell is created for each day, takes advantage of this referencing method. A new day is printed on every iteration of the loop. Note that the tags associated with the beginning and the end of the table's current row are not located inside the loop. A new row with all day names is started before the loop. The current row is terminated after the tags related to the cell of "Sat" are assigned to text.

The following portion of the function is:

```
var digit = 1
var curCell = 1
```

You will see the role of these variables later in the function.

By now, all tags associated with the table's header and the column headers have been assigned to the accumulative string variable `text`. The remaining part of the function assigns the tags associated with all the table's cells. As you know, the calendar is a rectangular table. Therefore, we prefer to use a nested loop structure to refer to its cells. If you want to practice your skills, try replacing this structure with a single loop, using the modulo operator to compute the location of new table rows.

The more difficult part of the loop is its terminating condition. Here it is again:

```
row <= Math.ceil((lastDate + firstDay - 1) / 7)
```

The `Math` object and its `ceil()` method are explained in detail in Chapter 11, "JavaScript Math." For now, you should just know that `Math.ceil(`*`num`*`)` evaluates to the nearest integer to *num* that is equal to or greater than *num* (rounding up). Here are some examples:

```
Math.ceil(15.15) == 16
Math.ceil(16) == 16
Math.ceil(16.0001) == 17
```

You may recall from the `setCal()` function that the value passed over to the parameter `firstDay` is from 1 to 7, not from 0 to 6. Therefore, 1 is subtracted from `firstDay` in this expression. `Math.ceil((lastDate + firstDay - 1) / 7)` represents the minimum number of rows needed in the calendar, or table. The number of cells in the calendar (not including the main header, column headers, and cells after the last day in the month) is `lastDate + firstDay - 1`, because `lastDate` is equal to the number of days in the month, and `firstDay - 1` is equal to the number of cells before the first date. The value is divided by 7, to get the exact minimum number of rows needed. However, the loop must execute a whole number of times. Therefore, the `Math.ceil()` method is needed.

Other, more simple, calendars just use five rows for every month, no matter what. However, this simple rule of five rows per month fails when (a) the first day of a non-leap year February occurs on Sunday, meaning only four lines are needed, and (b) the first day of a 31-day month is on Friday or Saturday, meaning six rows are needed. Although these situations seldom occur, you must take them into account. If the row computation is replaced by a simple 5 in this script, a month such as February 1987 does not appear properly.

The nested loop is not nearly as difficult, because it always executes seven times, once for each day of the week. Throughout the entire loop construct, including inner and outer loops, `digit` holds the current cell to be created. The variable `curCell` holds the accumulative number of cells in the table created (assigned) thus far. This variable is only needed until the cell of the first day of the month is created, and is not handled afterward; that is, after the first day of the month, it is not incremented anymore.

The `<TD>` and `</TD>` tags are used to create blank cells that are used as placeholders. These are only needed before the first day of the month, because the loop is terminated via a `break` statement after the last day of the month, and the remaining place in the line is filled in the same way as blank cells (placeholders). Each execution of the inner loop creates the current cell of the table. There are basically two types of cells:

- A cell representing the current day, which uses a special font color and displays the time inside the cell
- All other cells

The HTML tags used are obvious and are not dealt with in depth here.

There are two statements outside the inner loop but inside the containment loop. The first one creates a new table row and the second one ends the current row. Each execution of the inner loop (seven executions or its command block) is responsible for the creation of an entire row, or a partial one if it is the last row and the last day of the month is encountered before the last cell of the row—in this case the loop is terminated via a `break` statement. The term "create" refers to the concatenation of the proper strings and values and assignment to the variable `text`.

The last, but definitely not least, statement of the function is the one that actually prints the table to the HTML document. Up to that statement, the HTML document was stored as a string in the variable `text`.

Random Quotes

The finale for this chapter is a simple, yet interesting script to display a different message each time the page is loaded. Here is the script:

```
<HTML>
<HEAD>
<TITLE>Random quote</TITLE>
<SCRIPT LANGUAGE = "JavaScript">
<!--
function getMessage()
{
   // create array of Murphy's laws
   var ar = new Array(20)
   ar[0] = "Nothing is as easy as it looks."
   ar[1] = "Everything takes longer than you think."
   ar[2] = "Anything that can go wrong will go wrong."
   ar[3] = "If there is a possibility of several things going wrong, the one
            that will cause the most damage will be the one to go wrong."
   ar[4] = "If there is a worse time for something to go wrong, it will happen
            then."
   ar[5] = "If anything simply cannot go wrong, it will anyway."
   ar[6] = "If you perceive that there are four possible ways in which a
            procedure can go wrong, and circumvent these, then a fifth way,
            unprepared for, will promptly develop."
   ar[7] = "Left to themselves, things tend to go from bad to worse."
   ar[8] = "If everything seems to be going well, you have obviously
            overlooked something."
   ar[9] = "Nature always sides with the hidden flaw."
   ar[10] = "Mother nature is a bitch."
   ar[11] = "It is impossible to make anything foolproof because fools are
             so ingenious."
```

```
    ar[12] = "Whenever you set out to do something, something else must be
             done first."
    ar[13] = "Every solution breeds new problems."
    ar[14] = "Trust everybody ... then cut the cards."
    ar[15] = "Two wrongs are only the beginning."
    ar[16] = "If at first you don't succeed, destroy all evidence that you
             tried."
    ar[17] = "To succeed in politics, it is often necessary to rise above
             your principles."
    ar[18] = "Exceptions prove the rule ... and wreck the budget."
    ar[19] = "Success always occurs in private, and failure in full view."

    var now = new Date()
    var sec = now.getSeconds()
    alert("Murphy's Law:\r" + ar[sec % 20])
}
//-->
</SCRIPT>
</HEAD>
<BODY onLoad = "getMessage()">
</BODY>
</HTML>
```

Example 10-4 (ex10-4.htm). *A script to display a random message each time the page is loaded*

The first statement in the function creates an array, an instance of the built-in Array object. The array includes 20 elements, starting from ar[0] and ending with ar[19]. Each element is assigned a string, or to be exact, a Murphy's law. An instance of the Date object, now, is then created. The number of seconds in the current time is retrieved from now via the getSeconds() method. As you know, the value of sec is an integer from 0 to 59, with a random possibility for each. In total there are 60 consecutive integers. Due to this fact, the expression sec % 20 returns an integer from 0 to 19, with an equal chance for each, because 60 is divisible by 20 (60 / 20 = 3!). The ability to create a random number from 0 to 19 using this technique enables us to randomly choose a Murphy's law from the array. The selected Murphy's law is displayed by an alert box.

The most important part of the script to pay attention to is the use of an event handler to respond to the load event—onLoad. When the event handler is triggered (when the page has completed loading), the function getMessage() is called to display an alert message as described earlier. Also notice the use of an escape sequence, the carriage return character (\r).

Summary

In this chapter we discussed date- and time-related concepts in JavaScript. Such concepts are based on the `Date` object. We learned about this built-in object, the only one in JavaScript without any properties. After a thorough look at the object, we saw how its instances can be created and used in scripts. By now, you should have enough tools to create interesting scripts of various types. As we look further into the language in the following chapters, you will be able to grasp the power of JavaScript to enhance HTML documents. In this chapter you have seen that without much effort, you can add a graphical digital clock to any page. This may seem amazing, but the best is yet to come, including animated clocks and more.

Chapter 11
JavaScript Math

Math in JavaScript

One of the primary capabilities that computers are renowned for is their ability to perform math very accurately and very quickly. All programming languages include features, constants, functions, and other math elements that allow the programmer to perform mathematics. Likewise, JavaScript includes many features related to math, enabling JavaScript programmers to invoke numeric calculations in our scripts. In this chapter we will explore these mathematical operations and show you ways to implement them in your web pages.

Math in JavaScript is based on two general elements of the language:

- Mathematical operators
- The built-in `Math` object

Mathematical operators (+, –, *, /, %) are common to almost every language, and were discussed earlier in Chapter 3, so we won't cover operator basics again in this chapter. However, I have not yet introduced you to the `Math` object, which can perform a variety of mathematical operations. In this chapter I will familiarize you with this object, including its properties and methods. We will also take a look at some possible uses of this object. If there are any mathematical operations covered that you are not familiar with, don't be too concerned since that simply means you probably won't be needing to use that level of mathematics in your scripts. It is important to note that the `Math` object has functions that many people may not need in their web pages, but are important to math.

The Math Object

JavaScript's `Math` object provides many arithmetic and trigonometric functions. Most of these are functions you probably already know. These functions expand the mathematical ability of JavaScript beyond the basic arithmetic operators.

You already know how to create instances of JavaScript objects such as the `Date` object. Objects that you have to instantiate are referred to as *dynamic* objects. However, some objects in JavaScript are static objects. You don't need to instantiate them, as they are already there waiting to be used. You can refer directly to the object's methods and properties. This is different from dynamic objects such as `Date`. Recall that to retrieve the current year, you must first create an instance of the object, and then refer to the instance's methods.

JavaScript's `Math` object is a static object, so you won't need to instantiate it. Its properties are actually basic constants, such as pi (π) and the square root of 2. Its methods are mathematical functions, such as `pow()` (power), `sin()`, `cos()`, and others. These methods and properties are encapsulated in an object because objects are meant to be entities constructed of related data and functions. The requirements from mathematical functions and constants led JavaScript's developers to create a built-in object for mathematics—`Math`.

To access elements of the `Math` object, you do not need to create an instance. You access them via messages sent directly by the `Math` object itself. For example, the `PI` constant is a property of the `Math` object, and can be accessed via the following syntax:

```
var pi = Math.PI
```


Constants

Constants are defined with the full precision of floating-point numbers in JavaScript. In this section we shall outline these properties for your reference and understanding. Notice that all properties are specified with capital letters, although this convention is not common in the mathematical community. All properties refer to well-known constants (read your math books if you don't remember!); that is, they do not change. Therefore, these properties are read-only properties, and accessing them for the purpose of modification results in a JavaScript error.

E

A very important constant in mathematics is Euler's constant. Its approximate value is 2.718281828459045. It is rounded off to 15 digits after the decimal point. For your reference, the equation is:

$$e^{i} + 1 = 0$$

In JavaScript you refer to it with a capital "E"; that is, `Math.E`.

Note: In mathematics this is usually referred to with a lowercase "e".

LN2

Another constant featured as a property of the Math object is the natural logarithm of 2. Its approximate value is 0.6931471805599453. A defining equation is:

$$e^{LN2} = 2$$

JavaScript refers to this number as LN2. Because it is a property of the Math object, you should specify them together, as in Math.LN2.

You can use the pow method to assure that the preceding equation is true:

```
document.write(Math.pow(Math.E, Math.LN2))
```

Because both Euler's constant and the natural logarithm of 2 are approximate, the output of this statement is also approximate:

```
1.9999999999999998
```

LN10

The natural logarithm of 10 is also featured as a property of the static Math object. Its value, as stored in its corresponding property, is 2.302585092994046. Once again, you can understand this value via an equation:

$$e^{LN10} = 10$$

In JavaScript this value is referred to as Math.LN10.

Here is a JavaScript statement to define the natural logarithm of 10:

```
document.write(Math.pow(Math.E, Math.LN10))
```

Since both Euler's constant and the natural logarithm of 10 are approximate, the output of this statement is also approximate:

```
10.000000000000002
```

Note: Some browsers will round this number to 10.

LOG2E

Another important constant in the math arena is the base-2 logarithm of Euler's constant. Its approximate value is 1.4426950408889634. In math that is:

$$2^{LOG2E} = e$$

As you can see, you refer to this constant in JavaScript as Math.LOG2E. Here is a simple statement to confirm the value:

```
document.write(Math.pow(2, Math.LOG2E) – Math.E)
```

This time the output is apparently exact:

```
0
```

LOG10E

The base-10 logarithm is also widely used in complex mathematical calculations. Its value in JavaScript is approximately 0.4342944819032518. The following equation demonstrates the definition of the constant:

$$10^{\text{LOG10E}} = e$$

As you can see, the equation is built according to one of the basic logarithm rules. In JavaScript, log base-10 of Euler's constant is a property of the `Math` object: `Math.LOG10E`.

Here is a simple script for confirmation:

```
document.write(Math.pow(10, Math.LOG10E) - Math.E)
```

Once again, the output is exact:

```
0
```

PI

Probably the most well-known value among all constants featured by JavaScript is `PI`. Its approximate value, as enabled by the precision limits of real numbers in JavaScript, is 3.141592653589793.

As you could expect, you refer to pi in JavaScript as `Math.PI`. For example, to obtain the circumference of a circle you can use the following function:

```
function circumference(diameter)
{
   if (typeof diameter == "number" && diameter >= 0)
      return Math.PI * diameter
}
```

Note that the function does not return a value if the diameter is not a number or is not positive.

SQRT1_2

The square root of 0.5, as stored in JavaScript's object model, is 0.7071067811865476. You can also reach this value by calculating the square root of 0.5 (using the `sqrt()` method of the `Math` object), but accessing an existing property is somewhat faster and more obvious than calculating it via an execution of a method.

You refer to this property as `Math.SQRT1_2`. The reason an underscore is used for the property name is that the name of a property must follow the identifier rules, which allow only letters, numbers, and underscores in the middle of a name.

Here is an obvious statement to confirm that the value is correct:

```
document.write(Math.pow(Math.SQRT1_2, 2))
```

The not-so-obvious output is:

```
0.5000000000000001
```

SQRT2

The square root of 2 is also a well-known constant. Its approximate value is 1.4142135623730951. You refer to it as `Math.SQRT2`. You can use the following statement to confirm the value:

```
document.write(Math.pow(Math.SQRT2, 2))
```

As you could expect, the result is not exact:

```
2.0000000000000004
```

Math Methods

Constant values make up only a fraction of the entire strength of mathematical implementation in JavaScript. To harness the power of the `Math` object you have to familiarize yourself with the set of methods available.

JavaScript tends to organize functions and values in object structures to enable easy reference and simple understanding. For this reason, all functions related to math are implemented as methods of the `Math` object.

The methods of the `Math` object can be divided into two categories, each related to a different branch of mathematics:

- Arithmetic methods
- Trigonometric methods

All methods of the `Math` object are specified in lowercase letters, as opposed to constants, which are properties of this object and are specified in uppercase letters.

Arithmetic Methods

We use the term "arithmetic methods" to describe all methods that do not relate in any way to trigonometric math.

abs()

You can calculate the absolute value of any number, integer or floating point, via this method. The absolute value of a number is its corresponding positive number; that is, if the number is positive, its absolute value is the number itself, whereas if it is negative, its absolute value is the same number with a + sign instead of a –. You can simulate this method easily:

```
function abs(num)
{
   if (num < 0)
```

```
        return -num
    return num
}
```

For example, the absolute value of –5 is 5. The absolute value of 5 is also 5. In JavaScript you can calculate the absolute value of a number via the method `Math.abs()`. This method returns the absolute value of its argument. You can use this method to compute the absolute value of only one argument. If you call the method with more than one argument, only the absolute value of the first is returned.

If you want the corresponding negative value of a number, as opposed to the positive value, you can negate the returned value. For example:

```
var neg1 = -Math.abs(-3.7)
var neg2 = -Math.abs(3.7)
```

You can use the `Math.abs()` method for many purposes, not just in mathematical algorithms.

ceil()

The `Math.ceil()` method accepts a single numeric argument and returns the next integer greater than or equal to the argument (rounding up). Therefore, the returned value is never less than the argument. Here are a few examples:

```
Math.ceil(16) == 16
Math.ceil(16.01) == 17
Math.ceil(-15.01) == -15
```

Let's say you need to fit `num1` cars into parking lots, where each parking lot has space for `num2` cars. You can use the `Math.ceil()` method along with a function to calculate the minimum number of parking lots:

```
function getNumLots(num1, num2)
{
    return Math.ceil(num1 / num2)
}
```

The reason we need to use this method in the above function is that you can only use a whole parking lot, not a fractional part; that is, we are trying to calculate the minimum number of parking lots needed, not the exact space.

exp()

This method returns Euler's constant to the power of the specified argument ($e^{argument}$). It is approximately equivalent to the following function:

```
function exp(num)
{
    return Math.pow(Math.E, num)
}
```

You refer to this function as `Math.exp()`. Here is an example:

```
document.write(Math.exp(4))
```

Its output is:

```
54.598150033144236
```

floor()

The `Math.floor()` method returns the greatest integer less than or equal to the value passed to it. This is equivalent to integral division when dealing with non-negative numbers. It is also equivalent to rounding down to the nearest integer. Here are a few expressions, each evaluating to true:

```
Math.floor(16) == 16
Math.floor(16.01) == 16
Math.floor(-15.01) == -16
```

log()

This method returns the natural logarithm of the argument passed to it. For example, the natural log (base e) of e (Euler's constant) is 1. You can confirm this via the following statement:

```
document.write(Math.log(Math.E))
```

And indeed, the output is 1.

max(), min()

Both of these methods accept two numeric arguments. `max()` returns the greater of two numbers, whereas `min()` returns the lesser of the two. Here is a function that prints the lesser of two numbers followed by the greater:

```
function printInOrder(num1, num2)
{
   document.write(Math.min(num1, num2) + ", " + Math.max(num1, num2))
}
```

The following function call prints the string `-5, 1` to the document:

```
printInOrder(1, -5)
```

Here are a few true expressions to demonstrate the basic `min()` and `max()` methods:

```
Math.max(1, 2) == 2
Math.min(2, Math.abs(-2)) == 2
Math.min(2, -2) == -2
```

pow()

Given two numeric arguments, this method returns the first one to the power of the second. Here are a few true expressions demonstrating the method:

```
Math.pow(10, 2) == 100
Math.pow(0.5, 0.5) == 0.7071067811865476
Math.pow(Math.SQRT2, 4) == 4.000000000000001
```

random()

This method returns a random number between 0 and 1. It is obviously a floating-point number. The returned number's precision is a maximum of 16 digits after the decimal point. Here is a simple example:

```
for (var i = 0; i < 5; ++i)
{
   document.write(Math.random() + "<BR>")
}
```

The output of this loop depends on the output of `random()` and it is guaranteed that your results will not be the same as the following:

```
.924853870611902
.8248305636609181
.9539277224126104
.9806934571332098
.7639888801207115
```

This method is mostly used to create random integer numbers between x and y. Suppose x is 0 and y is a given number. You would multiply the value that `random()` returns by y and then round it off. For example, to generate a random number between 0 and 37 you can use the following expression:

```
Math.round(Math.random() * 37)
```

If you want an integer between 15 and 37, you can create a random integer between 0 and 22 and then add 15. Be very careful when attempting to create random numbers.

round()

The `Math.round()` method returns the nearest integer to the argument. If the argument's decimal part is equal to 0.5, the number is rounded up. Here are a few true expressions to demonstrate the method:

```
Math.round(3.7) == 4
Math.round(4.5) == 5
Math.round(16.1) == 16
Math.round(0) == 0
```

sqrt()

This method returns the square root of the argument. For example:

```
Math.sqrt(4) == 2
Math.sqrt(0) == 0
Math.sqrt(0.25) == 0.5
```

If the argument is a negative number, the method returns zero, which happens to be the wrong answer. It would be better if an error were generated instead, because this wrong answer can go undetected.

Trigonometric Methods

Trigonometric methods are obviously those that deal with trigonometry.

You should also know how to convert an angle from degrees to radians, and vice versa. Here is the basic conversion table:

Table 11-1. Degree-radian conversion table

Degrees	Radians
360	2π
270	1.5π
180	1π
90	0.5π

All angles in JavaScript are measured in radians, so the conversion table should help you visualize the size of an angle in radians.

cos()

The `Math.cos()` method accepts one argument, the angle of a triangle. It returns the cosine of that value, which must be specified in radians. The following statement prints –1:

```
document.write(Math.cos(Math.PI))
```

acos()

The `Math.acos()` method also accepts one argument. It returns the arc cosine of the argument in radians; that is, it accepts the cosine of a certain value and returns that value—the opposite of the `Math.cos()` method. Therefore, the following statement prints the value of `PI`:

```
document.write(Math.acos(-1))
```

sin()

The `Math.sin()` function returns the sine of its argument. Keep in mind that the argument must be in radian units. Here is a statement that prints 1:

```
document.write(Math.sin(0.5 * Math.PI))
```

asin()

The `Math.asin()` method accepts one argument and returns its arc sine in radians. The following statement prints half the value of `PI`:

```
document.write(Math.asin(1))
```

tan()

The `Math.tan()` method returns the tangent of its argument, which is equal to the quotient of the value's sine and cosine. Take a look at the following script segment:

```
var val = 0.25 * Math.PI
document.write("sine = " + Math.sin(val) + "<BR>")
```

```
document.write("cosine = " + Math.cos(val) + "<BR>")
document.write("tangent = " + Math.tan(val))
```

The output of these statements in Netscape Navigator is:

```
sine = .7071067811865475
cosine = .7071067811865476
tangent = .9999999999999999
```

From this script you can learn:

- The sine of ¼ * PI is equal to its cosine, which is also equal to the square root of ½.
- The cosine and sine methods sometimes return inaccurate results.

Take extra caution regarding the issue of inaccuracy. The following statements:

```
var val = 0.25 * Math.PI
if (Math.tan(val) == 1)
   do_this
else
   do_that
```

should be replaced by:

```
var val = 0.25 * Math.PI
if (Math.tan(val) > 0.99 && Math.tan(val) < 1.01)
   do_this
else
   do_that
```

Inaccuracy is more obvious in this case, because the result differs even from browser to browser. The following is the output received from Microsoft Internet Explorer:

```
sine = 0.707106781186547
cosine = 0.707106781186548
tangent = 1
```

Notice that the sine and cosine values differ. Also notice that Internet Explorer appends a leading zero digit to all numbers between –1 and 1 (not inclusive).

atan()

As you could expect, the `Math.atan()` method returns the arc tangent of its argument. For example, the following returns one-fourth of the value of `PI`:

```
document.write(Math.atan(1))
```

atan2()

The `Math.atan2()` method returns the angle (theta component) of the polar coordinate (r, theta) that corresponds to the specified Cartesian coordinate. You probably know that the normal x, y coordinates of a point are called Cartesian coordinates. Another measurement system is the polar system. You need to specify the point's radius (distance from the pole) and angle (theta component).

The Number Object

The Number object is a built-in JavaScript object that is very similar to the Math object in that it encapsulates several primitive numeric values. It is different from the Math object in that the Number object is dynamic and requires a creation step, while the Math object is static and does not require any instantiation.

The primary use for the Number object is to access its constant properties, including the largest and smallest representable numbers, positive and negative infinity, and the not-a-number value. You can also use the Number object to create numeric objects that you can add properties to. It is unlikely that you will need to use the Number object, but it is given here for the sake of completion.

To create a Number object, use the following statement:

```
numberObjectName = new Number()
```

where *numberObjectName* is either the name of a new object or a property of an existing one. To access Number's properties, use the following format:

```
numberObjectName.propertyName
```

where *numberObjectName* is either the name of an existing Number object or a property of an existing object. *propertyName* is one of the properties listed in the next section.

Number Properties

The Number object has several properties.

MAX_VALUE

This is the maximum numeric value representable in JavaScript. The MAX_VALUE property has a value of approximately 1.79E+308. Values larger than MAX_VALUE are represented as "infinity." Because MAX_VALUE is a constant, it is a read-only property of Number. The following code demonstrates the use of MAX_VALUE. The code multiplies two numeric values. If the result is less than or equal to MAX_VALUE, the func1 function is called; otherwise, the func2 function is called.

```
if (num1 * num2 <= Number.MAX_VALUE)
   func1()
else
   func2()
```

MIN_VALUE

The MIN_VALUE property is the number closest to zero, not the lowest number that JavaScript can represent. MIN_VALUE has a value of approximately 2.22E–308. Values smaller than MIN_VALUE ("underflow values") are converted to zero. Because MIN_VALUE is a constant, it is a read-only property of Number. The following code divides two numeric values. If the result is greater than or equal to MIN_VALUE, the func1 function is called; otherwise, the func2 function is called.

```
if (num1 / num2 >= Number.MIN_VALUE)
   func1()
else
   func2()
```

NaN

The unquoted literal constant NaN is a special value representing not-a-number. Since NaN always compares unequal to any number, including NaN, it is usually used to indicate an error condition for a function that should return a valid number. Notice, then, that you cannot check for not-a-number value by comparing to Number.NaN. Use the isNaN() function instead. Because NaN is a constant, it is a read-only property of Number. In the following code segment, dayOfMonth is assigned NaN if it is greater than 31, and a message is displayed indicating the valid range:

```
if (dayOfMonth < 1 || dayOfMonth > 31)
{
   dayOfMonth = Number.NaN
   alert("Day of Month must be from 1 to 31.")
}
```

NEGATIVE_INFINITY

This is a special numeric value representing negative infinity. This value is represented as "–Infinity" and resembles an infinity in its mathematical behavior. For example, anything multiplied by NEGATIVE_INFINITY is NEGATIVE_INFINITY, and anything divided by NEGATIVE_INFINITY is zero. Because NEGATIVE_INFINITY is a constant, it is a read-only property of Number.

The following code extract checks a number for NEGATIVE_INFINITY and calls a different function if it is:

```
if (smallNumber == Number.NEGATIVE_INFINITY)
   func1()
else
   func2()
```

POSITIVE_INFINITY

This is a special numeric value representing infinity. This value is represented as "Infinity" and resembles an infinity in its mathematical behavior. For example, anything multiplied by POSITIVE_INFINITY is

POSITIVE_INFINITY, and anything divided by POSITIVE_INFINITY is zero. Because POSITIVE_INFINITY is a constant, it is a read-only property of Number.

The following code extract checks a number for POSITIVE_INFINITY and calls a different function if it is:

```
if (bigNumber == Number.POSITIVE_INFINITY)
   func1()
else
   func2()
```

Number Methods

The Number object has no specific methods; however, you can use the generic methods eval(), toString(), and valueOf(), which are applicable to every object.

Math-Related Functions

Although the functions presented in this section are also discussed later in the book, it is important that you attain a basic understanding, so do not skip the following explanation. These functions are used in examples later in the chapter.

parseInt()

This built-in function accepts a numeric string of an integer and returns its corresponding numeric value. The following example is worth a thousand words:

```
var numStr = "99"
document.write("The initial " + typeof numStr + " is " + numStr)
document.write("<BR>")
var num = parseInt(numStr)
document.write("The converted " + typeof num + " is " + num)
```

The script's output is:

```
The initial string is 99
The converted number is 99
```

The data types are not provided to the document.write() method as literals, but as values. Note that the parseInt() function accepts a string and returns an integer. If a noninteger numeric string is given to the function, it returns the nearest integer as a number (as opposed to a string).

parseFloat()

This function is exactly the same as the preceding one, except that it does not round off any number. It converts the numeric string to a number without changing the numeric value at all. You should use this function with floating-point numeric strings, or when you are not sure what type of number is being used.

eval()

The eval() function is both powerful and useful. For now, you just need to know that upon acceptance of a string representing a numeric value or mathematical expression, it returns the value to which the expression evaluates. The following script segment prints 13:

```
var str = "6 + 7"
document.write(eval(str))
```

The function returns a number, not a string. Note that this function acts differently on Netscape Navigator than it does on Microsoft Internet Explorer. An example for such different behavior is seen in the following statement, which works fine under Internet Explorer, but generates an error under Navigator:

```
var str = "+7"
document.write(eval(str))
```

However, it works fine when the sign is minus (–) rather than plus (+).

Math Examples

Creating a Curve

Although JavaScript does not correspond very well with custom-created graphics, it is possible to create simple graphs, plots, and curves. In this section we shall plot a sine curve using JavaScript. The following example is very interesting, although a bit long and complex. First, just take a look at the script. Then we will discuss the various elements and how they fit together.

```
<HTML>
<HEAD>
<TITLE>Sine curve</TITLE>
</HEAD>
<BODY>
<FONT COLOR="blue" SIZE=+4>JavaScript Sine Curve</FONT><BR><BR>
<SCRIPT LANGUAGE="JavaScript">
<!--

function drawBlank(num)
{
   // draw num blank dots
   for (var i = 0; i < num; ++i)
   {
      document.write("<IMG SRC='blank.gif' HEIGHT=6 WIDTH=6>")
   }
}

function drawDot()
{
   document.write("<IMG SRC='dot.gif' HEIGHT=6 WIDTH=6>")
```

```
}

function getRadian(deg) {
   // return deg in radians
   return Math.PI * deg / 180
}

function getSpot(deg)
{
   // convert from degrees to radians
   var rad = getRadian(deg)

   // assign sine to variable
   var sine = Math.sin(rad)

   // return spot in graph
   return Math.round(sine * 30)
}

function get3DigitNum(num)
{
   // convert num to string
   num += ""

   // assign number of digits in num to variable
   var length = num.length

   // add preceding zero digits to reach three digits
   for (var i = 0; i < 3 - length; i++)
   {
      num = "0" + num
   }

   // return three-digit number
   return num // do not parse number!
}

function printDeg(deg)
{
   // print degree in purple font
   document.write("<FONT COLOR='purple' SIZE=1>" + get3DigitNum(deg) +
                  "</FONT>")
}

function drawLine(deg)
{
   // assign spot (-30 to 30)
   var spot = getSpot(deg)

   // if sine is negative
   if (spot < 0)
   {
      // draw blank images up to spot, not inclusive
      drawBlank(30 + spot)
```

```
      // draw dot image
      drawDot()

      // draw remaining images until axis
      drawBlank(-spot - 1) // 30 - ((30 + spot) + 1)

      // print current degree
      printDeg(deg)
   } else
      // if sine is positive
      if (spot > 0)
      {
         // draw 30 blank images = left of axis
         drawBlank(30)

         // print current degree
         printDeg(deg)

         // draw blank images up to spot, not inclusive
         drawBlank(spot - 1)

         // draw dot image
         drawDot()
      } else {
         // draw 30 blank images = left of axis
         drawBlank(30)

         // print current degree
         printDeg(deg)
      }
   // move to next line
   document.write("<BR>")
}

function drawCurve(lastDeg, jump)
{
   // loop through plot vertically
   for (var deg = 0; deg <= lastDeg; deg += jump)
   {
      drawLine(deg)
   }
}

drawCurve(720, 15)

// -->
</SCRIPT>
</BODY>
</HTML>
```

Example 11-1 (ex11-1.htm). *A simple script to plot the sine curve*

When you run the script you should see the image shown in Figure 11-1.

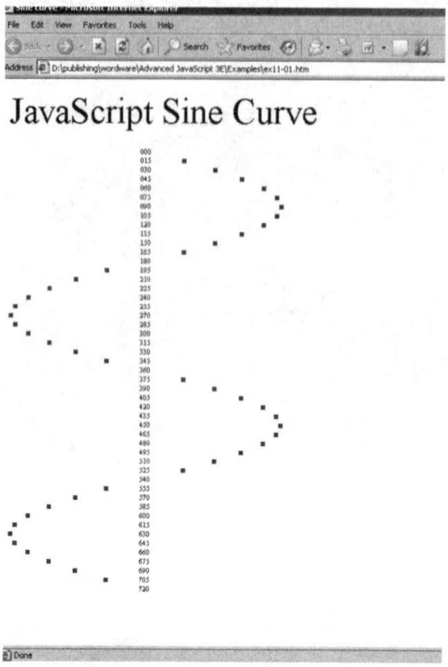

Figure 11-1. *The sine curve*

The script is intentionally divided into many short functions for better understanding by the reader. Let's analyze each function to see how it works.

drawBlank(num)

```
function drawBlank(num)
{
   // draw num blank dots
   for (var i = 0; i < num; ++i)
   {
      document.write("<IMG SRC = 'blank.gif' HEIGHT = 6 WIDTH = 6>")
   }
}
```

This function uses a `for` loop to print the transparent image the number of times indicated by `num`. Note that the transparent (blank) image's height and width are both equal to 6.

drawDot()

```
function drawDot()
{
   document.write("<IMG SRC = 'dot.gif' HEIGHT = 6 WIDTH = 6>")
}
```

This function simply draws the dot image.

getRadian(deg)

```
function getRadian(deg)
{
   // return deg in radians
   return Math.PI * deg / 180
}
```

This function accepts a number (actually the size of an angle in degrees) and returns it in radians. The conversion is based on a simple linear equation.

getSpot(deg)

```
function getSpot(deg)
{
   // convert from degrees to radians
   var rad = getRadian(deg)
   // assign sine to variable
   var sine = Math.sin(rad)
   // return spot in graph
   return Math.round(sine * 30)
}
```

This function accepts the size of an angle in degrees and returns its sine value multiplied by 30. At first, it assigns the radian measurement of the angle to the local variable `rad`. It then assigns the sine of that angle to the local variable `sine`. The function then multiplies the sine by 30 and returns the rounded-off value of that number. The reason for the multiplication by 30 is that the sine of any angle is a value between –1 and 1. The curve we are plotting generally consists of 30 images, transparent or not, at each side of the center axis. If you increase this number, the horizontal width of the curve becomes larger. As you can see, 30 images looks good. By multiplying a value between –1 and 1 by 30, we receive a value between –30 and 30. By rounding it off using the `Math.round()` method, the function returns an integer between –30 and 30.

Note that the plot acts like a 2D array because it consists of rows of images.

get3DigitNum(num)

```
function get3DigitNum(num)
{
   // convert num to string
   num += ""
   // assign number of digits in num to variable
   var length = num.length
   // add preceding zero digits to reach three digits
   for (var i = 0; i < 3 - length; i++)
   {
      num = "0" + num
   }
```

```
    // return three-digit number
    return num // do not parse number!
}
```

This function accepts any single-digit, double-digit, or triple-digit number, and returns a triple-digit number, appending preceding zeros when needed. At first, it converts the number to a string, which is required when using the `length` property. A string type is also required because numbers with leading 0 digits are considered octal. The length, or the number of digits in the original number, is assigned to the local variable `length`. The next statement is a loop whose command block is executed once for each digit missing to complete a triple-digit number. For example, if the number consists of two digits, the loop's command block is executed once (3 – 2 = 1, 1 – 0 = 1).

printDeg(deg)

```
function printDeg(deg)
{
    // print degree in purple font
    document.write("<FONT COLOR = 'purple' SIZE = 1>" + get3DigitNum(deg)
                   + "</FONT>")
}
```

This function accepts a number, converts it to a triple-digit number, and prints it in a purple font.

drawLine(deg)

```
function drawLine(deg)
{
    // assign spot (-30 to 30)
    var spot = getSpot(deg)
    // if sine is negative
    if (spot < 0)
    {
        // draw blank images up to spot, not inclusive
        drawBlank(30 + spot)
        // draw dot image
        drawDot()
        // draw remaining images until axis
        drawBlank(-spot - 1) // 30 - ((30 + spot) + 1)
        // print current degree
        printDeg(deg)
    } else
        // if sine is positive
        if (spot > 0)
        {
            // draw 30 blank images = left of axis
            drawBlank(30)
            // print current degree
            printDeg(deg)
            // draw blank images up to spot, not inclusive
            drawBlank(spot - 1)
            // draw dot image
```

```
            drawDot()
        } else
        {
            // draw 30 blank images = left of axis
            drawBlank(30)
            // print current degree
            printDeg(deg)
        }
    // move to next line
    document.write("<BR>")
}
```

The rounded-off sine value multiplied by 30 is assigned to the variable `spot`. The function is basically divided into three sections, only one of which is executed. The first deals with a situation in which the sine value is negative, the second deals with positive sine values, and the third deals with the remaining situations, that is, when the sine is zero.

When the sine (sine multiplied by 30) is negative, `30 – spot` transparent images are printed. For example, if the value of `spot` is –20, 10 transparent images are printed. The dot image is printed after these transparent images. The function then prints `–spot – 1` transparent images, up to the center axis. So far `30 + spot` transparent images were printed, as well as one more image representing the dot on the curve. In total, there are `31 + spot` images. Remember that each side of the axis consists of 30 images, so `30 – (31 + spot)` images still need to be printed; that is `–spot – 1`. The current degree is then printed via a call to the function `printDeg()`.

When the sine of the current angle is positive, 30 transparent images are printed to fill up the left side of the center axis. The current degree is then printed to continue the vertical span of the axis. Then `spot – 1` images are printed, up to the place where the dot on the curve needs to be placed. The dot image is then printed. When the sine of the current angle is zero, a row of 30 transparent images is printed, followed by the current angle in degrees.

The last statement of the function appends a line break to the document, opening a new row of images.

drawCurve(lastDeg, jump)

```
function drawCurve(lastDeg, jump)
{
    // loop through plot vertically
    for (var deg = 0; deg <= lastDeg; deg += jump)
    {
        drawLine(deg)
    }
}
```

This function accepts two arguments. The first parameter, `lastDeg`, accepts the last value included in the curve; that is, the last angle whose sine appears. The second argument specifies the difference between each two angles.

Global Statements

The script includes only one global statement, a function call. It calls the `drawCurve()` function with the desired arguments.

General Plotting Utility

As you can see, it is not difficult to plot a specific curve in JavaScript using two different images. The following example enables you to plot the curve of almost any function. Obviously, if you are not familiar with the mathematics involved, this script may be hard to follow. The purpose of this script is to illustrate the power of JavaScript's `Math` object.

```
<HTML>
<HEAD>
<TITLE>Function Plotting Utility</TITLE>
</HEAD>
<BODY>
<SCRIPT LANGUAGE = "JavaScript">
<!--
function root(a, b)
{
   // return b to the root of a
   return Math.pow(b, 1 / a)
}
function logab(a, b)
{
   // return log base-a of b
   return Math.log(b) / Math.log(a)
}
function factorial(a)
{
   // set recursion termination condition
   if (a == 0)
      return 1
   return a * factorial(a - 1)
}
function startWizard()
{
   // create array to hold messages
   var ar = new Array()
   ar[0] = "\r\rWelcome to the easy JavaScript function plotter!\r\r"
   ar[0] += "Press OK to continue, or CANCEL to exit the wizard...\r\r"
   ar[1] = "\r\rYou can plot almost any function you wish with this script.\r"
   ar[1] += "The plotter supports common arithmetic and trigonometric
             functions.\r"
   ar[1] += "It also supports widely used mathematical constants.\r"
   ar[1] += "For a list of the supported functions press OK...\r\r"
   ar[2] = "\r\r"
   ar[2] += "abs(val) = absolute value of val\r"
```

```
   ar[2] += "acos(val) = arc cosine of val\r"
   ar[2] += "asine(val) = arc sine of val\r"
   ar[2] += "atan(val) = arc tangent of val\r"
   ar[2] += "atan2(val) = angle (theta component) of the polar "
   ar[2] += "coordinate (r,theta) that corresponds to the specified "
   ar[2] += "cartesian coordinate (x,y).\r"
   ar[2] += "ceil(val) = next integer greater than or equal to val\r"
   ar[2] += "cos(val) = cosine of val\r"
   ar[2] += "exp(val) = Euler's constant to the power of val\r"
   ar[2] += "factorial(val) = val factorial (val!)\r"
   ar[2] += "floor(val) = next integer less than or equal to val\r"
   ar[2] += "log(val1, val2) = logarithm base-val1 of val2\r"
   ar[2] += "loge(val) = natural logarithm of val\r"
   ar[2] += "max(val1, val2) = greater of val1 and val2\r"
   ar[2] += "min(val1, val2) = lesser of val1 and val2\r"
   ar[2] += "pow(val1, val2) = val1 to the power of val2\r"
   ar[2] += "root(val1, val2) = val1-root of val2\r"
   ar[2] += "round(val) = val rounded off to the nearest integer\r"
   ar[2] += "sin(val) = sine of val\r"
   ar[2] += "sqrt(val) = square root of val\r"
   ar[2] += "tan(val) = tangent of val\r"
   ar[2] += "\r* all trigonometric functions deal with radians only *\r\r"
   ar[2] += "Click OK to view the supported constants...\r\r"
   ar[3] = "\r\r"
   ar[3] += "e = Euler's constant\r"
   ar[3] += "ln2 = Natural log of 2\r"
   ar[3] += "ln10 = Natural log of 10\r"
   ar[3] += "log2e = log base-2 of Euler's constant\r"
   ar[3] += "log10e = log base-10 of Euler's constant\r"
   ar[3] += "pi = pi (3.14...)\r"
   ar[3] += "sqrt1_2 = square root of 0.5\r"
   ar[3] += "sqrt2 = square root of 2\r"
   ar[3] += "\r\rEnjoy the plotter...\r\r"
   for (var i = 0; i < ar.length; ++i)
   {
      if (!confirm(ar[i]))
         break
   }
}
function drawBlank(num)
{
   // draw num blank dots
   for (var i = 0; i < num; ++i)
   {
      document.write("<IMG SRC = 'blank.gif' HEIGHT = 4 WIDTH = 4>")
   }
}
function drawDot(x, y)
{
   // print dot image
   document.write("<A HREF = \"javascript:alert(\'X = " + x + ", Y = " + y +
      "\')\"><IMG SRC = 'dot.gif' HEIGHT = 4 WIDTH = 4 BORDER = 0></A>")
}
function replaceSpecialSequence(str)
```

Chapter 11

```
{
   // replace all specified sequences with other sequences
   str = str.split("cos").join("Math.cos")
   str = str.split("sin").join("Math.sin")
   str = str.split("tan").join("Math.tan")
   str = str.split("acos").join("Math.acos")
   str = str.split("asin").join("Math.asin")
   str = str.split("atan").join("Math.atan")
   str = str.split("pi").join("Math.PI")
   str = str.split("ln2").join("Math.LN2")
   str = str.split("ln10").join("Math.LN10")
   str = str.split("log2e").join("Math.LOG2E")
   str = str.split("log10e").join("Math.LOG10E")
   str = str.split("sqrt1_2").join("Math.SQRT1_2")
   str = str.split("sqrt2").join("Math.SQRT2")
   str = str.split("abs").join("Math.abs")
   str = str.split("ceil").join("Math.ceil")
   str = str.split("exp").join("Math.exp")
   str = str.split("floor").join("Math.floor")
   str = str.split("loge").join("Math.log")
   str = str.split("max").join("Math.max")
   str = str.split("min").join("Math.min")
   str = str.split("pow").join("Math.pow")
   str = str.split("round").join("Math.round")
   str = str.split("log").join("logab")
   str = str.split("sqrt").join("Math.sqrt")
   str = str.split("e").join("Math.E")
   // return string
   return str
}
function splitFunc(func)
{
   // exclude "y =" from func
   var expr = func.substring(func.indexOf("=") + 1, func.length)
   // replace regular trigonometric functions with JavaScript convention
   expr = replaceSpecialSequence(expr)
   // split argument to *global* array, excluding "x" chars
   funcArray = expr.split("x")
}
function getInput()
{
   // ask user for function via prompt box
   var input = prompt('Enter function (example: "y = x * x + sin(x) - 5"):', '')
   // if user enters value in field
   if (input)
   {
      // split function to global array
      splitFunc(input)
      // print function to document
      document.write("<TT><H1><B>" + input + "</B></H1></TT><BR>")
      // return true to indicate that user entered a value
      return true
   }
   // generate alert box to display error message
```

```
   alert("Error in input...")
   // return false to indicate cancellation
   return false
}
function yVal(xVal)
{
   // build expression with xVal instead of x in original equation
   var expr = funcArray.join(xVal)
   // return evaluated expression
   return eval(expr)
}
function makeArray(min, max, dif)
{
   // create properties of array-like object
   for (var i = min; i <= max; i += dif)
   {
      this[i] = yVal(i)
   }
}
function printUnit(num)
{
   // print number in specified font and size, inside a table cell
   document.write("<FONT SIZE = 1 COLOR = 'purple'>" + num + "</FONT>")
}
function drawCurve()
{
   for (var x = minX; x <= maxX; x += dif)
   {
      // print opening table attributes and cell to hold current unit
      document.write("<TABLE BORDER = 0><TR><TD WIDTH = 90>")
      // print current number on axis
      printUnit(x)
      // close table cell and open new one
      document.write("</TD><TD>")
      // assign Y value to variable
      var y = ar[x]
      // get y value as integer from 1 to 100
      var ySpot = (y - minY) / (maxY - minY) * 100
      // draw transparent images
      drawBlank(ySpot - 1)
      // draw dot on curve
      drawDot(x, y)
      // close cell, row, and table (new line is automatic)
      document.write("</TD></TR></TABLE>")
   }
}
function main()
{
   // start wizard
   startWizard()
   // get input from user; if user cancels, function is terminated
   if (!getInput())
      return
   // accept minimum X value from user and assign to global variable
```

```
   minX = prompt("Enter minimum value on X axis:", "")
   // if user pressed "cancel" terminate function
   if (!minX)
      return
   // accept maximum X value from user and assign to global variable
   maxX = prompt("Enter maximum value on X axis:", "")
   // if user pressed "cancel" terminate function
   if (!maxX)
      return
   // assign difference between numbers on X axis global variable
   dif = prompt("Enter difference between each value on X axis:", "")
   // if user pressed "cancel" terminate function
   if (!dif)
      return
   // convert all input to numbers, replacing special sequences
   maxX = eval(replaceSpecialSequence(maxX))
   minX = eval(replaceSpecialSequence(minX))
   dif = eval(replaceSpecialSequence(dif))
   // create global array and assign Y values via function call
   ar = new makeArray(minX, maxX, dif)
   // assign maxY and minY (global variables) property of ar
   maxY = ar[minX]
   minY = ar[minX]
   // determine maximum and minimum Y values
   for (var i in ar)
   {
      if (ar[i] < minY)
         minY = ar[i]
      else
         if (ar[i] > maxY)
            maxY = ar[i]
   }
   // draw the final curve
   drawCurve()
}
main()
// -->
</SCRIPT>
</BODY>
</HTML>
```

Example 11-2 (ex11-2.htm). *A general function plotter*

When you load the page, the "wizard" pops up. The wizard displays the basic features and usage instructions via a few confirm boxes. Here are two of them:

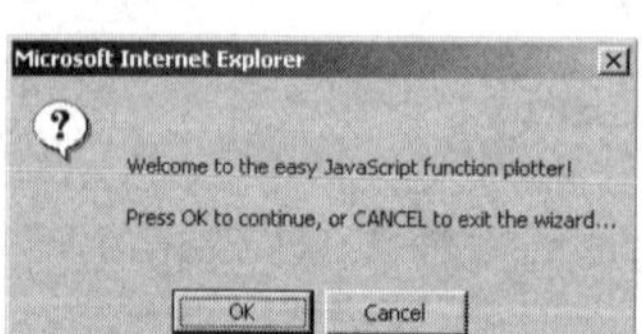

Figure 11-2. *A confirm box presented by the wizard displays a welcome message.*

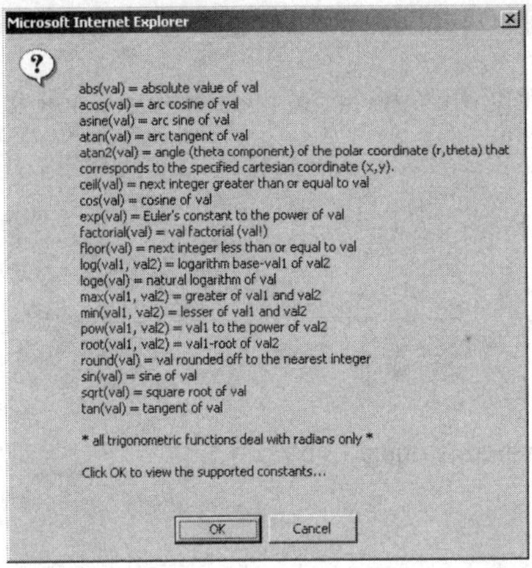

***Figure 11-3.** A confirm box that displays a list of supported functions*

Note: Some browsers may not line wrap automatically, so you may have to manually code the line wraps.

If the user presses Cancel on any of the confirm boxes, the wizard is terminated, and the actual plotting application begins. The first output of the plotter is a confirm box requesting the function, which may be constructed out of JavaScript's supported mathematical functions, constants, and operators.

If the user selects Cancel, an alert box displays an error message. Otherwise, the execution continues, and JavaScript asks the user to enter the minimum value on the X axis.

Cancellation of this box results in the termination of the script. If the user selected OK, the execution continues, and another prompt box is presented.

Once again, if the user presses Cancel, the script is terminated. Otherwise, the user is asked to enter the difference between two consecutive ticks on the X axis (e.g., if the user wants to see –4, –2, 0, 2, 4, 6, then the difference is 2).

The script now has all the needed information and is ready to plot the function's curve.

First of all, notice that the X axis is the vertical one. With some modification of the script you can swap the X axis with the Y axis (the unseen horizontal axis). The script automatically fits the script to a constant width, so you should not have to scroll horizontally under normal circumstances (a reasonable window width). However, this automatic setting requires that you plot functions whose Y values are proportional. For example, if you enter data to plot a curve consisting of one Y value equal to 10,000 and the other values less than 100, the single Y value (10,000) will be placed on the right, whereas all the other values will seem to be on the same spot. There is another feature to solve this problem. You can click on a point to view its coordinates via an alert box.

Now that we know exactly what the script does, let's see how it does that by analyzing each function.

root(a, b)

```
function root(a, b)
{
   // return b to the root of a
   return Math.pow(b, 1 / a)
}
```

This function returns a√b, which is equal to $b^{1/a}$.

logab(a, b)

```
function logab(a, b)
{
   // return log base-a of b
   return Math.log(b) / Math.log(a)
}
```

This function returns `log base-a` of `b`. This value is equal to `log base-x` of `b` divided by `log base-x` of `a`. In this case, we use the natural logarithm, where the base is Euler's constant. The following statement explains this computation:

$\log_e b / \log_e a = \log_a b$

factorial(a)

```
function factorial(a)
{
   // set recursion termination condition
   if (a == 0)
      return 1
   return a * factorial(a - 1)
}
```

This function returns a factorial (`a!`). Its algorithm is recursive.

startWizard()

```
function startWizard()
{
   // create array to hold messages
   var ar = new Array()
   ar[0] = "\r\rWelcome to the easy JavaScript function plotter!\r\r"
   ar[0] += "Press OK to continue, or CANCEL to exit the wizard...\r\r"
   ar[1] = "\r\rYou can plot almost any function you wish with this script.\r"
   ar[1] += "The plotter supports common arithmetic and trigonometric
            functions.\r"
   ar[1] += "It also supports widely used mathematical constants.\r"
```

```
    ar[1] += "For a list of the supported functions press OK...\r\r"
    ar[2] = "\r\r"
    ar[2] += "abs(val) = absolute value of val\r"
    ar[2] += "acos(val) = arc cosine of val\r"
    ar[2] += "asine(val) = arc sine of val\r"
    ar[2] += "atan(val) = arc tangent of val\r"
    ar[2] += "atan2(val) = angle (theta component) of the polar "
    ar[2] += "coordinate (r,theta) that corresponds to the specified "
    ar[2] += "cartesian coordinate (x,y).\r"
    ar[2] += "ceil(val) = next integer greater than or equal to val\r"
    ar[2] += "cos(val) = cosine of val\r"
    ar[2] += "exp(val) = Euler's constant to the power of val\r"
    ar[2] += "factorial(val) = val factorial (val!)\r"
    ar[2] += "floor(val) = next integer less than or equal to val\r"
    ar[2] += "log(val1, val2) = logarithm base-val1 of val2\r"
    ar[2] += "loge(val) = natural logarithm of val\r"
    ar[2] += "max(val1, val2) = greater of val1 and val2\r"
    ar[2] += "min(val1, val2) = lesser of val1 and val2\r"
    ar[2] += "pow(val1, val2) = val1 to the power of val2\r"
    ar[2] += "root(val1, val2) = val1-root of val2\r"
    ar[2] += "round(val) = val rounded off to the nearest integer\r"
    ar[2] += "sin(val) = sine of val\r"
    ar[2] += "sqrt(val) = square root of val\r"
    ar[2] += "tan(val) = tangent of val\r"
    ar[2] += "\r* all trigonometric functions deal with radians only *\r\r"
    ar[2] += "Click OK to view the supported constants...\r\r"
    ar[3] = "\r\r"
    ar[3] += "e = Euler's constant\r"
    ar[3] += "ln2 = Natural log of 2\r"
    ar[3] += "ln10 = Natural log of 10\r"
    ar[3] += "log2e = log base-2 of Euler's constant\r"
    ar[3] += "log10e = log base-10 of Euler's constant\r"
    ar[3] += "pi = pi (3.14...)\r"
    ar[3] += "sqrt1_2 = square root of 0.5\r"
    ar[3] += "sqrt2 = square root of 2\r"
    ar[3] += "\r\rEnjoy the plotter...\r\r"
    for (var i = 0; i < ar.length; ++i)
    {
        if (!confirm(ar[i]))
            break
    }
}
```

This function is responsible for the wizard. At first, an array is created as an instance of the `Array` object. Four different messages are assigned to the array as elements. The first is stored in `ar[0]`, the second in `ar[1]`, and so on. Note that the assigned strings are very long, so the assignment operator concatenates them by assigning them, one after the other, to the element of the array. The function uses a `for` loop to print the messages to the confirm boxes. If the user presses Cancel, the confirm box evaluates to false, and the `break` statement is executed, causing the loop to terminate immediately.

drawBlank(num)

```
function drawBlank(num)
   {
   // draw num blank dots
   for (var i = 0; i < num; ++i)
   {
      document.write("<IMG SRC = 'blank.gif' HEIGHT = 4 WIDTH = 4>")
   }
}
```

This function prints the transparent image num times, num being handed to the function as its sole argument. The image is repeatedly printed via a simple `for` loop.

drawDot(x, y)

```
function drawDot(x, y)
{
   // print dot image
   document.write("<A HREF = \"javascript:alert(\'X = " + x + ", Y = " +
      y + "\')\"><IMG SRC = 'dot.gif' HEIGHT = 4 WIDTH = 4 BORDER = 0></A>")
}
```

This function basically prints the dot image, but it prints it as a hypertext link. The URL specified as the link is a JavaScript statement. When the user clicks the image, an alert box is displayed, presenting the coordinates of that dot. The coordinates are given to this function as arguments. For example, if the arguments are –5 and 10, then the following string is printed to the document:

```
<A HREF = "javascript:alert('X = -5, Y = 10')"><IMG SRC = 'dot.gif'
HEIGHT = 4 WIDTH = 4 BORDER = 0></A>
```

Decoding this string is a good exercise for escaping quotes.

You may recall that a hypertext link's URL can be a JavaScript statement, provided that the statement is preceded by `"javascript:"`.

replaceSpecialSequence(str)

```
function replaceSpecialSequence(str)
{
   // replace all specified sequences with other sequences
   str = str.split("cos").join("Math.cos")
   str = str.split("sin").join("Math.sin")
   str = str.split("tan").join("Math.tan")
   str = str.split("acos").join("Math.acos")
   str = str.split("asin").join("Math.asin")
   str = str.split("atan").join("Math.atan")
   str = str.split("pi").join("Math.PI")
   str = str.split("ln2").join("Math.LN2")
   str = str.split("ln10").join("Math.LN10")
   str = str.split("log2e").join("Math.LOG2E")
   str = str.split("log10e").join("Math.LOG10E")
```

```
    str = str.split("sqrt1_2").join("Math.SQRT1_2")
    str = str.split("sqrt2").join("Math.SQRT2")
    str = str.split("abs").join("Math.abs")
    str = str.split("ceil").join("Math.ceil")
    str = str.split("exp").join("Math.exp")
    str = str.split("floor").join("Math.floor")
    str = str.split("loge").join("Math.log")
    str = str.split("max").join("Math.max")
    str = str.split("min").join("Math.min")
    str = str.split("pow").join("Math.pow")
    str = str.split("round").join("Math.round")
    str = str.split("log").join("logab")
    str = str.split("sqrt").join("Math.sqrt")
    str = str.split("e").join("Math.E")
    // return string
    return str
}
```

This function matches certain strings in the argument and replaces them with other strings. Here is an example:

```
str = str.split("max").join("Math.max")
```

The string is split into an array where the substring `max` is the delimiter, and the elements are joined back to a string with the delimiter `Math.max`. The final result is that, wherever the string `max` appears in the main string (`str`), it is replaced by the string `Math.max`. This is important because the string must be constructed as a valid JavaScript expression (the `eval()` function evaluates a string consisting of a valid JavaScript expression). The same process is done with all supported constants and mathematical functions. The function `factorial()` remains untouched, because its reference in the script is also `factorial()`.

An important point to notice is that the order in which substrings are replaced is vital. For example, you cannot replace the `sqrt` substring with `Math.sqrt` before you replace `sqrt2` with `Math.SQRT2`, because the result would be that the substring `sqrt2` is replaced by `Math.sqrt2`, which is not `Math.SQRT2`. The function must first replace subscripts that contain other subscripts that need to be replaced.

After all desired substrings are replaced, and provided the user entered a function in a valid format, the function returns the formatted string, which is now a valid JavaScript expression.

splitFunc(func)

```
function splitFunc(func)
{
    // exclude "y =" from func
    var expr = func.substring(func.indexOf("=") + 1, func.length)
    // replace regular trigonometric functions with JavaScript convention
    expr = replaceSpecialSequence(expr)
```

Chapter 11

```
   // split argument to *global* array, excluding "x" chars
   funcArray = expr.split("x")
}
```

This function accepts one parameter—the function. As you know, the general format of the function is `y = f(x)`. At first, the function assigns everything after the equal sign to the local variable `expr`. It then sends the value of `expr` to the function `replaceSpecialSequence()` and accepts a string in return in which the special substrings were replaced (see the explanation about that function). A global array, `funcArray`, is created by assigning it a value without using the keyword `var`. The string stored in the variable `expr` is split into the `funcArray` array, using the character `x` as a delimiter. Let's say the function's argument is `y = x * sin(x)`. The variable `expr` is assigned `x * sin(x)`. This value is sent to the function `replaceSpecialSequence()`, and the string `x * Math.sin(x)` is assigned to `expr`. This string is split by `x` to the global array, `funcArray`. Its elements are now:

```
funcArray[0] == " "
funcArray[1] == " * Math.sin("
funcArray[2] == ")"
```

getInput()

```
function getInput()
{
   // ask user for function via prompt box
   var input = prompt('Enter function (example: "y = x * x + sin(x) - 5"):', '')
   // if user enters value in field
   if (input)
   {
      // split function to global array
      splitFunc(input)
      // print function to document
      document.write("<TT><H1><B>" + input + "</B></H1></TT><BR>")
      // return true to indicate that user entered a value
      return true
   }
   // generate alert box to display error message
   alert("Error in input...")
   // return false to indicate cancellation
   return false
}
```

This function is responsible for prompting the user for the function he or she wants to plot. The function, as entered by the user in a prompt box, is first assigned to the local variable `input`. If the user entered a value and selected OK, the following command block is executed. This command block consists of a call to the function `splitFunc()`. It also includes a statement that prints the function to the document as a bold level-1 header. After the Boolean value true is returned to indicate that the user entered a value and pressed OK, the function is terminated. If the user selected Cancel, the command block is not executed, so the execution continues immediately after the block. An error message is displayed in an alert box, and the value false is returned.

yVal(xVal)

```
function yVal(xVal)
{
   // build expression with xVal instead of x in original equation
   var expr = funcArray.join(xVal)
   // return evaluated expression
   return eval(expr)
}
```

This function accepts a value representing the x coordinate of a dot on the curve and returns its corresponding y coordinate. The first statement declares a local variable, `expr`. It joins the elements of the global array `funcArray` back to a string, with the value of `xVal` between each two. Refer back to the function `splitFunc()` and read the example given (`y = x * sin(x)`). The values of the elements of the array are the following:

```
funcArray[0] == " "
funcArray[1] -- " * Math.sin("
funcArray[2] == ")"
```

The function `yVal()` joins these elements using the value of `xVal` as a glue between each two. Let's say the value of `xVal` is 5. The constructed string assigned to `expr` in this case is:

```
" 5 * Math.sin(5)"
```

The function returns the evaluated value of this string. For the preceding string, the value returned is:

```
" 5 * Math.sin(5)" == -4.794621373315692
```

makeArray(min, max, dif)

```
function makeArray(min, max, dif)
{
   // create properties of array-like object
   for (var i = min; i <= max; i += dif)
   {
      this[i] = yVal(i)
   }
}
```

`makeArray()` is a constructor function. It creates an object consisting of properties only. The names of the properties are the x values of the points that are to be drawn on the curve. Their value is the corresponding y coordinates of the points. The function accepts three arguments, which are all entered by the user via prompt boxes outside this function. The function creates the properties of the calling instance via a loop. The loop counter starts at `min`, and is incremented by `dif` after iteration. The loop continues as long as its counter is less than or equal to max. The corresponding y coordinate of each x coordinate is retrieved by the function yVal().

printUnit(num)

```
function printUnit(num)
{
   // print number in specified font and size, inside a table cell
   document.write("<FONT SIZE = 1 COLOR = 'purple'>" + num + "</FONT>")
}
```

This function accepts a numeric value and prints it in the specified font color and size.

drawCurve()

```
function drawCurve()
   {
   for (var x = minX; x <= maxX; x += dif)
   {
      // print opening table attributes and cell to hold current unit
      document.write("<TABLE BORDER = 0>><TR><TD WIDTH = 90>")
      // print current number on axis
      printUnit(x)
      // close table cell and open new one
      document.write("</TD><TD>")
      // assign Y value to variable
      var y = ar[x]
      // get y value as integer from 1 to 100
      var ySpot = (y - minY) / (maxY - minY) * 100
      // draw transparent images
      drawBlank(ySpot - 1)
      // draw dot on curve
      drawDot(x, y)
      // close cell, row, and table (new line is automatic)
      document.write("</TD></TR></TABLE>")
   }
}
```

This function does not accept any argument. It is responsible for printing the curve. To understand this function you must first understand how each row of the bitmap is printed. The entire row is placed inside an HTML table. The x value, or unit, is printed in the first cell of the table. This cell's width is fixed in order to preserve uniformity across rows. The second, and last, cell of the table is located on the same row, and contains all the images, both the transparent ones as well as the dot. The dot image is obviously the last image on the second cell of every row. Note that the left cell (the first in each table) is wide enough to hold almost any number.

The entire function is built of a single loop, which iterates through the points that are to be placed on the curve. See the explanation for the function makeArray() for information on the loop's algorithm. The function first prints the opening <TABLE>, <TR>, and <TD> tags. The border of the table is set to zero, so it is not seen. The width of the cell is set to 90 pixels. The value in the first cell is printed by the printUnit() function. The current cell of the table is then closed, and a new one is opened. The y value of the current point, which is stored as a property in the global object ar, is assigned to the local variable y for the sake of convenience. The minimum and maximum y coordinates of the whole curve are already stored in the global variables minY and maxY, respectively. A simple linear equation is used to convert the current y coordinate to a value between 1 and 100, where the minimum y coordinate in the entire curve is 1 and the maximum is 100. This value is assigned to the local variable yspot. The next statement calls the function drawBlank() to print ySpot - 1 transparent images, which is equal to the number of images up to ySpot, the spot where the dot image is placed. The function drawDot() is called with the current coordinates to print the current dot, or bullet, on the imaginary curve. The current cell and row of the table are then closed, and so is the table. When closing the table, a line break is automatically appended.

main()

The name of this function is drawn from traditional programming languages such as C, C++, and Java, where the function main() is executed automatically and is the starting point of the program. In JavaScript you have to call main() to draw the graph. The function first calls the startWizard() function to execute the wizard. The function getInput() is then executed. If it evaluates to false, meaning the user pressed Cancel when asked to enter a function, the function is terminated. Otherwise, execution continues. The function asks the user to enter additional information, including the minimum and maximum x coordinates and the difference between two consecutive ticks on the X axis. If the user selects Cancel on any of these requests, the function is terminated immediately, without executing any additional statements. After the user enters the values (and presses OK), the data is sent to the function replaceSpecialSequence from which a string is returned and converted to a number with the eval() function.

The next statement creates a global array-like object and assigns values by its constructor function, makeArray().

The function now needs to find the minimum and the maximum y coordinates of the curve. First, it assigns each variable, maxY and minY, an existing y coordinate. A for...in loop then iterates through the properties of the ar object, and if it finds a value less than the current minY or greater than the current maxY, it updates that value.

The last statement of the function draws the curve itself.

Global Statements

The only global statement is a call to the main() function.

Summary

In this chapter you learned about math usage in JavaScript. We have focused almost entirely on the `Math` object and its properties and methods. Among the methods discussed are the arithmetic and trigonometric ones. Arithmetic methods are found in almost every JavaScript script, whereas trigonometric methods are rather rare. You also learned the basics of some built-in functions that are closely related to JavaScript. These functions are discussed later in depth, so do not worry if you do not understand them very well. To spice things up, we have also shown an interesting example related to math involving curve plotting. If you understood all the scripts, or at least the curve plotting one, you are surely on the right track. However, don't worry if they seem very difficult at this stage, because knowledge comes with practice. In fact, some of the examples were purposefully a bit more advanced than you will probably need in the real world, simply to illustrate to you the power of the JavaScript `Math` object.

Chapter 12

Handling Strings

Strings are an important part of any programming language. Whether you are storing a person's last name or the name of a product in inventory, a string is often the best way to store that value. But what is a string really? Essentially, a string is simply an array of individual characters. This is true in all programming languages. Some languages, such as C and JavaScript, have you deal directly with the array of characters, while other languages, such as Visual Basic, hide that level of detail from the programmer. Each character has its position, or index. The indexing of strings, like that of arrays, is zero-based. The index of the first character of a string is 0, the index of the second one is 1, that of the third one is 2, and so on.

Characters

JavaScript, unlike some languages, does not include an explicit character (`char`) data type. A character is simply a string constructed of only one character. Characters of a string must be visual. That is, each symbol that appears in a string is a character that can actually be printed. This may seem obvious to you, but not all characters that appear in the ASCII table can be characters of a string, because some are not visual. An escape sequence is a sequence of characters that represents a single special character that is usually difficult to enter via the keyboard. For example, take a look at the following string:

```
"car\'s wheel"
```

It appears as if the string contains 12 characters (c, a, r, \, ', s, , w, h, e, e, l). However, when you print the string you can see only 11 characters (c, a, r, ', s, , w, h, e, e, l). Therefore, the string consists of 11 characters. The fourth character is an apostrophe (or single quote), not a backslash, because the sequence “\'” is shorthand for an apostrophe. This sequence is referred to as an *escape sequence* because it escapes the normal character processing and instead executes a special command.

Creating Strings

`String` is a very special built-in object because of the way you can create it. All strings belong to the built-in `String` object, so you can create strings as instances of the `String` object:

```
var str = new String("Hello!")
```

The general syntax is:

```
stringObjectName = new String(string)
```

`stringObjectName` is the name of the object you are creating, and *`string`* is any string, including literal strings in quotations as in the example. Strings created via this constructor function are considered objects. If you test their data type using the `typeof` operator you will find that they are objects, not strings. However, all the string properties and methods work on such objects.

Another way to create a string is by simply quoting a sequence of characters. If you want to use it as an object, you can follow the identifier by the desired property or method.

String Length

The `String` object combines many methods and one property, `length`. This property reflects the number of characters, including blanks, that it contains. Here are a few examples:

```
var str1 = "abc"
var str2 = "a b c"
var str3 = "\"abc\""
document.write(str1.length + "<BR>")
document.write(str2.length + "<BR>")
document.write(str3.length)
```

The output of this script is:

```
3
5
5
```

The index of a string's last character is equal to its length (number of characters) minus one. The string's length is the index of the nonexistent character following the string's last character.

HTML Formatting Methods

You have seen a great amount of HTML formatting throughout the book. You can print HTML tags by combining strings to receive the desired tag and attribute values. Here is an example:

```
var openBold = "<B>"
var closeBold = "</B>"
var message = "Something"
document.write("<B>Something</B>")
```

The result of this script is that the string `Something` is printed in bold. JavaScript provides methods to simplify this process. For example, you can create the same output using the following statement:

```
document.write("Something".bold())
```

The following table lists all these methods along with the HTML they generate:

Table 12-1. *HTML formatting methods*

Method Name	Example	Returned Value
anchor	"text".anchor("anchorName")	<A NAME="anchorName"> text</A>
big	"text".big()	<BIG>text</BIG>
blink	"text".blink()	<BLINK>text</BLINK>
bold	"text".bold()	<BOLD>text</BOLD>
fixed	"text".fixed()	<TT>text</TT>
fontcolor	"text".fontcolor("red")	<FONT COLOR="red"> text</FONT>
fontsize	"text".fontsize(-1)	<FONT SIZE=-1>text</FONT>
italics	"text".italics()	<I>text</I>
link	"text".link("URL")	<A HREF="URL">text</A>
small	"text".small()	<SMALL>text</SMALL>
strike	"text".strike()	<STRIKE>text</STRIKE>
sub	"text".sub()	_{text}
sup	"text".sup()	^{text}
toLowerCase	"TexT".toLowerCase()	text
toUpperCase	"TexT".toUpperCase()	TEXT

You can also "chain" methods together in order to apply more than one formatting conversion. For example, if you want an italic bold uppercase string, you can use the following expression: `toUpperCase().bold().italics()`. The evaluation here is done from left to right. The following list outlines the stages of the evaluation, where the calling string is the literal `"text"`:

```
"text".toUpperCase().bold().italics()
"TEXT".bold().italics()
"<B>TEXT</B>".italics()
"<I><B>TEXT</B></I>"
```

The value processed by a specific method is the accumulative value returned by the expression to the left of the method; that is, the expression that is implemented as the calling object, or string. Therefore, you must make sure that the expression to the left of a method returns a value that is valid for that method.

HTML text formatting tags usually consist of two tags that enclose the text. The nested structure is very clear in HTML, because a set of tags can enclose another set of tags. In the previous example, the `<I></I>` set encloses the <B></B> set. When creating HTML via JavaScript's `String` methods, keep in mind that the far-left specified method appears as the inner set of tags when formatted to HTML, whereas the far-right method is responsible for the outer set of tags.

General String Methods

As you already know, the `String` object has many methods. Those that convert strings to constant HTML formats (and listed in Table 12-1) are only some of the methods JavaScript offers. In this section, we'll take a look at the rest of the `String` methods.

charAt()

This method returns the character whose index is equal to the argument of the method. The characters of a string are indexed from 0 to `length - 1`. The general syntax is:

```
anyString.charAt(index)
```

Here is an example:

```
var pres = "Kennedy"
document.write(pres.charAt(1))
```

This script segment prints the character "e", because it is the second character in the string. You can also call this method with a literal as in the following example:

```
document.write("Kennedy".charAt(1))
```

You can print the characters of a string via a simple loop:

```
var str = "I am a string!"
for (var i = 0; i < str.length; ++i)
{
   document.write(str.charAt(i))
}
```

First, a string literal is assigned to the variable `str`. The loop then iterates `length` times. It starts at 0 and ends at `str.length - 1` (notice the less than operator, not less than or equal to). The `i` indexed character is printed in the `i`th iteration of the loop. Since the command block is executed once for each integer value of `i`, each character of the string is printed once and only once. The output of the preceding script segment is actually the string itself, printed one character at a time (no, you cannot notice the difference!).

indexOf()

This method returns the index of the first occurrence of the specified substring in the calling `String` object, starting the search at the beginning of the string. An example will surely clear things up:

```
var str = "ababa"
document.write(str.indexOf("ba"))
```

This script's output is the number 1. The first occurrence of the substring `"ba"` in the calling `String` object is at the second character, whose index is 1. The search for the specified substring starts at index 0, the beginning of the string. However, you can also instruct JavaScript to start the search at a different index, such as somewhere in the middle of the string. The following script segment prints the number 3:

```
var str = "ababa"
document.write(str.indexOf("ba", 2))
```

The general syntax of this method is:

```
stringName.indexOf(searchValue, [fromIndex])
```

Note that *fromIndex* must be an integer between 0 and the string's length minus 1. *searchValue* does not have to be a string. The following script prints the number 8:

```
var str = "August 27, 1985"
document.write(str.indexOf(7))
```

If the index to start looking for the substring is not specified, the default value of 0 is used. If the specified substring is not found in the entire string, the method returns one less than the base, –1.

This method is equivalent to the `index` function in Perl.

lastIndexOf()

This method is identical to the `indexOf` method, except that it returns the index of the last occurrence of the specified value, rather than the first occurrence. Its syntax is, therefore, the same:

```
stringName.lastIndexOf(searchValue, [fromIndex])
```

The following script prints the number 3:

```
var str = "a/b/c"
document.write(str.lastIndexOf("/"))
```

See the `indexOf` method for more details on this method.

substring()

Strings are constructed of characters. The `substring()` method returns a set of characters within its calling `String` object. Its general syntax is:

```
stringName.substring(indexA, indexB)
```

`stringName` is any string. *`indexA`* and *`indexB`* are both integers between 0 and *`stringName`*`.length – 1`. *`indexA`* is the index of the first character in the substring, whereas *`indexB`* is the index of the last character in the substring plus 1. The following script assigns the string `"bc"` to the variable `seg`:

```
var str = "abcd"
var seg = str.substring(1, 3)
```

Notice that the length of the substring is *`indexA – indexB`*.

The substring whose arguments are 0 and *`stringName`*`.length` is equal to the string itself (*`stringName`*).

This method is similar to its equivalent function in C#—`substring`. Nonetheless, it is important to point out the differences. First of all, since Perl does not support objects, the plain `substr()` function accepts the string itself as the first argument and *`indexA`* as the second one. However, the third argument is not *`indexB`*, but the length of the substring. Another difference is that when you call the function with a negative value as the offset (*`indexA`*), the substring starts that far from the end of the string. In JavaScript, though, a negative index is equivalent to a zero index, the first character of the string. JavaScript prototypes enable us to reproduce the `substring` function in Perl as a JavaScript method using the following script segment:

```
function substr(offset, length)
{
   if (offset < 0)
      offset = this.length + offset
   return this.substring(offset, offset + length)
}
String.prototype.substr = substr
```

You can use this method with any string in the following way:

```
var str = "abcd"
document.write(str.substr(-3, 2))
```

This statement prints the string "`bc`".

escape() and unescape()

JavaScript provides us with some built-in functions that deal with strings, such as `escape()` and `unescape()`. Before we can present these functions, we must discuss the ISO Latin-1 character set. The ISO Latin-1 (ISO-8859-1) is the standard set of characters used over the Internet. This standard also serves as the basis for the ANSI character set of Microsoft Windows, but, naturally, Microsoft extended and improved the set. However, only the ISO Latin-1 characters are guaranteed to be supported on a web site. You already know the standard coding scheme of the ISO Latin-1 character set through HTML, which enables you to display a character by its number or name as an entity. For example, the character © can be displayed on a page via two different expressions:

- `©`
- `©`

The first expression is based on the character code in the ISO Latin-1 character set. The second method is based on the name given to the character. With only a few exceptions, almost all platforms are compatible with the glyphs of ISO Latin-1. If you are interested in character sets or ISO-8859-1, search the web for more information. The ISO-8859-1 character table can be found in Appendix C.

Now back to JavaScript. The `escape` function returns the ASCII encoding of an argument in the ISO Latin-1 character set. The general syntax is:

```
escape(string)
```

Like all methods, you can pass it a variable, a property of an existing object, or a plain string literal. The `escape()` function is not a method associated with any object, but is a part of the language itself. The value returned by the `escape()` function is the string argument, where all nonalphanumeric characters are replaced by a string in the form of "%*xx*", *xx* being the ASCII encoding of a character in the argument.

The `unescape()` function is responsible for the opposite conversion. That is, it converts the string from nonalphanumeric ASCII encoding to ISO Latin-1 characters. Its syntax is similar:

```
unescape(string)
```

The following example demonstrates the conversion in both directions:

```
var str1 = "My phone # is 123-456-7890"
var str2 = escape(str1)
var str3 = unescape(str2)
document.write("After escape: " + str2 + "<BR>")
document.write("After unescape: " + str3)
```

The script's output is self-explanatory:

```
After escape: My%20phone%20%23%20is%20123-456-7890
After unescape: My phone # is 123-456-7890
```

Chapter 12

Number-to-String Conversion

Occasionally, you need to convert a number to a string. For example, if you want to compute the number of digits in a number, you can convert it to a string and use the `length` property, which applies only to strings. In this section we take a look at a few ways to convert a number into a string.

Empty String Concatenation

The most obvious way to convert a number to a string is by concatenating an empty string to the number. Here is an example of such a conversion:

```
var num = 987
num += ""
```

You can also make sure that the value of the variable is a string by using the `typeof` operator in the following way:

```
var num = 987
document.write("num is a " + typeof num + "<BR>")
num += ""
document.write("num is a " + typeof num)
```

The expected output of this script segment is:

```
num is a number
num is a string
```

You can also convert the number to a string and assign the numeric string to another variable, or even better, do both operations in one statement:

```
var num = 987
var numericString = num + ""
```

This script results in two different variables; the first holds a pure numeric value and the second, `numericString`, holds a string type. The side of the variable to which the empty string is concatenated has no importance:

```
var num = 987
var numericString = "" + num
```

If you concatenate several different literals, where some are numbers and other are strings, the expression evaluates to a string. Here is an example:

```
var str = 99 + " bottles of beer on the wall"
```

However, scripts become tricky when you concatenate more than two values or literals, especially when the first few are numbers. Here is a tricky expression:

```
var str = 50 + 49 + " bottles of beer on the wall"
```

JavaScript evaluates from left to right. The accumulated value is converted to a string only when a string value or literal is encountered in the expression. In the preceding example, JavaScript adds 49 to 50 in the regular mathematical way, so `50 + 49` evaluates to 99, which is then concatenated to the following string. So the value of `str` in this case is `99 bottles of beer on the wall`. The following statement demonstrates a slightly different situation:

```
var str = "bottles of beer on the wall -- " + 50 + 49
```

Like always, evaluation is done from left to right. The string, `bottles of beer on the wall --` , is concatenated with 50 and evaluates to `bottles of beer on the wall -- 50`. This value in turn is concatenated with the number 49, and evaluates to `bottles of beer on the wall -- 5049`, which is certainly not the value we want. A simple workaround is to enclose the numeric operation in parentheses in the following form:

```
var str = "bottles of beer on the wall -- " + (50 + 49)
```

The parentheses instruct JavaScript to evaluate the enclosed expression first, so the value of `str` in this case is `bottles of beer on the wall -- 99`.

String Instance Construction

Another way to convert a number to a string is by providing the number to the `String()` constructor function, which returns a regular `String` object. Here is a simple example to demonstrate this:

```
var num = 987
num = new String(num)
```

The data type of the variable `num` in this case is not a string, but an object. As mentioned earlier, strings created via the `String()` constructor are regular objects. However, you can still use any property or method associated with strings on such objects. A more obvious way to convert a number to a string via the constructor function is to assign the new string, or object, to a new variable in the following form:

```
var num = 987
var numericString = new String(num)
```


The toString() Method

The `toString()` method belongs to all objects. Its general syntax is:

```
objectName.toString([radix])
```

`objectName` is the object to convert to a string, whereas *`radix`* is the base to use for representing numeric values when the calling object is a number. The following example prints the string equivalents of the numbers 0 through 9 in decimal and binary:

```
for (x = 0; x < 10; x++)
{
   document.write("Decimal: ", x.toString(10), " Binary: ", x.toString(2),
                  "<BR>")
}
```

The loop's output is:

```
Decimal: 0 Binary: 0
Decimal: 1 Binary: 1
Decimal: 2 Binary: 10
Decimal: 3 Binary: 11
Decimal: 4 Binary: 100
Decimal: 5 Binary: 101
Decimal: 6 Binary: 110
Decimal: 7 Binary: 111
Decimal: 8 Binary: 1000
Decimal: 9 Binary: 1001
```

All objects, numbers included, have a `toString()` method. If an object has no string value, the method returns `[object type]`, where *type* is the object type (e.g., `Date`, `Array`, `Object` (user-defined), `Image`). When used with an array, `toString()` joins the array elements and returns one string where elements are separated by commas. This operation is exactly like the `join()` method, which concatenates the elements with a specified delimiter, possibly a comma.

For functions, `toString()` decompiles the function back into a canonical source string. Take a look at the following script segment:

```
function foo()
{
   var a = 5
   alert(a)
   document.write("wow")
}
document.write(foo.toString())
```

The script's output is:

```
function foo() { var a = 5; alert(a); document.write("wow"); }
```

String-to-Number Conversion

Mathematical operators, for example, accept numeric strings as operands and handle them fine. Here is an example for such an operation:

```
var num1= "7"
var num2 = "2"
var result = num1 - num2
document.write(result)
```

This script prints 5, just as if both variables were assigned a plain numeric value rather than a numeric string (we use the term *numeric string* to characterize a string that encloses a number, such as `"911"`). An operation consisting of numeric string operands returns a plain numeric value, not a string. Therefore, you can theoretically convert a numeric string to a number by performing an arithmetical operation on it. If you want, you can even use a function to execute the conversion in the following form:

```
function convert(val)
{
   return val - 0
}
var num = "911"
num = convert(num)
```

Note that you cannot use the plus (+) operator because it is also a string concatenation operator in JavaScript. If you are not sure whether a value is a numeric string or a number, always convert it. It's better to stay on the safe side than to spend hours searching for such errors. Conversion via mathematical operations is somewhat annoying, because it looks like a workaround. Therefore, JavaScript provides us with a few conversion functions, each with its own attributes.

parseInt() and parseFloat()

These two functions were briefly discussed in Chapter 11, "JavaScript Math." They are built-in functions, so they do not belong to any object. They convert their argument from a numeric string to a number. If the argument is a string but not a numeric one, the function returns zero. The `parseFloat()` function is more general, because it works with floating-point numbers as well as integers. The `parseInt()` function works with integers only, and returns a rounded-off value when called with a floating-point numeric string. Both functions return the value they are given if it is a plain number, not a numeric string. Therefore, if you are not sure whether a value is a number or a numeric string, simply send it to the function. If a certain value in the script has a chance to be a floating-point number, use `parseFloat()`. It will also work if the value is an integer.

Here are a few expressions to demonstrate these functions, along with returned values:

```
parseInt("16")        // 16
parseInt("16.33")     // 16
parseFloat("16")      // 16
parseFloat("16.33")   // 16.33
parseInt("Howdy!")    // 0
```

These functions are very useful when accepting input from the user via forms or prompts because they always return a string, even if it represents a number.

Note that both functions return zero when the argument is a Boolean value. Therefore, if you want to check whether the user canceled a prompt box by pressing the Cancel button, you must evaluate the condition before parsing the value. Here is an example:

```
var num = prompt("Enter a number from 0 to 9:")
if (num = false)
   alert("You must enter a value to continue.")
else
   num = parseInt(num)
```

A common but mistaken practice is to parse the value immediately. The result is that you cannot check if the user canceled the box, because he or she might have entered the number 0, which is parsed to the same value as a Boolean value.

Determining if a Value is a Number or Not

The `isNaN()` function evaluates an argument to determine if it is not a number, or NaN. The functions `parseFloat()` and `parseInt()` return `NaN` when they evaluate a value that is not a number or a numeric string. `NaN` is not a number in any string. If `NaN` is passed on to arithmetic operations, the result is also `NaN`. The `isNaN()` function returns a Boolean value, according to the argument. Bear in mind that Internet Explorer 3.0 does not support this feature—`parseFloat()` and `parseInt()` both return 0 if their argument is neither a number nor a numeric string.

`NaN` is not a string, nor is it a data type of its own. It is primarily a number! You can prove that to yourself via the following statement:

```
alert(typeof parseInt("something"))
```

The following construct demonstrates how to implement the `isNaN()` function (with the `parseFloat()` function for the sake of the example):

```
var floatValue = parseFloat(valueToBeConvertedToFloat)
if isNaN(floatValue)
{
   functionToBeCalledIfFloat()
}
else
{
   functionToBeCalledIfNotFloat()
}
```

The `isNaN()` function is not as important as `parseInt()` and `parseFloat()`, but we have discussed it here for completeness.

Evaluating Text Expressions

JavaScript supports evaluation and execution of text expressions via the `eval()` method. Here are some examples:

```
var str = "5 + 2"
var num = eval(str)
alert(num)
var al = "alert('This is an evaluated string.')"
eval(al)
```

This script segment pops up two alerts. The first one displays the number 7, because the expression `"5 + 2"` evaluates to 7. The second call to the `eval()` function does not cause it to return a value, but to execute the statement encapsulated in a string.

You can also use the `eval()` function to convert strings representing numbers to regular numbers. The `eval()` function accepts any valid JavaScript piece of code in the form of a string. You can store an entire script as a string and then hand it over to this function. The classic example for the function is to let the user enter a mathematical expression in a form field or a prompt box, and to display the result. Here is a simple example:

```
var inp = prompt("Enter mathematical expression", "")
alert(inp + " = " + eval(inp))
```

String Handling Example

In this section we focus on a script that takes advantage of the various built-in functions and other elements of the `String` object in JavaScript.

String Enciphering

The following script prompts the user for a short string. It then asks for a numeric key. The key has 63 possible values—all integers from 1 to 63. The ciphering technique used in this script is known as XORing, because it is primarily based on the bitwise XOR (exclusive OR) operator. The numeric value of each character of the input string, or password, is mixed with the numeric key value. A reverse process can be used to convert the enciphered string back to the original one. Since the conversion simply swaps the same two characters according to the key, the same JavaScript script is used as the decoder and the encoder. Enough theory—let's get to the point! Here is the script:

```
<HTML>
<HEAD>
<TITLE>Enciphering</TITLE>
<SCRIPT LANGUAGE="JavaScript">
<!--
// create list of valid characters
var list = "0123456789abcdefghijklmnopqrstuvwxyz._~ABCDEFGHIJKLMNOPQRSTUVWXYZ"
function encipher()
{
   // prompt user for string
   var str = prompt("Enter string:", "")
   // terminate function if user selects CANCEL
   if (!str)
      return
   // check that each character of input string is valid
   for (var i = 0; i < str.length; ++i)
   {
      if (list.indexOf(str.charAt(i)) == -1)
      {
         alert("script terminated -- invalid character found")
         return
      }
   }
```

```
    // prompt user for key
    var key = prompt("Enter key (1-63):", "")
    // terminate function if user selects CANCEL
    if (!key)
        return
    // convert key to integer (number)
    key = parseInt(key)
    // alert enciphered string
    alert(encode(str, key))
}
function encode(str, key)
{
    // initialize accumulative string variable
    var code = ""
    // encipher all characters
    for (var i = 0; i < str.length; ++i)
    {
        var ind = list.indexOf(str.charAt(i))
        var converted = list.charAt(ind ^ key)
        code += converted
    }
    // return enciphered value
    return code
}
encipher()
// -->
</SCRIPT>
</HEAD>
<BODY>
</BODY>
</HTML>
```

Example 12-1 (ex12-1.htm). *A simple ciphering script*

The output of this script is shown in Figures 12-1 through 12-3.

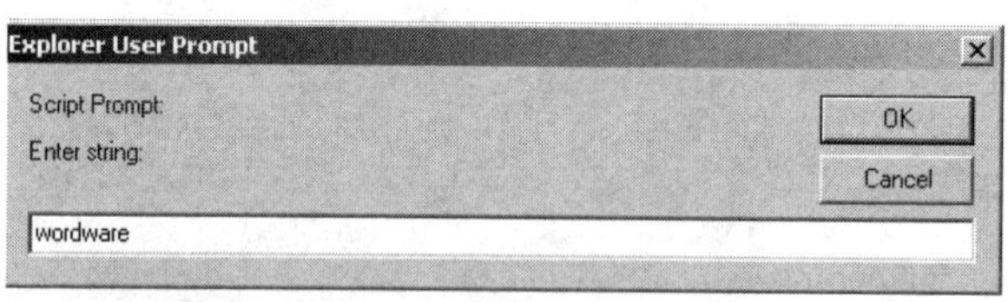

Figure 12-1. *Encryption input*

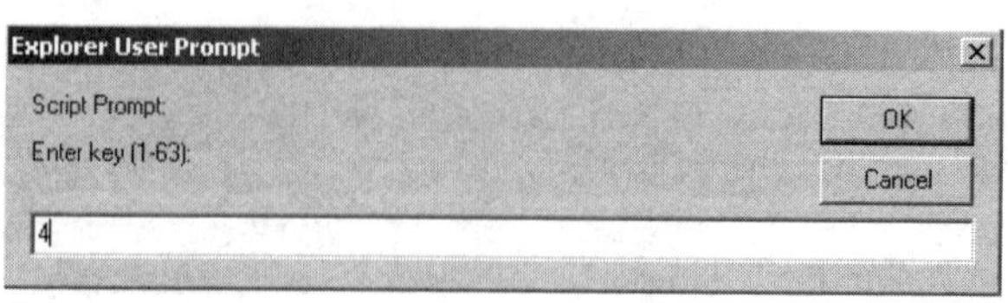

Figure 12-2. *Encryption seed*

Figure 12-3.
Encryption output

Warning: This is an incredibly primitive encrypting scheme and can easily be broken. It is presented here only as an example of how to use JavaScript and is not meant to be used to encrypt sensitive data.

Now let's see how this script works.

encipher()

First the `encipher()` function prompts the user for the string he or she wants to encode. It is stored in the variable `str`. If the value of the variable is a Boolean false, the function and the script itself are terminated. The logic behind terminating the function is that a Boolean false value can only be the result of the user pressing Cancel. A `for` loop is then used to check that all characters of the string are also located in the string held by `list`. The loop iterates through every character of the input string. Take a look at the condition used to test if the character is supported:

```
list.indexOf(str.charAt(i)) == -1
```

`str.charAt(i)` is the character for which the loop's block is currently being executed. The variable `i` starts at 0, the index of the string's first character, and is incremented each time until it is equal to the index of the string's last character. Suppose the current character is "t." The condition looks like this then:

```
list.indexOf("t") == -1
```

If the character "t" is not found in the string list, the method `indexOf()` whose argument is "t" returns –1—exactly the number against which the returned value is tested.

If a character is not valid (not found in `list`), a message is displayed and the function is terminated, indirectly causing the script's execution to end.

The function then asks the user to enter the key number, which must be an integer from 1 to 63. Because this is just an example, the input value is not tested. If the user clicks Cancel, the function is terminated. Otherwise, the function continues, and the key number is converted from a numeric string to a number via the `parseInt()` function. The encoded string, which is returned by the function `encode()`, is displayed.

encode(str, key)

First an empty string is assigned to the variable code. A loop is used to replace every character of the input string with another character. The index of the current character (the one whose index in str is equal to the loop's counter, i) in the list string is assigned to the variable ind. The bitwise OR operator is given the key number and the value of ind as operands. The character whose index in list is equal to the value returned by the bitwise OR operation is the one used to replace the current character in the new string, so it is assigned to the variable that holds the encoded string. The new string is returned by the function.

Summary

Strings are a very useful data type in JavaScript. JavaScript tends to organize its elements in the form of objects, so all string-related functions and data are grouped together to form the String object. In this chapter we discussed the methods of the String object, as well as its single property, length. Because strings are direct or indirect (based on the way you create them) instances of this object, you can create prototypes to extend the object's capabilities. The JavaScript example provided at the end of the chapter gives a clear view of the String object's strength. We did not provide many examples in this chapter because string manipulation and handling can be found in almost every example later on in this book.

Chapter 13
The Document Object Model

The Document Object Model (DOM), one of the most powerful tools available to a web developer, is a hierarchy of objects that represent the web browser, the browser's history, the currently loaded web page, and other important elements. You can see this hierarchy depicted in Figure 13-1.

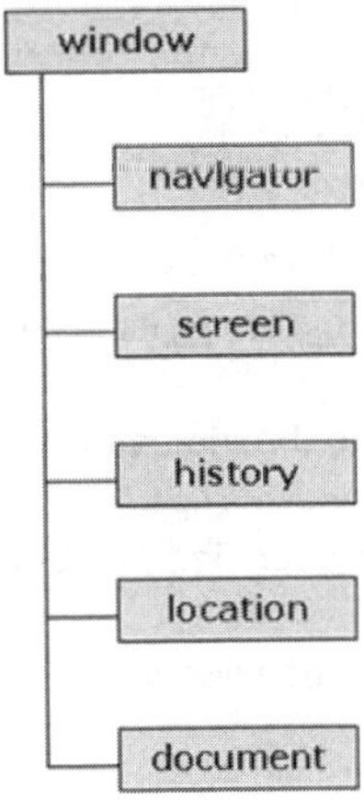

Figure 13-1. *The Document Object Model*

In this chapter and the next we will be exploring the DOM and giving you examples of how to use the various aspects of it. I think you will find these features exciting and very useful. Each of the objects within the DOM have a specific purpose, and we will explore most of them in this chapter.

The window Object

The `window` object is at the top of the DOM hierarchy. This object represents the browser window. You will find that you don't often deal directly with the `window` object, but rather as the container for the other objects you use directly on a regular basis. This doesn't mean that you never use the `window` object directly, merely that it is not as commonly used as other objects.

The `window` object contains properties that apply to the entire window. For example, the status bar of the browser is a property of this object. It also includes a property that is actually the object itself. Sound strange? Not really. You will find out more about this reference when we discuss windows and frames. When the document features frames, there can be several `window` objects in a single HTML document. Frames actually divide the page into "child" windows, so each frame has its own browser object hierarchy. You must be careful with such child windows because they can cause collisions due to the fact that several `window` objects have a shared property. For example, there is only one status bar in the browser, no matter which page you load (unless you open a window without a status bar).

Table 13-1 shows some of the various methods and properties of the `window` object.

Table 13-1. *Methods and properties of the `window` object*

Method/Property	Purpose
focus()	This function sets the focus to the current window.
resizeBy(x,y)	Adjusts the window size relative to its current width and height.
resizeTo(x,y)	Adjusts the window size to the indicated x and y width and height values.
moveBy(x,y)	Moves the window by the specified number of pixels in the x and y direction.
moveTo(x,y)	Moves the window to the specified x and y pixel location.

Table 13-2 shows a few examples of ways you might use the `window` object.

Table 13-2. *Using the `window` object*

Example	Purpose
var newwindow = window.open("http://www.chuckeasttom.com")	Open a new browser window.
newwindow.focus	Set focus to that window.
newwindow.close	Close that window.

The navigator Object

This object provides information about the browser being used. This can be quite useful in gathering information about people who visit your web site. In fact, the amount of information you can derive from this object is really rather astounding.

Table 13-3 shows some of the methods and properties of the `navigator` object.

Table 13-3. *Methods and properties of the* `navigator` *object*

Method/Property	Purpose
appName	The name of the end user's browser.
appVersion	The version number of the end user's browser.
cookieEnabled	Whether or not the end user's browser has cookies enabled.
platform	The end user's operating system.
javaEnabled()	A method that returns a Boolean telling if the browser has JavaScript enabled.

Following are examples of code snippets using the `navigator` object. In these examples, the `document` object is used to display the properties of the `navigator` object in the browser. We will be looking at the `document` object itself in the next section.

```
document.write(navigator.appName)
document.write(navigator.appVersion)
document.write(navigator.platform)
document.write(navigator.cpuClass)
```

As you can see, these methods and properties can provide a rich source of information about visitors to your site.

The document Object

By far the most useful object of the DOM is the `document` object. It contains properties for the current page loaded in the window. The properties of this object are content-dependent because each and every page has its own outline and elements. Almost everything in the page is a property of the `document` object, including links, images, forms and their elements, anchors, and more. Because each frame is a window (`window` object), it contains a `document` object as well. Even the background and the title are properties of this object. We will give you an overview of the `document` object here, but you will find even more details about this object later in this book. Table 13-4 lists some of the properties and methods of the `document` object.

***Table 13-4.** Methods and properties of the `document` object*

Method/Property	Purpose
write()	This is a very commonly used method and writes to the HTML page whatever is passed to the write function.
fileCreatedDate	This property shows when the loaded HTML file was created.
linkColor	This property shows the color of HTML links in the document. It is specified in the <BODY> tag.
open()	This method opens a new document in a new window.
embeds	An array containing all the plug-ins in a document.

Let's take a look at an example that uses the `document` object, since it is such a commonly used object.

```
<HTML>
<HEAD>
<TITLE>Sample Color Cube</TITLE>
</HEAD>
<BODY>
<SCRIPT LANGUAGE="JavaScript">
<!--
// create six-element array
var hex = new Array(6)
// assign non-dithered descriptors
hex[0] = "FF"
hex[1] = "CC"
hex[2] = "99"
hex[3] = "66"
hex[4] = "33"
hex[5] = "00"
// accept triplet string and display as background color
function display(triplet)
{
   // set color as background color
   document.bgColor = '#' + triplet
   // display the color hexadecimal triplet
   alert('Background color is now ' + triplet)
}
// draw a single table cell based on all descriptors
function drawCell(red, green, blue)
{
   // open cell with specified hexadecimal triplet background color
   document.write('<TD BGCOLOR = "#' + red + green + blue + '">')
   // open a hypertext link with javascript: scheme to call display function
   document.write('<A HREF = "javascript:display(\'' + (red + green + blue) +
             '\')">')
   // print transparent image (use any height and width)
   document.write('<IMG SRC="place.gif" BORDER=0 HEIGHT=12 WIDTH=12>')
```

```
   // close link tag
   document.write('</A>')
   // close table cell
   document.write('</TD>')
}
// draw table row based on red and blue descriptors
function drawRow(red, blue)
{
   // open table row
   document.write('<TR>')
   // loop through all non-dithered color descripters as green hex
   for (var i = 0; i < 6; ++i)
   {
      drawCell(red, hex[i], blue)
   }
   // close current table row
   document.write('</TR>')
}
// draw table for one of six color cube panels
function drawTable(blue)
{
   // open table (one of six cube panels)
   document.write('<TABLE CELLPADDING=0 CELLSPACING=0 BORDER=0>')
   // loop through all non-dithered color descripters as red hex
   for (var i = 0; i < 6; ++i)
   {
      drawRow(hex[i], blue)
   }
   // close current table
   document.write('</TABLE>')
   }
// draw all cube panels inside table cells
function drawCube()
{
   // open table
   document.write('<TABLE CELLPADDING=5 CELLSPACING=0 BORDER=1><TR>')
   // loop through all non-dithered color descripters as blue hex
   for (var i = 0; i < 6; ++i)
   {
      // open table cell with white background color
      document.write('<TD BGCOLOR="#FFFFFF">')
      // call function to create cube panel with hex[i] blue hex
      drawTable(hex[i])
      // close current table cell
      document.write('</TD>')
   }
   // close table row and table
   document.write('</TR></TABLE>')
}
// call function to begin execution
drawCube()
// -->
```

```
</SCRIPT>
</BODY>
</HTML>
```

Example 13-1 (ex13-1.htm). *`document` object example*

You should note that in this example the `write` method is used repeatedly. As I stated earlier, it is one of the most commonly used methods of the `document` object. You can see the output of Example 13-1 in Figure 13-2.

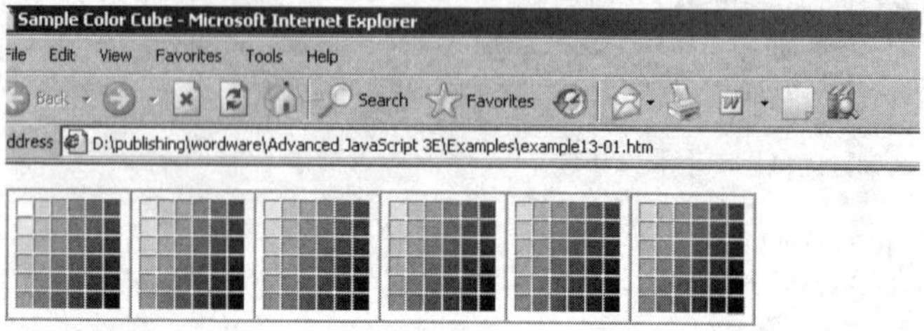

Figure 13-2. *Output from Example 13-1*

The history Object

The `history` object is also a property of the `window` object. It contains properties of the URLs the user has previously visited. This information is stored in a history list, and is accessible through the browser's menu. If the document consists of child documents in frames, each frame has its own history list, or `history` object. This object also contains methods enabling you to send the user's browser to a URL found in the history list. Table 13-5 lists some of the `history` object's most important properties and methods.

Table 13-5. *Methods and properties of the `history` object*

Methods/Properties	Purpose
current	The current document URL.
previous	The URL of the last document in the history list.
next	The URL of the next document in the history list.
length	The number of entries currently stored in the history object.

The following code snippet shows an example of how you might use the `history` object.

```
<FORM>
<INPUT TYPE="button" VALUE="Go Back" onClick="history.back()">
</FORM>
```

The location Object

The `location` object contains properties of the current URL. Although you may think of URLs as simple standard structures, they are far more than that. There are many types of protocols and various sections in every URL. There are also optional sections in the URL, such as anchor names and queries. It may seem as though the `history` object and the `location` object are similar, but the properties and methods shown in Table 13-6 should show you how different they are.

Table 13-6. *Methods and properties of the `location` object*

Method/Property	Purpose
host	The URL hostname and port.
href	The entire URL.
port	The port being used.
search	The URL query string section (i.e., the section after and including the question mark).

The following code snippets show ways you might use the `location` object.

```
document.write(location.href)
document.write(window.location.protocol)
```

Summary

In this chapter we have introduced you to the Document Object Model and explored the more important aspects of it. Mastering this object model is key to success in JavaScript, because JavaScript is primarily designed to enable interaction with the user via these objects. In the following chapters, we will discuss various concepts related to these objects, including their methods, properties, and event handlers, in more detail.

Chapter 14
The Document Object Model (Continued)

In the previous chapter we introduced you to the Document Object Model and examined the most important and widely used objects in that model. We also looked at some simple applications of those objects and their properties and methods. In this chapter we will take a closer look at the DOM and practical applications of it.

The power of the the Document Object Model stems from its position as a standard of the World Wide Web Consortium (W3C), which is responsible for most of the standards on the web. This position ensures that most browsers and platforms will support it eventually. The development of the DOM aligns with the trend to provide more interactive content on the web. The only way to provide this interactive content is by allowing HTML to be dynamically manipulated. The Document Object Model makes this challenge much easier to achieve.

The Document Object Model provides programmers with a standard set of objects for representing HTML or even XML documents. The DOM also provides a standard interface for accessing and manipulating these documents and their constituent objects. The Document Object Model is basically a representation of the various component parts of the browser and of the web that JavaScript can access. Since the Document Object Model is a W3C specification, this means its behavior and usage are not dependent on a particular vendor. The DOM should be the same with Internet Explorer, Mozilla, or any browser. An important objective for any W3C standard and for the Document Object Model is to provide a standard that can be used in a wide variety of environments and applications. The DOM is designed to be used with any programming language.

Within the DOM, documents have a logical structure that is designed like a tree. This means objects sometimes branch into subobjects. These subobjects can be described as *nodes*. In Chapter 13 we worked with some objects of the DOM. These objects were presented as individual objects, and not in relationship to the DOM tree. In this section we will examine that tree a bit closer. You can certainly continue to work with objects such as the `document`, `navigator`, and `history` objects without understanding the structure of the DOM tree, but it might help you with more advanced scripting if you do. It is also important to keep in mind that the DOM is language independent and is not specific to JavaScript.

Each document contains zero or one document type nodes, one document element node, and zero or more comments or processing instructions. The document element serves as the root of the element tree for the document. However, the DOM does not specify that documents must be implemented as a tree or a grove, nor does it specify how the relationships among objects should be implemented. This tree structure allows for "tree-walking" methods. This simply means the ability to move from one object in the tree to the next, and traverse all the relevant objects.

The DOM originated as a specification to allow JavaScript scripts and Java programs to be portable among web browsers. It originated with the Dynamic HTML model, which was used to make web pages more dynamic. Now the Document Object Model is a standard that is used in almost all web development technologies. Though our focus in this book is on how to use the DOM within JavaScript, its application is not limited to JavaScript.

The W3C DOM specifications are divided into levels, each of which contains required and optional modules. For an application or technology to claim to be at a given DOM level, it must implement all the requirements of that level. An application can also support vendor-specific extensions if they do not conflict with the W3C standards. Microsoft frequently makes use of vendor-specific extensions in its web development tools. Table 14-1 shows the various DOM levels and their requirements.

Table 14-1. DOM levels

Level	Description
Level 0	The application supports an intermediate DOM, which existed before the creation of DOM Level 1. An example would be the DHTML Object Model. Level 0 is not a formal specification published by the W3C but just a description of what existed before the standardization process.
Level 1	Applications at this level support navigation of the DOM document tree and content manipulation. HTML-specific elements are included as well.
Level 2	This level supports XML namespace support, filtered views, and events. This specification defines the Document Object Model Level 2 Core. The Document Object Model Level 2 Core builds on the Document Object Model Level 1 Core and is therefore inclusive of Level 1.
Level 3	This level is basically an enhancement to the DOM Level 2 Core. It completes the mapping between DOM and the XML information, including support for XML Base. It also adds the ability to attach user information to DOM nodes.

One goal of the DOM specification is to define a programmatic interface for both XML and HTML. We saw in Table 14-1 an overview of the various levels; however, there are a few details that table does not address.

The DOM Level 1 specification is separated into two parts: Core and HTML. The Core DOM Level 1 section provides a set of basic interfaces that can represent any structured document. The Core Level 1 also defines extended interfaces for representing an XML document. These extended XML interfaces don't need to be implemented by a DOM implementation that only provides access to HTML documents.

Accessing a Document's Structure with the DOM

The primary function of the Document Object Model is to view, access, and change the structure of an HTML document. You saw in Chapter 13 how you can access parts of the browser and even write to the HTML page using the Document Object Model. You can access certain HTML elements based on their `id` identifier, or allocate arrays of elements by their tag or CSS class type. All transformations are done according to the most recent HTML specification. More importantly, they happen dynamically—any transformation will happen without reloading the page. Some of the most commonly-used elements are listed in Table 14-2.

Table 14-2. *Common DOM elements*

DOM Element	Description
document	Returns the document object for the page. It also is the root node of the DOM tree.
element	Represents an instance of most structures and substructures in the DOM tree. For example, a text block can be an element or an item in an HTML form.
nodeList	A nodeList is basically an array of elements. You can access items in a nodeList through common syntax like myList[n], where n is an integer.

There are a number of JavaScript methods specified by the Document Object Model that allow you to access its structure. Some of the most commonly used methods are listed in Table 14-3.

Table 14-3. *Commonly used DOM methods*

DOM Method	Description
element getElementById(id)	Returns the element uniquely identified by its `id` identifier.
nodeList getElementsByTag-Name(name)	Returns a nodeList of any elements that have a given tag (such as a `<p>` tag), specified by `name`.

DOM Method	Description
element createElement(type)	Creates an element with the type specified by type (such as a <p> tag).
void appendChild(node)	Appends the node specified by node onto the receiving node or element.
string style	Returns the style rules associated with an element, in string form.
string innerHTML	Returns the HTML that contains the current element and all the content within it. You can also use this to set the innerHTML of an element.
void setAttribute(name, value)	Adds or changes an attribute of the target element.
string getAttribute(name)	Returns the value of the element attribute specified by name.

Using the Document Object Model

This section introduces some code examples to familiarize you with the Document Object Model. These examples should help you become more comfortable with using the DOM.

To work with DOM code examples, you need to create a sample HTML file. The following code represents the HTML file you will use in the examples:

```
<HTML>
<HEAD>
   <TITLE>Open a New Window</TITLE>
   <SCRIPT LANGUAGE="JavaScript">
   function OpenWindow()
   {
      var NewWindow = window.open("advjscript.jpg", "NewWindow",
                                  "width=350,height=400")
   }
   </SCRIPT>
</HEAD>
<BODY BGCOLOR=White>
   <A HREF="javascript:OpenWindow()">Advanced JavaScript</A>
</BODY>
</HTML>
```

The meat of this script is the single line of code found inside the OpenWindow function. The first parameter passed to this function is what you wish to open. This can be another HTML document or an image. The second parameter passed is the name of the variable that is going to represent this new window. In our case, that is NewWindow. The last parameter is the height and width of the new window we are opening.

This script is fairly simple and easy to use and can be very useful. For example, if you have a list of products on your web site and you do not wish to clutter the HTML document with all the details of every product, you can use this script to allow the user to view a page with those details after clicking on the name of a product.

The only real problem with our example for launching a new window is that if the item you are launching is larger than the size parameters you give it, we don't have scroll bars to let us see the whole image. Example 14-1 is very similar to the previous code, except that it adds something to the window.open method call to include scroll bars.

```
<HTML>
<HEAD>
   <TITLE>Open a New Window</TITLE>
   <SCRIPT LANGUAGE="JavaScript">
   function OpenWindow()
   {
      var NewWindow = window.open("anypage.htm", "NewWindow",
                                  "width=350,height=200,scrollbars=yes")
   }
   </SCRIPT>
</HEAD>
<BODY BGCOLOR=White>
   <A HREF="javascript:OpenWindow()">Advanced JavaScript</A>
</BODY>
</HTML>
```

Example 14-1 (ex14-1.htm). *Script that creates a window with scroll bars*

Simply adding `scrollbars=yes` right after the dimension parameters will give the new window you launch scroll bars! You can also add the line `toolbar = yes` so that your new window will have your browser's standard toolbar, if you wish.

The next example combines the scroll bars, the toolbar, and a method for the original window to close the window it launched.

```
<HTML>
<HEAD>
<TITLE>Close Windows</TITLE>
<SCRIPT LANGUAGE="JavaScript">
   var childwindow = null
   function opennewwindow()
   {
      childwindow = window.open("anypage.htm","childwindow",
                  "width=300,height=200,toolbar=yes,scrollbars=yes,")
   }
   function closenewwindow()
   {
      if (childwindow && !childwindow.closed)
      {
         childwindow.close()
      }
   }
```

```
</SCRIPT>
</HEAD>
<BODY BGCOLOR=White>
   <CENTER>
   <H3>
      <A HREF="javascript:opennewwindow()">View Advanced JavaScript</A>
      <BR>
      <A HREF="javascript:closenewwindow()">Close Advanced JavaScript</A>
   </H3>
   </CENTER>
</BODY>
</HTML>
```

Example 14-2 (ex14-2.htm). *Script that closes the window*

The only real difference in this script is the `closenewwindow` function. In that function, I simply use the name of the variable that represents the new window that was launched and call the `closewindow()` method. Although this difference is small, it is significant. Allowing the user to close the child window from the parent window that launched it is very important.

The following example shows you how to use the Document Object Model to detect what browser the client is using. This can be very important since some browsers may not support all the features of JavaScript you wish to implement.

```
<HTML>
<HEAD>
   <TITLE>Browser Detection</TITLE>
</HEAD>
<BODY BGCOLOR=White>
<SCRIPT LANGUAGE="JavaScript">
var browsername= navigator.appName
var browserversion = navigator.appVersion
   if (browsername == "Microsoft Internet Explorer")
   {
      document.write("You are using MS Internet Explorer version " +
                     browserversion)
   }
   else
   {
      document.write("You are using Netscape Navigator version " +
                     browserversion)
   }
</SCRIPT>
</BODY>
</HTML>
```

Example 14-3 (ex14-3.htm). *Script that detects the browser version*

These rather simple examples illustrate some of the practical things you can do with the `navigator` object.

Summary

In this chapter we expanded upon the material in Chapter 13. We looked more closely at the architecture of the Document Object Model and worked with some simple examples. With the material in this chapter and the preceding chapter you should have a basic working knowledge of the Document Object Model. Many subsequent chapters will be utilizing elements of the DOM, beginning with Chapter 15.

Mozilla Firefox has an interesting tool called DOM Inspector you may wish to use. You will find it under the Tools > Web Development menu in any Mozilla window. DOM Inspector is a tool that can be used to view the actual DOM objects of any web document. The DOM hierarchy can be navigated using a two-paned window that allows for a variety of different views on the document and all nodes within.

Chapter 15
Utilizing the Status Bar

The Status Bar

As we learned in Chapters 13 and 14, you can access the various elements of the web page or browser using the Document Object Model. The status bar is one of those elements you can access and utilize. The status bar is found at the bottom of the browser's window. It exists in all browsers, including Mozilla Firefox and Internet Explorer. It normally displays the current status of the document being loaded. The status bar is present in every window, unless the window is opened by a script that explicitly disables the status bar. Figure 15-1 shows the status bar from Mozilla.

Figure 15-1. The Mozilla Firefox status bar

The status bar is the gray bar at the bottom that shows the string "Document: Done."

In terms of the Document Object Model, the status bar is a direct property of the `window` object. In multiple-frame documents, each frame has a property representing the status bar, but you should only reference one of them to avoid an unwanted collision. The status bar in JavaScript is generally represented by the `status` property—`window.status`. You can also refer to the status bar of the current window via `self.status`, because `self` is actually a property of the `window` object that is the `window` object itself.

Note: You can also refer to the status bar as `status` instead of `window.status`; however, we shall stick with the latter for clarity.

Never try to read the status bar code, as such action usually generates an error. Setting the value of the status bar is permitted, with some restrictions.

Writing to the Status Bar

You can assign values to `window.status` via buttons, links, and every other event that is triggered by the user. For example, to have a message displayed when the user clicks a button, you can use the following form:

```
<HTML>
<HEAD>
<TITLE>status bar</TITLE>
<SCRIPT LANGUAGE = "JavaScript">
<!--
function showMessage()
{
   window.status = "Fascinating!"
}
// -->
</SCRIPT>
</HEAD>
<BODY>
<FORM>
<INPUT TYPE = "button" VALUE = "show message" onClick = "showMessage()">
</FORM>
</BODY>
</HTML>
```

Example 15-1 (ex15-1.htm). *You can display any string you like in the status bar as a reaction to a user-initiated event such as a button click. You can see the output of this script in Figure 15-2.*

Note: This script, and some others, may not function the same in Firefox as in Internet Explorer. Also note that Internet Explorer 7.0 was released as this book was being written and many scripts were not tested with that browser.

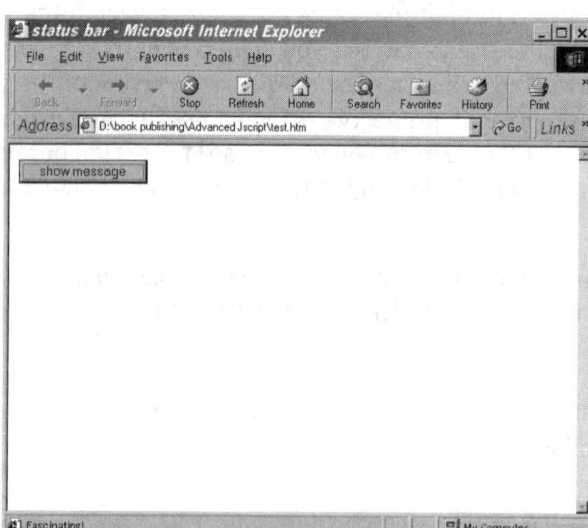

Figure 15-2. *Text in the status bar*

Many web pages implement a technique that displays a short description in the status bar rather than the URL when you place the mouse's pointer over a link. A description is usually much more meaningful than a URL. The event handler that is triggered when the user places the mouse's pointer over a link is `onMouseOver`. The event handler should always return the Boolean value true after the message is placed in the status bar. The only correct way to assign a message corresponding to a link in the status bar is to use the following syntax for the link:

```
<A HREF = "URL" onMouseOver = "window.status = 'any string'; return true">
```

Don't forget to return true—it's essential.

The following statement creates a link to Wordware Publishing's site and displays a short message when you place the pointer over it:

```
<A HREF = "http://www.wordware.com" onMouseOver = "window.status = 'Get
more cool computer books from Wordware'; return true">Wordware</A>
```

Take a look at the following example:

```
<HTML>
<HEAD>
<TITLE>status bar</TITLE>
<SCRIPT LANGUAGE = "JavaScript">
<!--
function showMessage(txt)
{
   window.status = txt
   setTimeout("clearMessage()", 2500)
}
function clearMessage()
{
   window.status = ""
}
// -->
</SCRIPT>
</HEAD>
<BODY>
<A HREF = "http://www.wordware.com" onMouseOver = "showMessage('Get more
cool computer books from Wordware'); return true">Wordware</A>
</BODY>
</HTML>
```

Example 15-2 (ex15-2.htm). *A script that displays the string in the status bar for 2.5 seconds*

The `setTimeout()` method is a possible replacement for the need to return true. This script is very simple. When the user places the pointer over the link, the function `showMessage()` is called with the desired string. The string is assigned to the `status` property, and the function `clearMessage()` is called to clear the status bar after 2.5 seconds, by replacing the current message with an empty string.

A much better way to erase a string written by `onMouseOver` from the status bar is to implement the `onMouseOut` event handler. This event handler serves as an attribute of a link or client-side image map area, and it is triggered when the mouse pointer leaves an area or link from inside that area (see Chapter 19, "Links, Anchors, and Image Maps"). This outside movement enables us to assign an empty string to the status bar when the user removes the pointer from the link.

Here is another example:

```
<A HREF = "http://www.wordware.com" onMouseOver = "window.status = 'Get
another cool computer book from Wordware'; return true" onMouseOut = "window.
        status = ''; return true">Wordware</A>
```

Setting a Default Value to the Status Bar

You have seen that it is possible to write one-line strings to the status bar via the `status` property. It is also possible to set a default value to the status bar. This value is kept in the status bar as long as no value is written to it by the `status` property. The general syntax of this property is `window.defaultStatus` or `defaultStatus`. When using this property with an event handler, you must return true.

Take a look at the following example:

```
<HTML>
<HEAD>
<TITLE>status bar</TITLE>
<SCRIPT LANGUAGE = "JavaScript">
<!--
function statusSetter()
{
   window.defaultStatus = "Click the link for the Wordware Publishing home page"
   window.status = "Wordware home page"
}
// -->
</SCRIPT>
</HEAD>
<BODY>
<A HREF = "http://www.wordware.com" onMouseOver = "statusSetter();
          return true">Wordware</A>
</BODY>
</HTML>
```

Example 15-3 (ex15-3.htm). *Sets a default value for the status bar*

When you load the page in the browser, you see a link. At that moment, the status bar does not contain any string (it might contain a string to report that the page has been loaded). When you place the pointer over the link, the message "Wordware home page" is written to the status bar. When the pointer is taken off the link, the string is replaced by another string—"Click the link for the Wordware Publishing home page." This is a nice alternative to using the `onMouseOut` event handler.

Banners

You can use the status bar to create banners. Banners are classic JavaScript scripts. They were, and still are, an attractive addition to any web page. Originally banners appeared in the status bar, scrolling several messages in sequence. Some programmers prefer to place the banner in a text box, because they feel that status bar-based banners are annoying to the common surfer. Banners are sometimes very unsteady; their speed is not uniform and they sometimes blink. There is no workaround to make them better. But, all in all, they are still a lot of fun. In this section we take a look at a few different banner-like scripts, most of which were created exclusively for this book.

T-banner

The T-banner simulates a typewriter and is one of my favorite banners. The typewriter style display catches the user's eye and ensures the message will be noticed. It displays each message by typing it in, one character at a time. It seems as if someone is typing the message at a certain speed and deleting it upon completion. First, take a look at the script:

```
<HTML>
<HEAD>
<TITLE>T-banner</TITLE>
<SCRIPT LANGUAGE = "JavaScript">
<!--
// set speed of banner (pause in milliseconds between characters)
var speed = 100 // decrease value to increase speed (must be positive)
// set pause between completion of message and beginning of following one
var pause = 1000 // increase value to increase pause
// set initial values
var timerID = null
var bannerRunning = false
// create global array
var ar = new Array()
// assign the strings to the array's elements
ar[0] = "Welcome to this JavaScript page"
ar[1] = "I hope you enjoy the T-banner script"
ar[2] = "It's kind of a cool banner"
ar[3] = "Don't forget to check out my other scripts"
// set index of first message to be displayed first
var currentMessage = 0
// set index of last character to be displayed first
var offset = 0
// stop the banner if it is currently running
function stopBanner()
{
   // if banner is currently running
   if (bannerRunning)
```

```
      // stop the banner
      clearTimeout(timerID)
   // timer is now stopped
   bannerRunning = false
}
// start the banner
function startBanner()
{
   // make sure the banner is stopped
   stopBanner()
   // start the banner from the current position
   showBanner()
}
// type in the current message
function showBanner()
{
   // assign current message to variable
   var text = ar[currentMessage]
   // if current message has not finished being displayed
   if (offset < text.length)
   {
      // if last character of current message is a space
      if (text.charAt(offset) == " ")
         // skip the current character
         offset++
      // assign the up-to-date to-be-displayed substring
      // second argument of method accepts index of last char plus one
      var partialMessage = text.substring(0, offset + 1)
      // display partial message in status bar
      window.status = partialMessage
      // increment index of last character to be displayed
      offset++
      // recursive call after specified time
      timerID = setTimeout("showBanner()", speed)
      // banner is running
      bannerRunning = true
   } else
   {
      // reset offset
      offset = 0
      // increment subscript (index) of current message
      currentMessage++
      // if subscript of current message is out of range
      if (currentMessage == ar.length)
         // wrap around (start from beginning)
         currentMessage = 0
      // recursive call after specified time
      timerID = setTimeout("showBanner()", pause)
      // banner is running
      bannerRunning = true
   }
}
```

```
// -->
</SCRIPT>
</HEAD>
<BODY onLoad = "startBanner()">
</BODY>
</HTML>
```

Example 15-4 (ex15-4.htm). *A T-banner*

Global Statements

```
// set speed of banner (pause in milliseconds between characters)
var speed = 100 // decrease value to increase speed (must be positive)
// set pause between completion of message and beginning of following one
var pause = 1000 // increase value to increase pause
// set initial values
var timerID = null
var bannerRunning = false
// create global array
var ar = new Array()
// assign the strings to the array's elements
ar[0] = "Welcome to this JavaScript page"
ar[1] = "I hope you enjoy the T-banner script"
ar[2] = "It is designed to be more stable than regular banners"
ar[3] = "Don't forget to check out my other scripts"
// set index of first message to be displayed first
var currentMessage = 0
// set index of last character to be displayed first
var offset = 0
```

At first, the speed of the banner is set to 100. This is equal to the pause between each character of a message in milliseconds. The pause (in milliseconds) between the completion of a message (string) and its deletion is assigned to the variable `pause`. The identifier for the current timeout is assigned null, because no timeout is set yet. The current state of the banner (false because it is not running yet) is assigned to the variable `bannerRunning`. An array is then created to hold the strings that are to be displayed as banner messages. The first string is assigned to the first element of the array, `ar[0]`, and so on. The number `0` is assigned to `currentMessage` because the first message displayed is `ar[0]`. The index of the last character displayed at a given moment in the status bar is assigned to the global variable `offset`. It is set to zero because the first appearance of the banner consists of only one character—the first one—whose index is zero.

stopBanner()

```
// start the banner
function startBanner()
{
   // make sure the banner is stopped
```

```
    stopBanner()
    // start the banner from the current position
    showBanner()
}
```

This function is called to stop the banner. If the banner is running, the current timeout is cleared. The variable `bannerRunning` is set to false because the banner is stopped.

startBanner()

```
// start the banner
function startBanner()
{
    // make sure the banner is stopped
    stopBanner()
    // start the banner from the current position
    showBanner()
}
```

This function calls the `stopBanner` function to make sure the banner is stopped, and then calls the function `showBanner` to start running the T-banner.

showBanner()

```
// type in the current message
function showBanner()
{
    // assign current message to variable
    var text = ar[currentMessage]
    // if current message has not finished being displayed
    if (offset < text.length)
    {
        // if last character of current message is a space
        if (text.charAt(offset) == " ")
            // skip the current character
            offset++
        // assign the up-to-date to-be-displayed substring
        // second argument of method accepts index of last char plus one
        var partialMessage = text.substring(0, offset + 1)
        // display partial message in status bar
        window.status = partialMessage
        // increment index of last character to be displayed
        offset++
        // recursive call after specified time
        timerID = setTimeout("showBanner()", speed)
        // banner is running
        bannerRunning = true
    } else
    {
        // reset offset
        offset = 0
        // increment subscript (index) of current message
```

```
        currentMessage++
        // if subscript of current message is out of range
        if (currentMessage == ar.length)
           // wrap around (start from beginning)
           currentMessage = 0
        // recursive call after specified time
        timerID = setTimeout("showBanner()", pause)
        // banner is running
        bannerRunning = true
    }
}
```

The current message is assigned to the local variable `text`. The function then continues in one of two directions. The first is selected if the current message is still being displayed; that is, if the index of the last character that was displayed of the current message is the last character or less. In that case, the expression `offset < text.length` evaluates to true. If the last character to be displayed during this pass through the function is a space, the value of `offset` is incremented, and no time is wasted on typing the space character. The substring that needs to be displayed during the current iteration is assigned to the local variable `partialMessage`. Since the second argument of the `substring` method is the index of the last character plus one, it is set to `offset + 1`. The current substring is displayed in the status bar, and the value of `offset` is incremented. The function is called once more after `speed` milliseconds.

When the end of the current message has been reached, another execution path is taken. In this case, the variable `offset` is assigned zero, the index of the first character of a string. To allow posting of the next message in the array, the index of the array element holding the current message is incremented. If the new value of `currentMessage` is out of range, it is set to zero, so the following message is the first one. The function is called recursively after `pause` milliseconds. This time the function should take the first route, because the message is only at its beginning.

Event Handlers

The `startBanner` function is called by the `onLoad` event handler when the document has finished loading.

R-banner

While T stands for "typewriter," R stands for "random," denoting the flavor of this special banner. The messages appear by popping up various characters of the message in a random order. Another special effect involved in this banner is the scrolling motion from right to left. This effect is achieved by simply letting each character that pops up take a three-character space. Take a look at the script:

```
<HTML>
<HEAD>
<TITLE>R-banner</TITLE>
<SCRIPT LANGUAGE = "JavaScript">
<!--
// set speed of banner (pause in milliseconds between addition of new character)
var speed = 10 // decrease value to increase speed (must be positive)
// set pause between completion of message and beginning of following one
var pause = 1500 // increase value to increase pause
// set initial values
var timerID = null
var bannerRunning = false
// create array
var ar = new Array()
// assign the strings to the array's elements
ar[0] = "Welcome to my JavaScript page"
ar[1] = "I hope you enjoy the R-banner script"
ar[2] = "It is pretty cool"
ar[3] = "Don't forget to check out my other scripts"
// assign index of current message
var message = 0
// empty string initialization
var state = ""
// no value is currently being displayed
clearState()
// stop the banner if it is currently running
function stopBanner()
   // if banner is currently running
   if (bannerRunning)
      // stop the banner
      clearTimeout(timerID)
   // banner is now stopped
   bannerRunning = false
}
// start the banner
function startBanner()
{
   // make sure the banner is stopped
   stopBanner()
   // start the banner from the current position
   showBanner()
}
// assign state a string of "0" characters of the length of the current message
function clearState()
{
   // initialize to empty string
   state = ""
   // create string of same length containing 0 digits
   for (var i = 0; i < ar[message].length; ++i)
{
      state += "0"
   }
}
// display the current message
```

```
function showBanner()
{
   // if the current message is done
   if (getString())
   {
      // increment message
      message++
      // if new message is out of range wrap around to first message
      if (ar.length <= message)
         message = 0
      // new message is first displayed as empty string
      clearState()
      // display next character after pause milliseconds
      timerID = setTimeout("showBanner()", pause)
      // banner is now running
      bannerRunning = true
   } else
   {
      // initialize to empty string
      var str = ""
      // build string to be displayed (only characters selected thus far
      // are displayed)
      for (var j = 0; j < state.length; ++j)
      {
         str += (state.charAt(j) == "1") ? ar[message].charAt(j) : "     "
      }
      // partial string is placed in status bar
      window.status = str
      // add another character after speed milliseconds
      timerID = setTimeout("showBanner()", speed)
      // banner is now running
      bannerRunning = true
   }
}
function getString()
{
   // set variable to true (it will stay true unless proven otherwise)
   var full = true
   // set variable to false if a free space is found in string (a
   // not-displayed char)
   for (var j = 0; j < state.length; ++j)
   {
      // if character at index j of current message has not been
      // placed in displayed string
      if (state.charAt(j) == 0)
         full = false
   }
   // return true immediately if no space found (avoid infinite loop later)
   if (full)
   return true
   // search for random until free space found (broken up via break statement)
   while (1)
   {
      // a random number (between 0 and state.length - 1 == message.length - 1)
```

```
        var num = getRandom(ar[message].length)
        // if free space found, break infinite loop
        if (state.charAt(num) == "0")
            break
    }
    // replace the 0 character with 1 character at place found
    state = state.substring(0, num) + "1" + state.substring(num + 1,state.length)
    // return false because the string was not full (free space was found)
    return false
}
function getRandom(max)
{
    return Math.round((max - 1) * Math.random())
}
// -->
</SCRIPT>
</HEAD>
<BODY onLoad = "startBanner()">
</BODY>
</HTML>
```

Example 15-5 (ex15-5.htm). *An R-banner*

Global Statements

```
// set speed of banner (pause in milliseconds between addition of new character)
var speed = 10 // decrease value to increase speed (must be positive)
// set pause between completion of message and beginning of following one
var pause = 1500 // increase value to increase pause
// set initial values
var timerID = null
var bannerRunning = false
// create array
var ar = new Array()
// assign the strings to the array's elements
ar[0] = "Welcome to my JavaScript page"
ar[1] = "I hope you enjoy the R-banner script"
ar[2] = "It is pretty cool"
ar[3] = "Don't forget to check out my other scripts"
// assign index of current message
var message = 0
// empty string initialization
var state = ""
// no value is currently being displayed
```

clearState()

First, the number 10 is assigned to the variable `speed`, representing the pause in milliseconds between the popping up of two consecutive characters in the current message. A longer pause is assigned to the variable `pause`, representing the number of milliseconds between the completion of the current message and its deletion. A null value is assigned to the global variable `timerID` and the Boolean value false is assigned to the variable `bannerRunning`. Predefined messages are stored in an array. The variable message is assigned zero, the index of the first element of the array to be displayed, ar[0].

The second section of the global statement section consists of only two statements, but they are important for understanding the entire script. The first statement in this section assigns an empty string to the global variable state. The clearState() function is called next. It modifies the value of the global variable state, by assigning it *n* "0" characters, where *n* is the length of the current message. The variable state is basically constructed of 0s and 1s. Suppose the first character is a 0. That means that the first character of the current message has not been popped up yet. The same applies to the second character and all the following ones. Therefore, the string starts off at all 0s, and the message is finished when all characters are 1s.

stopBanner()

See the explanation of this function in the T-banner section.

startBanner()

See the explanation of this function in the T-banner section.

clearState()

See the "Global Statements" section above for information regarding this function.

getRandom(max)

This simply returns an integer between 0 and max – 1. (See the explanation of Math.random() in Chapter 11.)

getString()

```
function getString()
{
   // set variable to true (it will stay true unless proven otherwise)
   var full = true
   // set variable to false if a free space is found in string (a
   // not-displayed char)
   for (var j = 0; j < state.length; ++j)
   {
      // if character at index j of current message has not been
      // placed displayed string
      if (state.charAt(j) == 0)
         full = false
   }
   // return true immediately if no space found (avoid infinite loop later)
   if (full)
      return true
   // search for random until free space found (broken up via break statement)
   while (1)
   {
      // a random number (between 0 and state.length - 1 == message.length - 1)
      var num = getRandom(ar[message].length)
```

```
        // if free space found, break infinite loop
        if (state.charAt(num) == "0")
            break
    }
    // replace the 0 character with 1 character at place found
    state = state.substring(0, num) + "1" + state.substring(num + 1,
            state.length)
    // return false because the string was not full (free space was found)
    return false
}
```

First, the variable `full` is initialized to true. An infinite loop (terminated by the `break` statement) is employed to go over all 0 and 1 characters of the `state` string. If a 0 character is found, the variable `full` is changed to false. It is not mandatory to break up the loop (as done above in `getString()`) when a free space, or 0, is found, because efficiency is not a concern in a random banner.

The remaining part of the function is executed only if a free space is available.

An infinite loop generates a new random index every iteration and checks if the space at that index is taken up. The loop continues to execute as long as the space at the random index is taken up. When a free space is finally found, the loop breaks up, returning the index `num` of the free space.

The value of `state` is updated by replacing the 0 character at index `num` with a 1 character. The function returns false upon termination, indicating that the message was not completed.

showBanner()

Like in the T-banner script, this is the main function. The function `getString()` is called to update the value of `state` and to check if the message has been completed. If it has, the current message is updated to the following one by incrementing the value of `message`, representing the index of the array's element where the current message is. If the new value is out of range, it is reset to the initial zero value. The function `clearState()` is called to set up the variable `state`, as explained above in the "Global Statements" section. The function is then called recursively after `pause` milliseconds.

In an ordinary case in which the message is not complete yet, the special display effects are generated. An empty string is assigned to the local variable `str`, ready to accumulate characters for display. A `for` loop iterates through the characters of the string `ar[message]`. If there is a 1 at the same index of the string `state`, the character from `ar[message]` is appended to the end of `str`. An alternative string is appended if a 0 character is found in the string `state`. The only way to create a right-to-left scrolling effect is to use a fairly long alternative string of a few spaces. Since a space has a very small horizontal span (characters are not uniform in width), a single-space alternative string will create a friendly left-to-right movement! Using an empty alternative string squeezes the string and creates a different right-to-left movement. The built-up string is placed in the status bar, and the function is called recursively after a pause of `speed` milliseconds.

Event Handlers

When the document is completely loaded, the `startBanner()` function is called by the `onLoad` event handler.

N-banner

The N-banner (for "normal") scrolls from right to left in the status bar. You have probably seen hundreds of these banners on the web. Here is a script to implement such a banner:

```
<HTML>
<HEAD>
<TITLE>N-banner</TITLE>
<SCRIPT LANGUAGE = "JavaScript">
<!--
function scrollBanner(seed)
{
   // set pause in milliseconds between each movement
   var speed = 10
   // assign one-space string to variable (space pads left side of status bar)
   var str = " "
   // create global array
   var ar = new Array()
   // assign the strings to the array's elements
   ar[0] = "Welcome to my JavaScript page. "
   ar[1] = "I hope you enjoy the N-banner script. "
   ar[2] = "It is kind of cool. "
   ar[3] = "Don't forget to check out my other scripts. "
   // join all messages to one string variable with no delimiter
   var total = ar.join("")
   // if message has not yet reached the left side of the status bar
   if (seed > 0)
   {
      // assign string of seed spaces to variable
      for (var i = 0; i < seed; ++i)
      {
         str += " "
      }
      // append message to end of output string
      str += total
      // message moved one position to the left
      seed--
      // assign expression containing recursive call with literal
      // argument in form of string
      var cmd = "scrollBanner(" + seed + ")"
      // place computed message in status bar
      window.status = str
```

```
            // recursive call after speed milliseconds
        timerID = setTimeout(cmd, speed)
    } else
        // if a substring of the total message still remains in status bar
        if (-seed < total.length)
        {
            // assign part of message that has not slid off the left
            str += total.substring(-seed, total.length)
            // message has moved one position to the left seed--
            // assign expression containing recursive call with
            // literal argument in form of string
            var cmd = "scrollBanner(" + seed + ")"
            // place computed message in status bar
            window.status = str
            // recursive call after speed milliseconds
            timerID = setTimeout(cmd, speed)
        } else
        {
            // assign a one-space string to status bar
            window.status = str
            // recursive call after speed milliseconds at initial position
            timerID = setTimeout("scrollBanner(100)", speed)
        }
}
// -->
</SCRIPT>
</HEAD>
<BODY onLoad = "scrollBanner(100)">
</BODY>
</HTML>
```

Example 15-6 (ex15-6.htm). *An N-banner*

A major advantage of this banner is that it does not include any global statements and has only one function.

scrollBanner(seed)

The banner's speed and messages are specified as in the previous banners. A single-space string is assigned to the variable `str`. It pads the left side of the status bar by leaving a space between the border and the far-left side of the message. Since this banner scrolls the messages one after the other, all messages are combined to a single string via the `join()` method of the `Array` object.

The function accepts one argument, which is assigned to the parameter `seed`. The value of `seed` determines the message's distance from the left side of the status bar. Space characters are used as spaceholders. It is common to start the banner 100 spaces from the left, so the function is initially called with the value of 100.

The function chooses one of three routes. The first is selected if the value of seed is positive; that is, if the message has not reached the left panel of the status bar. In this case, a loop is used to concatenate a string of seed space characters to the variable str. The entire message is then concatenated to str. Note that if a string placed in the status bar exceeds the maximum length of the bar, the excess characters are not displayed. After concatenating the entire message to the accumulative string, the value of seed decrements, creating a scrolling effect on the next iteration. A recursive call is constructed in a string in the following form:

```
var cmd = "scrollBanner(" + seed + ")"
```

Suppose the value of seed is 50. The value of cmd is then "scrollBanner(50)". A literal is used here because local variables or parameters cannot be evaluated by setTimeout as arguments of a function. The accumulative string is then placed in the status bar, and the function is called recursively, following a pause of speed milliseconds.

The second route is taken if part of the message has been dropped to the left, but some of it still remains in the status bar. This state is checked via the following expression:

```
seed < total.length
```

If the absolute value of seed exceeds the message's length, this expression evaluates to false. It means that the length of the message that has gone out of range to the left is greater or equal to the length of the message, meaning that no part of the message actually remains in the status bar. If this expression evaluates to true, only part of the message has gone past the left barrier.

If the expression above evaluates to true, the substring total.substring(–seed, total.length) is concatenated to the variable str. This substring represents the part of the message that has not gone overboard (|seed| is equal to the number of characters disposed). The remaining part of the command block is identical to the one used when the first route of the function is taken.

The third route that can be taken by the function is the most simple one. It places the value of str, a single-space string, in the status bar. It then calls the function recursively with the initial argument of 100.

Summary

While Chapters 13 and 14 gave you a theoretical introduction to the Document Object Model, this chapter showed you practical ways to use one part of that model. Remember that the status bar is just a single property of the `document` object, and you saw in this chapter several ways to use that property. This should illustrate to you the sheer power of the Document Object Model.

In this chapter we saw how to display link-related messages in the status bar, as well as default values. We emphasized one of JavaScript's pioneer scripts, the banner. We discussed some unique banners developed exclusively for this book, as well as other common banners. In terms of JavaScript, we have discussed two properties of the `window` object: `status` and `defaultStatus`. Besides enabling fun stuff like banners, the status bar can be used as an additional output device for displaying critical values while debugging the script.

Chapter 16

URLs and JavaScript

A Crash Course in URLs

Web addresses, more technically known as URLs, are an important part of web development. Fortunately, JavaScript includes a number of properties and methods that can be used to manipulate these URLs. Before discussing JavaScript's support, a general description of URLs is in order.

URL is an acronym that stands for Uniform Resource Locator, a standard way to specify the location of an electronic resource. In short, it is a web address, such as http://www.wordware.com. The definition of a URL is derived from concepts introduced by the World Wide Web Global Information Initiative that have been in use since 1990. URLs make Internet resources available to different Internet protocols. When surfing the net, you often run into URLs in your browser's "location" box. Such URLs usually start with "http:", but other protocols such as FTP and Gopher are also supported. Even e-mail addresses can be specified as URLs.

A URL is a very convenient, succinct way to direct people and applications to a file or other electronic resource. If the web did not use URLs, then you would have to memorize the IP address of every web site you wish to visit. That would make the web almost too difficult to use.

General URL Syntax

In general, URLs are written as follows:

```
<scheme>:<scheme-specific-part>
```

A URL includes the name of the scheme being used, followed by a colon and a string. `scheme` refers to the protocol being used. Valid schemes include FTP (File Transfer Protocol) and HTTP (Hypertext Transfer Protocol). The characters supported as schemes are lowercase letters, "a" to "z", and the characters plus (+), period (.), and hyphen (-). Web browsers such as Internet Explorer and Mozilla Firefox treat uppercase letters as lowercase ones. For example, both HTTP and http are accepted. Examples of schemes are "http," "ftp," "gopher," and "news." The scheme instructs the application or person how to treat that specific resource.

Most schemes include two different types of information:

- The Internet machine where the resource resides
- The full path to that resource

Such schemes are usually separated from the machine address by two slashes (//), whereas the machine address is separated from the full path via only one slash (/). Therefore, the common format is:

`scheme://machine.domain/full-path-of-file`

As an exercise, let's take a look at a simple URL:

`http://www.chuckeasttom.com/index.htm`

The URL's scheme is `http`, for the Hypertext Transfer Protocol. The Internet address of the machine is `www.chuckeasttom.com`, and the path to the specific file is `/index.htm`. You will find that the path portion sometimes ends with a slash. This indicates that the path is pointing to a directory rather than a file. In this case, the server returns either a directory listing of all the files or a default file, if one is available. The default filename is either `index.htm` or `home.htm`, but other variants are also used.

The URL Schemes

The "scheme" of a URL is another way to say its protocol. As you probably already know, all network, and thus all Internet, communication is accomplished via protocols. A *protocol* is an agreed-upon standard for communicating a particular type of data.

Hypertext Transfer Protocol (HTTP)

HTTP is the Internet protocol specifically designed for use with the World Wide Web, and therefore is the one most often seen by web surfers. Its general syntax is:

`http://<host>:<port>/<path>?<searchpart>`

The *host* is the Internet address of the WWW server, such as `www.geocities.com`, and the *port* is the port number to connect to. In most cases the port can be omitted along with the colon delimiter, and it defaults to the standard "80." The *path* tells the server which file is requested. The *searchpart* is very important. It may be used to pass information on to the server. It can also be referenced by other languages, including JavaScript as you will soon find out. Another frequently used character is the pound sign (#). It is used for referencing a named anchor. Anchors are often used on web pages to enable linking from one section of the page to another.

File Transfer Protocol (FTP)

FTP is commonly used for distributing and transmitting files over the Internet. Its general syntax is:

```
ftp://<user>:<password>@<host>:<port>/<cwd1>/<cwd2>/.../
<cwdN>/<name>;type=<typecode>
```

When contacting a site providing anonymous login, the *user* and *password* may be omitted, including the separating colon and the following @ symbol. The *host* and *port* are exactly the same as in the HTTP URL specification. The <*cwd1*>/<*cwd2*>/.../<*cwdN*> refers to the series of "change directory" (cd in Unix) commands a client must use to move from the main directory to the directory in which the desired file resides. Since most servers use Unix operating systems, you can print the working (current) directory by typing pwd at the command line. The *name* is the desired file's full name, as it is recognized by the operating system. The portion ;type=<*typecode*> allows you to specify the transmission mode (ASCII vs. binary). Most systems are not configured to work properly with this trailing specification, and some are even misled by it.

Gopher Protocol (Gopher)

The Gopher protocol is not used very much these days, but was once a common way to get files from the Internet. Its syntax is very similar to HTTP's:

```
gopher://<host>:<port>/<gopher-path>
```

Electronic Mail (Mailto)

The Mailto URL scheme is different from the previous three schemes in that it does not identify the location of a file but rather someone's e-mail address. Its syntax differs widely as well:

```
mailto:<account@site>
```

The *account@site* is the Internet e-mail address of the person you wish to mail to. Most WWW browsers, including the leaders, Navigator and Internet Explorer, support this scheme when encoded in an HTML document.

Usenet News (News)

The News URL scheme allows you to refer to Usenet newsgroups or specific articles in such a newsgroup. The syntax is either one of the following:

```
news:<newsgroup-name>
news:<message-id>
```

The *newsgroup-name* is the Usenet's newsgroup name (e.g., comp.lang.javascript) from which all title articles will be retrieved by the browser (a maximum number may be specified in the browser setup). *message-id* corresponds to the message-ID of a specific article to obtain. It is found in the article's header information.

Today, most people who read Usenet newsgroups do so through a web interface such as groups.google.com.

Host-Specific Filenames (File)

The File URL scheme indicates a file that can be obtained by the client machine. The syntax for the File scheme is:

```
file://<host>:<path>
```

The *host* is the fully qualified domain name of the system, and the *path* is the hierarchical directory path to the required file. Leave *host* empty or specify `localhost` to refer to the client's local files.

JavaScript Statements (javascript)

The JavaScript URL scheme is quite different. Its general syntax is:

```
javascript:<valid-javascript-statement-expression-command>
```

This scheme evaluates the expression after the colon. If the expression can be evaluated to a string, a new page is opened and the string displayed. If the expression is undefined, a new page does not open.

Other Schemes

There are several other schemes that are far beyond the scope of this book. Bear in mind that we are dealing with JavaScript, so we only focus on schemes that might be needed in a script. For most of your web development you will work with http and ftp, so the others are simply not that important to you in JavaScript.

The location Object

As you may have guessed, the `location` object is part of the Document Object Model. It is quite useful and, since it represents a complete URL, it is a property of the `window` object. As always, specifying the `window` object when referring to a property or a method of location is optional. Each property of the `location` object represents a different portion of the URL. The following syntax of a URL shows the relationship between the object's properties:

```
protocol//hostname:port pathname search hash
```

The `location` object belongs to the window containing the JavaScript script. Single-frame pages have only one `location` object. However, pages that use multiple frames consist of a `window.location (location)` object for each frame, as well as one for the main frameset document. For example, a page with two frames consists of three URLs, and a `location` object is available for each.

Because `window` is a default object in scripts, you can use `location` rather than `window.location`. However, if you use this object to specify an event handler script, you must specify the full `window.location`. Due to the scoping of static HTML objects in JavaScript, a call to `location` without specifying an object name is equivalent to `document.location`, which is currently a synonym for `document.URL`. You should avoid `document.location` because it will not be supported in the future.

location Properties

The `location` object, like any other object, consists of both properties and methods. The methods were added back in Navigator version 3.0. That means you are very unlikely to encounter a browser that does not support the methods of the `location` object. In this section we take a look at the object's properties, basing the discussion on an earlier section, "A Crash Course in URLs."

href

The `href` property is the most popular one in HTML scripting. The identifier HREF stands for "hypertext reference." This property supplies a string of the entire URL of the calling `window` object. This property is for both reading and setting. By assigning a string to this property, you can change the URL of the page in the window. For example, if you want to load Wordware's home page when the user clicks a button, you can use the following syntax:

```
<HTML>
<SCRIPT LANGUAGE="JavaScript">
<!--
function load()
{
   location.href = 'http://www.wordware.com'
}
// -->
</SCRIPT>
<FORM>
<INPUT TYPE="button" VALUE=" load page " onClick="load()">
</FORM>
</HTML>
```

Example 16-1 (ex16-1.htm). *Script that loads Wordware's home page when button is clicked*

The output of this script can be seen in Figure 16-1.

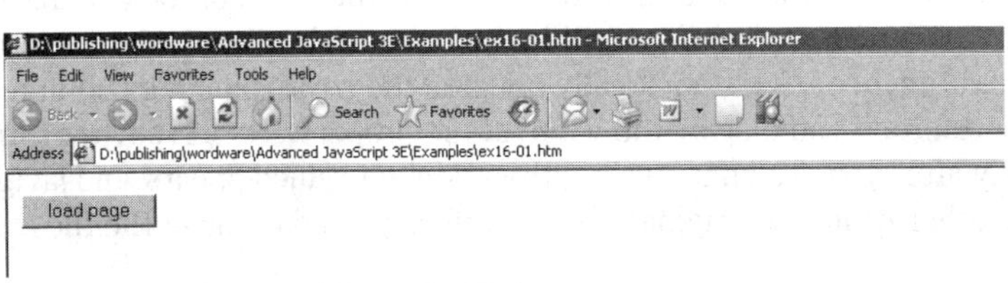

Figure 16-1. *Output of Example 16-1*

You can also retrieve the full URL of the current window (the current `window` object to be exact) by reading the URL value. For example, if you want the full URL of the current file, not including the filename itself, you can use the following script segment:

```
var url = location.href
var lastSlash = url.lastIndexOf("/")
var partialURL = url.substring(0, lastSlash + 1)
```

Take a look at the following script:

```
var location = "Ben"
```

This statement does not generate any error because "location" is not a reserved word. However, it deletes the `location` object inside the function in which `location` is assigned. Since `location` is not a browser object but rather a simple variable, it is fully accessible from outside the function.

Microsoft Internet Explorer and Netscape Navigator deal differently with the `location.href` property, and with the `location` object in general. The following code segment shows the difference:

```
<HTML>
<HEAD>
<TITLE>location test</TITLE>
</HEAD>
<SCRIPT LANGUAGE="JavaScript">
<!--
function load()
{
   location.href = "http://www.microsoft.com"
   alert(location.href)
}
// -->
</SCRIPT>
<BODY onLoad="load()">
</BODY>
</HTML>
```

Suppose this file is located at `http://www.geocities.com`. When Netscape Navigator loads a page, it holds the loaded URL in a cell somewhere in memory. Only when another page has begun loading (data is being transferred) is the value of that cell modified to match the new URL. When you read the value of `location.href`, you are reading the value of that cell. However, when you assign it a string representing another URL, the value held in that cell does not change immediately. Only if and when the page at the specified URL is found on the server is the value of the cell updated. Microsoft's browser differs in this case. When the user assigns a string to `location.href`, it automatically updates the corresponding cell in memory. Therefore, if you display the value of the property `location.href` immediately after you assign it a value, the assigned value appears. In Navigator, on the other hand, the original URL is still displayed because the file at the new

URL has not been found yet. Let's sum things up. The displayed value of the preceding script on each of the leading browsers is as follows:

- Netscape Navigator—`http://www.geocities.com`
- Microsoft Internet Explorer—`http://www.microsoft.com`

Depending on your browser, the value of `location.href` may be encoded with ASCII equivalents of nonalphanumeric characters. Such characters appear as a percent sign (%) followed by the ASCII code of that character. The most commonly encoded character is the space, `%20`. You can run such URLs under the `unescape()` function to convert them to ISO Latin-1 format.

Suppose you have an HTML file named `foo.html` located in a certain directory or folder. Loading the full path of this directory in the browser should normally show the listing of all the directory's files, provided that a default filename supported by the server is not included in that directory. You can use the following script to allow the user to view the listing of the files just by clicking a button:

```
<HTML>
<HEAD>
<TITLE>Directory listing</TITLE>
</HEAD>
<SCRIPT LANGUAGE="JavaScript">
<!--
function getListing()
{
   var url = location.href
   var lastSlash = url.lastIndexOf("/")
   location.href = url.substring(0, lastSlash + 1)
}
// -->
</SCRIPT>
<BODY>
<FORM>
<INPUT TYPE="button" VALUE=" view directory listing " onClick="getListing()">
</FORM>
</BODY>
</HTML>
```

Example 16-2 (ex16-2.htm). *Script that displays a list of files with a button click*

You can see what this web page would look like in Figure 16-2.

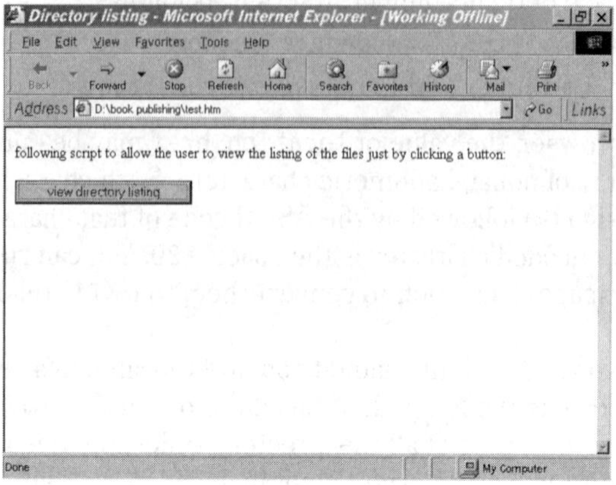

Figure 16-2. *Directory listing example*

hash

An anchor is a mark for other data to point to. It enables you to create a link to a specific place somewhere in a given web page. Suppose you have a web page that provides information on various DVD player models of different brands. A user who is looking for specific information on Sony DVD players should not have to scroll through other makes such as JVC. Therefore, you can create a named anchor somewhere near the name Sony. An anchor is created using the following syntax:

```
<A NAME="sony1">Sony DVD players</A>
```

The text “Sony DVD players” appears on the page as normal, but it serves as an anchor. You can direct the user to the “Sony DVD players” section via a simple link to the anchor, in the following fashion:

```
<A HREF="#sony1">Get information on Sony DVD players</A>
```

In this case, the link’s URL is the anchor’s name preceded by a hash mark (#). When the user clicks on the link “Get information on Sony DVD players,” the browser automatically “scrolls” down to the anchor named “sony1” (you can’t see the scrolling, of course). You can also direct the user to that anchor from within another page. For example, suppose the full URL of the DVD player page is `http://www.dvdplayer.com/information/index.html`. Now, let’s say you want to provide a link from the page `http://www.electronics.com/dvdplayerlinks/new.html` to the page containing information on DVD players, and, in particular, to the Sony section. You can accomplish this task by including the URL of the DVD player file, as well as the Sony anchor name, somewhere in the electronics file:

```
<A HREF=" http://www.dvdplayer.com/information/index.html#sony1">Get
        information on Sony DVD players</A>
```

This form enables you to specify the document URL as well as the specific anchor name. By specifying only the anchor name, it is assumed that the anchor resides in the current document, just as if you specify a filename without a full path, it is assumed to reside in the same directory as the HTML document. Such URL references are known as *relative* or *partial*.

When you click on a link to a URL containing a named anchor reference, the new URL, or location, consists of the hash mark (#) followed by the anchor name. This portion of the URL is considered a part of the URL, just like the path or filename. After linking to an anchor, user-initiated scrolling does not affect the URL (or the `location.href` value).

JavaScript provides a property for the current anchor reference in the URL. This property is named `hash (location.hash)`, because anchor references are stored in a hash table. You can assign a string to `location.hash` in order to direct the browser to a specified anchor within the current page. Like the `href` property, `hash` is also readable. You should use this property only when dealing with local anchors residing within the current document. Suppose the following document is saved as an .html file on a server or on your computer:

```
<HTML>
<HEAD>
<TITLE>status bar</TITLE>
<SCRIPT LANGUAGE="JavaScript">
<!--
function loadPage()
{
   location.href = "http://www.chuckeasttom.com/index.htm"
   location.hash = "authors"
}
// -->
</SCRIPT>
</HEAD>
<BODY onLoad="loadPage()">
</BODY>
</HTML>
```

The function `loadPage()` (called via the `onLoad` event handler) attempts to load the page `http://www.chuckeasttom.com/index.htm`. Since the browser does not wait until the page is loaded, the function continues to execute, advancing to the following statement. However, this statement also attempts to modify the URL of the page by specifying an anchor, via the `location.hash` property. Since the anchor resides on the current page, it is loaded immediately. By trying to allocate an anchor, the `onLoad` event handler is triggered, executing the function once again. The encountered loop is obviously infinite, and continues until the user presses the big red Stop button. It is very important to remember not to assign `location.hash` separately from `location.href`. You must assign them in the same statement:

```
function loadPage()
{
   location.href = " http://www.chuckeasttom.com/index.htm #certifications"
}
```

Rather than attempt to modify multiple properties of `href`, you should assign the property `href`, as it refers to a complete URL, including anchor references, search specifications, and all other properties of the `location` object. In general, the `location.hash` property is the only one that can be assigned separately to adjust the current anchor referencing position within the current document. Also, bear in mind that a page reload will follow the property assignment.

A common problem for beginners is that the value of the `hash` property seems to be inconsistent at times. For example, `location.hash` evaluates to an empty string if no anchor is referenced. If an anchor is specified, though, both the hash mark (#) and the anchor name are part of this property. When changing the value of an anchor, do not include the hash mark.

The following HTML document will clear up this matter:

```
<HTML>
<HEAD>
<TITLE>location.hash property</TITLE>
<SCRIPT LANGUAGE="JavaScript">
<!--
function goNext(nextAnchor)
{
   location.hash = nextAnchor
}
// -->
</SCRIPT>
</HEAD>
<BODY>
<A NAME="anchor1">Top</A>
<BR>
<FORM>
<INPUT TYPE="button" VALUE="advance" onClick="goNext('anchor2')">
</FORM>
<BR>
<HR>
<BR>
<A NAME="anchor2">Middle</A>
<BR>
<FORM>
<INPUT TYPE="button" VALUE="advance" onClick="goNext('anchor3')">
</FORM>
<BR>
<HR>
<BR>
<A NAME="anchor3">Bottom</A>
<BR>
<FORM>
```

```
<INPUT TYPE="button" VALUE="advance" onClick="goNext('anchor1')">
</FORM>
</BODY>
</HTML>
```

Example 16-3 (ex16-3.htm). *A script that jumps to anchors without using common links*

In order to observe the effect of the script in Example 16-3, you must resize the browser window to make it smaller than the full document (the scroll bar should appear), because referencing a named anchor has no effect if the anchor is already in view. By clicking each of the four buttons on the page, the focus is placed on a corresponding anchor and on a different button. Clicking the fourth button scrolls the page to the first anchor and to the beginning of the page. Since HTML does not support linking form buttons to anchors, you must use JavaScript to accomplish such a task.

host

The `location.host` property is not commonly used, but we shall cover it for completeness. This property represents the *<host>*:*<port>* part of a URL, not just the *<host>* (see `location.hostname`). When the scheme is `file` and the file is local, this property is an empty string. When no port is specified, the value of `location.host` is equal to `location.hostname`, or *<host>*. Suppose the complete URL of a page is `http://www.geocities.com:80/SiliconValley/9000/index.html`. The value of `location.host`, if queried on that page, is `www.geocities.com:80`. This value is always equal to the expression `location.hostname + ":" + location.port`. The colon is included only when a port is explicitly specified. The basic rule is that if the browser's "location" box does not include the port, it is not part of the `location.host` string.

Since 80 is considered the default port, the following function displays the full *<host>*:*<port>* portion of the URL:

```
function alertHost()
{
   var colonIndex = location.host.lastIndexOf(":")
   var port = (colonIndex == -1) ? ":80" : ""
   alert("The complete host specification is: " + location.host + port)
}
```

If you call this function from the page `http://www.chuckeasttom.com/index.htm`, the value displayed in the alert box is `www.geocities.com:80`. The same value is displayed if the page is loaded directly via the full host specification: `http://www.chuckeasttom.com/index.htm`.

hostname

The `location.hostname` property is almost identical to `location.host`, except that it does not include the port number if specified in the URL. That is, it consists of only the `<host>` portion of the complete URL (see the section "A Crash Course in URLs"). The `location.hostname` is simply the Internet address of the hosting machine. This property evaluates to `www.geocities.com` on the following two URLs:

```
http://www.chuckeasttom.com/index.htm
http://www.80/~chuckeasttom.com/index.htm
```

pathname

The pathname component of the URL consists of a directory structure, relative to the hosting server's root volume. In terms of http, this is the *<path>* portion of the URL. If the file is located in the root directory of the server, the `pathname` property evaluates to a single slash (/), followed by the complete filename. The `pathname` property always includes the name of the file where the script is located. This property returns a nonstandard value in Internet Explorer. When the file is on the client's computer, backslashes are used in place of slashes to separate directory names in the path.

For example, if the complete URL of the hosting document is `http://www.chuckeasttom.com/index.htm`, the value of `location.pathname` is `/~chuckeasttom.com/index.htm`.

port

As expected, the `location.port` property holds the port number, or the *<port>* portion of the general URL syntax. These days, few web sites require an explicit specification of the port number as part of their URL. When a port is not specified, it defaults to the standard 80, which is not part of the `location.port` property. If you intend to construct a URL from the values of the `port` and `hostname` properties, remember to separate them with a colon.

protocol

The protocol component of a URL is more commonly known as the scheme (*<scheme>*). The `location.protocol` property holds the scheme component of the document's URL, followed by a colon. The scheme component should normally be `http:`, but other schemes are also supported. For more information on the most popular schemes, see the section "A Crash Course in URLs" at the beginning of this chapter.

You can display the `mocha:` or `javascript:` protocols by loading one of them as the URL of the document and then typing `alert(location.protocol)`. You can also try loading the following strings as URLs instead:

- `javascript:alert(location.protocol)`
- `mocha:alert(location.protocol)`

search

When you submit a form, you sometimes find that the URL of the retrieved document is followed by a question mark (?) and an encoded string. For example, a typical search in Yahoo! looks like `http://search.yahoo.com/bin/search?p=perl+book&a=n`. The value of `location.search` is precisely that, including the question mark. Each part of the search specification (`?p=perl+book&a=n`) is usually delimited by an ampersand (&), as seen in the above string. Nonalphanumeric characters are encoded and replaced by their corresponding two-digit ASCII code, preceded by a percent sign (%). If text fields or text areas consist of space characters, then they are replaced by plus operators (+). The string following the question mark is known as the *search query,* although it does not serve as a query submitted to a search engine.

Although the usefulness of the `location.search` property may not be apparent, it is truly one of the most important properties supported by JavaScript. The reason for its importance is that you can use it for many purposes that are not related to CGI scripts or search engines.

First of all, remember that if a search query is specified (including the question mark), the URL of the page is actually the string preceding the query. For example, you can load Intel's home page via the URL `http://www.intel.com/index.htm?Intel+home+page` rather than the standard URL for that page, `http://www.intel.com/index.htm`. Since Intel's page does not use any search queries, a query specification is extraneous. You can load every page on the web by entering its regular URL followed by any search query. This feature enables the usage of search queries in JavaScript. For example, you can prompt the user for his or her name, and pass it on to all other pages on your site as a search query. Along with cookies (explained in Chapter 20, "Implementing Cookies"), the `location.search` property serves as a way to store permanent data acquired from an outside resource. The following example consists of two pages—page1.html and page2.html:

```
<HTML>
<HEAD>
<TITLE>User first name input</TITLE>
</HEAD>
<BODY>
<SCRIPT LANGUAGE="JavaScript">
<!--
var usernm = prompt("Enter your first name:", "")
location.href = "page2.html?" + usernm
// -->
</SCRIPT>
</BODY>
</HTML>
```

page1.html

```
<HTML>
<HEAD>
<TITLE>User first name output</TITLE>
</HEAD>
<BODY>
<SCRIPT LANGUAGE="JavaScript">
<!--
function getQuery()
{
   var query = location.search.substring(1, location.search.length)
   return query
}
alert("I know your name -- " + getQuery())
// -->
</SCRIPT>
</BODY>
</HTML>
```

page2.html

The script for page1.html prompts the user for his or her first name, and then, using a search query preceded by a question mark, loads page2.html with the input first name. The script for page2.html calls a function that strips off the question mark, returns the bare query, and then displays the user's first name. The `location.search` property serves as a convenient way to pass small pieces of information between documents, as shown in this example.

Example 16-4 demonstrates the use of this property in a more complex script:

```
<HTML>
<HEAD>
<TITLE>Matches game</TITLE>
</HEAD>
<BODY>
<SCRIPT LANGUAGE="JavaScript">
<!--
// return the current search query excluding question mark
function stripQuery()
{
   // assign value of location.search and length to local variables
   var search = location.search
   var length = search.length
   // if no query specified
   if (search == "")
      // return number of matches at beginning of game
      return "25"
   // strip question mark off string
   var query = search.substring(1, length)
   // return the stripped-off query
   return query
}
```

```
// print the desired row of match images
function placeMatches(num)
{
   // place num matches via loop
   for (var i = 1; i <= num; ++i)
   {
      document.write('<A HREF="' + getURL(i, num) + '">
            <IMG SRC="match.gif" BORDER=0></A>')
   }
}
// return computed URL for match image link
function getURL(pos, num)
{
   // assign position of match in row from right
   var distance = num - pos + 1
   // e.g., 19th match among 20 in row, 20-19+1 = 2nd match from right
   // if the match is not one of the last three in row
   if (distance > 3)
      // link does not do anything
      return "javascript:alert('Choose one of last three matches')"
   // else not required because return statement terminates function
   // return number of matches needed in following load of page
   return "ex16-4.htm?" + (num - 4)
}
// number of matches to be displayed
var num = parseInt(stripQuery())
// assign instructions to variable
var instructions = ""
instructions += "The objective of the game is to force the other Player "
instructions += "(the computer) to pick up the last match. On each turn "
instructions += "you may pick up some matches, but only 1, 2, or 3. The "
instructions += "computer does the exact same on its turn. Play smart, "
instructions += "or else you will be devastated."
// if no query specified
if (num == 25)
   // display instructions
   alert(instructions)
// if only one match remains
if (num == 1)
{
   // print the match image and a link to enable a new game
   document.write('<IMG SRC="match.gif"><BR><BR><A HREF="ex16-4.htm">Play
            again?</A>')
   // tell the human he / she lost
   alert("I win -- come back when you improve!")
} else
   // impossible condition
   if (num < 1)
      // tell the user he / she cheated
      alert("You cheated!")
   else
      // place the required number of matches
      placeMatches(num)
```

```
// -->
</SCRIPT>
</BODY>
</HTML>
```

Example 16-4 (ex16-4.htm). *A simple game*

Let's explain the rules of the game in Example 16-4. The game starts when the user first loads the page and 25 matches are displayed in a row. The user must pick up one, two, or three matches by clicking on the corresponding match. For example, to pick up only one match, the user must click on the far-right match. Clicking on the second match from the right is equivalent to picking up two matches, and the same applies to three. After the user picks up some matches, the computer plays its turn, following the same rules as the user. The objective of the game is to force the other player to pick up the last match. That is, the one who picks up the last match loses the game.

This game was designed to prove that computers are smarter than humans, because you cannot win. The real reason that it is impossible to defeat the computer is that the user makes the first move. The number of matches selected by the computer is equal to four minus the number of matches selected by the user. For example, if the user picked up two matches, the computer also picks up two. If the user selected three matches, the computer goes with one. Finally, if the user selects one match, the computer selects three. Therefore, each dual move (user and computer sequence) ends up with four matches lifted. After six dual moves, 24 (4 * 6) matches have been removed, and only one remains. It is then the user's turn, which means that the computer records another victory.

The `stripQuery()` function is very simple; it returns the search query without the question mark. If no query is specified, then the user has not begun the game, and the returned string is defaulted to `25`.

The `placeMatches()` function is also very simple; it accepts the number of matches to be printed and uses a loop to print the corresponding number of `match.gif` images. Each image is also a hypertext link, where the specified URL is retrieved by the `getURL()` function, based on the index of the current match (a positive integer `i`) and the total number of matches that are placed (`num`).

The function `getURL()` accepts the index of a given match as well as the total number of matches to be placed. The match's index corresponding to the far-right match is assigned to the variable `distance`. For example, if there are 25 matches, and the value of `pos` is 23, the value assigned to `distance` is 25 – 23 + 1 = 3. If the assigned value is greater than 3, the data of the given match indicates that it is not one of the last three matches in the row, so the returned URL is a JavaScript `alert` statement (using the `javascript:` scheme, or protocol). The function is terminated if the given match is not one of the last three, so the remaining portion applies only to matches that are one of the last three in the row. In this case, the returned URL is the bare URL of the document with a search query equal to the remaining number of matches (the current number of matches minus four, because the computer always completes the user's move to four—see explanation of algorithm above).

The global statements are also a very important part of the script. At first, the query of the current page is converted from a numeric string to a number and then assigned to the variable `num`. If the value of `num` is 25, the game has just begun, and the instructions are displayed in the form of an alert box. If the value of `num` is 1, the game is over (the computer wins), and a corresponding message is displayed, followed by a link to restart the game by loading the current document without a query. If the value of `num` is less than 1, an impossible state has been encountered, meaning that the user has tried to cheat or override the script by modifying the search query and an alert box reports this finding. The game is currently underway for all other values of `num`, so the function `placeMatches()` is called to place the matches according to the given situation.

location Methods

The `location` object (`window.location`) also has several methods. They are supported by the latest Netscape and Microsoft browsers.

reload

The `location.reload` method forces a reload of the window's current document. Its general syntax is:

```
location.reload([true])
```

Specifying the Boolean value true as the method's optional argument forces an unconditional HTTP `get` of the document from the server. An unconditional `get` retrieves a document directly from the server, ignoring the content of the browser's cache, which might already contain the desired data from that document. Therefore, true should not be specified unless you have reason to believe that either disk or memory cache is broken, or the server has a new version of the document. If such a version is available, you must force an unconditional HTTP `get` because the version of the document stored in cache is different from the new version on the server. This situation is common to CGI-generated documents.

The `reload()` method simply reloads the document its URL stored in `location.href`. It uses the same policy as the Reload or Refresh button. Microsoft has opted to label the button "refresh" rather than "reload," but will probably keep the same method names. The exact reload policy depends on the cache handling menu option. In Netscape Navigator, the user sets the default value of this policy by choosing Network Preferences from the Options menu, and specifying Verify Documents on the Cache tab of the Preferences dialog box.

The `reload()` method does not force a transaction with the server under normal conditions. However, if the user has set the preference to "Every Time," the request is an unconditional `get` using an "if-modified-since" HTTP header. HTTP headers are passed to the browser when a document is retrieved from the server. It contains important information regarding the current document. If the user sets the preference to "Every Time," the browser checks the transmitted HTTP header to see if the document has been updated according to the "last-modified time" property. If it has, the document cannot be loaded from the cache that holds a previous version of the file. In short, `reload()` will bring the cache's version unless the user has specified "Every Time" and the document has changed on the server since the last time it was loaded and saved in the cache. Since its size is limited, the cache might lose a document version that has not been reloaded for a long time. In this case, the document needs to be fully loaded from the server, even if it has not been changed since the previous load.

In event handlers, you must specify `window.location.reload()` instead of simply using `location.reload()`. Due to the static objects' scoping in JavaScript, a call to `location` without specifying an object name is equivalent to a call to `document.location`, which is a synonym for `document.URL`. This concept is explained later in the chapter in greater detail.

You have probably experienced situations in which you leave your computer connected to a host and go out for a break, then come back to find that the connection has been dumped. The usual cause is that the host (server) has disconnected you because you have not transmitted any data via the server for a long time. You can overcome this problem by periodically reloading a JavaScript document from the server. Next time you go out for lunch, load the following document in the browser's window:

```
<HTML>
<HEAD>
<TITLE>stay connected</TITLE>
</HEAD>
<!-- 200000 milliseconds == 200 seconds -->
<BODY onLoad="timerID = setTimeout('window.location.reload(true)', 200000)">
</BODY>
</HTML>
```

Example 16-5 (ex16-5.htm). *A simple HTML document that keeps the connection alive*

The `onLoad` event handler is used to call the `reload()` method. A `setTimeout()` method delays the reload procedure for 200,000 milliseconds, or 200 seconds, from the moment the document is completely loaded. Since it is used in the form of an event handler, the `reload()` method must be fully specified, including the `window` object reference. The `true` argument forces the transaction with the server.

replace

The `replace()` method is also a property of the `location`, or `window.location`, object. It overwrites the current history entry with the specified URL. The current history entry is the most recent URL added to the history list or the URL of the previous page loaded. This is the URL that is retrieved when the user presses Back, provided that the Forward button is grayed out. The general syntax of the `replace()` method is as follows:

```
location.replace("URL")
```

After the `replace()` method is used, the user cannot navigate to the previous URL via the Back button. Once again, bear in mind that event handlers require a full method specification.

Suppose you want the user to load page B by clicking a link on page A. Instead of using a plain hypertext link, you can invoke this method to load page B (using the URL of page B as the argument). Once page B has loaded, the user cannot return to page A via the Back button.

Another Location—document.location (document.URL)

So far, any reference to the `location` object defaulted to `window.location`. But there is another `location` in JavaScript—`document.location`. To avoid confusion, Netscape decided to change `document.location` to `document.URL`.

The `document.URL` property holds the complete URL of the current document. In contrast to `window.location(.href)`, it is a read-only value. It does not know windows from frames; it only recognizes the document that contains the script and the reference to this property. Keep in mind that the URL belongs to the document, not to the window. Therefore, when a window consists of multiple documents including frame structures, a single frame's `document.URL` is different from `window.location(.href)`, from any other frame's `document.URL`, and from the main frameset's `document.URL`.

If you want to load a new document into the browser's window, you have to use the write-enabled `window.location (==window.location.href)`. If you want the URL of a specific frame, you should use `document.URL`. You can also use this property to retrieve the URL of the window if the document does not have frames and you are sure you do not want to change the URL (to load another page).

Since `document.location` is still in use (especially with Internet Explorer 3.0), you must be very careful when using the `location` property. If you are not a very experienced scripter or do not fully understand object scoping in JavaScript, it is a good practice to always specify the calling object, `window` or `document`. When you refer to `location` in a script, it defaults to `window.location`, because `window` is the default object inside scripts. However, when you specify the bare `location` in an event handler script, the calling object defaults to `document`; that is, `location` defaults to `document.location`.

Search Utilities

You may have noticed that multiengine search utilities are beginning to rule the web. For example, you can use one form to search Infoseek, AltaVista, and Yahoo!. There are basically two ways to create such search interfaces:

- Via server-side CGI scripts
- Via client-side JavaScript scripts

Since CGI is beyond the scope of this book, we are only going to discuss the second method. JavaScript is a very flexible cross-platform language. You can perform a specific task with many completely different scripts. For example, you can put a long script in your page to enable a multiengine search interface. You can also place a form in the page to submit the query to another page that contains the script. You can even call a function located in an external script to do the work.

You have probably been exposed to advanced HTML for quite a while, so you should know how forms are submitted. There are generally two submission methods:

- `get`
- `post`

The `get` method calls a specified file along with the content of the form's fields. The `ACTION` attribute specifies the name of the document or script to be called when the form is submitted. Take a look at the following form:

```
<FORM METHOD="get" ACTION="file1.html">
<INPUT TYPE="text" SIZE=50 NAME="userid">
<INPUT TYPE="text" SIZE=30 NAME="passwd">
<INPUT TYPE="submit" VALUE="submit form">
</FORM>
```

This construct creates a form with three elements. The first two are simple text boxes, or fields. The latter is a submit button, which triggers the submission. That is, when the user clicks the button, the form is submitted according to the `ACTION` of the `METHOD`. Suppose the user enters "input of first box" in the first field, and "input of second box" in the second field, and then clicks the Submit Form button. The form is submitted. In this case, the method is `get`, so the browser "gets" the specified file, `file1.html`. The file, including a search query, is retrieved. The full URL retrieved by the browser in this case is `file1.html?userid=input+of+first+box&passwd=input+of+second+box`. Notice that each value in the search query is separated by an ampersand. In addition, the value entered by the user in each field, or the element's value in general, is preceded by the element's name followed by an equal sign (=). The constructed URL is loaded, and the search query can be used if the loaded file is an HTML document with a JavaScript script. Now let's take a look at an actual example:

```
<HTML>
<HEAD>
```

```
<TITLE>Multiple engine search</TITLE>
</HEAD>
<BODY>
<FORM METHOD="get" ACTION="ex16-6b.htm">
   <STRONG><FONT SIZE=+1>Search</FONT> the Web for information about:</STRONG>
   <BR>
   <INPUT TYPE="text" SIZE=40 MAXLENGTH=80 VALUE="" NAME="query">
   <BR>
   <STRONG>via the </STRONG>
   <SELECT NAME="engine" ALIGN="right">
      <OPTION VALUE="altavista" SELECTED>AltaVista
      <OPTION VALUE="excite">Excite
      <OPTION VALUE="infoseek">Infoseek
      <OPTION VALUE="lycos">Lycos
      <OPTION VALUE="magellan">Magellan
      <OPTION VALUE="yahoo">Yahoo
   </SELECT>
   <STRONG>engine. Click </STRONG>
   <INPUT TYPE="submit" VALUE="search">
</FORM>
</BODY>
</HTML>
```

Example 16-6a (ex16-6a.htm). *The search interface can be added to any page.*

This form is a bit more complex than the previous one. It consists of two value-contributing elements, a field (text box) and a `SELECT` object, enabling the user to choose an option from a list. The value of the selected `OPTION` is the contributed value of the `SELECT` element. Take a look at Figure 16-3, which demonstrates a possible user input:

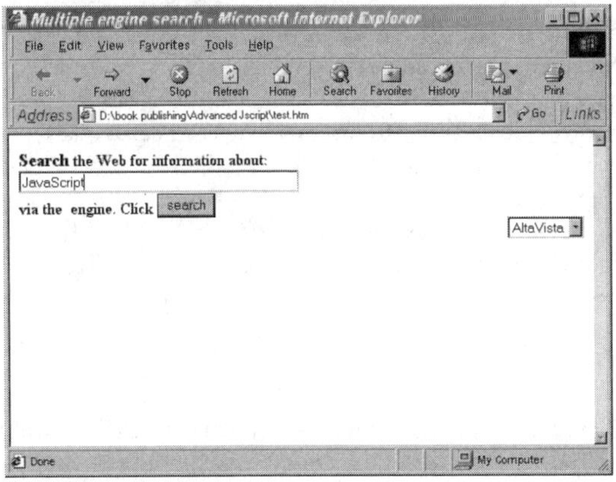

Figure 16-3. *Possible user input screen*

For the output demonstrated in Figure 16-3, the loaded URL is `ex16-6a.htm?query=JavaScript&engine=infoseek`. The name of the text box element is "query," which is the first substring of the loaded URL's search query. The value in this case is `JavaScript`, where all space characters are replaced by plus signs—this is the common encoding. The submitted form includes the SELECT object as well. Its name is engine and it follows the delimiting ampersand. Its value is the selected OPTION, infoseek. You now understand all the components of the retrieved URL, so we can go on to analyze the script itself.

```
<HTML>
<HEAD>
<TITLE>Please wait</TITLE>
<SCRIPT LANGUAGE="JavaScript">
<!--
// create object of all prefixes
var prefix = new prefixObject()
// create object of query prefixes
function prefixObject()
{
   // lycos prefix
   this.lycos = "http://www.lycos.com/cgi-bin/pursuit?query="
   // altavista prefix
   this.altavista = "http://www.altavista.digital.com/cgi-bin/query?pg=q&q="
   // infoseek prefix
   this.infoseek = "http://guide-p.infoseek.com//Titles?qt="
   // yahoo prefix
   this.yahoo = "http://av.yahoo.com/bin/search?p="
   // magellan prefix
   this.magellan = "http://searcher.mckinley.com/searcher.cgi?query="
   // excite prefix
   this.excite = "http://www.excite.com/search.gw?search="
}
// execute search
function callSearch()
{
   // create array to hold search engine and search query
   var queryArray = location.search.split("=")
   // assign search query
   var query = queryArray[1].substring(0, queryArray[1].indexOf("&"))
   // assign search engine
   var engine = queryArray[2]
   // load the desired page to display search results
   location.href = prefix[engine] + query
}
// -->
</SCRIPT>
</HEAD>
<BODY BGCOLOR="white" onLoad="timerID = setTimeout('callSearch()', 3000)">
<CENTER>
<BR>
<B>P<FONT SIZE=-1>LEASE </FONT>W<FONT SIZE=-1>AIT...</FONT></B>
<BR>
<BR>
Click the button to terminate search...
<FORM>
<INPUT TYPE="button" VALUE="terminate search" onClick="clearTimeout(timerID)">
</FORM>
```

```
</CENTER>
</BODY>
</HTML>
```

Example 16-6b (ex16-6b.htm). *The script that interprets the user's input and calls the appropriate search engine*

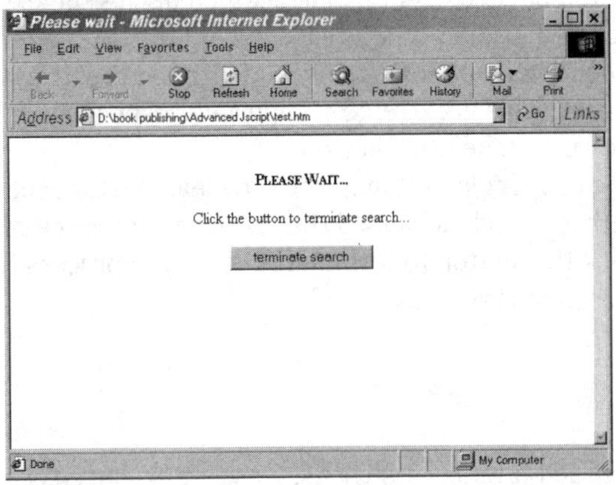

Figure 16-4. *Calling the appropriate search engine*

The script consists of only two functions. The first one, `prefixObject()`, is a constructor. It creates an object whose properties are the query prefixes for the supported search engines. A *query prefix* is the URL by which a query can be submitted to a search engine. The prefix is followed by the encoded inquiry (e.g., the user's keywords). For example, you can look up the keyword "JavaScript" in Infoseek by loading `http://guide-p.infoseek.com//Titles?qt=JavaScript`. Each search engine has its own unique prefix, so the prefix for each of the supported engines must be explicitly specified. The constructor function `prefixObject()` assigns each prefix to a property, named according to the search engine with which the prefix is associated. For example, Infoseek's prefix is assigned to a property named `infoseek` in the following fashion:

```
this.infoseek = "http://guide-p.infoseek.com//Titles?qt="
```

If you know the prefixes, you can easily extend the script to support additional search engines. It is not difficult to find such a prefix—just run a normal search on the desired engine and then extract the desired prefix. Since prefixes are sufficient for most engines, suffixes are only occasionally used. Search engines' prefixes are subject to change and should be maintained by the script owner (webmaster).

The global variable `prefix` is an instance of this object, so its properties are the search engines' prefixes.

The `callSearch()` function is also very simple. At first, it assigns the encoded user input (keywords) to the variable `query`. It also assigns the selected search engine to the variable `engine`. The expression `prefix[engine]` is equal to the selected search engine's prefix, because the values of the form's `OPTION`s (see Example 16-6a) are equivalent to the names of the properties used in this script. The expressions stored in `prefix[engine]` and `query` are combined to construct the full desired URL. The combined string is then loaded as the new URL via assignment to the `location.href` property.

You have probably noticed that the function is not called as an immediate script. It is called via the `onLoad` event handler, which delays the execution until the page has finished loading. In this case, a `setTimeout` statement is used to delay the execution another three seconds, giving the user a chance to terminate the process. This is extremely important, especially if the user is surfing in "reverse" using the Back button.

A form consisting of a single button is used to clear the timeout via the `clearTimeout()` method, which is handed the identifier of the initial timeout. The user can click this button to terminate the search process before the specified search engine is actually called.

Summary

In this chapter I discussed JavaScript's URLs. First, I introduced common URL terms, including the various supported schemes (http, ftp, gopher, etc.). I then presented the `window.location` object with all its properties and methods. The `href` property is used to link documents to each other. I have also discussed a URL-processing-based multiple-engine search utility and introduced another URL-related element, the `document.URL` property, also known as `document.location`. You should be mastering URL handling by now, because we will move on to more advanced URL-related concepts, such as frames, later in the book.

Chapter 17

The Document Object and the History List

The document Object

The `document` object is a property of the `window` object. Every `window` object, whether it is a full browser window, a frame, or a JavaScript-generated window, has a `document` property. This property is actually an object itself; you can think of it as a subobject of the `window` object. The `document` object encapsulates everything that exists in the content region of the browser's window or frame. It is the parent object of the web page's content, including links, anchors, colors, titles, and so forth. The `document` object's properties are spread over the entire HTML document. Some are commonly placed in the head portion, while others are normally found in the body portion. The `document` object does not consist of any event handlers. You might have thought that `onLoad`, `onUnload`, and `onError` belong to this object, but they are actually properties of the `window` object.

While it is common to use the `document` object to work with the HTML content, you should remember that not all of the `document` object's properties are HTML-driven content. For example, the `lastModified` property provides the date on which the document was last modified, even though this date is not provided explicitly in the document but rather in the document's unseen header.

The `document` object groups many content-related properties, such as text color, background color, and others. It also includes more complex properties that are actually objects, such as forms, links, and image maps.

The title Property

The document's title is set by default to its complete URL. Most web page authors replace this title with their own text, which is specified in the `<TITLE></TITLE>` tag pair in the head portion. The title, which usually appears in the title bar, also identifies the browser in the operating system's environment. When the web page includes frames, the title bar displays the title of the document that contains the frameset. Documents providing the content of the frames may include their own titles, but they don't affect the title bar.

The document's title can be scripted via JavaScript as well. Its general reference is `document.title`. If the document does not make up the main browser window, the reference must be preceded by the specific window to which the document belongs. The title of a frame document is also accessible via JavaScript by using the same procedure.

The `document.title` property cannot be set by just any JavaScript script, but only during construction of the entire document. You can use the `title` property in many different ways. Suppose you want your document to have a large header containing the document's title. Here is such a page's outline:

```
<HTML>
<HEAD>
<TITLE>Chuck's Home Page</TITLE>
</HEAD>
<BODY>
<SCRIPT LANGUAGE="JavaScript">
<!--
document.write("<CENTER><H1>" + document.title + "</H1></CENTER>")
// -->
</SCRIPT>
</BODY>
</HTML>
```

You can see the output of this script in Figure 17-1.

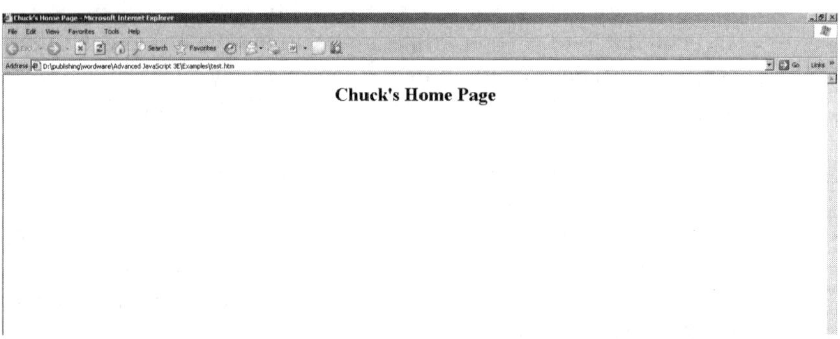

Figure 17-1. *The title property*

If you do not include the `<TITLE></TITLE>` tag pair, the title defaults to the complete URL of the document, including any search query if one is specified. If you place the `<TITLE></TITLE>` tag pair without text in between, the title still defaults to the URL. If the text between the opening and closing tags does not include any characters besides one or more space characters, the document is assumed untitled, and `document.title` remains an empty string, or a space-filled string in the case of Microsoft Internet Explorer. The property `document.title` never evaluates to the URL unless you specifically write the URL between the `<TITLE></TITLE>` tags.

Because the value of the title bar also identifies the browser application in the operating system environment, neither Netscape nor Microsoft have made it possible to explicitly modify it. Since it would not make any sense to identify an application as scrolling text, for example, the value of the title bar can be assigned only via the `document.title` property.

Colors

JavaScript supports several web page color properties, such as background colors and activated link colors. They are all constructed by the same method. There are generally two ways to construct color specifications:

- Netscape color names
- Hexadecimal triplets

The tendency among web page designers is to use Netscape color name specification, which is more intuitive and easier to maintain. For example, you can set the document's background color in the following fashion:

```
<BODY BGCOLOR="white">
```

Before Netscape and Microsoft implemented such color names, the only way to specify a color was via hexadecimal triplets. These are still supported, so you can set the background color to white, for instance, in the following way:

```
<BODY BGCOLOR="#ffffff">
```

Even though this method is not necessary any longer, you will still see it used frequently so it is a good idea to have a basic understanding of how it works. As you can see, the triplet is constructed of three two-digit hexadecimal numbers. They represent the red, green, and blue elements of the color descriptor. In total, there are approximately 17 million combinations, which is equal to the number of colors supported by a typical Macintosh or SVGA color display. However, Netscape uses a much more limited color cube. The cube consists of all the combinations of 00, 33, 66, 99, CC, and FF for each of the color descriptors. The result is 216 (6 * 6 * 6) distinct colors. The cube occasionally varies. On Macs, it includes the full 256-color palette. On Windows systems, if more than 40 (256 – 216) colors are already in use, the cube is minimized to only 125 (5 * 5 * 5) colors. For now, we will base our discussion on the standard 216-color cube. Colors that are the result of dithering, or mixing, are beyond the standard cube.

An HTML document may consist of several color specifications. The following script segment demonstrates them:

```
<BODY
   [BGCOLOR="#backgroundColor"]
   [TEXT="#foregroundColor"]
   [LINK="#unfollowedLinkColor"]
   [ALINK="#activatedLinkColor"]
   [VLINK="#followedLinkColor"]>
</BODY>
```

All color attributes are scripted via JavaScript as properties of the `document` object.

bgColor

The `document.bgColor` property is expressed as a hexadecimal RGB triplet or as a string literal (such as "white," "blue," etc.). This property is the JavaScript reflection of the `BGCOLOR` attribute of the `<BODY>` tag. You can change the background color at any time, even via a deferred script. If you express the color as a hexadecimal RGB triplet, you must use the format *rrggbb* (case insensitive).

The `bgColor` property is a commonly scripted property. You can set it to create fade effects, color cubes, and so forth, as will be demonstrated in this chapter. The following script creates a sample color cube and sets the background color to the one the user selected from the cube:

```
<HTML>
<HEAD>
<TITLE>Sample Color Cube</TITLE>
</HEAD>
<BODY>
<SCRIPT LANGUAGE="JavaScript">
<!--
// create 6-element array
var hex = new Array(6)
// assign non-dithered descriptors
hex[0] = "FF"
hex[1] = "CC"
hex[2] = "99"
hex[3] = "66"
hex[4] = "33"
hex[5] = "00"
// accept triplet string and display as background color
function display(triplet)
{
   // set color as background color
   document.bgColor = '#' + triplet
   // display the color hexadecimal triplet
   alert('Background color is now ' + triplet)
}
// draw a single table cell based on all descriptors
function drawCell(red, green, blue)
{
   // open cell with specified hexadecimal triplet background color
   document.write('<TD BGCOLOR="#' + red + green + blue + '">')
   // open a hypertext link with javascript: scheme to call display function
   document.write('<A HREF="javascript:display(\'' + (red + green + blue)
                 + '\')">')
   // print transparent image (use any height and width)
   document.write('<IMG SRC="place.gif" BORDER=0 HEIGHT=12 WIDTH=12>')
```

```
   // close link tag
   document.write('</A>')
   // close table cell
   document.write('</TD>')
}
// draw table row based on red and blue descriptors
function drawRow(red, blue)
{
   // open table row
   document.write('<TR>')
   // loop through all non-dithered color descripters as green hex
   for (var i = 0; i < 6; ++i)
   {
      drawCell(red, hex[i], blue)
   }
   // close current table row
   document.write('</TR>')
}
// draw table for one of six color cube panels
function drawTable(blue)
{
   // open table (one of six cube panels)
   document.write('<TABLE CELLPADDING=0 CELLSPACING=0 BORDER=0>')
   // loop through all non-dithered color descripters as red hex
   for (var i = 0; i < 6; ++i)
   {
      drawRow(hex[i], blue)
   }
   // close current table
   document.write('</TABLE>')
   }
// draw all cube panels inside table cells
function drawCube()
{
   // open table
   document.write('<TABLE CELLPADDING=5 CELLSPACING=0 BORDER=1><TR>')
   // loop through all non-dithered color descripters as blue hex
   for (var i = 0; i < 6; ++i)
   {
      // open table cell with white background color
      document.write('<TD BGCOLOR="#FFFFFF">')
      // call function to create cube panel with hex[i] blue hex
      drawTable(hex[i])
      // close current table cell
      document.write('</TD>')
   }
   // close table row and table
   document.write('</TR></TABLE>')
}
// call function to begin execution
drawCube()
// -->
```

```
</SCRIPT>
</BODY>
</HTML>
```

Example 17-1. (ex17-1.htm). *A color cube*

You can see the output of this in Figure 17-2.

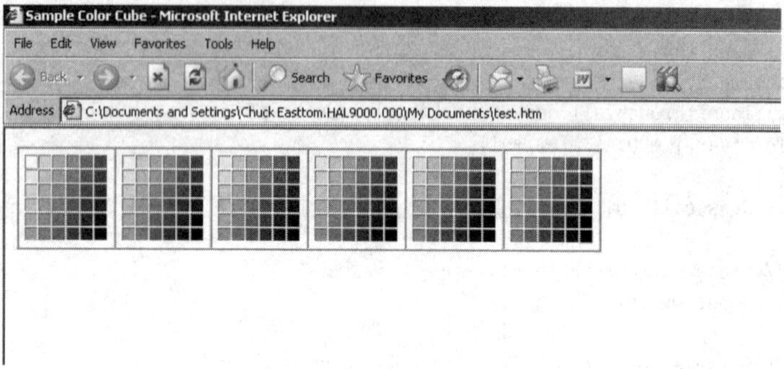

Figure 17-2. *A color cube*

This script basically prints tables. Each table cell contains a transparent image that defines the size of the cell. Each cell is also assigned a background color that determines the color that fills that cell. When you click on the image, the hexadecimal triplet is displayed via an alert box, and the background color is set to the selected color.

The main outline of the cube is a table with one row and six cells (columns). Each cell contains a table of all non-dithered colors with a given blue descriptor. There are six tables in total, one for each of the non-dithered colors: 00, 33, 66, 99, CC, FF. Since there are six non-dithered hexadecimal values, each table is 6 x 6. Each row presents a red hexadecimal value and each column represents a green one.

Now let's analyze the script itself.

Global Statements

```
// create 6-element array
var hex = new Array(6)
// assign non-dithered descriptors
hex[0] = "FF"
hex[1] = "CC"
hex[2] = "99"
hex[3] = "66"
hex[4] = "33"
hex[5] = "00"
```

A six-element array is created as an instance of the `Array` object. The elements of the array are assigned the six values from which the 216 non-dithered colors, which are supported on all platforms, can be combined. The `drawCube()` function call at the end of the script is also global.

display(triplet)

```
// accept triplet string and display as background color
function display(triplet)
{
   // set color as background color
   document.bgColor = '#' + triplet
   // display the color hexadecimal triplet
   alert('Background color is now ' + triplet)
}
```

This function's single argument is a six-character string representing the hexadecimal RGB triplet of a color. The document's background color is set, and an alert box displays the selected color's exact RGB triplet.

drawCell(red, green, blue)

```
// draw a single table cell based on all descriptors
function drawCell(red, green, blue)
{
   // open cell with specified hexadecimal triplet background color
   document.write('<TD BGCOLOR="#' + red + green + blue + '">')
   // open a hypertext link with javascript: scheme to call display function
   document.write('<A HREF="javascript:display(\'' + (red + green +blue)
                  + '\')">')
   // print transparent image (use any height and width)
   document.write('<IMG SRC="place.gif" BORDER=0 HEIGHT=12 WIDTH=12>')
   // close link tag
   document.write('</A>')
   // close table cell
   document.write('</TD>')
}
```

This function accepts three arguments: the red, green, and blue descriptors. It creates a table cell with the combined triplet as the background color. The content of each cell is a gif89 transparent image, `place.gif`. The image's height and width specification determines the size of each cell. Each image is also a hypertext link to a `"javascript:"`-scheme URL, which calls the `display()` function. The argument to this function is a hexadecimal triplet that is also used for the cell's background. Note that all the global array descriptors are strings, so the plus sign is used to concatenate the three double-digit hexadecimal values.

drawRow(red, blue)

```
// draw table row based on red and blue descriptors
function drawRow(red, blue)
{
   // open table row
   document.write('<TR>')
   // loop through all non-dithered color descriptors as green hex
   for (var i = 0; i < 6; ++i)
   {
      drawCell(red, hex[i], blue)
```

```
    }
    // close current table row
    document.write('</TR>')
}
```

This function accepts the red and blue descriptors and prints a table row. The content of the table is created by six calls to the drawCell() function, passing the red and blue descriptors "as is" and a different green descriptor (from the global hex array) on each call.

drawTable(blue)

```
// draw table for one of six color cube panels
function drawTable(blue)
{
    // open table (one of six cube panels)
    document.write('<TABLE CELLPADDING=0 CELLSPACING=0 BORDER=0>')
    // loop through all non-dithered color descriptors as red hex
    for (var i = 0; i < 6; ++i)
    {
        drawRow(hex[i], blue)
    }
    // close current table
    document.write('</TABLE>')
}
```

This function is very similar to the drawRow() function. The only difference is that it draws a 6 x 6 table instead of a 6 x 1 row. It calls the drawRow() function six times, each time with a different red descriptor. All table attributes are set to 0 in order to avoid boundaries between the cells, creating the appearance of gradually changing colors across the cube.

drawCube()

```
// draw all cube panels inside table cells
function drawCube()
{
    // open table
    document.write('<TABLE CELLPADDING=5 CELLSPACING=0 BORDER=1><TR>')
    // loop through all non-dithered color descripters as blue hex
    for (var i = 0; i < 6; ++i)
    {
        // open table cell with white background color
        document.write('<TD BGCOLOR="#FFFFFF">')
        // call function to create cube panel with hex[i] blue hex
        drawTable(hex[i])
        // close current table cell
        document.write('</TD>')
    }
    // close table row and table
    document.write('</TR></TABLE>')
}
```

Unlike the other functions, this one does not accept any arguments. It creates the outline table of a single six-cell row with a white background color. The function calls `drawTable()` six times, once for each given blue descriptor. Setting the `CELLPADDING` attribute to a positive number separates the tables.

Another classic example that takes advantage of the ability to set background colors via JavaScript is a script that creates a fade-in or fade-out effect when the page is loaded or unloaded. Here is the script:

```
<HTML>
<HEAD>
<TITLE>Fade in and out</TITLE>
<SCRIPT LANGUAGE="JavaScript">
<!--
// convert decimal value (0 - 255) to hexadecimal
// (use .toString(16) method supported by Internet Explorer)
function toHex(dec)
{
   // create list of hex characters
   var hexCharacters = "0123456789ABCDEF"
   // if number is out of range return limit
   if (dec < 0)
      return "00"
   if (dec > 255)
      return "FF"
   // decimal equivalent of first hex character in converted number
   var i = Math.floor(dec / 16)
   // decimal equivalent of second hex character in converted number
   var j = dec % 16
   // return hexadecimal equivalent
   return hexCharacters.charAt(i) + hexCharacters.charAt(j)
}
// set background color to specified descriptors
function setbgColor(red, green, blue)
{
   document.bgColor = "#" + toHex(red) + toHex(green) + toHex(blue)
}
// fade from start to end descriptors (increase step to increase transition
// speed)
function fade(sred, sgreen, sblue, ered, egreen, eblue, step)
{
   // loop to create fade effect
   for(var i = 0; i <= step; ++i)
   {
      // set current red descriptor
      var red = Math.floor(sred * ((step - i) / step) + ered * (i / step))
      // set current green descriptor
      var green = Math.floor(sgreen * ((step - i) / step) + egreen * (i / step))
      // set current blue descriptor
      var blue = Math.floor(sblue * ((step - i) / step) + eblue * (i / step))
      // set background color according to descriptors
      setbgColor(red, green, blue)
   }
```

```
}
// -->
</SCRIPT>
</HEAD>
<BODY onLoad="fade(0, 0, 0, 255, 255, 255, 64)" onUnload="fade(255, 255,
                    255, 0, 0, 0, 64)">
<H1>Is this totally cool or what!!</H1>
</BODY>
</HTML>
```

Example 17-2 (ex17-2.htm). *A script to create a fade effect*

The script gradually changes the document's background color from a given color to another specified color. It works with any colors represented in a hexadecimal triplet format. Let's analyze the script.

toHex(dec)

```
// convert decimal value (0 - 255) to hexadecimal
// (use .toString(16) method supported by Internet Explorer)
function toHex(dec)
{
   // create list of hex characters
   var hexCharacters = "0123456789ABCDEF"
   // if number is out of range return limit
   if (dec < 0)
      return "00"
   if (dec > 255)
      return "FF"
   // decimal equivalent of first hex character in converted number
   var i = Math.floor(dec / 16)
   // decimal equivalent of second hex character in converted number
   var j = dec % 16
   // return hexadecimal equivalent
   return hexCharacters.charAt(i) + hexCharacters.charAt(j)
}
```

This function accepts a single argument representing a decimal number, normally from 0 to 255. It converts it to its hexadecimal equivalent. A list of the hexadecimal digits is assigned to the string variable `hexCharacters`. It returns the minimum `00` string if the decimal argument is less than 0, and the maximum `FF` if the decimal argument is greater than 255, the equivalent to "FF" in hex representation. The value `Math.floor(dec / 16)` is equal to the decimal representation of the first hexadecimal digit in the converted number. The value `Math.floor(dec % 16)` is equal to the decimal value of the second hex digit of the converted number. The hexadecimal value of a decimal number from 0 to 15 is that `hexCharacter`'s character, the index of which is equal to the decimal number.

setbgColor(red, green, blue)

```
// set background color to specified descriptors
function setbgColor(red, green, blue)
{
   document.bgColor = "#" + toHex(red) + toHex(green) + toHex(blue)
}
```

This function accepts three RGB descriptors and assigns the color combination to the `document.bgColor` property, setting the document's background color. The arguments are in decimal notation, so first they are converted to hex numbers.

fade(sred, sgreen, sblue, ered, egreen, eblue, step)

```
// fade from start to end descriptors (increase step to increase transition
// speed)
function fade(sred, sgreen, sblue, ered, egreen, eblue, step)
{
   // loop to create fade effect
   for(var i = 0; i <= step; ++i)
   {
      // set current red descriptor
      var red = Math.floor(sred * ((step - i) / step) + ered * (i / step))
      // set current green descriptor
      var green = Math.floor(sgreen * ((step - i) / step) + egreen * (i / step))
      // set current blue descriptor
      var blue = Math.floor(sblue * ((step - i) / step) + eblue * (i / step))
      // set background color according to descriptors
      setbgColor(red, green, blue)
   }
}
```

This function is responsible for the fade effect. It accepts seven arguments; the first three represent the RGB descriptors of the initial background color, the next three represent the RGB values of the target one, and the last argument determines the speed of the fade. The function consists of a single loop that iterates from 0 to `step` in increments of one. The RGB descriptors of the current background are computed and assigned to local variables on each iteration of the loop. A computed red, green, or blue color is a weighted average between the initial color value and the target one. During the first iteration, `step - i` is equal to `step`, so the initial color descriptor is actually multiplied by 1 in the expression `Math.floor(s`*`col`*` * ((step - i) / step)`. Since `i` is 0, the descriptor of the target color is multiplied by 0 in the expression `e`*`col`*` * (i / step)` where *`col`* is `red`, `green`, or `blue`. Therefore, the background color is set to the initial color during the first pass, and to the target color during the last pass. The last statement in the loop actually sets the background color by passing the computed descriptors to `setbgColor()`.

Chapter 17

Event Handlers

It is common to use the fading effect with the `onLoad` and `onUnload` event handlers. If you prefer to use it with both, it is recommended that you generate the reversed transition for each.

fgColor

The `document.fgColor` property represents the color of the document text (foreground color). It reflects the `<BODY>` tag's `TEXT` attribute. The property is expressed as a hexadecimal RGB triplet or as one of the supported color names. When you assign it a triplet, the crosshatch mark (#) is optional.

Setting a value to the `fgColor` property is equivalent to setting a value to the `<BODY>` tag's `TEXT` attribute, enclosing the entire text with the `<FONT COLOR="setColor"></FONT>` tag pair, or using the `String` object's `fontcolor` method.

alinkColor

The `document.alinkColor` property is JavaScript's reflection of the `<BODY>` tag's `ALINK` attribute. It is a string specifying the color of an active link (after the mouse button is pressed down over a link but before it goes back up). The string must represent the hexadecimal RGB triplet of a color or one of the supported color names.

Aside from a few exceptions, you cannot set the value of this property after the page has finished loading, because there is no way to modify a page's content after it has been laid out.

linkColor

The `document.linkColor` property is JavaScript's reflection of the `<BODY>` tag's `LINK` attribute. It specifies the color of the document's hypertext links that the user has not visited. The color must be represented in the form of a hexadecimal RGB triplet or one of the supported color names. As explained above, you cannot set this property after the HTML source has gone through the layout stage. You can still read the property's value at any time via an immediate script or a deferred one.

vlinkColor

The `document.vlinkColor` property is JavaScript's reflection of the `<BODY>` tag's `VLINK` attribute. The color must be represented in the form of a hexadecimal RGB triplet or one of the supported color names. This property represents the color of already-followed hypertext links. You can set it as long as the HTML source has not been through layout yet.

Output Methods and Streams

write and writeln

The `document.write` method displays any number of expressions in a document window. Expressions to be printed can be of any type, including numerics, strings, and logicals.

This method prints its arguments to the plain HTML document window. It does not append any external character to the printed arguments. The method `document.write`, also accessible as `window.document.write`, can be used from either a plain script (`<SCRIPT LANGUAGE="JavaScript">... </SCRIPT>`) or an event handler.

Bear in mind that event handler scripts are executed only after the HTML source has been through layout. The `write()` method implicitly opens a new document of *mimeType* `text/html` if you do not explicitly invoke a `document.open()` method prior to the `document.write()` call.

The `writeln()` method acts exactly like the `write()` method, except that it appends a new line character to the end of the output. HTML generally ignores this character, but certain tags, such as <PRE>, use it:

```
<PRE>
one
two
three
<PRE>
```

After interpretation, the web page appears as:

```
one
two
three
```

You can create the same output via JavaScript in the following fashion:

```
document.write("<PRE>")
document.writeln("one")
document.writeln("two")
document.writeln("three")
document.write("</PRE>")
```

Data Streams

The `document.open()` method opens a stream to collect the output of the `write()` and `writeln()` methods. Its general syntax is:

```
document.open(["mimeType"])
```

mimeType specifies the type of document, which is one of the following:

```
text/html
text/plain
image/gif
image/jpeg
```

```
image/x-bitmap
plugIn
```

`plugIn` is any two-part plug-in supported by the user's browser.

Generally speaking, if the `mimeType` is one of the text or image types, the stream is opened to layout, which is generated by instructions from the browser. Otherwise, the stream is opened to a target plug-in that you are sure understands the data you provide. Since `document` is a property of `window`, `document.open()` or `window.document.open()` opens a stream specific to the document in the target window. If a document already exists in the target window, the open method clears it. If you do not specify `mimeType` as the method's argument, the most common one, `text/html`, is assumed. Note that you should never use this method to open a stream in the document that includes the JavaScript method itself. It is always used to open data streams to documents in other windows.

After you complete supplying data to the opened stream, you should close it via the `document.close()` method. Its syntax is simply the following:

```
document.close()
```

This method primarily closes a stream opened with the `document.open()` method. If not explicitly closed by the script, all font style tag pairs are closed implicitly. For example, if you provide a `<BIG>` tag but do not provide a closing `</BIG>` tag later, JavaScript provides it automatically. The `close()` method also stops the "meteor shower" in the Netscape icon or the rotation of the Internet Explorer icon, and displays "Document: Done" in the status bar.

The `document.close()` method is extremely important because it instructs the browser's interpreter to display the data stream. If you do not invoke it, the output might not have any influence on the content of the page.

Since we have not discussed windows yet, this discussion seems a bit theoretical. We will refer to these methods later, when the subject of windows is dealt with in depth.

Another related method is `document.clear()`. Clearing a document via this method clears all HTML outputs in that document and resets the object model corresponding to that document. Normally, since JavaScript automatically clears the old document when you open a new stream, you don't have to clear a document prior to its opening or rewriting. The only case in which you should clear a document is after you close the stream to it. Since the method `document.clear()` does not work in versions of Netscape prior to 4.5, you can clear a document by opening it, writing a line break to it, and then closing it. Look at the following example:

```
windowReference.document.open("text/html")
windowReference.document.write("<BR>")
windowReference.document.close()
```

For some reason, this clearing method requires writing at least one character to the stream. The line break is used here because it is transparent to the user.

What Is a History List?

As you surf the web, you will load many different pages, each with its own URL. The browser maintains a list of the most recent URLs, which can be viewed with ease in Mozilla Firefox, Netscape Navigator, and Internet Explorer. This history allows you to go back to sites you have previously visited. This history list is very simple to use, but also very informative.

The history list behaves like a LIFO (Last In First Out) queue, where the Back button climbs up the list so URLs loaded by the Back button are not entered into the history list. Therefore, the history list does not always contain all the recently visited pages. For example, if you reach a page named "a.html" and you press the Back button to load a page named "b.html," its URL replaces the URL of "a.html."

The history Object

The history list is represented in JavaScript by the `window.history` object. This object lets you deal with the history list but not with its exact data. That is, actual URLs maintained in that list cannot be extracted or otherwise modified by a script. The only property of this object is `length`. Its methods enable you to load the list's entries but not to manipulate the URL explicitly.

You can take advantage of this object to automatically navigate the user's browser backward. Another possible application is to create the equivalent of the browser's Back button directly in the document.

Since the `history` object is a property of the topmost `window` object, you have the option to refer to it as `window.history` or simply `history`.

History List Length

You can access the number of entries in the history list via the `history.length` property. It works exactly like the `length` property for `String` and `array` objects. You can use this property to find how many pages the user has visited lately:

```
// display message according to number of entries
if (history.length > 10)
   alert("You've already accessed " + history.length + " web pages this
         session")
else
   alert("You've only accessed " + history.length + " web pages this session")
```

This script displays an alert message that depends on the number of entries in the history list.

History List Entry Indexing

As in arrays, each entry of the history list has an index that differentiates it from the other elements of the list. However, the indexing method is quite different from character indexing in strings and element indexing in arrays. As opposed to these indexing algorithms, the history list indexing scheme does not feature a minimum value. The index of the document currently loaded into the browser's window is 0. The index of the document that was loaded before the current document, the one that can be reached by pressing the Back button, is –1. The document before that is indexed at –2, and so on. Similarly, documents that were first loaded after the current document are indexed positively. The index of the first document loaded after the current one, the one that can be retrieved via the Forward button, is 1. The following one is indexed at 2, and so on. The complete index resembles an axis with no limit at either end.

The history list is dynamic (changes rapidly) because whenever the page in the browser's window is replaced by a new document, the current entry becomes the previous one, and a new document takes its place. The desired shifting in terms of indexing is performed automatically by the browser, so you don't have to worry about it.

Since most people tend to surf different places at different times, the content of the history list almost never repeats itself. You might think that by creating a very structured site, you can control the way the user surfs your site and thus be able to forecast the content of the history list. This is generally impossible, and you should not even try to do it.

history Methods

You can implement the `history` object's methods in your script to enable the user to navigate among the list's URLs. You cannot access the string value of any URL, but you can load any of them into the browser's window.

back

This method performs the same action as the Back button in the browser's toolbar. It loads the most recent entry in the history list—the entry with index –1. The following HTML code can be used to create a Back button in a web page:

```
<FORM>
<INPUT TYPE="button" VALUE="Back" onClick="history.back()">
</FORM>
```

forward

The history.forward method is equivalent to the Forward button in the browser's toolbar. It loads the entry with index 1. It is less useful than the preceding method because the current document is usually the most recent in the list, so there is no URL that can be loaded when this method is invoked. You must take special precautions when using this method, because it normally does not have any effect. It should be used only when you are sure that you have full control over the user's navigational path. The following sequence creates a Forward button for a web page:

```
<FORM>
<INPUT TYPE="button" VALUE="Back" onClick="history.forward()">
</FORM>
```

go

The go method is also one of those less useful methods featured in JavaScript. It enables you to load a history list entry in the browser's window. You must have full control over the user's navigating path in order to implement this method for useful purposes.

This method accepts one argument, the index of the history list that you want to retrieve. This can be any integer number that has a corresponding history list entry. If the argument is 0, the current page is loaded, or better said, reloaded. For example, the following call is equivalent to invoking the history.back() method:

```
history.go(-1)
```

When you want to jump back to the entry with index –1, use history.go(–1) rather than history.back(), because, among other reasons, you can just change the argument in order to jump back a few steps instead of only one. The same applies to history.forward(), which is equivalent to the following call:

```
history.go(1)
```

Also bear in mind that this method does not return any value but causes immediate navigation.

Alternatively, you can specify one of the URLs as the argument of this method. A portion of the desired URL is also sufficient, provided that it is a unique substring of only one entry. In both cases, the specified string (literal or value) is compared against all entries, and the one whose URL includes the specified substring will be loaded.

Unfortunately, you cannot extract the URL; you can only load it. The following script segment retrieves Netscape's home page (www.netscape.com or home.netscape.com) if it is resident in the history list:

```
<FORM>
<INPUT TYPE="button" VALUE="Go" onClick="history.go('netscape.com')">
</FORM>
```

The following call reloads the current document:

```
history.go(0)
```

For quite some time Netscape Navigator has also offered this method to reload the current page:

```
location.reload()
```

Security Aspects of the history Object

It would be very useful to be able to extract and process URLs that reside in the history list. For security reasons, this functionality has been excluded thus far. First of all, nobody should use the back door to know where the user has been and, secondly, data can be easily submitted from the client to the server via e-mail. Netscape has solved the e-mail breach of security by displaying a warning whenever an e-mail is sent (other than that sent explicitly by the user from the mail window). Netscape's solution is not foolproof since the user might have disabled this warning, might not pay attention, or might ignore it altogether.

The problem with the history list's entries is that they contain complete URLs. A URL may contain extremely confidential information, especially in the form of a search query. For example, the user might have recently submitted a form with a field containing a credit card number. The form may have loaded another page with a search query containing the credit card number. Thus, credit card numbers or other secure information may be revealed and gleaned by malicious individuals.

Summary

This chapter focused first on the `document` object and ended with the history list. In this chapter I showed you several properties and methods of the `document` object. The focus was on colors, and naturally on hexadecimal triplets that define them. You learned how to script the various document colors such as background color, link color, and so forth. Two interesting examples dealing with colors were also analyzed. We have discussed other properties and methods as well. I have presented the basic output methods, `document.write()` and `document.writeln()`, as well as data streams. Data streams and document clearing play an important role in scripting windows and frames, as will be explained later.

Since the `history` object is not as important and does not have many uses, we kept the discussion short. The most important property of the `history` object is the `go` method. Besides having a unique functionality of its own, the `go` method can replace the other history methods. Because it is closely related to URLs, the history-related function `replace` was discussed in the previous chapter.

Chapter 18
Forms

What Are HTML Forms?

HTML forms, consisting of buttons, menus, and text boxes, are the means by which the client computer can gather information from the user. They create a graphical interface whereby the user can enter data in a logical and easy-to-follow method. Forms are supported by all the major browsers, so you can use them with confidence. You have undoubtedly used forms on many pages. Most often when you fill out "contact us" fields on a business's web site you are using an HTML form.

Form tags have been part of HTML since HTML 2.0 (the current specification as of this writing is HTML 4.01) and are supported by all the well-known browsers (Internet Explorer, Netscape, Mozilla Firefox, Opera, Galleon, and others). This is one of the reasons why forms are heavily supported by JavaScript. As you will see in this chapter, JavaScript provides a convenient means of form content manipulation and validation through the use of a client-side application.

An HTML form by itself is of minimal use. Without some code to execute when the form's buttons are clicked or when you wish to load data into the form, the form is not very useful. That is where JavaScript comes in, providing the code to work with the form. And as you will see it is really not very difficult.

JavaScript Form Reference

JavaScript enables you to interact with the user via forms. You must know how forms are referenced in order to implement them in scripts. A form in terms of JavaScript is an object. It has properties, methods, and even event handlers. There are quite a few possible references from which you may choose. In this section I will outline all of these possibilities so you will have the freedom to select the most convenient method.

forms Array

Suppose you have an HTML document that includes several forms, each defined by a regular `<FORM></FORM>` tag pair. You can refer to each form by its index in the `forms` array. The `forms` array is a property of the `document` object, so it is referred to as `document.forms`. The object representing the first form in the page is `document.forms[0]`, the second form is `document.forms[1]`, the third one is `document.forms[2]`, and so forth. The `forms` array includes an entry for each of the document's forms (`<FORM>` tag), in source order. The general reference to a form is as follows:

```
document.forms[index]
```

As with all of JavaScript's arrays, the `forms` array includes a `length` property representing the number of forms on the page. The last form in the document, therefore, is:

```
document.forms[document.forms.length - 1]
```

Elements in the `forms` array can be set only by the HTML document and, hence, they are read-only for JavaScript. The following statement, for example, has no effect:

```
document.forms[0] = "work hard"
```

The string value of a form is `<object` *`nameAttribute`*`>`, where *`nameAttribute`* is the `NAME` attribute of the form.

Form Name

You can refer to a form by its name, rather than by its index:

```
document.formName
```

In order to take advantage of this referencing method, you have to explicitly assign a name to the form, via the `NAME` attribute. I strongly recommend using this method. If your HTML page has more than one form, indices to the `forms` array are less meaningful than form names.

Note: The term *reference* is used to describe an object's scripting protocol. A single object can be referenced via different but equivalent protocols.

form Object

HTML Syntax

All forms are basically just another set of HTML tags. The top-level tags are the <FORM></FORM> tag pair. All form elements must be placed within these tags in order to be interpreted correctly. The general syntax of the <FORM> tag is as follows:

```
<FORM
   [NAME="formName"]
   [TARGET="windowName"]
   [ACTION="serverURL"]
   [METHOD="get" | "post"]
   [ENCTYPE="encodingType"]
   [onSubmit="handlerText"]
   [onReset="handlerText"]>
</FORM>
```

The attributes are:

- NAME—specifies the name of the form. This attribute is seldom used because it does not have any effect when using a server-side script. When using client-side JavaScript, though, it is recommended you name the form for easier referencing. Since a form's name will be mostly used by JavaScript's scripts, it is also preferred to use the JavaScript identifier naming standards.
- TARGET—specifies the window to which form responses go. This attribute instructs the browser to display the server responses in the specified window rather than in the default window where the form resides. The specified value cannot be a JavaScript reference to a window—it must be a plain HTML frame or a window reference.
- ACTION—specifies the URL of the server-side script that processes the data submitted by the form. This attribute is necessary only when the processing script resides on the server. In this case, the script will be written in either C or Perl and will adhere to the CGI (Common Gateway Interface) protocol. The URL scheme must be HTTP.
- METHOD—specifies how to submit the form. It can be either `get` or `post`. The latter is more popular because it enables the client to send a greater amount of data to the processing script. Nonetheless, `get` is much easier to use and is also suitable for JavaScript scripts. If a form is returned with `get`, the data is placed in the `QUERY_STRING` environment variable. `post`, on the other hand, instructs the client to pass the data to the server via its operating system's standard input method.
- ENCTYPE—specifies the MIME type of the submitted data, such as `"text/plain"` for plain text. The default MIME encoding of the data sent is `"application/x-www-form-urlencoded"`.

Although the <FORM></FORM> tag pair represents an HTML form, you can still place any other valid HTML tags within it. Mixing tables with forms, for example, is often used to enable simple layout. Although syntactically valid, nesting a form inside another form does not make any sense and you should avoid doing so.

Note: Microsoft Internet Explorer allows you to place form elements outside the <FORM></FORM> tag pair. You should avoid using such elements, however, because they are not accessible via a full object hierarchy. They are accessible, though, via JavaScript's `this` scheme (see the explanation on `this` later in this chapter).

Event Handlers

onSubmit

A submit event occurs when a form is submitted, an event reflected by the `onSubmit` event handler. This attribute is a must; otherwise, there won't be any response to the form's submission.

The `onSubmit` event handler is an attribute of the <FORM> tag because its action relates to the entire form, not just to its Submit button. A form can be submitted in several ways; the Submit button is only one of many.

The submit event occurs immediately upon clicking the Submit button, pressing Enter, or via any other method. Since JavaScript triggers the event prior to sending the data to the server, the event handler's script is executed before the form's data is actually submitted to the server for further processing. Timing is very important here. For example, suppose you ask the user to send you comments by filling a text box in a form you place on your page. One would want to thank the user by replacing his comments in the text area box with a "Thank You" notice. You cannot use the `onSubmit` event handler to do that because the "Thank You" notice will replace the user's input before it would have a chance to be submitted to the server. The net effect would be that you will receive the "Thank You" notice instead of the user's comments. One way to work around the problem is to use an alert box instead of overwriting the form's text area box.

The `onSubmit` event handler is commonly used to validate the content of a form's element. Client-side form validation is gaining popularity because, rather than waiting for a server-side CGI script to respond, the user receives an immediate response regarding invalid entries. Let's say you have a form with a text box in which the user is asked to type his or her e-mail address. You can use a simple JavaScript script that will make sure (upon submission) that the user's entry is a string containing an "at" sign (@), which is necessary for all e-mail addresses.

You can use the `onSubmit` event handler not only to validate the form's elements but also to cancel its submission altogether. The form's submission is aborted when the event handler returns a false value, as in the following example:

```
<FORM NAME="form1" onSubmit="return false">
```

Obviously, this example is not very useful because it disables the form submission unconditionally. Usually, a function validates the form and returns a true or false value accordingly. You can use the following structure to cancel or proceed with the form submission, according to the value returned by the function:

```
<FORM NAME="form1" onSubmit="return checkData()">
```

The following example shows how to create a form with a text area box and a Submit button that e-mails you the contents of the text area after prompting the user for confirmation:

```
<SCRIPT LANGUAGE="JavaScript">
<!--
function proceedSubmission()
{
   return confirm("Click OK to mail this information")
}
// -->
</SCRIPT>
<FORM ACTION="mailto:chuckeasttom@yahoo.com" METHOD="post" ENCTYPE=
            "text/plain" onSubmit="return proceedSubmission()">
<TEXTAREA NAME="inputField" COLS=40 ROWS=10></TEXTAREA><BR>
<INPUT TYPE="submit" VALUE="mail it!">
</FORM>
```


The output of this script is shown in Figure 18-1.

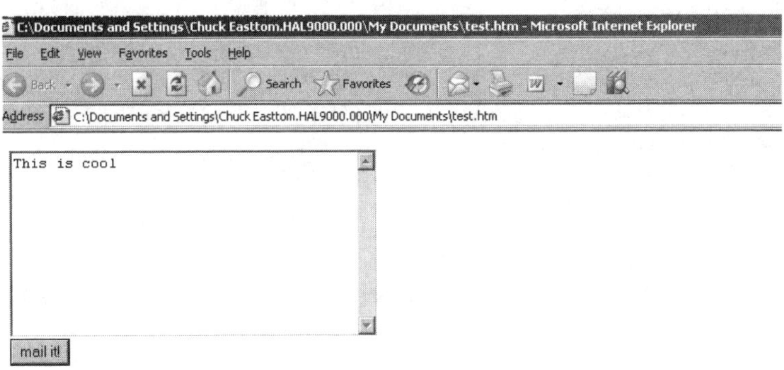

Figure 18-1. *Using the Submit button*

The Boolean value returned by the `onSubmit` event handler is actually the result of a confirm box presented to the user. Although some elements of this form are discussed later, you should be aware that, in order to receive the form's content as plain, unscrambled e-mail, you need to assign a `"text/plain"` value to the `ENCTYPE` attribute.

onReset

Another event handler of the <FORM> tag is onReset. A reset event usually occurs when the user clicks the Reset button. Except for the triggering event, the onReset event handler behaves like the onSubmit event handler.

The following example asks the user to confirm the resetting process before executing it:

```
<FORM ACTION="mailto:chuckeasttom@yahoo.com" METHOD="post" ENCTYPE="text/plain"
    onReset="return confirm('Click OK to reset form to default status')">
<TEXTAREA NAME="input" COLS=40 ROWS=10></TEXTAREA><BR>
<INPUT TYPE="reset" VALUE="reset it!">
</FORM>
```

Note: The onReset event handler was first implemented years ago in Navigator 3.0.

Methods

submit()

The submit() method submits a form much the same way as the Submit button. The submit() method sends data back to the HTTP server via get or post submission schemes. The general syntax is as follows:

```
formName.submit()
```

formName is the exact reference of the form object. You can invoke this method when the user clicks a given hypertext link. Take a look at the following example:

```
<HTML>
<HEAD>
<TITLE>hypertext link submission</TITLE>
<SCRIPT LANGUAGE="JavaScript">
<!--
function submitForm(sub)
{
   document.forms[sub].submit()
}
function proceedSubmission()
{
   return confirm("Click OK to mail this information")
}
// -->
</SCRIPT>
</HEAD>
<BODY>
<FORM METHOD="post" ACTION="mailto:chuckeasttom@yahoo.com" ENCTYPE=
          "text/plain" onSubmit="return proceedSubmission()">
<TEXTAREA NAME="inputField" COLS=40 ROWS=10></TEXTAREA><BR>
<A HREF="example18-01b.htm" onClick="submitForm(0)">Mail it!</A>
```

```
</FORM>
</BODY>
</HTML>
```

Example 18-1a (ex18-1a.htm)*. A hypertext link used to submit a form just like a Submit button*

In Example 18-1a the form is submitted by the `submitForm` function, which is invoked via the `onClick` event handler of a `link` object. After prompting the user for confirmation via the `onSubmit` event handler, the form, referenced as `document.forms[0]` (it is the first and only form in the page), is submitted through its `submit()` method. Example 18-1b shows the file ex18-1b.htm, which displays the "Thank You" notice referenced in Example 18-1a:

```
<HTML>
<HEAD>
<TITLE>Thank you</TITLE>
</HEAD>
<BODY>
Thank you very much for your feedback
</BODY>
</HTML>
```

Example 18-1b (ex18-1b.htm)*. The "Thank You" message displayed after submitting the mail in Example 18-1a*

Note: The `submit` method is broken in many versions of Navigator prior to 4.5 and Internet Explorer prior to 4.0. Test every new release before usage.

reset()

The `reset()` method resets a given form and is equivalent to clicking the Reset button. Its syntax and usage is exactly the same as the `submit()` method. See the `onReset` event handler for more information on resetting a form.

Properties

action

The `action` property reflects the value of the `<FORM>` tag's `ACTION` attribute. Its value is the URL of a CGI or LiveWire application on the server that needs to execute upon submission. If no explicit URL for the server-side application is specified, the value of `action` in Navigator defaults to the URL of the current document (the one containing the form). Microsoft Internet Explorer defaults the property to an empty string.

The *`formReference`*`.action` property can also be assigned a value by JavaScript. You can take advantage of this feature to modify the form's behavior after the page has been laid out, according to the user's preferences.

In general, you can assign the form's properties by JavaScript, instead of HTML attributes. Take a look at the following form example:

```
<FORM NAME="form1" METHOD="post" ACTION="http://www.foo.com/trash.cgi">
</FORM>
```

An alternative to this construct is the following combination of HTML and JavaScript:

```
<FORM NAME="form1" METHOD="post">
</FORM>
<SCRIPT LANGUAGE="JavaScript">
<!--
document.form1.action = "http://www.foo.com/trash.cgi"
// -->
</SCRIPT>
```

elements

The `elements` property is an array of objects corresponding to the form elements. It is a property of any form and is referenced as *`formReference`*`.elements`.

As you already know, since all `form` objects are elements of the `document.forms` object, it is possible to refer to a specific form within a document if you know its index in relationship to the other forms in the document. Similarly, a specific form's elements are elements of the `elements` array. The first element of this array is a reference to the first form element (`button`, `checkbox`, `hidden`, `password`, `radio`, `reset`, `select`, `submit`, `text`, or `textarea` object), the second entry is a reference to the second form element, and so on, in source order. For example, if a form has one text box and three radio buttons, you can reference these elements as *`formReference`*`.elements[0]`, *`formReference`*`.elements[1]`, *`formReference`*`.elements[2]`, and *`formReference`*`.elements[3]`.

Like the `forms` array, the `elements` array is an alternative to referencing by name. Some programmers prefer to use array reflection, whereas others prefer to trace elements by their names. It is convenient to implement the `elements` array when a form contains many elements that are related to indices. A form with ten text boxes that each accept a telephone number, for example, should be referenced via the `elements` array. Such referencing will allow you to use a loop to iterate through the ten different elements.

Usually, though, you will use forms to collect data fields of different meanings that are not similar to each other as the phone numbers in the previous example. In such cases, referencing by name is much more convenient and easier to understand, follow, and maintain. You can easily redesign the physical layout of the form or even add new elements in the middle while keeping the old references. If you use the `elements` array, on the other hand, any layout modification causes the indices to shift, invalidating all previous references.

The number of elements in a form is *formReference*.`elements.length`. Therefore, the last element in a form is reflected by the *formReference*.`elements[formReference.elements.length - 1]` entry.

Elements in the `elements` array are read-only, so the following statement, for example, has no effect:

```
formReference.elements[0] = "do not do this"
```

The first few elements of the `elements` array represent the form elements. The following property, `length`, reflects the number of form elements.

Suppose a form element evaluates to `foo`. Then, the following references all evaluate to `foo`:

```
document.forms[0].elements[0].value
document.forms[0].elements.elements[0].value
document.forms[0].elements.elements.elements[0].value
```

These bizarre references are possible due to the fact that an `elements` object contains all the properties of its form, in addition to the form's elements. A form, say `document.forms[0]`, can also have a property named `name` reflecting the value of the `NAME` attribute of the corresponding `<FORM>` tag. You can also reference this property in Navigator using one of the following known methods:

```
document.forms[0].name
document.forms[0].elements.name
document.forms[0].elements.elements.name
```

You may recall from Chapter 5 that the `for...in` loop statement provides the capability to list an object's properties, top to bottom. The following function can be used to list the properties of a typical `elements` object by name (not index):

```
function printElements(form, formString)
{
   // initialize output string
   var result = ""
   for (var i in form.elements)
   {
      result += formString + ".elements." + i + " = " + form.elements[i] + "\r"
   }
   alert(result)
}
```

You can use this function by invoking it with a specific form's reference and a name. Consider the following simple HTML form:

```
<FORM NAME="form1" ACTION="http://www.yourserver.com/filename.cgi"
         METHOD="post">
<INPUT TYPE="text" NAME="num1" VALUE="bla">
<INPUT TYPE="hidden" NAME="num2" VALUE="foo">
<TEXTAREA NAME="num3">wow</TEXTAREA>
</FORM>
```

The preceding `printElements()` function returns the following output when provided with the arguments `document.forms[0]` and `"document.forms[0]"`:

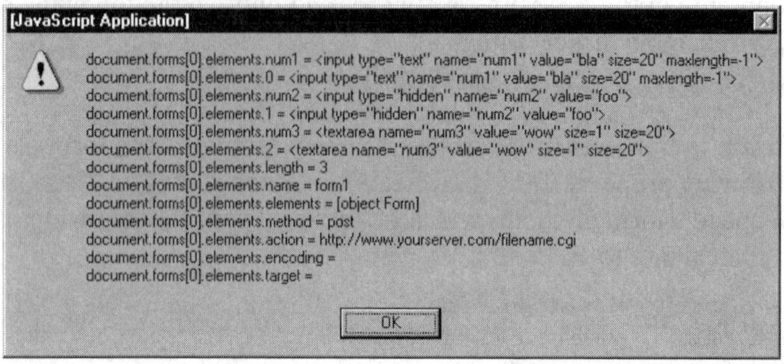

Figure 18-2. *A list of the `elements` object's properties*

Notice that the first four lines list the exclusive properties of the `elements` object. The following lines represent properties of elements that are identical to those of the form itself, `document.forms[0]` in this case. Theoretically, you can reference all `forms` properties of a given form as properties of its `elements` object.

If you think this wealth of referencing methods is confusing, you are right. The best solution is to stick to some standards. Suppose you have a form in a document that is referenced as `document.forms[`*`index`*`]`, `document.`*`formName`*, or *`formReference`*. The following objects include all `forms` properties:

```
formReference
formReference.elements
```

The `elements` property of *`formReference`* is just another interface to the same object. Since Netscape originally documented the above two objects as different ones (and still does), it is common to refer to *`formReference`* when accessing a form's general properties and to *`formReference`*`.elements` when accessing the properties of the form's elements. Theoretically, you can also access the first element of the form by:

```
formReference[0]
```

As you already know, any form element object can be referenced by its name. For example, a `text` object whose name is `field1` in the first form of a page can be accessed as follows:

```
document.forms[0].field1
```

When two or more elements have the same name, they form an array in which the indices are determined according to their layout order. For example, if there are three `text` objects in one form, all named `inputField`, you can reference these elements in the following fashion:

```
document.forms[0].inputField[0]
```

```
document.forms[0].inputField[1]
document.forms[0].inputField[2]
```

encoding

The content of a form is encoded before it is submitted to the server. There are various types of encoding, or MIME encoding—some suitable for files, while others are suitable for plain text or other purposes. The encoding method is initially specified by assigning it to the `<FORM>` tag's `ENCTYPE` attribute. The default encoding method is `application/x-www-form-urlencoded`, but others such as `multipart/form-data` and `text/plain` are also available.

Every HTML form has a MIME encoding specification, even if it is not explicitly shown. The value of JavaScript's *formReference*`.encoding` is initially the value assigned to the HTML `ENCTYPE` attribute. This property is not read-only, so it can be set at any time, even after layout has been completed. Setting `encoding` overrides the `ENCTYPE` attribute and instructs the browser (primarily Navigator) to use the new MIME encoding method.

For your reference, the general syntax of this property is:

```
formReference.encoding
```

If no value is specified as the `ENCTYPE` attribute of a form, it is defaulted to `application/x-www-form-urlencoded`. Nevertheless, the value of *formReference*`.encoding` remains an empty string.

method

The `METHOD` attribute of a `<FORM>` tag accepts either a `get` or a `post` value. JavaScript reflects the value of this attribute in the form of a `method` property. You can use this property like all other form properties. It can be read or set at any time, even after layout has been completed. The term "method," in this case, has no relation whatsoever to the object-oriented interpretation of the word (a function associated with an object).

The *formReference*`.method` property is active when the client-side JavaScript script interacts with a specific server-side CGI or LiveWire application. In this case, you can set the `method` property along with other form-related properties to modify the form's layout on the fly. The general syntax to reference this property is:

```
formReference.method
```

The default value of the HTML `METHOD` attribute is `get`. The value of the JavaScript `method` property, however, has no default and stays empty.

target

When you "surf the web," you often encounter HTML forms that submit data to the server and return a result, such as a list of sites or a simple "Thank You" page. Since most forms serve as a means to interact with the user, you will seldom find forms that submit to the server and do not respond. Furthermore, even forms that just receive input from the user and submit it to a server-side script are expected to respond and give the user an indication that the content of the form was correctly submitted.

Most server-side applications return a new HTML page in the same window as the form. Sometimes, however, you may prefer to receive the results in a different window or frame. You can specify the target of the returned page by setting the `TARGET` attribute of the `<FORM>` tag. This value is reflected by JavaScript's `target` property, which belongs to the `form` object. The general syntax for referencing this property is:

```
formReference.target
```

This property can be both read and set at any time, even after the page has been laid out. Despite the fact that the `TARGET` attribute defaults to the current window or frame's HTML document, the JavaScript's `target` property does not default to any string.

The value of the JavaScript's `target` property, like the HTML's `TARGET` attribute, can be either a window or a frame name. In addition to these obvious values, there are several common references: `_top`, `_parent`, `_self`, and `_blank`. These values will be covered again when we discuss frames and windows and, for detailed information, you may also refer to HTML documentation. It may seem convenient to assign `window` or `frame` objects to this property, but unfortunately it only accepts HTML specifications.

Element Types

Each and every form element (`button`, `radio`, `text area`, etc.) features a `type` property that reflects the type of that form element. As usual in JavaScript syntax, the `type` property follows the element reference. For example, you can access the type of the first element of the first form in the following fashion:

```
document.forms[0].elements[0].type
```

Table 18-1 lists the various form elements with their corresponding types.

Table 18-1. *Form elements*

HTML Element	Value of type Attribute
INPUT TYPE="button"	"button"
INPUT TYPE="checkbox"	"checkbox"
INPUT TYPE="file"	"file"
INPUT TYPE="hidden"	"hidden"
INPUT TYPE="password"	"password"
INPUT TYPE="radio"	"radio"
INPUT TYPE="reset"	"reset"
INPUT TYPE="submit"	"submit"
INPUT TYPE="text"	"text"
SELECT	"select-one"
SELECT MULTIPLE	"select-multiple"
TEXTAREA	"textarea"

All values listed in the right column are plain strings representing the element type.

Using this with Event Handlers

When you call a function via an event handler, you may refer to the form element that triggered the event handler, such as a `text` object or a button. The following script segment and figure demonstrate this concept:

```
<SCRIPT LANGUAGE="JavaScript">
<!--
function process()
{
   document.forms[0].elements[0].value = "thank you"
}
// -->
</SCRIPT>
<FORM>
<INPUT TYPE="text" NAME="myField" VALUE="email..." onChange="process()">
</FORM>
```

You can see the output of this script in Figure 18-3.

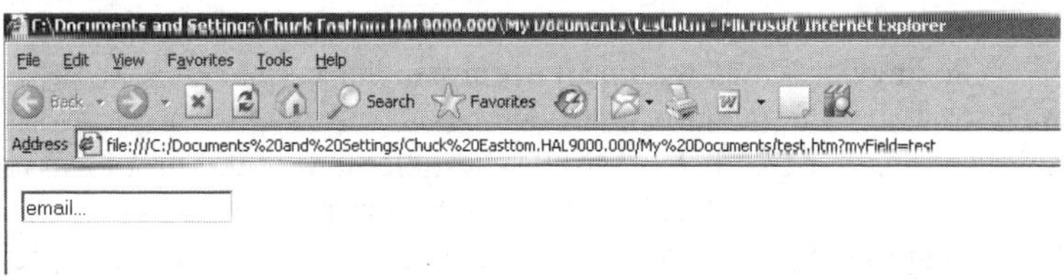

***Figure 18-3.** Calling a function via an event handler*

At this point, it is not so important to understand exactly what this script does. The `INPUT TYPE="text"` definition creates a simple text box in which the user can enter a value. The text box (or `text` object) is assigned the string `"email..."` as its default value (the form comes up with this text inside the box). The `onChange` event handler captures the change event that occurs when the user changes the value of the `text` object and clicks outside of it. When such an event occurs, the function process is invoked and assigns the string `"thank you"` to that `text` object's `value` property. Notice that a full object path specification, from the document browser object downward, is used to access the `text` object. Such referencing has two disadvantages:

- The path is fairly long and complex.
- If you change the position or the name of either a form or an element, the path must be modified to reflect this change, making the maintenance very difficult.

The answer to this problem is using the keyword `this` to refer to the "current" object. For example, you can simplify the preceding code by implementing the `this` reference in the following way:

```
<SCRIPT LANGUAGE="JavaScript">
<!--
function process(callingElement)
{
   callingElement.value = "thank you"
}
// -->
</SCRIPT>
<FORM>
<INPUT TYPE="text" NAME="myField" VALUE="email..." onChange="process(this)">
</FORM>
```

Using the above scheme, you can change the element's position, name, or any other optional attribute (other than the event handler) and the script will still work without any modifications. The keyword `this` refers to the element providing the event handler. In this case, the value of `this` is equal to `document.forms[0].elements[0]`. When the function process is called, the value assigned to the `callingElement` parameter is `this`, so `callingElement.value` is equivalent to `document.forms[0].elements[0].value`.

The keyword `this` within an event handler script refers to the form element to which the event handler belongs. For example, the keyword `this` in an event handler that belongs to the first element of the first form in a document can be safely replaced by `document.form[0].element[0]`.

Using the object `this` is very convenient when you use a single function to refer to different form elements.

You can use `this` in an event handler script for purposes other than a function's argument. You can also hand any property of the `this` object to a function, as demonstrated by the following script segment:

```
<SCRIPT LANGUAGE="JavaScript">
<!--
function display(str)
{
   alert(str)
}
// -->
</SCRIPT>
<FORM>
<INPUT TYPE="text" NAME="myField1" VALUE="d" onChange="display(this.value)">
<INPUT TYPE="text" NAME="myField2" VALUE="f" onChange="display(this.value)">
</FORM>
```

Note: Object, property, and method references can be passed as function arguments. Just like assigning any other value, they can be assigned to a variable as well. For example, you can use the following script segment instead of a `window.document.write` statement:

```
var obj = window.document
obj.write("Cool<BR>")
```

Be careful not to enclose an object reference in quotation marks—it is not a string.

Until now, the special object `this` was used as a substitute for a form element's full path. JavaScript also allows you to reference a form from an element's event handler script via the `form` property of this object. The previous source can be rewritten in the following form:

```
<SCRIPT LANGUAGE="JavaScript">
<!--
function process(callingElement)
{
   callingElement.elements[0].value = "thank you"
}
// -->
</SCRIPT>
<FORM>
<INPUT TYPE="text" NAME="myField" VALUE="email..." onChange=
         "process(this.form)">
</FORM>
```

The object representing the form is equivalent to `document.forms[0]`.

Generally speaking, every form element includes a `form` property that enables reverse access; that is, the ability to reach the form from its element (although the element is really the form's property). Therefore, you can use any one of the following expressions to access the first element of the first form in a given document:

```
document.forms[0].elements[0]
document.forms[0].elements[0].form.elements[0]
document.forms[0].elements[0].form.elements[0].form.elements[0]
```

You will probably never use this property independently in a script, because you can always refer to a form directly as a property of a window's `document` object. However, such a reference is used often with forms, because an event handler's script references the event handler as `this`, and the `form` property enables you to reference the form through a back door.

In addition to event handlers associated with form elements, you can also use `this` with event handlers of the `<FORM>` tag. In this case, `this` represents the object encompassing the entire form (such as `document.forms[0]`). Suppose you want to call a function from an `onSubmit` event handler. You can use the following outline to hand an object reference representing the `form` object to the function:

```
<FORM ... onSubmit="functionName(this)">
```

In this case, the expression `this.form` has no logical meaning.

Utilizing the form Property

In this chapter we discuss the various objects reflecting HTML form elements. Each form element is a direct property of the form to which it belongs. Take a look at the following example:

```
<FORM NAME="myForm">
<INPUT TYPE="text" NAME="myField" SIZE=10>
</FORM>
```

In this simple example, the `text` object may be referenced as `document.myForm.myField`. This top-to-bottom hierarchy enables you to access any form element object if you already have access to the `form` object itself. However, you may encounter a situation in which you pass a form element object to a function, for instance, and you want to reference the `form` object through a back door. JavaScript enables you to do so with the `form` property. For example, suppose you have a variable `myField` that holds a form element object. (For now, simply ignore how the object was assigned to the variable.) Assume the variable is named `objRef` and the object reference was explicitly assigned to it by the following statement:

```
var objRef = document.myForm.myField
```

Bear in mind that you do not have this statement in the script—all you have is the variable `objRef`, and you are attempting to reference the `form` object, `myForm`. You can use the `form` property to do so:

```
var formObjRef = objRef.form
```

`form` is a property of every form element object, with no exceptions. It is very convenient to invoke a function from an event handler with `this` as an argument. For example, consider the following script segment:

```
<SCRIPT LANGUAGE="JavaScript">
<!--
function getValue(otherElement)
{
   alert(otherElement.form.elements[1].value)
}
// -->
</SCRIPT>
<FORM>
<INPUT TYPE="button" VALUE="click me" onClick="getValue(this)">
<INPUT TYPE="text" VALUE="Baruch Spinoza" SIZE=10>
</FORM>
```

The output of this script is shown in Figure 18-4.

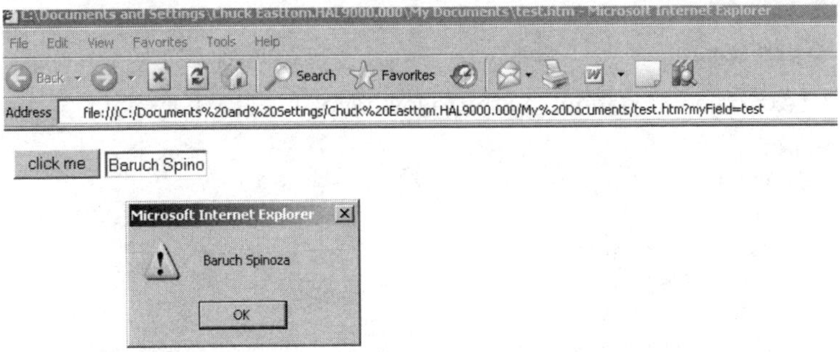

Figure 18-4. *Form elements*

The first `text` object (form element) invokes the `getValue` function with this object as the argument. The function is designed to print the value of the second element, `elements[1]`. The only relation between the value handed to the function (the object representing the first form element) and the second form element is that they are both "children" of the same "parent." The function accepts the object reflecting the first element, so it must access the second element through the common parent, the `form` object. Therefore, the correct syntax must include the `form` property (which is an object as well):

```
firstElement.form.secondElement
```

The `form` property acts like a connector in this case. If you implement a function that references various elements of a form, you may want to initially use `this.form` as the function's argument. You should then use the following code in place of the preceding script segment:

```
<SCRIPT LANGUAGE="JavaScript">
<!--
function getValue(form)
{
   alert(form.elements[1].value)
}
// -->
</SCRIPT>
<FORM>
<INPUT TYPE="button" VALUE="click me" onClick="getValue(this.form)">
<INPUT TYPE="text" VALUE="Baruch Spinoza" SIZE=10>
</FORM>
```

text Object

HTML Syntax

A text object is defined by the following plain HTML syntax:

```
<INPUT
   TYPE="text"
   NAME="textName"
   [VALUE="contents"]
   [SIZE="integer"]
   [MAXLENGTH="integer"]
   [onBlur="handlerStatement"]
   [onChange="handlerStatement"]
   [onFocus="handlerStatement"]
   [onSelect="handlerStatement"]>
```

The NAME attribute enables you to assign this HTML object a name that identifies it in both server-side queries and JavaScript scripts. The VALUE attribute accepts the initial string that should appear in the box when the page loads. Not only is this string the initial one in the text box, but it is also the default string. When you reset the form via a Reset button or the reset() method, this string reappears in the text box. The SIZE attribute is essential because it determines the size (in characters) of the text box. The MAXLENGTH attribute specifies the maximum input length allowed in this field. If the user enters a string that is longer than MAXLENGTH, only the first MAXLENGTH characters are entered. This option is especially handy when requesting a specific string, such as a password, which is naturally limited to a given length. The following script segment demonstrates the use of the text object in an HTML document:

```
Processor: <INPUT TYPE="text" NAME="comp" SIZE=15 MAXLENGTH=20
VALUE="Intel Xeon">
```

A text object can hold a maximum of one line. You can use a textarea object to display multiple lines.

JavaScript Access

There are basically four ways to access a text object via JavaScript:

```
[window.]document.formName.textName
[window.]document.formName.elements[index]
[window.]document.forms[index].textName
[window.]document.forms[index].elements[index]
```

You already know that a form can be accessed through its name or via the forms object when the form's index is known. Similarly, you can access a form's element by its name or through the elements array if the element's index is known.

The preceding expressions show how to access a `text` object by itself. Usually, you will not access the `text` object, but rather its properties, methods, or event handlers.

Event Handlers

The `text` object is a very convenient means for both input and output. A `text` object has a wealth of event handlers you can use.

onBlur

A blur event occurs when a text field loses focus. A field gains focus when the user clicks inside the text box, and the focus is lost when the user clicks outside the box, anywhere on the page. The `onBlur` event handler executes JavaScript code when a blur event occurs. Take a look at the following form and function:

```
<SCRIPT LANGUAGE="JavaScript">
<!--
function checkInput(element)
{
   if (element.value == "")
      alert("Please enter a value!")
}
// -->
</SCRIPT>
<FORM>
<INPUT TYPE="text" NAME="myField" VALUE="" onBlur="checkInput(this)">
</FORM>
```


The output of this script is shown in Figure 18-5.

Figure 18-5. Working with the element value property

If the box is left empty, an alert dialog box informs the user that he or she must enter a value. The dialog box is displayed only if the user first accesses the field and then exits it without entering any value.

onChange

A change event occurs when a blur event occurs and the value of the `text` object has been modified. The `onChange` event handler, also defined as an HTML tag attribute, executes JavaScript code when a change event occurs.

The `onChange` event handler is probably the most commonly used event handler with the `text` object (box or field). You can use this event handler when validating data entered by the user. That is, when the user modifies the text box content, a function is invoked to validate the changes. Validation via JavaScript instead of CGI or LiveWire saves precious network transmission time.

In order to demonstrate the `onBlur` event handler, a simple `form` element and a corresponding function have been implemented. The problem with this example is that the value of the text box is validated whenever it loses focus. It is generally better to validate the form only after changes are made. Therefore, the `onChange` event handler is superior for such tasks. The previous example is much better when rewritten as follows:

```
<SCRIPT LANGUAGE="JavaScript">
<!--
function checkInput(element)
{
   if (element.value == "")
      alert("Please enter a value!")
}
// -->
</SCRIPT>
<FORM>
<INPUT TYPE="text" NAME="myField1" VALUE="" onChange="checkInput(this)">
</FORM>
```

The following dual rule is very important in order to fully understand this event handler:

- A blur event naturally takes place whenever a change event occurs.
- A change event takes place only when a blur event occurs and the value of the `text` object has been modified and gained focus.

onFocus

A focus event occurs when a field receives input focus by tabbing on the keyboard or clicking with the mouse. The `onFocus` event handler obviously executes a prespecified code when a focus event occurs.

In addition, a focus event occurs in many browsers when the page loads. This behavior is not common to all browsers, so you should check the script with the various browsers you use to make sure it works the way you want.

The following script scrolls a T-banner in a `text` object. It starts when the user clicks somewhere inside the text box (`text` object), triggering the `onFocus` event handler. Here is the script:

```
<HTML>
<HEAD>
<TITLE>T-banner</TITLE>
<SCRIPT LANGUAGE="JavaScript">
<!--
// set speed of banner (pause in milliseconds between characters)
var speed = 100 // decrease value to increase speed (must be positive)
// set pause between completion of message and beginning of following one
var pause = 1000 // increase value to increase pause
```

```
// set initial values
var timerID = null
var bannerRunning = false
// create global array
var ar = new Array()
// assign the strings to the array's elements
ar[0] = "Welcome to our JavaScript page"
ar[1] = "We hope you enjoy the T-banner script"
ar[2] = "It is designed to be more stable than regular banners"
ar[3] = "Don't forget to check out my other scripts"
// set index of first message to be displayed first
var currentMessage = 0
// set index of last character to be displayed first
var offset = 0
// stop the banner if it is currently running
function stopBanner()
{
   // if banner is currently running
   if (bannerRunning)
      // stop the banner
      clearTimeout(timerID)
   // timer is now stopped
   bannerRunning = false
}
// start the banner
function startBanner()
{
   // make sure the banner is stopped
   stopBanner()
   // start the banner from the current position
   showBanner()
}
// type in the current message
function showBanner()
{
   // assign current message to variable
   var text = ar[currentMessage]
   // if current message has not finished being displayed
   if (offset < text.length)
   {
      // if last character of current message is a space
      if (text.charAt(offset) == " ")
         // skip the current character
         offset++
      // assign the up-to-date to-be-displayed substring
      // second argument of method accepts index of last character plus one
      var partialMessage = text.substring(0, offset + 1)
      // display partial message in text field
      document.bannerForm.bannerField.value = partialMessage
      // increment index of last character to be displayed
      offset++ // IE sometimes has trouble with "++offset"
      // recursive call after specified time
      timerID = setTimeout("showBanner()", speed)
      // banner is running
```

```
        bannerRunning = true
    } else
    {
        // reset offset
        offset = 0
        // increment subscript (index) of current message
        currentMessage++
        // if subscript of current message is out of range
        if (currentMessage == ar.length)
            // wrap around (start from beginning)
            currentMessage = 0
        // recursive call after specified time
        timerID = setTimeout("showBanner()", pause)
        // banner is running
        bannerRunning = true
    }
}
// -->
</SCRIPT>
</HEAD>
<BODY>
<FORM NAME="bannerForm">
<INPUT TYPE="text" NAME="bannerField" VALUE="Click here..." SIZE=50
            onFocus="if (!bannerRunning) { startBanner() }">
</FORM>
</BODY>
</HTML>
```

Example 18-2 (ex18-2.htm). *A T-banner starts in a text box when the user clicks in the box*

First of all, notice the form named `bannerForm` in the HTML body. The form consists of only one element, a `text` object named `bannerField`. Its size is set to 50 characters, and its default value is the string `"Click here..."`. The `onFocus` event handler is provided. When the user clicks inside the text box, a focus event occurs and the `startBanner()` function is invoked to start the scrolling. Notice that this statement is executed only if the banner is not running. The variable `bannerRunning` holds the banner's current state and is already true when the page loads.

The only difference between the original status bar-based T-banner script earlier in this book and the text box-based one in Example 18-2 is that the property `window.status` is replaced by `document.bannerForm.bannerField.value`, which is the reference to the `text` object's content-reflecting property.

onSelect

A select event occurs when the user selects part of the text within a text field. The `onSelect` event handler enables you to respond to such an event.

Here is the general syntax for implementing this event handler:

```
<INPUT TYPE="text" VALUE="" NAME="valueField" onSelect="selectState()">
```

Since the select event is rather rare and insignificant, this event handler is not commonly used. It was also broken in some versions of Navigator prior to version 4.5.

Methods

blur()

You already know what a blur event is. You can explicitly blur a `text` object using the object's `blur()` method, which removes focus from the field. This method deselects any text that might be selected in the field and removes the text insertion pointer from the field. At this point, no fields or form elements are focused. A manual way to blur a `text` object is to press the Tab key, which advances focus to the next field in order and removes it from the current field (blurring it). However, the JavaScript `blur()` method only removes focus from its object, without giving focus to any other field in the form or in the page.

A read-only text field is a classic example for using the `blur()` method. The algorithm to create such a field is very simple. When the user explicitly gives focus to a field in order to write in it, an event handler (`onFocus`) invokes the `blur()` method to instantly remove the focus. Here is a read-only text field example:

```
<INPUT TYPE="text" NAME="myField" VALUE="" SIZE=15 onFocus="this.blur()">
```

You can consider the expression `onFocus="this.blur()"` an attribute of a read-only `<INPUT TYPE="text">` element.

focus()

The `focus()` method focuses on a `text` object (or other form element object). Focusing on a form element usually means that the window scrolls until the text field is viewable and the cursor is positioned at the beginning of the text in the field.

Although not mandatory, it is a good practice to give focus to a `text` object before accessing it. It will have a positive contribution to the script's robustness.

When the page contains many fields, you can use the script-driven `focus()` method to emphasize one of them, thus "attracting" the user to it. The `focus()` method resembles the camera's focus: It emphasizes a specific object and prepares it for further use.

The following HTML tag can be used to maintain focus on a `text` object (it may be useful if you have multiple `text` objects and the user is allowed to modify only one of them):

```
<INPUT TYPE="text" NAME="myField" VALUE="" SIZE=15 onBlur="this.focus()">
```

When the text field loses focus, a blur event occurs, the `onBlur` event handler is triggered, and focus is given once again to the field.

The `focus()` method usually belongs to `text` objects (fields), but, as will be explained later in this chapter, other kinds of objects use it as well.

select()

The most useful method of the `text` object is the `select()` method. When you select a field via JavaScript, all the text in the field is selected.

In Navigator on some platforms, you must give focus to a text field before selecting it. Suppose you have a document with one form that contains one element, a `text` object. The following script segment is needed in order to select that text field via JavaScript:

```
document.forms[0].elements[0].focus()
document.forms[0].elements[0].blur()
```

The `select()` method is extremely useful and very convenient when validating a form on the client side. For example, let's say you have a form that accepts inputs from the user for several elements and validates each element in turn before submitting the data to the server. The most basic way to report an error is to display a message in an alert dialog box. More sophisticated error reporting includes automatic preparation of the form for the user's corrections. Such preparation can be implemented by using the `focus()` and `select()` methods together. When the script encounters a text field that contains invalid data, you can direct the cursor to that field and automatically highlight the interior text. The user can then write the new, correct value without having to delete the invalid entry. Sounds quite complicated on the programmer's behalf, but it is actually very simple. The following script and form demonstrate simple validation and handy error reporting:

```
<HTML>
<HEAD>
<TITLE>Simple form validation</TITLE>
</HEAD>
<SCRIPT LANGUAGE="JavaScript">
<!--
function checkName(field)
{
   if (field.value == "")
   {
      alert("Value is required")
      field.focus()
      field.select()
   } else
      if (field.value.split(" ").length < 2)
      {
         alert("Enter full name")
         field.focus()
         field.select()
      }
```

```
}
function checkEmail(field)
{
   if (field.value.indexOf("@") == -1)
   {
      alert("Enter a valid e-mail address")
      field.focus()
      field.select()
   }
}
// -->
</SCRIPT>
<BODY>
<FORM>
Full name: <INPUT TYPE="text" NAME="userName" VALUE="" SIZE=15
                      onChange="checkName(this)">
<BR>
Email address: <INPUT TYPE="text" NAME="email" VALUE="" SIZE=15
                      onChange="checkEmail(this)">
</FORM>
</BODY>
</HTML>
```

***Example 18-3 (ex18-3.htm)**. A simple form validation and error handling script*

The form in Example 18-3 includes two `text` objects: the user's full name and e-mail address. The element (text field) object is passed as an argument to the two different event handler functions. The `value` property reflects the current string in the text field.

`checkName()` checks that the value of its calling object (text field) is not empty and that it contains exactly two words (with a separating space). If one of these rules is violated, an appropriate message is displayed, and the calling element (the `userName text` object) is focused and selected, indicating the invalid text field.

`checkEmail()` checks if the value of its calling `text` object contains an "at" character (@). If one is not found, an appropriate message is displayed, and the calling element (the `email text` object) is focused and selected. The text within the field is highlighted by the `select()` method of the second `text` object in the form. As you can see, the script conveniently uses this for all references to the form element objects. Also notice that the field checking is done per mouse click anywhere inside the window.

Properties

defaultValue

The `defaultValue` property is a string indicating the default value of a `text` object. The default value is initially assigned to the `VALUE` attribute of the HTML tag, reflected also by JavaScript's `defaultValue` property. Setting this property in JavaScript overrides the initial HTML values. You can set and read the `defaultValue` property at any time, even after layout has been completed. Since it reflects the field's default value only (the one seen when the page loads or after resetting the form), this property cannot be used to dynamically update the text in the field.

If the HTML attribute `VALUE` is not specified, `defaultValue` defaults to an empty string, as if explicitly specifying `VALUE=""`.

The following script segment demonstrates a simple use of the `defaultValue` property to reset only a specific form element (a `text` object in this case), rather than resetting the entire form with the Reset button or the `reset()` method. Note that this script uses the `value` property, which we discuss later.

```
<SCRIPT LANGUAGE="JavaScript">
<!--
function resetField(sub)
{
   document.forms[0].elements[sub].value = document.forms[0]
                     .elements[sub].defaultValue
}
// -->
</SCRIPT>
<FORM NAME="fields">
<INPUT TYPE="text" NAME="field1" VALUE="enter first" SIZE=15>
<A HREF="javascript:resetField(0)">reset</A><BR>
<INPUT TYPE="text" NAME="field2" VALUE="enter second" SIZE=15>
<A HREF="javascript:resetField(1)">reset</A><BR>
<INPUT TYPE="text" NAME="field3" VALUE="enter third" SIZE=15>
<A HREF="javascript:resetField(2)">reset</A><BR>
</FORM>
```

Since we haven't discussed buttons yet, this script uses links for invoking JavaScript functions. A link is not a form element, so you cannot refer to `this` or `this.form` inside the `resetField()` function. To work around this problem, each link is identified by the index of the corresponding `text` object and is handed to the function as an argument. The first link, for example, is responsible for resetting the first `text` object in the form, so it hands a `0` to the `resetField()` function. Instead of resetting the form element, the function sets the current value of the corresponding text field to its default value.

name

It is generally a good practice to name every form element, especially the `text` objects. Names are mandatory for CGI scripts, which use them for field identification and value extraction. Since it allows more logical and convenient access to JavaScript `text` objects, identifying `text` objects by name contributes significantly to the script's robustness and ease of maintenance. All names, therefore, should be meaningful and adhere to JavaScript's naming conventions.

The `name` property initially reflects the value of the HTML's `NAME` attribute. Changing the value of this property overrides the initial HTML setting. By assigning a new string to the `name` property, you can set the name of a `text` object at any time.

Do not confuse this property with the text that appears in the field. A field's content is represented by the `VALUE` attribute, rather than the `NAME` attribute. Hence, if you modify the value of `name`, you will notice no change in the page's appearance.

You should recall that a form element can be referenced by its index or by its name. If a form contains multiple elements with identical names, they form an array. Although this situation is especially common to radio buttons, as you will see later in this chapter, you may encounter it with `text` objects as well. The following example demonstrates the use of such arrays to handle complex forms:

```
<HTML>
<HEAD>
<TITLE>Form element arrays</TITLE>
<SCRIPT LANGUAGE="JavaScript">
<!--
function correctName()
{
   for (var i = 0; i < document.fields.username.length; ++i)
   {
      var field = document.fields.username[i]
      field.value = field.value.charAt(0).toUpperCase() + field
                 .value.substring(1, field.value.length)
   }
}
function checkEmail()
{
   for (var i = 0; i < document.fields.email.length; ++i)
   {
      var field = document.fields.email[i]
      if (field.value.indexOf("@") == -1)
      {
         alert("Error in email address!")
         field.focus()
         field.select()
         return
      }
   }
}
// -->
</SCRIPT>
</HEAD>
<BODY>
<FORM NAME="fields">
Employee #1: <INPUT TYPE="text" NAME="username" VALUE="first name" SIZE=10>
<INPUT TYPE="text" NAME="username" VALUE="last name" SIZE=10>
<INPUT TYPE="text" NAME="email" VALUE="email" SIZE=10><BR>
Employee #2: <INPUT TYPE="text" NAME="username" VALUE="first name" SIZE=10>
<INPUT TYPE="text" NAME="username" VALUE="last name" SIZE=10>
<INPUT TYPE="text" NAME="email" VALUE="email" SIZE=10><BR>
Employee #3: <INPUT TYPE="text" NAME="username" VALUE="first name" SIZE=10>
<INPUT TYPE="text" NAME="username" VALUE="last name" SIZE=10>
<INPUT TYPE="text" NAME="email" VALUE="email" SIZE=10><BR>
```

```
<P>
<A HREF="javascript:checkEmail()">Check email addresses</A>.
<A HREF="javascript:correctName()">Correct names</A>.
</FORM>
</BODY>
</HTML>
```

Example 18-4 (ex18-4.htm). *A form validation script based on arrays reflecting elements with identical names*

In order to understand this listing you must be aware of the page's initial appearance:

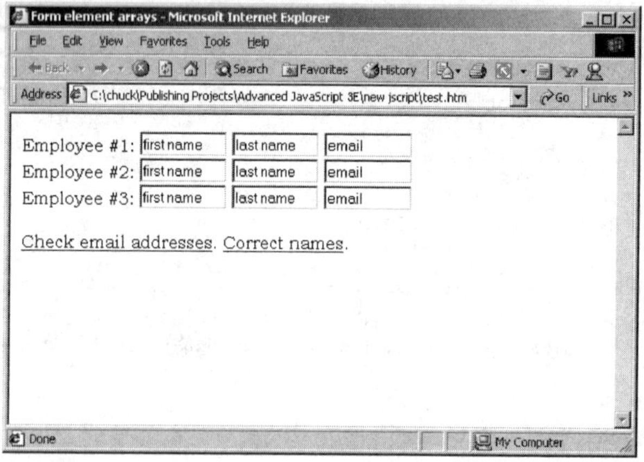

Figure 18-6. *A form that collects data about several people*

As you can see, this form is divided into nine `text` objects. All six `text` objects for entering first and last names are named `username`. The value of `document.forms[0].elements[0].name`, for example, is equal to the string `"username"`. The three `text` objects for entering e-mail addresses are named `email`.

There are basically two element groups, `username` and `email`. Since all form elements are named fields, you can reference these two groups as arrays via the following syntax:

```
document.fields.username
document.fields.email
```

Both arrays have a `length` property, representing the number of elements sharing the given name. The `length` and elements of the `username` array, for example, can be referenced as follows:

```
document.fields.username.length  // number of name-related elements
document.fields.username[0]      // first First Name object
document.fields.username[1]      // first Last Name object
document.fields.username[2]      // second First Name object
document.fields.username[3]      // second Last Name object
document.fields.username[4]      // third First Name object
document.fields.username[5]      // third Last Name object
```

The same syntax is also used to reference elements of the `email` array. Take another look at the script in Example 18-4. It includes two functions, one for handling name input fields and one for e-mails. The first function, `correctName()`, loops through all username elements and capitalizes their first letters. The second function uses the same technique to alert the user if any of the e-mail addresses do not include the "at" character (@). If such a field is found, the function focuses on and selects it, in order to attract the user's attention to the invalid field.

You should normally assign a distinct name to each and every form element. Example 18-4 demonstrates that in some cases, however, it is much more convenient to reuse a specific name in order to enable a loop-based processing of elements that share similar characteristics.

value

The `value` property reflects the current text located in a given `text` object (field). It is not equivalent to any HTML attribute. You can read and set this property at any time. The field's content is updated immediately upon setting. Although we have been using this property throughout this chapter, here is another example that shows how to reference the `value` attribute of the first element of the first form in a page:

```
document.forms[0].elements[0].value
```


password Object

HTML Syntax

Another possible value for the `TYPE` attribute is `"password"`. It is similar to the `"text"` option except that, instead of displaying the user's input, it responds to any typed character with a predefined single character, such as an asterisk (*). The general syntax of this object is as follows:

```
<INPUT
   TYPE="password"
   NAME="passwordName"
   [VALUE="contents"]
   [SIZE="integer"]
   [MAXLENGTH="integer"]
   [onBlur="handlerStatement"]
   [onChange="handlerStatement"]
   [onFocus="handlerStatement"]
   [onSelect="handlerStatement"]>
```

The `value` property is an asterisk character (or any other character chosen by the browser). The additional properties are identical to those of the text input type. Here is a simple password box code:

```
Password: <INPUT TYPE="password" NAME="pswrd" SIZE=15 MAXLENGTH=20 VALUE="">
```

The value of the password box is the typed-in string, not the asterisks (or other characters) that appear. The value is hidden so it cannot be seen by someone near the user.

JavaScript Access

Like all other elements, there are four ways to access a password object via JavaScript:

```
[window.]document.formName.passwordName
[window.]document.formName.elements[index]
[window.]document.forms[index].passwordName
[window.]document.forms[index].elements[index]
```

All methods and element references adhere to one of these alternatives.

Event Handlers

The `password` event handlers are identical to those of the `text` object in all aspects. Refer to earlier discussion in this and other chapters.

Properties and Methods

The `password` object's properties are:

- `defaultValue`
- `name`
- `value`

The `password` object's methods are identical to those of the `text` object:

- `focus`
- `blur`
- `select`

The `password` object was not very useful in Netscape Navigator 2.0 because JavaScript was not allowed to access its value. Starting with version 3.0, JavaScript on Navigator and Internet Explorer can freely access the `VALUE` attribute as if it were a `text` object. In terms of JavaScript, the `password` object is identical to the `text` object. The only difference is that the value of the password field is never displayed.

textarea Object

HTML Syntax

Multiple lines of text can be entered into a form via text areas, which are defined by the `<TEXTAREA></TEXTAREA>` tag pair. You should always name a text area and specify its size. The general syntax of the `<TEXTAREA>` tag is as follows:

```
<TEXTAREA
   NAME="textareaName"
   ROWS="integer"
   COLS="integer"
   WRAP="off | virtual | physical"
   [onBlur="handlerStatement"]
   [onChange="handlerStatement"]
   [onFocus="handlerStatement"]
   [onSelect="handlerStatement"]>
   textToDisplay
</TEXTAREA>
```

The attributes are:

- NAME—specifies the name (label) of the text area element. It is very difficult to work with unnamed text areas, so always name your text areas according to JavaScript naming conventions.
- ROWS—specifies the number of text rows in the text area. Since Netscape Navigator and Microsoft Internet Explorer use different size fonts in text fields, you cannot set the text area size in pixels by setting ROWS.
- COLS—specifies the number of text columns in the text area. It is equal to the number of characters in one text line.

It is possible to initialize the text area by placing text between the <TEXTAREA> and </TEXTAREA> tags in the following fashion:

```
<TEXTAREA NAME="comments" COLS=35 ROWS=5>
Write any comments regarding this page here.
Don't forget to mention your e-mail address.
</TEXTAREA>
```

Carriage return characters are interpreted as new lines in this text zone. Netscape Navigator enables you to write HTML tags in the text area by simply placing the script between the opening and closing <TEXTAREA> tags.

Another attribute accepted by the <TEXTAREA> tag is WRAP. It can be set to one of the following values:

- off—do not wrap lines (default value).
- virtual—wrap lines on the screen but refer to them as one line otherwise.
- physical—insert actual line breaks (CR characters) in the string.

JavaScript Access

There are four ways to access a textarea object via JavaScript:

```
[window.]document.formName.textareaName
[window.]document.formName.elements[index]
[window.]document.forms[index].textareaName
[window.]document.forms[index].elements[index]
```

Event Handlers

The `textarea` object's event handlers are identical to those of the `text` object.

Properties and Methods

Like the event handlers, all properties and methods of the `textarea` object are exactly the same as those of the `text` object and `password` object. Please refer to previous listings for the `text` object in order to learn about its properties, methods, and event handlers.

Inserting New Line Characters

A text area field is actually a multiline text field. Printing output to a `textarea` object is somewhat more complicated than printing to a `text` object due to the extra complication of new line insertion. This is especially important when the `WRAP` attribute is set to `off` and you are interested in avoiding a long horizontal text span.

Since the new line character is not uniform across different platforms, inserting a new line is not as simple as inserting any other printable character. The new line character on Unix- and Macintosh-based machines is `"\n"`, while Windows operating systems require the `"\r\n"` pair. The simplest way to work around the problem is to test the actual platform and insert the corresponding new line character. Here is a function that automatically returns the correct string for the user's platform:

```
function getNL()
{
   if (navigator.appVersion.lastIndexOf('Win') != -1)
      return "\r\n"
   /* else */
      return "\n"
}
```

You can assign the new line character in the following fashion:

```
var NL = getNL()
```

Now, you can use the function's return value to place multiple-line text in a `textarea` object. Here is a simple example:

```
document.forms[0].elements[0].value = "line 1" + NL + "line 2"
```

Important Note: Netscape Navigator supports "\n" as a new line character on all platforms.

Handling textareas by Line

In general, you cannot deal with specific lines of text area content. The following function overcomes this deficiency by assigning the text to an array, line by line:

```
function getLines(textareaReference)
{
   var str = escape(textareaReference.value)
   var ar = str.split("%0D%0A") // "%0D%0A" <=> "\r\n"
   if (ar.length == 0)
      ar = str.split("%0A") // "%0A" <=> "\n"
   for (var i = 0; i < ar.length; ++i)
   {
      ar[i] = unescape(ar[i])
   }
   return ar
}
```

The function is a bit tricky. It first encodes the `textarea`'s value via the `escape` function and assigns the "escaped" string to a local variable, `str`. You may recall that after `escape`, any nonalphanumeric characters are represented in a "*%XX*" format. The escape sequence `"\n"` is represented as `"%0A"` (zero + A), whereas `"\r"` is converted to `"%0D"` (zero + D). The entire encoded string is then spliced with the `split()` method, using either the `"%0D%0A"` or the `"%0A"` string as the delimiter. The "trick" is to use the second delimiter (`"%0A"`) only after the first one (`"%0D%0A"`) fails to split the text. At the end, each element of the `ar` array is decoded back by the `unescape` function and the final array of lines is returned.

hidden Object

HTML Syntax

A hidden form field is one that is not displayed on an HTML page. It is used for passing unique identification values upon submission. Since the user cannot modify or interact with a hidden element, the initial value given when the page loads stays the same throughout the life of the page. The `hidden` object, then, is not useful for the user but rather for the programmer. For example, on a large web site, a server-side application can use a `hidden` object to distinguish between different forms submitted to the server.

Except that it is not viewable, you should basically treat the hidden element exactly like the text type. The element's general syntax is:

```
<INPUT
   TYPE="hidden"
   NAME="hiddenName"
   [VALUE="textValue"]>
```

The NAME property specifies the name of the hidden object, whereas VALUE specifies the value of the field. Although not viewable, they are part of the form's content, as any other element type's attributes.

JavaScript Access

There are four ways to reference a hidden object:

```
[window.]document.formName.hiddenName
[window.]document.formName.elements[index]
[window.]document.forms[index].hiddenName
[window.]document.forms[index].elements[index]
```

Event Handlers

Since a hidden object cannot be seen on a page, no events can be associated with it, and hence there is no support for event handlers for hidden objects.

Properties and Methods

Since all methods associated with form element objects emulate events, a hidden object does not have any methods.

A hidden object does have several properties that you can access via JavaScript. The object's properties are:

- defaultValue
- name
- value

These properties are equivalent to those of the text, password, and textarea objects. You can read and set the value property, for example, at any time. The value property can be used to earmark forms submitted to the server for identification by a server-side application.

button, submit, and reset Objects

HTML Syntax

The most precise input event is a button click. submit, reset, and button objects are all buttons that feature identical properties and attributes. The general syntax of a button object is as follows:

```
<INPUT
   TYPE="button" | "submit" | "reset"
   NAME="buttonName"
   VALUE="buttonText"
   [onClick="handlerText"]>
```

Although a plain button (<INPUT TYPE="button">) does not have any explicit meaning in HTML, it is extremely useful in JavaScript scripts. A

Submit button plays a very important role in all forms that are submitted to a server. A Reset button resets the form in which it is located.

A button's style depends on the client's platform. Macintosh buttons, for example, are different from Windows buttons. The only control you have over a button's appearance is by determining its label, initially defined by the VALUE attribute. Since the button size is determined solely by the label string, you can only modify its width by padding it with spaces on both ends. This "sophisticated" technique may be very annoying, but it is the only way to explicitly control a button's size.

A Submit button's syntax differs from plain buttons and Reset buttons only in the value assigned to the TYPE attribute, "submit". This button is primarily designed for server-side applications. When the user clicks such a button, the form's data is sent to the URL specified in the <FORM> tag's ACTION attribute. A Reset button's TYPE is "reset" and, when clicked, it resets the entire form. A plain button (with no HTML meaning) is defined by assigning "button" to the TYPE attribute.

JavaScript Access

The four ways you can reference a button via JavaScript are:

```
[window.]document.formName.buttonName
[window.]document.formName.elements[index]
[window.]document.forms[index].buttonName
[window.]document.forms[index].elements[index]
```


Event Handlers

All button objects (button, reset, and submit) are associated with a single event, and therefore support only one event handler. This event handler is probably the most important of all form-related event handlers.

onClick

A button, by definition, has only one designation—to be clicked. Its event handler, therefore, responds only to a click event. Such an event occurs when the user presses the button and then releases it while the pointer is still atop the button. The event does not take place immediately when the user presses the button, in order to give the user a chance to cancel the clicking action by releasing it outside the button area.

You can also use this event handler with Submit and Reset buttons. The onClick event handler script is executed prior to performing the built-in action associated with a button. You can use this event, for example, to compute a certain expression and assign its value to the value property of an existing form element object.

The general syntax for this event handler is as follows:

```
<INPUT TYPE=... onClick="handlerScript">
```

Netscape Navigator supports an option to cancel a click event. This is also supported in Mozilla Firefox. This can be done by having the event handler return false, much the same way you cancel a form's submission or resetting. The canceled action is the one defined by the button (or other objects that support this event handler). Canceling a click event of a Submit button, for example, cancels the form's submission.

Example 18-5 demonstrates the usage of the `onClick` event handler for invoking a function that handles other elements of the form:

```
<HTML>
<HEAD>
<TITLE>Expression evaluator</TITLE>
<SCRIPT LANGUAGE="JavaScript">
<!--
function compute(form)
{
   form.result.value = eval(form.expression.value)
}
// -->
</SCRIPT>
</HEAD>
<BODY>
<FORM>
<INPUT TYPE="text" NAME="expression" VALUE="" SIZE=15> =
<INPUT TYPE="text" NAME="result" VALUE="" SIZE=8 onFocus="this.blur()">
<P>
<INPUT TYPE="button" NAME="computeButton" VALUE="compute" onClick=
                 "compute(this.form)">
<INPUT TYPE="button" NAME="clear" VALUE="clear result" onClick=
                 "this.form.result.value = ''">
</FORM>
</BODY>
</HTML>
```

Example 18-5 (ex18-5.htm). *A simple expression evaluation script*

The user types any numeric expression (such as 4 + 6 * 15) in the upper-left field, and, after pressing "compute," the result appears in the upper-right field. The "clear result" button deletes the value in that field.

The form contains four elements. The first two are `text` objects—each with its own unique attributes. The first button, named `computeButton`, uses an `onClick` event handler to call the `compute` function with the object reflecting the entire form. The second button provides the only means for clearing the result field (the upper-right one).

The `onClick` event handler of this object is a single, immediate statement. Its `onFocus` event handler creates a read-only field by calling the `blur` method.

Since the entire form object is assigned to `compute`'s `form` parameter, the property `form.result.value` refers to the content of the top-right `text` object, whereas `form.expression.value` refers to the text inside the first field. The text in the first field is evaluated, and the numeric result becomes its value. If the left field contains the expression `5 * 3 - 2`, for example, then eval returns 13, which is placed in the second text object by assigning 13 to its value property.

Methods

click()

A button's click() method simulates the user's action of clicking that button. It causes the same action as would a human click, except that the button's onClick event handler is not triggered. Since their only usefulness is in triggering the onClick event handler, this method is not useful for TYPE="button" buttons. On some platforms, a visual border effect is created when invoking this method.

You will probably never need to use this method, but here is an example for your reference:

```
document.forms[0].elements[0].click()
```

Properties

name

A button's name property is an exact reflection of the NAME attribute and is read-only. In order to respond correctly to an event, the onClick event handler function commonly uses this property to figure out which button was clicked. Here is an example of how to reference this property:

```
var buttonName = document.forms[0].elements[0].name
```

value

A button's value is the visual label you give the button by assigning it to the VALUE attribute of the <INPUT> tag. All form elements defined by the <INPUT> tag feature this attribute. As far as buttons are concerned, the length of the string determines the button's size. The VALUE attribute can be more than one word, and should generally be enclosed by quotation marks.

The VALUE attribute is reflected in JavaScript by the value property. Although it is unlikely you will ever need to extract the property's value, its modification may be useful. Suppose you have a single button on a web page, and you want its label to change whenever the user clicks the button. You can implement such behavior by modifying the value property as a response to the click event. Netscape Navigator began enabling explicit JavaScript setting of event handlers in version 3.0, so you can even modify the event handler's script along with the button's label to create a "new" button on the fly (without reloading the page). Example 18-6 uses these features to create a simple stopwatch.

```
<HTML>
<HEAD>
<TITLE>stopwatch (timer)</TITLE>
<SCRIPT LANGUAGE="JavaScript">
<!--
```

```
// set initial values
var timerRunning = false
var timerID = null
// create instance of Date object representing current time
var initial = new Date()
// start timer
function start()
{
   // set the button's label to "stop"
   document.forms[0].general.value = "stop"
   // assign the stop function reference to the button's onClick event handler
   document.forms[0].general.onclick = stop
   // ask if the user wants to reset the timer
   if (confirm("Would you like to reset the timer?"))
      // set global variable to new time
      initial = new Date()
   // assign milliseconds since 1970 to global variable
   startTime = initial.getTime()
   // make sure the timer is stopped
   stopTimer()
   // run and display timer
   showTimer()
}
// set button to initial settings
function stop()
{
   // set the button's label to "start"
   document.forms[0].general.value = "start"
   // assign the start function reference to the button's onClick event handler
   document.forms[0].general.onclick = start
   // stop timer
   stopTimer()
}
// stop timer
function stopTimer()
{
   // if the timer is currently running
   if (timerRunning)
      // clear the current timeout (stop the timer)
      clearTimeout(timerID)
      // assign false to global variable because timer is not running
   timerRunning = false
}
function showTimer()
{
   // create instance of Date representing current timer
   var current = new Date()
   // assign milliseconds since 1970 to local variable
   var curTime = current.getTime()
   // assign difference in milliseconds since timer was cleared
   var dif = curTime - startTime
   // assign difference in seconds to local variable
   var result = dif / 1000
   // if result is not positive
```

```
    if (result < 1)
        // attach an initial "0" to beginning
        result = "0" + result
        // convert result to string
    result = result.toString()
    // if result is integer
    if (result.indexOf(".") == -1)
        // attach ".00" to end
        result += ".00"
    // if result contains only one digit after decimal point
    if (result.length - result.indexOf(".") <= 2)
        // add a second digit after point
        result += "0"
    // place result in text field
    document.forms[0].display.value = result
    // call function recursively immediately (must use setTimeout to
    // avoid overflow)
    timerID = setTimeout("showTimer()", 0)
    // timer is currently running
    timerRunning = true
}
// -->
</SCRIPT>
</HEAD>
<BODY>
<FORM>
<INPUT TYPE="text" NAME="display" VALUE="" onFocus="this.blur()">
<INPUT TYPE="button" NAME="general" VALUE="start" onClick="start()">
</FORM>
</BODY>
</HTML>
```

Example 18-6 (ex18-6.htm). *A simple timer with an adjusting button*

Look through the script for a few minutes, and make sure you understand the recursive flow and the handling of time-related features. Since most of the features in this script should be well known to you by now, we'll just cover the new and difficult ones.

Take a look at the following statements from the `start()` function:

```
// set the button's label to "stop"
document.forms[0].general.value = "stop"
// assign the stop function reference to the button's onClick event handler
document.forms[0].general.onclick = stop
```

The first statement adjusts the button's label by assigning it a new value—`stop`. The second statement assigns a function reference (no parentheses because it is a function reference, not a function call) to the button's `onClick` event handler. Notice that the event handler must be specified in lowercase letters. These statements convert the Start button to a Stop button. The following statements from the `stop()` function convert the Stop button back to a Start button, on the fly:

```
// set the button's label to "start"
document.forms[0].general.value = "start"
// assign the start function reference to the button's onClick event handler
document.forms[0].general.onclick = start
```

Notice that the button is labeled "stop" when the timer is running and is labeled "start" otherwise.

The form in Example 18-6 consists of two elements. The first one is a read-only `text` object (set via an event handler), whereas the second one is a simple button.

Setting the value of a button is somewhat problematic. First, the button size is not adjusted to the new label, so any excess text is dropped on both sides. Another problem is that since the button label is centered, you do not have control over its alignment with other buttons of different form elements. If you initialize a button to a very long string via its HTML attribute (try assigning a string with many spaces to `VALUE`), you can even run a T-banner on the button!

checkbox Object

HTML Syntax

A check box is a small box that reflects an "on" or "off" state. An HTML check box is a form element that closely resembles a check box on a paper form. If a mark is placed in the box, the current state is considered true. If the check box is unchecked, the current state is false.

Check boxes are used a lot in server-based forms. If a box is checked, it is included in the submitted data, whereas if it is empty it is excluded from the data submitted to the server. Since a check box is an individual form element that is not grouped with other elements, you should apply a distinct name to every check box in a form. The user can check or uncheck a box at any time after the page has been laid out.

The general syntax of a `checkbox` object is as follows:

```
<INPUT
   TYPE="checkbox"
   NAME="checkboxName"
   VALUE="checkboxValue"
   [CHECKED]
   [onClick="handlerText"]>
```

Both the `NAME` and `VALUE` attributes specify internal values that are not displayed on the page. In order to label a check box, you should simply place the label directly after the check box, so it appears as if connected to the object. The following piece of code demonstrates this trick:

```
Select all the computers used at your business:
<P>
<INPUT TYPE="checkbox" NAME="PC">PC
<P>
<INPUT TYPE="checkbox" NAME="Mac">Macintosh
<P>
<INPUT TYPE="checkbox" NAME="Unix">Unix (X-Windows)
```

In order to create a check box that is initially checked, you simply specify the `CHECKED` attribute, without assigning it any value. Its presence determines the initial state of the check box when the page loads.

A JavaScript `checkbox` provides a wide variety of functionality, but you should not use it as a regular button (supporting, for example, an `onClick` event handler); rather use it only as a yes/no selection interface. You can, however, use the click event to trigger a side-effect statement. It is important to recognize that a check box is primarily a toggle switch.

JavaScript Access

There are basically four ways to reference a `checkbox`:

```
[window.]document.formName.checkboxName
[window.]document.formName.elements[index]
[window.]document.forms[index].checkboxName
[window.]document.forms[index].elements[index]
```


Event Handlers

onClick

Since a check box responds to only the click event, the `checkbox` object does not support event handlers other than `onClick`. Use this event handler when you want to invoke a function or execute a statement immediately when the user clicks a check box. A click event occurs when the user clicks a check box, regardless of whether it is checked or empty.

Again, be extremely conservative when using this event handler. A check box should be used only for yes/no selection.

Methods

click()

The `checkbox` object supports only the `click()` method, which is equivalent to manually clicking the check box. You can use this method to implement a nonmodifiable check box, for example, by clicking the check box whenever the user clicks it, thus always reversing the user's action and leaving the check box untouched. Here is how to define such a "read-only" check box:

```
<INPUT TYPE="checkbox" onClick="this.click()">
```

Another useful implementation of this method is to open an invisible connection between two or more check boxes. Here is an example script that always keeps two check boxes at the same state (checked or unchecked):

```
<SCRIPT LANGUAGE="JavaScript">
<!--
function connectMe(destination)
{
   document.forms[0].elements[destination].click()
}
// -->
</SCRIPT>
</HEAD>
<BODY>
<FORM>
<INPUT TYPE="checkbox" onClick="connectMe(1)"> Number 1<BR>
<INPUT TYPE="checkbox" onClick="connectMe(0)"> Number 2
</FORM>
```

Each check box's `onClick` event handler invokes the `connectMe()` function with the target check box's index as the argument. The second check box's event handler, for example, calls `connectMe()` with a `0` value because it is connected to the first check box (its index is `0`). The `connectMe()` function simply emulates a click event for the form element at the given index.

The `click()` method does not trigger the `onClick` event handler so you should not worry about the script getting into an infinite loop here. You can generalize the `connectMe()` function to handle an array of check boxes with a `for` loop.

Properties

checked

The `checkbox`'s Boolean property `checked` reflects the button's current state. A true value means that the specified check box is checked, whereas a false one represents an unchecked box. Of the properties supported by the `checkbox` object, this property is both the simplest and the most useful. You can read and adjust this property at any time, even after layout has been completed.

Checking and unchecking a check box is accomplished by simply assigning the corresponding Boolean value to the object's `checked` property. The following statement unchecks a box:

```
document.forms[0].elements[0].checked = false
```

Since a check box can be set to either of the two possible states regardless of the current one, you do not have to use an `if` statement to determine the current state and then invoke the action accordingly. Be aware that setting the state of a check box by assigning `checked` is much more efficient than probing the current state and calling the check box's `click()` method.

Example 18-7 demonstrates the use of the `checked` property in a simple game. It features both reading the `checked` property as well as setting it. The objective of the game is to check as many boxes as possible within 20 seconds (20,000 milliseconds). The accumulated number of currently checked boxes is displayed in a `text` object at the top. When the time has elapsed, all check boxes become read-only, and a Start button is placed at the bottom for restarting the game.

```
<HTML>
<HEAD>
<TITLE>Checkbox game</TITLE>
<SCRIPT LANGUAGE="JavaScript">
<!--
// assign initial values to global variables
var total = 0
var play = false
// react to a click in a checkbox (element == clicked checkbox object)
function display(element)
{
   // assign instance of Date object representing current time
   var now = new Date()
   // if the game has not started yet
   if (!play)
   {
      // game starts now
      play = true
      // milliseconds since 1970 for time at beginning
      startTime = now.getTime()
   }
   // if more than 20 seconds have passed since startTime was last set
   if (now.getTime() - startTime > 20000)
   {
      // reject modification (make "read-only")
      element.checked = !element.checked
      // terminate function
      return
   }
   // if the clicked checkbox is now checked
   if (element.checked)
      // increment total
      total++
   else
      // decrement total
      total--
   // display total in text object
   element.form.num.value = total
}
function restart(form)
{
   // set global variables back to initial values
   total = 0
   play = false
   // uncheck all 100 check boxes
   for (var i = 1; i <= 100; ++i)
   {
      // uncheck current check box
      form.elements[i].checked = false
   }
}
```

```
// -->
</SCRIPT>
</HEAD>
<BODY>
<SCRIPT LANGUAGE="JavaScript">
<!--
// immediate script (executed before the other script because it is deferred)
document.write("<FORM><CENTER>")
document.write('<INPUT TYPE="text" VALUE="0" NAME="num" SIZE=10 onFocus=
                            "this.blur()"><BR>')
document.write("<HR SIZE=1 WIDTH=40%>")
// use loop to create a 10 x 10 square of check boxes
for (var i = 0; i < 10; ++i)
{
   for (var j = 0; j < 10; ++j)
   {
      // write check box with "display(this)" as event handler script
      document.write('<INPUT TYPE="checkbox" onClick="display(this)">')
   }
   document.write("<BR>")
}
document.write("<HR SIZE=1 WIDTH=40%>")
// create button to call restart function to restart game
document.write('<INPUT TYPE="button" VALUE="restart" onClick=
                            "restart(this.form)">')
document.write("</CENTER></FORM>")
// -->
</SCRIPT>
</BODY>
</HTML>
```

***Example 18-7 (ex18-7).** A game demonstrating the use of check boxes*

The global statements in the <HEAD></HEAD> portion define the variable `total`, which holds the accumulated number of checked check boxes, and the variable `play`, which holds a Boolean indication as to whether or not the game is currently being played (timer is running).

Since its statements are all immediate ones, the first script segment to be executed is the one within the <BODY></BODY> portion of the page. That script simply prints the HTML interface of the game: a `text` object, 100 check boxes, a button, and two horizontal rules. All check boxes have an `onClick` event handler that calls the `display()` function with the `checkbox` object itself (`this`) as an argument.

The `display()` function accepts one argument—the triggered `checkbox` object. First, an instance of the `Date` object, representing the time at which the `display()` function was called, is assigned to the local variable `now`. The next segment of the function checks if the game is already being played. If not, `play` is set to true and the number of milliseconds since 1970 is assigned to the global variable `startTime`. If the difference between the current time and the time at the beginning of the game is greater than 20 seconds, the `checked` property of the calling `checkbox` is reversed (rejecting the user's attempts to continue playing after time is out), and the function terminates immediately. The rest of the function deals with a normal event of the user clicking the check box. The total number of check boxes is incremented if the calling check box is currently checked, and is decremented if the check box is currently unchecked. The total number of checked check boxes is assigned to `element.form.num.value`, the `text` object's `value` property.

The `restart()` function simply resets all global variables and `checkbox` states to their initial settings.

```
<INPUT TYPE="checkbox" onClick="this.checked = !this.checked">
```

defaultChecked

A check box definition may include a `CHECKED` specification to signal that the default state of the check box is "on," or true. If you do not specify this HTML attribute, it defaults to false. You can access a check box's default state via JavaScript's `defaultChecked` property. You can set `default-Checked` at any time, thus overriding the `CHECKED` attribute. Use the following statement to reset a check box's state to its default:

```
this.checked = this.defaultChecked
```

`this` is the specific check box you want to reset.

name

A `checkbox` object's `name` property reflects the `NAME` attribute of the `<INPUT>` element definition. It is a read-only property, so you cannot modify it. You should be as descriptive as possible when choosing a `NAME` attribute, especially for server-side applications that access the box's value only through its name. If your form is primarily for JavaScript processing, you can use the `NAME` attribute to mimic the functionality of a second `VALUE` attribute.

value

The `value` property initially reflects the `VALUE` attribute of the `<INPUT>` definition, but it can be adjusted via a JavaScript script at any time.

Just like a `text` object's `string` value, the `value` property represents the `checkbox` object's value, and as such is very important for forms processed by the server. By setting the `VALUE` attribute, you explicitly affect the content of the form submitted to the server.

Although you can accomplish many tasks without using the `value` property, it is sometimes very convenient to use this property instead. The following example demonstrates how to use a check box list to print all operating systems your business uses:

```
<HTML>
<HEAD>
<TITLE>Checkbox value property</TITLE>
<SCRIPT LANGUAGE="JavaScript">
<!--
function displayList(list)
{
   var total = ""
```

```
   for (var i = 0; i < list.length; ++i)
   {
      if (list[i].checked)
         total += list[i].value + "\r"
   }
   if (total == "")
      alert("No OS selected!")
   else
      alert(total)
}
// -->
</SCRIPT>
</HEAD>
<BODY>
<FORM>
<INPUT TYPE="checkbox" VALUE="DOS / Windows" NAME="computer">DOS /
         Windows XP<BR>
<INPUT TYPE="checkbox" VALUE="Windows Vista" NAME="computer">Windows Vista<BR>
<INPUT TYPE="checkbox" VALUE="Macintosh" NAME="computer">Macintosh<BR>
<INPUT TYPE="checkbox" VALUE="Linux" NAME="computer">Linux<BR>
<INPUT TYPE="button" VALUE="display list" onClick=
         "displayList(this.form.computer)">
</FORM>
</BODY>
</HTML>
```

First of all, notice that the form consists of four check boxes and one button. The button's `onClick` event handler invokes the `displayList()` function, passing the computer form element as an argument. Since there are four elements matching that name, `this.form.computer` is actually an array of four check box elements. A `checkbox`'s `VALUE` attribute specifies the operating system associated with that check box.

The `displayList()` function is based on a simple `for` loop that concatenates the check box values inside the local variable `total`, inserting new line characters as delimiters. When the loop terminates, `total` holds a list of all the operating systems that the user checked. If the value of `total` is an empty string, the user did not check any of the boxes, and an appropriate message is displayed. Otherwise, the list of the checked operating systems is displayed in an alert box.

radio Object

HTML Syntax

A radio button provides an interface to select an option among multiple choices. Unlike check boxes, which are rectangular in shape, radio buttons are circular. Another difference between the two types of buttons is that radio buttons belong to a group of buttons and are not independent. A group of radio buttons behaves exactly like the station buttons on an old car radio. It has two possible states: one button is pressed (on) or all buttons are released (off). When a button is pressed, the button that was pressed is automatically released.

All buttons of the same group share the same name. In fact, the identical name is an indication to the browser to restrict the number of checked radio buttons to one. Clicking a button automatically deselects the currently selected button of the same group. The general syntax of a single radio button is as follows:

```
<INPUT
   TYPE="radio"
   NAME="groupName"
   VALUE="buttonValue"
   [CHECKED]
   [onClick="handlerText"]>
```

Keep in mind that you should only use this type of button to enable a single selection among multiple choices. The following construct, for example, provides the means to choose a computer type from three options:

```
What computer do you most often use:
<P>
<INPUT TYPE="radio" NAME="computers" VALUE="unix">Unix (X-Windows)
<P>
<INPUT TYPE="radio" NAME="computers" VALUE="pc">PC
<P>
<INPUT TYPE="radio" NAME="computers" VALUE="mac">Macintosh
```


JavaScript Access

Although a radio button is a simple form element, its reference is an unusual one. You can reference a radio button group via one of the following expressions:

```
[window.]document.formName.radioGroupName
[window.]document.formName.elements[ElementIndex]
[window.]document.forms[FormIndex].radioGroupName
[window.]document.forms[FormIndex].elements[ElementIndex]
```

As explained at the beginning of this chapter, elements with the same names are combined and indexed into a single array. Therefore, the above references are actually arrays, where each element is a single radio button. Hence, the four ways to reference a specific radio button are as follows:

```
[window.]document.formName.radioGroupName[ButtonIndex]
[window.]document.formName.elements[ElementIndex][ButtonIndex]
[window.]document.forms[FormIndex].radioGroupName[ButtonIndex]
[window.]document.forms[FormIndex].elements[ElementIndex][ButtonIndex]
```

You can look up the number of radio buttons in a group by accessing the group's `LENGTH` attribute. For more details, check the section about the `name` property of the `text` object earlier in this chapter.

Some versions of Internet Explorer do not work perfectly with the `radio` object, so be sure to test your script.

When a radio button group consists of only one radio button, it is not considered a group. Therefore, you cannot access the array, and references such as the following ones are not valid:

```
[window.]document.formName.radioGroupName[index]
[window.]document.formName.radioGroupName.length
```

Instead, you must access the radio button directly, without an array:

```
[window.]document.formName.radioButtonName
```

The difference in referencing a single button and a multiple-button group complicates scripts quite a bit. If the radio buttons are created with plain HTML, you obviously know if the number of radio buttons is greater than one and access them accordingly. If the radio buttons are automatically generated by a script, then you have to add a counter that will indicate if the number of buttons is greater than one.

Event Handlers

onClick

A `radio` object supports only one event handler—the `onClick` event. When the user checks (fills) a radio button, a click event occurs, and the specified statements are executed. See the listings for the `checkbox` object for more details, syntax, and examples.

Methods

click()

The `click()` method emulates a button click on the calling `radio` object. It does not, however, trigger the button's `onClick` event handler. Example 18-8 demonstrates the use of this method to create a "Christmas lights" effect.

```
<HTML>
<HEAD>
<TITLE>Blinking lights</TITLE>
</HEAD>
<BODY onLoad="animate()">
<SCRIPT LANGUAGE="JavaScript">
<!--
// create row of radio buttons
lay(20)
// set index of lamp to start animation
var current = 0
// set speed (pause in milliseconds between each movement)
var speed = 100
function lay(num)
{
   // assign "greater than" character to variable
   var gt = unescape("%3e")
   // open form
```

```
   document.write("<FORM NAME='animation'" + gt)
   // use loop to lay radio buttons down (all buttons in same group)
   for (var i = 0; i < num; ++i)
   {
      document.write("<INPUT TYPE='radio' NAME='lamps'" + gt)
   }
   // close form
   document.write("</FORM" + gt)
}
function animate()
{
   // click next radio button
   document.animation.lamps[current].click()
   // if radio button is the last one reset variable to 0 (otherwise increment)
   current = (current == document.animation.lamps.length - 1) ? 0 : ++current
   // recursive call after speed milliseconds
   timerID = setTimeout("animate()", speed)
}
// -->
</SCRIPT>
</BODY>
</HTML>
```

Example 18-8 (ex18-8.htm). *A radio button animation*

The function `lay()` prints a form with a given number of `radio` objects. Notice a very important technique to encode the greater than character. This character (>) is assigned to the variable `gt` via the `unescape()` function. You may recall from Chapter 2, "Getting Started with JavaScript," that Netscape uses a different HTML comment than other browsers. While standard browsers terminate a comment with a greater than character (>), Navigator uses a three-character string (-->) instead. Therefore, if a greater than character is really placed in the script, it terminates the comment that hides the script from browsers that do not support JavaScript (specified by the `<SCRIPT>` tag). When creating a JavaScript-powered web page, you should be sure to use this technique whenever possible, especially to close HTML tags that are printed via `document.write`. You can also use less than operators instead of greater than operators, simply by reversing the order of the operands of a conditional statement. If your page is based on JavaScript, though, you may choose to disregard other browsers because they probably won't be able to display the page anyway. Nevertheless, if you are using JavaScript only to add some special effects, you should use this technique to make it clearly viewable with any browser, even with those that do not feature JavaScript. Yahoo!, for example, used this technique to create a "Yahoo Remote" for its page. The button that launched this JavaScript device was printed by a script, so browsers without JavaScript didn't even see the button. Had the greater than character not been encoded, the whole page (not just one button) would have been scrambled for users without JavaScript-enabled browsers.

Back to the `lay()` function. It is important to name the form for later access—`animation` is chosen. A simple `for` loop is executed to print `num` (the parameter) radio objects named lamps (belong to the same group). Notice that all HTML tags are printed in the following fashion:

```
document.write("<TAG ATTRIBUTES" + gt)
```

As explained above, the value of gt is a greater than character (a one-character string). See the previous page for a complete explanation on the motivation for this encoding.

The second function, animate(), is responsible for the actual animation. A global variable, current, is already defined and initialized to 0. The function's main task is to invoke the click() method associated with the radio object of index current. Note that all radio objects are elements of a unique array—document.animation.lamps. The second statement handles the boundary case when the checking loop needs to advance from the last button of the row to the first one (wraparound). The expression current == document.animation.lamps.length - 1 evaluates to true when the value of current is equal to the index of the last element in the document.animation.lamps array (the last radio button). In this case, current is set to 0, forcing the first button on the row to be checked next. In all other cases, the value of current is incremented, advancing the checked radio button. Note that when a radio button belonging to a group is clicked, any previously selected button is deselected. The last statement of the function recursively calls itself after a pause of speed milliseconds (speed is a global variable).

Properties

checked

The checked property evaluates to a Boolean value. If its calling radio object is checked (highlighted), the value of checked is true; otherwise it is false. Due to the structure of a radio object group, the checked property of a single radio object in a group is always true.

You can set the value of checked in order to modify the radio object's display. Since all buttons of a group can be deselected, setting a checked property to false simply deselects the calling radio object, without causing any side effects to the other buttons. Checking an empty radio object, however, does deselect any previously highlighted member of the group. See the section on the checkbox object for full coverage of this property.

defaultChecked

The defaultChecked property reflects the HTML CHECKED attribute. Refer to the section on the checkbox object for further details.

name

The name property initially reflects the NAME attribute in the HTML definition. See the section on the checkbox object's name property for a complete explanation.

value

The `value` property initially corresponds to the `VALUE` attribute of a radio button HTML tag, but it can be adjusted to any valid string. Once again, refer to the section on the `checkbox` object for the syntax and a full description.

select Object

HTML Syntax

Scrolling menus are a flexible means of input you can use on your forms. The `<SELECT>` tag is used to create various types of scrolling menus. This is the common way to enable the user to select an option from a list.

The `<SELECT>` tag is specified by a `<SELECT></SELECT>` pair. You should always specify the menu's name in the following fashion:

```
<SELECT NAME="anyName">
```

It is preferred to use a name that meets the JavaScript identifier naming conventions. As you might expect, the interior of the `<SELECT></SELECT>` portion includes the list's options. An option is specified in the following form:

```
<OPTION VALUE="optionValue">optionText
```

For example, the following element creates a simple menu of computer firms:

```
<SELECT NAME="comp">
<OPTION VALUE="http://www.microsoft.com/">Microsoft
<OPTION VALUE="http://www.mozilla.org//">Firefox
<OPTION VALUE="http://www.sun.com/">Sun
</SELECT>
```

You can use the `SELECTED` attribute (no value is necessary) to automatically select a default option when the page loads. For example, the following script creates a menu, where the default option (which is also the value that appears highlighted in the box) is "Sun":

```
<SELECT NAME="comp">
<OPTION VALUE="http://www.microsoft.com/">Microsoft
<OPTION VALUE="http://www.mozilla.org//">Firefox
<OPTION VALUE="http://www.sun.com/" SELECTED>Sun
</SELECT>
```

The text in the box is not the `VALUE` attribute specified inside the `<OPTION>` tag, but rather the string placed outside the `<OPTION>` tag. The string has no effect other than being the menu label.

Chapter 18

The main advantage of this menu is that, due to its pop-up configuration, it does not take up much space on the page. Its disadvantage is that the user can select only one option. To work around this deficiency, you can specify the MULTIPLE attribute, but, since all options are laid out instead of popping up, you lose the space advantage. Here is a simple example:

```
<SELECT NAME="comp" MULTIPLE>
<OPTION VALUE="http://www.microsoft.com/">Microsoft
<OPTION VALUE="http://www.mozilla.org/">Firefox
<OPTION VALUE="http://www.sun.com/" SELECTED>Sun
</SELECT>
```

You can select multiple options by holding the Shift key down and selecting or deselecting options from the menu. The Control key can also be held in order to select each option individually. These keys are commonly used in all major operating systems.

The complete syntax for the `select` object is as follows:

```
<SELECT
   NAME="selectName"
   [SIZE="integer"]
   [MULTIPLE]
   [onBlur="handlerText"]
   [onChange="handlerText"]
   [onFocus="handlerText"]>
   <OPTION VALUE="optionValue" [SELECTED]>textToDisplay
   [...<OPTION VALUE="optionValue" [SELECTED]>textToDisplay]
</SELECT>
```

You should recognize all attributes except for the event handlers, which are explained later.

JavaScript Access

There are several ways to reference a `select` object:

```
[window.]document.formName.selectName
[window.]document.formName.elements[index]
[window.]document.forms[index].selectName
[window.]document.forms[index].elements[index]
```

You can access a specific option in a `select` object by appending an `options` property to its reference. This property is actually an array of options starting at index 0. You can reference, for example, the first option of a `select` object in the following fashion:

```
[window.]document.formName.selectName.options[0]
```

The `options` array is discussed later as one of the `select` object's properties.

Event Handlers

onBlur

A blur event occurs when a `select` object loses focus. The `onBlur` event handler's script executes upon a blur event. There are a few ways to generate a blur event:

- Select an option from the list and then click outside the `select` object, either on the page's body or in another form element.
- Select an option from the menu and then send the browser's window to the background. The new window you focus on may be a different browser window or a window associated with any foreign application.

This event handler is not very useful because it relies on the user to remove focus from the object, which is not that intuitive.

onChange

A change event associated with a `select` object occurs when the user changes the selected option. Unlike change events associated with other objects, the `select` object does not have to lose focus in order to generate the event. The `onChange` event handler executes when a change event occurs.

The `onChange` event handler is commonly used for exchanging information with the user. We will demonstrate this event handler in later examples, when we discuss the `select` object's methods and properties.

onFocus

A focus event associated with a `select` object occurs when the user gives it focus; that is, when the user attempts to select an option from the menu, but before the menu pops up or modifies the currently selected option. The `onFocus` event handler responds to a focus event. When the user clicks somewhere inside the `select` object, you can, for example, pop up an alert box with user instructions for that particular menu. The following source demonstrates this suggestion:

```
<FORM>
<SELECT NAME="comp" onFocus="alert('Simply select the desired home')">
<OPTION VALUE="http://www.microsoft.com/">Microsoft
<OPTION VALUE="http://www.mozilla.org//">Firefox
<OPTION VALUE="http://www.sun.com/" SELECTED>Sun
</SELECT>
</FORM>
```

Methods

blur, focus

The only explicit methods of the `select` object are `blur()` and `focus()`. See the listings for the `text` object at the beginning of this chapter for complete coverage of these methods.

Properties (select Object)

The select object features various properties, but the most useful are actually properties of the options array, as you will find out later. In this section we discuss only the properties that belong directly to the select object.

length

You can access the number of options in a select object through the length property. Since this value is also referenced as the length property of the options array, you have the freedom to choose which length to use. Since length is known to be a standard property of all arrays in JavaScript, we personally prefer referencing length via the options array. Netscape Navigator accepts any of the following references to the number of options in the select object:

```
selectName.length
selectName.options.length
selectName.options.options.length
selectName.options.options.options.length
```

Microsoft Internet Explorer (since version 3.0) has accepted only the first two, but, since the third one does not make any sense, you should avoid using it anyway.

The value of the length property should not be assigned by a script. It is dynamic, so it changes whenever an option is added to the corresponding select object.

name

The name property reflects the NAME attribute of the <SELECT> tag. You can modify this property freely. Adjusting it via a script overrides the initial HTML setting. The following script segment shows how to display the name property ("products") via an alert dialog box:

```
<SCRIPT LANGUAGE="JavaScript">
<!--
function sayName(selectObject)
{
   alert(selectObject.name)
}
// -->
</SCRIPT>
<FORM>
<SELECT NAME="products" onChange="sayName(this)">
<OPTION VALUE="sny">Sony
<OPTION VALUE="jvc">JVC
<OPTION VALUE="tsh">Toshiba
</SELECT>
</FORM>
```

options

You can reference the options in a `select` object by the `options` property. Generally speaking, this array contains an entry for each option (<OPTION>) in a `select` object (<SELECT>). Suppose the first element of the first form in a document is a `select` object with three options. These options can be referenced in JavaScript as:

```
document.forms[0].elements[0].options[0]
document.forms[0].elements[0].options[1]
document.forms[0].elements[0].options[2]
```

As always, the length of the array, which is equal to the number of options in the given `select` object, is stored in the array's `length` property. In the preceding examples that would be:

```
document.forms[0].elements[0].options.length
```

Elements of the `options` array are read-only. Although it does not generate a JavaScript error, assigning a value to any of the elements has no effect.

The bare-bones *`selectObject`*`.options` reference evaluates to the full HTML syntax used to create the specified *`selectObject`*.

Note that you can also access the properties of the `select` object as if they were direct properties of the `options` array.

selectedIndex

The `selectedIndex` property is an integer specifying the index of the selected option in a `select` object. Options in a `select` object are indexed in the order of definition, i.e., in the same order they are entered in the `options` array. You can also set the value of `selectedIndex` in a script to immediately update the state (the selected option) of a `select` object.

The `selectedIndex` property is not useful with multiple `select` objects because it can only refer to the first selected option in the list. You can work around this problem by using the `selected` property of the `options` array and a simple loop. See the `selected` property in the next section, "Properties (options Array)" for further details.

Example 18-9 demonstrates the `selectedIndex` property. Although we have not discussed the `value` property yet, its role is obvious. If needed, refer to its description later in this chapter.

```
<HTML>
<HEAD>
<TITLE>URL option</TITLE>
<SCRIPT LANGUAGE="JavaScript">
<!--
function loadPage(list)
{
   location.href = list.options[list.selectedIndex].value
}
// -->
</SCRIPT>
</HEAD>
```

```
<BODY>
<FORM>
<SELECT onChange="loadPage(this)">
<OPTION VALUE="http://www.cnn.com/">CNN
<OPTION VALUE="http://www.msnbc.com/">MSNBC
<OPTION VALUE="http://www.usatoday.com/">USA TODAY
</SELECT>
</FORM>
</BODY>
</HTML>
```

Example18-9 (ex18-9.htm). *A URL picker*

When the user selects an option in the `select` object, the `loadPage()` function is invoked by the `onChange` event handler, passing the `select` object as an argument. The URL associated with each option is stored as the option's `VALUE` attribute, or `value` property in terms of JavaScript. The selected option is `list.options[list.selectedIndex]` because `list.selectedIndex` is an integer representing the index of the selected option. The `value` property is used to access the URL of the selected object, which is then assigned to `location.href`, in order to load that page to the browser window. You may prefer to use a button in place of the `onChange` event handler:

```
<HTML>
<HEAD>
<TITLE>URL option with button</TITLE>
<SCRIPT LANGUAGE="JavaScript">
<!--
function loadPage(list)
{
  location.href = list.options[list.selectedIndex].value
}
// -->
</SCRIPT>
</HEAD>
<BODY>
<FORM>
<SELECT>
<OPTION VALUE="http://www.cnn.com/">CNN
<OPTION VALUE="http://www.msnbc.com/">MSNBC
<OPTION VALUE="http://www.usatoday.com/">USA TODAY
</SELECT>
<INPUT TYPE="button" VALUE="load page" onClick=
            "loadPage(this.form.elements[0])">
</FORM>
</BODY>
</HTML>
```

Example 18-10 (ex18-10.htm). *Another version of the URL picker—this one uses a button*

The only difference between Example 18-9 and Example 18-10 is that in Example 18-9 the event handler is attached to a `select` object, while in Example 18-10 it is attached to a `button` object. In order to avoid changing the function, we have modified the argument handed to the function to keep passing the `select` object. The expression `this.form` references the form and `elements[0]` references the `select` object, which is the first element in the form.

Properties (options Array)

An element in the `options` array reflects a `select` object's option defined by the `<OPTION>` tag in HTML. Properties of the `options` array are properties of specific options in a `select` object.

defaultSelected

The `defaultSelected` property evaluates to a Boolean value. If the specified option is defined with a `SELECTED` attribute (`<OPTION...SELECTED>`), the value of `defaultSelected` is true. Otherwise, it is false.

`defaultSelected` initially reflects whether the `SELECTED` attribute is used within an `<OPTION>` tag. Setting the `defaultSelected` property via a script overrides the initial HTML setting.

In a `select` object without a `MULTIPLE` specification you can only have one option selected by default. Therefore, setting the `defaultSelected` property of a given option to true clears any previous default selections, including those set with `SELECTED`. Nevertheless, if you set `default-Selected` in a `select` object defined with the `MULTIPLE` attribute, previous default selections are not cleared.

index

The `index` property of a single option in a `select` object is the number identifying the position of the object in the selection list, starting from zero. Under normal circumstances, there is no justification for the existence of the `index` property, because in order to reference an option, you need to know its index:

```
document.selectObject.options[indexValue]
```

and when you reference the `index` property, you supposedly know the index already:

```
document.selectObject.options[indexValue].index
```

length

See the listings for the `length` property in the preceding section—"Properties (select Object)."

selected

The `selected` property is a Boolean value specifying the current selection state of an option in a `select` object. Its general syntax is as follows:

```
selectName.options[index].selected
```

If an option in a `select` object (*`selectName`*`.options[`*`index`*`]`) is selected, the `selected` property evaluates to true. Otherwise, it evaluates to false. You can set this property at any time, which immediately affects the display of the `select` object.

The `selected` and `defaultSelected` properties are very useful. Suppose you want to create a button by which the user can reset the `select` object. Using the Reset button is not desirable because it resets the entire form, not just the `select` object. You can solve the problem by using a simple JavaScript function to revert the `select` object to its default state. Here is the function that the button should invoke:

```
<HTML>
<HEAD>
<TITLE>Reset select object</TITLE>
<SCRIPT LANGUAGE="JavaScript">
<!--
function setDefault(selectName)
{
   for (var i = 0; i < selectName.options.length; ++i)
   {
      selectName.options[i].selected = selectName.options[i].defaultSelected
   }
}
// -->
</SCRIPT>
</HEAD>
<BODY>
<FORM>
<SELECT NAME="myMenu" MULTIPLE>
<OPTION> First option
<OPTION SELECTED> Second option
<OPTION> Third option
<OPTION> Fourth option
<OPTION SELECTED> Fifth option
</SELECT>
<INPUT TYPE="button" VALUE="reset menu" onClick="setDefault(this.form.myMenu)">
</FORM>
</BODY>
</HTML>
```

Example 18-11 (ex18-11.htm). *A simple function to reset a `select` object*

The `setDefault()` function works with any type of `select` object, whether it is a multiple one or not. It simply loops through the options of the `select` object and sets the `selected` property of each to its `defaultSelected` property, reverting all options to their default selection state. The value handed to the function is the `select` object, referenced as `this.form.myMenu`.

Note: Microsoft Internet Explorer does not fully support the `select` object. This entire discussion is based on Navigator because it simply does not work for Microsoft's browser. As you can see, Microsoft has focused on the user interface of its browser but did not pay much attention to script-level access via JavaScript. The average web surfer does not feel the disadvantages because web content providers use only features that are supported by both browsers.

text

There is no HTML attribute that defines the option's label. Take a look at Example 18-11. The strings "First option," "Second option," and so forth are not specified in any HTML attribute as you could expect. They are simply appended to the `<OPTION>` definitions.

The `text` property can be set at any time, immediately affecting the display. Example 18-12 demonstrates the use of this property. When the user selects an option from the list, that option is automatically placed at the top of the list, shifting all other options downward. See the listings for the `value` property if this is not completely clear.

```
<HTML>
<HEAD>
<TITLE>Swapping options</TITLE>
<SCRIPT LANGUAGE="JavaScript">
<!--
var choiceIndex = -1
function swap(opt1, opt2)
{
   var tempText = opt1.text
   var tempValue = opt1.value
   var tempDefault = opt1.defaultSelected
   opt1.text = opt2.text
   opt1.value = opt2.value
   opt1.defaultSelected = opt2.defaultSelected
   opt2.text = tempText
   opt2.value= tempValue
   opt2.defaultSelected = tempDefault
}
function shift(selectName)
{
   if (choiceIndex == -1)
   {
      choiceIndex = selectName.selectedIndex
      swap(selectName.options[choiceIndex], selectName.options[0])
   }
   else
   {
      swap(selectName.options[choiceIndex], selectName.options[0])
      choiceIndex = selectName.selectedIndex
      swap(selectName.options[choiceIndex], selectName.options[0]
   }
```

```
    selectName.options[0].selected = true
}
// -->
</SCRIPT>
</HEAD>
<BODY>
<FORM>
<SELECT onChange="shift(this)">
<OPTION VALUE="val1"> First option
<OPTION VALUE="val2" SELECTED> Second option
<OPTION VALUE="val3"> Third option
<OPTION VALUE="val4"> Fourth option
<OPTION VALUE="val5"> Fifth option
</SELECT>
</FORM>
</BODY>
</HTML>
```

Example 18-12 (ex18-12.htm). *You can swap options in a `select` object by swapping their values.*

When the user selects an option from the `select` object, the top option is swapped back to its original position and then the selected option is swapped with the top option that the first swap yielded.

At first, when the page loads and the `select` object has not been through layout yet, the global variable `choiceIndex` is initialized to –1. Since the index of an option in a `select` object is always non-negative, –1 is used to indicate that this is the first execution and that the current state of the `select` object is its initial one.

The `swap()` function accepts two options associated with a `select` object and simply swaps them by swapping their three properties:

- `text`
- `value`
- `defaultSelected`

You cannot directly swap two options because the `options` array is read-only.

The `shift()` function accepts one argument—a `select` object. If the value of `choiceIndex` is –1, then `choiceIndex` is assigned the index of the selected option, and the selected option is swapped with the option at the top of the list (index is 0). Since `choiceIndex` is a global variable, its value will remain intact until the next invocation of the `shift()` function. When the value of `choiceIndex` is not –1, the function runs a different set of statements. First, it swaps the option at the top of the menu with option number `choiceIndex`. Since `choiceIndex` has not been set yet during the current execution of the function, it holds the index of the option that the user selected on the previous round. That is, the function simply returns the `select` object to the state that preceded the previous function's execution. The following two statements are identical to those executed when the value of `choiceIndex` is –1. It is unnecessary to specify these statements twice. Instead, you may conditionally execute the first statement (if `choiceIndex` is not –1) and then unconditionally execute the other two.

value

The `value` property initially reflects the `VALUE` attribute of an `<OPTION>` definition. You can override the initial setting at any given time by assigning this property a value. We have seen this property in action before. For working examples, see the listings for the `defaultSelected` property of the `select` object and the preceding listings for the `text` property.

The Option Object—Adding Options Using the Option Constructor

JavaScript for Netscape Navigator (beginning back with version 3.0) enables you to explicitly create options via the `Option` constructor. Options you create are instances of the `option` object. The syntax for creating an option is as follows:

```
var optionName = new Option([optionText, optionValue, defaultSelected,
                  selected])
```

Here is a brief explanation of the arguments you should normally hand to the constructor function:

- *optionText*—a string representing the option's `text` property.
- *optionValue*—a string representing the option's `value` property.
- *defaultSelected*—a string representing the option's `defaultSelected` property.
- *selected*—a string representing the option's `selected` property.

See the listings for each of these properties for more details.

You can add an option to an existing `select` object in the following fashion:

```
selectName.options[index] = optionName
```

After you create an option and add it to a `select` object, you must refresh the document. You can do that via JavaScript using the following statement:

```
history.go(0)
```

You can also refresh a document using the browser control options either by clicking in the Location box and pressing Enter, or by selecting Refresh from the View menu.

You can delete an option from a `select` object by assigning it a null value. The general syntax is as follows:

```
selectName.options[index] = null
```

Once again, you must refresh the document via `history.go(0)` in order to see the updated appearance of the `select` object.

An option created as an instance of the `option` object includes the same properties as an option associated with a `select` object.

Example 18-13 demonstrates the use of the Option constructor to create a nested select object structure.

```
<HTML>
<HEAD>
<TITLE>Nested select structure</TITLE>
<SCRIPT LANGUAGE="JavaScript">
<!--
var menu = new Array(3)
for (var i = 0; i < menu.length; ++i)
{
   menu[i] = new Array()
}
menu[0][0] = new Option("Option 1-1", "", true, true)
menu[0][1] = new Option("Option 1-2")
menu[0][2] = new Option("Option 1-3")
menu[0][3] = new Option("Option 1-4")
menu[0][4] = new Option("Option 1-5")
menu[1][0] = new Option("Option 2-1", "", true, true)
menu[1][1] = new Option("Option 2-2")
menu[1][2] = new Option("Option 2-3")
menu[2][0] = new Option("Option 3-1", "", true, true)
menu[2][1] = new Option("Option 3-2")
menu[2][2] = new Option("Option 3-3")
menu[2][3] = new Option("Option 3-4")
function updateSub(index, subMenu)
{
   // delete all options in submenu
   for (var j = 0; j < subMenu.options.length; ++j)
   {
      subMenu.options[j] = null
   }
   // add options to submenu
   for (var k = 0; k < menu[index].length; ++k)
   {
      subMenu.options[k] = menu[index][k]
   }
   history.go(0)
}
// -->
</SCRIPT>
</HEAD>
<BODY>
<FORM>
<SELECT NAME="main" onChange= "updateSub(this.selectedIndex, this.form.sub)">
<OPTION SELECTED> Option 1
<OPTION> Option 2
<OPTION> Option 3
</SELECT>
<SELECT NAME="sub">
<SCRIPT LANGUAGE="JavaScript">
<!--
for (var ind = 0; ind < menu[0].length; ++ind)
{
```

```
    document.write("<OPTION> Option 1-" + (ind + 1))
}
// -->
</SCRIPT>
</SELECT>
</FORM>
</BODY>
</HTML>
```

Example 18-13 (ex18-13.htm). *"Nested"* `select` *objects connected via JavaScript*

When the page first loads, two `select` objects are created. The first one includes three options and is not modified at any stage. The second one is a dynamic `select` object, i.e., its options and length change. The script in the `<HEAD></HEAD>` portion of the page defines a two-dimensional array. The first index is of the first `select` object (an integer from 0 to 2). The second index is an integer between 0 and the index of the last option of the second `select` object. The number of options in the second `select` object depends on the option selected from the first `select` object.

Sounds difficult, but it's not! First you must understand what the script does. When the user selects an option from the first menu (`select` object), the second `select` object is updated with the corresponding option list. For example, if the second option in the main menu is selected, the script uses its index (1) to determine the array of elements (`menu[1]`) that should constitute the options of the second `select` object. For the sake of the example, we used text properties to identify the structure (`1-1`, `0-3`, etc.).

When the user first loads the page, the first `select` object is laid out according to its HTML definition, while the second `select` object is generated via a JavaScript `for` loop that iterates over the `menu[0]` array and writes out its elements.

The first `select` object includes an `onChange` event handler that invokes the `updateSub()` function, passing, as arguments, the form and the selected index. The function is based on two loops. The first one deletes the current options of the second menu by assigning each a null value. The second loop adds new options to the second menu, according to the elements of the selected menu array. Notice that we did not add properties for all options, but rather only for the first option of each menu array (a value, a default property, and a `defaultSelected` property). The elements of the menu array are obviously instances of the `option` object. The document is refreshed by `history.go(0)`.

An instance of the `option` object has the same structure as an element of a `select` object's element array. Both objects include the same properties and none have methods.

fileUpload Object

HTML Syntax

A file upload element of an HTML form enables the user to supply a local file as input. Generally speaking, its syntax is as follows:

```
<INPUT
   TYPE="file"
   NAME="fileUploadName">
```

Note that *fileUploadName* is not the name of the file, but rather the name of the form element that enables the user to supply the file.

JavaScript Access

The regular syntax is as follows:

```
[window.]document.formName.fileUploadName
[window.]document.formName.elements[index]
[window.]document.forms[index].fileUploadName
[window.]document.forms[index].elements[index]
```

Event Handlers and Methods

A discussion of the various event handlers and methods for this object are out of the scope of this book.

Properties

The `fileUpload` object includes these two properties.

name

The `name` property initially reflects the `NAME` attribute of the HTML definition. You may set its value at any time.

value

This read-only property reflects the current value of the `fileUpload` element's field—the name of the file to upload.

Summary

You deserve a reward if you had the motivation to read through this lengthy chapter. I believe that you have already been rewarded with the knowledge to implement interactive forms including their event handlers. Forms are a convenient means of collecting user's input without producing annoying dialog boxes. Some form elements such as `text` and `textarea` objects also come in handy when you need to display changing output, such as a clock or a banner. Don't worry if you do not remember every single method and property of the objects discussed in this chapter. This book will serve as an easy-to-use reference when you actually need to create a JavaScript-powered form. At this point, you should know the basics of and how to use form elements in JavaScript, and the properties, methods, and event handlers of `text` objects and regular buttons.

Chapter 19
Links, Anchors, and Image Maps

Defining a Link

A *link* is basically a piece of HTML code that allows you to redirect the browser to a different resource on the Internet. That redirection can be to another page on your site, a different site entirely, an e-mail address, or even an FTP address for file download. Here is the general HTML syntax:

```
<A HREF="locationOrURL"
   [NAME="anchorName"]
   [TARGET="windowName"]>
   linkText
</A>
```

The `HREF` attribute defines the document or anchor to which you are linking. HREF literally stands for HyperText Reference. The `NAME` attribute specifies a tag that becomes an available hypertext target within the current document. If this attribute is present, the `link` object is also an `anchor` object. The `TARGET` attribute specifies the window the linked document should load (e.g., a name of a window, a name of a frame, a special literal frame name such as `_top`, `_parent`, `_self`, and `_blank`).

You can create a link with a plain HTML tag as shown above, but you can also use JavaScript for that. The following script segment demonstrates how to create a link with JavaScript:

```
document.write(linkText.link(hrefAttribute))
```

This statement uses the `link()` method of the `String` object. See Chapter 12, "Handling Strings," for instructions on using this method.

Another obvious way to create a link with JavaScript is by printing the plain HTML syntax via `document.write` in the following form:

```
document.write('<A HREF="locationOrURL" [NAME="anchorName"]
              [TARGET="windowName"]>linkText</A>')
```

Although this syntax works on a JavaScript-enabled browser, it contains several flaws that will spoil the appearance of the page when viewed with a browser that does not support JavaScript. The problem is that greater than (>) characters in a script terminate code hiding. Most of the common browsers currently support JavaScript, however.

Defining an Anchor

The plain HTML definition of an anchor is as follows:

```
<A [HREF=locationOrURL]
   NAME="anchorName"
   [TARGET="windowName"]>
   anchorText
</A>
```

The attributes are the same as those of a link.

You can also use the String object's anchor() method to create an anchor using the following format:

```
text.anchor(nameAttribute)
```

Defining an Image Map Area

The general syntax of a client-side image map is as follows:

```
<MAP NAME="mapName">
   <AREA
      [NAME="areaName"]
      COORDS="x1,y1,x2,y2,..." | "x-center,y-center,radius"
      HREF="location"
      [SHAPE="rect" | "poly" | "circle" | "default"]
      [TARGET="windowName"]>
</MAP>
```

The first NAME attribute specifies the name of the image map that contains various areas, whereas the second one specifies the name of a single area in the image map. An image map can consist of any number of areas. The COORDS attribute specifies the coordinates of a specific area in a map. This attribute consists of either four coordinates, if the area is defined as a rectangle (an *x* and *y* for the top-left and bottom-right corners), or three coordinates, if the area is a circle (*x* and *y* for the center and the radius). HREF specifies the URL of the document to load when the user clicks the area. Any area of the image map that does not have this attribute does not act as a hypertext link. You can use any scheme (protocol) for the location, including a JavaScript statement via javascript:. The SHAPE attribute determines the shape of an area in an image map. If not specified, the shape defaults to rect. TARGET specifies the window or frame in which the destination document is loaded. See the section above on link definition for additional information regarding this attribute.

links Array

The only way to reference a link object in your code is by using the links array. This array is similar to the forms array you saw in the previous chapter. It is also a property of the document object, so you can access this array in the following fashion:

```
[window.]document.links
```

This links array contains an entry for each link (<A HREF="...">) and area (<AREA HREF="...">) object in the document. Suppose you have a document containing three links. You can reference these links using the following syntax:

```
document.links[0]
document.links[1]
document.links[2]
```

These references can equally apply to a document with three area objects (within a single map or multiple image maps), as well as for a document with two links and one image map area. The total number of qualifying links and image map areas is reflected by the length property of the array:

```
document.forms.length
```

This is probably the most useful link-related property. Elements in the links array are obviously read-only, but assigning a value to a given element does not cause an error—it simply doesn't work.

anchors Array

You can reference the anchors in your code via the anchors array. This array contains an entry for each tag containing a NAME attribute in a document, in source order. If a document contains three named anchors, for example, these anchors are reflected as document.anchors[0], document.anchors[1], and document.anchors[2]. You can use this array in one of two ways, exactly like you use the links array or the forms array:

```
document.anchors[index]
document.anchors.length
```

Each element of the document.anchors array holds a null value and does not feature any methods or properties. The value of document.anchors[0], for example, is null, regardless of whether there are anchors in the document. The anchors array does not play a role in any script, but its length property occasionally does. If you use a systematic naming scheme for all anchors in a document, you can take advantage of the length property (document.anchors.length). Suppose a document contains a variable number of anchors. You can name these anchors anchor0, anchor1, anchor2, and so forth, or, alternatively, test0, test1, and test2, if you so desire. The latter anchors would use the following syntax:

```
<A ... NAME="test0" ...></A>
<A ... NAME="test1" ...></A>
<A ... NAME="test2" ...></A>
```

Take a look at the following function:

```
function goAnchor(num)
{
   if (num >= document.anchors.length)
      alert("Anchor does not exist!")
   else
      location.hash = "test" + num
}
```

This function accepts an existing anchor's index and scrolls the page to that anchor by assigning its name to the `location.hash` property. It also demonstrates a possible usage of the `anchors` array, or its `length` property, to be exact. See Chapter 16, "URLs and JavaScript," for details on the `location.hash` property.

Link and Area Event Handlers

Anchors do not feature any event handlers, but links and image map areas do provide them. Some of the event handlers are very useful, so it is important that you know how to use them.

Calling Event Handlers Explicitly

Since the `document.links` array holds an entry for every link and image map area in a document, it is fairly straightforward to explicitly call an event handler for a specific link or area by assigning it to the corresponding array element. You can use the following statement to explicitly call the event handler `doSomething` for the first link or area (whichever is first in source order):

```
document.links[0].onmouseover = doSomething
```

onClick

You can add an `onClick` event handler in the following fashion:

```
<A ... onClick="validJavaScriptCode">
<AREA ... onClick="validJavaScriptCode">
```

A click event associated with a `link` object or an `area` object occurs when the user clicks the content of the link, which can be plain text, an image, and so forth. In the case of an `area` object, the link content is (usually) a portion of an image.

The JavaScript statements you specify for the `onClick` event handler are executed prior to loading the URL defined by the `HREF` attribute. They can be used to do any last-minute preparations.

Usually, you simply want a link or image map area to execute a JavaScript code when the user clicks it. You can accomplish this task by simply using a URL based on a `javascript:` scheme with the `HREF` attribute. When the user clicks it, the following link calls a function named `register`:

```
<A HREF="javascript:register()">Register Profile</A>
```

If you wish to create a link that does not respond at all to a link but still enables `onMouseOver` and `onMouseOut` event handlers, you can use the `void` operator (only compatible with Netscape Navigator 3.0 and above and Internet Explorer 5.5. and above):

```
<A HREF="javascript:void(0)">Register Profile</A>
```

onMouseOver

A `mouseOver` event occurs each time the mouse pointer moves into an object or an area from outside that object or area. Upon this event, the `onMouseOver` event handler executes JavaScript code. The syntax of a general script to do this is as follows:

```
<A ... onMouseOver="validJavaScriptCode">
<AREA ... onMouseOver="validJavaScriptCode">
```

If the mouse moves from one area of a client-side image map to another, it is the `onMouseOver` event handler of the destination area (the one you are moving to) that is being triggered.

Instead of having its URL displayed by default in the status bar whenever the user places the mouse over it, this event handler is often used to display a message associated with a link. (You must return true from the event handler.) The following link, for example, displays "Cool shareware stuff" in the status bar when the user places the mouse over the link labeled "Jumbo":

```
<A HREF="http://www.jumbo.com" onMouseOver="window.status = 'Cool
                                shareware stuff'; return true">Jumbo</A>
```

If you prefer to use a function, you should return true in the following fashion:

```
<SCRIPT LANGUAGE="JavaScript">
<!--
function displayStatus(str)
{
   window.status = str
   return true
}
// -->
</SCRIPT>
<A HREF="http://www.jumbo.com" onMouseOver="return displayStatus('Cool
                                shareware stuff')">Jumbo</A>
```

Alternatively, you may choose to explicitly return a true value by adding a statement to the event handler code.

onMouseOut

A mouseOut event occurs each time the mouse pointer leaves an area within a client-side image map or a link from inside that area or link. The `onMouseOut` event handler executes JavaScript code upon this event.

If the mouse moves from one area to another in a client-side image map, the `onMouseOut` event handler of the source area is triggered, and the `onMouseOver` event handler of the destination area is triggered.

If you want an area to use the `onMouseOut` or the `onMouseOver` event handler, you should specify the `HREF` attribute of the `<AREA>` tag. Nice effects can be achieved by using `onMouseOver` and `onMouseOut` together. Upon placing the pointer over a link or an image map area, for example, you can display a message in the status bar, and then, instead of waiting for an arbitrary number of seconds, you can delete it immediately upon the removal of the mouse pointer. The following code demonstrates how to implement such an effect:

```
<A HREF="http://www.jumbo.com" onMouseOver="window.status = 'Cool
          shareware stuff'; return true" onMouseOut="window.status
          = ''; return true">Jumbo</A>
```

Note that a similar effect can be achieved with an image map area instead of a link. Example 19-1 demonstrates both `onMouse` event handlers for a client-side image map. The image map is shown in Figure 19-1.

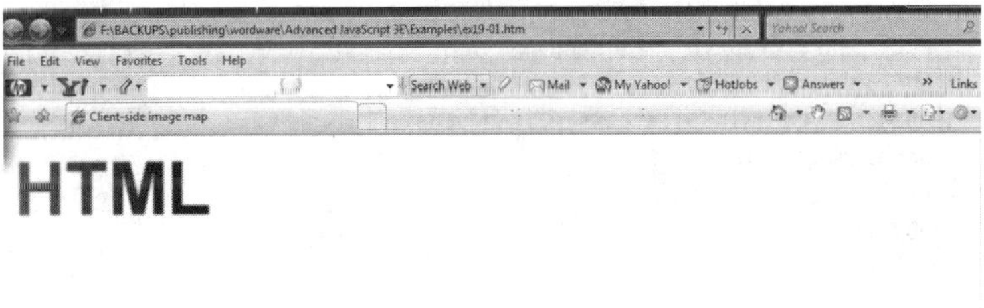

Figure 19-1. *The image used for the client-side image map*

When the user clicks the "H" area, the word "Hyper" is displayed in an alert box. When he or she clicks the "T" area, "Text" is displayed, and so forth with "Markup" and "Language." When the mouse pointer is over a certain letter, the corresponding word ("Hyper," "Text," "Markup," "Language") is displayed in the status bar. When the mouse pointer is removed from the image map, the status bar is blanked. Now, take a look at Example 19-1 to find out how this works.

```
<HTML>
<HEAD>
<TITLE>Client-side image map</TITLE>
</HEAD>
<BODY BGCOLOR="#ffffff">
```

```
<IMG SRC="img19-1.gif" HEIGHT=69 WIDTH=194 ALT="HTML" BORDER=0
                       USEMAP="#html_map">
<MAP NAME="html_map">
<AREA
   NAME="H"
   COORDS="0, 0, 55, 69"
   HREF="javascript:alert('Hyper')"
   SHAPE="rect"
   onMouseOver="window.status = 'Hyper'; return true"
   onMouseOut="window.status = ''; return true">
<AREA
   NAME="T"
   COORDS="56, 0, 101, 69"
   HREF="javascript:alert('Text')"
   SHAPE="rect"
   onMouseOver="window.status = 'Text'; return true"
   onMouseOut="window.status = ''; return true">
<AREA
   NAME="M"
   COORDS="102, 0, 161, 69"
   HREF="javascript:alert('Markup')"
   SHAPE="rect"
   onMouseOver="window.status = 'Markup'; return true"
   onMouseOut="window.status = ''; return true">
<AREA
   NAME="L"
   COORDS="161, 0, 194, 69"
   HREF="javascript:alert('Language')"
   SHAPE="rect"
   onMouseOver="window.status = 'Language'; return true"
   onMouseOut="window.status = ''; return true">
</MAP>
</BODY>
</HTML>
```

Example 19-1 (ex19-1.htm). *JavaScript to handle the image map areas*

First, notice the HTML tag that creates the image:

```
<IMG SRC="img19-1.gif" HEIGHT=69 WIDTH=194 ALT="HTML" BORDER=0
                       USEMAP="#html_map">
```

Except for the last one, all attributes are self-explanatory. USEMAP specifies the name of the image map definition (<MAP>) for the image, preceded by a hash character. The image map definition itself uses the following opening tag:

```
<MAP NAME="html_map">
```

You should set the name of the map as shown above; otherwise, the image won't be able to refer to it. There are basically four areas in Figure 19-1's image map, one for each letter of the "HTML" banner. Since, except for the triggered message and coordinates, all four areas are alike, only one will be discussed here. Let's take a look at the last area:

```
<AREA
   NAME="L"
   COORDS="161, 0, 194, 69"
   HREF="javascript:alert('Language')"
   SHAPE="rect"
   onMouseOver="window.status = 'Language'; return true"
   onMouseOut="window.status = ''; return true">
```

First, notice that this area is defined as a rectangle (`SHAPE="rect"`). The *x* and *y* coordinates of the upper-left corner are 161 and 0, respectively. Coordinates are measured in pixels starting at (0, 0), the first pixel in the image. The *x* and *y* coordinates of the bottom-right corner are 194 and 69, respectively, which are the `HEIGHT` and `WIDTH` attributes of the image. When the user places the mouse pointer over this area, the status bar displays the string "Language" (for "L") (the string is assigned to the `status` property), and the Boolean value true is returned. When the user removes the mouse from this area, the status bar is blanked (assigned an empty string). Since the `onMouseOver` event handler of the destination area immediately overtakes the `onMouseOut` operation of the source area, the user usually won't notice this interim state when moving the pointer to one of the adjacent image map areas. When the user removes the mouse pointer from this area to outside of the entire image, the status bar is cleared and remains empty, until either a different value is explicitly assigned to the status bar or the mouse moves back into the image map area. When the user clicks this area, the location specified in `HREF` is loaded, and since the value of this attribute is a JavaScript statement preceded by the `javascript:` scheme, it does not load a new document but rather pops up an alert dialog box with the string "Language."

Link and Area Properties

Location-Equivalent Properties

Most of the properties that belong to a `link` or an `area` object (`document.links[`*`index`*`]`) are associated with the URL of the `HREF` definition. These are all properties of the `window.location` object, which we describe briefly below. The only way to reference a property of a `link` or an `area` object is to use the following syntax:

```
document.links.propertyName
```

Note that links do not have any methods.

Here is the equivalence list between the properties of `document.links` and those of `window.location`:

- `hash` specifies an anchor name in the URL.
- `host` specifies the *`hostname`*`:`*`port`* portion of the URL.
- `hostname` specifies the host and domain name, or IP address, of a network host.

- `href` specifies the entire URL.
- `pathname` specifies the *`url-path`* portion of the URL.
- `port` specifies the communications port that the server uses for communications (80 by default).
- `protocol` specifies the beginning of the URL, including the colon (also known as the scheme).
- `search` specifies a query.

target

The `target` property initially reflects the `TARGET` attribute of the `<A HREF="...">` or `<AREA HREF="...">` HTML definitions. Setting the value of this property overrides the initial definition.

The `target` property (`document.links[`*`index`*`].target`) cannot be assigned a JavaScript expression or variable.

Referring Documents

When a user clicks a link in one document and causes a new page to load in the same or another window, the calling document is known as the *referring document.* When a user arrives at a page via a link from another page (and not from his or her bookmark, history list, favorites, etc.), the URL of the referring page is reflected in the new page as a read-only property, `document.referrer`. A referring document is also called the *source document*, whereas the new page the referrer document links to is known as the *destination document.*

The property `document.referred` is very useful for tracking a user's movement inside a large site you maintain by yourself. It is not helpful at all if the user surfs to foreign pages, so, unless *Playboy* provides a link to your page, you won't be able to greet the user with a message such as "Naughty boy—*Playboy* is for grown-ups only!"

Suppose you have a page on your site, C.html, that is linked from two different pages, A.html and B.html. Let's say A.html includes important copyright information on a shareware product available on C.html, and B.html provides important instructions on installing the software package. You can use the following JavaScript script on C.html to check where the user came from and to print a link to the third page:

```
<SCRIPT LANGUAGE="JavaScript">
<!-- begin JavaScript *immediate* script
// assign greater than character without literally displaying it
var gt = unescape("%3E")
if (document.referred.indexOf("A.html") == -1)
   document.write('<A HREF="A.html"' + gt + 'Copyright notice</A>' + gt)
```

```
if (document.referred.indexOf("B.html") == -1)
   document.write('<A HREF="B.html"' + gt + 'Installation instructions
                 </A>' + gt)
// -->
</SCRIPT>
```

This script prints links to the documents the user has not come from. It prints A.html it the user has not come from A.html, B.html if the user has not come from B.html, or both links if the user has apparently arrived from a different document or not from a link at all.

Summary

In this chapter, we discussed the `link`, `area`, and `anchor` objects. You learned that the only way to reference one of these objects is by either `document.links` or `document.anchors`. There are three important concepts you should remember from this chapter:

- The `javascript:` protocol specifies a JavaScript statement for the `HREF` attribute of a link or image map area.
- The `onMouseOver` event handler of links and image map areas can execute a JavaScript statement. When the user places the mouse pointer over the link, it is an indication of his or her interest in it, so displaying related information in the status bar may be very helpful in such a scenario.
- The `onMouseOut` event handler is also an attribute of a link or image map area. Its usage is similar to that of the `onMouseOver` event handler.

Chapter 20
Implementing Cookies

Maintaining a State

When you create a web site, you expect the user to load HTML documents, view them, navigate from one page to another, etc. Occasionally, it is important to enable the web page to maintain a *state*. That is, the page "remembers" certain actions executed by the user during previous sessions.

A classic example of maintaining a given state is a shopping cart application, as you might see on almost any commercial web site. The user travels from one product review to another via simple HTML links. When he or she comes across an interesting product, clicking a button puts the selected product's data in a "shopping cart." The *shopping cart*, which is sometimes displayed visually on the page, is basically a name for a storage mechanism. Since it is not possible to store the data for each user on the server, the data is kept on the client side, in what is called a shopping cart.

Cookies are a general mechanism that server-side applications (such as CGI) and client-side JavaScript scripts can use to store textual data on the client side for the purpose of retrieving it later. The name "cookies" does not have any technically significant meaning. It is simply a name that the inventors thought was cool. You probably are aware that cookies have gained a bad reputation in recent years. Some unscrupulous web site developers have created cookies to store information that many people feel should be private. A common tactic for legitimate web developers is to put a policy statement on their web sites stating exactly what the site stores in cookies and why it does so, which may help alleviate customer concerns. As you will see in this chapter, cookies are a very useful tool.

Cookies are tidbits of information, stored in a browser-dependent format on the client machine. Netscape Navigator, for example, holds all cookies in a regular text file named cookies.txt (in the directory where Navigator is installed), whereas Internet Explorer stores cookies in multiple files, located in a user-provided directory.

Cookies and HTTP

The connection established between the server and the client uses Hypertext Transfer Protocol (HTTP). Although this protocol is very complicated at the implementation level, it is fairly easy to understand conceptually. When a user requests a page, an *HTTP request* is sent to the server, specifying the user's exact request with some additional attributes. As a user, you are not aware of any data sent to the server as a result of your request. Among its elements, an HTTP request includes a header that defines the most important attributes, such as the URL of the requested page. An HTTP request includes all valid cookies as well.

When the server replies to the client's request, it returns an *HTTP response* that also features a header. This header contains important information about the file being returned, such as its MIME type (discussed in detail in Chapter 25).

The general syntax of an HTTP header is as follows:

```
Field-name: Information
```

When the server returns an HTTP object to the client, it may also transmit some state information for the client to store as cookies. Since a cookie is basically simple text, the server-side script does not have the ability to abuse the client machine in any way. In addition to its textual value, a cookie contains several attributes, such as the range of URLs for which the cookie is valid. Any future HTTP requests from the client to one of the URLs in the above range will transmit back to the server the current cookie's value on the client.

Setting an HTTP Cookie

An HTTP cookie is introduced to the client in an HTTP request, usually by a CGI script, using the following syntax:

```
Set-Cookie: NAME=VALUE; expires=DATE; path=pathName; domain=DOMAIN_NAME; secure
```

The attributes are as follows:

- *name=value*—*name* is the name of the cookie by which you can reference it later. Notice that the only way to access the cookie is by this name. *value* is the regular string to be stored as a cookie. It is recommended that the string be encoded using the "%XX" style (equivalent to JavaScript's `escape` function's output). Generally speaking, the *name=value* is the only required attribute of the Set-Cookie field.
- `expires`=*date*—`expires` is an optional attribute that specifies the expiration date of the cookie. The cookie will no longer be stored or retrieved beyond that date. The date string is formatted as follows:

  Wdy, DD-Mon-YYYY HH:MM:SS GMT

You will see later that this date format is equivalent to the value returned by the `toGMTString()` date's method. If `expires` is not specified, the cookie will expire when the user's session ends.

- `path=`*`pathName`*—`path` specifies a subset of URLs in a domain for which a cookie is valid. After domain matching, the pathname component of the URL is compared with the `path` attribute, and, if successful, the cookie is considered valid and is sent along with the URL requests. The path `/foo`, for example, would match `/foobar` and `/foo/bar/html`. The path / is the most general one. If the path is not specified, it is assumed to be the same path as the document specified in the cookie's header.
- `domain=`*`domainName`*—When searching for valid cookies, your browser compares the domain attributes of each cookie to the Internet domain name of the host from which the URL will be retrieved. If there is a tail match, then the cookie will go through a full path matching. *Tail matching* means that the `domain` attribute is matched against the tail of the fully qualified domain name of the host. A `domain` attribute of `ac.il`, for example, would tail match `mis.study.ac.il` as well as `mba.haifa.ac.il`.

  The `domain` attribute makes sure that only hosts within the specified domain can set a cookie for the domain. There are seven common top-level domains—"com", "edu", "net", "org", "gov", "mil", and "int"—along with several others that have been proposed recently.

  The default value of `domain` is the host name of the server that generated the cookie response.
- `secure`—If a cookie is marked `secure`, it will only be transmitted across a secured communication channel between the client and the host. If `secure` is not specified, the cookie will be sent over unsecured channels.

Getting an HTTP Cookie

When a script (client-side or server-side) requests a URL from an HTTP server, the browser will match the URL against all cookies, and if any of them matches, a line containing the name and value pairs of all matching cookies will be included in the HTTP request. The format is straightforward:

```
Cookie: name1=value1; name2=value2 ...
```

Notice that the `Cookie` field in a request header contains only the names and values of all valid cookies. The `Set-Cookie` field in the response header includes additional attributes such as expiration date. These attributes are not actually part of the cookie, but rather are used to determine if a specific cookie is valid for the purpose of entering the HTTP request header.

Notes and Limitations

The only way to overwrite a cookie is by creating another cookie with the same name and path as an existing one. Creating a cookie with the same name but with a different path than that of an existing one will add an additional cookie. The only way to instantly delete a cookie is by overwriting it with an expired cookie. A cookie may be deleted by the browser before its expiration date but only if the number of cookies exceeds its internal limit.

When sending cookies to a server, all cookies with more specific path mapping should be sent before cookies with less-specific path mapping. If both are sent, the cookie `name1=foo` with a path mapping of `/`, for example, should be sent after the cookie `name1=foo2` with a path mapping of `/bar`.

There are several extremely important limitations on the size and number of cookies a client can store at any given time:

- The client can hold up to 300 cookies.
- A cookie can be up to 4KB, including its name and values. Cookies that exceed this length are trimmed to fit, so remember to keep within this length.
- A maximum of 20 cookies per server or domain are allowed.

A client is not expected to exceed these limits. The oldest cookies are deleted in case this rule is violated.

Proxy servers should propagate the `Set-Cookie` header to the client, regardless of whether the response was 304 ("not modified") or 200 ("OK"). Proxy servers work fine with cookies.

Examples

Here are some sample exchanges from Netscape documentation that illustrate the use of cookies.

First Transaction Sequence Example

Client requests a document and receives in the response:

```
Set-Cookie: CUSTOMER=WILE_E_COYOTE; path=/; expires=Wednesday,
            09-Nov-11 23:12:40 GMT
```

When client requests a URL in the path / on this server, it sends:

```
Cookie: CUSTOMER=WILE_E_COYOTE
```

Client requests a document and receives in the response:

```
Set-Cookie: PART_NUMBER=ROCKET_LAUNCHER_0001; path=/
```

When client requests a URL in the path / on this server, it sends:

```
Cookie: CUSTOMER=WILE_E_COYOTE; PART_NUMBER=ROCKET_LAUNCHER_0001
```

Client receives:

```
Set-Cookie: SHIPPING=FEDEX; path=/foo
```

When client requests a URL in the path / on this server, it sends:

```
Cookie: CUSTOMER=WILE_E_COYOTE; PART_NUMBER=ROCKET_LAUNCHER_0001
```

When client requests a URL in the path /foo on this server, it sends:

```
Cookie: CUSTOMER=WILE_E_COYOTE; PART_NUMBER=ROCKET_LAUNCHER_0001; SHIPPING=FEDEX
```

Second Transaction Sequence Example

Assume all mappings from above have been cleared.

Client receives:

```
Set-Cookie: PART_NUMBER=ROCKET_LAUNCHER_0001; path=/
```

When client requests a URL in the path / on this server, it sends:

```
Cookie: PART_NUMBER=ROCKET_LAUNCHER_0001
```

Client receives:

```
Set-Cookie: PART_NUMBER=RIDING_ROCKET_0023; path=/ammo
```

When client requests a URL in the path /ammo on this server, it sends:

```
Cookie: PART_NUMBER=RIDING_ROCKET_0023; PART_NUMBER=ROCKET_LAUNCHER_0001
```

Note that there are two attributes named `PART_NUMBER` due to the two different paths, / and /ammo.

Cookies and JavaScript

Setting and getting cookies with a server-side application relies on HTTP headers. You cannot set a cookie or retrieve one after the page has loaded. However, a JavaScript script is a client-side application and thus enables you to process cookies at any time, without contacting the server.

The `cookie` property of the `document` object reflects all cookies that are valid for the web page hosting the script; that is, `document.cookie` is equivalent to the `Cookie` field in the HTTP request header.

In the same way you set a cookie via the `Set-Cookie` field in an HTTP response header, you can do so with JavaScript, by assigning a value to `document.cookie`.

Cookie Functions

You should have noticed that we neither demonstrated nor emphasized the usage of cookies with JavaScript. The reason for this is that it is difficult and almost useless to explicitly deal with the `document.cookie` property. Furthermore, there are only three defined actions related to cookies:

- Retrieving the value of a cookie according to its name
- Setting a cookie to a desired attribute
- Deleting a cookie

You may find the following functions useful when you want to perform one of the above actions. All functions are self-explanatory and are fully commented:

```
// Boolean variable specified if alert should be displayed if cookie exceeds 4KB
var caution = false
// name - name of the cookie
// value - value of the cookie
// [expires] - expiration date of the cookie (defaults to end of current
session)
// [path] - path for which the cookie is valid (defaults to path of calling
document)
// [domain] - domain for which the cookie is valid (defaults to domain of
calling document)
// [secure] - Boolean value indicating if the cookie transmission requires
a secure transmission
// * an argument defaults when it is assigned null as a placeholder
// * a null placeholder is not required for trailing omitted arguments
function setCookie(name, value, expires, path, domain, secure)
{
   var curCookie = name + "=" + escape(value) +
      ((expires) ? "; expires=" + expires.toGMTString() : "") +
      ((path) ? "; path=" + path : "") +
      ((domain) ? "; domain=" + domain : "") +
      ((secure) ? "; secure" : "")
   if (!caution || (name + "=" + escape(value)).length <= 4000)
      document.cookie = curCookie
   else
      if (confirm("Cookie exceeds 4KB and will be cut!"))
         document.cookie = curCookie
}
// name - name of the desired cookie
// * return string containing value of specified cookie or null if cookie does
not exist
function getCookie(name)
{
   var prefix = name + "="
   var cookieStartIndex = document.cookie.indexOf(prefix)
   if (cookieStartIndex == -1)
      return null
   var cookieEndIndex = document.cookie.indexOf(";", cookieStartIndex +
                        prefix.length)
   if (cookieEndIndex == -1)
      cookieEndIndex = document.cookie.length
   return unescape(document.cookie.substring(cookieStartIndex +
                  prefix.length, cookieEndIndex))
}
// name - name of the cookie
// [path] - path of the cookie (must be same as path used to create cookie)
// [domain] - domain of the cookie (must be same as domain used to create
cookie)
// * path and domain default if assigned null or omitted if no explicit
argument proceeds
```

```
function deleteCookie(name, path, domain)
{
   if (getCookie(name))
   {
      document.cookie = name + "=" +
      ((path) ? "; path=" + path : "") +
      ((domain) ? "; domain=" + domain : "") +
      "; expires=Thu, 01-Jan-70 00:00:01 GMT"
   }
}
// date - any instance of the Date object
// * you should hand all instances of the Date object to this function for
"repairs"
// * this function is taken from Chapter 10, "Time and Date in JavaScript,"
in " Advanced JavaScript, Third Edition"

function fixDate(date)
{
   var base = new Date(0)
   var skew = base.getTime()
   if (skew > 0)
      date.setTime(date.getTime() – skew)
}
```

Read through the functions and comments so you understand how to use them. The most basic demonstration of these functions is a script that counts the number of times a user has visited the page that hosts the code:

```
<HTML>
<HEAD>
<TITLE>Remember number of visits</TITLE>
<SCRIPT LANGUAGE="JavaScript">
<!--
// Boolean variable specified if alert should be displayed if cookie exceeds 4KB
var caution = false
// name - name of the cookie
// value - value of the cookie
// [expires] - expiration date of the cookie (defaults to end of current
session)
// [path] - path for which the cookie is valid (defaults to path of calling
document)
// [domain] - domain for which the cookie is valid (defaults to domain of
calling document)
// [secure] - Boolean value indicating if the cookie transmission requires a
secure transmission
// * an argument defaults when it is assigned null as a placeholder
// * a null placeholder is not required for trailing omitted arguments
function setCookie(name, value, expires, path, domain, secure)
{
   var curCookie = name + "=" + escape(value) +
      ((expires) ? "; expires=" + expires.toGMTString() : "") +
      ((path) ? "; path=" + path : "") +
      ((domain) ? "; domain=" + domain : "") +
      ((secure) ? "; secure" : "")
```

```
   if (!caution || (name + "=" + escape(value)).length <= 4000)
      document.cookie = curCookie
   else
      if (confirm("Cookie exceeds 4KB and will be cut!"))
         document.cookie = curCookie
}
// name - name of the desired cookie
// * return string containing value of specified cookie or null if cookie does
not exist
function getCookie(name)
{
   var prefix = name + "="
   var cookieStartIndex = document.cookie.indexOf(prefix)
   if (cookieStartIndex == -1)
      return null
   var cookieEndIndex = document.cookie.indexOf(";", cookieStartIndex +
                        prefix.length)
   if (cookieEndIndex == -1)
      cookieEndIndex = document.cookie.length
   return unescape(document.cookie.substring(cookieStartIndex +
                   prefix.length, cookieEndIndex))
}
// name - name of the cookie
// [path] - path of the cookie (must be same as path used to create cookie)
// [domain] - domain of the cookie (must be same as domain used to create
cookie)
// * path and domain default if assigned null or omitted if no explicit
argument proceeds
function deleteCookie(name, path, domain)
{
   if (getCookie(name))
   {
      document.cookie = name + "=" +
      ((path) ? "; path=" + path : "") +
      ((domain) ? "; domain=" + domain : "") +
      "; expires=Thu, 01-Jan-70 00:00:01 GMT"
   }
}
// date - any instance of the Date object
// * you should hand all instances of the Date object to this function for
"repairs"
function fixDate(date)
{
   var base = new Date(0)
   var skew = base.getTime()
   if (skew > 0)
      date.setTime(date.getTime() - skew)
}
var now = new Date()
fixDate(now)
now.setTime(now.getTime() + 365 * 24 * 60 * 60 * 1000)
var visits = getCookie("counter")
if (!visits)
   visits = 1
```

Chapter 20

```
else
   visits = parseInt(visits) + 1
setCookie("counter", visits, now)
document.write("You have been here " + visits + " time(s).")
// -->
</SCRIPT>
</HEAD>
</HTML>
```

Example 20-1 (ex20-1.htm). *A simple cookie-based counter*

You can see the output of this script in Figure 20-1.

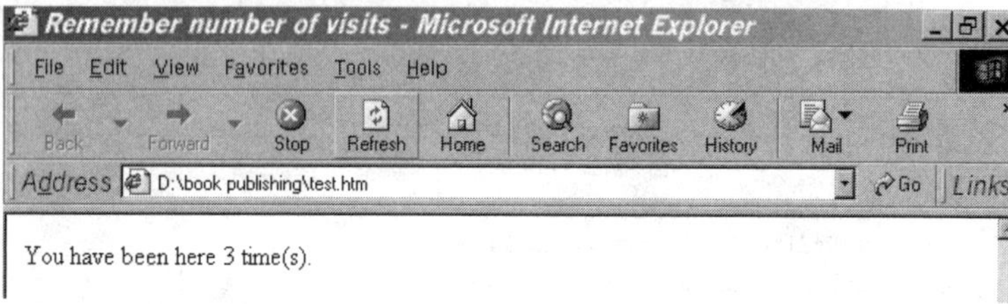

Figure 20-1. *A cookie-based counter*

Bear in mind that this script does not emulate a regular counter that counts the number of visitors to a given site. Because cookies are stored on the client side, they can only be used to count the number of visits by a specific client. At first, an instance of the `Date` object reflecting the current date is assigned to the variable `now`. The instance is then handed to the `fixDate()` function, which is needed to properly format the date values for Macintosh OS users. The `now.setTime(now.getTime() + 365 * 24 * 60 * 60 * 1000)` statement sets the cookie expiration date to one year in the future. This expiration date is used later when setting the cookie. The script gets a cookie named `counter` and retrieves the number of visits from it. If there is no cookie by the specified name, the variable `visits` is initialized to one; otherwise, the number of visits in the cookie is incremented by one. The script then writes the new number of visits back to the cookie by `setCookie()`. The last statement of the script informs the user how many visits the user had in the current page.

The following script is similar to the preceding one, but it asks the user for his or her name and "remembers" it. Here is the script:

```
<HTML>
<HEAD>
<TITLE>Remember user's name</TITLE>
<SCRIPT LANGUAGE="JavaScript">
<!--
// Boolean variable specified if alert should be displayed if cookie exceeds 4KB
var caution = false
// name - name of the cookie
// value - value of the cookie
// [expires] - expiration date of the cookie (defaults to end of current
```

```
session)
// [path] - path for which the cookie is valid (defaults to path of calling
document)
// [domain] - domain for which the cookie is valid (defaults to domain of
calling document)
// [secure] - Boolean value indicating if the cookie transmission requires a
secure transmission
// * an argument defaults when it is assigned null as a placeholder
// * a null placeholder is not required for trailing omitted arguments
function setCookie(name, value, expires, path, domain, secure)
{
   var curCookie = name + "=" + escape(value) +
      ((expires) ? "; expires=" + expires.toGMTString() : "") +
      ((path) ? "; path=" + path : "") +
      ((domain) ? "; domain=" + domain : "") +
      ((secure) ? "; secure" : "")
   if (!caution || (name + "=" + escape(value)).length <= 4000)
      document.cookie = curCookie
   else
      if (confirm("Cookie exceeds 4KB and will be cut!"))
         document.cookie = curCookie
}
// name - name of the desired cookie
// * return string containing value of specified cookie or null if cookie does
not exist
function getCookie(name)
{
   var prefix = name + "="
   var cookieStartIndex = document.cookie.indexOf(prefix)
   if (cookieStartIndex == -1)
      return null
   var cookieEndIndex = document.cookie.indexOf(";", cookieStartIndex +
                        prefix.length)
   if (cookieEndIndex == -1)
      cookieEndIndex = document.cookie.length
   return unescape(document.cookie.substring(cookieStartIndex +
                  prefix.length, cookieEndIndex))
}
// name - name of the cookie
// [path] - path of the cookie (must be same as path used to create cookie)
// [domain] - domain of the cookie (must be same as domain used to create
cookie)
// * path and domain default if assigned null or omitted if no explicit argument
proceeds
function deleteCookie(name, path, domain)
{
   if (getCookie(name))
   {
      document.cookie = name + "=" +
      ((path) ? "; path=" + path : "") +
      ((domain) ? "; domain=" + domain : "") +
      "; expires=Thu, 01-Jan-70 00:00:01 GMT"
   }
}
```

```
// date - any instance of the Date object
// * you should hand all instances of the Date object to this function for
"repairs"
function fixDate(date)
{
   var base = new Date(0)
   var skew = base.getTime()
   if (skew > 0)
      date.setTime(date.getTime() - skew)
}
var now = new Date()
fixDate(now)
now.setTime(now.getTime() + 31 * 24 * 60 * 60 * 1000)
var name = getCookie("name")
if (!name)
   name = prompt("Please enter your name:", "John Doe")
setCookie("name", name, now)
document.write("Hello " + name + "!")
// -->
</SCRIPT>
</HEAD>
</HTML>
```

Example 20-2 (ex20-2.htm). *A script that remembers the user's name and displays a greeting each time*

Figure 20-2. *Asking for the user name*

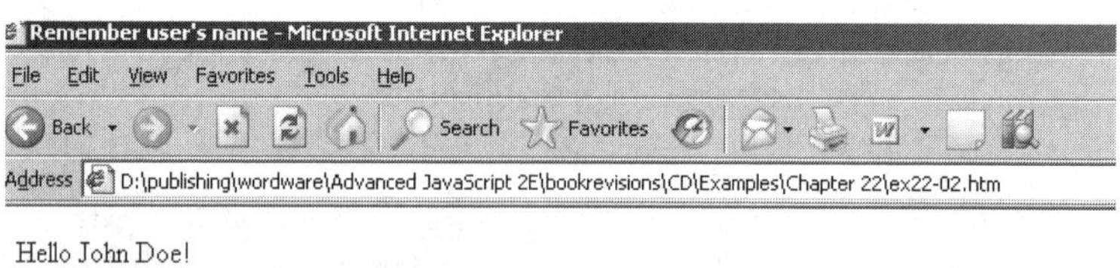

Figure 20-3. *Displaying a greeting*

The output of this example is shown in Figures 20-2 and 20-3.

The differences between this script and the previous one are confined to the last five statements of the script. In the current script, the name of the cookie is `name` and it is the user's name that is being retrieved from it. Notice that the variable to which you assign the value of `getCookie()` does not have to have the same name as the cookie, as is done here. If the cookie is not found, the user is prompted for his or her name. The script then sets the cookie with the user's name and prints a personalized welcome message.

Examples 20-1 and 20-2 were rather simple, because they only set and read a cookie. Example 20-3 demonstrates using cookies in a slightly different way. It creates a calendar that enables the user to enter reminders for specific days of the month. This reminder calendar stores the data for the entire month, even if the user turns off his or her computer. Since there are up to 31 days in a month, and since you are limited to 20 cookies per domain or server, the script stores all reminders in a single cookie, with special delimiting sequences. Assuming a reminder does not exceed 100 characters, storing 31 values takes up 31 * 100, or 3100 characters, which is less than the 4KB upper limit. Here is the script:

```
<HTML>
<HEAD>
<TITLE>
JavaScript calendar
</TITLE>
</HEAD>
<BODY>
<SCRIPT LANGUAGE="JavaScript">
<!--
//
// Cookie functions to store and retrieve cookies
//
// Boolean variable specified if alert should be displayed if cookie exceeds 4KB
var caution = false
// name - name of the cookie
// value - value of the cookie
// [expires] - expiration date of the cookie (defaults to end of current
session)
// [path] - path for which the cookie is valid (defaults to path of calling
document)
// [domain] - domain for which the cookie is valid (defaults to domain of
calling document)
// [secure] - Boolean value indicating if the cookie transmission requires a
secure transmission
// * an argument defaults when it is assigned null as a placeholder
// * a null placeholder is not required for trailing omitted arguments
function setCookie(name, value, expires, path, domain, secure)
{
   var curCookie = name + "=" + escape(value) +
      ((expires) ? "; expires=" + expires.toGMTString() : "") +
      ((path) ? "; path=" + path : "") +
      ((domain) ? "; domain=" + domain : "") +
      ((secure) ? "; secure" : "")
   if (!caution || (name + "=" + escape(value)).length <= 4000)
      document.cookie = curCookie
   else
      if (confirm("Cookie exceeds 4KB and will be cut!"))
         document.cookie = curCookie
}
```

Chapter 20

```
// name - name of the desired cookie
// * return string containing value of specified cookie or null if cookie does
not exist
function getCookie(name)
{
   var prefix = name + "="
   var cookieStartIndex = document.cookie.indexOf(prefix)
   if (cookieStartIndex == -1)
      return null
   var cookieEndIndex = document.cookie.indexOf(";", cookieStartIndex
                        + prefix.length)
   if (cookieEndIndex == -1)
      cookieEndIndex = document.cookie.length
   return unescape(document.cookie.substring(cookieStartIndex +
                prefix.length, cookieEndIndex))
}
// name - name of the cookie
// [path] - path of the cookie (must be same as path used to create cookie)
// [domain] - domain of the cookie (must be same as domain used to create
cookie)
// * path and domain default if assigned null or omitted if no explicit
argument proceeds
function deleteCookie(name, path, domain)
{
   if (getCookie(name))
   {
      document.cookie = name + "=" +
      ((path) ? "; path=" + path : "") +
      ((domain) ? "; domain=" + domain : "") +
      "; expires=Thu, 01-Jan-70 00:00:01 GMT"
   }
}
// date - any instance of the Date object
// * you should hand all instances of the Date object to this function for
"repairs"
function fixDate(date)
{
   var base = new Date(0)
   var skew = base.getTime()
   if (skew > 0)
      date.setTime(date.getTime() - skew)
}
function initCookie(monthName)
{  // initializes cookie with the following format:
   // ^1^^2^^3^^4^...^30^^31^
   // initialize accumulative variable
   var text = ""
   for (var i = 1; i <= 31; ++i)
   {
      text += "^" + i + "^"
   }
   var now = new Date()
   fixDate(now)
   // set time to one month (31 days) in the future
```

```
   now.setTime(now.getTime() + 1000 * 60 * 60 * 24 * 31)
   setCookie(monthName + "Calendar", text, now)
}
function getSpecificReminder(num, monthName)
{
   var prefix = "^" + num + "^"
   var totalCookie = getCookie(monthName + "Calendar")
   var startIndex = totalCookie.indexOf(prefix, 0)
   var startData = totalCookie.indexOf("^", startIndex + 1) + 1
   if (num == 31)
      var endData = totalCookie.length
   else
      var endData = totalCookie.indexOf("^", startData)
   return totalCookie.substring(startData, endData)
}
function setSpecificReminder(num, monthName, newValue)
{
   var prefix = "^" + num + "^"
   var totalCookie = getCookie(monthName + "Calendar")
   var startIndex = totalCookie.indexOf(prefix, 0)
   var startData = totalCookie.indexOf("^", startIndex + 1) + 1
      if (num == 31)
      var endData = totalCookie.length
   else
      var endData = totalCookie.indexOf("^", startData)
   var now = new Date()
   fixDate(now)
   // set time to one month (31 days) in the future
   now.setTime(now.getTime() + 1000 * 60 * 60 * 24 * 31)
   setCookie(monthName + "Calendar", totalCookie.substring(0, startData)
   + newValue + totalCookie.substring(endData, totalCookie.length), now)
}
function getInput(num, monthName)
{
   if (!getCookie(monthName + "Calendar"))
      initCookie(monthName)
   var newValue = prompt("Enter reminder for current date:",
            getSpecificReminder(num, monthName))
   if (newValue)     // user did not cancel
      setSpecificReminder(num, monthName, newValue)
}
function getTime()
{
   // initialize time-related variables with current time settings
   var now = new Date()
   var hour = now.getHours()
   var minute = now.getMinutes()
   now = null
   var ampm = ""
   // validate hour values and set value of ampm
   if (hour >= 12)
   {
      hour -= 12
      ampm = "PM"
```

```
   }
   else
      ampm = "AM"
   hour = (hour == 0) ? 12 : hour
   // add zero digit to a one-digit minute
   if (minute < 10)
      minute = "0" + minute   // do not parse this number!
   // return time string
   return hour + ":" + minute + " " + ampm
}
function leapYear(year)
{
   if (year % 4 == 0)          // basic rule
      return true              // is leap year
   return false                // is not leap year
}
function getDays(month, year)
{
   // create array to hold number of days in each month
   var ar = new Array(12)
   ar[0] = 31  // January
   ar[1] = (leapYear(year)) ? 29 : 28  // February
   ar[2] = 31  // March
   ar[3] = 30  // April
   ar[4] = 31  // May
   ar[5] = 30  // June
   ar[6] = 31  // July
   ar[7] = 31  // August
   ar[8] = 30  // September
   ar[9] = 31  // October
   ar[10] = 30 // November
   ar[11] = 31 // December
   // return number of days in the specified month (parameter)
   return ar[month]
}
function getMonthName(month)
{
   // create array to hold name of each month
   var ar = new Array(12)
   ar[0] = "January"
   ar[1] = "February"
   ar[2] = "March"
   ar[3] = "April"
   ar[4] = "May"
   ar[5] = "June"
   ar[6] = "July"
   ar[7] = "August"
   ar[8] = "September"
   ar[9] = "October"
   ar[10] = "November"
   ar[11] = "December"
   // return name of specified month (parameter)
   return ar[month]
}
```

```
function setCal()
{
   // standard time attributes
   var now = new Date()
   var year = now.getYear()
   var month = now.getMonth()
   var monthName = getMonthName(month)
   var date = now.getDate()
   now = null
   // create instance of first day of month, and extract the day
             on which it occurs
   var firstDayInstance = new Date(year, month, 1)
   var firstDay = firstDayInstance.getDay()
   firstDayInstance = null
   // number of days in current month
   var days = getDays(month, year)
   // call function to draw calendar
   drawCal(firstDay + 1, days, date, monthName, 1900 + year)
}
function drawCal(firstDay, lastDate, date, monthName, year)
{
   // constant table settings
   var headerHeight = 50           // height of the table's header cell
   var border = 2                  // 3D height of table's border
   var cellspacing = 4             // width of table's border
   var headerColor = "midnightblue" // color of table's header
   var headerSize = "+3"           // size of table's header font
   var colWidth = 60               // width of columns in table
   var dayCellHeight = 25          // height of cells containing days of the
                                   // week
   var dayColor = "darkblue"       // color of font representing weekdays
   var cellHeight = 40             // height of cells representing dates in the
                                   // calendar
   var todayColor = "red"          // color specifying today's date in the
                                   // calendar
   var timeColor = "purple"        // color of font representing current time
   // create basic table structure
   var text = ""                   // initialize accumulative variable to
                                   // empty string
   text += '<CENTER>'
   text += '<TABLE BORDER=' + border + ' CELLSPACING=' + cellspacing + '>'
   // table settings
   text += '<TH COLSPAN=7 HEIGHT=' + headerHeight + '>'
   // create table header cell
   text += '<FONT COLOR="' + headerColor + '" SIZE=' + headerSize+ '>'
   // set font for table header
   text += monthName + ' ' + year
   text += '</FONT>'               // close table header's font settings
   text += '</TH>'                 // close header cell
   // variables to hold constant settings
   var openCol = '<TD WIDTH=' + colWidth + ' HEIGHT=' + dayCellHeight + '>'
   openCol += '<FONT COLOR="' + dayColor + '">'
   var closeCol = '</FONT></TD>'
   // create array of abbreviated day names
```

```
var weekDay = new Array(7)
weekDay[0] = "Sun"
weekDay[1] = "Mon"
weekDay[2] = "Tues"
weekDay[3] = "Wed"
weekDay[4] = "Thu"
weekDay[5] = "Fri"
weekDay[6] = "Sat"
// create first row of table to set column width and specify week day
text += '<TR ALIGN="center" VALIGN="center">'
for (var dayNum = 0; dayNum < 7; ++dayNum)
{
   text += openCol + weekDay[dayNum] + closeCol
}
text += '</TR>'
// declaration and initialization of two variables to help with tables
var digit = 1
var curCell = 1
   for (var row = 1; row <= Math.ceil((lastDate + firstDay - 1) / 7);++row)
   {
      text += '<TR ALIGN="right" VALIGN="top">'
      for (var col = 1; col <= 7; ++col)
      {
         if (digit > lastDate)
            break
         if (curCell < firstDay)
         {
            text += '<TD></TD>';
            curCell++
         }
         else
         {
            if (digit == date) { // current cell represents today's date
               text += '<TD HEIGHT=' + cellHeight + '>'
               text += '<FONT COLOR="' + todayColor + '">'
               text += '<A HREF="javascript:getInput(' + digit +
                  ', \'' + monthName + '\')"onMouseOver
                  ="window.status = \'Store or retrieve data
                  for ' + monthName + ' ' + digit + '\';
                  return true"><FONT COLOR="' + todayColor +
                  '">' + digit + '</FONT></A>'
               text += '<BR>'
               text += '<FONT COLOR="' + timeColor + '" SIZE=2>'
               text += '<CENTER>' + getTime() + '</CENTER>'
               text += '</FONT>'
               text += '</TD>'
         }
         else
            text += '<TD HEIGHT=' + cellHeight + '><A HREF=
               "javascript:getInput(' + digit + ', \'' +
               monthName + '\')" onMouseOver="window.
               status = \'Store or retrieve data for
               ' + monthName + ' ' + digit + '\';
               return true">' + digit + '</A></TD>'
```

```
            digit++
         }
      }
      text += '</TR>'
   }
   // close all basic table tags
   text += '</TABLE>'
   text += '</CENTER>'
   // print accumulative HTML string
   document.write(text)
}
setCal()
// -->
</SCRIPT>
</BODY>
</HTML>
```

***Example 20-3 (ex20-3.htm).** A cookie-based reminder calendar*

The `setCal()` function creates the calendar. The calendar is created by the same functions as those in Example 10-3 (Chapter 10, "Time and Date in JavaScript"). The only difference is the following:

```
if (digit == date)
{ // current cell represents today's date
   text += '<TD HEIGHT=' + cellHeight + '>'
   text += '<FONT COLOR="' + todayColor + '">'
   text += '<A HREF="javascript:getInput(' + digit + ', \'' + monthName +
         '\')" onMouseOver="window.status = \'Store or retrieve
         data for ' + monthName + ' ' + digit + '\'; return true">
         <FONT COLOR="' + todayColor + '">' + digit + '</FONT></A>'
   text += '<BR>'
   text += '<FONT COLOR="' + timeColor + '" SIZE=2>'
   text += '<CENTER>' + getTime() + '</CENTER>'
   text += '</FONT>'
   text += '</TD>'
}
else
   text += '<TD HEIGHT=' + cellHeight + '><A HREF="javascript:getInput('
         + digit + ', \'' + monthName + '\')" onMouseOver="window
         .status = \'Store or retrieve data for ' + monthName + ' '
         + digit + '\'; return true">' + digit + '</A></TD>'
```

This statement differs from its corresponding one in Example 10-3 in that, instead of writing the date as a plain number, it makes each number a link that invokes the `getInput()` function, using the `javascript:getInput()` URL. The exact syntax of the URL is as follows:

```
javascript:getInput(digit, monthName)
```

The first argument is the digit that serves as a link (an integer from 1 to 28, 29, 30, or 31). The second argument is a string—the full name of the current month reflected by the calendar.

Note that when the user places the mouse pointer over a link, a related message is assigned to the status bar. We will only discuss the functions that are responsible for the cookie handling and storage because the functions that create the calendar are discussed in Chapter 10, "Time and Date in JavaScript."

getInput(num, monthName)

```
function getInput(num, monthName)
{
   if (!getCookie(monthName + "Calendar"))
      initCookie(monthName)
   var newValue = prompt("Enter reminder for current date:",
                  getSpecificReminder(num, monthName))
   if (newValue) // user did not cancel
      setSpecificReminder(num, monthName, newValue)
}
```

The `getInput()` function, in general, reads the reminder from the cookie, asks the user to modify it or enter it for the first time, and then saves the reminder back to the cookie. First, it gets the reminder text from the cookie, the name of which is composed of the name of the current month and the "Calendar" string. The name selection algorithm prevents mixing cookies between different months or different applications. If the cookie is not found, the function `initCookie()` is called to create a cookie with empty reminders, one for each day of the month. The script then prompts the user for a reminder, displaying the old one in the form's input field. Notice that the reminder is displayed in the field of a prompt dialog box by specifying the value returned by `getSpecificReminder()`, as the second argument for the `prompt()` method. If the user did not press Cancel as a response to the request form, the new information is saved in the cookie by the `setSpecificReminder()` function.

initCookie(monthName)

```
function initCookie(monthName)
{
   // initializes cookie with the following format:
   // ^1^^2^^3^^4^...^30^^31^
   // initialize accumulative variable
   var text = ""
   for (var i = 1; i <= 31; ++i)
   {
      text += "^" + i + "^"
   }
   var now = new Date()
   fixDate(now)
   // set time to one month (31 days) in the future
   now.setTime(now.getTime() + 1000 * 60 * 60 * 24 * 31)
   setCookie(monthName + "Calendar", text, now)
}
```

The initCookie() function creates a cookie with empty reminders, one for every day of the month. The cookie's text is a string concatenation of all 31 reminders, delimited by "^" from each other. The function builds the empty string, fixes the date for Mac computers, computes the time, and finally sets the cookie, saving the empty reminders, date, and time in it.

getSpecificReminder(num, monthName)

```
function getSpecificReminder(num, monthName)
{
   var prefix = "^" + num + "^"
   var totalCookie = getCookie(monthName + "Calendar")
   var startIndex = totalCookie.indexOf(prefix, 0)
   var startData = totalCookie.indexOf("^", startIndex + 1) + 1
   if (num == 31)
      var endData = totalCookie.length
   else
      var endData = totalCookie.indexOf("^", startData)
   return totalCookie.substring(startData, endData)
}
```

This function retrieves the specific reminder of the month from the cookie. It first builds the "search key" in prefix. It is built of a "^" followed by the day number of the month and another "^". After getting the cookie and reading the string into the totalCookie string object, the function searches for the position of the relevant reminder, according to prefix "search key," yielding the startIndex position. Looking for the next "^" skips over the number of the day itself and leaps onto the string index of the reminder's first character, startData. The last character of the reminder is found via a search for the next "^" character or by reaching the end of the cookie. Once the startData and endData are known, the substring between these two indices is returned. Note that because the indexing relies on "^" characters, that character should not be provided by the user in a reminder text.

setSpecificReminder(num, monthName, newValue)

```
function setSpecificReminder(num, monthName, newValue)
{
   var prefix = "^" + num + "^"
   var totalCookie = getCookie(monthName + "Calendar")
   var startIndex = totalCookie.indexOf(prefix, 0)
   var startData = totalCookie.indexOf("^", startIndex + 1) + 1
      if (num == 31)
      var endData = totalCookie.length
   else
      var endData = totalCookie.indexOf("^", startData)
   var now = new Date()
   fixDate(now)
   // set time to one month (31 days) in the future
   now.setTime(now.getTime() + 1000 * 60 * 60 * 24 * 31)
   setCookie(monthName + "Calendar", totalCookie.substring(0,
```

```
            startData) + newValue + totalCookie.substring
            (endData, totalCookie.length), now)
}
```

As in `setSpecificReminder()`, the first section determines the indices of the first and last character of the relevant reminder (`startData` and `endData`, respectively). An instance of the `Date` object is then created and fixed for Mac computers. The expiration date is computed to one month in the future. The last statement of the function sets the cookie. The first parameter is the name of the cookie, while the second one is the reminder string, composed of the substring before the new reminder (all previous days are not modified), the `newValue` of the current day, and the rest of the old string (all following days are not modified as well). The expiration date is handed to the function as the last argument.

Outliner

As you have seen in this chapter, you can use JavaScript to store data in the form of client-side cookies. The *outliner* is another example for using cookies. It is an expanding/collapsing structure used to store an index or table of contents. The user can expand or collapse items in the outline. Outliners first became popular in Windows 3.1 and are still used today. An outliner written in JavaScript enables the user to take advantage of the structure for convenient navigation among many web pages and anchors. The main topics of a web site are the topmost items in the outline, while the more detailed items are usually deeply nested. Take a look at the following:

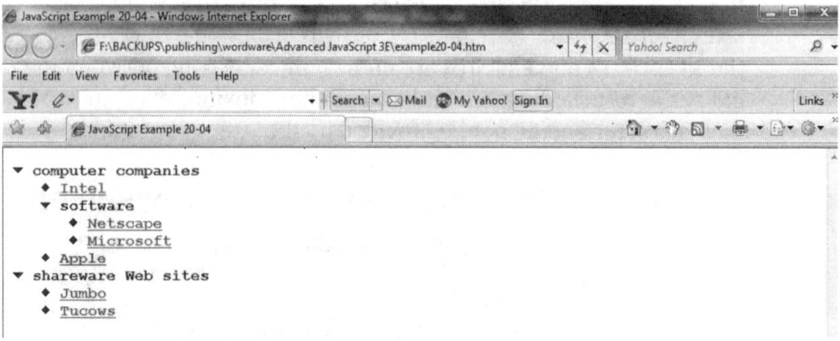

Figure 20-4. *A fully expanded outline*

Figure 20-4 illustrates a fully expanded outline. When the user clicks the downward triangle to the left of "software," the icon becomes a triangle facing right. The "Netscape" and "Microsoft" items then disappear, because their parent was collapsed. The basic idea should be clear. You can toggle a single item (only if it is a parent) between two different states (either expanded or collapsed).

Before we discuss the script itself, it is important that you understand exactly what the script does and how it differs from other JavaScript outliners available. Compared to other variants you might find on the web, our outliner script has the following advantages:

- You can use any HTML tag for an item. You can use colored text, hypertext links, and even small images.
- The current state of the outline structure is stored in the form of a cookie, so it is safe, even if you leave the page.
- You can use as many nested items as you wish. Some outline designs limit you to two levels, which is very restrictive.
- The outliner design is not limited to frame documents. Since you can use any HTML for the text of an item, you can target any link to any frame or window you wish.

First, study the script (Example 20-4) and try to understand as much as you can:

```
<HTML>
<HEAD>
<TITLE>Outliner</TITLE>
<SCRIPT LANGUAGE="JavaScript">
<!--
// Boolean variable specified if alert should be displayed if cookie exceeds 4KB
var caution = false
// name - name of the cookie
// value - value of the cookie
// [expires] - expiration date of the cookie (defaults to end of current
session)
// [path] - path for which the cookie is valid (defaults to path of calling
document)
// [domain] - domain for which the cookie is valid (defaults to domain of
calling document)
// [secure] - Boolean value indicating if the cookie transmission requires a
secure transmission
// * an argument defaults when it is assigned null as a placeholder
// * a null placeholder is not required for trailing omitted arguments
function setCookie(name, value, expires, path, domain, secure)
{
   var curCookie = name + "=" + escape(value) +
      ((expires) ? "; expires=" + expires.toGMTString() : "") +
      ((path) ? "; path=" + path : "") +
      ((domain) ? "; domain=" + domain : "") +
      ((secure) ? "; secure" : "")
   if (!caution || (name + "=" + escape(value)).length <= 4000)
      document.cookie = curCookie
   else
      if (confirm("Cookie exceeds 4KB and will be cut!"))
         document.cookie = curCookie
}
// name - name of the desired cookie
// * return string containing value of specified cookie or null if
         cookie does not exist
```

```
function getCookie(name)
{
   var prefix = name + "="
   var cookieStartIndex = document.cookie.indexOf(prefix)
   if (cookieStartIndex == -1)
      return null
   var cookieEndIndex = document.cookie.indexOf(";", cookieStartIndex +
prefix.length)
   if (cookieEndIndex == -1)
      cookieEndIndex = document.cookie.length
   return unescape(document.cookie.substring(cookieStartIndex + prefix.length,
cookieEndIndex))
}
// name - name of the cookie
// [path] - path of the cookie (must be same as path used to create cookie)
// [domain] - domain of the cookie (must be same as domain used to create
cookie)
// * path and domain default if assigned null or omitted if no explicit
argument proceeds
function deleteCookie(name, path, domain)
{
   if (getCookie(name))
   {
      document.cookie = name + "=" +
      ((path) ? "; path=" + path : "") +
      ((domain) ? "; domain=" + domain : "") +
      "; expires=Thu, 01-Jan-70 00:00:01 GMT"
   }
}
// date - any instance of the Date object
// * you should hand all instances of the Date object to this function for
 "repairs"
function fixDate(date)
{
   var base = new Date(0)
   var skew = base.getTime()
   if (skew > 0)
      date.setTime(date.getTime() - skew)
}
// constructor function to create an entry (parent or child)
function item(parent, text, depth)
{
   this.parent = parent       // is this item a parent?
   this.text = text           // text for link (may include HTML)
   this.depth = depth         // nested depth
}
// constructor function to create array (compatible with all browsers)
function makeArray(length)
{
   this.length = length       // length of array (integer)
}
// create items of outline
function makeDatabase()
{
```

```
   outline = new makeArray(9) // create global object
   // create items in outline
   outline[0] = new item(true, 'computer companies', 0)
   outline[1] = new item(false, '<A HREF="http://www.intel.com">Intel</A>', 1)
   outline[2] = new item(true, 'software', 1)
   outline[3] = new item(false, '<A HREF="http://www.netscape.com">
                Netscape</A>', 2)
   outline[4] = new item(false, '<A HREF="http://www.microsoft.com">
                Microsoft</A>', 2)
   outline[5] = new item(false, '<A HREF="http://www.apple.com">Apple</A>', 1)
   outline[6] = new item(true, 'shareware web sites', 0)
   outline[7] = new item(false, '<A HREF="http://www.jumbo.com">Jumbo</A>', 1)
   outline[8] = new item(false, '<A HREF="http://www.tucows.com">
                Tucows.com</A>', 1)
   // determine current state of each item and assign to state properties
   setStates()
   // set image for each item (only items with true state)
   setImages()
}
function setStates()
{
   // assign current cookie to local variable
   var storedValue = getCookie("outline")
   // if desired cookie not found (null)
   if (!storedValue)
   {
      // set states to default if no cookie found
      for (var i = 0; i < outline.length; ++i)
      {
         // only topmost level is visible by default
         if (outline[i].depth == 0)
            outline[i].state = true
         else
            outline[i].state = false
      }
   }
   else
   {
      // extract current states from cookie (0 => false, 1 => true)
      for (var i = 0; i < outline.length; ++i)
      {
         if (storedValue.charAt(i) == '1')
            outline[i].state = true
         else
            outline[i].state = false
      }
   }
}
function setImages()
{
   // loop through all elements of the outline "array" (object)
   for (var i = 0; i < outline.length; ++i)
   {
      if (outline[i].state)
```

Chapter 20

```
         if (outline[i].parent)        // outline[i] is a parent
            if (outline[i + 1].state)  // outline[i] is exploded
               outline[i].pic = '<A HREF="javascript:toggle(' +
               i + ')"><IMG SRC="exploded.gif" BORDER=0></A>'
            else // outline[i] is collapsed
               outline[i].pic = '<A HREF="javascript:toggle(' +
               i + ')"><IMG SRC="collapsd.gif" BORDER=0></A>'
         else // outline[i] is only a child (not a parent)
            outline[i].pic = '<IMG SRC="child.gif" BORDER=0>'
   }
}
// change from expanded to collapsed and vice versa
function toggle(num)
{
   // loop starts at item following argument
   // terminate loop when:
   // a) last element of outline "array" reached
   // b) current item (outline[i]) is not deeper than toggled item
               (outline[num])
   for (var i = num + 1; i < outline.length && outline[i].depth >=
               outline[num].depth + 1; ++i)
   {
      // if current item (outline[i]) is a direct child of
               outline[num]
      if (outline[i].depth == outline[num].depth + 1)
         outline[i].state = !outline[i].state // toggle state
   }
   // store new states in cookie
   setStorage()
   // reload page
   history.go(0)
}
function setStorage()
{
   // initialize local variable to empty string
   var text = ""
   // loop through all properties of outline "array"
   for (var i = 0; i < outline.length; ++i)
   {
      // use "1" character to represent true state, and "0" for
                false state
      text += (outline[i].state) ? "1" : "0"
   }
   // create cookie named "outline" with "binary" string
   setCookie("outline", text)
}
// update database
makeDatabase()
// -->
</SCRIPT>
</HEAD>
<BODY>
<SCRIPT LANGUAGE="JavaScript">
<!--
```

```
// use <PRE> to enable indentation via spaces
document.write('<PRE><H4>')
// loop through elements of outline "array"
for (var i = 0; i < outline.length; ++i)
{
   // if current item's state is true
   if (outline[i].state)
   {
      // place three spaces for each nesting (depth * 3 spaces)
      for (var j = 0; j < outline[i].depth * 3; ++j)
      {
         document.write(' ')
      }
      // follow indentation with picture, another space, text, and
               new line
      document.write(outline[i].pic, ' ', outline[i].text, '<BR>')
   }
   else
   {
      // current item's state is false (skip all its children)
      var previous = i
      for (var k = i + 1; k < outline.length && outline[k].depth >=
               outline[previous].depth; ++k)
      {
         ++i
      }
   }
}
// end <PRE> to return to normal formatting
document.write('</H4></PRE>')
// -->
</SCRIPT>
</BODY>
</HTML>
```

Example 20-4 (ex20-4.htm). *The outliner script includes deferred script and immediate script.*

A quick look at Example 20-4 is enough to conclude that the script uses cookies. Our set of cookie-related functions is embedded in the script. Although not all are invoked, we feel that you should always provide all the functions, regardless of whether you require all of them. Also notice that the HTML document includes two scripts—one in the <HEAD></HEAD> portion and one in the <BODY></BODY> portion. The first script is responsible for setting up the outline-style table and contents, and for performing the calculations and manipulations. The second script simply interprets the data and prints it to the web page. First let's take a look at the script in the <HEAD></HEAD> portion.

item(parent, text, depth)

```
// constructor function to create an entry (parent or child)
function item(parent, text, depth)
{
   this.parent = parent    // is this item a parent?
   this.text = text        // text for link (may include HTML)
   this.depth = depth      // nested depth
}
```

The constructor function `item()` accepts three arguments and creates three properties with the same names as the function's parameters: `parent`, `text`, and `depth`. The first parameter (and property), `parent`, accepts a Boolean value indicating whether or not the item is a parent. An item is considered a parent only if it has children, or nested items. The function's second argument, `text`, accepts an HTML-valid string such as `<A HREF="http://www.jumbo.com">Jumbo</A>` for the "Jumbo" entry in Figure 20-4. You can use virtually any HTML-valid string such as plain text, a link (as in the "Jumbo" example), or even a small image. The last argument, `depth`, is the depth of the item being created, i.e., it specifies how deep the item is nested. The topmost level item's `depth` property is 0, whereas its children's `depth` property is 1, and so forth.

makeArray(length)

```
// constructor function to create array (compatible with all browsers)
function makeArray(length)
{
   this.length = length    // length of array (integer)
}
```

This function is an alternative to the built-in `Array()` constructor of Navigator and Internet Explorer. We decided to write an array constructor on our own in order to make the script compatible with all JavaScript-enabled browsers. We used JavaScript's support for adding properties to an object to explicitly create `length`, which holds the number of elements in the array, or the number of its properties (not counting `length` itself), to be exact.

makeDatabase()

```
// create items of outline
function makeDatabase()
{
   outline = new makeArray(9) // create global object
   // create items in outline
   outline[0] = new item(true, 'computer companies', 0)
   outline[1] = new item(false, '<A HREF="http://www.intel.com">Intel</A>', 1)
   outline[2] = new item(true, 'software', 1)
   outline[3] = new item(false, '<A HREF="http://www.netscape.com">
                Netscape</A>', 2)
   outline[4] = new item(false, '<A HREF="http://www.microsoft.com">
```

```
               Microsoft</A>', 2)
   outline[5] = new item(false, '<A HREF="http://www.apple.com">Apple</A>', 1)
   outline[6] = new item(true, 'shareware web sites', 0)
   outline[7] = new item(false, '<A HREF="http://www.jumbo.com">Jumbo</A>', 1)
   outline[8] = new item(false, '<A HREF="http://www.tucows.com">
               Tucows.com</A>', 1)
   // determine current state of each item and assign to state properties
   setStates()
   // set image for each item (only items with true state)
   setImages()
}
```

This function creates the main array used for the outline structure. Notice that the `outline` array is declared without the keyword `var` and thus is global. Try adding `var` to this statement to find out how important "one small word" can be. The next portion of this function deals with the properties (elements) of the `outline` array. Each property becomes an instance of the `item` object. The order of the elements in the array is very important. An item's children should immediately follow the item, so the order in the `outline` array is the order in which the entries appear, from top to bottom, in a fully expanded table of contents.

The function then calls `setStates()` and `setImages()`.

setStates()

```
function setStates()
{
   // assign current cookie to local variable
   var storedValue = getCookie("outline")
   // if desired cookie not found (null)
   if (!storedValue)
   {
      // set states to default if no cookie found
      for (var i = 0; i < outline.length; ++i)
      {
         // only topmost level is visible by default
         if (outline[i].depth == 0)
            outline[i].state = true
         else
            outline[i].state = false
      }
   }
   else
   {
      // extract current states from cookie (0 => false, 1 => true)
      for (var i = 0; i < outline.length; ++i)
      {
         if (storedValue.charAt(i) == '1')
            outline[i].state = true
         else
            outline[i].state = false
      }
```

```
   }
}
```

The `setStates()` function adds a `state` property to all properties of the `outline` object (array). If no cookie by the name of "outline" is found, the default states are used, i.e., the entire outline structure is collapsed, and only the topmost level is viewable. If the desired cookie is found, the current states are extracted. The cookie is basically a string of "0" and "1" characters, the first representing a false state, and the latter representing a true one. The first character of the string is associated with the first element of the array (`outline[0].state`), and so on. An item's state determines whether or not that item's parent is expanded. Therefore, on a two-level outline-style table of contents, if an item has a true state it is viewable.

setImages()

```
function setImages()
{
   // loop through all elements of the outline "array" (object)
   for (var i = 0; i < outline.length; ++i)
   {
      if (outline[i].state)
         if (outline[i].parent)        // outline[i] is a parent
            if (outline[i + 1].state)  // outline[i] is exploded
               outline[i].pic = '<A HREF="javascript:toggle
                  (' + i + ')"><IMG SRC="exploded.gif"
                  BORDER=0></A>'
            else // outline[i] is collapsed
               outline[i].pic = '<A HREF="javascript:toggle
                  (' + i + ')"><IMG SRC="collapsd.gif"
                  BORDER=0></A>'
         else // outline[i] is only a child (not a parent)
            outline[i].pic = '<IMG SRC="child.gif" BORDER=0>'
   }
}
```

This function loops through all elements of the `outline` object and assigns an image to the `pic` property of each element whose state is true. Note that this property is an extension of the original instance of the `item` object. If an element is a parent, there are two possible images—one to represent an expanded item and the other to reflect a collapsed one. Notice that if the Boolean expression `outline[i + 1].state` is true, `outline[i]` is expanded. You may recall that an element's `state` property is true if its parent is expanded (by definition). Since `outline[i]` is surely a parent in this case (`if (outline[i].parent)...`), `outline[i + 1]` is its child. If `outline[i + 1]`'s current state is false, the image representing a collapsed item is chosen. If `outline[i]` is not a parent at all, there is only one option for the image—the one representing a child item. The immediate conclusion from this function is that in order to use the outliner, you must have three images:

- exploded.gif
- collapsd.gif
- child.gif

toggle(num)

```
// change from expanded to collapsed and vice versa
function toggle(num)
{
   // loop starts at item following argument
   // terminate loop when:
   // a) last element of outline "array" reached
   // b) current item (outline[i]) is not deeper than toggled
            item (outline[num])
   for (var i = num + 1; i < outline.length && outline[i].depth >=
            outline[num].depth + 1; ++i)
   {
      // if current item (outline[i]) is a direct child of
            outline[num]
      if (outline[i].depth == outline[num].depth + 1)
         outline[i].state = !outline[i].state // toggle state
   }
   // store new states in cookie
   setStorage()
   // reload page
   history.go(0)
}
```

When the user clicks an image (exploded.gif or collapsd.gif), the item associated with it either collapses or explodes, depending on its current status. The `toggle()` function accepts an integer reflecting the index of the item whose icon the user clicked, and then toggles the `state` property of all the item's direct children. By definition, when an item has no children with a true state, the item is collapsed, and when all children of an item have a true state, the item is expanded. Therefore, toggling the `state` property of the selected item's children toggles that item's current status (exploded or collapsed). After all manipulations, the function invokes the `setStorage()` function to store the current status in a cookie, overwriting any previous cookie used for the outliner. After the cookie is written, the function reloads the page via the `history.go()` method, with the argument 0 to indicate that the current page should be loaded. We chose to use `go(0)` rather than `reload()` because it works with all JavaScript-compatible browsers, and it is perfect for refreshing a document, which is exactly what the script does.

setStorage()

```
function setStorage()
{
   // initialize local variable to empty string
   var text = ""
   // loop through all properties of outline "array"
   for (var i = 0; i < outline.length; ++i)
   {
      // use "1" character to represent true state, and "0" for false state
      text += (outline[i].state) ? "1" : "0"
   }
   // create cookie named "outline" with "binary" string
   setCookie("outline", text)
}
```

The `setStorage()` function creates a string with binary characters (0s and 1s). The first character of the string is associated with the first element of the `outline` array, and so forth. The character `"0"` indicates that the value of the item's `state` property is false, and a `"1"` character means that the item's `state` property is true. The last statement of this function sets the cookie via the `setCookie()` function, using "outline" as the name and the accumulative string as the value. No path or expiration date is specified, so the cookie is specific to the creating page and expires at the end of the user's current session.

Global Statements

The only global statement in the first script is the one invoking the `makeDatabase()` function. The second script, on the other hand, consists of global statements only and is responsible for printing the outline-style table of contents. The `<PRE></PRE>` tags are important because they enable us to use regular spaces for indentation.

The most important statement in the second script is the loop itself, which iterates through all elements of the global `outline` array (created by the `makeDatabase()` function in the first script). Each indentation level consists of three spaces and can be configured to any other integer for customized indentation. The topmost level items are not indented at all ($0 * 3 = 0$), the second level is indented by three spaces ($1 * 3 = 3$), the third level by six spaces ($2 * 3 = 6$), and so on. Note that an item is only printed if the value of its `state` property is true (by definition, if it is false, its parent is collapsed so you are not supposed to see the item). Each printed item consists of its small image (`outline[i].pic`), followed by one space and its text (`outline[I].text`). A new line (`<BR>`) is appended to each item. When an element whose `state` property is false is encountered, `i` is incremented the desired amount of times until its index is that of the next item at its level or a higher one. It passes over all items at lower levels because they do not appear.

Summary

In this chapter you have learned the fundamentals and usage of cookies, one of the most powerful features of JavaScript. It enables the programmer of a web page to store information in one session and retrieve it later in another session. I have provided three important functions by which you can get a cookie, set a cookie, and delete a cookie. All operations, as well as storage, are handled on the client side. Cookies are transparent to the server. The client imposes two limitations on cookies: a maximum of 20 cookies per server or domain that are 4KB each. I have shown several scripts in this chapter: one using cookies to remember the number of visits to a web site, one using cookies to store the user name, and one using cookies to remember a user's reminders for every day of the month. I also included an advanced collapsing/expanding outline-style table of contents that uses cookies as well.

Chapter 21

Images and Graphics

Defining Images in HTML

Without images web pages would be pretty dull. In fact, it is hard to imagine a modern web site without graphics. Inserting images into HTML is very simple. However, the images inserted via HTML simply sit there; they don't do anything dynamic. Thankfully, adding that dynamic behavior with JavaScript is not a difficult task. The syntax to define an image in HTML is as follows:

```
<IMG
   [NAME="imageName"]
   SRC="Location"
   [LOWSRC="Location"]
   [HEIGHT="Pixels" | "Value"%]
   [WIDTH="Pixels" | "Value"%]
   [SPACE="Pixels"]
   [BORDER = "Pixels"]
   [ALIGN = "left" | "right" |"top" | "absmiddle" | "absbottom"
            |"texttop" | "middle" | "baseline" | "bottom" ]
   [ISMAP]
   [USEMAP="Location#MapName"]
   [onAbort="handlerText"]
   [onError="handlerText"]
   [onLoad="handlerText"]>
```

The attributes are:

- `NAME="imageName"` specifies the name of the image object.
- `SRC="Location"` specifies the URL of the image to be displayed in the document.
- `LOWSRC="Location"` specifies the URL of a low-resolution version of the image to be displayed in the document. When this argument is provided, the smaller image is loaded first, and is then replaced by the larger image specified by `SRC`. Loading a low-resolution version first gives the user the impression of a shorter turnaround time.

- HEIGHT="*Pixels*" | "*Value*"% specifies the height of the image, either in pixels or as a percentage of the window height. If necessary, the image is scaled to fit the space specified by this attribute.
- WIDTH="*Pixels*" | "*Value*"% specifies the width of the image, either in pixels or as a percentage of the window width. If necessary, the image is scaled to fit the space specified by this attribute.
- HSPACE="*Pixels*" specifies the margin in pixels between the left and right edges of the image and the surrounding text. This attribute applies only to images that use "left" or "right" as the value of the ALIGN attribute.
- VSPACE="*Pixels*" specifies the margin in pixels between the top and bottom edges of the image and the surrounding text. This attribute applies only to images that use "top" or "bottom" as the value of the ALIGN attribute.
- BORDER="*Pixels*" specifies the width in pixels of the image border. You can suppress the border by setting its value to 0. If, however, it appears within an anchor, users will not see the colored border indicating a hyperlink.
- ALIGN specifies the alignment of the image in relation to the surrounding text. Images that are aligned left or right float into the next available space on the left or right side of the page, respectively, while text fills the empty space next to the image. The rest of the ALIGN values specify the alignment of the image with respect to a line of text in which it is placed (no filling). If omitted, "bottom" is used, which means that the bottom of the image is aligned with the line of text.
- ISMAP specifies the image as a server-side image map.
- USEMAP="*Location#MapName*" specifies the image as a client-side image map. This attribute must specify the URL of the file that contains the map definition, followed by a # symbol, and then the name of the map. For example, USEMAP="http://www.HomeWorld.com/maplist.html #areamap". The URL can be omitted if the image map specifications reside in the same document as the reference.

The image Object

The image object enables you to create instances that reflect a given image in any supported format (usually GIF or JPG). By introducing movement and animation, the image object immensely increased JavaScript's capabilities. You can take advantage of this object to create an animation, for example, with full control over timing and order of events. You can also create animation-based games such as Tetris, MineSweeper, and so forth.

The primary incentive for using the image object is to accelerate image displaying in the browser window. Instead of waiting for the image to be transmitted from the server to the client when the display is needed, it is loaded and stored in the browser's cache ahead of time, and displayed immediately upon request. In order to use the `image` object, you must create an instance associated with a given image. The general syntax is as follows:

```
var imageName = new Image([width, height])
```

width is the width of the image in pixels, and *height* is its height.

An instance of the `image` object can be associated with one image at any given time. In order to associate an instance with an existing image, you must assign it a source in the following fashion:

```
var imageName = new Image([width, height])
imageName.src = "imageLocation"
```

imageLocation is the full URL of the image. The second statement in the preceding script segment assigns a value to the instance's `src` property. The browser will retrieve the image from the server and will keep it in the cache until needed. Note that the *width* and *height* attributes are optional.

The images Array

When you create an HTML document you usually include several images (defined by the <IMG> definition). JavaScript features an array that reflects all images in a document—`document.images`. Each element of the array reflects an existing image. The first image in a document, for example, is `document.images[0]`. Obviously, the total number of images in a document is stored in the `length` property—`document.images.length`. Using the array within a deferred script ensures that all images have been loaded and the array reflects all images of a document.

An alternative way to reference an image is by its name, which is defined by the NAME attribute of the <IMG> HTML tag. See Example 21-5 for further details and explanations.

The size and position of an image in a document are set when the document is displayed in the browser window, and cannot be changed. Therefore, when creating an animation, you should generally use images of the same height and width. You can only change the image itself by setting the `src` and `lowsrc` properties. (See the description of SRC and LOWSRC in the previous section, "Defining Images in HTML.")

Consider the following HTML document:

```
<HTML>
<HEAD>
<TITLE>images</TITLE>
<SCRIPT LANGUAGE="JavaScript">
<!--
function swapImages(a, b)
{
   var asource = document.images[a].src
   document.images[a].src = document.images[b].src
   document.images[b].src = asource
}
// -->
</SCRIPT>
```

```
</HEAD>
<BODY>
<IMG SRC="comp1.gif" HEIGHT=60 WIDTH=70>
<IMG SRC="comp2.gif" HEIGHT=60 WIDTH=70><P>
<FORM>
<INPUT TYPE="button" VALUE="swap" onClick="swapImages(0, 1)">
</FORM>
</BODY>
</HTML>
```

Example 21-1 (ex21-1.htm). *A button enables the user to swap two given images.*

You can see the output of this script in Figure 21-1.

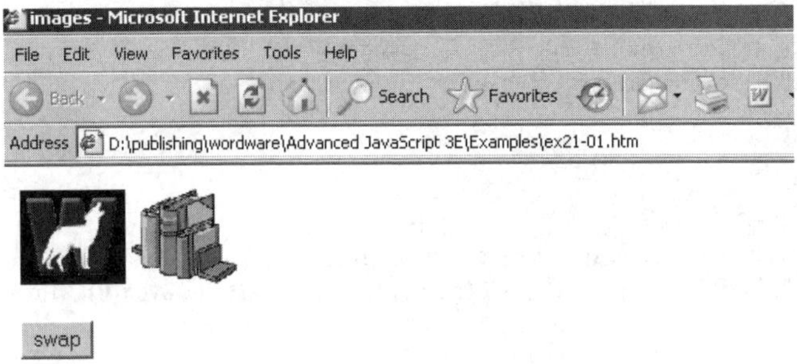

Figure 21-1. *Swapping images*

When the user clicks the button, the `swapImages()` function is invoked with two arguments: 0 and 1. The `src` property of the image whose index is the first argument is assigned to the local variable `asource`. The `src` property of the second image is assigned to the `src` property of the first image, and the `src` property of the second image is assigned the previous `src` property of the first image, stored locally in `asource`.

The `document.images` array is read-only—you cannot explicitly assign a value to any of its elements. Nevertheless, you can assign values to properties of an array element, as the preceding example demonstrates with the `src` property.

As mentioned earlier, an animation should consist of images of the same size. Example 21-2 demonstrates a simple animation with seven images of identical dimensions. Note that recent browser developments may make this example not function in some browsers.

```
<HTML>
<HEAD>
<TITLE>images</TITLE>
<SCRIPT LANGUAGE="JavaScript">
<!--
var pause = 250
var on = new Array()
on[0] = new Image(12, 12)
on[1] = new Image(12, 12)
on[2] = new Image(12, 12)
on[3] = new Image(12, 12)
```

```
on[2] = new Image(12, 12)
on[3] = new Image(12, 12)
on[4] = new Image(12, 12)
on[5] = new Image(12, 12)
on[6] = new Image(12, 12)
for (var i = 0; i < 7; ++i)
{
   on[i].src = "1" + i + ".gif"
}
timerID = setTimeout("", 0)
function animate(num, imageIndex)
{
   document.images[imageIndex].src = on[num].src
   num = (num == on.length - 1) ? 0 : (++num)
   var str = "animate(" + num + ", " + imageIndex + ")"
   timerID = setTimeout(str, pause)
}
// -->
</SCRIPT>
</HEAD>
<BODY onLoad="timerID = setTimeout('animate(1, 0)', pause)">
<IMG SRC="&{on[0].src};" HEIGHT="&{on[0].height};" WIDTH="&{on[0].width};">
</BODY>
</HTML>
```

Example 21-2 (ex21-2.htm). *A simple animation with images of identical size*

The script consists of a few immediate statements as well as a deferred code. First, an array named on is created to store the images of the animation. Each element is actually an instance of the `image` object.

Take a look at the following statement:

```
timerID = setTimeout("", 0)
```

This statement sets the value of `timerID` to null, but it does not explicitly assign that value. This syntax is useful with Internet Explorer because it generates an error if you use `clearTimeout()` with a variable that holds a null value.

```
function animate(num, imageIndex)
{
   document.images[imageIndex].src = on[num].src
   num = (num == on.length - 1) ? 0 : (++num)
   var str = "animate(" + num + ", " + imageIndex + ")"
   timerID = setTimeout(str, pause)
}
```

The `animate()` function accepts two arguments. The first specifies the index of the first image in the animation according to the on array. Take a look at the following statement from `animate()`, which is the most important one:

```
document.images[imageIndex].src = on[num].src
```

The current image that appears in the document at the imageIndex index of the document.images array is replaced by the image in the on array whose index is equal to the first argument handed to the function. The second statement in this function sets the value of num to 0 if the current value exceeds the index of the last entry in the on array. Otherwise, it increments the value of num, so the next image is displayed during the next execution of the function.

Properties

Instances of the image object feature many properties, some of which are more useful than others. You can also add more properties by creating prototypes. This section describes each property in depth.

border

An image's border appears only when the image is used in a hypertext link and when the value of the BORDER attribute is set to a positive integer. The general reference is as follows:

```
imageName.border
```

imageName is either the name of an image object's instance or an element in the document.images array. The border property is read-only. The following function displays the image's border if it is not 0:

```
function checkBorder(theImage)
{
   if (theImage.border == 0)
      alert('The image has no border!')
   else
      alert('The image's border is ' + theImage.border)
}
```

complete

The complete property is a Boolean value that indicates whether the browser has completed its attempt to load an image. The general specification is as follows:

```
imageName.complete
```

imageName is either the name of an image object's instance or an element in the document.images array.

height

The height property specifies the height of an image, either in pixels or as a percentage of the window's total height. The general syntax is as follows:

```
imageName.height
```

imageName is either the name of an image object's instance or an element in the document.images array. The height property reflects the HEIGHT attribute of the <IMG> tag. For images created with the Image() constructor, the value of the `height` property is the actual height, not the displayed height. The `height` property is read-only.

The script in Example 21-3 shows how an alert box can display, upon clicking a button, the height, width, and space around an image.

```
<HTML>
<HEAD>
<TITLE>images</TITLE>
<SCRIPT LANGUAGE="JavaScript">
<!--
function showImageSize(theImage)
{
   alert('height=' + theImage.height +
      '; width=' + theImage.width +
      '; hspace=' + theImage.hspace +
      '; vspace=' + theImage.vspace)
}
// -->
</SCRIPT>
</HEAD>
<BODY>
<IMG SRC="computer2.jpg" HEIGHT=60 WIDTH=70 VSPACE=30 HSPACE=10>
<FORM>
<INPUT TYPE="button" VALUE="show image size" onClick=
            "showImageSize(document.images[0])">
</FORM>
</BODY>
</HTML>
```

Example 21-3 (ex21-3.htm). *A script to display the height, width, and space around an image*

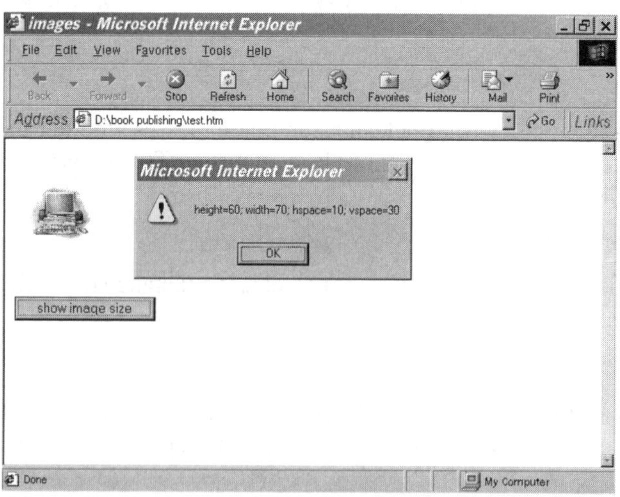

Figure 21-2. *An alert box that displays the height, width, and space around an image*

hspace

The hspace property specifies the margin in pixels between the left and right edges of an image and the surrounding text. The general syntax is as follows:

```
imageName.hspace
```

imageName is either the name of an image object's instance or an element in the document.images array. The hspace property reflects the HSPACE attribute of the <IMG> tag. For images created with the Image() constructor, the value of the hspace property is 0. The hspace property is read-only. The script in Example 21-3 shows how an alert box can display, upon clicking a button, the height, width, and space around an image.

lowsrc

lowsrc is a string specifying the URL of a low-resolution version of an image to be displayed in a document. The general syntax is as follows:

```
imageName.lowsrc
```

imageName is either the name of an image object's instance or an element in the document.images array. The lowsrc property initially reflects the LOWSRC attribute of the <IMG> tag. The browser loads the smaller image specified by lowsrc and then replaces it with the larger image specified by the src property. You can change the lowsrc property at any time.

The script in Example 21-4 lets the user display one image out of three available ones. There are two versions ready for each of the three selections: low resolution and high resolution. When loading the requested selection, the low-resolution image is loaded first and then the high-resolution one:

```
<HTML>
<HEAD>
<TITLE>Aircraft</TITLE>
<SCRIPT LANGUAGE="JavaScript">
<!--
function displayImage(lowRes, highRes)
{
   document.images[0].lowsrc = lowRes
   document.images[0].src = highRes
}
// -->
</SCRIPT>
</HEAD>
<BODY>
<FORM NAME="imageForm">
<B>Choose an image:</B>
<BR><INPUT TYPE="radio" NAME="imageChoice" VALUE="image1" CHECKED
   onClick="displayImage('img1l.gif', 'img1h.gif')"> IMAGE 1
```

```
<BR><INPUT TYPE="radio" NAME="imageChoice" VALUE="image2"
   onClick="displayImage('img2l.gif', 'img2h.gif')"> IMAGE 2
<BR><INPUT TYPE="radio" NAME="imageChoice" VALUE="image3"
   onClick="displayImage('img3l.gif', 'img3h.gif')"> IMAGE 3
<BR>
<IMG NAME="firstImage" SRC="img1h.gif" LOWSRC="img1l.gif" ALIGN="left"
         VSPACE="10"><BR>
</FORM>
</BODY>
</HTML>
```

Example 21-4 (ex21-4.htm). *A script to display one of three images, with low-resolution images loaded first*

name

The name property reflects the NAME attribute of the <IMG> HTML definition. The name property is read-only. As with forms, you can use an image's name to reference it. If the first image in a document is defined by the following syntax, for instance, you can reference it as document.myImage as well as document.images[0]:

```
<IMG SRC="myPicture.gif" NAME="myImage">
```

src

src specifies the URL of an image to be displayed in a document. The general syntax is:

```
imageName.src
```

imageName is either the name of an image object's instance or an element in the document.images array. The src property is used in almost all this chapter's examples. Consider the following statement:

```
var myImage = new Image()
```

An instance of the image object, named myImage, is created with the Image() constructor. When you create an instance of the image object in this fashion, it is not associated with any image. In order to associate it with an existing image, you must assign a value to its src property in the following manner:

```
myImage.src = "myPicture.gif"
```

You can use either a full or relational URL. When you associate an image with an instance in this fashion, the image is cached. Since it is already stored on the client side (where the cache normally is), the user does not have to wait for the image to be received from the server when you decide to display the image. When you adjust the src property of an element from the document.images array (or an image that is viewable on the page), the image immediately changes to the image at the new URL.

vspace

This property is a string specifying the margin in pixels between the top and bottom edges of an image and the surrounding text. The general syntax is as follows:

```
imageName.vspace
```

imageName is either the name of an `image` object's instance or an element in the `document.images` array. The `vspace` property reflects the `VSPACE` attribute of the `<IMG>` tag. For images created with the `Image()` constructor, the value of the `vspace` property is `0`. The `vspace` property is read-only. The script in Example 21-3 shows how an alert box can display, upon clicking a button, the height, width, and space around an image.

width

`width` is a string specifying the width of an image either in pixels or as a percentage of the window width. The general syntax is as follows:

```
imageName.width
```

imageName is either the name of an `image` object's instance or an element in the `document.images` array. The `width` property reflects the `WIDTH` attribute of the `<IMG>` tag. For images created with the `Image()` constructor, the value of the `width` property is the actual, not the displayed, width of the image. The `width` property is read-only. The script in Example 21-3 shows how an alert box can display, upon clicking a button, the height, width, and space around an image.

Event Handlers

onAbort

An abort event occurs when the user aborts the loading of an image (for example, by clicking a link or the Stop button). The `onAbort` event handler executes JavaScript code when an abort event occurs. In Example 21-5, an `onAbort` handler belonging to an `image` object displays a message when the user aborts the image's loading:

```
<HTML>
<HEAD>
<TITLE>Aircraft</TITLE>
<SCRIPT LANGUAGE="JavaScript">
<!--
function displayImage(lowRes, highRes)
{
   document.images[0].lowsrc = lowRes
   document.images[0].src = highRes
}
// -->
</SCRIPT>
</HEAD>
<BODY>
```

```
<FORM NAME="imageForm">
<B>Choose an image:</B>
<BR><INPUT TYPE="radio" NAME="imageChoice" VALUE="image1" CHECKED
  onClick="displayImage('img1l.gif', 'img1h.gif')"> IMAGE 1
<BR><INPUT TYPE="radio" NAME="imageChoice" VALUE="image2"
  onClick="displayImage('img2l.gif', 'img2h.gif')"> IMAGE 2
<BR><INPUT TYPE="radio" NAME="imageChoice" VALUE="image3"
  onClick="displayImage('img3l.gif', 'img3h.gif')"> IMAGE 3
<BR>
<IMG NAME="onAbort" SRC="img1h.gif" LOWSRC="img1l.gif" ALIGN="left"
        VSPACE="10" onAbort="alert('You didn\'t get to see the
        image!')"><BR>
</FORM>
</BODY>
</HTML>
```

Example 21-5 (ex21-5.htm). *The script from Example 21-4 with the onAbort event handler*

onError

An error event occurs when the loading of an image causes an error. The `onError` event handler executes JavaScript code when an error event occurs.

The `onError` event handler can be assigned a null value to suppress all error dialogs. When you set *imageName*`.onerror` to null, your user won't see any JavaScript errors caused by the image.

An error event occurs only when a JavaScript syntax or run-time error occurs, and not when a browser error occurs. If you try to set *image-Name*`.src = 'notThere.gif'`, for instance, and `notThere.gif` does not exist, the resulting error message is a Navigator error message, and an `onError` event handler would not intercept that message.

In the following `<IMG>` tag, the `onError` event handler calls the function `badImage` if errors occur when the image loads:

```
<SCRIPT LANGUAGE="JavaScript">
<!--
function badImage(theImage)
{
  alert('Error: ' + theImage.name + ' did not load properly.')
}
// -->
</SCRIPT>
<IMG NAME="imageBad2" SRC="orca.gif" ALIGN="left" BORDER=2
onError="badImage(this)">
```

onLoad

The `onLoad` event handler is triggered when an image is displayed. Do not confuse displaying an image with loading one. You can load several images and then, by setting the instance's `src` property, you can display them one by one in the same `image` object instance. If you change a displayed image this way, the onLoad event handler executes every time an image is displayed, not just when the image is loaded into memory.

If you specify an onLoad event handler for an image object that displays a looping GIF animation (multi-image GIF), each loop of the animation triggers the onLoad event, and the event handler executes once for each loop.

By repeatedly setting the src property of an image's JavaScript reflection, you can use the onLoad event handler to create a JavaScript animation.

Demonstration 1: Updating Digital Clock

The following JavaScript script displays a digital clock on your page that is updated every minute. The clock includes two digits for the hour, delimiting colon, two digits for the minute, and am/pm subscript:

```
<HTML>
<HEAD>
<TITLE>
JavaScript clock
</TITLE>
</HEAD>
<BODY>
<!-- JavaScript immediate script -->
<SCRIPT LANGUAGE="JavaScript">
<!--
// create array of all digit images
var digit = new Array()
digit[0] = new Image(16, 21)
digit[1] = new Image(16, 21)
digit[2] = new Image(16, 21)
digit[3] = new Image(16, 21)
digit[4] = new Image(16, 21)
digit[5] = new Image(16, 21)
digit[6] = new Image(16, 21)
digit[7] = new Image(16, 21)
digit[8] = new Image(16, 21)
digit[9] = new Image(16, 21)
digit[10] = new Image(16, 21) // am
digit[11] = new Image(16, 21) // pm
digit[12] = new Image(9, 21)  // colon
digit[13] = new Image(9, 21)  // blank
// assign sources to digit image objects (0 - 9)
for (var i = 0; i < 10; ++i)
{
   digit[i].src = getPath(location.href) + "dg" + i + ".gif"
}
// assign sources to other image objects
digit[10].src = getPath(location.href) + "dgam.gif"
digit[11].src = getPath(location.href) + "dgpm.gif"
digit[12].src = getPath(location.href) + "dgc.gif"
digit[13].src = getPath(location.href) + "dgb.gif"
// set initial time values to impossible ones
```

```
var hour1 = getHour(0)
var hour2 = getHour(1)
var minute1 = getMinute(0)
var minute2 = getMinute(1)
var ampm = getAmpm()
var colon = false
// get array substring of first clock image in document.images array
var start = document.images.length // number of images in document
// print initial clock
var openImage = "<IMG SRC=\"" + getPath(location.href) + "dg"
var closeImage = ".gif\" HEIGHT=21 WIDTH=16>"
document.write(openImage + hour1 + closeImage)
document.write(openImage + hour2 + closeImage)
document.write(openImage + "c.gif\" HEIGHT=21 WIDTH=9>")
document.write(openImage + minute1 + closeImage)
document.write(openImage + minute2 + closeImage)
document.write(openImage + ((ampm == 10) ? "am" : "pm") + closeImage)
var timerID = null
var timerRunning = false
update()
function setClock()
{
   if (getHour(0) != hour1)
   {
      // not getHours()!
      hour1 = getHour(0)
      document.images[start].src = digit[hour1].src
   }
   if (getHour(1) != hour2)
   {
      // not getHours()!
      hour2 = getHour(1)
      document.images[start + 1].src = digit[hour2].src
   }
   colon = !colon
   if (!colon)
      document.images[start + 2].src = digit[13].src
   else
      document.images[start + 2].src = digit[12].src
   if (getMinute(0) != minute1)
   {
      // not getMinutes()!
      minute1 = getMinute(0)
      document.images[start + 3].src = digit[minute1].src
   }
   if (getMinute(1) != minute2)
   {
      // not getMinutes()!
      minute2 = getMinute(1)
      document.images[start + 4].src = digit[minute2].src
   }
   if (getAmpm() != ampm)
   {
```

```
      ampm = getAmpm()
      document.images[start + 5].src = digit[ampm].src
   }
   timerID = setTimeout("setClock()",1000)
   timerRunning = true
}
function update()
{
   stopClock()
   setClock()
}
function stopClock()
{
   if (timerRunning)
      clearTimeout(timerID)
   timerRunning = false
}
function getHour(place)
{
   var now = new Date()
   var hour = now.getHours()
   if (hour >= 12)
      hour -= 12
   hour = (hour == 0) ? 12 : hour
   if (hour < 10)
      hour = "0" + hour        // do not parse number!
   hour += ""
   return parseInt(hour.charAt(place))
}
function getMinute(place)
{
   var now = new Date()
   var minute = now.getMinutes()
   if (minute < 10)
      minute = "0" + minute   // do not parse number!
   minute += ""
   return parseInt(minute.charAt(place))
}
function getAmpm()
{
   var now = new Date()
   var hour = now.getHours()
   if (hour >= 12)
      return 11   // pm
   /* else */
      return 10   // am
}
function getPath(url)
{
   lastSlash = url.lastIndexOf("/")
   return url.substring(0, lastSlash + 1)
}
// -->
```

```
</SCRIPT>
</BODY>
</HTML>
```

Example 21-6 (ex21-6.htm). *An updating clock*

Global Statements

The script starts by creating the `digits` array, holding 14 instances of the `image` object, for the digits 0 through 9, am, pm, colon, and blank symbols. All images are 21 pixels high and 16 pixels wide, except for the colon and the blank images, which are thinner (9 pixels):

```
// create array of all digit images
var digit = new Array()
digit[0] = new Image(16, 21)
digit[1] = new Image(16, 21)
digit[2] = new Image(16, 21)
digit[3] = new Image(16, 21)
digit[4] = new Image(16, 21)
digit[5] = new Image(16, 21)
digit[6] = new Image(16, 21)
digit[7] = new Image(16, 21)
digit[8] = new Image(16, 21)
digit[9] = new Image(16, 21)
digit[10] = new Image(16, 21) // am
digit[11] = new Image(16, 21) // pm
digit[12] = new Image(9, 21)  // colon
digit[13] = new Image(9, 21)  // blank
```

Since the artistic representation of each symbol is given in a GIF format, we assign a GIF filename to the `src` property of each element of the `digit` array. The GIF files are located in the same directory as the URL, and the naming algorithm is based on concatenating the `dg` substring to the characters represented by the image (0 to 9, am, pm). The colon symbol is denoted by a "c" character, and the blank by a "b."

```
// assign sources to digit image objects (0 - 9)
for (var i = 0; i < 10; ++i)
{
   digit[i].src = getPath(location.href) + "dg" + i + ".gif"
}
// assign sources to other image objects
digit[10].src = getPath(location.href) + "dgam.gif"
digit[11].src = getPath(location.href) + "dgpm.gif"
digit[12].src = getPath(location.href) + "dgc.gif"
digit[13].src = getPath(location.href) + "dgb.gif"
```

Then, we find the current time and store it in six variables, four digits for the hour and minute, one for the `ampm` value, and one Boolean variable for the blinking colon. After initializing the time variables, the script turns off the colon, ready to be turned on next time:

```
// set initial time values to current time
var hour1 = getHour(0)
var hour2 = getHour(1)
var minute1 = getMinute(0)
var minute2 = getMinute(1)
var ampm = getAmpm()
var colon = false
```

We need to probe and remember the number of images already displayed in the document:

```
// get array substring of first clock image in document.images array
var start = document.images.length // number of images in document
```

When the page is loaded, the script displays the clock. Since JavaScript does not support image creation, all images are constructed via HTML:

```
// print initial clock
var openImage = "<IMG SRC=\"" + getPath(location.href) + "dg"
var closeImage = ".gif\" HEIGHT=21 WIDTH=16>"
document.write(openImage + hour1 + closeImage)
document.write(openImage + hour2 + closeImage)
document.write(openImage + "c.gif\" HEIGHT=21 WIDTH=9>")
document.write(openImage + minute1 + closeImage)
document.write(openImage + minute2 + closeImage)
document.write(openImage + ((ampm == 10) ? "am" : "pm") + closeImage)
```

The `timerID` variable, which holds the elapsed time before the next clock updating, is initialized to null before the clock starts running. For the same reason, the `timerRunning` variable is set to false. The `update()` function starts the infinite loop of running the clock:

```
var timerID = null
var timerRunning = false
update()
```

setClock()

```
function setClock()
{
   if (getHour(0) != hour1)
   {
      // not getHours()!
      hour1 = getHour(0)
      document.images[start].src = digit[hour1].src
   }
   if (getHour(1) != hour2)
   {
      // not getHours()!
      hour2 = getHour(1)
      document.images[start + 1].src = digit[hour2].src
   }
   colon = !colon
   if (!colon)
      document.images[start + 2].src = digit[13].src
```

```
    else
       document.images[start + 2].src = digit[12].src
    if (getMinute(0) != minute1)
    {
       // not getMinutes()!
       minute1 = getMinute(0)
       document.images[start + 3].src = digit[minute1].src
    }
    if (getMinute(1) != minute2)
    {
       // not getMinutes()!
       minute2 = getMinute(1)
       document.images[start + 4].src = digit[minute2].src
    }
    if (getAmpm() != ampm)
    {
       ampm = getAmpm()
       document.images[start + 5].src = digit[ampm].src
    }
    timerID = setTimeout("setClock()",1000)
    timerRunning = true
}
```

This function retrieves the current value of each digit (and symbol) in the clock and updates only the necessary images, i.e., only those digits that have been changed since the previous iteration. The blinking colon effect is accomplished by simply reversing the value of `colon`. Notice that the index of the `images` array is an offset from the last image of the document, not counting the clock's images. The variable `timerID` is now modified to recursively execute the function `setClock()` after 1000 milliseconds.

update()

```
function update()
{
   stopClock()
   setClock()
}
```

The function `update()` stops the clock and then restarts it.

stopClock()

```
function stopClock()
{
   if (timerRunning)
      clearTimeout(timerID)
   timerRunning = false
}
```

This function clears the timeout and sets the `timerRunning` variable to false, indicating that the timer is not running because no timeout is set.

getHour(place)

```
function getHour(place)
{
   var now = new Date()
   var hour = now.getHours()
   if (hour >= 12)
      hour -= 12
   hour = (hour == 0) ? 12 : hour
   if (hour < 10)
      hour = "0" + hour // do not parse number!
   hour += ""
   return parseInt(hour.charAt(place))
}
```

The `getHour()` function has been mentioned a lot before. It finds the digit in `place` position of a two-digit hour representation. Notice the computation to convert a 24-hour military time notation to 12-hour notation. Pay attention, also, to the concatenation of a null string to force the conversion to a string, which is needed for the `charAt()` method. The returned value is converted back to integer format.

getMinute(place)

```
function getMinute(place)
{
   var now = new Date()
   var minute = now.getMinutes()
   if (minute < 10)
      minute = "0" + minute // do not parse number!
   minute += ""
   return parseInt(minute.charAt(place))
}
```

This function is similar to the `getHour()` function. See the listings for that function.

getAmpm()

```
function getAmpm()
{
   var now = new Date()
   var hour = now.getHours()
   if (hour >= 12)
      return 11 // pm
   /* else */
      return 10 // am
}
```

The `getAmpm()` function returns 11 if the current time is P.M., and 10 if it is A.M. Notice that, since a `return` statement immediately terminates a function, the `else` keyword is not needed here and is commented out.

getPath(url)

```
function getPath(url)
{
   lastSlash = url.lastIndexOf("/")
   return url.substring(0, lastSlash + 1)
}
```

The script's last function, `getPath()`, extracts the full URL of the document's directory (or folder). It simply finds the last slash in the URL and returns the substring, starting at the beginning of the URL and ending at its last slash.

Demonstration 2: LED Sign

You have probably seen LED signs in airports and ticker-type bulletin boards. This LED sign displays a given number of messages, one after the other, and returns to the first one when the list is exhausted. Each character is built of on and off dots, where each dot (or light) is a small 5 x 5 GIF image.

```
<HTML>
<HEAD>
<TITLE>LED sign</TITLE>
</HEAD>
<BODY>
<SCRIPT LANGUAGE="JavaScript">
<!--
// set messages (specify backslash in double form (i.e., \\)
var messages = new Array()
messages[0] = "welcome to my page"
messages[1] = "free scripts are available"
messages[2] = "new scripts by request"
messages[3] = "this site is updated..."
messages[4] = "almost every day"
messages[5] = "I love javascript..."
messages[6] = "And I love..."
messages[7] = "wordware publishing!!!"
messages[8] = "contact me for more info"
// number of milliseconds to pause between two messages
var pause = 3000
// set normal spacing between two characters (no whitespace in between)
var space = 1
// set height and width of each character
var height = 5
var width = 3
// create object of all supported characters in font
var letters = new letterArray()
// initialize image variables
var on = new Image(5, 5)
var off = new Image(5, 5)
// set image URLs
```

```
on.src = "on.gif"
off.src = "off.gif"
// get number of images already laid out in page
var imageNum = document.images.length
// compute width of board
// var boardWidth = longest * (width + space) - space
// set maximum message length in images
var boardWidth = 0
for (var i = 0; i < messages.length; ++i)
{
   var lengthWithNoSpaces = messages[i].split(" ").join("").length
   var numberOfSpaces = messages[i].length - lengthWithNoSpaces
   var currentBoardWidth = lengthWithNoSpaces * (width + space) -
               space + numberOfSpaces * space * 2
   if (boardWidth < currentBoardWidth)
      boardWidth = currentBoardWidth
}
// sign is currently not running
var running = false
var timerID = null
function letterArray()
{
   this.a = new Array(height)
   this.a[0] = " * "
   this.a[1] = "* *"
   this.a[2] = "***"
   this.a[3] = "* *"
   this.a[4] = "* *"
   this.b = new Array(height)
   this.b[0] = "** "
   this.b[1] = "* *"
   this.b[2] = "** "
   this.b[3] = "* *"
   this.b[4] = "** "
   this.c = new Array(height)
   this.c[0] = "***"
   this.c[1] = "*  "
   this.c[2] = "*  "
   this.c[3] = "*  "
   this.c[4] = "***"
   this.d = new Array(height)
   this.d[0] = "** "
   this.d[1] = "* *"
   this.d[2] = "* *"
   this.d[3] = "* *"
   this.d[4] = "** "
   this.e = new Array(height)
   this.e[0] = "*** "
   this.e[1] = "*  "
   this.e[2] = "***"
   this.e[3] = "*  "
   this.e[4] = "***"
   this.f = new Array(height)
   this.f[0] = "***"
```

```
this.f[1] = "*  "
this.f[2] = "***"
this.f[3] = "*  "
this.f[4] = "*  "
this.g = new Array(height)
this.g[0] = "***"
this.g[1] = "*  "
this.g[2] = "***"
this.g[3] = "* *"
this.g[4] = "***"
this.h = new Array(height)
this.h[0] = "* *"
this.h[1] = "* *"
this.h[2] = "***"
this.h[3] = "* *"
this.h[4] = "* *"
this.i = new Array(height)
this.i[0] = "***"
this.i[1] = " * "
this.i[2] = " * "
this.i[3] = " * "
this.i[4] = "***"
this.j = new Array(height)
this.j[0] = "  *"
this.j[1] = "  *"
this.j[2] = "  *"
this.j[3] = "* *"
this.j[4] = "***"
this.k = new Array(height)
this.k[0] = "* *"
this.k[1] = "* *"
this.k[2] = "** "
this.k[3] = "* *"
this.k[4] = "* *"
this.l = new Array(height)
this.l[0] = "*  "
this.l[1] = "*  "
this.l[2] = "*  "
this.l[3] = "*  "
this.l[4] = "***"
this.m = new Array(height)
this.m[0] = "* *"
this.m[1] = "***"
this.m[2] = "***"
this.m[3] = "* *"
this.m[4] = "* *"
this.n = new Array(height)
this.n[0] = "* *"
this.n[1] = "***"
this.n[2] = "***"
this.n[3] = "***"
this.n[4] = "* *"
this.o = new Array(height)
this.o[0] = "***"
```

```
this.o[1] = "* *"
this.o[2] = "* *"
this.o[3] = "* *"
this.o[4] = "***"
this.p = new Array(height)
this.p[0] = "** "
this.p[1] = "* *"
this.p[2] = "** "
this.p[3] = "*  "
this.p[4] = "*  "
this.q = new Array(height)
this.q[0] = "***"
this.q[1] = "* *"
this.q[2] = "* *"
this.q[3] = "***"
this.q[4] = "***"
this.r = new Array(height)
this.r[0] = "** "
this.r[1] = "* *"
this.r[2] = "** "
this.r[3] = "* *"
this.r[4] = "* *"
this.s = new Array(height)
this.s[0] = "***"
this.s[1] = "*  "
this.s[2] = "***"
this.s[3] = "  *"
this.s[4] = "***"
this.t = new Array(height)
this.t[0] = "***"
this.t[1] = " * "
this.t[2] = " * "
this.t[3] = " * "
this.t[4] = " * "
this.u = new Array(height)
this.u[0] = "* *"
this.u[1] = "* *"
this.u[2] = "* *"
this.u[3] = "* *"
this.u[4] = "***"
this.v = new Array(height)
this.v[0] = "* *"
this.v[1] = "* *"
this.v[2] = "* *"
this.v[3] = "* *"
this.v[4] = " * "
this.w = new Array(height)
this.w[0] = "* *"
this.w[1] = "* *"
this.w[2] = "***"
this.w[3] = "***"
this.w[4] = "***"
this.x = new Array(height)
this.x[0] = "* *"
```

```
this.x[1] = "* *"
this.x[2] = " * "
this.x[3] = "* *"
this.x[4] = "* *"
this.y = new Array(height)
this.y[0] = "* *"
this.y[1] = "* *"
this.y[2] = "***"
this.y[3] = " * "
this.y[4] = " * "
this.z = new Array(height)
this.z[0] = "***"
this.z[1] = "  *"
this.z[2] = " * "
this.z[3] = "*  "
this.z[4] = "***"
this['!'] = new Array(height)
this['!'][0] = " * "
this['!'][1] = " * "
this['!'][2] = " * "
this['!'][3] = "   "
this['!'][4] = " * "
this[':'] = new Array(height)
this[':'][0] = "   "
this[':'][1] = " * "
this[':'][2] = "   "
this[':'][3] = " * "
this[':'][4] = "   "
this['.'] = new Array(height)
this['.'][0] = "   "
this['.'][1] = "   "
this['.'][2] = "   "
this['.'][3] = "   "
this['.'][4] = " * "
this['='] = new Array(height)
this['='][0] = "   "
this['='][1] = "***"
this['='][2] = "   "
this['='][3] = "***"
this['='][4] = "   "
this['='] = new Array(height)
this['='][0] = "   "
this['='][1] = "***"
this['='][2] = "   "
this['='][3] = "***"
this['='][4] = "   "
this['+'] = new Array(height)
this['+'][0] = "   "
this['+'][1] = " * "
this['+'][2] = "***"
this['+'][3] = " * "
this['+'][4] = "   "
this['-'] = new Array(height)
this['-'][0] = "   "
```

```
this['-'][1] = "   "
this['-'][2] = "***"
this['-'][3] = "   "
this['-'][4] = "   "
this['/'] = new Array(height)
this['/'][0] = "  *"
this['/'][1] = "  *"
this['/'][2] = " * "
this['/'][3] = "*  "
this['/'][4] = "*  "
this['\\'] = new Array(height)
this['\\'][0] = "*  "
this['\\'][1] = "*  "
this['\\'][2] = " * "
this['\\'][3] = "  *"
this['\\'][4] = "  *"
this['\\'] = new Array(height)
this['\\'][0] = "*  "
this['\\'][1] = "*  "
this['\\'][2] = " * "
this['\\'][3] = "  *"
this['\\'][4] = "  *"
this['"'] = new Array(height)
this['"'][0] = "* *"
this['"'][1] = "* *"
this['"'][2] = "* *"
this['"'][3] = "   "
this['"'][4] = "   "
this["'"] = new Array(height)
this["'"][0] = " * "
this["'"][1] = " * "
this["'"][2] = " * "
this["'"][3] = "   "
this["'"][4] = "   "
this['('] = new Array(height)
this['('][0] = "  *"
this['('][1] = " * "
this['('][2] = " * "
this['('][3] = " * "
this['('][4] = "  *"
this[')'] = new Array(height)
this[')'][0] = "*  "
this[')'][1] = " * "
this[')'][2] = " * "
this[')'][3] = " * "
this[')'][4] = "*  "
this['*'] = new Array(height)
this['*'][0] = "   "
this['*'][1] = "***"
this['*'][2] = "***"
this['*'][3] = "***"
this['*'][4] = "   "
this['?'] = new Array(height)
this['?'][0] = "** "
```

```
this['?'][1] = "  *"
this['?'][2] = " * "
this['?'][3] = "   "
this['?'][4] = " * "
this['0'] = new Array(height)
this['0'][0] = " * "
this['0'][1] = "* *"
this['0'][2] = "* *"
this['0'][3] = "* *"
this['0'][4] = " * "
this['1'] = new Array(height)
this['1'][0] = " * "
this['1'][1] = " * "
this['1'][2] = " * "
this['1'][3] = " * "
this['1'][4] = " * "
this['2'] = new Array(height)
this['2'][0] = "***"
this['2'][1] = "  *"
this['2'][2] = "***"
this['2'][3] = "*  "
this['2'][4] = "***"
this['3'] = new Array(height)
this['3'][0] = "***"
this['3'][1] = "  *"
this['3'][2] = "***"
this['3'][3] = "  *"
this['3'][4] = "***"
this['4'] = new Array(height)
this['4'][0] = "* *"
this['4'][1] = "* *"
this['4'][2] = "***"
this['4'][3] = "  *"
this['4'][4] = "  *"
this['5'] = new Array(height)
this['5'][0] = "***"
this['5'][1] = "*  "
this['5'][2] = "***"
this['5'][3] = "  *"
this['5'][4] = "** "
this['6'] = new Array(height)
this['6'][0] = "** "
this['6'][1] = "*  "
this['6'][2] = "***"
this['6'][3] = "* *"
this['6'][4] = "***"
this['7'] = new Array(height)
this['7'][0] = "***"
this['7'][1] = "  *"
this['7'][2] = " * "
this['7'][3] = "*  "
this['7'][4] = "*  "
this['8'] = new Array(height)
this['8'][0] = "***"
```

```
   this['8'][1] = "* *"
   this['8'][2] = "***"
   this['8'][3] = "* *"
   this['8'][4] = "***"
   this['9'] = new Array(height)
   this['9'][0] = "***"
   this['9'][1] = "* *"
   this['9'][2] = "***"
   this['9'][3] = "  *"
   this['9'][4] = "***"
}
function drawBlank()
{
   // assign greater than symbol to variable
   var gt = unescape("%3e")
   document.write('<TABLE BORDER=2 CELLPADDING=8' + gt + '<TR' + gt +
      '<TD BGCOLOR ALIGN="center" VALIGN="center"' + gt)
   // print entire board of off images
   for (var y = 0; y < height; ++y)
   {
      for (var x = 0; x < boardWidth; ++x)
      {
         document.write('<IMG SRC="' + off.src + '" HEIGHT=5
                          WIDTH=5' + gt)
      }
      document.write('<BR' + gt)
   }
   document.write('</TD>' + gt + '</TR>' + gt + '</TABLE>' + gt)
}
function setLight(state, x, y)
{
   // set a specific light in sign to on (true) or off (false)
   if (state)
      document.images[computeIndex(x, y)].src = on.src
   else
      document.images[computeIndex(x, y)].src = off.src
}
function drawLetter(letter, startX)
{
   // draws a letter at the given x coordinate
   for (var x = 0; x < width; ++x)
   {
      for (var y = 0; y < height; ++y)
      {
         setLight(letters[letter][y].charAt(x) == "*", startX + x, y)
      }
   }
}
function drawSpace(startX)
{  // create a small space between each two characters
   for (var x = 0; x < space; ++x)
   {
      for (var y = 0; y < height; ++y)
      {
```

```
         setLight(false, startX + x, y)
      }
   }
}
function computeIndex(x, y)
{
   // compute the document index of an image in the sign, based on the x-y
coordinates
   return (y * boardWidth + x) + imageNum
}
function floodBoard(startX)
{
   // set all lights from startX to off
   for (var x = startX; x < boardWidth; ++x)
   {
      for (var y = 0; y < height; ++y)
      {
         setLight(false, x, y)
      }
   }
}
function drawMessage(num)
{
   // initialize variable to current message
   var text = messages[num]
   // initialize two counters (j - current character in message, i -
current x coordinate)
   var i = 0
   var j = 0
   while (1)
   {
      if (text.charAt(j) != " ")
      {
         // draw current letter
         drawLetter(text.charAt(j), i)
         // increment i by the constant width of an image
         i += width
      } else
      {
         // add an extra space (do not advance j yet)
         drawSpace(i)
         i += space
      }
      // if j is less than index of last character
      if (j < text.length - 1)
      {
         drawSpace(i)
         i += space
      } else // j is the index of the last character (last character already
                  printed)
         break
      // increment j by one because one letter was printed
      ++j
   }
```

```
   // flood the remaining piece of the sign (turn it off)
   floodBoard(i)
   // if message printed this time was not the last one in the array
   if (num < messages.length - 1)
      // val *must* be a global variable for use with the timeout
      val = ++num
   else
      val = 0 // start cycle over again
   // recursive call after waiting 3 seconds (some of the time already
            passed during printing)
   timerID = setTimeout("drawMessage(val)", pause)
}
function startSign()
{
   running = true
   // wait 3 seconds and then call function to print first message
   drawMessage(0)
}
function stopSign()
{
   if(running)
      clearTimeout(timerID)
   running = false
}
// open form
document.write('<FORM>')
// create initial sign (all signs are off)
drawBlank()
document.write('<INPUT TYPE="button" VALUE="start" onClick="startSign()">')
document.write('<INPUT TYPE="button" VALUE="stop" onClick="stopSign();
              floodBoard(0)">')
document.write('</FORM>')
// -->
</SCRIPT>
</BODY>
</HTML>
```

Example 21-7 (ex21-7.htm). *A JavaScript-only LED sign*

Global Statements

The script starts by filling the `messages` array with nine messages:

```
// set messages (specify backslash in double form (i.e., \\)
var messages = new Array()
messages[0] = "welcome to my page"
messages[1] = "free scripts are available"
messages[2] = "new scripts by request"
messages[3] = "this site is updated..."
messages[4] = "almost every day"
messages[5] = "I love javascript..."
messages[6] = "And I love..."
messages[7] = "wordware publishing!!!"
messages[8] = "contact me for more info"
```

Note that all messages must be written in lowercase.

The definition of the following variables are documented inline:

```
// number of milliseconds to pause between two messages
var pause = 3000
// set normal spacing between two characters (no whitespace in between)
var space = 1
// set height and width of each character
var height = 5
var width = 3
// create object of all supported characters in font
var letters = new letterArray()
// initialize image variables
var on = new Image(5, 5)
var off = new Image(5, 5)
```

The on and off images represent the on and off lights. The artistic presentations of these dots are stored in on.gif and off.gif:

```
on.src = "on.gif"
off.src = "off.gif
```

As in Demonstration 1, we load all images to the browser before we start to display the LED sign:

```
// get number of images already laid out in page
var imageNum = document.images.length
```

The next section computes the length of the longest message by multiplying the number of nonblank characters with the combined width of a normal character and an intercharacter space, and then adding the width of blanks. The number of nonblank characters is computed by first splitting the message on blanks, then joining the pieces, and finally extracting the concatenated length:

```
// set maximum message length in images
var boardWidth = 0
for (var i = 0; i < messages.length; ++i)
{
   var lengthWithNoSpaces = messages[i].split(" ").join("").length
   var numberOfSpaces = messages[i].length - lengthWithNoSpaces
   var currentBoardWidth = lengthWithNoSpaces * (width + space) -
                           space + numberOfSpaces * space * 2
   if (boardWidth < currentBoardWidth)
      boardWidth = currentBoardWidth
}
```

After setting the `running` variable to false and `timerID` to null (see Demonstration 1), we define the dots of each character of the alphabet by the function `letterArray()`.

letterArray()

`letterArray()` is a constructor function. The general syntax to create an instance of this object is as follows:

```
var instanceName = new letterArray()
```

This object has many properties but no methods. Each property represents a single character supported by the script. For example, the "A" character is defined as follows:

```
   this.a = new Array(height)
   this.a[0] = " * "
   this.a[1] = "* *"
   this.a[2] = "***"
   this.a[3] = "* *"
   this.a[4] = "* *"
```

Notice that each property is defined as an array of five three-character strings. You will see how to use an instance of this object later in the chapter.

drawBlank()

```
function drawBlank()
{
   // assign greater than symbol to variable
   var gt = unescape("%3e")
   document.write('<TABLE BORDER=2 CELLPADDING=8' + gt + '<TR' + gt +
                  '<TD BGCOLOR ALIGN="center" VALIGN="center"' + gt)
   // print entire board of off images
   for (var y = 0; y < height; ++y)
   {
      for (var x = 0; x < boardWidth; ++x)
      {
         document.write('<IMG SRC="' + off.src + '" HEIGHT=5 WIDTH=5' + gt)
      }
      document.write('<BR' + gt)
   }
   document.write('</TD>' + gt + '</TR>' + gt + '</TABLE>' + gt)
}
```

The next function, `drawBlank()`, draws the border around the LED sign and then covers the entire board with off dots (GIF images). Notice that the board's width and height are stored in global variables and thus are not passed as arguments to the `drawBlank()` function. Also, notice how `unescape()` is used to avoid the ">" literal.

setLight(state, x, y)

```
function setLight(state, x, y)
{
   // set a specific light in sign to on (true) or off (false)
   if (state)
```

```
      document.images[computeIndex(x, y)].src = on.src
   else
      document.images[computeIndex(x, y)].src = off.src
}
```

The `setLight()` function accepts three arguments. The first one is either a Boolean value or a binary digit (0 or 1). The second parameter accepts the x coordinate of the light, and the third specifies its y coordinate. For example, the following statement replaces the second image from the left and third from the top of the LED sign with an on image, regardless of which image is currently displayed there:

```
setLight(true, 1, 2)
```

It is correct to define this function as one that turns on or off a specific light in the LED sign.

drawLetter(letter, startX)

```
function drawLetter(letter, startX)
{
   // draws a letter at the given x coordinate
   for (var x = 0; x < width; ++x)
   {
      for (var y = 0; y < height; ++y)
      {
         setLight(letters[letter][y].charAt(x) == "*", startX + x, y)
      }
   }
}
```

This function accepts two arguments:

- The letter that it is supposed to draw
- The x coordinate of the letter in the entire LED sign

This function reads the letter's coordinates by scanning the appropriate properties of the `letters` object.

The LED sign is updated by adding characters consecutively, creating the effect of a top-to-bottom, left-to-right motion.

drawSpace(startX)

```
function drawSpace(startX)
{
   // create a small space between each two characters
   for (var x = 0; x < space; ++x)
   {
      for (var y = 0; y < height; ++y)
      {
         setLight(false, startX + x, y)
      }
   }
}
```

This function is very similar to the `drawLetter()` function. It simply creates space columns of off images, mimicking the space characters of the message.

computeIndex()

```
function computeIndex(x, y)
{
   // compute the document index of an image in the sign, based on the
   // x-y coordinates
   return (y * boardWidth + x) + imageNum
}
```

The `computeIndex()` function accepts x and y coordinates of a dot and returns the corresponding index of the image in the `document.images` 1D array.

floodBoard(startX)

```
function floodBoard(startX)
{
   // set all lights from startX to off
   for (var x = startX; x < boardWidth; ++x)
   {
      for (var y = 0; y < height; ++y)
      {
         setLight(false, x, y)
      }
   }
}
```

The function `floodBoard()` sets all dots (images) to the right of a given coordinate, one column at a time, from top to bottom and from left to right.

drawMessage(num)

```
function drawMessage(num)
{
   // initialize variable to current message
   var text = messages[num]
   // initialize two counters (j - current character in message,
            i - current x coordinate)
   var i = 0
   var j = 0
   while (1)
   {
      if (text.charAt(j) != " ")
      {
         // draw current letter
         drawLetter(text.charAt(j), i)
         // increment i by the constant width of an image
         i += width
      } else
```

```
      {
         // add an extra space (do not advance j yet)
         drawSpace(i)
         i += space
      }
      // if j is less than index of last character
      if (j < text.length - 1)
      {
         drawSpace(i)
         i += space
      } else // j is the index of the last character (last character already
                   printed)
         break
      // increment j by one because one letter was printed
      ++j
   }
   // flood the remaining piece of the sign (turn it off)
   floodBoard(i)
   // if message printed this time was not the last one in the array
   if (num < messages.length - 1)
      // val *must* be a global variable for use with the timeout
      val = ++num
   else
      val = 0 // start cycle over again
   // recursive call after waiting 3 seconds (some of the time already
             passed during printing)
   timerID = setTimeout("drawMessage(val)", pause)
}
```

The next function, `drawMessage()`, is probably the most important but is still straightforward. After initializing some variables, the `while` statement loops over the message characters and displays them with the `drawLetter()` or the `drawSpace()` functions. After the message is exhausted, the rest of the board is flooded with off dots. The function ends, after determining the index of the next message to be displayed (either next or first one), by recursively calling itself after a pause of `pause` milliseconds.

startSign()

```
function startSign()
{
   running = true
   // wait 3 seconds and then call function to print first message
   drawMessage(0)
}
```

This function simply sets the value of the global variable `running` to true, indicating that the ticker has started, and then invokes the `drawMessage()` function to actually start displaying the first message (0).

stopSign()

```
function stopSign()
{
   if(running)
      clearTimeout(timerID)
   running = false
}
```

This function stops the LED ticker by clearing the last timeout via the `clearTimeout()` method. Reflecting the status of the banner, the value of `running` is set to false. Note that the `stopSign()` function does not clear the current LED sign display.

More Global Statements

```
// open form
document.write('<FORM>')
// create initial sign (all signs are off)
drawBlank()
document.write('<INPUT TYPE="button" VALUE="start" onClick="startSign()">')
document.write('<INPUT TYPE="button" VALUE="stop" onClick="stopSign();
              floodBoard(0)">')
document.write('</FORM>')
```

The second segment of global statements at the end of the script creates the form where the Start and Stop buttons reside (they are form elements). We then define the buttons and their `onClick` event handler script. Notice that the Stop button event handler includes two function calls, one to stop the LED sign and the other to clear (flood) it. It is important to open the form before the `drawBlank()` function creates the LED sign, because the `<FORM>` tag starts a new line with some vertical space from the HTML elements above it. In order to assure that the buttons touch the border of the LED sign, we include the LED sign in the form itself.

To get rid of the buttons and make the LED sign start on its own, simply delete the lines that open and close the form, as well as the lines that define the buttons:

```
1. document.write('<FORM>')
2. document.write('<INPUT TYPE="button" VALUE="start"
   onClick="startSign()">')
3. document.write('<INPUT TYPE="button" VALUE="stop"
   onClick="stopSign(); floodBoard(0)">')
4. document.write('</FORM>')
```

You should then use an `onLoad` event handler to start the LED sign when the document finishes loading:

```
<BODY onLoad="startSign()">
```

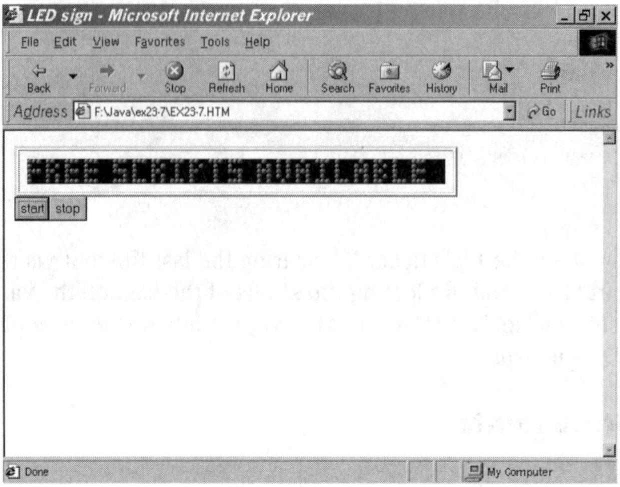

Figure 21-3. *An LED sign*

Demonstration 3: Netris Deluxe

"Netris Deluxe" is the name of our JavaScript-only Tetris game. The Netris Deluxe script is approximately 1,000 lines of code, including comments, and we suggest you read its entire description. Although we have more efficient versions, we decided to include the original version because it demonstrates a larger variety of JavaScript features and concepts. First, take a look at the script and find functions you are familiar with:

```
<HTML>
<HEAD>
<TITLE>Tetris</TITLE>
<SCRIPT LANGUAGE="JavaScript">
<!--
// array to hold number of shapes used from each type
var statistics = new Array(7)
for (var shapeNum = 0; shapeNum < 7; ++shapeNum)
{
   statistics[shapeNum] = 0
}
// set pause to false
var paused = false
// game is currently running
var timerRunning = false
// no shape currently falling
var shape = -1
// timer is not running
var timerID = null
// initialize image variables for seven shapes
var on = new Array()
on[0] = new Image(12, 12)
```

```
on[1] = new Image(12, 12)
on[2] = new Image(12, 12)
on[3] = new Image(12, 12)
on[4] = new Image(12, 12)
on[5] = new Image(12, 12)
on[6] = new Image(12, 12)
// create a transparent block
var off = new Image(12, 12)
// set image URLs
on[0].src = "10.gif"
on[1].src = "11.gif"
on[2].src = "12.gif"
on[3].src = "13.gif"
on[4].src = "14.gif"
on[5].src = "15.gif"
on[6].src = "16.gif"
off.src = "0.gif"
// get number of images already laid out in the page
var firstImage = document.images.length
// create initial screen
drawScreen()
// array of screen (10 x 19)
var ar = new Array()
for (var i = 0; i < 10; ++i)
{
   ar[i] = new Array(19)
   for (var j = 0; j < 19; ++j)
   {
      ar[i][j] = 0
   }
}
// draw initial empty screen
function drawScreen()
{
   with (document)
   {
      // center entire game
      write('<CENTER>')
      // start main table
      write('<TABLE BORDER=1 CELLPADDING=0 CELLSPACING=0><TR><TD>')
      // create board (10 x 19)
      for (var i = 0; i < 19; ++i)
      {
         for (var j = 0; j < 10; ++j)
         {
            write('<IMG SRC=' + off.src + ' HEIGHT=' + off.height +
                        ' WIDTH=' + off.width + '>')
         }
         write('<BR>')
      }
      // close table cell
      write('</TD><TD VALIGN="top" ALIGN="center">')
      // make small header ("Netris Deluxe")
      write('<B><FONT SIZE=+2>N</FONT>ETRIS <FONT SIZE=+2>D</FONT>
```

Chapter 21

```
        ELUXE</B><BR>')
   // create form for lines and level displays
   write('<FORM NAME="lineslevel"><TABLE BORDER=0 CELLPADDING=5
        CELLSPACING=0>')
   // make "LINES" table cell and header
   write('<TR><TD WIDTH=100 ALIGN="center"><FONT SIZE=2>LINES</FONT>
        <BR><INPUT TYPE="text" NAME="lines" VALUE="" SIZE=5></TD>')
   // make "LEVEL" table cell and header
   write('<TD WIDTH=100 ALIGN="center"><FONT SIZE=2>LEVEL</FONT><BR>
      <INPUT TYPE="text" NAME="level" VALUE="" SIZE=5></TD></TR>')
   // create start button link
   write('<TR><TD WIDTH=100 ALIGN="center"><A HREF="javascript:start()"
        onMouseOver="window.status=\'Start game\'; return true">')
   // create start button image
   write('<IMG SRC="start.gif" WIDTH=72 HEIGHT=24 BORDER=0></A></TD>')
   // create pause button link
   write('<TD WIDTH=100 ALIGN="center"><A HREF="javascript:pause()"
        onMouseOver="window.status=\'Pause / unpause game\'; return true">')
   // create pause button image
   write('<IMG SRC="pause.gif" WIDTH=72 HEIGHT=24 BORDER=0></A></TD></TR>')
   // close start + pause table and form
   write('</TABLE></FORM>')
   // create table for shape statistics (two rows, seven columns)
   write('<FORM NAME="stats"><TABLE BORDER=0 CELLPADDING=5
        CELLSPACING=0><TR>')
   // put one block of each type in each cell of upper row
   for (var k = 0; k < 7; ++k)
   {
      write('<TD ALIGN="center"><IMG SRC="' + on[k].src + '" HEIGHT='
           + on[k].height + ' WIDTH=' + on[k].width + '></TD>')
   }
   // start new table row
   write('</TR><TR>')
   // create 7 text fields named "0", "1", "2", ..., "6"
   for (var l = 0; l < 7; ++l)
   {
      write('<TD ALIGN="center"><INPUT TYPE="text" SIZE=2 VALUE="0" NAME="'
           + l + '"></TD>')
   }
   // close statistics table and form
   write('</TR></TABLE></FORM>')
   // close table cell for header, start + pause buttons, and statistics,
              and start new row in main table
   write('</TD></TR><TR><TD>')
   // center control panel (left, right, down, rotate)
   write('<CENTER>')
   // organize control panel in a table
   write('<TABLE BORDER=0>')
   // create left table cell and button
   write('<TR><TD><A HREF="javascript:moveX(-1)" onMouseOver="window
        .status=\'Move left\'; return true" onMouseOut="window.
        status=\'\'; return true"><IMG SRC="left.gif" WIDTH=24
        HEIGHT=24 BORDER=0></A></TD>')
   // create rotate table cell and button
```

```
    write('<TD><A HREF="javascript:rotate()" onMouseOver="window
          .status=\'Rotate\'; return true" onMouseOut="window.
          status=\'\'; return true"><IMG SRC="rotate.gif" WIDTH=24
          HEIGHT=24 BORDER=0></A></TD>')
    // create right table cell and button
    write('<TD><A HREF="javascript:moveX(1)" onMouseOver="window
          .status=\'Move right\'; return true" onMouseOut="window.
          status=\'\'; return true"><IMG SRC="right.gif" WIDTH=24
          HEIGHT=24 BORDER=0></A></TD></TR>')
    // create down table cell and button, preceded and proceeded by a
            black cell (placeholder)
    write('<TR><TD></TD><TD><A HREF="javascript:moveY()" onMouseOver=
          "window.status=\'Move down\'; return true" onMouseOut=
          "window.status=\'\'; return true"><IMG SRC="down.gif"
          WIDTH=24 HEIGHT=24 BORDER=0></A></TD><TD></TD></TR>')
    // close table for control panel
    write('</TABLE>')
    // close center of control panel
    write('</CENTER>')
    // close control panel table cell (main table) and create another
            main table cell with credits
    write('</TD><TD ALIGN="center">JavaScript code: Tomer Shiran<BR>
          <FONT SIZE=2>Graphics: Dr. Clue</FONT><BR><FONT SIZE=2>
          Music: Brian Kobashikawa</FONT></TD></TR></TABLE>')
    // close center of main table
    write('</CENTER>')
  }
}
// return index of image according to given x and y coordinates
function computeIndex(x, y)
{
  return (y * 10 + x) + firstImage
}
// returns state of square (true / false)
function state(x, y)
{
  // assign URL of image at given coordinates to local variable
  var source = document.images[computeIndex(x, y)].src
  // expression evaluates to 0 or 1
  return (source.charAt(source.lastIndexOf('/') + 1) == '0') ? false : true
}
// set square to 1 / 0
function setSquare(x, y, state)
{
  if (state == 0)
    document.images[computeIndex(x, y)].src = off.src
  else
    document.images[computeIndex(x, y)].src = on[shape].src
  // if state is 1 square is active, so 1 is assigned to ar[x][y]
  // otherwise square is not active so 0 is assigned to ar[x][y]
  ar[x][y] = state
}
// clear array so no active squares exist
function clearActive()
```

```
{
   // scan entire array and assign 0 to all elements (no active squares)
   for (var i = 0; i < 10; ++i)
   {
      for (var j = 0; j < 19; ++j)
      {
         ar[i][j] = 0
      }
   }
   // no shape is currently in screen
   shape = -1
}
// check if specified move (left or right) is valid
function checkMoveX(step)
{
   // scan screen (direction does not matter)
   for (var x = 0; x < 10; ++x)
   {
      for (var y = 0; y < 19; ++y)
      {
         // if current square is active
         if (ar[x][y] == 1)
         {
            // check all conditions:
            // not out of range and not colliding with existing not
            // block
            if (x + step < 0 || x + step > 9 || (state(x + step, y) &&
                        ar[x + step][y] == 0))
               // return false if move (new situation) is not legal
               return false
         }
      }
   }
   // return true if no invalid state has been encountered
   return true
}
// check if specified move (down) is valid
function checkMoveY()
{
   // only possible step is one to the bottom
   var step = 1
   // scan screen (direction does not matter)
   for (var x = 0; x < 10; ++x)
   {
      for (var y = 0; y < 19; ++y)
      {
         // if current square is active
         if (ar[x][y] == 1)
         {
         // check all conditions:
         // not out of range and not colliding with existing notactive block
            if (y + step > 18 || (state(x, y + step) && ar[x][y + step] == 0))
               // return false if move (new situation) is not legal
               return false
```

```
            }
         }
      }
      // return true if no invalid state has been encountered
      return true
   }
   // move all active squares step squares on the x axis
   function moveX(step)
   {
      // if specified move is not legal
      if (!checkMoveX(step))
         // terminate function (active blocks are not moved)
         return
      // if left movement then scan screen from left to right
      if (step < 0)
      {
         for (var x = 0; x < 10; ++x)
         {
            for (var y = 0; y < 19; ++y)
            {
               // if current square is active
               if (ar[x][y] == 1)
                  // call function to handle movement
                  smartX(x, y, step)
            }
         }
      } else
      // if right movement then scan screen from right to left
      if (step > 0)
      {
         for (var x = 9; x >= 0; --x)
         {
            for (var y = 0; y < 19; ++y)
            {
               // if current square is active
               if (ar[x][y] == 1)
                  // call function to handle movement
                  smartX(x, y, step)
            }
         }
      }
   }
   // responsible for the blocks' horizontal movement
   function smartX(x, y, step)
   {
      // if moving one step to the left
      if (step < 0)
         // if the destination square needs to be turned on explicitly
         if (ar[x + step][y] == 0)
            // if there is a block to the right of the current block
            if (x != 9 && ar[x - step][y] == 1)
               // set square to the left on without clearing current block
               setSquare(x + step, y, 1)
            else
```

```
                // clear current block and turn square to the left on
                warp(x, y, x + step, y)
        else
            // if there is no block to the right of the current block
            if (x == 9 || ar[x - step][y] == 0)
                // clear current block
                setSquare(x, y, 0)
    // if moving one step to the right
    if (step > 0)
        // if the destination square needs to be turned on explicitly
        if (ar[x + step][y] == 0)
            // if there is a block to the left of the current block
            if (x != 0 && ar[x - step][y] == 1)
                // set square to the right on without clearing current block
                setSquare(x + step, y, 1)
            else
                // clear current block and turn square to the right on
                warp(x, y, x + step, y)
        else
            // if there is no block to the left of the current block
            if (x == 0 || ar[x - step][y] == 0)
                // clear current block
                setSquare(x, y, 0)
}
// move all active squares step squares on the y axis
function moveY()
{
    // if specified move is not legal (shape is laid down on block or bottom
            panel)
    if (!checkMoveY())
    {
        // active squares are not active anymore (should not be moved later)
        clearActive()
        // terminate function (active blocks are not moved)
        return
    }
    // scan screen from bottom to top
    for (var y = 18; y >= 0; --y)
    {
        for (var x = 0; x < 10; ++x)
        {
            // if current square is active
            if (ar[x][y] == 1)
                // call function to handle movement
                smartY(x, y)
        }
    }
}
// responsible for the blocks' vertical (downward) movement
function smartY(x, y)
{
    // if the destination square needs to be turned on explicitly
    if (ar[x][y + 1] == 0)
        // if there is a block above current block
```

```
      if (y != 0 && ar[x][y - 1] == 1)
         // set square below on without clearing current block
         setSquare(x, y + 1, 1)
      else
         // clear current block and turn square below on
         warp(x, y, x, y + 1)
   else
      // if there is no block above the current block
      if (y == 0 || ar[x][y - 1] == 0)
         // clear current block
         setSquare(x, y, 0)
}
// construct object containing shape
function shapeMap()
{
   // set minimum and maximum coordinates to opposite (minimum and maximum
   // found thus far)
   var minX = 9
   var minY = 18
   var maxX = 0
   var maxY = 0
   // scan screen to find actual minimum and maximum coordinates of active
            squares
   for (var y = 0; y < 19; ++y)
   {
      for (var x = 0; x < 10; ++x)
      {
         // if current coordinates reflect active square
         if (ar[x][y] == 1)
         {
            if (x < minX)
               minX = x
            if (x > maxX)
               maxX = x
            if (y < minY)
               minY = y
            if (y > maxY)
               maxY = y
         }
      }
   }
   // create a length property representing the x coordinate span
   this.length = maxX - minX + 1
   // create properties to hold minimum coordinates of both axes
   this.offsetX = minX
   this.offsetY = minY
   // construct minimum array containing all active squares respectively
   for (x = 0; x <= maxX - minX; ++x)
   {
      this[x] = new Array()
      for (y = 0; y <= maxY - minY; ++y)
      {
         this[x][y] = ar[x + minX][y + minY]
      }
```

```
   }
}
// random function to return an integer from 0 to 6
function getRandom()
{
   // use random number method to find integer from 0 to 8
   var randomNum = Math.round(Math.random() * 8)
   // call function again if random number is 0 or 8.
   if (randomNum == 0 || randomNum == 8)
      return getRandom()
   // 1 to 7 => 0 to 6
   randomNum--
   // update selected shape's statistics
   statistics[randomNum]++
   // update statistics display form (update *all* fields so user cannot
   // enter any value in fields)
   for (var shape = 0; shape < 7; ++shape)
   {
      document.stats[shape].value = statistics[shape]
   }
   // return the random number
   return randomNum
}
// inserts a shape when there is no active shape
function insertShape()
{
   // initialize *global* variable
   shape = getRandom()
   // The following segment checks if the selected shape has room to enter.
   // If there is no room, the game is over (function returns false).
   // If there is room, the function inserts the shape by setting its initial
            coordinates.
   if (shape == 0)
   {
      if (state(3, 2) || state(3, 2) || state(3, 2) || state(3, 2))
         return false
      setSquare(3, 2, 1)
      setSquare(4, 2, 1)
      setSquare(5, 2, 1)
      setSquare(6, 2, 1)
   } else
   if (shape == 1)
   {
      if (state(4, 2) || state(5, 2) || state(4, 3) || state(5, 3))
         return false
      setSquare(4, 2, 1)
      setSquare(5, 2, 1)
      setSquare(4, 3, 1)
      setSquare(5, 3, 1)
   } else
   if (shape == 2)
   {
      if (state(3, 2) || state(4, 2) || state(5, 2) || state(3, 3))
         return false
```

```
    setSquare(3, 2, 1)
    setSquare(4, 2, 1)
    setSquare(5, 2, 1)
    setSquare(3, 3, 1)
  } else
  if (shape == 3)
  {
    if (state(3, 2) || state(4, 2) || state(4, 3) || state(5, 3))
      return false
    setSquare(3, 2, 1)
    setSquare(4, 2, 1)
    setSquare(4, 3, 1)
    setSquare(5, 3, 1)
  } else
  if (shape == 4)
  {
    if (state(4, 2) || state(5, 2) || state(3, 3) || state(4, 3))
      return false
    setSquare(4, 2, 1)
    setSquare(5, 2, 1)
    setSquare(3, 3, 1)
    setSquare(4, 3, 1)
  } else
  if (shape == 5)
  {
    if (state(3, 2) || state(4, 2) || state(5, 2) || state(4, 3))
      return false
    setSquare(3, 2, 1)
    setSquare(4, 2, 1)
    setSquare(5, 2, 1)
    setSquare(4, 3, 1)
  } else
  if (shape == 6)
  {
    if (state(3, 2) || state(4, 2) || state(5, 2) || state(5, 3))
      return false
    setSquare(3, 2, 1)
    setSquare(4, 2, 1)
    setSquare(5, 2, 1)
    setSquare(5, 3, 1)
  }
  // return true because shape was able to enter screen
  return true
}
// warp several squares if possible
// initial x1, initial y1, destination x1, destination y1, initial x2, initial
// y2, destination x2, destination y2, etc.
function complexWarp()
{
  // loop through arguments checking that each warp is valid
  for (var i = 0; i < arguments.length; i += 4)
  {
    // if warp is not valid
    if (!checkWarp(arguments[i], arguments[i + 1], arguments[i + 2],
```

```
                    arguments[i + 3]))
            // terminate the function -- no squares warped
            return
    }
    // loop through arguments again -- warp squares
    for (var i = 0; i < arguments.length; i += 4)
    {
        // call function to warp the current square corresponding to argument
        //coordinates
        warp(arguments[i], arguments[i + 1], arguments[i + 2], arguments[i + 3])
    }
}
// check if warp is valid (used by complexWarp function)
function checkWarp(startX, startY, endX, endY)
{
    // if a destination coordinate is invalid or destination square is off
    // state(endX, endY) must be last due to short-circuit evaluation
    if (endX < 0 || endX > 9 || endY < 0 || endY > 18 || state(endX, endY))
        // return false because warp is invalid
        return false
    // return true because warp has not been proved to be invalid (it is valid)
    return true
}
// rotate the current active shape
function rotate()
{
    // create instance of shapeMap object (similar to minimum 2D array
    // reflecting active shape)
    var curMap = new shapeMap()
    // note: all arguments handed to complexWarp are explained in that function
    // if shape is 4 x 1 line
    if (shape == 0)
        // if line is in horizontal state
        if (curMap.length == 4) complexWarp(curMap.offsetX, curMap.offsetY,
            curMap.offsetX + 1, curMap.offsetY + 1, curMap.offsetX + 2,
            curMap.offsetY, curMap.offsetX + 1, curMap.offsetY - 1,
            curMap.offsetX + 3, curMap.offsetY, curMap.offsetX + 1,
            curMap.offsetY - 2)
        // else line is in vertical state
        else
            complexWarp(curMap.offsetX, curMap.offsetY + 3, curMap.offsetX - 1,
                curMap.offsetY + 2, curMap.offsetX, curMap.offsetY + 1,
                curMap.offsetX + 1, curMap.offsetY + 2, curMap.offsetX,
                curMap.offsetY, curMap.offsetX + 2, curMap.offsetY + 2)
    // if shape is square
    if (shape == 1)
        // do not rotate shape because square does not change appearance after
                rotation
        return
    // if shape is L
    if (shape == 2)
        // if shape is L tilted 90 degrees to the right
        if (state(curMap.offsetX, curMap.offsetY) && curMap.length == 3)
            complexWarp(curMap.offsetX, curMap.offsetY + 1, curMap.offsetX + 1,
```

```
         curMap.offsetY + 1, curMap.offsetX + 2, curMap.offsetY,
         curMap.offsetX + 1, curMap.offsetY - 1, curMap.offsetX,
         curMap.offsetY, curMap.offsetX, curMap.offsetY - 1)
   else
      // if shape is L tilted 180 degrees
      if (state(curMap.offsetX + 1, curMap.offsetY) && curMap.length == 2)
         complexWarp(curMap.offsetX + 1, curMap.offsetY + 2, curMap.offsetX,
            curMap.offsetY + 1, curMap.offsetX + 1, curMap.offsetY,
            curMap.offsetX + 2, curMap.offsetY, curMap.offsetX,
            curMap.offsetY, curMap.offsetX + 2, curMap.offsetY + 1)
      else
         // if L is tilted 90 degrees to the left
         if (curMap.length == 3)
            complexWarp(curMap.offsetX, curMap.offsetY + 1,
               curMap.offsetX + 1, curMap.offsetY, curMap.offsetX + 2,
               curMap.offsetY, curMap.offsetX + 2, curMap.offsetY + 2,
               curMap.offsetX + 2, curMap.offsetY + 1,
               curMap.offsetX + 1, curMap.offsetY + 2)
         // else L is not tilted
         else
            complexWarp(curMap.offsetX, curMap.offsetY,
               curMap.offsetX + 1, curMap.offsetY + 1,
               curMap.offsetX, curMap.offsetY + 2,
               curMap.offsetX - 1, curMap.offsetY + 2,
               curMap.offsetX + 1, curMap.offsetY + 2,
               curMap.offsetX - 1, curMap.offsetY + 1)
if (shape == 3)
   if (curMap.length == 3)
      complexWarp(curMap.offsetX + 1, curMap.offsetY + 1,
         curMap.offsetX, curMap.offsetY + 1, curMap.offsetX + 2,
         curMap.offsetY + 1, curMap.offsetX + 1, curMap.offsetY - 1)
   else
      complexWarp(curMap.offsetX, curMap.offsetY + 2,
         curMap.offsetX + 1, curMap.offsetY + 2,
         curMap.offsetX + 1, curMap.offsetY,
         curMap.offsetX + 2, curMap.offsetY + 2)
if (shape == 4)
   if (curMap.length == 3)
      complexWarp(curMap.offsetX, curMap.offsetY + 1,
         curMap.offsetX, curMap.offsetY, curMap.offsetX + 2,
         curMap.offsetY, curMap.offsetX, curMap.offsetY - 1)
   else
      complexWarp(curMap.offsetX, curMap.offsetY, curMap.offsetX + 2,
         curMap.offsetY + 1, curMap.offsetX, curMap.offsetY + 1,
         curMap.offsetX, curMap.offsetY + 2)
if (shape == 5)
   if (curMap.length == 3 && state(curMap.offsetX, curMap.offsetY))
      complexWarp(curMap.offsetX + 2, curMap.offsetY, curMap.offsetX
         + 1, curMap.offsetY - 1)
   else
      if (curMap.length == 2 && state(curMap.offsetX + 1,
         curMap.offsetY))
         complexWarp(curMap.offsetX + 1, curMap.offsetY + 2,
            curMap.offsetX + 2, curMap.offsetY + 1)
```

```
            else
               if (curMap.length == 3)
                  complexWarp(curMap.offsetX, curMap.offsetY + 1,
                     curMap.offsetX + 1, curMap.offsetY + 2)
               else
                  complexWarp(curMap.offsetX, curMap.offsetY, curMap
                     .offsetX - 1, curMap.offsetY + 1)
   if (shape == 6)
      if (curMap.length == 3 && state(curMap.offsetX + 1, curMap.offsetY))
         complexWarp(curMap.offsetX, curMap.offsetY, curMap.offsetX,
            curMap.offsetY + 1, curMap.offsetX + 2, curMap.offsetY + 1,
            curMap.offsetX + 1, curMap.offsetY + 1, curMap.offsetX + 2,
            curMap.offsetY, curMap.offsetX + 1, curMap.offsetY - 1)
      else
         if (curMap.length == 2 && state(curMap.offsetX + 1,
                                    curMap.offsetY + 1))
            complexWarp(curMap.offsetX, curMap.offsetY + 2,
               curMap.offsetX, curMap.offsetY, curMap.offsetX + 1,
               curMap.offsetY + 2, curMap.offsetX, curMap.offsetY + 1,
               curMap.offsetX + 1, curMap.offsetY, curMap.offsetX + 2,
               curMap.offsetY + 1)
      else
         if (curMap.length == 3)
            complexWarp(curMap.offsetX + 1, curMap.offsetY + 1,
               curMap.offsetX + 1, curMap.offsetY, curMap.offsetX + 2,
               curMap.offsetY + 1, curMap.offsetX, curMap.offsetY + 2)
         else
            complexWarp(curMap.offsetX, curMap.offsetY, curMap.offsetX + 1,
               curMap.offsetY + 1, curMap.offsetX + 1, curMap.offsetY,
               curMap.offsetX + 2, curMap.offsetY + 1, curMap.offsetX,
               curMap.offsetY + 2, curMap.offsetX + 2, curMap.offsetY + 2)
}
// flood entire screen with given state
function flood(state)
{
   for (var x = 0; x < 10; ++x)
   {
      for (var y = 0; y < 19; ++y)
      {
         if (state == 0)
            document.images[computeIndex(x, y)].src = off.src
         else
            document.images[computeIndex(x, y)].src = on[3].src
      }
   }
}
// return true if no active squares are found and false otherwise
function noActive()
{
   // scan board from top to bottom
   for (var y = 0; y < 19; ++y)
   {
      for (var x = 0; x < 10; ++ x)
      {
```

```
            if (ar[x][y] == 1)
               return false
         }
      }
      // no active square found on the board
      return true
}
// return true if the line with the given coordinate is completed
function isLine(y)
{
   // horizontal scan of current line
   for (var x = 0; x < 10; ++x)
   {
      // if a square is off the line is not completed
      if (!state(x, y))
         return false
   }
   // no square was found off
   return true
}
// move block from one position to another
function warp(startX, startY, endX, endY)
{
   document.images[computeIndex(endX, endY)].src = document.images
                  [computeIndex(startX, startY)].src
   document.images[computeIndex(startX, startY)].src = off.src
   // block in new position is now active
   ar[endX][endY] = 1
   // previous position is no longer active
   ar[startX][startY] = 0
}
// function that starts game (*works with global variables only*)
function start()
{
   // accept level from user (no validation to save space)
   tempLevel = prompt("Enter level to begin game (0 – 10):", "0")
   // if user cancelled prompt
   if (!tempLevel)
      // abort function
      return
   // tempLevel is the actual level
   level = tempLevel
   // clear states, blocks, and timer
   clearActive()
   flood(0)
   clearTimeout(timerID)
   // clear statistics
   for (var i = 0; i < 7; ++i)
   {
      statistics[i] = 0
   }
   // convert input from string to integer
   level = parseInt(level)
   // calculate speed
```

```
   speed = 800 - (level * 80)
   // game begins with no lines completed!
   lines = 0
   // game starts
   timerRunning = true
   // game is not paused for sure
   paused = false
   // start actual playing
   play()
}
// check if lines have been completed and drop accordingly
function dropLines()
{
   // on line has been found
   var aLine = -1
// scan screen from top to bottom and stop when first complete line is found
            and assigned
   for (var y = 0; y < 19; ++y)
   {
      if (isLine(y))
      {
         aLine = y
         break
      }
   }
   // if a complete line has been found
   if (aLine != -1)
   {
      // increment lines
      lines++
      // if enough lines have been made increment level
      if (lines > level * 10 + 9)
         level++
      if (level == 11)
         alert("You are a champion!")
      // scan screen from one line above the complete one to top of screen
      for (y = aLine - 1; y >= 0; --y)
      {
         for (var x = 0; x < 10; ++x)
         {
            // if current square is on
            if (state(x, y))
               // call function to warp it down
               warp(x, y, x, y + 1)
            else
            {
            // clear square below (similar to a warp because
            // initial square is off)
               setSquare(x, y + 1, 0)
            }
         }
      }
      // recursive call (maybe more than one line was completed)
      dropLines()
```

```
   }
   // no square should be active
   clearActive()
}
// main function responsible for game action
function play()
{
   // place values in form fields (display)
   document.lineslevel.lines.value = lines
   document.lineslevel.level.value = level
   // if no shape is falling
   if (noActive())
   {
      // check for line completions and drop them
      dropLines()
      // insert a new shape (if shape is not able to enter)
      if (!insertShape())
      {
         // flood screen to black
         flood(1)
         // flood screen to blank
         flood(0)
         // display final results
         alert('Game over!\r\rlevel = ' + level + '\rlines = '+ lines)
         // clear timeout
         clearTimeout(timerID)
         // timer is not running
         timerRunning = false
         // terminate function (and game)
         return
      }
   } else
      // a shape is currently falling so move it one square downward
      moveY()
   // call after speed milliseconds
   timerID = setTimeout('play()', speed)
}
// constructs an object representing a specific position
function characteristics(x, y)
{
   // create property to hold status (block or empty)
   this.state = state(x, y)
   // if block found in specified position
   if (state(x, y))
   {
      // local variable to hold URL of image at specified location
      var src = document.images[computeIndex(x, y)].src
      // local variable to hold color (0, 1, 2, ..., 6)
      var color = src.charAt(src.lastIndexOf('/') + 2)
   } else
      // no color because no block found at specified position
      color = -1
   // convert color from string to integer and assign to property
   this.color = parseInt(color)
```

```
   // create property to hold square's current state (active or not, 1 or 0)
   this.activity = ar[x][y]
}
// contructs a map of entire board and status
function fullMap()
{
   for (var x = 0; x < 10; ++x)
   {
      this[x] = new Array(10)
      for (var y = 0; y < 19; ++y)
      {
         this[x][y] = new characteristics(x, y)
      }
   }
   this.shape = shape
}
// pause and unpause game
function pause()
{
   // if game is not paused
   if (!paused)
   {
      // stop timer
      clearTimeout(timerID)
      // game is now paused
      paused = true
      // create global map of board
      map = new fullMap()
      // flood board so player cannot see current status
      flood(1)
      // no active blocks so user cannot move anything with buttons
      clearActive()
      alert('Oh no, not the boss...')
   } else
   {
   // return board to status before game was paused, according to the map object
      for (var x = 0; x < 10; ++x)
      {
         for (var y = 0; y < 19; ++y)
         {
            if (!map[x][y].state)
              document.images[computeIndex(x, y)].src = off.src
            else
              document.images[computeIndex(x, y)].src = on[map
                           [x][y].color].src
            ar[x][y] = map[x][y].activity
         }
      }
      shape = map.shape
      // game is no longer paused
      paused = false
      // play ball!
      play()
   }
```

```
}
// -->
</SCRIPT>
</HEAD>
<BODY>
<EMBED SRC="tetrisla.mid" AUTOSTART=TRUE LOOP=TRUE HIDDEN=TRUE>
</BODY>
</HTML>
```

Example 21-8 (ex21-8.htm). *A 1,000-line script creates a Tetris game on a web page.*

Global Statements

```
// array to hold number of shapes used from each type
var statistics = new Array(7)
for (var shapeNum = 0; shapeNum < 7; ++shapeNum)
{
   statistics[shapeNum] = 0
}
```

Tetris is based on seven shapes, so an array of seven elements named `statistics` is created first, and its elements are zero-initialized. The first element, `statistics[0]`, is associated with the first shape, and so forth. The array holds the shape statistics from the beginning of the game, so the element `statistics[2]`, for example, holds the number of times shape 3 appeared.

```
// set pause to false
var paused = false
// game is currently running
var timerRunning = false
// no shape currently falling
var shape = -1
// timer is not running
var timerID = null
```

Since the game is paused only when the user clicks the Pause button, we set the `paused` variable to false. The second variable, `timerRunning`, is also set to false, as no timeout has been set by the `setTimeout()` method. The `shape` variable normally holds the index of the shape that is currently falling down on the screen. It is initialized to –1, indicating that no shape is falling yet (the game has not started). Another global variable, `timerID`, is initialized to null.

```
// initialize image variables for seven shapes
var on = new Array()
on[0] = new Image(12, 12)
on[1] = new Image(12, 12)
on[2] = new Image(12, 12)
on[3] = new Image(12, 12)
on[4] = new Image(12, 12)
on[5] = new Image(12, 12)
on[6] = new Image(12, 12)
```

```
// create a transparent block
var off = new Image(12, 12)
```

Like the LED sign, Netris Deluxe is based on image manipulations. In this script we create a seven-element global array named on and a variable named off, and assign an instance of the image object to each element of the array and to the variable. Notice that all images are the same size, 12 pixels by 12 pixels. The off variable holds a transparent GIF image for the background.

```
// set image URLs
on[0].src = "10.gif"
on[1].src = "11.gif"
on[2].src = "12.gif"
on[3].src = "13.gif"
on[4].src = "14.gif"
on[5].src = "15.gif"
on[6].src = "16.gif"
off.src = "0.gif"
```

After creating the Image instances, we set the src property of each instance to the URL of its image. The images for the seven color blocks (those used to construct shapes) are 10.gif through 16.gif. The URL of the transparent image is 0.gif. Notice that the first character of all block images is "1", whereas the first character of the "off image" (the transparent one) is "0".

```
// get number of images already laid out in the page
var firstImage = document.images.length
// create initial screen
drawScreen()
// array of screen (10 x 19)
var ar = new Array()
for (var i = 0; i < 10; ++i)
{
   ar[i] = new Array(19)
   for (var j = 0; j < 19; ++j)
   {
      ar[i][j] = 0
   }
}
```

Once the essential instances of the image object are ready, we compute the document index of the first image. Since the document.images array starts from index 0, the index of the last image in the document, before loading the game, is document.images.length – 1. The value assigned to firstImage, then, is the index of the first image of the game and is equal to document.images.length. The function drawScreen() creates the initial screen of the game.

The last portion of the global statements creates a simple 10 x 19 2D array. Since the actual height of a Tetris screen is 17 squares instead of 19, all shapes enter two lines above the top. This two-line margin enables the user to see the entire shape, even if he or she rotates it immediately upon entering the game (17th row).

drawScreen()

The drawScreen() function simply uses document.write() statements to generate the game. Notice that we use the with(document) construct so that we can use write() rather than document.write(). The function creates several forms and buttons:

- The first form includes the LINES and LEVEL text fields, referenced as document.lineslevel.lines and document.lineslevel.level, respectively.
- The Start and Pause buttons are images linked with the start() and pause() functions, respectively.
- The second form is named "stats." It includes seven two-character text fields, named 0 through 6.
- The control panel includes direction and rotation buttons as well. The left movement button calls moveX() with the argument –1, the right movement button invokes moveX() with the argument 1, the downward movement button calls the moveY() function with no argument, and the rotation button calls the rotate() function.

computeIndex(x, y)

See the listings for Demonstration 2 for a detailed explanation of this function.

state(x, y)

```
// returns state of square (true / false)
function state(x, y)
{
   // assign URL of image at given coordinates to local variable
   var source = document.images[computeIndex(x, y)].src
   // expression evaluates to 0 or 1
   return (source.charAt(source.lastIndexOf('/') + 1) == '0') ? false : true
}
```

This function first finds the URL of the image located at the given x and y coordinates and assigns it to the local variable source. You may recall from the beginning of our discussion that the filename of an image starts with either a "0" (for the off image) or a"1" (for a color block). Since source.lastIndexOf('/') + 1 is the index of the first character of the image's filename, the following expression evaluates to either a "1" or a "0":

```
source.charAt(source.lastIndexOf('/') + 1)
```

This computation also applies to the case when the images are stored in the same directory in which the document resides (there is no slash in the URL expression). The source.lastIndexOf('/') evaluates to –1, and source.lastIndexOf('/') + 1 yields a 0 value, the index of the first character.

The state() function returns true if the image at the given coordinates is a block (its filename starts with a "1"), and false if it is a transparent image (its filename starts with a "0").

setSquare(x, y, state)

```
// set square to 1 / 0
function setSquare(x, y, state)
{
   if (state == 0)
      document.images[computeIndex(x, y)].src = off.src
   else
      document.images[computeIndex(x, y)].src = on[shape].src
   // if state is one square is active, so 1 is assigned to ar[x][y]
   // otherwise square is not active so 0 is assigned to ar[x][y]
   ar[x][y] = state
}
```

The setSquare() function accepts three arguments: the x coordinate of a square, its y coordinate, and a state (0 or 1) assignment. If the value of state is 0, the square at the given position is cleared by assigning off.src to its src property. On the other hand, if state is 1 (or any other value), the box at the given position is assigned the block image whose index is shape, where shape is a global integer from 0 to 6. The current state of the square, at the specified position, is stored in the global array ar. See the inline comments for additional explanations regarding this statement.

clearActive()

```
// clear array so no active squares exist
function clearActive()
{
   // scan entire array and assign 0 to all elements (no active squares)
   for (var i = 0; i < 10; ++i)
   {
      for (var j = 0; j < 19; ++j)
      {
         ar[i][j] = 0
      }
   }
   // no shape is currently in screen
   shape = -1
}
```

The ar array, which is 10 x 19, keeps track of all current "active" blocks, i.e., those that belong to a falling shape. Moving blocks around is done simply by visiting all active ones and assigning their next locations. Whenever a block hits the bottom of the board or lies on top of another block, the falling shape is inactivated by the clearActive() function, which clears the entire board.

The last statement of the function sets shape to –1, signaling that there is no falling shape on the board.

checkMoveX(step)

```
// check if specified move (left or right) is valid
function checkMoveX(step)
{
   // scan screen (direction does not matter)
   for (var x = 0; x < 10; ++x)
   {
      for (var y = 0; y < 19; ++y)
      {
         // if current square is active
         if (ar[x][y] == 1)
         {
         // check all conditions:
         // not out of range and not colliding with existing not active block
            if (x + step < 0 || x + step > 9 || (state(x + step,
                     y) && ar[x + step][y] == 0))
            // return false if move (new situation) is notlegal
               return false
         }
      }
   }
   // return true if no invalid state has been encountered
   return true
}
```

This function accepts one argument, either 1 or –1, and checks if it is possible to move the active shape one square to the right (if the argument is 1) or to the left (if the argument is –1). The function looks for all active squares on the board and the following condition is evaluated for each active one:

```
x + step < 0 || x + step > 9 || (state(x + step, y) && ar[x + step]
[y] == 0)
```

This expression yields true if the active square, after moving it `step` positions to the right, finds itself out of the board's range or in the territory of an inactive block (an active block obviously belongs to the same shape). If the specified movement is not valid, the function returns false. Otherwise, it returns true.

The efficiency of this function can be improved in two ways. First, to reduce the number of checks, the function can be spliced into `CheckMoveXright()` and `CheckMoveXleft()`. Second, instead of searching the whole board for active squares, a more localized algorithm that takes advantage of the current shape and position information can be devised.

checkMoveY()

```
// check if specified move (down) is valid
function checkMoveY()
{
   // only possible step is one to the bottom
   var step = 1
   // scan screen (direction does not matter)
   for (var x = 0; x < 10; ++x)
   {
      for (var y = 0; y < 19; ++y)
      {
         // if current square is active
         if (ar[x][y] == 1)
         {
         // check all conditions:
         // not out of range and not colliding with existing not active block
            if (y + step > 18 || (state(x, y + step) && ar[x]
                     [y + step] == 0))
               // return false if move (new situation) is not legal
               return false
         }
      }
   }
   // return true if no invalid state has been encountered
   return true
}
```

This function is very similar to `checkMoveX()`, except that, since the movement is always downward, it does not accept any argument. The `step` variable appears in this function for historical reasons; it could have been replaced by 1.

moveX(step)

```
// move all active squares step squares on the x axis
function moveX(step)
{
   // if specified move is not legal
   if (!checkMoveX(step))
      // terminate function (active blocks are not moved)
      return
   // if left movement then scan screen from left to right
   if (step < 0)
   {
      for (var x = 0; x < 10; ++x)
      {
         for (var y = 0; y < 19; ++y)
         {
            // if current square is active
            if (ar[x][y] == 1)
               // call function to handle movement
               smartX(x, y, step)
```

```
			}
		}
	} else
	// if right movement then scan screen from right to left
	if (step > 0)
	{
		for (var x = 9; x >= 0; --x)
		{
			for (var y = 0; y < 19; ++y)
			{
				// if current square is active
				if (ar[x][y] == 1)
					// call function to handle movement
					smartX(x, y, step)
			}
		}
	}
}
```

The moveX() function accepts one argument, specifying the number of positions that all active squares need to be moved. A positive value means that they should be moved to the right, while a negative value means that they should be moved to the left. The scanning algorithm is coordinated with the movement direction, so it does not visit the same square again (after it has been moved). The movement itself is accomplished by the smartX() function. Refer to the inline comments for statement-specific notes.

smartX(x, y, step)

```
// responsible for the blocks' horizontal movement
function smartX(x, y, step)
{
	// if moving one step to the left
	if (step < 0)
		// if the destination square needs to be turned on explicitly
		if (ar[x + step][y] == 0)
			// if there is a block to the right of the current block
			if (x != 9 && ar[x - step][y] == 1)
				// set square to the left on without clearing current block
				setSquare(x + step, y, 1)
			else
				// clear current block and turn square to the left on
				warp(x, y, x + step, y)
		else
			// if there is no block to the right of the current block
			if (x == 9 || ar[x - step][y] == 0)
				// clear current block
				setSquare(x, y, 0)
	// if moving one step to the right
	if (step > 0)
		// if the destination square needs to be turned on explicitly
		if (ar[x + step][y] == 0)
			// if there is a block to the left of the current block
```

```
        if (x != 0 && ar[x - step][y] == 1)
           // set square to the right on without clearing current block
           setSquare(x + step, y, 1)
        else
           // clear current block and turn square to the right on
           warp(x, y, x + step, y)
     else
        // if there is no block to the left of the current block
        if (x == 0 || ar[x - step][y] == 0)
           // clear current block
           setSquare(x, y, 0)
}
```

The smartX() function is responsible for the horizontal movement of the affected blocks. Notice that when you move a horizontal bar (four blocks) shape to the right, for example, you only need to move the far-right block to the right of the shape and clear the pre-movement far-left block. Moving a shape consisting of four blocks one step to the right requires the setting of two blocks and the clearing of two other blocks.

moveY()

```
// move all active squares step squares on the y axis
function moveY()
{
   // if specified move is not legal (shape is laid down on block or bottom
              panel)
   if (!checkMoveY())
   {
      // active squares are not active anymore (should not be moved later)
      clearActive()
      // terminate function (active blocks are not moved)
      return
   }
   // scan screen from bottom to top
   for (var y = 18; y >= 0; --y)
   {
      for (var x = 0; x < 10; ++x)
      {
         // if current square is active
         if (ar[x][y] == 1)
            // call function to handle movement
            smartY(x, y)
      }
   }
}
```

The moveY() function is identical to the moveX() function, except that if a move is not possible, the clearActive() function is called, inactivating the whole board. Also, since the movement is always downward, no argument is needed.

smartY(x, y)

```
// responsible for the blocks' vertical (downward) movement
function smartY(x, y)
{
   // if the destination square needs to be turned on explicitly
   if (ar[x][y + 1] == 0)
      // if there is a block above current block
      if (y != 0 && ar[x][y - 1] == 1)
         // set square below on without clearing current block
         setSquare(x, y + 1, 1)
      else
         // clear current block and turn square below on
         warp(x, y, x, y + 1)
   else
      // if there is no block above the current block
      if (y == 0 || ar[x][y - 1] == 0)
         // clear current block
         setSquare(x, y, 0)
}
```

This function is the y axis equivalent of the `smartX()` function presented earlier. See the listing for that function.

shapeMap()

```
// construct object containing shape
function shapeMap()
{
   // set minimum and maximum coordinates to opposite (minimum and maximum
             found thus far)
   var minX = 9
   var minY = 18
   var maxX = 0
   var maxY = 0
   // scan screen to find actual minimum and maximum coordinates of active
             squares
   for (var y = 0; y < 19; ++y)
   {
      for (var x = 0; x < 10; ++x)
      {
         // if current coordinates reflect active square
         if (ar[x][y] == 1)
         {
            if (x < minX)
               minX = x
            if (x > maxX)
               maxX = x
            if (y < minY)
               minY = y
            if (y > maxY)
               maxY = y
         }
```

```
      }
   }
   // create a length property representing the x coordinate span
   this.length = maxX - minX + 1
   // create properties to hold minimum coordinates of both axes
   this.offsetX = minX
   this.offsetY = minY
   // construct minimum array containing all active squares respectively
   for (x = 0; x <= maxX - minX; ++x)
   {
      this[x] = new Array()
      for (y = 0; y <= maxY - minY; ++y)
      {
         this[x][y] = ar[x + minX][y + minY]
      }
   }
}
```

Before the script rotates a shape, it must know which shape is currently active and its exact position. The `shapeMap()` constructor builds the minimum 2D array that encloses the current shape.

In addition to the array elements, an instance of `shapeMap` features the board's x and y coordinates (`offsetX` and `offsetY`) of the shape-enclosing rectangle's top-left square (*`shapeMapInstance`*`[0][0]`). The 2D array and these two properties are enough to determine the current active shape and its location. For a complete discussion of each statement in the function, refer to the comments.

getRandom()

```
// random function to return an integer from 0 to 6
function getRandom()
{
   // use random number method to find integer from 0 to 8
   var randomNum = Math.round(Math.random() * 8)
   // call function again if random number is 0 or 8.
   if (randomNum == 0 || randomNum == 8)return getRandom()
   // 1 to 7 => 0 to 6
   randomNum--
   // update selected shape's statistics
   statistics[randomNum]++
   // update statistics display form (update *all* fields so user cannot enter
            any value in fields)
   for (var shape = 0; shape < 7; ++shape)
   {
      document.stats[shape].value = statistics[shape]
   }
   // return the random number
   return randomNum
}
```

The `getRandom()` function returns a random integer from 0 to 6. First, it uses the `Math` object's `random()` method to generate a random number.

Peculiarly enough, we found out that the random generator prefers the inner integers (1, 2, 3, 4, and 5) over the boundary ones (0 and 6). To remedy the situation, we decided to generate random integers from 0 to 8, and then do some juggling to fit the result into the 0 to 6 range. If the integer is 0 or 8, the function invokes itself recursively until an integer from 1 to 7 is randomly generated. The number then decrements by 1 to fit the 0 to 6 range, and is returned by the function. After updating the `statistics` array, the text fields, representing the number of appearances of each shape, are updated as well.

insertShape()

This function inserts a new shape whose index is a random integer stored in the global variable `shape`. Take a look at the following code segment:

```
if (shape == 4)
{
   if (state(4, 2) || state(5, 2) || state(3, 3) || state(4, 3))
      return false
   setSquare(4, 2, 1)
   setSquare(5, 2, 1)
   setSquare(3, 3, 1)
   setSquare(4, 3, 1)
}
```

The `insertShape()` function includes such a script segment for each of the seven supported shapes.

The conditional statement uses the function `state()` to check whether all four squares are empty. If one of the four is blocked, the `insertShape()` function returns false and terminates. Otherwise, the function proceeds by invoking the `setSquare()` function four times, one for each block of the new shape.

complexWarp()

```
// warp several squares if possible
// initial x1, initial y1, destination x1, destination y1, initial x2,
initial y2, destination x2, destination y2, etc.
function complexWarp()
{
   // loop through arguments checking that each warp is valid
   for (var i = 0; i < arguments.length; i += 4)
   {
      // if warp is not valid
      if (!checkWarp(arguments[i], arguments[i + 1], arguments[i + 2],
                  arguments[i + 3]))
         // terminate the function -- no squares warped
         return
   }
   // loop through arguments again -- warp squares
   for (var i = 0; i < arguments.length; i += 4)
   {
```

```
      // call function to warp the current square corresponding to
              argument coordinates
      warp(arguments[i], arguments[i + 1], arguments[i + 2],
              arguments[i + 3])
   }
}
```

This function moves a shape's blocks from their current positions to their new ones. The argument list includes sets of four coordinates: x and y values of these positions. Since the number of sets depends on the shape type, the arguments are accessed via the `arguments` array, rather than as parameters.

First, the function calls `checkWarp()` to check if the destination squares are populated or not. The `complexWarp()` function terminates immediately whenever one of the squares is occupied. The warping itself is accomplished by calling the `warp()` function, once for each set of four arguments.

checkWarp(startX, startY, endX, endY)

```
// check if warp is valid (used by complexWarp function)
function checkWarp(startX, startY, endX, endY)
{
   // if a destination coordinate is invalid or destination square is off
   // state(endX, endY) must be last due to short-circuit evaluation
   if (endX < 0 || endX > 9 || endY < 0 || endY > 18 || state(endX,endY))
      // return false because warp is invalid
      return false
   // return true because warp has not been proved to be invalid (it is valid)
   return true
}
```

Out of the four arguments this function accepts, it uses the last two (`endX`, `endY`) to check if the given position is occupied.

rotate()

First, `rotate()` assigns an instance of the `shapeMap` object to a local variable, `curMap`. The `shapeMap` object is used to find out the current angle of the shape. The "L" shape, for example, has four different angles, whereas a "square" (2 x 2) shape has only one. It then calls the `complexWarp()` function with the coordinates of the blocks that need to be "warped" during rotation.

flood(state)

```
// flood entire screen with given state
function flood(state)
{
   for (var x = 0; x < 10; ++x)
   {
      for (var y = 0; y < 19; ++y)
      {
```

```
         if (state == 0)
            document.images[computeIndex(x, y)].src = off.src
         else
            document.images[computeIndex(x, y)].src = on[3].src
      }
   }
}
```

When its argument is 0, the `flood()` function clears the entire board by setting the URL of all images to `off.src`. If the argument is not 0, all board images are replaced with `on[3].src`. Note that, instead of the doubly nested loop, you can use a single loop to fill the `document.images` 1D array. Since you would not have to invoke the `computeIndex()` function for each position, the flooding would have been more efficient.

noActive()

```
// return true if no active squares are found and false otherwise
function noActive()
{
   // scan board from top to bottom
   for (var y = 0; y < 19; ++y)
   {
      for (var x = 0; x < 10; ++ x)
      {
         if (ar[x][y] == 1)
            return false
      }
   }
   // no active square found on the board
   return true
}
```

This function is self-explanatory.

isLine(y)

```
// return true if the line with the given coordinate is completed
function isLine(y)
{
   // horizontal scan of current line
   for (var x = 0; x < 10; ++x)
   {
      // if a square is off the line is not completed
      if (!state(x, y))
         return false
   }
   // no square was found off
   return true
}
```

This function looks for complete lines, i.e., lines with all squares checked.

warp(startX, startY, endX, endY)

```
// move block from one position to another
function warp(startX, startY, endX, endY)
{
   document.images[computeIndex(endX, endY)].src = document.images
                  [computeIndex(startX, startY)].src
   document.images[computeIndex(startX, startY)].src = off.src
   // block in new position is now active
   ar[endX][endY] = 1
   // previous position is no longer active
   ar[startX][startY] = 0
}
```

The `warp()` function "warps" a block from one position to another by setting the URL of the destination image to that of the source image, and then setting the URL of the source image to that of the transparent one, `off.src`. The `ar` array is also being updated with the recent changes in square assignments.

start()

```
// function that starts game (*works with global variables only*)
function start()
{
   // accept level from user (no validation to save space)
   tempLevel = prompt("Enter level to begin game (0 – 10):", "0")
   // if user cancelled prompt
   if (!tempLevel)
      // abort function
      return
   // tempLevel is the actual level
   level = tempLevel
   // clear states, blocks, and timer
   clearActive()
   flood(0)
   clearTimeout(timerID)
   // clear statistics
   for (var i = 0; i < 7; ++i)
   {
      statistics[i] = 0
   }
   // convert input from string to integer
   level = parseInt(level)
   // calculate speed
   speed = 800 – (level * 80)
   // game begins with no lines completed!
   lines = 0
   // game starts
   timerRunning = true
   // game is not paused for sure
   paused = false
```

```
   // start actual playing
   play()
}
```

This function is very well documented and explained. Use it as an example for how to comment a script.

dropLines()

```
// check if lines have been completed and drop accordingly
function dropLines()
{
   // on line has been found
   var aLine = -1
   // scan screen from top to bottom and stop when first complete
   // line is found and assigned
   for (var y = 0; y < 19; ++y)
   {
      if (isLine(y))
      {
         aLine = y
         break
      }
   }
   // if a complete line has been found
   if (aLine != -1)
   {
      // increment lines
      lines++
      // if enough lines have been made increment level
      if (lines > level * 10 + 9)
         level++
      if (level == 11)
         alert("You are a champion!")
      // scan screen from one line above the complete one to top of screen
      for (y = aLine - 1; y >= 0; --y)
      {
         for (var x = 0; x < 10; ++x)
         {
            // if current square is on
            if (state(x, y))
               // call function to warp it down
               warp(x, y, x, y + 1)
            else
            {
            // clear square below (similar to a warp because
            // initial square is off)
               setSquare(x, y + 1, 0)
            }
         }
      }
      // recursive call (maybe more than one line was completed)
```

```
      dropLines()
   }
   // no square should be active
   clearActive()
}
```

The `dropLines()` function loops over the board rows, from top to bottom, searching for fully blocked rows to clear. After finding a line, all blocks above the line are warped one position downward, and the `dropLines()` function is called recursively to search and clear other rows. Since there are no active shapes after clearing, the `clearActive()` function is invoked to clear all board squares. The script also checks if the user has completed enough lines to up the current level of play.

play()

```
// main function responsible for game action
function play()
{
   // place values in form fields (display)
   document.lineslevel.lines.value = lines
   document.lineslevel.level.value = level
   // if no shape is falling
   if (noActive())
   {
      // check for line completions and drop them
      dropLines()
      // insert a new shape (if shape is not able to enter)
      if (!insertShape())
      {
         // flood screen to black
         flood(1)
         // flood screen to blank
         flood(0)
         // display final results
         alert('Game over!\r\rlevel = ' + level + '\rlines = '+lines)
         // clear timeout
         clearTimeout(timerID)
         // timer is not running
         timerRunning = false
         // terminate function (and game)
         return
      }
   } else
      // a shape is currently falling so move it one square downward
      moveY()
   // call after speed milliseconds
   timerID = setTimeout('play()', speed)
}
```

characteristics(x, y)

```
// constructs an object representing a specific position
function characteristics(x, y)
{
   // create property to hold status (block or empty)
   this.state = state(x, y)
   // if block found in specified position
   if (state(x, y))
   {
      // local variable to hold URL of image at specified location
      var src = document.images[computeIndex(x, y)].src
      // local variable to hold color (0, 1, 2, ..., 6)
      var color = src.charAt(src.lastIndexOf('/') + 2)
   } else
      // no color because no block found at specified position
      color = -1
   // convert color from string to integer and assign to property
   this.color = parseInt(color)
   // create property to hold square's current state (active or not, 1 or 0)
   this.activity = ar[x][y]
}
```

fullMap()

```
// contructs a map of entire board and status
function fullMap()
{
   for (var x = 0; x < 10; ++x)
   {
      this[x] = new Array(10)
      for (var y = 0; y < 19; ++y)
      {
         this[x][y] = new characteristics(x, y)
      }
   }
   this.shape = shape
}
```

pause()

```
// pause and unpause game
function pause()
{
   // if game is not paused
   if (!paused)
   {
      // stop timer
      clearTimeout(timerID)
      // game is now paused
      paused = true
      // create global map of board
      map = new fullMap()
```

```
        // flood board so player cannot see current status
        flood(1)
        // no active blocks so user cannot move anything with buttons
        clearActive()
        alert('Oh no, not the boss...')
    }
    else
    {
        // return board to status before game was paused, according to the map
                object
        for (var x = 0; x < 10; ++x)
        {
            for (var y = 0; y < 19; ++y)
            {
                if (!map[x][y].state)
                    document.images[computeIndex(x, y)].src = off.src
                else
                    document.images[computeIndex(x, y)].src=
                            on[map[x][y].color].src
                ar[x][y] = map[x][y].activity
            }
        }
        shape = map.shape
        // game is no longer paused
        paused = false
        // play ball!
        play()
    }
}
```

The pause() function is responsible for pausing and unpausing the game, depending on its current state.

Music

The background music featured by Netris Deluxe is embedded via an HTML statement:

```
<EMBED SRC="tetris1a.mid" AUTOSTART=TRUE LOOP=TRUE HIDDEN=TRUE>
```

Summary

In this chapter I discussed the image object, and how it is implemented in client-side JavaScript. Mastering the usage of the image object and the document.images array is not trivial, but will become easier with experience. This is the reason I included three image-based comprehensive demonstrations, including a 1,000-line script (Netris Deluxe). JavaScript is very useful when you want to interact with the user (as in games), or when the animation is customized (as in the updating clock and in the LED sign). Plain animation is better created with gif89, rather than with JavaScript.

Chapter 22
Frames

What Are Frames?

Frames provide the ability to divide the browser's window into several sections, each containing a distinct HTML document. Although some developers and web development books recommend avoiding the use of frames, they are a perfectly valid and quite easy to use method for organizing a web site and allowing easy navigation. There are many different ways to use frames. You can display, for instance, the table of contents on one side of the window, and the content itself on the other side. You can then direct all links in the table of contents to load documents in the other frame, thus ensuring that the table of contents is present at all times. While surfing the web, you can occasionally recognize a frame-separated window by the frame's borders. Borderless frames, though, have become much more popular.

Creating Frames

Frames are basically plain HTML that is loaded by a parent document. In order to specify the frames in the top-level document, you must use the <FRAMESET> definition. This tag specifies how to divide the window. A single <FRAMESET> tag can divide a document into a set of rows or columns, depending on the desired design. For example, the following definition divides a document into two frames:

```
<FRAMESET COLS="50, *">
```

These two frames are organized in columns. The left frame is 50 pixels wide, whereas the other frame fills the rest of the document. An asterisk (*) represents the remaining space in a document, after allocating space for the other frames.

You can also specify the percentage width of a column frame out of the window's width, or the percentage height of a row frame out of the window's height. The following definition, for instance, divides a document into two frames (laid out as rows), where the upper one takes up one-quarter of the document, and the bottom one takes up three-quarters of it:

```
<FRAMESET ROWS="25%, *">
```

The following tags are equivalent to the preceding one:

```
<FRAMESET ROWS="*, 75%">
<FRAMESET ROWS="25%, 75%">
```

The `<FRAMESET>` tag must always be specified along with its closing counterpart, `</FRAMESET>`. The basic attributes of the `<FRAMESET>` tag are `COLS` and `ROWS` (they cannot be present simultaneously). Netscape Navigator 3.0 introduced two more attributes:

- `FRAMEBORDER`
- `BORDERCOLOR`

The `FRAMEBORDER` attribute accepts either a `no` or a `yes`. Alternatively, you can replace `no` with a `0` digit, and `yes` with a `1` digit. This attribute enables you to create a document that consists of frames with invisible borders. The `BORDERCOLOR` attribute accepts a color, either in the form of a hexadecimal triplet or a recognized color name. Since there is a plain gray transition line between two borderless frames, you should specify a white border even when setting `FRAMEBORDER` to `no`.

The `<FRAMESET>` tag specifies a set of frames, each defined by a `<FRAME>` tag and usually a URL that reflects the initial document in the frame. The following construct creates a document consisting of two frames:

```
<FRAMESET COLS="100, *">
  <FRAME SRC="frame1.html">
  <FRAME SRC="frame2.html">
</FRAMESET>
```

The `SRC` attribute specifies the URL of the document in the frame. You can always load a different document in that frame by clicking a link, submitting a form, and so forth. The preceding source requires three documents: the parent HTML document that includes the `<FRAMESET>` definition, frame1.html, and frame2.html (note that you can use either a relative or absolute URL). Take a look at the following documents:

```
<HTML>
<HEAD>
<TITLE>Frames</TITLE>
</HEAD>
<FRAMESET COLS="150, *">
  <FRAME SRC="example22-01a.htm">
  <FRAME SRC="example22-01b.htm">
</FRAMESET>
<NOFRAMES>
You must download a frame-capable browser in order to view this document.
</NOFRAMES>
</HTML>
```

Example 22-1 (ex22-1.htm). *The top-level <FRAMESET> document*

You can see the output of this in Figure 22-1.

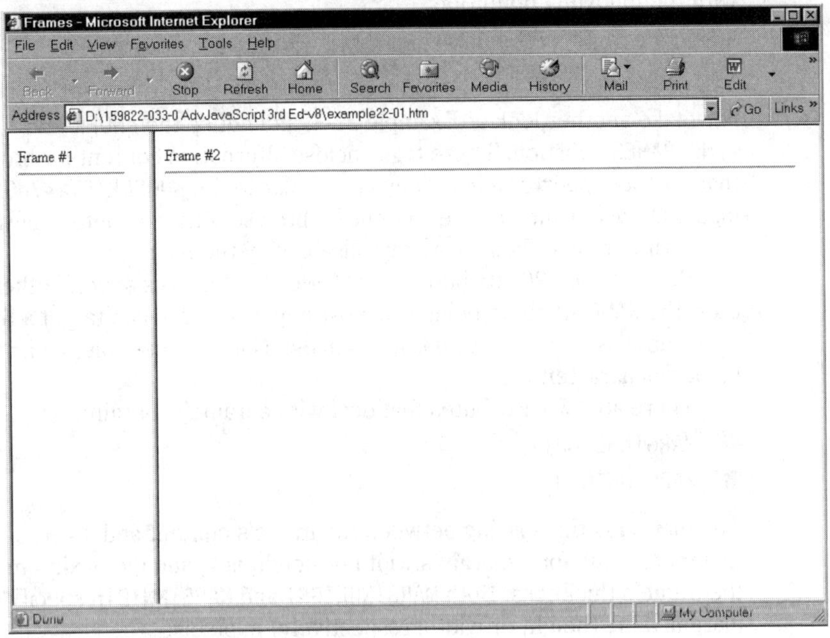

Figure 22-1. *The top level of the frameset*

```
<HTML>
<HEAD>
<TITLE>First frame</TITLE>
</HEAD>
<BODY BGCOLOR="white">
Frame #1
<HR>
</BODY>
</HTML>
```

Example 22-1a—first frame (ex22-1a.htm). *The initial document for the left frame*

```
<HTML>
<HEAD>
<TITLE>Second frame</TITLE>
</HEAD>
<BODY BGCOLOR="white">
Frame #2
<HR>
</BODY>
</HTML>
```

Example 22-1b—second frame (ex22-1b.htm). *The initial document for the right frame*

You can delete the borders by replacing the <FRAMESET> tag in Example 22-1 with the following definition:

```
<FRAMESET COLS="150, *" FRAMEBORDER="no" FRAMESPACING=0 BORDER="0"
              BORDERCOLOR="#ffffff">
```

Now take another look at Example 22-1, and notice the <NOFRAMES> </NOFRAMES> portion. These tags enclose alternative content for browsers that do not support frames. They are similar to the <NOSCRIPT></NOSCRIPT> tags that specify alternative content for browsers that do not support JavaScript or have their JavaScript disabled by the user.

Besides the SRC attribute, the <FRAME> tag features several other attributes, the NAME attribute being the most important. You can target a link or a form submission return by a frame's name. Names must start with an alphanumeric character.

There are two attributes that deal with a frame's margin:

- MARGINHEIGHT
- MARGINWIDTH

The margin is the spacing between the frame's content and its borders. The minimum value for a margin's width or height is 1, and its maximum value is the frame's thickness. Both MARGINHEIGHT and MARGINWIDTH specify the margin value (height or width, respectively) in pixels.

The SCROLLING attribute is another important one. It accepts one of three values:

- "yes"
- "no"
- "auto"

The default value "auto" instructs the browser to make a scrolling frame (with a scroll bar) whenever needed. The browser's algorithm is very simple—if the length or width of the frame's content exceeds the frame's physical size, a scroll bar is provided. The other options, "yes" and "no", force a decision on the browser.

A powerful feature of frames is that the user can resize them by dragging. You can disable this option by specifying the NORESIZE option.

Targeting Frames

Frames are powerful because they enable the content provider to direct various documents to specific frames. Directing a document to a frame is referred to as *targeting*. Targeting is supported in HTML via the TARGET attribute, which you can add to a variety of tags in the following fashion:

```
TARGET="windowName"
```

Since frames act as independent browser windows, they are often called as such. The classic usage of the TARGET attribute is with hypertext links, according to the following syntax:

```
<A HREF="URL" TARGET="windowName">text or image</A>
```

You should place such a link in a document that resides within a frame. *windowName* is the name of the frame in which the URL document should load.

You can use the <BASE> tag's TARGET attribute for targeting most of a document's links to a single common frame. The TARGET attribute establishes a default *windowName* to which all links in a document will be targeted. This default can be overridden by specific instances of the TARGET attribute in individual anchor tags. The general syntax of the <BASE> tag's TARGET attribute is as follows:

```
<BASE TARGET="windowName">
```

Note that this definition should be placed at the beginning of the HTML document.

As you can see, it is possible to target a document to a named frame. There are reserved names that define specific locations:

- TARGET="_blank" loads a new, empty window.
- TARGET="_self" loads the same window the anchor was clicked in.
- TARGET="_parent" loads the <FRAMESET> (parent) document.
- TARGET="_top" loads the full body of the browser window.

Nested Frames

There are basically two ways to nest frames.

The easiest way is to use a simple <FRAMESET> tag in the top-level document to define several rows or columns of frames, and then use another <FRAMESET> tag in one or more of the frame documents to further divide it. Suppose you want to divide a window into two columns, where the second column is divided into two rows. You can define a two-frame <FRAMESET COLS="..."> construct in the parent document as follows:

```
<FRAMESET COLS="50%, *">
   <FRAME SRC="left.html" NAME="left">
   <FRAME SRC="right.html" NAME="right">
</FRAMESET>
```

The document right.html would then need to be subdivided into frames by including the following definition:

```
<FRAMESET ROWS="50%,50%">
   <FRAME SRC="topRight.html" NAME="topRight">
   <FRAME SRC="bottomRight.html" NAME="bottomRight">
</FRAMESET>
```

You can see the output of this in Figure 22-2, which demonstrates the deeply nested frame hierarchy:

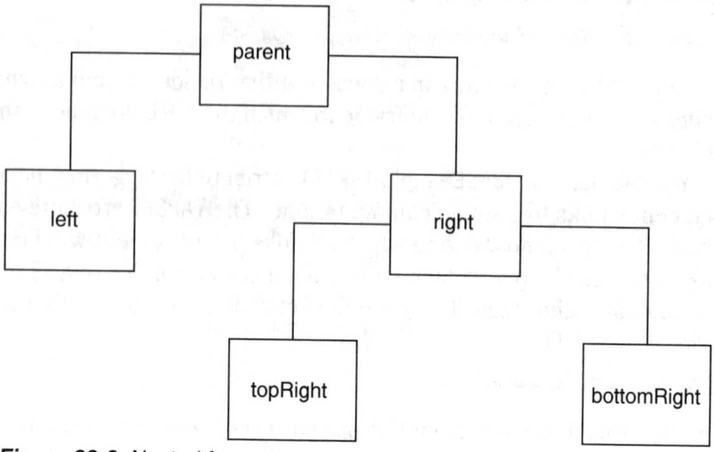

Figure 22-2. *Nested frameset*

A more convenient way to nest frames is as follows:

```
<FRAMESET COLS="50%, *">
   <FRAME SRC="left.html" NAME="left">
   <FRAMESET ROWS="50%,50%">
      <FRAME SRC="topRight.html" NAME="topRight">
      <FRAME SRC="bottomRight.html" NAME="bottomRight">
   </FRAMESET>
</FRAMESET>
```

In this code we define a set of two frames, where the second one is not specified via a <FRAME> tag but rather as another inner <FRAMESET> definition.

Notice that this technique differs from the previous one because all frames are directly defined in the top-level document. Figure 22-3 illustrates the structure of such a document.

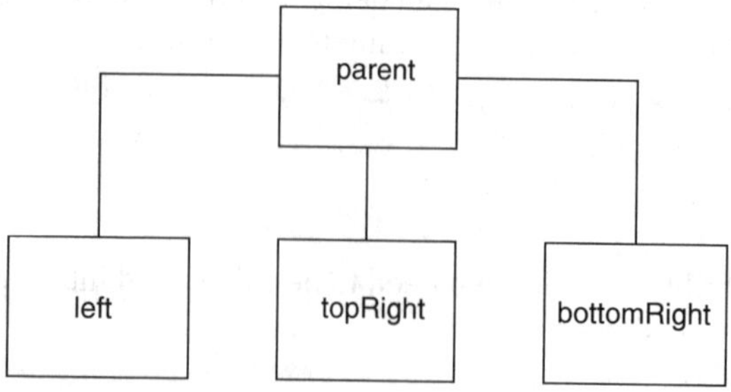

Figure 22-3. *Frameset structure*

Notice that frames in a document are not directly connected to each other. However, HTML enables you to reference one frame directly from another one.

JavaScript and Frames

In JavaScript, each frame acts as a full-fledged `window` object. A frame consists of a complete set of browser objects, including its own `document` object, `status` object (which is a bit tricky), and so forth.

self

The `self` object is similar to the "this" term in object-oriented languages. It refers to the window you are in. The background color of a document in a single-frame window can be referenced in one of the following ways:

```
window.document.bgcolor
self.document.bgcolor
document.bgcolor
```

Although it is technically possible to combine multiple references within a single-frame window, as in `window.self.document.bgcolor`, you should use such references only in a multiple-frame window.

Suppose you have a multiple-frame document, and you want to reference an object that belongs to a specific frame from that same frame. One option is to simply specify that object using a common syntax. Specifying the `self` object, however, can make the script crystal clear and its debugging much easier. You can use the following code, for instance, to display the title of that frame:

```
alert(self.document.title)
```

In summary, when the HTML document appears in one frame of a multiple-frame document, it is recommended to precede all `window` object references with the `self` object.

Note that you can also precede all function calls with the `self` object specification:

```
self.functionName()
```

parent

A script running in a frame of a multiple-frame document can reference objects or properties of its parent document (the one that sets the frames) via the `parent` property.

Note that the `window` object of the frame-setting document is equivalent to the `window.parent` (or `self.parent` or `parent`) of a document in one of the frames. In a way, since it points to a higher level of hierarchy, the `parent` property may seem to violate the object hierarchy rules.

A child window can also call a function of the parent window. The reference would be as follows:

```
parent.functionName([arguments])
```

The `parent` property of a frame's `window` object does not always point to the top-level window. If one of the children of the top-level window is also a frame-setting window, then you wind up with three levels of hierarchies. The `parent` property of the bottom level of hierarchy points to the second one.

I recommend that you draw flowcharts when you design a site with deeply nested frames. (See the section called "Nested Frames" earlier in this chapter for a discussion of the different types of nesting.)

top

The `window` object's `top` property refers to the topmost window in a JavaScript hierarchy. For a single-frame window, `top` is equivalent to `window`, which in turn is equivalent to `self` and `parent`. In a multiple-frame window, the `top` object always reflects the topmost window that defines the first frameset. In a window that contains several frames, where at least one of the frames also contains a frameset, the `top` property of all `window` objects (including all generations in the hierarchy) refers to the window with the first frameset. In terms of flowcharts, the `top` property always refers to the highest rectangle.

The top-level window can be referenced from the "youngest" child as `parent.parent`, `top`, `window.top`, or `self.top`.

frames

In a multiple-frame window, all frames act like full-fledged `window` objects. The `frames` property plays an important role when a statement in one frame must access an object or property located in a different frame.

The `frames` property is an array that reflects all direct children of a given `window` object. The property `window.frames.length` reflects the number of direct children from the point of view of that `window` object.

The browser stores information about all visible frames in an indexed array, where the first frame is stored in index `0`:

```
window.frames[0]
```

Since you should never deeply nest frames using several frame-setting documents, the `frames` array should usually be referenced as `parent.frames` or `top.frames`. Suppose you have a window divided into three frames. You can access the title of the second frame from a script in the first frame as `parent.frames[1].document.title`.

You can also access frames by their names. You can use the following syntax to retrieve (from any frame) the background color of a document in a frame named myFrame:

```
parent.myFrame.document.bgcolor
```

You can also refer to the `frames` array as an associative array, in the following fashion:

```
parent.frames["myFrame"].document.bgcolor
```

An Example: The Color Center

The Color Center is a JavaScript application that enables the user to test a variety of colors in order to find the best configurations for his or her web site. There are five distinct attributes that play a role in this tool:

- `bgcolor`—the background color
- `link`—the color of standard links
- `alink`—the color of active links
- `vlink`—the color of visited links
- `text`—the color of plain text

The Color Center is compatible with both Internet Explorer and Navigator. It is divided into three frames. The upper frame includes the red, green, and blue text fields that display the RGB values of the current color. It also features a menu enabling the user to select the attribute (one of five) that he or she wants to customize. A Save button stores the settings in a cookie, and a Load button retrieves them from the cookie.

The left frame displays the color cube—a complete set of 216 non-dithering colors. The user can select a color from the color cube and assign it to the attribute selected in the upper frame.

The right frame is the most simple one. Its initial document does not contain any data besides the basic HTML tags. Its content is generated by `document.write()` statements, executed in the parent frame-setting document.

The Frame-setting Window

Example 22-2 shows the frame-setting document.

```
<HTML>
<HEAD>
<TITLE>Color Center</TITLE>
<SCRIPT LANGUAGE="JavaScript">
<!--
// Boolean variable specified if alert should be displayed if cookie exceeds 4KB
var caution = false
deleteCookie("slot")
// name - name of the cookie
// value - value of the cookie
```

```
// [expires] - expiration date of the cookie (defaults to end of current
            session)
// [path] - path for which the cookie is valid (defaults to path of calling
            document)
// [domain] - domain for which the cookie is valid (defaults to domain of
            calling document)
// [secure] - Boolean value indicating if the cookie transmission requires a
            secure transmission
// * an argument defaults when it is assigned null as a placeholder
// * a null placeholder is not required for trailing omitted arguments
function setCookie(name, value, expires, path, domain, secure)
{
   var curCookie = name + "=" + escape(value) +
      ((expires) ? "; expires=" + expires.toGMTString() : "") +
      ((path) ? "; path=" + path : "") +
      ((domain) ? "; domain=" + domain : "") +
      ((secure) ? "; secure" : "")
   if (!caution || (name + "=" + escape(value)).length <= 4000)
      document.cookie = curCookie
   else
      if (confirm("Cookie exceeds 4KB and will be cut!"))
         document.cookie = curCookie
}
// name - name of the desired cookie
// * return string containing value of specified cookie or null if cookie does
            not exist
function getCookie(name)
{
   var prefix = name + "="
   var cookieStartIndex = document.cookie.indexOf(prefix)
   if (cookieStartIndex == -1)
      return null
   var cookieEndIndex = document.cookie.indexOf(";", cookieStartIndex +
                        prefix.length)
   if (cookieEndIndex == -1)
      cookieEndIndex = document.cookie.length
   return unescape(document.cookie.substring(cookieStartIndex + prefix.length,
                   cookieEndIndex))
}
// name - name of the cookie
// [path] - path of the cookie (must be same as path used to create cookie)
// [domain] - domain of the cookie (must be same as domain used to create
            cookie)
// * path and domain default if assigned null or omitted if no explicit
            argument proceeds
function deleteCookie(name, path, domain)
{
   if (getCookie(name))
   {
      document.cookie = name + "=" +
      ((path) ? "; path=" + path : "") +
      ((domain) ? "; domain=" + domain : "") +
      "; expires=Thu, 01-Jan-70 00:00:01 GMT"
```

```
   }
}
// date - any instance of the Date object
// * you should hand all instances of the Date object to this function for
          "repairs"
function fixDate(date)
{
   var base = new Date(0)
   var skew = base.getTime()
   if (skew > 0)
      date.setTime(date.getTime() - skew)
}
// updates the R, G, and B text fields (invoked as a method)
function display()
{
   frames[0].document.forms[0].red.value = this.r
   frames[0].document.forms[0].green.value = this.g
   frames[0].document.forms[0].blue.value = this.b
}
// constructs an attribute
function makeAttribute(r, g, b)
{
   this.r = r + ""
   this.g = g + ""
   this.b = b + ""
   this.display = display
}
// create instances for all attributes
var link = new makeAttribute("00", "00", "00")     // black
var alink = new makeAttribute("00", "00", "00")    // black
var vlink = new makeAttribute("00", "00", "00")    // black
var text = new makeAttribute("00", "00", "00")     // black
var bgcolor = new makeAttribute("FF", "FF", "FF")  // white
// invoked when user selects a color from swatches
function select(r, g, b)
{
   // assign string reflecting selected attribute ("text", "bgcolor", etc.)
   var attribute = curAttribute()
   // assign new descriptors
   eval(attribute).r = r
   eval(attribute).g = g
   eval(attribute).b = b
   // display new descriptors in R, G, and B text fields
   eval(attribute).display()
   // update main frame
   update()
}
// return string reflecting selected attribute ("text", "bgcolor", etc.)
function curAttribute()
{
   var list = frames[0].document.forms[0].attribute
   return list.options[list.selectedIndex].value
}
```

```
// returns <BODY> tag (excluding ">" and "<") reflecting all selections
function bodyDefinition()
{
   var str = 'BODY '
   str += 'BGCOLOR="#' + bgcolor.r + bgcolor.g + bgcolor.b + '" '
   str += 'LINK="#' + link.r + link.g + link.b + '" '
   str += 'ALINK="#' + alink.r + alink.g + alink.b + '" '
   str += 'VLINK="#' + vlink.r + vlink.g + vlink.b + '" '
   str += 'TEXT="#' + text.r + text.g + text.b + '"'
   return str
}
// update main window
function update()
{
   var bodyDef = bodyDefinition()
   var result = ""
   result += '<HTML><HEAD><TITLE>Main</TITLE></HEAD>'
   result += '<' + bodyDef + '>'
   result += '<CENTER>'
   result += 'Text <B>Text</B><HR WIDTH=50%>'
   result += '<FONT COLOR="#' + link.r + link.g + link.b + '">
             Link <B>Link</B><HR WIDTH=50%></FONT>'
   result += '<FONT COLOR="#' + alink.r + alink.g + alink.b + '">
             Alink <B>Alink</B><HR WIDTH=50%></FONT>'
   result += '<FONT COLOR="#' + vlink.r + vlink.g + vlink.b + '">
             Vlink <B>Vlink</B><HR WIDTH=50%></FONT>'
   result += '<BR><FONT SIZE=2>&lt;' + bodyDef + '&gt;</FONT>'
   result += '</CENTER></HTML>'
   // assign document object of main frame to local variable
   var doc = frames[2].document
   // close data stream to document
   doc.close()
   // open new data stream to document (text/html)
   doc.open('text/html')
   // print HTML content
   doc.write(result)
   // close data stream to document
   doc.close()
}
// stores all selections as a cookie
function save()
{
   var slot = link.r + link.g + link.b +
              alink.r + alink.g + alink.b +
              vlink.r + vlink.g + vlink.b +
              text.r + text.g + text.b +
              bgcolor.r + bgcolor.g + bgcolor.b
   var now = new Date()
   fixDate(now)
   now.setTime(now.getTime() + 31 * 22 * 60 * 60 * 1000) // one month
   setCookie("slot", slot, now)
}
// load values from cookie (concatenation order in save() matters!)
```

```
function load()
{
   var slot = getCookie("slot")
   if (slot != null)
   {
      link.r = slot.substring(0, 2)
      link.g = slot.substring(2, 4)
      link.b = slot.substring(4, 6)
      alink.r = slot.substring(6, 8)
      alink.g = slot.substring(8, 10)
      alink.b = slot.substring(10, 12)
      vlink.r = slot.substring(12, 14)
      vlink.g = slot.substring(14, 16)
      vlink.b = slot.substring(16, 18)
      text.r = slot.substring(18, 20)
      text.g = slot.substring(20, 22)
      text.b = slot.substring(22, 24)
      bgcolor.r = slot.substring(24, 26)
      bgcolor.g = slot.substring(26, 28)
      bgcolor.b = slot.substring(28, 30)
      eval(curAttribute()).display()
      update()
   }
}
// -->
</SCRIPT>
</HEAD>
<FRAMESET
   ROWS="50, *"
   BORDER="0"
   FRAMEBORDER="no"
   FRAMESPACING="0"
   BORDERCOLOR="#ffffff">
   <FRAME
      NAME="control"
      SRC="ex22-3.htm"
      NORESIZE
      SCROLLING="no">
   <FRAMESET
      COLS="80, *"
      BORDER="0"
      FRAMEBORDER="no"
      FRAMESPACING="0"
      BORDERCOLOR="#ffffff">
      <FRAME
         NAME="swatches"
         SRC="ex22-4.htm"
         NORESIZE
         SCROLLING="no">
      <FRAME
         NAME="main"
         SRC="ex22-5.htm"
         NORESIZE>
```

```
   </FRAMESET>
</FRAMESET>
<NOFRAMES>Please download a frames-capable browser!</NOFRAMES>
</HTML>
```

***Example 22-2 (ex22-2.htm).** Using the frame center as a control center*

The first portion of the script in Example 22-2 consists of a complete set of cookie functions, which are not repeated here. This chapter focuses on functions that are specific to the Color Center application.

display(r, g, b)

```
// updates the R, G, and B text fields (invoked as a method)
function display()
{
   frames[0].document.forms[0].red.value = this.r
   frames[0].document.forms[0].green.value = this.g
   frames[0].document.forms[0].blue.value = this.b
}
```

All attributes are defined as instances supporting the `display()` method. You can call this function, for example, to display the color of `bgcolor`:

```
bgcolor.display()
```

The `display()` method sets the values of the R, G, and B fields in the upper frame to the corresponding RGB values of the calling instance. Those values, named `r`, `g`, and `b`, are stored as properties of the calling instance.

The upper frame is the first frame to be defined, so we reference it as `frames[0]`. You can alternatively use `self.frames[0]`, `window.frames[0]`, `parent.frames[0]`, or `top.frames[0]`.

makeAttribute(r, g, b)

```
// constructs an attribute
function makeAttribute(r, g, b)
{
   this.r = r + ""
   this.g = g + ""
   this.b = b + ""
   this.display = display
}
```

`makeAttribute()` is a constructor function. All attributes are created as instances of this object, so each attribute has three properties (`r`, `g`, and `b`) and one method (`display()`). The function accepts three arguments representing the red, green, and blue descriptors. Just to be on the safe side, the arguments are converted to strings.

Global Statements

```
// create instances for all attributes
var link = new makeAttribute("00", "00", "00")      // black
var alink = new makeAttribute("00", "00", "00")     // black
```

```
var vlink = new makeAttribute("00", "00", "00")    // black
var text = new makeAttribute("00", "00", "00")     // black
var bgcolor = new makeAttribute("FF", "FF", "FF")  // white
```

We define five global variables in this script segment. All variables are defined as instances of the `makeAttribute` object. The arguments handed to the `makeAttribute()` function reflect the default colors for each attribute.

select(r, g, b)

```
// invoked when user selects a color from swatches
function select(r, g, b)
{
   // assign string reflecting selected attribute ("text", "bgcolor", etc.)
   var attribute = curAttribute()
   // assign new descriptors
   eval(attribute).r = r
   eval(attribute).g = g
   eval(attribute).b = b
   // display new descriptors in R, G, and B text fields
   eval(attribute).display()
   // update main frame
   update()
}
```

The `select()` function is invoked when the user selects a color from the swatches in the left frame, and it accepts the red, green, and blue descriptors of the selected color. The function first assigns the currently selected attribute to the local variable `attribute`. For example, if the current attribute (chosen from the menu in the upper frame) is "Visited link," the value of `attribute` is `"vlink"`. Therefore, `eval(attribute)` is an instance of the `makeAttribute` object, holding the red, green, and blue descriptors of the attribute.

curAttribute()

```
// return string reflecting selected attribute ("text", "bgcolor", etc.)
function curAttribute()
{
   var list = frames[0].document.forms[0].attribute
   return list.options[list.selectedIndex].value
}
```

This function returns the currently selected attribute in the form of a string. First, the object representing the select element of the form in the upper frame is assigned to the local variable `list`. The text value of the selected option is then returned. As shown above, it is often convenient to assign an object reference to a local variable, especially when that reference is extremely lengthy. In this case, we specify the variable `list` twice, instead of specifying the entire object reference (`frames[0].document.forms[0].attribute`) twice.

bodyDefinition()

```
// returns <BODY> tag (excluding ">" and "<") reflecting all selections
function bodyDefinition()
{
   var str = 'BODY '
   str += 'BGCOLOR="#' + bgcolor.r + bgcolor.g + bgcolor.b + '" '
   str += 'LINK="#' + link.r + link.g + link.b + '" '
   str += 'ALINK="#' + alink.r + alink.g + alink.b + '" '
   str += 'VLINK="#' + vlink.r + vlink.g + vlink.b + '" '
   str += 'TEXT="#' + text.r + text.g + text.b + '"'
   return str
}
```

The `bodyDefinition()` function constructs and returns a complete `<BODY>` tag, based on the current values of the descriptors of each attribute. For instance, the function might return the following string:

```
BODY BGCOLOR="#FFFFCC" LINK="#FF00CC" ALINK="#00FF99" VLINK="#006633"
            TEXT="#0000FF"
```

Notice that we do not include the less than (<) and greater than (>) characters in the final string.

update()

```
// update main window
function update()
{
   var bodyDef = bodyDefinition()
   var result = ""
   result += '<HTML><HEAD><TITLE>Main</TITLE></HEAD>'
   result += '<' + bodyDef + '>'
   result += '<CENTER>'
   result += 'Text <B>Text</B><HR WIDTH=50%>'
   result += '<FONT COLOR="#' + link.r + link.g + link.b + '">
              Link <B>Link</B><HR WIDTH=50%></FONT>'
   result += '<FONT COLOR="#' + alink.r + alink.g + alink.b + '">
              Alink <B>Alink</B><HR WIDTH=50%></FONT>'
   result += '<FONT COLOR="#' + vlink.r + vlink.g + vlink.b + '">
              Vlink <B>Vlink</B><HR WIDTH=50%></FONT>'
   result += '<BR><FONT SIZE=2>&lt;' + bodyDef + '&gt;</FONT>'
   result += '</CENTER></BODY></HTML>'
   // assign document object of main frame to local variable
   var doc = frames[2].document
   // close data stream to document
   doc.close()
   // open new data stream to document (text/html)
   doc.open('text/html')
   // print HTML content
   doc.write(result)
   // close data stream to document
   doc.close()
}
```

The update() function generates the HTML content of the main frame (the right one). The first portion of the function simply assigns the new HTML document to the local variable result. We then assign the document object of that frame window to the local variable doc. In order to replace the old HTML content with the newly generated content, we close the current data stream to the right frame document and reopen a new one to it. Since there is no apparent reason for the current data stream to be open, its closing is optional, and is done here just to be on the safe side. Forgetting to reopen the data stream, though, will crash the browser under certain situations. Since we are printing ASCII text with HTML formatting, we specify the MIME type as text/html, which is also the default MIME value. After printing the entire HTML content to the frame's document via the write() method, we close the data stream. Note that it is very important to open a stream before printing to a document, and to close the stream afterward. The close() method displays text or images that were previously sent to layout.

save()

```
// stores all selections as a cookie
function save()
{
   var slot = link.r + link.g + link.b +
              alink.r + alink.g + alink.b +
              vlink.r + vlink.g + vlink.b +
              text.r + text.g + text.b +
              bgcolor.r + bgcolor.g + bgcolor.b
   var now = new Date()
   fixDate(now)
   now.setTime(now.getTime() + 31 * 22 * 60 * 60 * 1000) // one month
   setCookie("slot", slot, now)
}
```

This function combines the descriptors of all attributes into one string and stores it as a cookie, set to expire one month later. Since the load() function relies on the order in which the descriptors are concatenated, the order cannot be altered.

load()

```
// load values from cookie (concatenation order in save() matters!)
function load()
{
   var slot = getCookie("slot")
   if (slot != null)
   {
      link.r = slot.substring(0, 2)
      link.g = slot.substring(2, 4)
      link.b = slot.substring(4, 6)
      alink.r = slot.substring(6, 8)
      alink.g = slot.substring(8, 10)
      alink.b = slot.substring(10, 12)
```

```
      vlink.r = slot.substring(12, 14)
      vlink.g = slot.substring(14, 16)
      vlink.b = slot.substring(16, 18)
      text.r = slot.substring(18, 20)
      text.g = slot.substring(20, 22)
      text.b = slot.substring(22, 24)
      bgcolor.r = slot.substring(24, 26)
      bgcolor.g = slot.substring(26, 28)
      bgcolor.b = slot.substring(28, 30)
      eval(curAttribute()).display()
      update()
   }
}
```

The load() function retrieves the descriptors for each attribute stored in the cookie. If the cookie does not exist, the function is terminated. Otherwise, the function extracts each descriptor from the string and assigns it to the corresponding property. The function then displays the new values in the upper frame and updates the main frame accordingly.

HTML

```
<FRAMESET
   ROWS="50, *"
   BORDER="0"
   FRAMEBORDER="no"
   FRAMESPACING="0"
   BORDERCOLOR="#ffffff">
   <FRAME
      NAME="control"
      SRC="ex22-3.htm"
      NORESIZE
      SCROLLING="no">
   <FRAMESET
      COLS="80, *"
      BORDER="0"
      FRAMEBORDER="no"
      FRAMESPACING="0"
      BORDERCOLOR="#ffffff">
      <FRAME
         NAME="swatches"
         SRC="ex22-4.htm"
         NORESIZE
         SCROLLING="no">
      <FRAME
         NAME="main"
         SRC="ex22-5.htm"
         NORESIZE>
   </FRAMESET>
</FRAMESET>
<NOFRAMES>Please download a frames-capable browser!</NOFRAMES>
```

As you can see, all frames are defined in one frame-setting document. The upper frame is named `"control"`, the bottom left frame is named `"swatches"`, and the bottom right frame is named `"main"`. Their URLs are ex22-3.htm, ex22-4.htm, and ex22-5.htm, respectively. Notice the configurations used to create "borderless" frames.

The "control" Frame

Example 22-3 shows that the upper frame consists of very little JavaScript. The only JavaScript in this document is used to interact with the JavaScript objects in the frame-setting window (`self.top` or `self.parent`).

```
<HTML>
<HEAD>
<TITLE>Control Panel</TITLE>
<SCRIPT LANGUAGE="JavaScript">
<!--
function display()
{
   top[top.curAttribute()].display()
}
// -->
</SCRIPT>
</HEAD>
<BODY BGCOLOR="#ffffff" onLoad="self.display()">
<FORM>
<FONT SIZE=2>
<FONT COLOR="#ff0000">R</FONT>:
<INPUT TYPE="text" SIZE=3 VALUE="" NAME="red" onFocus="this.blur()">
<FONT COLOR="#00ff00">G</FONT>:
<INPUT TYPE="text" SIZE=3 VALUE="" NAME="green" onFocus="this.blur()">
<FONT COLOR="#0000ff">B</FONT>:
<INPUT TYPE="text" SIZE=3 VALUE="" NAME="blue" onFocus="this.blur()">
Attribute:
<SELECT NAME="attribute" onChange="self.display()">
<OPTION VALUE="bgcolor">Background
<OPTION VALUE="text">Text
<OPTION VALUE="link">Link
<OPTION VALUE="alink">Active link
<OPTION VALUE="vlink">Visited link
</SELECT>
Save settings:
<INPUT TYPE="button" VALUE="save" onClick="top.save()">
Load settings:<INPUT TYPE="button" VALUE="load" onClick="top.load()">
</FONT>
</FORM>
</BODY>
</HTML>
```

Example 22-3 (ex22-3.htm). *The "control" frame*

display()

```
function display()
{
   top[top.curAttribute()].display()
}
```

The script in the "control" frame's document consists of just one function, display(). There is a function named display() in the frame-setting document as well, but due to JavaScript's object hierarchy, each function is actually a method of a different object. The display() function in the "control" frame document invokes the display() function of the frame-setting document as a method of the selected attribute's instance. For example, if the selected attribute is "Background," the function's statement is equivalent to:

```
top.bgcolor.display()
```

Event Handlers

The "control" frame's document features an onLoad event handler that invokes the local display() function. This is why the text fields in the upper frame are not empty when you first load the Color Center application. When the user selects a new option, the onChange event handler, associated with the select object, invokes the local display() function.

Notice that the text fields in this frame are read-only, thanks to the onFocus event handler which, whenever the user attempts to gain focus, immediately issues the blur() method to remove focus from the field.

The "swatches" Frame

```
<HTML>
<HEAD>
<TITLE>Swatches</TITLE>
</HEAD>
<BODY BGCOLOR="#ffffff">
<SCRIPT LANGUAGE="JavaScript">
<!--
// create 6-element array
var hex = new Array(6)
// assign non-dithered descriptors
hex[0] = "FF"
hex[1] = "CC"
hex[2] = "99"
hex[3] = "66"
hex[4] = "33"
hex[5] = "00"
// accept triplet string and display as background color
function display(triplet)
{
   // set color as background color
   self.document.bgColor = '#' + triplet
```

```
   // display the color hexadecimal triplet
   self.alert('Background color is now ' + triplet)
}
// draw a single table cell based on all descriptors
function drawCell(red, green, blue)
{
   // open cell with specified hexadecimal triplet background color
   self.document.write('<TD BGCOLOR="#' + red + green + blue + '">')
   // open a hypertext link with javascript: scheme to call display function
   self.document.write('<A HREF="javascript:top.select(\'' + (red + '\',
            \'' + green + '\', \'' + blue) + '\')">')
   // print transparent image (use any height and width)
   self.document.write('<IMG SRC="place.gif" BORDER=0 HEIGHT=7 WIDTH=7>')
   // close link tag
   self.document.write('</A>')
   // close table cell
   self.document.write('</TD>')
}
// draw table row based on red and blue descriptors
function drawRow(red, blue)
{
   // open table row
   self.document.write('<TR>')
   // loop through all non-dithered color descripters as green hex
   for (var i = 0; i < 6; ++i)
   {
      drawCell(red, hex[i], blue)
   }
   // close current table row
   self.document.write('</TR>')
}
// draw table for one of six color cube panels
function drawTable(blue)
{
   // open table (one of six cube panels)
   self.document.write('<TABLE CELLPADDING=0 CELLSPACING=0 BORDER=0>')
   // loop through all non-dithered color descripters as red hex
   for (var i = 0; i < 6; ++i)
   {
      drawRow(hex[i], blue)
   }
   // close current table
   self.document.write('</TABLE>')
}
// draw all cube panels inside table cells
function drawCube()
{
   // open table
   self.document.write('<TABLE CELLPADDING=0 CELLSPACING=5 BORDER=0>')
   // loop through all non-dithered color descripters as blue hex
   for (var i = 0; i < 6; ++i)
   {
      // open table cell with white background color
```

```
        self.document.write('<TR><TD>')
        // call function to create cube panel with hex[i] blue hex
        drawTable(hex[i])
        // close current table cell
        self.document.write('</TD></TR>')
    }
    // close table row and table
    self.document.write('</TABLE>')
}
// call function to begin execution
drawCube()
// -->
</SCRIPT>
</BODY>
</HTML>
```

Example 22-4 (ex22-4.htm). *The "swatches" frame*

The "main" Frame

Here is the complete source for the "`main`" frame:

```
<HTML>
<HEAD>
<TITLE>Main</TITLE>
</HEAD>
<BODY onLoad="top.update()">
</BODY>
</HTML>
```

Example 22-5 (ex22-5.htm). *The "main" frame*

Notice the `onLoad` event handler, which invokes the `update()` function of the frame-setting document's script.

Frames, Events, and Event Handlers

Using Event Handlers in a Frame

A child frame normally contains an HTML document. As opposed to a frame-setting document, an HTML document in a child frame is structured as a standard HTML document:

```
<HTML>
<HEAD>
<TITLE></TITLE>
</HEAD>
<BODY>
</BODY>
</HTML>
```

You can load any document in a frame, regardless of its content. If a frame does not contain another frame-setting document, you can use any event handler in its document. You can issue, for example, an `onLoad` event handler in the <BODY> tag, an `onSubmit` event handler in a <FORM> tag, and so forth.

HTML documents that users see in frames of a multiple-frame browser window are different from the frame-setting document, in that the latter remains in memory and is not otherwise visible to the user. It only instructs the browser to divide the window into sections, and assigns a visible document to each one of them. Since a child frame's document is visible, it can consist of forms, links, image maps, images, etc., which are rich in events and event handlers. As a document in a frame behaves exactly like a document in a single-frame browser window, the common event handler rules apply.

Using Event Handlers in a Frame-Setting Document

A frame-setting document differs from a regular HTML document in that it is not visible, and therefore does not include any output-generating HTML tags. Nevertheless, a frame-setting document can feature several event handlers that are very important for a frameset.

All event handlers that you normally issue within a <BODY> tag can be issued within a <FRAMESET> tag. An `onLoad` event handler within a <FRAMESET> tag, for example, specifies a JavaScript code to be executed when all frames defined in that frameset have finished loading. Therefore, the `onLoad` event handler in the <BODY> tag of a child frame triggers before the `onLoad` event handler in the <FRAMESET> tag. When all frames under its control have finished loading, the frameset that governs the frames receives a separate load event.

onFocus and onBlur

Netscape Navigator 3.0 introduced a new functionality to the `onFocus` and `onBlur` event handlers. You can use these event handlers to capture focus and blur events that are associated with a frame. A frame gains focus when the user clicks anywhere in that frame or issues a focus event in an element of that frame. A frame's blur event occurs when the frame loses focus.

There are two equivalent ways to specify an `onFocus` or an `onBlur` event handler for a single frame:

- In the <BODY> tag of the frame's document.
- In the <FRAMESET> tag of the frame-setting document. You can execute, for example, the statement `frames[0].onfocus = display` from a script within the frame-setting document. An event handler specified using this technique overrides an event handler issued in the child frame's <BODY> tag.

Never use an `alert()` method or any other dialog box within a frame's `onFocus` event handler. Doing so results in an endless loop: When you press OK to dismiss the alert, the underlying window gains focus again, and produces another focus event.

The following <BODY> definition of a frame's document demonstrates a common usage of the onBlur and onFocus event handlers:

```
<BODY BGCOLOR="lightgray" onBlur="document.bgColor='lightgray'"
              onFocus="document.bgColor='antiquewhite'">
```

The frame's background color depends on whether or not the frame has focus.

Emulating Events

As with many other events, you can emulate the blur and focus events via their corresponding methods. You can use, for instance, the following statement to focus on the first frame from the point of view of another frame:

```
self.parent.frames[0].focus()
```

The same applies to the blur() method:

```
self.parent.frames[0].blur()
```

Since it is barely noticeable when a frame gains or loses focus, these methods are not that useful.

Targeting Multiple Frames

Creating a link in one frame to load a document in a different frame requires a simple HTML attribute—TARGET. Consider the following frameset:

```
<FRAMESET ROWS="150, *">
   <FRAME NAME="one" SRC="docA.htm">
   <FRAMESET COLS="120, *">
      <FRAME NAME="two" SRC="docB.htm">
      <FRAME NAME="three" SRC="docC.htm">
   </FRAMESET>
</FRAMESET>
```

A link in docA.htm that loads Netscape's home page in the right frame ("three") would use the following syntax:

```
<A HREF="http://www.netscape.com/" TARGET="three">Netscape</A>
```

Now suppose you want a single link in docA.htm to load both Netscape's page in the frame named "three" and Microsoft's page in the frame named "two". JavaScript's object hierarchy enables such operations:

```
<SCRIPT LANGUAGE="JavaScript">
<!--
function loadPages()
{
   parent.two.location.href = 'http://www.microsoft.com/'
   parent.three.location.href = 'http://www.netscape.com/'
}
```

```
// -->
</SCRIPT>
<A HREF="javascript:loadPages()">Microsoft and Netscape</A>
```

Summary

While some prefer to avoid frames completely, they are widely used by others. And there is absolutely no logical reason not to use them. Frames are widely used because they enable web site designers to organize data in a pleasant, structured format. Frames are very easy to handle with JavaScript. An understanding of the JavaScript object model is required in order to take advantage of the language's powerful frame-handling features. Some frame operations can be accomplished only by JavaScript. The only way, for example, to load several documents in different frames when the user clicks a link is by scripting the link's event handler via JavaScript. Referencing objects in JavaScript can be done with `self`, `window`, or no prefix at all. Mastering frames requires practice. After creating a few JavaScript applications with frames, you will have the knowledge to do virtually anything with frames.

Chapter 23
Evaluation and Compilation

JavaScript is replete with functions that allow you to evaluate various items. The basic idea is that these built-in functions will allow you to extract data about something, such as a string. This is a somewhat advanced topic and many JavaScript developers work for years without ever having to use these functions. So if you have trouble with the functions in this chapter, don't worry—just do the best you can with them. In time as you encounter places to use them, their use will become more clear.

Evaluating a String

The `eval` function executes the JavaScript contained within the brackets. In some cases, this may return a value that can be assigned to a variable. It is used to evaluate whatever is passed to it and then to run it. The `eval()` function is the easiest way to evaluate a string expression. There are, however, several other ways:

```
var abc = "def"
document.write(abc)                // 1
document.write("<BR>")
document.write(eval("abc"))        // 2
document.write("<BR>")
document.write(window.abc)         // 3
document.write("<BR>")
document.write(window["abc"])      // 4
document.write("<BR>")
document.write(window.eval("abc")) // 5
```

In the preceding script segment, all five lines (1, 2, 3, 4, 5) print the same output: `def` (except for the fifth one in versions of Internet Explorer prior to 5.0).

- **Line 1** The `document.write()` method automatically evaluates its argument, whether it is stored in a variable or handed to the function in the form of a literal. In this particular case, I hand the function a data structure (a variable), which evaluates to `def`. This method always evaluates the argument, so you must surround a string literal with quotes (of any type).

- **Line 2** The `eval()` function evaluates its argument and returns it as is. Unlike the `document.write()` function, `eval()` does not do anything with the value except return it. In this case, the function returns `abc` (not `"abc"`), and `document.write(eval("abc"))` is then equivalent to `document.write(abc)`, which outputs `def`, as explained above.
- **Line 3** Since all variables in a document are actual properties of the `window` object, the variable `abc` can be specified with a complete object reference, as shown on this line.
- **Line 4** You can use the array notation instead of the dot syntax (`window["abc"]` is equivalent to `window.abc`). Since the square brackets evaluate their content, you should place a quoted string inside.
- **Line 5** Based on the preceding discussion, `window.eval("abc")` is equivalent to `window.abc`.

Here is another set of slightly more complicated statements:

```
var abc = "def"
var def = "abc"
document.write(eval('eval("abc")'))          // 1
document.write("<BR>")
document.write(eval(eval("abc")))            // 2
document.write("<BR>")
document.write(eval('window.eval("def")')) // 3
document.write("<BR>")
document.write(eval(window.eval("def")))    // 4
document.write("<BR>")
document.write(window[eval("def")])          // 5
document.write("<BR>")
document.write(eval(window[eval("def")]))  // 6
```

These statements output different strings, as explained below.

- **Line 1** `eval('eval("abc")')` evaluates to `eval("abc")` because the top-level `eval()` removes the quotes. The expression `eval("abc")` evaluates to `abc`, so the output of this statement is `"def"`.
- **Line 2** `eval("abc")` is evaluated first, because the innermost function call is always evaluated before any other function call in the same expression. (In the previous statement, as the "inner" function call is actually a string, there is only one function call besides the `document.write()` statement.) Therefore, `eval("abc")` evaluates to `abc`, and `eval(eval("abc"))` evaluates to `eval("def")`, which, in turn, evaluates to `def`. The statement's output is then `"def"`.
- **Line 3** You should have guessed that the output of this statement differs from browser to browser (Internet Explorer and Mozilla). On both browsers, `eval('window.eval("def")')` evaluates to `window.eval("def")`. This statement evaluates to `"def"` on Internet

Explorer, and "abc" on Netscape Navigator. (See the explanation for the last statement in the previous script segment.)

- **Line 4** I already know that `window.eval("def")` evaluates to "def" on Internet Explorer, and "abc" on Netscape Navigator. Therefore, `eval(window.eval("def"))` evaluates to the exact opposite: "abc" on Internet Explorer, and "def" on Netscape Navigator.
- **Line 5** `eval("def")` evaluates to `def`, so `window[eval("def")]` evaluates to `window[def]`, which evaluates to `window["abc"]`. Therefore, this statement prints "def".
- **Line 6** `eval(window[eval("def")])` is actually the value handed to the `document.write()` method in the previous statement, evaluated by another `eval()` function call. Therefore, it evaluates to `eval("def")`, which evaluates to `def`, so this statement prints "abc".

Function References and Calls

Take a look at the following function definition:

```
function multiply(op1, op2)
{
   var result = op1 * op2
   return result
}
```

A *function call* is an expression that invokes a function. The following statement, for example, consists of a function call:

```
var num = multiply(5, 8)
```

Function calls are very convenient because you can specify arguments for the function and accept the returned value. JavaScript, however, does not always permit function calls. You cannot, for example, use a function call as a constructor function's method. Instead, you should use a function reference:

```
function makeOperator()
{
   this.multiply = multiply // not multiply()
}
```

All functions in JavaScript are objects, so a function reference is actually an object reference. Suppose you want to use a function in one window as a method in a constructor function located in a different window. You should specify the full function reference, using the following format:

```
this.methodName = windowReference.functionName
```

A function reference, as opposed to a function call, is not a command—the JavaScript interpreter cannot execute it. You should treat a function like any other object in JavaScript: Assign it to a variable, hand it to a function, and so forth. Here's an example:

```
function myAlert(msg)
{
   alert("*** " + msg + " ***")
}
function test(func)
{
   func("Hello!")
}
test(myAlert)
```

In this script segment I invoke the `test()` function with the function `myAlert` (a reference) as an argument. I then refer to the function `myAlert` as `func`, because the parameter is named `func`. Since `func` is equivalent to `myAlert`, I can call it in the same fashion I would call the `myAlert()` function.

Compiling Code as a Function

The `function` object specifies a string of JavaScript code to be compiled as a function. The general syntax is:

```
var functionTarget = new Function ([arg1, arg2, ..., argn], functionBody)
```

`functionTarget` is the name of a variable or a property of an existing object. It can also be a browser object followed by an event handler such as `window.onerror`.

`arg1, arg2, ..., argn` are string arguments to be used by the function as formal parameter names.

`functionBody` is a string specifying the JavaScript code to be compiled as the function body.

The `function` object is supported in early versions of Netscape and Internet Explorer. An instance of the `function` object is evaluated each time it is used. This is much less efficient than declaring a function and invoking it within your code, because declared functions are compiled. Declared functions are evaluated as the page loads, and are stored in memory as machine code. Instances of the `function` object are stored in memory as objects (consisting of strings), and are converted to machine code for each execution.

Specifying the Function's Body

The function body, *`functionBody`*, is a string consisting of JavaScript statements. You could use, for example, the following string:

```
"document.bgColor='antiquewhite'"
```

Things become more complicated when you want to create an instance with a body of several statements. The string should then include all statements separated by semicolons. Although you will rarely use this feature, I show you how to write the function according to your personal preferences and have a distinct script convert it to valid, one-line JavaScript code.

Take a look at the following function:

```
function getCookie(name)
{
   var prefix = name + "="
   var cookieStartIndex = document.cookie.indexOf(prefix)
   if (cookieStartIndex == -1)
      return null
   var cookieEndIndex = document.cookie.indexOf(";", cookieStartIndex +
                        prefix.length)
   if (cookieEndIndex == -1)
      cookieEndIndex = document.cookie.length
   return unescape(document.cookie.substring(cookieStartIndex + prefix.length,
                   cookieEndIndex))
}
```

Example 23-1 prints the body of this function on one line, including semicolons where needed.

```
<HTML>
<HEAD>
<TITLE>Function body string</TITLE>
</HEAD>
<BODY>
<SCRIPT LANGUAGE="JavaScript">
<!--
function getCookie(name)
{
   var prefix = name + "="
   var cookieStartIndex = document.cookie.indexOf(prefix)
   if (cookieStartIndex == -1)
      return null
   var cookieEndIndex = document.cookie.indexOf(";", cookieStartIndex +
                        prefix.length)
   if (cookieEndIndex == -1)
      cookieEndIndex = document.cookie.length
   return unescape(document.cookie.substring(cookieStartIndex + prefix.length,
                   cookieEndIndex))
}
// print function body
document.write(getCookie)
// -->
</SCRIPT>
</BODY>
</HTML>
```

Example 23-1 (ex23-1.htm). *You can print a function reference to see its one-line equivalent.*

Using the function Object with a Variable

The following statement assigns a function to a variable:

```
var setBGColorBeige = new Function("document.bgColor = 'beige'")
```

Since it serves as a function, it is a good practice to include a verb form in the variable's name. You can call the variable as if it were a regular function:

```
setBGColorBeige()
```

Assigning a function to a variable is similar to declaring a function, with some differences, as expressed in Table 23-1.

Table 23-1. *The differences between declaring a function and assigning a function to a variable*

Assigning a function to a variable *functionName* = new Function("...")	**Declaring a function** function *functionName*() {...}
`functionName` is a variable for which the current value is a reference to the function created with `new Function()`.	`functionName` is the name of a function, not a variable.
The function's body is evaluated each time you call the function.	The function's body is evaluated only once—when the browser parses the script.
The function's parameters and body are specified as strings.	The function's parameters and body are plain code, not an explicit data type.

Specifying Arguments

As you already know, you can create an instance of the `function` object that takes arguments. Take a look at the following statement:

```
var multiply = new Function("x", "y", "return x * y")
```

The last argument handed to the `Function()` constructor is the function's body (in the form of a string). Preceding string arguments are formal parameter names that are used in the function's body. Although they do not act as strings in the function, the arguments must be specified as strings. If you do not specify them as string literals, JavaScript attempts to evaluate them. If you use the following statement, for example, JavaScript will look for two variables named `x` and `y`:

```
var multiply = new Function(x, y, "return x * y")
```

You can invoke a function reference created with the `Function()` constructor as if it were a declared function.

Using the function Object with an Event Handler

You have already seen how to assign a function reference to an event handler. Here is a simple example:

```
<SCRIPT LANGUAGE="JavaScript">
<!--
function bye()
{
   alert("Bye!")
}
window.onunload = bye
// -->
</SCRIPT>
```

I assign the window's `onunload` event handler a function reference, not a function call. Note that you cannot use arguments with an event handler. When you want to assign a statement to an event handler with this technique, you must use a function reference even if you want to specify only a single statement as demonstrated in the preceding script. It may seem very annoying to create a function for each event handler. Therefore, you can assign a function reference to an event handler via the `Function()` constructor. The preceding script would then be much more simple and organized:

```
<SCRIPT LANGUAGE="JavaScript">
<!--
window.onunload = new Function('alert("Bye!")')
// -->
</SCRIPT>
```

When the user unloads a document containing such a script, an alert dialog box pops up. When you assign a function reference to an event handler in this fashion, the event handler becomes a reference to a `function` object. When you use it as a function, the event handler method will be converted from an object to a function:

```
window.onunload()
```

Properties of the function Object

Instances of the `function` object do not feature any properties. But, like all other dynamic objects in JavaScript, you can use its `prototype` property to extend the object by adding properties to it. Here is an interesting example:

```
function execute(x, y)
{
   var now = new Date()
   if (now.getDay() == 5 && now.getDate() == 13) // Friday 13
      alert("This function does not execute on Friday the 13th")
   else
      this(x, y)
}
```

```
Function.prototype.exec = execute
var add = new Function("x", "y", "alert(x + y)")
add.exec(3, 4)
```

I use a function reference, execute, as a property (method) of Function.prototype, so the function execute() becomes a method of all instances of the function object. Note that I could have used Function() directly, instead of declaring a function and assigning its reference. Now, let's take a look at the execute() function. It first creates an instance of the Date object reflecting the current time and date. I check if the current date happens to be Friday the 13th, and if so, a corresponding message is displayed via the window.alert() method. If it is not Friday the 13th, the statement this(x, y) executes. I'll refer to our specific instance, add, in order to make this clear. When I assign an instance of the function object to the variable add, it becomes an object. You can invoke that object as a function:


```
add(3, 4)
```

You can also invoke its method, exec(), in the following fashion:

```
add.exec(3, 4)
```

When you call exec() as a method of the add object, its calling object is obviously add. Therefore, the keyword this refers to add, and this(x, y) is equivalent to add(x, y).

Summary

In this chapter, I dealt mostly with the eval function and function references. Bear in mind that all functions are objects, and parentheses are used only to invoke a function. As you will find out with practice, there are many things you can do with functions besides calling them.

Chapter 24
JavaScript Authoring Tools

Introduction

Frankly, I am an old-school programmer and do my HTML, JavaScript, Java, and even C in a simple text editor. However, this is not for everyone. Many people prefer an authoring tool to help smooth out the development process. Several authoring tools have shown up recently. These tools aim at helping you ramp up faster on HTML and JavaScript. Let's look at a couple of JavaScript authoring tools that are widely available today.

ScrypTik

This editor, which can be downloaded at http://www.scryptik.com/, is very easy to use. The main screen is shown in Figure 24-1. It has a simple interface with a work area that looks and behaves much like any basic text editor.

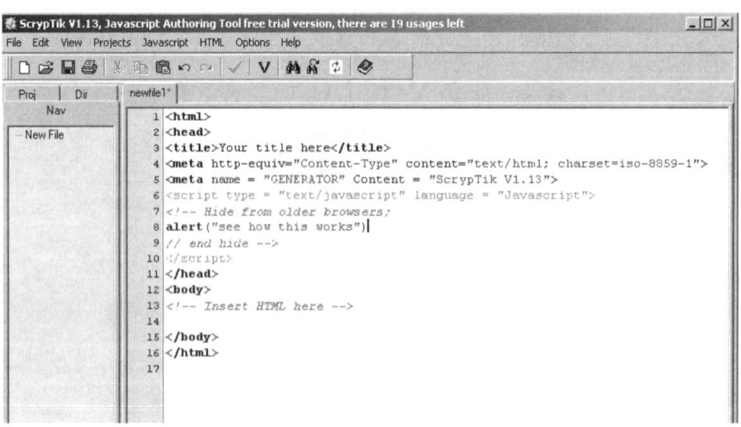

Figure 24-1. *ScrypTik user interface*

The toolbar, shown in Figure 24-2, is easy to work with and most of the tools are self-explanatory, but we will discuss a few of the less familiar here. Once you have typed in your HTML and JavaScript, simply click on the check mark button in the toolbar and ScrypTik will check your JavaScript code and give you the line numbers of any errors along with descriptive error messages. The V button you see on the toolbar allows you to view the output of your script in a web browser.

Figure 24-2. *ScrypTik toolbar*

In addition to the toolbar, the drop-down menus allow you to select a variety of settings. Particularly important is the Options menu, which allows you to set colors and properties of the visual interface. The Options window also allows you to choose the Errors and Warnings tab from which you can set the way the editor will handle errors. This screen is shown in Figure 24-3.

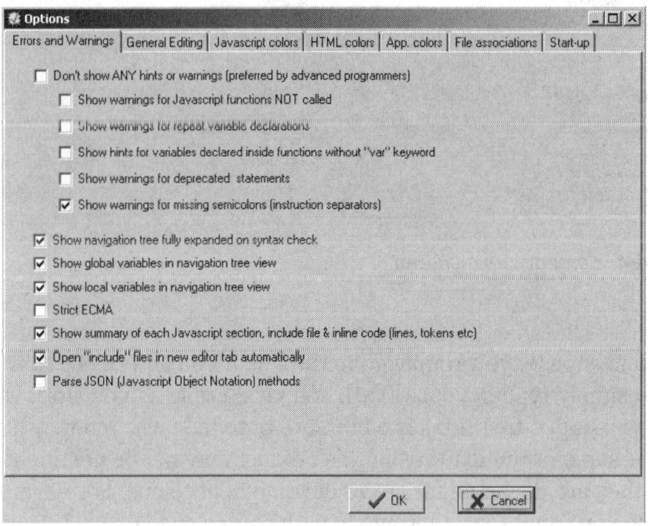

Figure 24-3. *Errors and Warnings settings*

ScrypTik is very easy to use and working with it for just a short time will allow you to be completely competent in its use. Tools like ScrypTik can be very useful in reducing debugging time.

Komodo

This product, available from ActiveState (www.activestate.com), is also available as a free trial download version. The opening page of Komodo, shown in Figure 24-4, has a number of useful links to things like an FAQ page and various helpful Komodo information links.

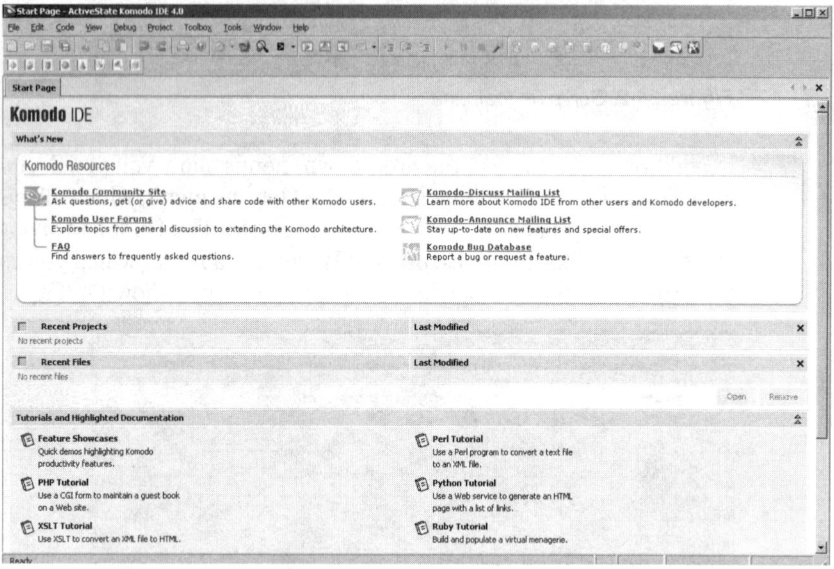

***Figure 24-4**. Komodo main screen*

To start a new page, you simply go to the File menu and select New. At that point you simply type in your HTML and JavaScript. As you work with this tool you will notice that it takes a bit more time to learn. You may also discover that some of the features in this product may not be pertinent to you because they are designed for larger development teams. For example, under File you can integrate Komodo with source code control tools. This tool is probably not the tool of choice for the beginner, but might be a solution for teams that are looking for a JavaScript editing solution.

1st JavaScript Editor Pro

You can get this product at http://www.yaldex.com/JSFactory_Pro.htm. The opening screen is shown in Figure 24-5. As you can see, this editor, like most editors, starts you off with a shell HTML/JavaScript page. It also displays line numbers to the left, which can be invaluable in debugging large scripts.

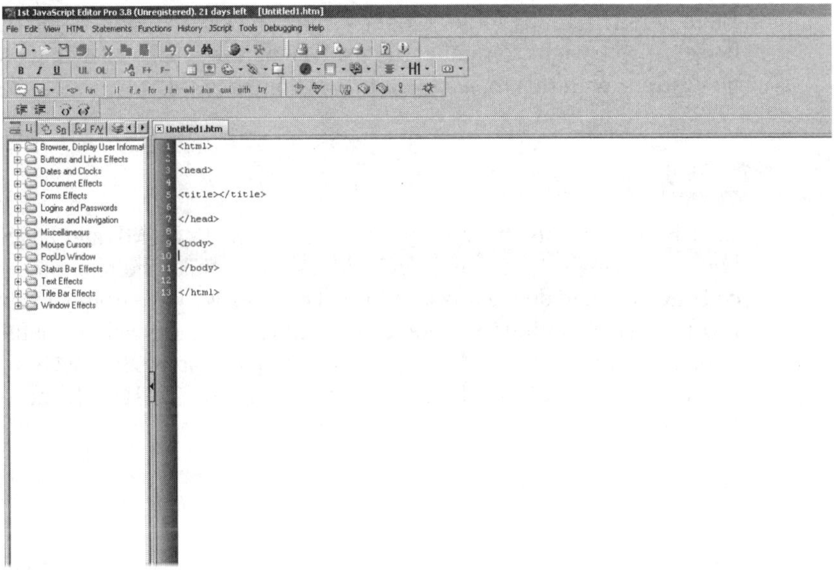

Figure 24-5. *1st JavaScript Editor Pro*

Perhaps the most important feature of this tool is that as you type it gives you tips. So if you forget a particular keyword or the specific syntax for a given function, it is shown to you (see Figure 24-6).

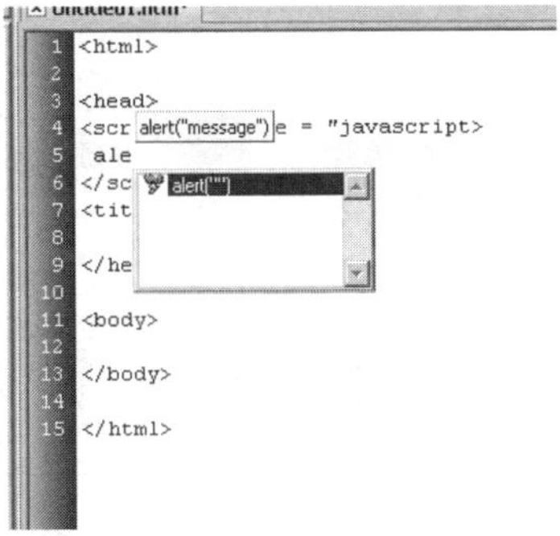

Figure 24-6. *Assistance for JavaScript is displayed as you type*

Even more helpful are the menus at the top. If you select the Functions menu you get a drop-down list of common functions such as `focus`, `alert`, and `document.write` that you can simply insert into your script. The Statements menu gives you similar functionality with statements (e.g., `if-end if`, etc.). The HTML menu does the same thing for HTML tags (bold, italics, etc.).

Because of these helpful tools for inserting HTML and JavaScript directly into your code, I feel that this is one of the best tools for the novice. Beginners frequently forget proper syntax and spend time looking through books or web pages to remind themselves of how a particular thing should be written. With this tool, a lot of that is done for you.

Summary

Clearly, one can simply use any text editor to write HTML and JavaScript; however, many programmers find editors are useful in helping them write code quicker and debug it faster. In this chapter we have briefly examined a few JavaScript editing tools you can download from the web. Hopefully, one of these will meet your editing needs. A simple search of the web will reveal many more products like these that you can use to edit HTML and JavaScript.

Chapter 25
Plug-ins

Plug-ins are very common parts of web pages. For example, you have probably seen Flash animations inserted into HTML pages. There are a variety of things that can be plugged into HTML. In this chapter we will discuss some of the more common plug-ins and methods of incorporating plug-in objects.

Embedding a Plug-in Object in HTML

A *plug-in* is a piece of software that the browser calls to process data referenced in an HTML document. In order to reference such data in an HTML tag, you must use the <EMBED> tag. This tag's general syntax is as follows:

```
<EMBED
   SRC=source
   NAME=appletName
   HEIGHT=height
   WIDTH=width>
   [<PARAM NAME=parameterName VALUE=parameterValue>]
   [...</PARAM>]
</EMBED>
```

SRC=*source* specifies the URL containing the source content to be interpreted by the plug-in.

NAME=*appletName* specifies the name of the embedded object in the document.

HEIGHT=*height* specifies the height of the applet in pixels within the browser window.

WIDTH=*width* specifies the width of the applet in pixels within the browser window.

<PARAM> defines a parameter for the embedded object.

NAME=*parameterName* specifies the name of the parameter.

VALUE=*parameterValue* specifies a value for the parameter (an argument).

We will refer to such <EMBED> definitions as plug-ins, although that is not entirely correct.

Referencing Plug-ins in JavaScript

You can reference the plug-ins in your code by using the `embeds` array, a property of the `document` object. This array contains an entry for each `plugin` object (<EMBED> tag) in a document, in source order. That is, the first `plugin` object in the document is reflected by the first element of the array, for example, `document.embeds[0]`. The `length` property of this array, `document.embeds.length`, holds the number of `plugin` objects in the document. Elements in the `embeds` array are read-only, so a statement such as the following has no effect:

```
document.embeds[0]="myVideo.avi"
```

It is important to understand that each element of the `embeds` array is a `plugin` object. As you will see later in this chapter, referencing a `plugin` object is very useful, because some plug-ins feature JavaScript methods.

You can also reference a `plugin` object by its name. Take a look at the following HTML definition:

```
<EMBED SRC="rabin.avi" AUTOSTART=FALSE LOOP=FALSE HEIGHT=120 WIDTH=159
        NAME="rabin">
```

Assuming this is the first plug-in in the HTML document, you can reference it via JavaScript in two ways:

- `document.embeds[0]`
- `document.rabin`

We recommend that you use the second method because it is more convenient. It does not rely on the order in which the plug-ins are defined, so you do not have to modify your scripts if you choose to change the order of the plug-ins in the document. Secondly, you can choose meaningful names for your plug-ins so your code becomes much easier to understand.

Determining Installed Plug-ins with JavaScript

You can use JavaScript to determine if a user has installed a plug-in (the software). You can then display embedded plug-in data if the plug-in is installed, or alternative content if it is not. You can also determine whether a client is capable of handling a particular MIME (Multipart Internet Mail Extension) type. The `navigator` object has two properties for checking installed plug-ins:

- The `mimeTypes` object is an array of all the MIME types supported by the client. A MIME type can be supported either internally, via a helper application, or by plug-ins. Each element of this array is an object that has properties for its type, description, file extensions, and enabled plug-ins. The array is named `mimeTypes`, and each element is a `mimeTypes` object.

- The `plugins` object is an array of all the plug-ins installed on the client. Each element of this array has properties for its name and description as well as an array of `mimeTypes` objects for the MIME types supported by that plug-in. Each element of the `plugins` array is a `plugins` object.

In order to check if a plug-in is supported, you must know that plug-in's name. The general syntax used to check if a specific plug-in is installed is as follows:

```
if (navigator.plugins["name of the plug-in"]) ...
```

The name often consists of space characters or other nonalphanumeric characters, so it is a common practice to use the array notation, even if the dot syntax is possible. The following script segment checks if the Shockwave plug-in is installed, and provides data for that plug-in if it is:

```
if (navigator.plugins["Shockwave"])
   document.writeln("<EMBED SRC='myMovie.dir' HEIGHT=100 WIDTH=100>")
else
   document.writeln("You don't have Shockwave installed!")
```

Once you have installed a plug-in on your computer, it is very easy to find its name.

Some JavaScript programmers prefer to write a simple Boolean function to assist in determining whether a given plug-in is installed. Here is an example:

```
function isInstalled(plugName)
{
   if (navigator.plugins[plugName])
      return true
   else
      return false
}
```

The following script checks whether the client is capable of displaying QuickTime movies.

```
if (navigator.mimeTypes["video/quicktime"])
   document.writeln("Click <A HREF='movie.qt'>here</A> to see a QuickTime
                    movie")
else
   document.writeln("Sorry, can't show you any movies.")
```

You should use such plug-in detection routines with care, because they often conflict with LiveConnect routines located in the same document.

Properties of the mimeTypes Object

A `mimeTypes` object, as found in the `mimeTypes` array (as an element), features the following properties:

- `type`—the name of the MIME type, such as `"video/mpeg"` or `"audio/x-wav"`. This property is obviously a string.

- description—a description of the MIME type, such as "JPEG image."
- enabledPlugin—a reference to the plugins object that handles the MIME type.
- suffixes—a string listing possible filename extensions (suffixes) for the MIME type. This property is a string consisting of any valid suffix, typically three letters long, separated by commas.
- length—the number of elements in the array.

Example 25-1 shows a list of the MIME types supported by the browser, including all three string properties of each mimeTypes object.

```
<HTML>
<HEAD>
<TITLE>Supported MIME types</TITLE>
</HEAD>
<BODY>
<SCRIPT LANGUAGE="JavaScript">
<!--
// notice that you do not have to issue </TH> and </TD> tags!
document.write("<TABLE BORDER=1><TR VALIGN=TOP>" +
        "<TH ALIGN=left><I>i</I>" +
        "<TH ALIGN=left><I>type</I>" +
        "<TH ALIGN=left><I>description</I>" +
        "<TH ALIGN=left><I>suffixes</I></TR>")
for (var i = 0; i < navigator.mimeTypes.length; ++i)
{
  document.writeln("<TR VALIGN=TOP><TD>" +
  i +
  "<TD>" +
  navigator.mimeTypes[i].type +
  "<TD>" +
  navigator.mimeTypes[i].description +
  "<TD>" +
  navigator.mimeTypes[i].suffixes +
  "</TR>")
}
document.writeln("</TABLE>")
// -->
</SCRIPT>
</BODY>
</HTML>
```

Example 25-1 (ex25-1.htm). *We use tables to organize the list of supported MIME types.*

You can see this demonstrated in Figure 25-1.

Try loading Example 25-1 in your browser. You should see a fairly long list of MIME types. Figure 25-1 shows the beginning of the list as it appeared on our computer.

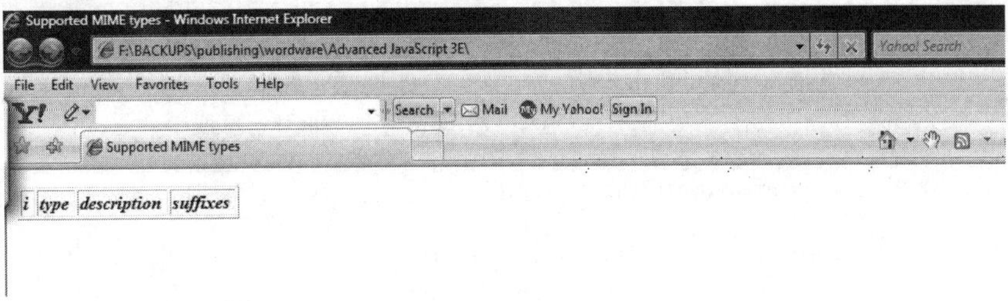

Figure 25-1. The plug-ins list

Notice that in Example 25-1 we referred to elements of the `mimeTypes` array by indices. You can also use the MIME type's name, as shown earlier in this chapter. Here are a few examples:

```
navigator.mimeTypes["image/jpeg"].type
navigator.mimeTypes["image/jpeg"].description
navigator.mimeTypes["image/jpeg"].suffixes
```

Properties of the plugins Object

The `plugins` object features the following properties:

- `name`—the name of the plug-in.
- `filename`—the name of the plug-in file on disk.
- `description`—a description supplied by the plug-in itself.
- `length`—the number of elements in the array.
- `[...]`—array of `mimeTypes` objects, indexed by number or type, that the plug-in can handle.

The following statement, for example, assigns shorthand variables for the predefined Shockwave properties:

```
var myPlugin = navigator.plugins["Shockwave"].name
var myPluginFile = navigator.plugins["Shockwave"].filename
var myPluginDesc = navigator.plugins["Shockwave"].description
```

Example 25-2 lists the installed plug-ins, including each plug-in's name, filename, description, and MIME types that it handles.

```
<HTML>
<HEAD>
<TITLE>Installed plug-ins</TITLE>
</HEAD>
<BODY>
<SCRIPT LANGUAGE="JavaScript">
<!--
// notice that you do not have to issue </TH> and </TD> tags!
document.write("<TABLE BORDER=1>")
for (i = 0; i < navigator.plugins.length; ++i)
{
   document.writeln("<TR><TD><FONT SIZE=2>" +
   "<U><B>" + navigator.plugins[i].name + "</B></U><BR>" +
```

```
    "<U>Filename:</U> " + navigator.plugins[i].filename + "<BR>" +
    "<U>Description:</U> " + navigator.plugins[i].description + "<BR>" +
    "<U>MIME types:</U> ")
    for (var j = 0; j < navigator.plugins[i].length; ++j)
    {
       document.write(navigator.plugins[i][j].type + "; ")
    }
    document.write("</FONT></TD></TR>")
}
document.write("</TABLE>")
// -->
</SCRIPT>
</BODY>
</HTML>
```

***Example 25-2**. I use navigator.plugins to list the installed plug-ins and their properties.*

The following statement assigns the string `"LiveAudio"` to a variable:

```
var audioPlugin = navigator.mimeTypes["audio/basic"].enabledPlugin.name
```

The `name` property belongs to a `plugins` object, because `navigator.mimeTypes["audio/basic"].enabledPlugin` is equivalent to `navigator.plugins["LiveAudio"]`.

LiveAudio and LiveVideo

LiveAudio and LiveVideo are plug-ins that are built into Netscape Navigator 6.0 and above. LiveAudio enables you to embed audio in a web page, whereas LiveVideo supports various video formats. Since both LiveAudio and LiveVideo are plug-ins, you include them in an HTML document via the standard `<EMBED>` tag.

LiveAudio

LiveAudio plays audio files in WAV, AIFF, AU, and MIDI formats. Audio controls appear according to the size specified in the `WIDTH` and `HEIGHT` parameters in the `<EMBED>` tag. You can create an audio console with any of the following controls:

- `console`—consisting of a Play, Pause, Stop, and volume control lever. This is the most complete suite of controls.
- `smallConsole`—consisting of a Play, Stop, and volume control lever. The buttons in this view are somewhat smaller than those in a console.
- `playButton`—a button that starts the sound playing.
- `pauseButton`—a button that pauses (without unloading) the sound while it is playing.
- `stopButton`—a button that ends the playing of sound and unloads it.
- `volumeLever`—a lever that adjusts the volume level for playback of the sound (and adjusts the system's volume level).

Here is the general HTML syntax for a LiveAudio control:

```
<EMBED SRC=[URL] AUTOSTART=[TRUE|FALSE] LOOP=[TRUE|FALSE|INTEGER]
STARTTIME=[MINUTES:SECONDS] ENDTIME=[MINUTES:SECONDS] VOLUME=[0-100]
WIDTH=[#PIXELS] HEIGHT=[#PIXELS] ALIGN=[TOP|BOTTOM|CENTER|BASELINE
|LEFT|RIGHT|TEXTTOP|MIDDLE|ABSMIDDLE|ABSBOTTOM] CONTROLS=[CONSOLE
|SMALLCONSOLE|PLAYBUTTON|PAUSEBUTTON|STOPBUTTON|VOLUMELEVER] HIDDEN=[TRUE]
MASTERSOUND NAME=[UNIQUE NAME TO GROUP CONTROLS TOGETHER SO THAT THEY CONTROL
ONE SOUND]...>
```

The syntax may seem very complicated, but a close look shows that it does not consist of many attributes. It's a bit misleading because there are many different values that can be given to each attribute. Here is a short description of each attribute and the values it accepts:

- SRC=[*URL*]—The URL of the source sound file. It can be either a relative URL or a full URL, including the server's identification.
- AUTOSTART=[TRUE|FALSE]—When set to TRUE, the sound will begin playing automatically upon loading the web page. The default is FALSE.
- LOOP=[TRUE|FALSE|*INTEGER*]—When set to TRUE, the sound will play continuously until the Stop button is clicked on the console or the user goes to another page. If an *INTEGER* value is used, the sound repeats the number of times indicated.
- STARTTIME=[*MINUTES:SECONDS*]—Use STARTTIME to specify where the playback should begin. If you want to begin the sound at 30 seconds, you would set the value to 00:30.
- ENDTIME=[*MINUTES:SECONDS*]—Use ENDTIME to specify where in the sound file you would like playback to end. If you want to stop the sound at 1.5 minutes, you would set the value to 01:30.
- VOLUME=[0-100]—This value must be a number from 0 to 100 to represent 0 to 100 percent. This attribute sets the volume for the sound that is playing or for the entire system if MASTERVOLUME (see NAME attribute below) is used. The default volume level is the current system volume.
- WIDTH=[*#PIXELS*]—Use WIDTH to change the width of the console or console element. For the CONSOLE and SMALLCONSOLE, the default is WIDTH=144. For VOLUMELEVER, the default is WIDTH=74. For a button, the default is WIDTH=37 (WIDTH=34 looks much better). We suggest that you specify this attribute regardless of whether it is the default value.
- HEIGHT=[*#PIXELS*]—Use HEIGHT to change the height of the console. For CONSOLE, the default is HEIGHT=60. For the SMALLCONSOLE, the default is HEIGHT=15. For VOLUMELEVER, the default is HEIGHT=20. For a button, the default is HEIGHT=22. We strongly recommend specifying this attribute even if it is the default.
- ALIGN=[TOP|BOTTOM|CENTER|BASELINE|LEFT|RIGHT|TEXTTOP|MIDDLE|ABSMIDDLE|ABSBOTTOM]—While RIGHT and LEFT specify the position of the console with respect to the page, the other options tell the browser how you want to align text as it flows around the consoles. It acts

similarly to the ALIGN attribute of the <IMG> tag. The default value is BOTTOM.

- CONTROLS=[CONSOLE|SMALLCONSOLE|PLAYBUTTON|PAUSEBUTTON|STOPBUTTON|VOLUMELEVER]—Use this attribute to select the control you want to place on your page. The default for this field is CONSOLE.
- HIDDEN=[TRUE]—The value for this attribute should be TRUE, or it should not be included in the <EMBED> tag. If it is specified as TRUE, no controls will load and the sound will act as a background one.
- MASTERSOUND—This value must be used when grouping sounds together in a NAME group. It takes no value (it must merely be present in the <EMBED> tag), but tells LiveAudio which file is a genuine sound file and allows it to ignore any stub files. In order to associate several <EMBED>s with one sound file, all <EMBED>s should have the same name (see the NAME attribute). The SRC attribute of one of those <EMBED>s should be the URL of the actual sound file, whereas the other SRC attributes should specify the URL of a stub file. A *stub file* is a text file containing a single space (that's the recommended content). Its name should consist of a sound extension (e.g., .mid, .wav, .aif). To create a page with four LiveAudio elements (Play, Pause, Stop, and Volume) all controlling the same file, you need to create three sound stubs and of course have one legitimate sound file (for a total of four <EMBED>s). Anytime you use the NAME attribute in a LiveAudio <EMBED>, you must also use a MASTERSOUND attribute. LiveAudio will play no sound when a NAME attribute exists without a corresponding MASTERSOUND attribute, even if that is the only <EMBED> with that name on the page. Since you do not want LiveAudio to attempt to play a stub file (it contains no sound data), you should specify a NAME attribute with no MASTERSOUND attribute. The <EMBED> reflecting the legitimate sound file, on the other hand, should feature MASTERSOUND in order to play.
- NAME=[*UNIQUE NAME*]—This attribute sets a unique ID for a group of <EMBED>s (each with a distinct CONTROLS attribute), so they all act on the same sound as it plays. The deficiency of <EMBED>'s syntax is that it takes only one value for CONTROLS. For example, if a content creator wishes to have one sound controlled by two embedded objects (a PLAYBUTTON and a STOPBUTTON), he or she must use two separate <EMBED>s and group them by the NAME attribute. In this case, MASTERSOUND is necessary to flag LiveAudio and let it know which of the two <EMBED> tags actually has the sound file you wish to control. LiveAudio ignores any <EMBED>(s) with no MASTERSOUND attribute.

  If you want one VOLUMELEVER to control multiple NAMEs (or the system volume), create an <EMBED> using VOLUMELEVER for CONTROLS. Then set NAME to "_MASTERVOLUME".

Example 25-3 is a nice summary of the LiveAudio features.

```
<HTML>
<HEAD>
<TITLE>LiveAudio</TITLE>
</HEAD>
<BODY>
<TABLE BORDER=1><TR>
<TD BGCOLOR="black" ALIGN="center">
<FONT COLOR="white" SIZE=2>Beverly Hills</FONT><BR>
<EMBED SRC="bh190210.mid"
   AUTOSTART=FALSE
   LOOP=FALSE
   CONTROLS=PLAYBUTTON
   WIDTH=34
   HEIGHT=22
   MASTERSOUND
   NAME="90210">
<EMBED SRC="stub1.aif"
   AUTOSTART=FALSE
   LOOP=FALSE
   CONTROLS=STOPBUTTON
   WIDTH=34
   HEIGHT=22
   NAME="90210">
<EMBED SRC="stub2.aif"
   AUTOSTART=FALSE
   LOOP=FALSE
   CONTROLS=PAUSEBUTTON
   WIDTH=34
   HEIGHT=22
   NAME="90210">
</TD>
<TD BGCOLOR="black" ALIGN="center">
<FONT COLOR="white" SIZE=2>Melrose</FONT><BR>
<EMBED SRC="melrose.mid"
   AUTOSTART=FALSE
   LOOP=FALSE
   CONTROLS=PLAYBUTTON
   WIDTH=34
   HEIGHT=22
   MASTERSOUND
   NAME="melrose">
<EMBED SRC="stub1.aif"
   AUTOSTART=FALSE
   LOOP=FALSE
   CONTROLS=STOPBUTTON
   WIDTH=34
   HEIGHT=22
   NAME="melrose">
<EMBED SRC="stub2.aif"
   AUTOSTART=FALSE
   LOOP=FALSE
   CONTROLS=PAUSEBUTTON
   WIDTH=34
   HEIGHT=22
```

```
   NAME="melrose">
</TD>
</TR><TR>
<TD COLSPAN=2 BGCOLOR="black" ALIGN="center">
<FONT COLOR="white" SIZE=2>Master Volume</FONT><BR>
<EMBED SRC="stub1.aif"
   CONTROLS=VOLUMELEVER
   WIDTH=74
   HEIGHT=20
   NAME="_MASTERVOLUME">
</TD>
</TR></TABLE>
</BODY>
</HTML>
```

Example 25-3 (ex25-3.htm). *Two sound files, with three <EMBED>s for each, and an <EMBED> to control the system volume*

Since each <EMBED> statement can specify one control object, we need three of them to place the PLAYBUTTON, STOPBUTTON, and PAUSEBUTTON. Here's the syntax for the Master Volume control:

```
<EMBED SRC="stub1.aif"
   CONTROLS=VOLUMELEVER
   WIDTH=74
   HEIGHT=20
   NAME="_MASTERVOLUME">
```

Notice that the first character in the object's name is an underscore.

LiveVideo

LiveVideo plays video files in AVI format. Use the <EMBED> tag to place AVI movies in your web page. The general syntax for this tag is as follows:

```
<EMBED SRC=[URL] AUTOSTART=[TRUE|FALSE] LOOP=[TRUE|FALSE] WIDTH=[#PIXELS]
HEIGHT=[#PIXELS] ALIGN=[TOP|BOTTOM|CENTER|BASELINE|LEFT|RIGHT|TEXTTOP|
MIDDLE|ABSMIDDLE|ABSBOTTOM]...>
```

We discussed the attributes in the LiveAudio section.

Once the AVI video loads, you can start it with a click (only if you didn't set AUTOSTART to TRUE). Click the right mouse button over the video panel for a list of operations.

Other Plug-ins

There are currently hundreds of plug-ins besides LiveAudio and LiveVideo. We decided to focus on these for several reasons:

- They come bundled with Netscape Navigator 6.0 and later, so anyone running this browser can view audio and video files without downloading any external software.
- Both LiveAudio and LiveVideo enable LiveConnect, so you can control them with JavaScript (and Java).

Live3D lets you access distributed 3D spaces rendered at maximum speed with adaptive rendering, background processing, hardware acceleration, and GZIP data compression. This plug-in also matches the preceding features, but it is beyond the scope of this book because it requires VRML.

Summary

In this chapter we focused on embedding plug-ins in HTML and referencing them with JavaScript. We also introduced LiveAudio and LiveVideo. Before you move on, be sure you know how to reference plug-ins with JavaScript, both with the `embeds` array and by name.

Chapter 26
Style Sheets

Introduction

In early versions of browsers, web page authors had limited control over the page style. They could not, for example, specify the left margin for their pages. The World Wide Web Consortium (W3C) solved this problem by introducing standards for defining stylistic attributes for web pages. Cascading style sheets are now a common aspect of many web pages.

Using style sheets, you can specify many such attributes, ranging from text color, margins, and element alignments to font styles and sizes.

Netscape Communicator supports two types of style sheets: cascading style sheets (CSS) and JavaScript-accessible style sheets. The W3C has defined a set of properties and syntax for CSS, and its proposal is posted at http://www.w3.org/pub/WWW/TR/PR-CSS1. Each style item is defined by a relevant attribute. The left margin, for example, is set by `margin-left`, and the interword spacing by `word-spacing`.

In this book, the JavaScript-accessible style sheet syntax will be used to manipulate style sheets. For each stylistic property, there is a JavaScript equivalent. Generally, property names are the same for both types, with some minor differences due to JavaScript naming restrictions.

Using JavaScript, you can specify styles for all elements of a particular kind (all paragraphs should be displayed in green, for example) or you can declare classes of styles to which you can assign any element you want. You can define, for instance, a class called `BAR` whose style is green, bold, large text. Any document element (paragraph, block quote, heading) can be a member of the class `BAR`, and it will be displayed in green, bold, large text. You can also specify local styles for individual instances of document elements. You can specify, for example, that the color for a single, particular paragraph is blue.

Content Layout

Using style sheets, you can determine margins for individual elements on a page, or for all elements on a page. The following code, for instance, specifies that all paragraphs will have a right margin of 20 pixels:

```
<STYLE>
tags.P.rightmargin=20;
</STYLE>
```

Font Properties

You can create styles that determine font size and font style (such as bold). The following code, for example, specifies that all block quote elements will appear in bold:

```
<STYLE>
document.blockquote.fontStyle="bold";
</STYLE>
```

Text Properties

The modifiable attributes of text properties include line height, text attribute (such as underlined), horizontal and vertical alignment of text, and text indent (which allows indented and outdented paragraphs). For example:

```
<STYLE>
// the line height for block quotes is increased by 150 percent
tags.blockquote.lineHeight* = 1.5
// level four headings are underlined
tags.H4.textDecoration = "underline"
// bold elements are vertically aligned with the top of their parent
tags.B.verticalAlign = "top"
// level five headings are displayed in uppercase
tags.H5.textTransform = "uppercase"
// the text in all paragraphs is centered
tags.P.align = "center"
// the first line of each paragraph is indented 20 pixels
tag.P.indent = 20
</STYLE>
```


Inheritance of Styles

JavaScript-based style sheets use the notion of parent and child elements. For example, in the following HTML source, the <H1> element is the parent, while the <EM> element is a child of the <H1> element.

```
<H1>The headline <EM>is</EM> important!</H1>
```

In general, child elements acquire or inherit the styles of their parent elements. Look at the following example:

```
<H1 CLASS="boldBlue">The headline <EM>is</EM> important!</H1>
```

The child element (the <EM> element) inherits the style of its parent, so the word "is" will appear emphasized in the boldBlue style. However, if you had previously set up a style that specified that the <EM> element should be displayed in red, then the word "is" would be displayed in red, since properties set on the child override properties inherited from the parent. Inheritance starts at the oldest ancestor, at the top-level element. In HTML, this is the <HTML> element that is followed by <BODY>.

To set default style properties, just define the style before the <BODY> element. For example, the following code sets the default text color to green:

```
<STYLE>document.tags.BODY.color="green";</STYLE>
```

If you want to change the color in a specific place, you can set styles for different kinds of elements, or you can set up classes of styles. Some style properties cannot be inherited from the parent, such as background color.

Creating Style Sheets and Assigning Styles

There are three ways to specify styles using JavaScript-based style sheets: (1) create external style sheets and link them into your document, (2) create style sheets within a document, or (3) specify specific styles for certain elements within a document.

The simplest way to assign styles is to apply them to all elements of a certain type. For example, the following code indicates that all level one headings will be displayed in green:

```
<STYLE>document.tags.H1.color = "green"</STYLE>
```

Setting up classes of styles within a document (boldBlue style, for example) will allow you to apply styles to some elements but not others. Then, whenever you want an element to be displayed in that style, you simply tell the browser what class of style to use. For example:

```
<STYLE TYPE="text/javascript">
   classes.boldBlue.all.color = "blue";
   classes.boldBlue.all.fontlight = "bold";
</STYLE>
<P CLASS="boldBlue">This paragraph appears in bold, blue style</P>
<P>This should be in the normal document color<P>
```

The rest of this section describes the different ways to assign styles.

Defining Styles with the <STYLE> Tag in the Header

You can use the <STYLE> tag within the header of a document to define styles for specified elements used in the document. You can specify, for instance, that all level one headings are blue, all block quotes are red, all paragraphs are emphasized, and so on. For example:

```
<HTML>
   <HEAD>
      <TITLE>A Grand Title</TITLE>
      <STYLE TYPE="text/javascript">
         tags.H1.color = "blue"
      </STYLE>
   </HEAD>
<BODY>
   <H1>This heading is in blue</H1>
```

Specifying Styles for Individual Elements

You can use the STYLE attribute to specify a style for a particular instance of an element. You can specify, for example, that a particular paragraph is green or a particular block quote is bold. This approach mixes style with content, as opposed to style sheets where they are separated. For example:

```
<BODY>
   <P STYLE="color = 'green'">This paragraph is green.</P>
   <P>This paragraph is in the usual color </P>
</BODY>
```

Defining Classes of Styles

You can declare classes of styles by using the CLASSES attribute inside the <STYLE> tag. You can define, for example, a green, bold class. Whenever you want an element to be green and bold, you can specify that the element is a member of the greenbold class. For example:

```
<HTML>
<HEAD>
   <TITLE>Title</TITLE>
   <STYLE TYPE="text/javascript">
      classes.greenbold.all.color = "#00FF00"
      classes.greenbold.all.fontlight = "bold"
   </STYLE>
</HEAD>
<BODY>
   <H1 CLASS=greenbold>This heading is way too green</H1>
```

You can use the keyword all to specify that all tags within the class are affected by the STYLE property, or you can selectively identify which elements belong to the class. The following code, for instance, creates a class called red1. Only paragraphs and block quotes will be displayed in this style:

```
<HTML>
   <HEAD>
      <TITLE>Title</TITLE>
      <STYLE TYPE="text/javascript">
         classes.red1.P.color = "red"
         classes.red1.blockquote.color = "red"
      </STYLE>
   </HEAD>
<BODY>
   <H1 CLASS=red1>This paragraph is in red</H1>
   <P>This paragraph is in the default color, since it is not a member of
         class red1.</P>
   <BLOCKQUOTE CLASS="red1">Oh what a beautifully red quote this is.
   </BLOCKQUOTE>
```

Format Properties

JavaScript-accessible style sheets treat each block level element as if it is surrounded by a box. (Block level elements start on a new line; for example, `<H1>` and `<P>` are block level elements, but `<EM>` is not.) Each box can have padding, border, and margins. You can set values for top, bottom, left, and right padding and margins. The padding area uses the same background as the element itself (which is set with the `background` property). The margins are always transparent, so the parent element shines through. The width of the box is the sum of the element width (that is, the width of the formatted text or image), the padding, and the border. Padding and margin properties are not inherited, but, since the placement of an element is relative to its ancestors and siblings, the parent's padding and margin properties affect its children.

Box Math

Seven length units influence the horizontal dimension of a box: left margin, left border, left padding, width, right padding, right border, right margin. The width of the element has to be equal to the sum of these units. Therefore, you cannot specify values for all seven properties and expect them to be honored.

By default, the value of the `width` property is automatically calculated based on the other properties' values (`auto`). If `width`, however, is assigned another value, or the dimensions do not add up for other reasons, the property with the lowest rank (closest to 7) will automatically be calculated (`auto`).

Replaced Elements

A replaced element is an element that is replaced by content pointed to from the element. For example, in HTML, the `<IMG>` element is replaced by the image pointed to by the `SRC` attribute.

Replaced elements often come with their own intrinsic width and height. If the value for `width` is `auto`, the intrinsic width is used as the width of the element. If a value other than `auto` is specified in the style sheet, this value is used and the replaced element should be resized accordingly (the resize method will depend on the media type). The height of the element is determined in a similar way.

Setting Margins

You can set the size of the margins for a block level element by specifying the `marginLeft`, `marginRight`, `marginTop`, and `marginBottom` properties. You can also use the predefined `margins()` method to set all four properties simultaneously. For example:

```
// manual assignment
with(tags.P)
{
   marginTop = 30;
   marginBottom = 40;
   marginRight = 50;
   marginLeft = 60;
}
```

The above manual assignment has the same result as the call to the `margins()` method shown below:

```
// assignment using a method
// margins(top, right, bottom, left)
tags.P.margins(30, 50, 40, 60);
```

To set the default margins for everything in a document, specify the `margins` properties for the `<BODY>` tag. The following code, for example, sets the left and right margins to 20:

```
tags.BODY.margins(0, 20, 0, 20);
```

The actual distances between boxes is equal to the sum of two adjoining margins. A box with no border, padding, or content is a legal element and may be used to increase the margin between two real boxes. If there are negative margins, the absolute maximum of the negative adjoining margins is deducted from the maximum of the positive adjoining margins.

Setting Border Width

You can set the width of the border surrounding a block level element by specifying the `borderTopWidth`, `borderRightWidth`, `borderBottomWidth`, and `borderLeftWidth` properties. You can also use the predefined `borderWidths()` method to set all four properties simultaneously. The style of the border can be specified using the `borderStyle` property.

Setting the Padding Size

You can set the size of the padding surrounding a block level element by specifying the `paddingTop`, `paddingRight`, `paddingBottom`, and `paddingLeft` properties. You can also use the predefined `padding()` method to set all four properties simultaneously.

Summary

In this chapter, I introduced new ways to specify a page's style via style sheets. You can specify specific styles for certain element types or instances. Style sheets can be specified outside the page and linked into it, or created within a document. The concepts of style class and style inheritance were explained. I described how to specify a page's padding and margins, and what the mathematical rules are for governing a page's settings. If it is your goal to be a professional programmer, I strongly recommend you delve deeper into the topic of style sheets.

Chapter 27
Security Issues

Security is a growing concern among all developers because it is a growing concern among all end users. Any web development tool must also give some attention to security. Since most of Microsoft's security efforts have been centered around ActiveX components rather than JavaScript, this chapter will focus on Netscape Navigator security. Some of the scripts shown will produce no result at all in Internet Explorer.

Security is every surfer's top concern when surfing the net or posting home pages to it. There are several types of security issues. This chapter deals with those issues related to protecting your private information such as e-mail address, directory structures, user session history, and objects and properties of a loaded page.

History

Netscape Navigator 2.0 was the first browser to include support for JavaScript. The language provided intranet managers with some very powerful methods to access user information for beneficial purposes. But JavaScript also allowed hackers to use these methods for not-so-beneficial purposes. They intercepted client computer information such as file directories, user history, and even passwords you may have entered to access secure sites. The trade and even popular press were all over Netscape for compromising users' privacy and security.

Netscape Navigator 3.0 and later warns you when a loaded document is about to reveal normally hidden information, even if the trigger for this action is your own action. A classic example is clicking on a Submit button, which, unless you don't approve it, will reveal your e-mail address to the site's author.

URL to URL Access Security

When you challenge the security of a URL that resides on a different server, an error message pops up, specifying your script's URL and the URL of the document you are trying to access without permission. Note that you can still load the document from another domain into any of your windows or frames, but you won't be able to read any information from this document, including its location properties or form element values. Let's demonstrate this situation by trying to get the title of Yahoo!'s index page, as shown in Example 27-1.

```
<HTML>
<HEAD>
<TITLE>Security</TITLE>
<SCRIPT LANGUAGE="JavaScript">
<!--
var URL = "http://www.yahoo.com/index.html"
function openYahoo()
{
   win = window.open(URL, "win")
}
function alertTitle()
{
   alert(win.document.title)
}
// -->
</SCRIPT>
</HEAD>
<BODY>
<FORM>
<INPUT TYPE="button" VALUE="open Yahoo!" onClick="openYahoo()">
<INPUT TYPE="button" VALUE="display title" onClick="alertTitle()">
</FORM>
</BODY>
</HTML>
```

Example 27-1 (ex27-1.htm). *A script that attempts to access properties of a document on a different server*

The `alert()` function tries to access the `title` property of Yahoo!'s window document.

The Concept of Tainting

Obviously, security measures make scripters' lives difficult, especially if a site consists of multiple servers, and documents from different servers need to interact with each other. Security upon demand is Netscape's answer to scripters' needs, and is achieved by the concept of *data tainting*. This feature allows the page's publisher to mark the specific properties he or she wants to secure. Data tainting is turned off by default and you can turn it on from within your script, as will be shown later. When data tainting is enabled, JavaScript in one window can see properties of another window, no matter what server the other window's document was loaded from. However, the author of the other window taints (marks) property values or other data that should be secure or private, and JavaScript cannot pass these tainted values on to any server without the user's permission. When data tainting is disabled, a script cannot access any properties. Again, notice that the page's reader has no control on data tainting; it's the publisher's exclusive right. Obviously, data tainting is supported only by tainting-enabled browsers.

Tainting terminology applies to both the page author and the browser. The publisher has tainting control over his or her document. The browser must be manually enabled by the individual browser user before it can recognize that data has been tainted. If the browser does not have data tainting enabled, it just ignores the tainting attributes of the document and access to the document properties is not allowed.

Values derived from tainted data elements are also tainted. If a tainted value is passed to a function, the return value of the function is tainted. If a string is tainted, any of its substrings will be tainted. If a script examines a tainted value in an `if`, `for`, or `while` statement, the script itself accumulates taint in what will be explained later in the section "Window Taint Accumulator."

Enabling Data Tainting

To enable data tainting, the end user sets the `NS_ENABLE_TAINT` environment variable as follows.

- On Unix, use the `setenv` command in csh—`setenv NS ENABLE_TAINT`.
- On Windows, use `set` in autocxcc.bat or NT user settings—`SET NS_ENABLE_TAINT=1`. Be sure not to include any spaces around the equal sign. The variable applies to all copies of Navigator (for different languages).
- On Macintosh, edit the resource with type "Envi" and number 128 in the Netscape application by removing the two ASCII slashes (//) before the `NS_ENABLE_TAINT` text at the end of the resource.

`NS_ENABLE_TAINT` can have any value; 1 will do. If the end user does not enable tainting and a script attempts to access properties of a window on another URL, a message is displayed, indicating that access is not allowed. To determine whether tainting is enabled, use the `taint Enabled()` method. The following code executes `function1()` if data tainting is enabled; otherwise it executes `function2()`:

```
if (navigator.taintEnabled())
{
   function1()
}
else function2()
```

You can also enable tainting interactively in your browser. Navigate to javascript: URL and enter `navigator.taintEnabled()`.

Specific Tainting

Navigator marks a specific set of objects, their properties, and their methods as tainted. The user should not care about the taint value Navigator assigned to them. These items are identified as a source for a potential security risk if abused. The following list shows items that are automatically tainted when in a document.

```
window.status                document.length
window.defaultStatus         document.element
                             document.forms[]
location.href                document.links[]
location.protocol            document.title
location.host                document.location
location.hostname            document.referrer
location.port                document.lastModified
location.pathname            document.cookie
location.hash                document.domain
location.search
location.toString()          form.action

history.previous             inputObject.name
history.current              inputObject.value
history.next                 inputObject.defaultValue
history.toString()           iputObject.status
                             inputObject.defaultStatus
option.text                  inputObject.toString()
option.value
option.defaultSelected
option.selected
```

Taint-enabled browsers can view tainted items, but they cannot send the information to any location on the Internet that is not on the same domain and server. If, on the other hand, you want some snoopy scripts to propagate your home page information (form entries, for example) to wherever they want, you can use the `untaint()` method to make an untainted reference of the object:

```
var prevHistoryFree = untaint(history.previous)
```

By making an untainted reference to your previous link, you have given the world explicit permission to take the data and propagate it wherever it wants. Of course, the author of such a snoopy script would have to study your HTML source to figure out how you have named the untainted data.

There are times when you want to secure more than what is tainted by default. You may have some custom functions or global variables that you do not want to share or allow some snoopy scripts to invoke. Sometimes, sensitive information about the document is hidden in one of your document's functions. Navigator helps you protect this function or other entities by tainting them via the `taint()` method. For example, if you define a function named `mySecretAlgorithm()`, you can taint it as follows:

```
function mySecretAlgorithm ()
{
   statements
}
taint(mySecretAlgorithm)
```

Foreign scripts may use `mySecretAlgorithm()`, but the result will be tainted. That is, the function or any result computed by the function must stay in the foreign script scope and cannot be communicated to other domains or servers.

Window Taint Accumulator

The browser keeps track of tainted data exchanges between windows by updating each window's taint accumulator. The taint accumulator is the mechanism that watches your window's tainting status as your scripts interact with items in other windows. When a document is loaded into a window, its taint accumulator is initialized to `identity`, which is the null value. Every time there is a tainted data exchange with another server, the accumulator mixes different taint codes to create new codes that identify the sources of data origins (server1, server2, server3, ...). Notice that all of the server's data elements share the same tainted code of the server.

The taint codes in the accumulator are checked whenever there is an attempt to pass data over the network. Three taint codes are checked: the script's accumulated taint, the taint code of the targeted server, and the taint code of the data. For the transfer operation to succeed, either two taint codes are equal, or at least one is `identity` (null). If an incompatibility is identified, a dialog box pops up, asking for a confirmation or cancellation of the URL load or form post.

The taint accumulator changes dynamically upon interaction with another server, but it can also be manipulated by the page author. In general, taint accumulates until the document is unloaded, and is reset to `identity` only if it contains the current document's original code. Also, all windows loading documents from the same server share the same taint accumulator. To manipulate the taint accumulator, call `taint()` or `untaint()` with no arguments. When calling `taint()`, JavaScript adds the current document's taint code to the accumulator. Calling `untaint()` removes taint from the accumulator only if it holds taint from the current window. If the current window has been tainted by other servers, `untaint()` will have no effect. Removing taint from the accumulator will reset the taint code to `identity`.

Summary

This chapter described the security issues of the Internet and Netscape's tainting mechanism, which answers some of those issues. Tainting can be applied to specific elements, to the whole document, or to a window. The concept of a taint accumulator was described. Users of Navigator 3.0 and up find themselves answering many more dialog boxes than with Navigator 2.0. There is no way to circumvent this situation except to untaint specific elements. Security on the web is critical for its growth and commercial usage. Netscape does not have the last word on it, so you can expect some changes in this direction. Changes may vary in range from revolutionary (adopting the digital signature algorithm) to evolutionary (improving on the current methods of tainting and taint accumulator).

Chapter 28
Debugging Scripts

The fact is it is impossible to program without some bugs creeping in. Finding those bugs and fixing them is a critical part of any programming project. This process is called *debugging*. Knowing how to debug in a given programming language or tool is critical to using that language or tool.

Development environments usually include at least one powerful debugger, and sometimes a multitude of them. In fact, experienced programmers, when introduced to a new language, are concerned first and foremost about the power and the productivity factor of the debugger. The debugger is the most powerful tool an advanced computer scientist uses to find his or her bugs, and we have yet to meet a programmer who does not have bugs in his or her code. Sources for bugs range from simple ones like typos to logic problems in very complex applications like the Tetris game.

There are a number of development environments, as we have seen in previous chapters. Most of these environments provide the programmer with all language features online, and thus can help you write better code with fewer bugs. But in the end, you can still end up with a script that has bugs and no debugger to find them with. You have to revert to the old way people used to debug their programs: printing messages and progressive commenting of lines.

Types of Errors

In a traditional language such as C there are two main types of errors: compile-time errors (syntax) and run-time errors. Since JavaScript is not a compiled language, the boundaries between these two types of errors are blurred. As the page loads, the first type of errors the browser is looking for are syntax errors. These are relatively easy to detect and fix. Misspelling `else` in the `if-else` construct is one example of a syntax error. Run-time errors involve mismatching between function definitions and function calls, undeclared variables located on the right-hand side of assignment operators, mismatches between object types, etc. If the script lines execute as the page loads, undeclared variables will be flagged immediately. Other errors will be detected when culprit functions execute, which may occur upon loading or while responding to user actions. In fact, some errors, if not invoked as a response to user actions, may never be detected. This kind of issue belongs to a wider field of coverage analysis. There are methodologies and tools for mainstream languages that measure the percentage of code covered by a specific testing suite, where the coverage can be measured by the percentage of lines or functions executed by the suite. Such a tool is yet to be developed for JavaScript.

Error Messages

Navigator and Internet Explorer behave very similarly when detecting a problem. They produce a large alert box specifying:

- The URL or filename of the document causing the problem
- The line number
- A description of the problem in a very condensed and terse statement
- An extract of the code that JavaScript could not handle
- An arrow marker pointing to the offending word

The line number shown in the alert box is exactly the line count of the code extract shown in the alert box, where the first line of the file is at line 1. Some authors mistakenly write that the line number is counted from the opening <SCRIPT> tag of the group that contains the code extract.

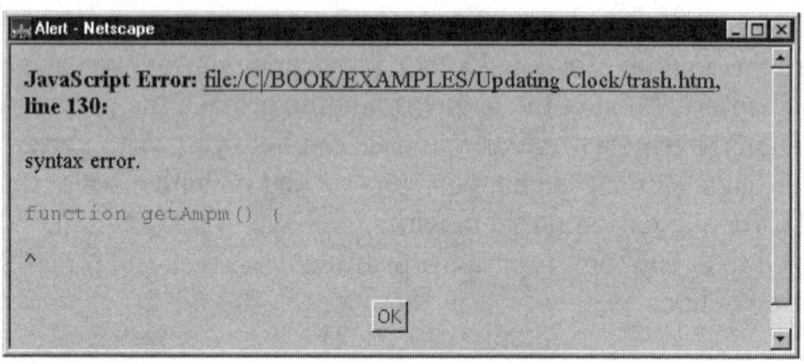

Figure 28-1a. *A typical Navigator error alert box*

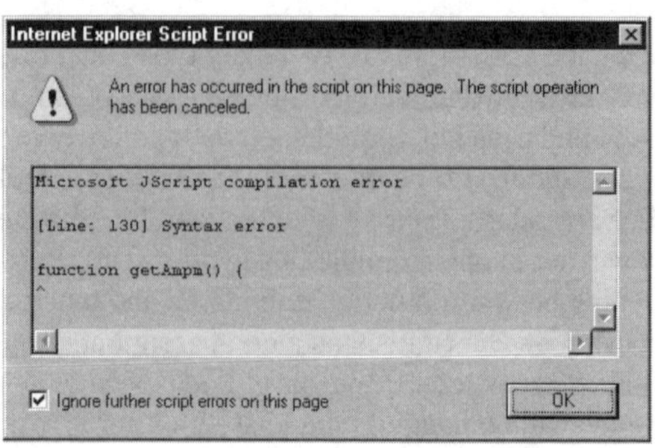

Figure 28-1b. *A typical Internet Explorer error alert box*

Debugging JavaScript may be tricky at times. You have to infer from the shown code extract what might be the real problem. In Figures 28-1a and 1b, for example, the problem is a missing closing brace for the function defined before the shown `getAmpm()` function. Some error messages, as Figure 28-2 shows, do not provide the code extract but rather the offending element (a property name, for example) instead.

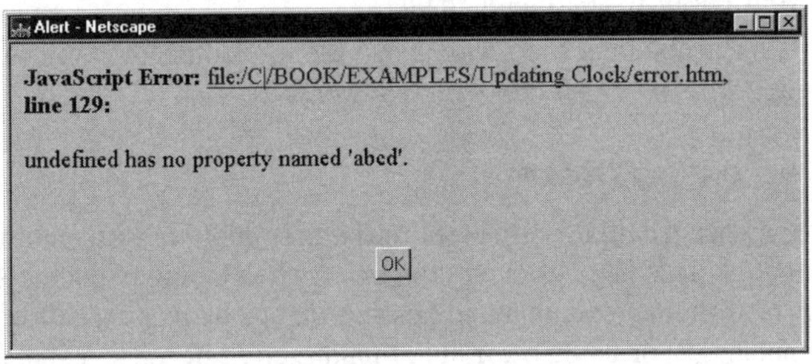

Figure 28-2. *The property 'abcd' is provided instead of the code extract.*

There are many error message types. The rest of this chapter discusses the most important ones with some explanations on proper remedies to the problems and also provides information on preventing errors in the first place.

"string is not defined"

This error usually points to an uninitialized variable being referenced to another variable (two-operand statement) or to itself (unary-operand statement). Obviously, this variable has not been declared or assigned a value prior to the line provided in the error message window. There may be several reasons for this bug:

1. The variable *string* has been initialized as a local variable in another function. Search for *string* in your file and check if this is the case.
2. You have intended to enclose *string* in quotes but forgot. Check if this is the case.
3. You have misspelled a variable that has been declared before. Check if you have a similar name for a variable that has been initialized before the culprit statement. Also, since JavaScript is case sensitive, see if the capitalization of the variable name is different from previously defined variable names. Use the case-insensitive option of your editor to search for such matches.
4. If the erroneous statement starts with a function, you either have a bug in the script above the flagged line (failed to balance braces, for example) or are calling a function that is defined in another window or frame, but you forgot to include the reference to that window or frame.

"string is not a function"

The following problems are the most common sources for such a bug:

1. There is a case mismatch of letters between the calling statement and function definition.
2. You are reusing a variable or HTML object name by the function name. Use your editor to search for *string*.
3. There is a problem in the script above the function named in the error message window. Do some detective work.

"unterminated string literal"

This error message will usually point to the first quote of a string it thinks is not terminated. This is a very common error when trying to concatenate strings or nest them. You can avoid nesting strings by using a pair of in-line quote symbols (`\"`) or using a variable to indirectly reference a string.

"missing } after function body"

A brace is missing somewhere in the function, but not necessarily where the error message says. When a function includes several nested items such as `if..else` or `for` loop constructs, it is not so obvious where the brace is missing. An intelligent editor can be of help here to match braces, pair by pair.

"string is not a number"

The erroneous line has an operator that requires a number, but a different type of variable has been found instead. You either have declared the variable (with the `var` statement) and not initialized it, or have not declared it. It is always preferred to use `parseInt()` or `parseFloat()` to convert strings to numbers.

"string has no property named property"

JavaScript did not find the property provided for the object referenced on the specified line number. There may be few explanations for this bug. You either are trying to reference a property that does not exist for the relevant object or are failing to reference the right object. The latter often occurs when you forget to specify the index of an arrayed object. Look closely at the error message to see if it includes a reference to an entire array rather than just one of its elements. Common arrays are forms, links, and buttons.

"string has no property indexed by [i]"

This error is the opposite of the previous one. Look at the last item and prove to yourself that it is not an element of an array. This is a very common mistake when references become very long and cumbersome, especially when creating radio buttons and select options. Just scan the reference elements one by one, and determine which are simple object names and which are arrays.

"string cannot be set by assignment"

You are either trying to assign a value to a read-only property or assigning a value to an object reference that must be created via a constructor function, rather than by simple assignment.

"test for equality (==) mistyped as assignment (=)? Assuming equality test"

JavaScript is usually right here. You meant to use the equality comparison test (==) but had typed a single equal sign.

"function does not always return a value"

JavaScript checks the organization of every function and verifies that a value is always returned. It is very common to focus on a single logic path while designing deeply nested `if..else` loops, and to overlook other cases in which the decision process "falls through" all the way to the bottom without returning any value.

"access disallowed from scripts at URL_1 to documents at URL_2"

This message indicates cross-domain security is being violated.

"Lengthy JavaScript still running. Continue?"

JavaScript provides a safeguard against the infamous infinite loop bug. After processing a large number of cycles, JavaScript asks the user whether the script should continue. This safety net is for developers and users both. Developers use it for debugging infinite loops and freeing up the browser that would have been locked up forever otherwise. The safety net also protects users against JavaScript's harmful hackers.

"syntax error"

This is every compiler's classic error message. The alert box provides you with the code extract and a pointer to the exact location of the error.

Manual Debugging Techniques

Sometimes, the error messages are of no help in finding the bug and you have to resort to manual and other techniques for debugging. This section describes some of those techniques.

Match Those Tag Pairs

Before checking the code itself, go over the document carefully and check that all tags have matching pairs. Be sure to check that each tag is closed by a closing angle bracket.

View the Intermediate HTML Source

Just click in a frame to select it and choose Frame Source from the View menu. The displayed results include the HTML code that the script generates. Debugging often involves examining intermediate results. The HTML source code is an excellent means for verifying that the computer does what you intend it to. You can also print and save this JavaScript-written HTML.

Reopen the File

Sometimes reloading a URL does not free the browser memory from a bug you are trying to debug. Try reopening the file via the File menu. It may clear the browser's memory completely and reload the fixed version of your source file. If this does not help, try quitting the browser and restarting it again. Rebooting the computer may also help if you are still not able to load your fixed source code.

Print Messages

Senior programmers may identify with this method, very popular in the days when we did not have debuggers. Just put alert dialog boxes in your script with a brief message that you will recognize (such as `alert("Just before calling function xyz")`). These dialog boxes will tell exactly which parts are working and which parts are disconnected and cannot be reached. You can either work your way from top to bottom or use the binary search mechanism. This method is very popular in classic searching and sorting algorithms. Insert an alert dialog box in the middle of the script. If the flow reaches this point of the script, then focus your effort on the second half, since the problem is somewhere there. If the flow does not reach the script's midpoint, insert an alert box in the middle of the first half, and keep going until you quarantine the bug.

Comment Out Statements

Sometimes, the line number provided by the error message does not exactly lead to the culprit code. To find the error, start commenting the lines, one by one, starting from the given line number. Reload the source file after every additional commented line and observe when the error message goes away (and usually substituted with the next in order). At this stage, you know exactly which is the offending source line.

Watching and Tracing Variables

Watching and *tracing* variables, as well as *single-stepping*, are among the most powerful features of any programming environment. Most serious bugs occur when a variable holds an unexpected value, and the only way to find it is to single-step through the code and examine every variable upon its assignment. Unfortunately, JavaScript does not support these basic features, and you need to mimic them via alert boxes. Every time you change a variable by an assignment or invocation of a `String`, `Math`, or `Date` method, insert an `alert()` method on the following line, and show the content of the variable in it. Repeat this sequence of edit-save-switch-reload until you find a variable content that is not what you expected.

This technique may seem very tedious and time-consuming, and indeed it is. But in some cases, you won't have any other way to find the bug. These cases usually involve a value coming back as `<undefined>` or null. Check for incomplete object reference (missing the top-level parent), misspelling an object name, or accessing an undefined property.

Sometimes you are not aware that an object property has been changed. To look for such cases, use the following function to list all object properties in your alert box:

```
function listProperties(object, objectName)
{
   var message = ""
   for (var i in object)
   {
      message += objectName + "." + i + " = " + object[i] + "\n"
   }
alert(message)
}
```

You invoke this function with the object type (unquoted) and the name of the instance (quoted string).

Getting It Right the First Time

Some bug prevention programming techniques are as valid for JavaScript as they are for any other languages, and they should always be used in order to prevent bugs in the first place. The lack of sophisticated debuggers in JavaScript only emphasizes the leverage you can get by using these techniques.

Build the Script's Skeleton First

Build your script in a top-down fashion. Start laying down your HTML parts first, including all form definitions. After you have designed the page layout, you can start filling in the JavaScript portions. When beginning a function, `repeat` loop, or `if` statement, fill out the entire structure before entering any details. For example, suppose you want to define a `showProperties()` function. First, enter the following structure:

```
function showProperties()
{

}
```

and then add the parameters and the `for` structure

```
function showProperties(object, objectName)
{
   var message = ""
   for ( )
   {
   }
}
```

and so on. This technique has two advantages. It assures you have the closing character always attached at the end of the structure, as well as aligning the indentations. If you want, you can prepare a file with all JavaScript structure templates to copy from and paste in your document. You can also use JavaScript editor applications.

Keep Testing While Developing

This technique cannot be overemphasized. Always test your code after an incremental development. Don't write pages of code and only then test it. Test the script whenever you have a new feature, function, algorithm, or any other complete chunk that can be tested by itself.

Evaluate Expressions Outside Your Source

Instead of printing variable contents via an alert box, it is much faster to evaluate certain expressions in an independent, isolated environment such as a separate document you write with a few `text` or `textarea` objects in it. You can also use the internal javascript: URL for testing out expressions. This technique is especially recommended for beginners who need to gain confidence in their knowledge of what different methods (such as `String`, `Math`, and `Date`) yield.

Test Your Functions Outside Your Source

The same arguments presented above for expressions are applicable to functions as well. It is much easier to debug a function in an independent, isolated environment than inside a complex scripted document. Develop your function in a separate document that includes the minimum number of user interface elements you need for the testing. Of course, you will find it more and more difficult to develop your functions in isolation, because they are usually tied to numerous objects in the original document. It will encourage you, though, to develop much more generalized functions that have fewer ties to the environment.

Testing Your Script

Writing JavaScript is development and should be treated as such when you come to test your piece of art. Management bodies of development projects often allocate 50 percent of the resources for testing. You should anticipate similar proportions in your own work plans.

Making a script robust for the World Wide Web audience is not an easy task and should not be taken lightly. You have to anticipate what the user can do at any point and make sure your code handles it correctly. You should not make any assumptions on either the sequence of operations the user is going to follow or the type of data the user is going to enter into forms. You should assume, on the contrary, that the user is not going to follow your instructions (accidentally or intentionally). The user will enter characters in numeric fields, and will fill the form bottom up. Your script should handle all weird and incorrect data, giving the proper feedback to the user. If a form field accepts character values only, give the user an error message. Make sure your script does not crash the system if the input is not valid. Specifically check for the following items:

- Unexpected reloading. Check how it affects the relationship between frames.
- Suspending a document loading. Does it affect your script?
- Bad data. Does the script crash when the data is not valid?

Test your pages extensively and on as many browsers as you can. Users expect the same robustness from your script as from the most professional software published on earth.

Summary

In this chapter, I gave some tips for debugging JavaScript scripts. I first listed common error messages, and explained what they mean and how you can use them to find bugs. I also provided some manual debugging techniques, which are very important in JavaScript, because, unlike other languages, it does not come with a debugger.

Appendix A
HTML Primer

This appendix is designed to give you the basics of HTML. If you have no prior knowledge of HTML, then it is critical that you thoroughly study this appendix before proceeding. However, if you are an experienced HTML programmer, you may wish to skim this appendix or skip it entirely. JavaScript is a scripting language that is embedded into HTML documents in order to add significant functionality to those web pages. For this reason, a working knowledge of HTML is integral to understanding and using JavaScript.

HTML, or Hypertext Markup Language, is a relatively simple scripting language that web browsers can use to display web pages. The beautiful part of HTML is that you don't need any special software; HTML can be written in any text editor including Windows Notepad. Just remember to save the file as an .htm or .html file. HTML has had a long history and has gone through a number of revisions. Each successive revision added more functionality to HTML, and the current version of HTML (Version 4.1) is a very powerful language that can take some time to learn. Fortunately, most work on web pages can be done with just the essentials of HTML and that is what this appendix will teach you. Now let's start with the basics of HTML.

HTML Tags

The first question is how do we get the web browser to know that our document has HTML codes for it to read? Simply put, there is more to creating a web page than simply taking a document and changing its extension to .htm. At the beginning of your document you place the `<HTML>` command (or tag) and at the end you put `</HTML>`; the web browser will know that the codes in between are supposed to be HTML.

```
<HTML>
   put code here
</HTML>
```

Now that is pretty simple you must admit. But this web page won't do much of anything at all. So let's do the obligatory "Hello World" sample that every programming book starts off with. It will show you how to input text with some basic HTML.

```
<HTML>
<HEAD>
<TITLE>My First HTML Page</TITLE>
</HEAD>
<BODY>
<P><CENTER>
<B><FONT SIZE="+2">Hello World</FONT></B>
</CENTER></P>
</BODY>
</HTML>
```

Believe it or not, this little snippet shows you most of what you need to know about HTML. To begin with, note that everything is contained between the <HTML> and </HTML> tags. These two commands define the beginning and end of the HTML document. The web browser will ignore any items outside these commands. Next, we have a section that is contained between the <HEAD> and </HEAD> commands. This is the header portion of your HTML document. The <TITLE> and </TITLE> commands contain the title that will actually appear in the title bar of your browser.

Then we have the <BODY> and </BODY> commands. As you might have guessed, this is the body of your HTML document. This is where all of your web page's code (including scripting code like JavaScript) is going to go. Inside the body section is some text and some additional commands that will define how the text will appear in the browser. The <P> and </P> commands define the beginning and end of a paragraph. The <B> and </B> commands tell the browser to make whatever text is between them bold. The <FONT SIZE="+2"> tells the browser how big the text should be (there are a variety of methods for doing this, as we shall see.). The </FONT> command ends the font section of the HTML code.

By now, I trust you have noticed a pattern. All the above commands have an opening command and a closing command. This is true for all but a very few HTML commands. Just remember this rule: You close the commands in the opposite order of how you opened them. In the above sample code, I opened the commands before the text like this: <P><CENTER><B> <FONT SIZE="+2">, and then closed them like this: </FONT></B></CENTER> </P>. This is important to remember. You can think of it as "backing out" of your commands.

Now this gives you a very simple web page that displays one phrase in bold. Admittedly not very impressive, but if you understand the concepts involved with using the HTML commands, then you understand HTML.

Let's move on to some more HTML. Usually web pages contain more than simply a title and some text. Other items you might put in a web page include images and links to other web pages. Placing an image on an HTML document is rather simple:

```
<IMG SRC="imagepath\imagename" WIDTH=52 HEIGHT=88 ALIGN=bottom>
```

You simply provide the path to the image and the name of the image, including its file extension (such as .gif, .bmp, .jpg, etc.). The other properties in this command allow you to alter the placement and size of the image. You can alter its width and height as well as its alignment.

Placing a hyperlink to another web site or to an e-mail address is just as simple:

```
<A HREF="http://www.wordware.com">
```

This link will connect to the URL (Uniform Resource Locator) contained inside the quotation marks. In order to use this methodology to create an e-mail link, simply use this:

```
<A HREF="mailto:sombody@somemail.com">
```

You simply have to change the "http://" portion to "mailto:". Notice that all three of the preceding methods have one thing in common: They do not close the command in the typical manner that other HTML commands are closed. Now let's examine the source code for a simple but complete HTML document:

```
<HTML>
<HEAD>
<TITLE>Example A-1</TITLE>
</HEAD>
<BODY BGCOLOR="white">
<P><CENTER><B><FONT SIZE="+2">My First web page </FONT></B>
</CENTER></P>
<P>I am learning HTML! I <B><I>LOVE</I></B> HTML!</P>
<P><CENTER><IMG SRC="comp1.gif" WIDTH=52 HEIGHT=88
ALIGN=bottom></CENTER></P>
<P><CENTER>You can e-mail me at</CENTER></P>
<P><CENTER><A HREF="mailto:myemail@someemail.com">Email ME</A>
</CENTER></P>
<P><CENTER>Or go to this publisher's Web Site </CENTER></P>
<P><CENTER><A HREF="http://www.wordware.com">Wordware Publishing</A>
        </CENTER></P>
</BODY>
</HTML>
```

You will note a new command at the beginning:

```
<BODY BGCOLOR="white">
```

You can change the background color of your page using this command and any standard color. You can also set a background image for your HTML document with a similar command:

```
<BODY background="mypicture.gif">
```

The comp1.gif image is included in the downloadable files. If you entered the code properly and used the image, your web page should look something like Figure A-1.

Figure A-1. *Your first web page*

Now I will be the first to admit that this sample web page is very trivial. But it does contain the basics of HTML. With the material we have covered so far, you can display images, text, links, e-mail links, background colors, and background images. Not too bad for just a few short pages. You may also want to look in the sample HTML folder in the companion files to see several sample HTML documents suited for various purposes. These can be used as templates for your own web pages. Examining these can give you a deeper understanding of basic HTML.

Let's examine a few other simple items we can add to our HTML documents. The first is altering text color. You can set the default text color for the entire document as well as alter the color of specific text. You alter the default text color for the entire document using a technique very similar to the one used to alter the background color of the document:

```
<BODY TEXT="blue">
```

This command simply tells the browser that unless otherwise specified, all text in this document should be blue. In addition to changing the default color of all text in a document, you may wish to simply change the color of a specific section of text. This is fairly easy to do as well. Instead of using the `<BODY TEXT>` command, we use the `<FONT COLOR>` command:

```
<FONT COLOR="red">This is red text</FONT>
```

This, like the other color commands, can specify any standard color.

There are a wide variety of tags you can use to alter the appearance and behavior of text and images. Just a few others for you to consider would be the `<BLINK>` and `</BLINK>` tags which, as the name implies, causes the text to blink (this is only supported by Netscape and will not work in Internet Explorer). Another example is `<STRIKE></STRIKE>`, which causes the text to appear with a line through it, a strikethrough.

The last HTML command we are going to examine is `<TABLE>`. Tables are a very good way to organize data on your web page. You can use the tables with or without a border, and I will explain the various reasons to use both.

Here is how to create a table with a border:

```
<TABLE BORDER=1>
   <TR>
      <TD>
         <P>This
      </TD><TD>
         <P>Is a
      </TD></TR>
   <TR>
      <TD>
         <P>Table
      </TD><TD>
         <P>With a border
      </TD></TR>
</TABLE></P>
```

By now you should be able to recognize that the <TABLE> and </TABLE> tags actually contain the table. Each <TR> tag designates another row in the table. The <TD> and </TD> tags create a cell within that row. Using those three tags you can create a table with any number of rows or columns you wish. Notice in the first line of this code that the BORDER property is set to 1. This means the border has a width and is therefore visible.

In some instances you may not want the border to show. Tables can be used simply to hold images and text in relative positions. In cases such as these you may not wish the border to show. Below is an example of a table whose borders will not show:

```
<P><TABLE BORDER=0 CELLSPACING=0 CELLPADDING=0>
   <TR>
      <TD>
         <P>This
      </TD><TD>
         <P>is a
      </TD></TR>
   <TR>
      <TD>
         <P>Table
      </TD><TD>
         <P>With no borders or padding
      </TD></TR>
</TABLE></P>
```

Notice that the BORDER, CELLPADDING, and CELLSPACING properties are all set to 0. This causes the table itself to not be displayed. However, the contents of the table will display. You should also notice that in both examples I have placed text in each cell.

Since the entire purpose of this book is to teach you JavaScript, the obvious question on your mind should be, how do I insert scripts into HTML? Well, fortunately that is not particularly difficult. The browser deals with script code (including JavaScript) like it handles HTML code, scanning the source from left to right and from top to bottom. JavaScript has "tags" of its own by which it instructs the browser and determines the layout. However, JavaScript is not read exactly like HTML. In HTML, the browser acts immediately according to the elements it recognizes. Not all JavaScript code refers to actions that take place while the page is loading. Some parts are just kept in memory until they are called. For instance, if you write a function and do not call it, the browser does not do anything with it. This part of the script stays in memory, and can be invoked later. But the real question you are wondering is, how do I put scripts into my HTML documents? Any script can be placed very easily by encasing the script you write inside two commands:

```
<SCRIPT LANGUAGE = "whateverscriptlanguageyouareusing">
```

and

```
</SCRIPT>
```

There are many scripting languages available for the web, including VBScript (based on the Visual Basic programming language), CGI, and, of course, JavaScript. Below is an example of JavaScript inserted into HTML code.

```
<SCRIPT LANGUAGE="JavaScript">
   alert("Wonderful!")
</SCRIPT>
```

Figure A-2. *An alert box*

Let me stress that I have only covered the essentials of writing HTML code. You can find a number of books that go into HTML in more depth than this.

Appendix B
JavaScript Object Specification Syntax

anchor Object

Creating

```
<A NAME="anchorName">
   textOrImageAnchor
</A>
```

applet Object

Creating

```
<APPLET
   CODE="AppletURL"
   HEIGHT="PixelCount"
   NAME="AppletName"
   WIDTH="PixelCount"
   [ALIGN="AlignmentLocation"]
   [ALT="AlternateTextDisplay"]
   [CODEBASE="ClassFileDirectory"]
   [HSPACE="MarginPixelCount"]
   [VSPACE="MarginPixelCount"]>
      <PARAM NAME="AppletParameterName" VALUE="ParameterValue">
      ...
      <PARAM NAME="AppletParameterName" VALUE="ParameterValue">
</APPLET>
```

Properties

```
name                (string)
(Java variables)
```

Event Handlers

```
onMouseOut=
onMouseOver=
```

Methods

(*Java methods*)

area Object

Creating

```
<MAP NAME="areaMapName">
  <AREA
   COORDS="x1,y1,x2,y2…." | "x-center,y-center,radius"
   HREF="URLorLocation"
   [NOHREF]
   [SHAPE="rect" | "poly" | "circle" | "default" ]
   [TARGET="windowName"]
   [onFocus="EventHandlerTextOrFunction"]
   [onMouseOut="EventHandlerTextOrFunction"]
   [onMouseOver="EventHandlerTextOrFunction"]>
</MAP>
```

Properties

```
links[index].target     (window name)
[location object properties]
```

Event Handlers

```
onMouseOut=
onMouseOver=
```

Array Object

Creating

```
var myArray = new Array([integer] | [val1 [ , val2 ... [ , valn]]])
```

Properties

```
length                  (integer)
prototype               (expression)
```

Methods

```
join("delimiterChar")
reverse()
sort(compareFunc)
```

button, submit, and reset Objects

Creating

```
<FORM>
  <INPUT
   TYPE="button" | "submit" |"reset"
   [NAME="buttonName]
   [VALUE="labelText"]
   [onClick="EventHandlerTextOrFunction"]
   [onFocus="EventHandlerTextOrFunction"]
   [onLoad="EventHandlerTextOrFunction"]
   [onUnLoad="EventHandlerTextOrFunction"]>
</FORM>
```

Properties

```
name            (string)
type            (string)
value           (string)
```

Methods

```
click()
```

Event Handlers

```
onClick=
```

checkbox Object

Creating

```
<FORM>
  <INPUT
   TYPE="checkbox"
   [CHECKED]
   [NAME="boxName]
   [VALUE="buttonValue"]
   [onClick="EventHandlerTextOrFunction"]>
   buttonText
</FORM>
```

Properties

```
checked         (Boolean)
defaultChecked  (Boolean)
name            (string)
type            (string)
value           (string)
```

Methods

```
click()
```

Event Handlers

```
onClick=
```

Date Object

Creating

```
var myDate = new Date("Month dd, yyyy, hh:mm:ss")
var myDate = new Date("Month dd, yyyy")
var myDate = new Date("yy,mm,dd,hh,mm,ss")
var myDate = new Date("yy, mm, dd")
var myDate = new Date(millisecondsInteger)
```

Properties

```
prototype          (expression)
```

Methods

```
myDate.getDate()               (1-31)
myDate.getDay()                (0-6)
myDate.getHours()              (0-23)
myDate.getMinutes()            (0-59)
myDate.getMonth()              (0-11)
myDate.getSeconds()            (0-59)
myDate.getTime()               (0-...)
myDate.getTimezoneOffset()     (0-...)
myDate.getYear()               (70-...)
myDate.setDate()               (1-31)
myDate.setDay()                (0-6)
myDate.setHours()              (0-23)
myDate.setMinutes()            (0-59)
myDate.setMonth()              (0-11)
myDate.setSeconds()            (0-59)
myDate.setTime()               (0-...)
myDate.setYear()               (70-...)
myDate.toGMTString()           (String)
myDate.toLocaleString()        (String)
Date.parse("dateString")
Date.UTC("date values")
```

document Object

Creating

```
<BODY
   [ALINK="#activatedLinkColor"]
   [BACKGROUND="backgroundImageURL"]
   [BGCOLOR="#backgroundColor"]
   [LINK="#unfollowedLinkColor"]
   [TEXT="#foregroundColor"]
   [VLINK="#followedLinkColor"]
   [onLoad="#handlerTextOrFunction"]
   [onUnload="#handlerTextOrFunction"]
</BODY>
```

Properties

```
alinkColor   (hexadecimal triplet or constant)
anchors      (array)
applets      (array)
bgColor      (hexadecimal triplet or constant)
cookie       (string)
domain       (string)
embeds       (array)
fgColor      (hexadecimal triplet or constant)
forms        (array)
images       (array)
lastModified (date string)
linkColor    (hexadecimal triplet or constant)
links        (array)
location     (string)
referrer     (string)
title        (string)
URL          (string)
vlinkColor   (hexadecimal triplet or constant)
```

Methods

```
write("string1" [,"string2",..., "stringn"])
write("string1" [,"string2",..., "stringn"])
write("string1" [,"string2",..., "stringn"])
open("mimeType")
close()
clear()
```

fileUpload Object

Creating

```
<FORM>
<INPUT
   TYPE="file"
   [NAME="fieldName"]
   [SIZE="numberOfCharacters"]>
</FORM>
```

Properties

```
name        (string)
value       (string)
type        (string)
```

Methods

```
blur()
focus()
select()
```

Event Handlers

```
onBlur=
onChange=
onFocus=
onSelect=
```

form Object

Creating

```
<FORM
   [ACTION="serverURL"]
   [ENCTYPE="MIMEType"]
   [METHOD=GET | POST]
   [NAME="formName"]
   [onSubmit="eventHandlerTextOrFunction"]
   [onReset="eventHandlerTextOrFunction"]
</FORM>
```

Properties

```
action      (URL)
elements    (array)
encoding    (MIME type)
method      (GET or POST)
name        (string)
target      (window name)
```

Methods

```
reset()
submit()
```

Event Handlers

```
onReset=
onSubmit=
```

function Object

Creating

```
function functionName( [parameter1]...[, parameterN] )
{
     statements
}
var myFunction = new function([parameter1]...[, parameterN],
                 statements)
```

Properties

```
arguments     (array)
caller        (function)
prototype     (expression)
```

Methods

```
reset()
submit()
```

Event Handlers

```
onReset=
onSubmit=
```

hidden Object

Creating

```
<FORM>
  <INPUT
   NAME="fieldName"
   TYPE="hidden"
   [VALUE="contents"]>
</FORM>
```

Properties

```
defaultValue  (string)
name          (string)
type          (string)
value         (string)
```

history Object

Properties

```
length        (integer)
```

Methods

```
back()
forward()
go(relativeNumber |"URLorTitleSubstring")
```

image Object

Creating

```
<IMG
   NAME="imageName"
   SRC="imageURL"
   [ALIGN="left" | "right" | "top" | "absmiddle" | "absbottom" |
          "texttop" | "middle" | "baseline" | "bottom" ]
   [BORDER="pixelCount"]
   [HEIGHT="pixelCount" | "percentageValue%"]
   [HSPACE="pixelCount"]
   [ISMAP]
   [LOWSRC="lowResImageURL"]
   [USEMAP="areaMapName"]
   [VSPACE="pixelCount"]
   [WIDTH="pixelCount" | "percentageValue%"]
   [onAbort="EventHandlerTextOrFunction"]
   [onError="EventHandlerTextOrFunction"]
   [onLoad="EventHandlerTextOrFunction"]>
```

Properties

```
border        (integer)
complete      (Boolean)
height        (integer)
hspace        (integer)
lowsrc        (string)
src           (string)
vspace        (integer)
```

Event Handlers

```
onAbort=
onError=
onLoad=
```

layer Object

Properties

```
above
background        (colorValue)
below             (layerObject)
bgColor           (colorValue)
clip.top          (pixelCount)
clip.left         (pixelCount)
clip.right        (pixelCount)
clip.bottom       (pixelCount)
clip.width        (pixelCount)
clip.height       (pixelCount)
height            (pixelCount)
left              (pixelCount)
layers            (array)
name              (string)
parentLayer       (layerObject)
siblingAbove      (layerObject)
siblingBelow      (layerObject)
top               (pixelCount)
visibility        (hide|show|inherit)
width             (pixelCount)
zIndex            (integer)
```

Methods

```
offset()
moveTo()
resize()
moveAbove()
moveBelow()
```

link Object

Creating

```
<A HREF="URLorLocation"
   [NAME="anchorName"]
   [TARGET="windowName"]
   [onClick="EventHandlerTextOrFunction"]
   [onMouseOut="EventHandlerTextOrFunction"]
   [onMouseOver="EventHandlerTextOrFunction"]>
```

```
   TextOrImageLink
</FORM>
```

Properties

```
links[index].target        (window name)
[location object properties]
```

Event Handlers

```
onClick=
onMouseOut=
onMouseOver=
```

Math Object

Properties

```
Math.E
Math.LN2
Math.LN10
Math.LOG2E
Math.LOG10E
Math.PI
Math.SQRT1_2
Math.SQRT2
```

Methods

```
Math.abs()
Math.acos()
Math.asin()
Math.atan()
Math.atan2()
Math.ceil()
Math.cos()
Math.exp()
Math.floor()
Math.log()
Math.max()
Math.min()
Math.pow()
Math.random()
Math.round()
Math.sin()
Math.sqrt()
Math.tan()
```

mimeType Object

Properties

```
description     (string)
enabledPlugin   (string)
type            (string)
suffixes        (string)
```

navigator Object

Properties

```
appName         (string)
appVersion      (string)
appCodeName     (string)
mimeTypes       (string)
plugins         (string)
userAgent       (string)
```

Methods

```
javaEnabled()
taintEnabled()
```

plugin Object

Properties

```
description     (string)
enabledPlugin   (string)
type            (string)
suffixes        (string)
```

Methods

```
javaEnabled()
taintEnabled()
```

radio Object

Creating

```
<FORM
   <INPUT
  NAME="buttonGroupName"
  TYPE="radio"
  [CHECKED]
  [VALUE="buttonValue"]
```

```
   [onClick="EventHandlerTextOrFunction"]
   buttonText
</FORM>
```

Properties

```
checked          (Boolean)
defaultChecked   (Boolean)
name             (string)
value            (string)
type             (string)
```

Methods

```
click()
```

Event Handlers

```
onClick=
```

select Object

Creating

```
<FORM
   <SELECT
   NAME="listName"
   [MULTIPLE]
   [SIZE="NumberOfCharacters"]
   [onBlur="EventHandlerTextOrFunction"]
   [onChange="EventHandlerTextOrFunction"]
   [onFocus="EventHandlerTextOrFunction"]>
   <OPTION [SELECTED] [VALUE="string"]>listItem
   […<OPTION [VALUE="string"]>listItem
   </SELECT>
</FORM> >
```

Properties

```
length                            (integer)
name                              (string)
options[index]                    (array)
options[index].defaultSelected    (Boolean)
options[index].index              (integer)
options[index].value              (string)
options[index].selected           (Boolean)
options[index].text               (string)
selectedIndex                     (integer)
type                              (string)
```

Methods

```
blur()
focus()
```

Event Handlers

```
onBlur=
onChange=
onFocus=
```

String Object

Creating

```
var myString = new String(["stringExpression"])
```

Properties

```
length          (integer)
prototype       (expression)
```

Methods

```
myString.anchor("anchorName")
myString.big()
myString.blink()
myString.bold()
myString.charAt(index)
myString.fixed()
myString.fontcolor(colorValue)
myString.fontsize(integer1to7)
myString.indexOf(searchString [ , startIndex])
myString.italics()
myString.lastIndexOf(searchString [ , startIndex])
myString.link(locationOrURL)
myString.small()
myString.split("delimitingChar")
myString.strike()
myString.sub()
myString.substring(beginIndex, endIndex)
myString.sup()
myString.toLowerCase()
myString.toUpperCase()
```

text, textarea, and password Objects

Creating

```
<FORM>
   <INPUT
   NAME="fieldName"
   TYPE="text"
   [MAXLENGTH="MaxLengthAllowed"]
   [SIZE="NumberOfCharacters"]
   [VALUE="contents"]
   [onBlur="EventHandlerTextOrFunction"]
   [onChange="EventHandlerTextOrFunction"]
   [onFocus="EventHandlerTextOrFunction"]
   [onSelect="EventHandlerTextOrFunction"]>
</FORM>

<FORM>
   <TEXTAREA
   COLS="NumberOfColumns"
   NAME="fieldName"
   ROWS="NumberOfRows"
   [WRAP="off" | "virtual" | "physical"]
   [onBlur="EventHandlerTextOrFunction"]
   [onChange="EventHandlerTextOrFunction"]
   [onFocus="EventHandlerTextOrFunction"]
   [onSelect="EventHandlerTextOrFunction"]>
   defaultText
   </TEXTAREA>
</FORM>

<FORM>
   <INPUT
   NAME="fieldName"
   TYPE="password"
   [MAXLENGTH="MaxLengthAllowed"]
   [SIZE="CharacterLength"]
   [VALUE="contents"]>
</FORM>
```

Properties

```
defaultValue    (string)
name            (string)
value           (string)
type            (string)
```

Methods

```
blur()
focus()
select()
```

Event Handlers

```
onBlur=
onChange=
onFocus=
onSelect=
```

window and frame Objects

Creating

```
windowObject = window.open([parameters])

<BODY
   ...
   [onBlur="EventHandlerTextOrFunction"]
   [onFocus="EventHandlerTextOrFunction"]
   [onLoad="EventHandlerTextOrFunction"]
   [onUnLoad="EventHandlerTextOrFunction"]>
</BODY>

<FRAMESET
   COLS="valueList"
   ROWS="valueList"
   [BORDER=pixelSize]
   [BORDERCOLOR=colorSpecs]
   [FRAMEBORDER=YES | NO]
   [onBlur="EventHandlerTextOrFunction"]
   [onFocus="EventHandlerTextOrFunction"]
   [onLoad="EventHandlerTextOrFunction"]
   [onUnLoad="EventHandlerTextOrFunction]>
      <FRAME
         SRC="locationOrURL"
         NAME="firstFrameName"
         [BORDER=pixelsize]
         [BORDERCOLOR=colorSpecs]>
         ...
</FRAMESET>
```

Properties

```
defaultStatus   (string)
frames          (array)
name            (string)
onerror         (function)
opener          (window object)
parent          (window object)
self            (window object)
status          (window object)
top             (window object)
window          (window object)
```

Methods

```
alert(message)
blur()
clearTimeout(timeoutIDnumber)
close()
confirm(message)
focus()
open("URL", "windowName"[,,"windowSpecification"])
prompt(message,defaultReply)
scroll(horizontalPixel, verticalPixel)
setTimeout("expression", millisecondsDelay)
```

Event Handlers

```
onBlur=
onFocus=
onLoad=
onUnload=
```

Control Structures

```
if (condition)=
{
  statements
}
if (condition)=
{
  statements
}
else
{
  statements
}
variable = (condition) ? val1 : val2

for ( [ initial expression]; [condition]; [update expression])
{
  statements
```

```
}
while (condition)
{
  statements
}
for (var in object)
{
  statements
}
with (object)
{
  statements
}
```

Operators

Comparison

```
==    Equals
!=    Does not equal
>     Is greater than
>=    Is greater than or equal to
<     Is less than
<=    Is less than or equal to
```

Binary and Unary

```
+     Plus
-     Minus
*     Multiply
/     Divide
%     Modulo
++    Increment
--    Decrement
-val  Negation
```

Assignment

```
=     Equals
+=    Add the RHS (Right Hand Side)
-=    Subtract the RHS
*=    Multiply by the RHS
/=    Divide by the RHS
%=    Modulo by the RHS
<<=   Left shift by the RHS
>>=   Right shift by the RHS
>>>=  Right shift by the RHS, zero fill
&=    Bitwise AND by the RHS
|=    Bitwise OR by the RHS
^=    Bitwise XOR by the RHS
```

Boolean

```
&&   And
||   Or
!    Not
```

Bitwise

```
&    Bitwise And
|    Bitwise Or
^    Bitwise XOR
~    Bitwise Not
<<   Left Shift
>>   Right Shift
>>>  Zero-Fill Right Shift
```

Miscellaneous

```
new
typeOf
void
```

JavaScript Functions and Methods

```
eval("string")
isNan(expression)
object.toString()
parseFloat("string")
parseInt("string")
taint([object])
untaint([object])
```

Appendix C

ASCII Character Set

Char	Oct	Dec	Hex	Ctrl-key	Control Action
NUL	0	0	0	^@	Null character
SOH	1	1	1	^A	Start of heading, = console interrupt
STX	2	2	2	^B	Start of text, maintenance mode on HP console
ETX	3	3	3	^C	End of text
EOT	4	4	4	^D	End of transmission; not the same as ETB
ENQ	5	5	5	^E	Enquiry; goes with ACK (old HP flow control)
ACK	6	6	6	^F	Acknowledge; clears ENQ logon hang
BEL	7	7	7	^G	Bell; rings the bell
BS	10	8	8	^H	Backspace; works on HP terminals/computers
HT	11	9	9	^I	Horizontal tab; move to next tab stop
LF	12	10	a	^J	Line feed
VT	13	11	b	^K	Vertical tab
FF	14	12	c	^L	Form feed, page eject
CR	15	13	d	^M	Carriage return
SO	16	14	e	^N	Shift Out, alternate character set
SI	17	15	f	^O	Shift In, resume default character set
DLE	20	16	10	^P	Data link escape
DC1	21	17	11	^Q	XON, with XOFF to pause listings; " okay to send"
DC2	22	18	12	^R	Device control 2, block-mode flow control
DC3	23	19	13	^S	XOFF, with XON is TERM=18 flow control

Char	Oct	Dec	Hex	Ctrl-key	Control Action
DC4	24	20	14	^T	Device control 4
NAK	25	21	15	^U	Negative acknowledge
SYN	26	22	16	^V	Synchronous idle
ETB	27	23	17	^W	End transmission block; not the same as EOT
CAN	30	24	18	^X	Cancel line; MPE echoes
EM	31	25	19	^Y	End of medium; Control-Y interrupt
SUB	32	26	1a	^Z	Substitute
ESC	33	27	1b	^[	Escape; next character is not echoed
FS	34	28	1c	^\	File separator
GS	35	29	1d	^]	Group separator
RS	36	30	1e	^^	Record separator, block-mode terminator
US	37	31	1f	^_	Unit separator
SP	40	32	20		Space
!	41	33	21		Exclamation mark
"	42	34	22		Quotation mark (" in HTML)
#	43	35	23		Cross hatch (number sign)
$	44	36	24		Dollar sign
%	45	37	25		Percent sign
&	46	38	26		Ampersand
'	47	39	27		Closing single quote (apostrophe)
(	50	40	28		Opening parenthesis
)	51	41	29		Closing parenthesis
*	52	42	2a		Asterisk (star, multiply)
+	53	43	2b		Plus
,	54	44	2c		Comma
-	55	45	2d		Hypen (dash, minus)
.	56	46	2e		Period
/	57	47	2f		Slant (forward slash, divide)
0	60	48	30		Zero
1	61	49	31		One
2	62	50	32		Two
3	63	51	33		Three
4	64	52	34		Four
5	65	53	35		Five
6	66	54	36		Six
7	67	55	37		Seven
8	70	56	38		Eight
9	71	57	39		Nine

Char	Oct	Dec	Hex	Ctrl-key	Control Action
:	72	58	3a		Colon
;	73	59	3b		Semicolon
<	74	60	3c		Less than sign (< in HTML)
=	75	61	3d		Equal sign
>	76	62	3e		Greater than sign (> in HTML)
?	77	63	3f		Question mark
@	100	64	40		At sign
A	101	65	41		Uppercase A
B	102	66	42		Uppercase B
C	103	67	43		Uppercase C
D	104	68	44		Uppercase D
E	105	69	45		Uppercase E
F	106	70	46		Uppercase F
G	107	71	47		Uppercase G
H	110	72	48		Uppercase H
I	111	73	49		Uppercase I
J	112	74	4a		Uppercase J
K	113	75	4b		Uppercase K
L	114	76	4c		Uppercase L
M	115	77	4d		Uppercase M
N	116	78	4e		Uppercase N
O	117	79	4f		Uppercase O
P	120	80	50		Uppercase P
Q	121	81	51		Uppercase Q
R	122	82	52		Uppercase R
S	123	83	53		Uppercase S
T	124	84	54		Uppercase T
U	125	85	55		Uppercase U
V	126	86	56		Uppercase V
W	127	87	57		Uppercase W
X	130	88	58		Uppercase X
Y	131	89	59		Uppercase Y
Z	132	90	5a		Uppercase Z
[	133	91	5b		Opening square bracket
\	134	92	5c		Reverse slant (backslash)
]	135	93	5d		Closing square bracket
^	136	94	5e		Caret (circumflex)
_	137	95	5f		Underscore
`	140	96	60		Opening single quote
a	141	97	61		Lowercase a
b	142	98	62		Lowercase b

Char	Oct	Dec	Hex	Ctrl-key	Control Action
c	143	99	63		Lowercase c
d	144	100	64		Lowercase d
e	145	101	65		Lowercase e
f	146	102	66		Lowercase f
g	147	103	67		Lowercase g
h	150	104	68		Lowercase h
i	151	105	69		Lowercase i
j	152	106	6a		Lowercase j
k	153	107	6b		Lowercase k
l	154	108	6c		Lowercase l
m	155	109	6d		Lowercase m
n	156	110	6e		Lowercase n
o	157	111	6f		Lowercase o
p	160	112	70		Lowercase p
q	161	113	71		Lowercase q
r	162	114	72		Lowercase r
s	163	115	73		Lowercase s
t	164	116	74		Lowercase t
u	165	117	75		Lowercase u
v	166	118	76		Lowercase v
w	167	119	77		Lowercase w
x	170	120	78		Lowercase x
y	171	121	79		Lowercase y
z	172	122	7a		Lowercase z
{	173	123	7b		Opening curly brace
|	174	124	7c		Vertical line
}	175	125	7d		Closing curly brace
~	176	126	7e		Tilde (approximate)
DEL	177	127	7f		Delete (rubout), cross-hatch box

Appendix D
Online Resources

This appendix contains a list of what I consider to be the best JavaScript sites on the web. You can consult these sites in order to get tutorials, source code, and much more. I strongly recommend that you familiarize yourself with these sources.

JavaScript Web Sites

JavaScript.com is one of the premier JavaScript sites. It has hundreds of tutorials and samples. You will really want to use this one.

http://www.javascript.com/

Doc JavaScript is another excellent site you would do well to reference.

http://www.webreference.com/js/

A1 JavaScripts is a site with some interesting source code you might wish to review.

http://www.a1javascripts.com/

JavaScript.com is an excellent site with lots of source code and tutorials.

http://www.javascript.com/

Webdeveloper.com contains articles, a resource directory, and an extensive web developer forum on a multitude of topics, including JavaScript.

http://webdeveloper.com/

JavaScript Games is a page with a number of games written in JavaScript. It's a good page to see what you can do with JavaScript.

http://plaza.harmonix.ne.jp/~jimmeans/

HTML Web Sites

WebMonkeys HTML cheat sheet is a very good site.

http://www.webmonkey.com/webmonkey/reference/html_cheatsheet/

The official HTML 4.01 Specification is an excellent resource to find out exactly what is included in HTML 4 and 4.01.

http://www.w3.org/TR/REC-html40/

Organizational Web Sites

The HTML Writers Guild is an association of HTML writers.

http://www.hwg.org/

The International Webmasters Association is an association of webmasters and web developers. They have a variety of interesting membership benefits.

http://www.irwa.org/

Certification Web Sites

If you are looking to prove that you have learned JavaScript, BrainBench has a JavaScript certification test you can take online.

www.brainbench.com

Employment Web Sites

If you are seeking employment in the programming field, there are several web sites you should check out.

Computer Jobs.com www.computerjobs.com
Jobs for Programmers www.prgjobs.com

Index

Looking for more?

Check out Wordware's market-leading Applications Library featuring the following titles.

Recent Releases

Essential LightWave v9
1-59822-024-1 • $49.95
6 x 9 • 992 pp.

LightWave v9 Texturing
1-59822-029-2 • $44.95
6 x 9 • 648 pp.

LightWave v9 Lighting
1-59822-039-X • $44.95
6 x 9 • 616 pp.

Managing Virtual Teams: Getting the Most From Wikis, Blogs, and Other Collaborative Tools
1-59822-028-4 • $29.95
6 x 9 • 400 pp.

Microsoft Excel Functions & Formulas
1-59822-011-X • $29.95
6 x 9 • 416 pp.

Advanced SQL Functions in Oracle 10*g*
1-59822-021-7 • $36.95
6 x 9 • 416 pp.

SQL for Microsoft Access
1-55622-092-8 • $39.95
6 x 9 • 360 pp.

Word 2003 Document Automation with VBA, XML, XSLT and Smart Documents
1-55622-086-3 • $36.95
6 x 9 • 464 pp.

Access 2003 Programming by Example with VBA, XML, and ASP
1-55622-223-8 • $39.95
6 x 9 • 704 pp.

Excel 2003 VBA Programming with XML and ASP
1-55622-225-4 • $36.95
6 x 9 • 968 pp.

Camtasia Studio 4: The Definitive Guide
1-59822-037-3 • $39.95
6 x 9 • 600 pp.

Introduction to Game Programming with C++
1-59822-032-2 • $44.95
6 x 9 • 392 pp.

Don't Miss

FileMaker Web Publishing A Complete Guide to Using the API for PHP
1-59822-041-1 • $49.95
6 x 9 • 472 pp.

FileMaker Pro Business Applications
1-59822-014-4 • $49.95
6 x 9 • 648 pp.

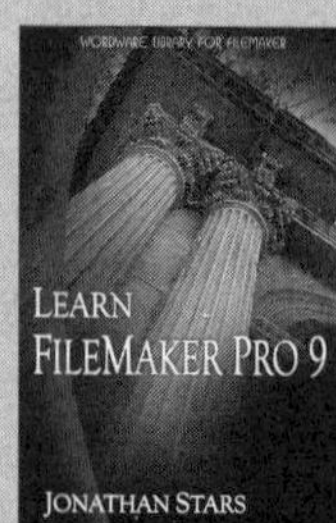

Learn FileMaker Pro 9
1-59822-046-2 • $39.95
6 x 9 • 550 pp.

Visit us online at www.wordware.com for more information.
Use the following coupon code for online specials: Java0330